PLAN YOUR TRIP

WITOLD SKRYPCZAK / GETTY IMAGES ©

CANCÚN P54

MARK D CALLANAN / GETTY IMAGES ©

MAYA WOMAN WEAVING, YUCATÁN P140

ON THE ROAD

MICHELE FALZONE / GETTY IMAGES ©

SAN CRISTÓBAL DE LAS CASAS P223

Contents

UNDERSTAND

SURVIVAL GUIDE

SPECIAL FEATURES

Welcome to Cancún, Cozumel & the Yucatán

The Yucatán Peninsula captivates visitors with its endless offerings of natural wonders and an ancient culture that's still very much alive today.

Life's a Beach

Without a doubt, this corner of Mexico has some of the most beautiful stretches of coastline you'll ever see – which explains in large part why beaches get top billing on the peninsula. On the east coast you have the famous coral-crushed white sands and turquoise-blue waters of the Mexican Caribbean, while up north you'll find sleepy fishing villages with sandy streets and wildlife-rich surroundings. For the ultimate beach-bumming experience you can always hit one of several low-key islands off the Caribbean coast.

Maya Ruins Galore

You can't help but feel awestruck when standing before the pyramids, temples and ball courts of one of the most brilliant pre-Hispanic civilizations of all time. Yes, those Maya certainly knew a thing or two about architecture and they were no slouchers when it came to astronomy, science and mathematics either. Witnessing their remarkable achievements firsthand leaves a lasting impression on even the most jaded traveler – and the peninsula is chock-full of these mind-blowing Maya archaeological sites.

Nature's Playground

The Yucatán is the real deal for nature enthusiasts. With colorful underwater scenery like none other, it offers some of the best diving and snorkeling sites in the world. Then you have the many biosphere reserves and national parks that are home to a remarkably diverse variety of animal and plant life. Just to give you an idea of what's in store: you can swim with whale sharks, spot crocodiles and flamingos, help liberate sea turtles and observe hundreds upon hundreds of bird species.

Culture & Fun

In case you need a little something more than pretty beaches, ancient ruins and outdoor adventures, you'll be glad to know that culture and fun-filled activities abound in the Yucatán. On any given day you may come across soulful dance performances, free concerts, interesting museums or art exhibits – particularly in Mérida, the peninsula's cultural capital. For all-out fun, the Yucatán is one big splashfest after another with thousands of underground natural pools, theme parks with subterranean rivers, and all kinds of thrilling boat tours.

Why I Love Cancún, Cozumel & the Yucatán

By John Hecht, Author

Above all, I love the colors. Maybe I've been living in smog-choked Mexico City *waaay* too long now but every time I visit the peninsula I find myself asking: can an ocean really have that many shades of intense blue, or can jungles and mangroves really be so chlorophyll green? I also love that there are so many things to do. Had your fill of Maya ruins? No problem - have a dip in a gorgeous cenote (limestone sinkhole) or explore amazing coral reefs. And don't even get me started about the Yucatán's wonderful regional cuisine.

For more about our authors, see page 320

Above: Tulum beach and ancient Maya ruins

Cancún, Cozumel & the Yucatán

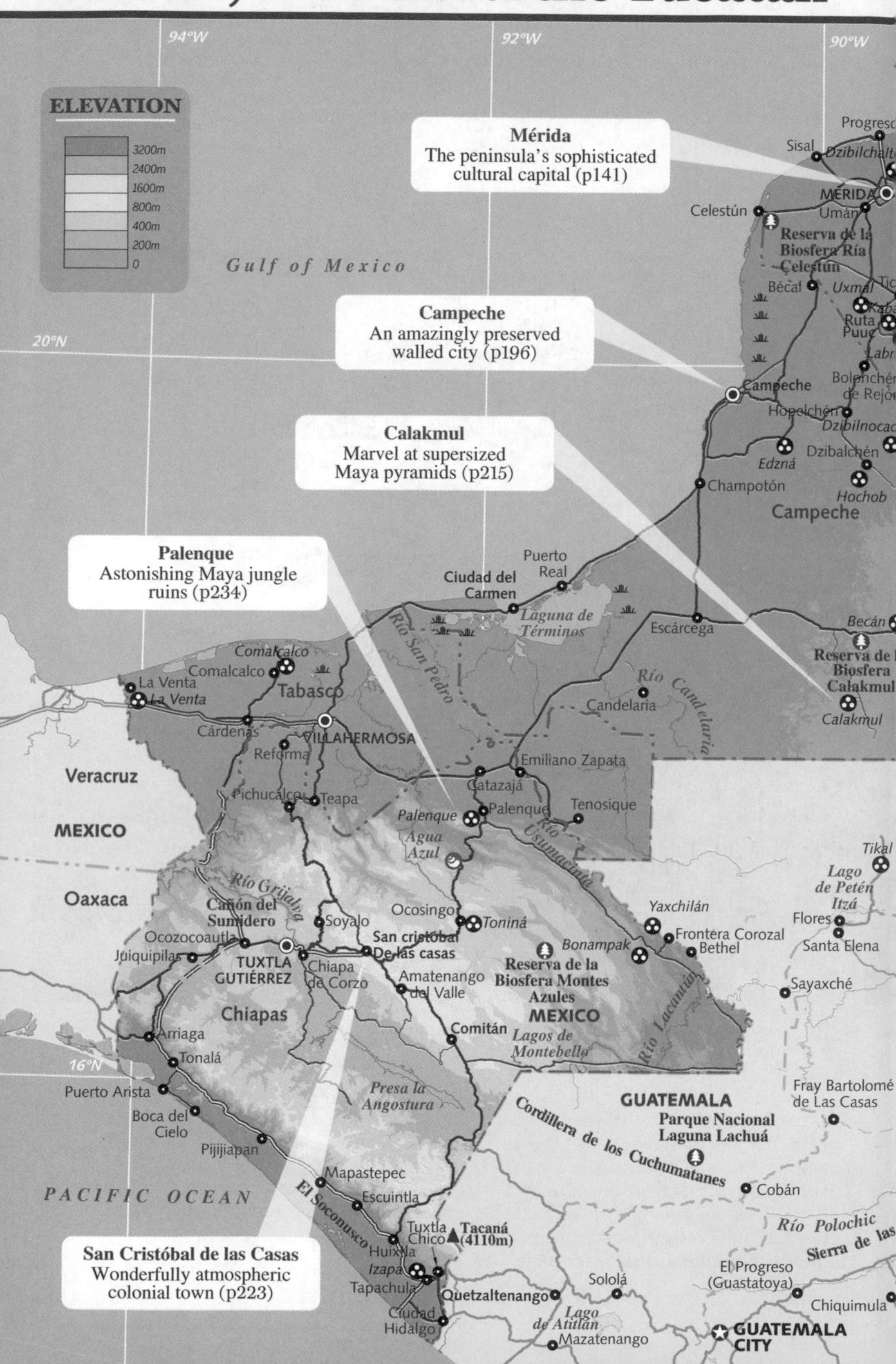

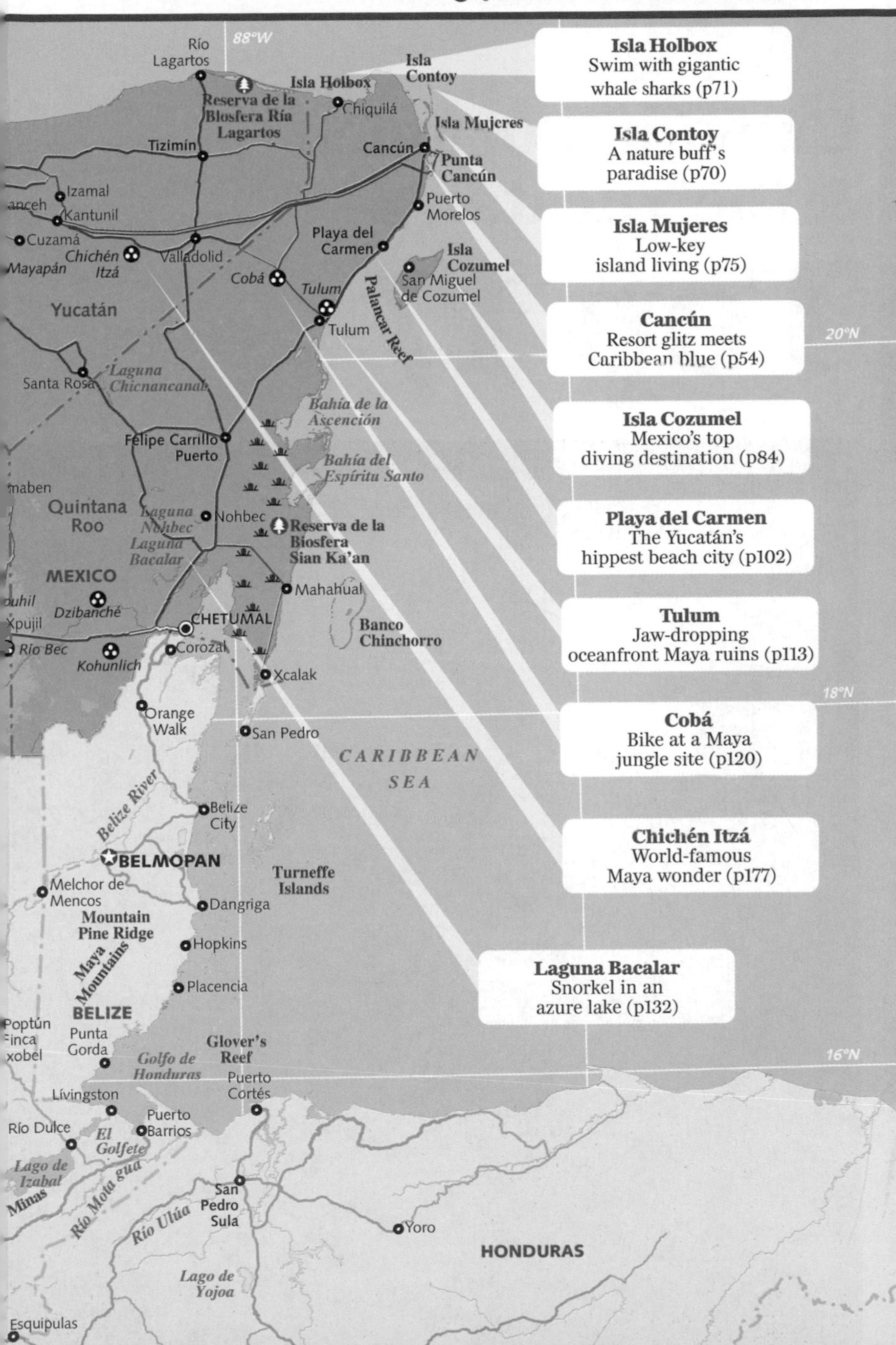

0 200 km
0 120 miles
Isla Holbox
Swim with gigantic whale sharks (p71)
Isla Contoy
A nature buff's paradise (p70)
Isla Mujeres
Low-key island living (p75)
Cancún
Resort glitz meets Caribbean blue (p54)
Isla Cozumel
Mexico's top diving destination (p84)
Playa del Carmen
The Yucatán's hippest beach city (p102)
Tulum
Jaw-dropping oceanfront Maya ruins (p113)
Cobá
Bike at a Maya jungle site (p120)
Chichén Itzá
World-famous Maya wonder (p177)
Laguna Bacalar
Snorkel in an azure lake (p132)
Río Lagartos
88°W
Isla Holbox
Isla Contoy
Reserva de la Biosfera Ría Lagartos
Chiquilá
Isla Mujeres
Tizimín
Cancún
Punta Cancún
Izamal
Kantunil
Puerto Morelos
Cuzamá
Playa del Carmen
Isla Cozumel
Chichén Itzá
Valladolid
Mayapán
Cobá
Tulum
San Miguel de Cozumel
Palancar Reef
Yucatán
Tulum
20°N
Santa Rosa
Laguna Chicnancanab
Bahía de la Ascención
Felipe Carrillo Puerto
Bahía del Espíritu Santo
Quintana Roo
Laguna Nohbec
Nohbec
Reserva de la Biosfera Sian Ka'an
Laguna Bacalar
MEXICO
Mahahual
Dzibanché
CHETUMAL
Banco Chinchorro
Xpujil
Río Bec
Corozal
Kohunlich
Xcalak
18°N
Orange Walk
San Pedro
CARIBBEAN SEA
Belize River
Belize City
BELMOPAN
Turneffe Islands
Melchor de Mencos
Dangriga
Mountain Pine Ridge
Hopkins
Maya Mountains
Placencia
BELIZE
Poptún
Punta Gorda
Glover's Reef
Golfo de Honduras
16°N
Puerto Cortés
Lívingston
Puerto Barrios
Río Dulce
El Golfete
Lago de Izabal
Río Motagua
San Pedro Sula
Río Ulúa
Yoro
HONDURAS
Lago de Yojoa
Esquipulas

Cancún, Cozumel & the Yucatán's Top 17

1

Swimming in Cenotes

1 The Maya considered them sacred gateways to the underworld. OK, so maybe they had a flair for the dramatic, but once you visit a cenote (a limestone sinkhole) you'll better understand where the Maya were coming from. An estimated 6000 cenotes dot the peninsula; some, like the spectacular pair of caverns at Cenote Dzitnup (p186), make for refreshing, fun-filled swimming holes, while others, such as the underground cave system at Dos Ojos (p111), draw divers from far and wide.

Savor the Flavors

2 If you've never tried regional *yucateco* cuisine, you're in for a real treat. Even by Mexican standards, with its strong culinary tradition, the Yucatán is a foodie's haven. *Yucatecos* (people of the Yucatán Peninsula) are famous for their marinated *pollo* (chicken) and *cochinita* (pork) *pibiles*. Often wrapped in banana leaves and cooked underground for what seems an eternity, this meaty traditional dish reigns supreme on the peninsula. And a visit wouldn't be complete without sampling a delicious homestyle *sopa de lima* (a brothy lime soup). *Buen provecho*!

Below: Tortilla soup

PAUL NICKLEN / GETTY IMAGES ©

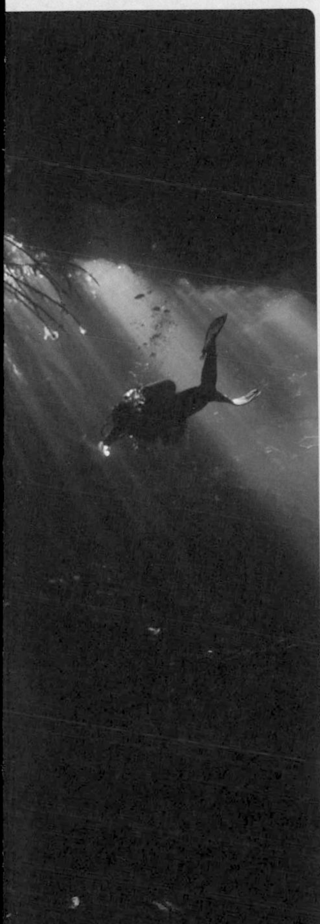

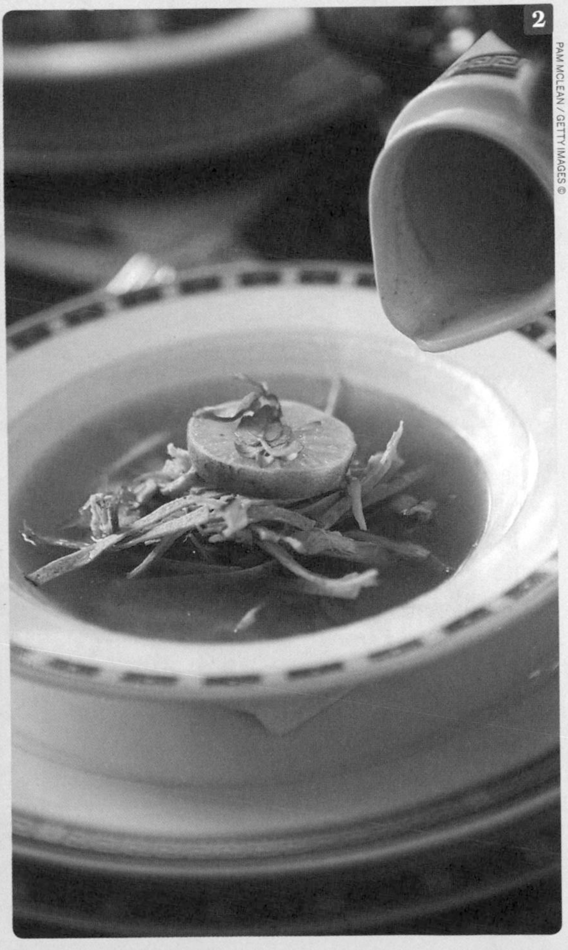

2

PAM MCLEAN / GETTY IMAGES ©

Magical San Cristóbal

3 Wander through the cobblestone streets of San Cristóbal de las Casas (p223), the high-altitude colonial city in the heart of indigenous Chiapas. A heady mix of modern and Maya, with cosmopolitan cafes and traditional culture, it's also a jumping-off point for fascinating Tzotzil and Tzeltal villages. Spend sunny days exploring captivating churches and shopping at markets for amber or chocolate, then dine at one of many gourmet restaurants in town. Late nights are best whiled away by the fireplace of a cozy watering hole.

Calakmul, Jungle Ruins

4 The 'Kingdom of the Serpent's Head' was one of the most powerful Maya cities that ever existed. What has survived the ravages of time here is very impressive – some of the Maya's largest and tallest pyramids, with awesome views of expansive surrounding jungle alive with birds, monkeys and jaguars. And relatively recent excavations at Calakmul (p215) have unearthed an amazing rarity in the Maya world – incredibly well-preserved painted murals and a spectacular stucco frieze.

3

4

WITOLD SKRYPCZAK / GETTY IMAGES ©

NATHAN BLANEY / GETTY IMAGES ©

Diving in Cozumel

5 Don't miss the opportunity to plunge into the colorful waters surrounding Isla Cozumel, one of the world's best diving and snorkeling destinations. While the spectacular coral reefs are undeniably the main draw, the island's beautiful beaches and pleasant town square keep nondiver types sufficiently entertained. If you're planning on visiting in February, don't miss the annual Carnaval (p90), a street celebration infused with lively music, dancing and plenty of partying.

Cancún

6 Cancún may not appeal to everyone, but the resort city certainly has its charms. The Zona Hotelera, for instance, straddles some of the most precious Caribbean coastline in the Yucatán and it boasts the new Museo Maya de Cancún (p56), plus several small Maya ruins. For local flavor, stay in downtown Cancún, where the happening nightlife scene is within stumbling distance of most hotels and the Zona Hotelera's beaches are just a short bus ride away.

Top right: Playa Chac-Mool, Zona Hotelera, Cancún

Morning in Cobá

7 Everyone will tell you to get to the ruins of the Yucatán early to beat the crowds, but at the ruins of Cobá (p120) it really makes a difference. To be there as the jungle awakens – with bird calls and the morning light filtering through the canopy – is magical. The experience of climbing the massive Nohoch Mul pyramid and looking out over the surrounding jungle on your own is unbeatable. Make it even more memorable and explore the ruins on a rented bike.

Above right: Nohoch Mul Pyramid, Cobá

STUART DEE / GETTY IMAGES ©

Playa del Carmen

8 European chic. Nightlife extraordinaire. Rivera Maya boomtown. Oh yeah, Playa del Carmen (p102) has some pretty nice beaches too. And if at any moment you grow tired of wining, dining and dancing under the moon at beachside discos, you'll be happy to know that Playa makes for a convenient base to explore nearby sinkholes, such as Cristalino cenote (p110), and it's also a prime spot for scuba diving and snorkeling.

Isla Mujeres

9 Isla Mujeres (p75) doesn't have the mega-resort mindset of nearby Cancún across the bay, and therein lies its appeal. Even though it's a fairly small island, you should have no problem finding things to do. Scuba diving and snorkeling are big, and it has some of the most swimmable beaches on the Yucatán, making it perfect for kids. The island is also home to the Isla Mujeres Turtle Farm (p77), which releases tens of thousands of turtles each year and has a nice little aquarium.

Top right: Sea turtle

Wonderful Chichén Itzá

10 Ever since Chichén Itzá (p177) was named one of the new seven wonders of the world, it started making its way onto many bucket lists. The massive El Castillo pyramid, Chichén Itzá's most iconic structure, will knock your socks off, especially at vernal and autumnal equinoxes, when morning and afternoon sunlight cast a shadow of a feathered serpent on the staircase.

Above: El Castillo (p180), Chichén Itzá

Isla Contoy

11 Parque Nacional Isla Contoy (p70), an uninhabited island just a short distance from Cancún and Isla Mujeres, allows only 200 visitors a day in order to retain its mostly pristine environment. Home to more than 150 bird species and nesting sea turtles during summer months, the island will definitely appeal to nature lovers and those simply looking to get in a little hiking and snorkeling.

Peerless Palenque

12 Gather all your senses and dive headfirst into these amazing ruins (p234), one of the Maya world's finest. Here pyramids rise above jungle treetops and howler monkeys sound off like monsters in the dense canopy. Wander the mazelike Palace, gazing up at its iconic tower. Scale the stone staircases of the Templo de las Inscripciones, the lavish mausoleum of Pakal. Following the Otulum river and its pretty waterfalls, and end by visiting Palenque's excellent museum.
Bottom: Templo de la Cruz, Palenque

11

12

Campeche's Walled City

13 This lovely colonial city (p196) is a pleasant antidote to the larger, more bustling tourist-filled destinations in other parts of the Yucatán. And since relatively few tourists make it here you'll get more of that real Mexican experience. Campeche's Unesco-listed historic center is like a pastel wonderland, surrounded by high stone walls and home to narrow cobbled streets with well-preserved buildings. Nearby, the *malecón* (beachside promenade) provides a fine place to stroll, people-watch and say goodnight to the setting sun.

Scenic Laguna Bacalar

14 Known as 'the lake of seven colors' for its intense shades of blue and aqua-green, it doesn't get any more scenic for an afternoon swim than sparkling Laguna Bacalar (p132). Resort hotel Rancho Encantado (p133) has quite possibly the best view on the shore, and at the lake's south end you can take a plunge into the 90m-deep Cenote Azul (p132).

Bottom: Cenote Azul

13

14

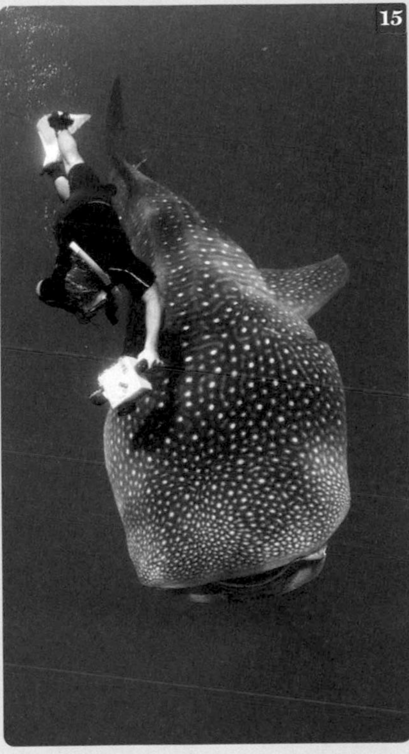

KEREN SU / GETTY IMAGES ©

PAUL THOMPSON / GETTY IMAGES ©

Isla Holbox

15 You gotta love a place with no cars and no banks. Granted, you may see some golf carts humming up and down Holbox's sandy streets for the dinner-hour rush, but that's about as hectic as it gets on this low-key fisherfolks' island (p71). Snorkeling with 15-ton whale sharks is all the rage at Holbox these days. Even if you miss whale-shark season, boat tours go to a freshwater spring and nearby islands for some excellent bird-watching.

Above left: whale shark

Mérida, Cultural Capital

16 Everyone who goes to Cancún or Playa del Carmen should carve off a couple days to get to Mérida (p141), a town with awesome Spanish colonial architecture unlike anything you'll find by the sea. The weekends see great citywide parties: the city center closes to cars and you can munch on *yucateco* street eats as you watch all sorts of spirited song-and-dance around the main plaza, aka Plaza Grande. And living up to its fame as the peninsula's cultural capital, Mérida abounds with museums and art galleries.

Tulum, Scenic Ruins

17 Talk about your prime beachfront real estate! The dramatically situated Tulum ruins (p113) sit pretty, atop a high cliff overlooking a spectacular white-sand beach. After marveling at the sun-baked Maya ruins, and dodging iguanas and distracted tourists, you can cap off your history lesson with a refreshing dip in the azure waters of the Mexican Caribbean. Come nighttime, join in on soulful fiestas in bars along Tulum Pueblo's main strip or escape to the Zona Hotelera for a quiet oceanfront dinner.

Bottom right: El Castillo and ruins, Tulum

Need to Know

For more information, see Survival Guide (p277)

Currency
Mexican peso (M$)

Language
Spanish, Maya

Visas
Tourist permit required; some nationalities also need visas

Money
ATMs widely available in big cities and most towns. Credit cards accepted in many midrange and top-end hotels and restaurants.

Cell Phones
Many US cell-phone companies offer Mexico roaming deals. Local SIM cards can only be used on phones that have been unlocked.

Time
Central Standard Time (GMC/UTC minus six hours)

When to Go

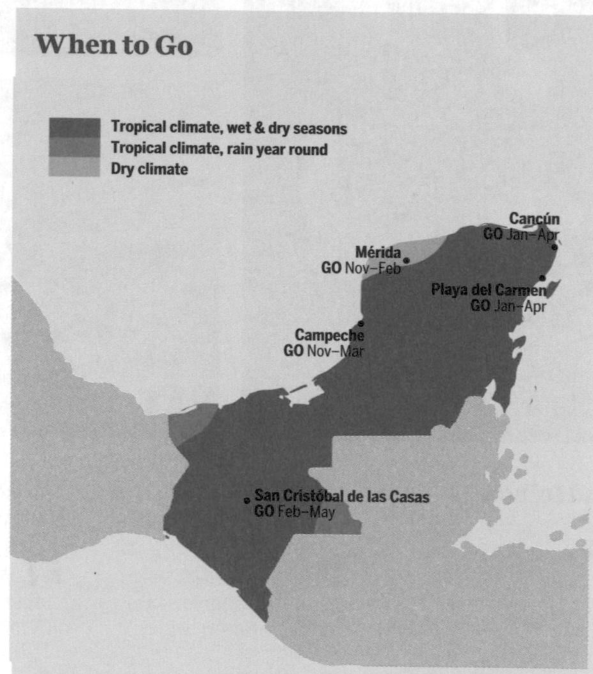

High Season
(Dec-Apr)

- Remains dry for the most part, but so-called *'nortes'* bring northerly winds and occasional showers.
- Hotel rates increase considerably, even more so during 'ultra' high-season periods around Christmas and Easter.

Shoulder Season
(Jul & Aug)

- Very hot and humid throughout the peninsula. Hurricane season begins.
- Vacationing Mexicans flock to the beaches to beat the heat.

Low Season
(May, Jun, Sep-Nov)

- Weather cools down from September to November. Hurricane and rainy seasons end in October.
- Great deals on hotels. Crowds thin out at ruins, beaches and other popular attractions.

Websites

Yucatán Today (www.yucatantoday.com) Online version of free monthly magazine covering Yucatán and Campeche states.

Loco Gringo (www.locogringo.com) A good site to book homes and hotels on the Riviera Maya.

Lonely Planet (www.lonelyplanet.com/mexico) Lonely Planet's Mexico portal.

Yucatán Tierra de Maravillas (www.yucatan.travel) Yucatan state tourism site.

Riviera Maya (www.rivieramaya.com) Has info on the Riviera Maya's sights and activities.

Campeche Travel (www.campeche.travel) Campeche state tourism board site.

Important Numbers

Police	☎066
Fire	☎068
Tourist assistance	☎078
Country code	☎52
International access code	☎00

Exchange Rates

Australia	A$1	M$13.13
Canada	C$1	M$12.70
Euro zone	€1	M$17.01
Japan	¥100	M$13.74
New Zealand	NZ$1	M$10.63
UK	UK£1	M$21.60
USA	US$1	M$12.73

Daily Costs

Budget: Less than M$500

- Dorm bed: M$130-200
- Double room in budget hotel: M$350-400
- Street eats or economical set menu: M$20-50
- City bus: M$5-10

Midrange: M$1000-1500

- Double room in comfortable hotel: M$600-1200
- Lunch or dinner in decent restaurant: M$150-250
- Short taxi trip: M$20-50
- Sightseeing, activities: M$200

Top End: More than M$2000

- Double room in upscale hotel: from M$1200
- Dining in fine restaurant: M$250-500
- Car rental: from M$600 per day
- Tours: M$1000-2500

Opening Hours

Here we've provided high-season opening hours; hours at some places may decrease during shoulder and low seasons. Some shops, restaurants and hotels may close for several weeks – or several months – during low season.

Banks 9am-4pm Monday to Friday, 10am-2pm Saturday (some banks do not open Saturday and hours may vary)

Bars and clubs 10pm-3am

Stores & shops 9am-8pm Monday to Saturday

Archaeological sites 8am-5pm

Museums 9am-5pm Tuesday to Sunday

Arriving in Cancún, Cozumel & Yucatán

Aeropuerto Internacional de Cancún Yellow Transfers shuttles, with ticket offices inside the terminal, cost M$160 per person to Ciudad Cancún or the Zona Hotelera. ADO buses (M$52) go to the downtown bus station. Regular taxis and private vans charge M$450 to M$500.

Cozumel Airport Shared shuttle vans from the airport into town cost M$60. For hotels on the island's north end, the shuttles charge M$96 and to the south side expect to pay between M$97 and M$140.

Mérida airport Curbside Transporte Terrestre taxis charge M$180 per carload to downtown. Buses (M$8) do not enter the airport; catch one on the main road if you don't mind walking.

Getting Around

Shared Van *Colectivos* (shared vans) are quicker and cheaper than buses. Most have frequent departures.

Bus 1st- and 2nd-class buses go pretty much everywhere in the Yucatán.

Car Great option for traveling outside big cities. Expect to pay about M$750 a day for rental and gas.

For much more on getting around, see p290

First Time Cancún, Cozumel & the Yucatán

For more information, see Survival Guide (p277)

Checklist

- Make sure you have a valid passport
- Check if your country requires a visa to enter Mexico (p287)
- Inform your debit/credit card company of your travels
- Get necessary vaccinations (p282)
- Book hotels in advance
- Look in to travel insurance options (p283)
- Check if you can use your cell phone (p286)
- Check your airline's baggage restrictions

What to Pack

- Passport
- Credit and/or debit card
- Driver's license (if driving)
- Scuba or snorkel gear
- Sunscreen
- Insect repellent
- Swim suit
- Phrasebook
- Camera
- Pocketknife
- Cell phone and charger

Top Tips for Your Trip

- For beaches and scuba diving, visit the peninsula's Caribbean side. For culture, Maya ruins and nature experiences, go west.
- Avoid staying in accommodations where mosquitoes may be a problem. If you're unfortunate enough to get pricked by one carrying the dengue virus, expect to spend several days in bed.
- Visiting Maya communities brings money into local economies and the experience leaves you with a lasting impression.
- Driving at night in Mexico can be very dangerous. If you must do it, toll highways have better lighting and fewer potholes than the *libre* (free) roads.

What to Wear

Keep in mind that the Yucatán, especially in Mérida, gets very hot in the months of April and May, so bring light and loose-fitting clothes to stay cool. If you're staying on the coast or in cool inland areas, bring a light sweater or jacket for evenings. Take long-sleeve shirts and long pants/skirts for protection against mosquitoes, especially if you plan to be near mangrove swamps or jungles; this attire is also good for formal restaurants and for visiting nonbeach towns, where you'll see fewer people wearing shorts and tank tops.

Sleeping

If you're planning on visiting during high season (mid-December to April), it's a good idea to book your accommodation in advance. See p278 for more information.

- **Hotels** Range from budget digs to all-inclusive resorts
- **Guesthouses** Family-run houses that usually provide good value and more personable service.
- **Hostels** The most affordable option and a great way to meet other travelers.
- **Bungalows** From cheap cabins to elegant, boutique setups.
- **B&Bs** A little more intimate and slightly more upscale than some guesthouses.

Money

ATMs can be found in all major and medium-size cities and most small towns. In towns with just one or two ATMs, the machines might run out of money, so bring extra cash just in case. For security, use ATMs during the day; also be aware that every time you pull out money you'll be charged 'service fees.' Most midrange and top-end hotels and restaurants accept major credit cards; Visa is the most commonly accepted. Plan on making all cash purchases with Mexican pesos. You can exchange cash at banks or money-exchange offices.

For more information, see p284.

Bargaining

Most stores and shops have set prices. You can do some friendly haggling in some arts and crafts markets, but don't get carried away – most of the artisans are just trying to make a living.

Tipping

- **Hotels** About 5% to 10% of room costs for staff
- **Restaurants** Leave 15% if service is not already included in the check
- **Supermarkets** Baggers usually get M$3 to M$5
- **Porters** Tip M$20 per bag
- **Taxis** Drivers don't expect tips unless they provide an extra service
- **Bars** Bartenders usually don't get tipped, so anything is appreciated

Language

English is widely spoken in Cancún and the Riviera Maya. Elsewhere on the peninsula, you can get by with English in the main tourist centers, but outside of these Spanish is useful. Any effort to speak Spanish is appreciated. See Language for more information.

Phrases to Learn Before You Go

Where can I buy handicrafts?
¿Dónde se puede comprar artesanías?
don·de se *pwe*·de kom·*prar* ar·te·sa·*nee*·as

Star buys in Mexico are the regional handicrafts produced all over the country, mainly by the indigenous people.

Which *antojitos* do you have?
¿Qué antojitos tiene? ke an·to·*khee*·tos *tye*·ne

'Little whimsies' (snacks) can encompass anything – have an entire meal of them, eat a few as appetisers, or get one on the street for a quick bite.

Not too spicy, please.
No muy picoso, por favor. no mooy pee·*ko*·so por fa·*vor*

Not all food in Mexico is spicy, but beware – many dishes can be fierce indeed, so it may be a good idea to play it safe.

Where can I find a *cantina* nearby?
¿Dónde hay una cantina cerca de aquí?
don·de ai *oo*·na kan·*tee*·na *ser*·ka de a·*kee*

Ask locals about the classical Mexican venue for endless snacks, and often dancing as well.

How do you say ... in your language?
¿Cómo se dice ... en su lengua?
ko·mo se *dee*·se ... en su *len*·gwa

Numerous indigenous languages are spoken around Mexico, primarily Mayan languages and Náhuatl. People will appreciate it if you try to use their local language.

Etiquette

- **Greetings** A handshake is standard when meeting people for the first time. Among friends, men usually exchange back-slapping hugs; for women it's usually an (air) kiss on the cheek.
- **Conversation** *Yucatecos* are generally warm and entertaining conversationalists. As a rule, they express disagreement more by nuance than by contradiction. The Maya can be more reserved.

Safety

Is it safe to go to the Yucatán, given all the news about Mexico's drug-related violence? The answer is yes. Yucatán has barely been touched by the violence, which is mostly in northern Mexico. Safety precautions are as they would be for anywhere else in the world (such as avoiding hitch-hiking and not putting up resistance if mugged).

If You Like...

Maya Ruins

The peninsula boasts some of the best-preserved and most remarkable ruins in all of Mexico.

Chichén Itzá Recently named one of the 'new seven wonders of the world.' Enough said. (p177)

Tulum Maya ruins perched atop a cliff with jaw-dropping views of the Caribbean blue down below. (p113)

Cobá A sprawling site in a jungle setting that's best explored on a bicycle. (p121)

Calakmul High pyramids sit pretty in a huge Maya city tucked away in a rainforest. (p215)

Palenque Exquisite Maya temples backed by steamy, jungle-covered hills. (p234)

Uxmal Set in the hilly Puuc region, this site contains some of the most fascinating structures you'll ever see. (p159)

Yaxchilán Half the fun is getting there on a riverboat adventure deep in the Chiapas jungle. (p240)

Beach Resorts

There's more to the beach resort experience than white sands and turquoise waters. Each destination has its own unique vibe.

Cancún The mother of all megaresorts is part glitzy hotel zone, part downtown scene with local flavor. (p56)

Isla Cozumel A popular divers' destination with a pleasant town square and surprisingly quiet beaches. (p84)

Isla Mujeres Has some of the most gorgeous beaches around but is more low-key than Cancún and Cozumel. (p75)

Playa del Carmen The hippest beach town on the coast – European chic meets the Mexican Caribbean. (p102)

Tulum Idyllic beachside bungalows coupled with a buzzing, friendly inland town. (p113)

Puerto Morelos Calm, small-town feel, plus great diving and snorkeling. (p99)

IF YOU LIKE... TURTLES

Check out the Isla Mujeres Turtle Farm, which liberates more than 100,000 of these little guys each year. (p77)

Colonial Towns

The 300-year period of Spanish rule left behind awesome plazas and opulent mansions and haciendas.

Mérida Even if you're not big on architecture, the stately mansions in the peninsula's cultural capital never cease to amaze. (p141)

Campeche The protective walls once used to fend off pirate attacks still stand today. (p196)

Valladolid Think Mérida without the grandeur. Colonial flavor here comes on a smaller, more intimate scale. (p184)

San Cristóbal de las Casas The cobbled streets of San Cristóbal lead to splendid colonial-era churches. (p223)

Izamal Smack in the middle of town rises the imposing Convento de San Antonio de Padua. (p175)

Diving & Snorkeling

Not only does this region have some of the best reef diving in the world it also offers fascinating dives in cave systems.

Isla Cozumel The famed reefs of this island draw diving

Top: Tulum (p113), Riviera Maya
Bottom: Cathedral, Campeche (p196)

aficionados from all over the world. (p84)

Banco Chinchorro The largest coral atoll in the western hemisphere; known for its colorful underwater scenery and sunken ships. (p129)

Isla Holbox During summer months you can snorkel with whale sharks off the coast of this low-key island. (p71)

Isla Mujeres Offers excellent reef diving and there's a new underwater sculpture museum in the area. (p77)

Tulum Nearby cenotes (limestone sinkholes) provide wonderful opportunities to snorkel and dive in caverns and caves. (p115)

Puerto Morelos Get in some wreck diving here; the barrier reef is just 600m offshore. (p99)

Regional Cuisine

The Yucatán is unquestionably one of Mexico's most remarkable culinary destinations.

Kinich Exquisitely prepared traditional dishes – try the *papadzules* (egg enchiladas) and you'll understand why. (p176)

La Chaya Maya A trip to Mérida wouldn't be complete without a meal or three at the Chaya. (p152)

La Fuente Well-known in Ciudad del Carmen for its *pibipollo* (chicken tamales cooked underground). (p213)

Manjar Blanco Offers a contemporary take on classic *yucateco* dishes, such as *poc-chuc* (grilled pork). (p152)

La Cueva del Chango Uses fresh, natural ingredients accented with local flavors of the peninsula. (p107)

Arts & Crafts

Hamacas El Aguacate Who doesn't like to catch a siesta on a quality hammock? Buy one here, then it's sweet dreams baby. (p155)

Artisans' Market A main attraction in Puerto Morelos, this market sells authentic Tixkokob hammocks and fine jewelry at fair prices. (p101)

Bazar Artesanal Campeche's Folk Art Bazaar is a one-stop shop for regional crafts. (p204)

Los Cinco Soles Pick up black ceramics from Oaxaca and Talavera pottery at this Isla Cozumel crafts store. (p94)

Mercado Municipal Ki-Huic A labyrinthine downtown Cancún market carrying a wide variety of handicrafts. (p67)

Centro Cultural y Artesanal Crafts purchases here help support rural indigenous families. (p176)

Nature Experiences

The peninsula spoils nature lovers silly with its wide array of wildlife in biosphere reserves and national parks.

Reserva de la Biosfera Ría Celestún Head out to the mangroves here to spy flamingos and crocs. (p170)

Reserva de la Biosfera Ría Lagartos Experienced guides lead bird-watching and snorkeling tours in this magnificent reserve. (p190)

Parque Nacional Isla Contoy An uninhabited island that's home to more than 150 bird species and provides nesting grounds for sea turtles as well. (p70)

Reserva de la Biosfera Pantanos de Centla This massive reserve in Tabasco has glorious lakes, marshes, rivers and, of course, abundant wildlife. (p228)

Reserva de la Biosfera Sian Ka'an A sprawling jungle – the dwelling of howler monkeys, jaguars, pumas and hundreds of bird species. (p124)

Nightlife & Dancing

Mambo Café Groove to live Cuban salsa music at this downtown Cancún nightclub. (p66)

Papaya Playa Project The Tribal Room at this hotel has been known to throw a fair number of wild beach parties. (p119)

La Fundación Mezcalería Sip some smoky *mezcals* (alcoholic agave drink) at this happening Mérida retro bar. (p153)

Fusion The beach often becomes an impromptu stage for fire dancers at this cool Playa del Carmen bar. (p108)

Salón Rincón Colonial An atmospheric Cuban-style drinking establishment that served as a location for the Antonio Banderas flick *Original Sin*. (p204)

Swimming

Between cenotes, swimmable beaches and spectacular pools, you can enjoy a perfectly amphibious existence here.

Cenote Dzitnup A lovely cavern pool near Valladolid with *álamo* (poplar) roots stretching down many meters. (p186)

Playa Norte Swimming in the shallow, crystalline waters of this Isla Mujeres beach is heavenly. (p76)

Le Blanc This Cancún resort hotel boasts a gorgeous azure infinity pool overlooking the Caribbean Sea. (p64)

Cristalino Cenote A quiet spot with mangrove on one side and a large open section you can dive into. (p110)

Xcaret Kids love swimming and snorkeling in underground rivers and caves in this Riviera Maya fun park. (p102)

Getaway Destinations

Xcalak No cruise ships, no gas stations, no banks and a wonderful barrier reef – the Caribbean coast as it once was. (p131)

Río Lagartos Nature tours and whiling away the time in a sleepy fishing village on the northern coast. (p190)

Punta Allen The road to this remote beach community ain't pretty but the village sure is. (p124)

San Crisanto Palm groves; quiet, white-sand beaches; and a few rustic cabins: it's the ultimate escapist's retreat. (p175)

Corozal, Belize Not much happens in this small coastal

IF YOU LIKE... SPICY FOOD

The Yucatán is home to the four-alarm habanero chili, one of the hottest peppers on the planet. (p262)

Ceramic skulls, Chichén Itzá

community and that's what makes it so darn appealing. (p138)

Family-Friendly Trips

Riviera Maya The land of theme parks, swimming opportunities galore and excellent diving. (p97)

Cancún Plenty of water-related activities, hotels with kids' clubs and tours geared toward children. (p54)

Valladolid The nearby cenotes make a big splash with the little ones and the town's pyramids are fun to climb. (p184)

Campeche Pirate-themed cruises and a walled city full of swashbuckler legends makes for good family entertainment. (p194)

Progreso A popular family beach destination, first and foremost because you can holiday on the cheap here. (p173)

Studying Spanish

Take classes in the Yucatán's cultural capital of Mérida at the non-profit **Instituto Benjamín Franklin**. (p148)

Head down to the lovely San Cristóbal de las Casas and brush up on your skills at **El Puente Spanish Language School**. (p227)

Between beach-bumming and scuba diving, squeeze in a few hours of class at the **Puerto Morelos Language Center**. (p100)

Ask about very affordable homestays at the **International House** in Playa del Carmen. (p103)

Once you've mastered Spanish, take a Maya language course at **Playa Lingua del Caribe** in the Riviera Maya. (p105)

Month by Month

TOP EVENTS

Vernal Equinox, March

Swimming with Whale Sharks, June

Carnaval, February

Día de Muertos, November

Mérida Fest, January

January

The first week of January is one of the busiest times of the year, meaning hotel rates spike. Weather-wise, it's relatively cool.

Mérida Fest

This cultural event, running most of January across the city, celebrates the founding of Mérida with art exhibits, concerts, plays and book presentations.

Día de los Reyes Magos

(Three Kings' Day) On January 6, this is the day when Mexican children traditionally receive gifts, rather than at Christmas. A good place to be at this time is Tizimín.

February

Temperatures rise slightly and it stays fairly dry. It's still considered high season but most destinations have quietened down significantly.

Día de la Candelaría

Held on February 2, Candlemas commemorates the presentation of Jesus in the temple 40 days after his birth; celebrated in many towns with processions, bullfights and dancing.

Carnaval

A big street bash preceding the 40-day penance of Lent, Carnaval is usually in February or March. It's festively celebrated in Mérida, Campeche and Isla Cozumel with parades, music, dancing and fun.

March

The thermometer rises a few notches in more ways than one as US spring breakers flock to the peninsula for tequila-fueled revelry.

Spring Break

Bust out that beer bong. Most university students get midterm break in March and Cancún is the preferred destination – so either join the party or head for the hills.

Vernal Equinox

On the day of the spring equinox (March 20) and about a week thereafter, thousands head to Chichén Itzá to witness the shadow formation of a serpent appear on the staircase of the El Castillo pyramid. (p177)

April

One of the hottest and driest months of the year on the peninsula. Semana Santa brings out Mexican tourists in droves as they look to cool off at the beach.

Semana Santa

Held throughout Holy Week (starting on Palm Sunday, in March or April), solemn processions move through the streets. On Good Friday (Viernes Santo) there are dramatic re-enactments of the Passion Play.

Feria de San Cristóbal

Starting on Easter Sunday, the week-long Feria de la Primavera y de la Paz in San Cristóbal de las Casas features art shows, song and dance, amusement rides, bullfights, fireworks and, of course, lots of food.

May

A scorcher of a month, especially in Mérida where the daily high averages around 35°C. Not surprisingly, great hotel deals can be found.

Feria del Cedral

On Isla Cozumel, the entertaining Feria del Cedral honors a group of Caste War refugees who settled on the island in 1848. The fairgrounds have rides, rodeo events and you can see the time-honored 'Dance of the Pigs' Heads.' (p90)

June

It's still very hot and it's the beginning of hurricane season, which runs to November. Tourism slows down considerably.

Swimming with Whale Sharks

A good time to swim with these gentle giants off the coasts of Isla Holbox and Isla Mujeres.

July

Expect warm, wet and humid weather. This is a summer holiday month for both Mexicans and foreigners so don't be surprised to find a lot of activity in tourist centers.

Fiesta de la Virgen del Carmen

For the last two weeks of July, the patron saint of Ciudad del Carmen, Campeche, is taken on a journey over land and across the harbor. The fiesta features artistic and cultural events and craft shows.

August

Summer holiday season continues, as do the rains. Inland spots tend to be sticky this time of year.

Festival Jats'a Já

Held the third weekend of August in Mahahual, this festival is a prayer offering of sorts to the hurricane gods. Traditional Maya dancing, art exhibits and culinary events.

September

The height of the hurricane season, though it shouldn't present a problem if you keep an eye out for alerts. It's also Mexico's most patriotic month of the year.

Día de la Independencia

(Independence Day; September 16) The anniversary of the start of Mexico's War of Independence in 1810. On the evening of the 15th, the famous call to rebellion is repeated from the balcony of every town hall in the land.

October

Cooler climes and slightly less rainfall. If you visit during the last days of October and the first days of November it's interesting to compare Halloween to Day of the Dead celebrations.

Halloween

Playa del Carmen is the scene of a wild, all-night costume party that draws more than its fair share of inebriated zombies.

November

The rainy season has passed and temperatures are subsiding. Some accommodations drop prices by as much as 50%.

Día de Muertos

(Day of the Dead; November 2) Families build altars in their homes and visit graveyards to commune with their dead, taking garlands and gifts. Theme park Xcaret in the Riviera Maya arranges beautiful altars. (p102)

December

***Nortes* (northerly winds that bring showers) are prevalent along the coast from November to January. The first two weeks of December are quiet on the peninsula ahead of the big Christmas rush.**

Plan Your Trip Itineraries

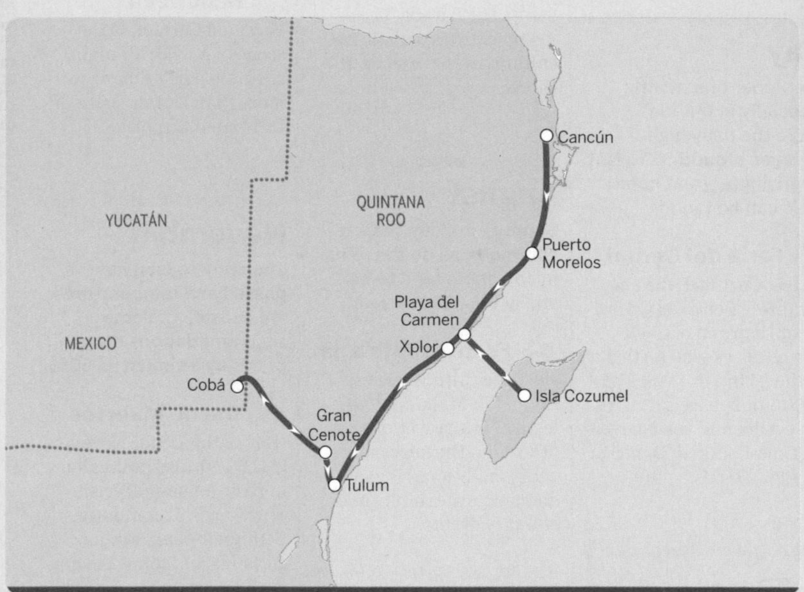

Cancún & the Riviera Maya

The road from Cancún to Cobá is chock full of coast-hugging surprises. Along the way you'll find fun-filled cenotes (limestone sinkholes), astonishing Maya ruins and happening little beach towns with sugar-white sands.

Get things started with a dip in the sapphire waters along the Zona Hotelera (hotel zone) of **Cancún** (p56), then hit downtown and see the other side of the city over dinner and dancing.

Make your way south about 30km and stop in **Puerto Morelos** (p99) to duck out to the beach, then browse for handmade crafts in the small town's artisans market. Spend a day or so beach-bumming and dining in uberchic **Playa del Carmen** (p102). Playa, as it's called, is a good jumping-off point for **Isla Cozumel** (p84), where you'll enjoy amazing diving and snorkeling, quiet beaches on the island's windswept side and a pleasant town plaza. If you've brought kids, head back to the mainland and visit one of the theme parks just south of Playa, such as **Xplor** (p102) with its underground river-raft rides.

You'll definitely want to visit Maya ruins and it's hard to imagine a more

El Castillo, Tulum

spectacular location than **Tulum** (p113), where structures are perched atop a cliff overlooking the Mexican Caribbean. While at the site, take the stairs down to the beach and have a refreshing swim to cool off. Tulum's town and its coastal Zona Hotelera are destinations in their own right. Stay in a bungalow on the sand and at night paint the town red along the buzzing main strip.

With an early start, head for the Maya ruins of **Cobá** (p120; find the road to Cobá at Tulum's north end). Once inside this archaeological site, rent a bicycle and marvel at jungle ruins connected by ancient paths. Before heading back to Tulum, have lunch at one of Cobá's lakeside restaurants. On the return, drop by the **Gran Cenote** (p120) for a little swimming and snorkeling action.

This easy 170km trip stays close to Cancún and there's frequent bus service to all of these destinations, or just rent a car.

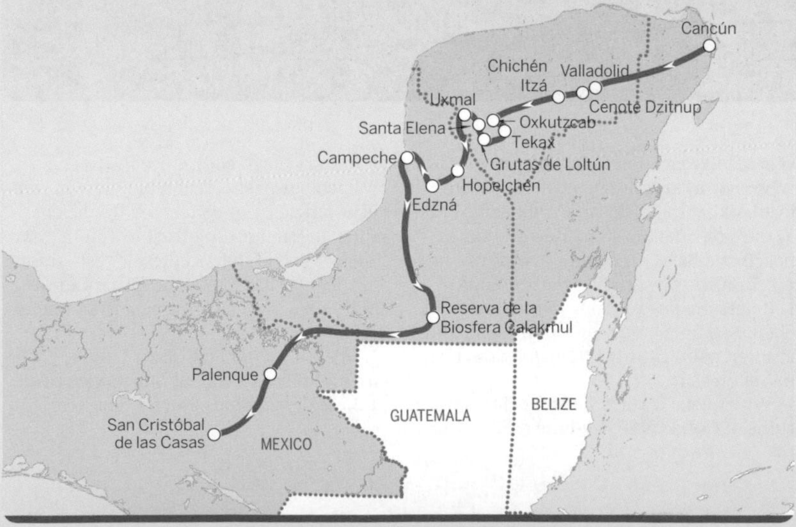
Cancún
Chichén Itzá
Valladolid
Cenote Dzitnup
Uxmal
Santa Elena
Oxkutzcab
Tekax
Grutas de Loltún
Campeche
Hopelchén
Edzná
Reserva de la Biosfera Calakmul
Palenque
San Cristóbal de las Casas
MEXICO
GUATEMALA
BELIZE

PHILIPPE COLOMBI / GETTY IMAGES ©

COSMO CONDINA / GETTY IMAGES ©

Top: Ruins, Palenque
Bottom: Folkloric dancers

Maya Country

The architectural and artistic achievements of the Maya are prominently dotted across the peninsula. Though the ancient cities are long abandoned, the Maya people and their traditions are still very much present. One can spend weeks, even months, visiting all of the ruins, archaeological museums and small Maya towns – this itinerary assumes you have a life to get back to.

For background, visit the shiny new **Museo Maya de Cancún** (p56) in the heart of the resort city's Zona Hotelera. The price of admission includes access to the adjoining **San Miguelito** (p56) archaeological site, which features Maya ruins that were just recently unveiled. Hit the road the next day and spend a day or two in the colonial town of **Valladolid** (p184), a former Maya ceremonial center. For some respite from your Maya itinerary, drop by the **Cenote Dzitnup** (p186) on your way out of town and take a plunge into a spectacular limestone sinkhole. Next up is must-see **Chichén Itzá** (p177), Maya ruins that were recently named one of the 'new seven wonders of the world.' Get an early start to beat the tour bus crowds.

A route then leads to **Oxkutzcab** and **Tekax**, offering glimpses of traditional Maya life. While in Oxkutzcab, be sure to check out the nearby **Grutas de Loltún** (p164), the largest cave system on the peninsula. Move on to **Santa Elena**, a fine base for exploring the impressive ruins of **Uxmal** (p159) and other archaeological sites tucked away in the rolling Puuc hills.

After crossing the Yucatán-Campeche border, stop at **Hopelchén** (p207), where you can witness the ancient arts of beekeeping and herbal medicine. Make your way to the walled city of **Campeche** (p196), a good base for visiting **Edzná** (p209), a formidable Maya site with a five-story temple. The peninsula's south harbors fascinating but scarcely visited remnants of classic Maya civilization in the vast **Reserva de la Biosfera Calakmul** (p215). Serious Maya buffs should visit the ruins of **Palenque** (p234) and the contemporary Maya domain of **San Cristóbal de las Casas** (p223), both in Chiapas.

Most destinations here are accessible by bus or shared transport vehicles, but for some, such as the Ruta Puuc ruins, you'll need to hire a rental car or taxi, or go with a tour operator.

Off the Beaten Track: Cancún, Cozumel & the Yucatán

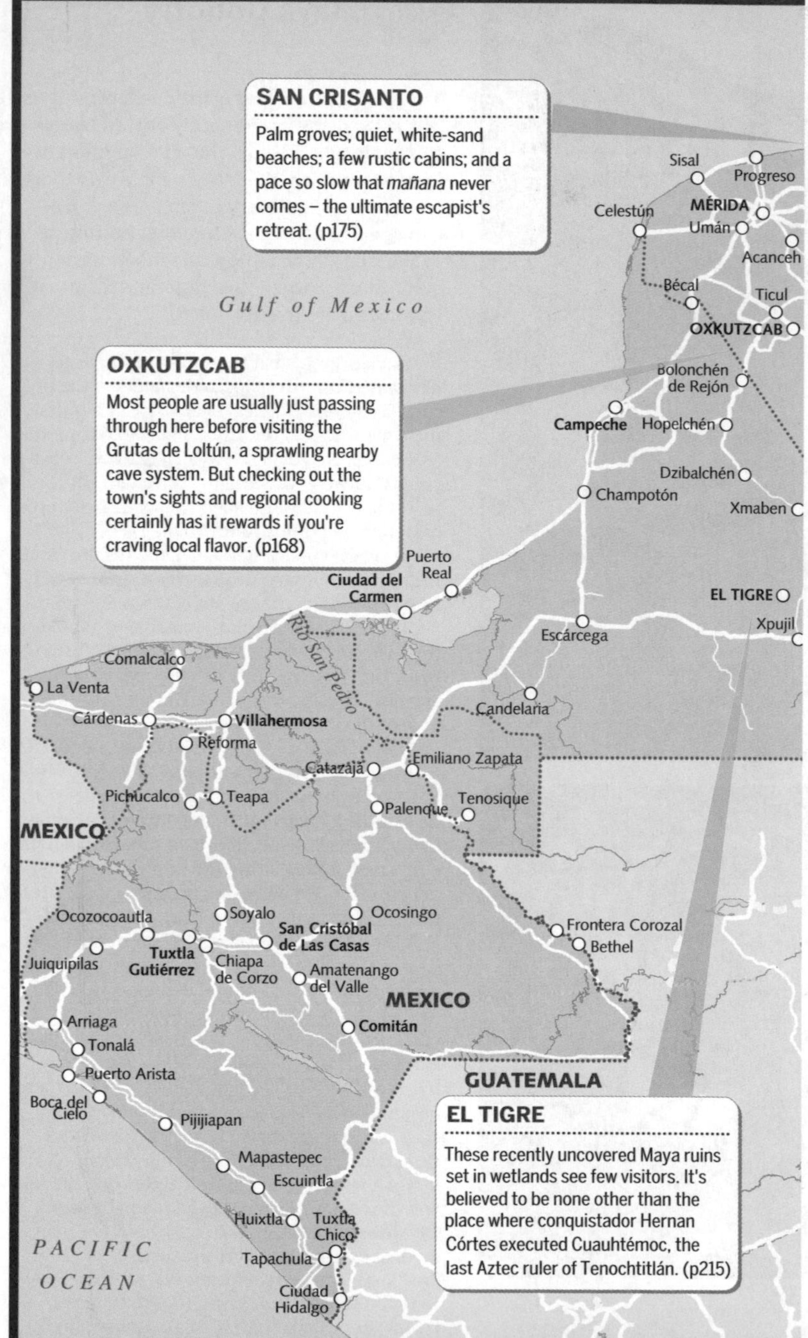

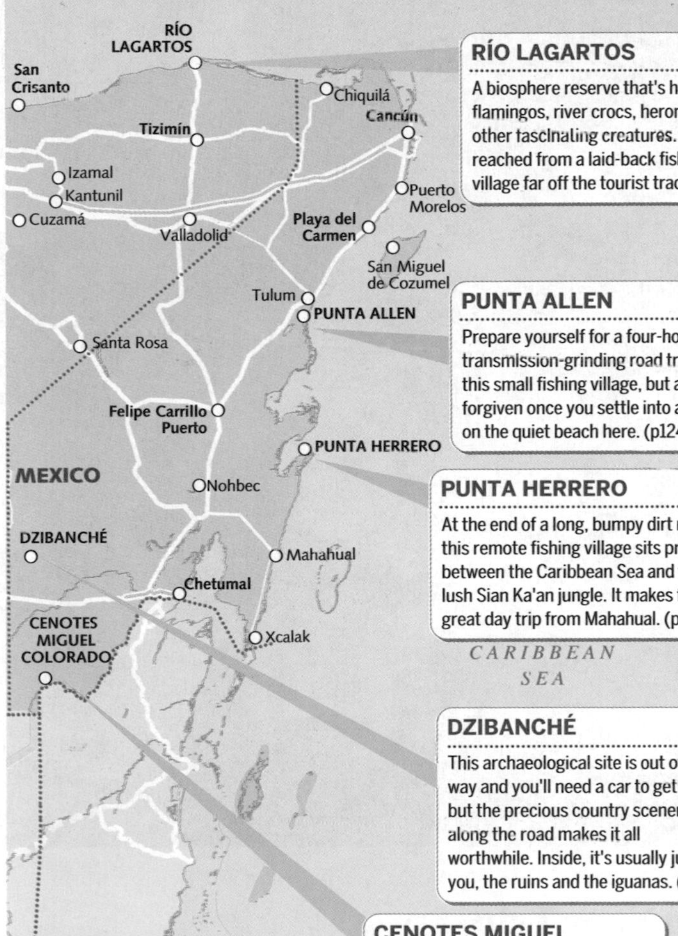

RÍO LAGARTOS

A biosphere reserve that's home to flamingos, river crocs, herons and other fascinating creatures. It's reached from a laid-back fishing village far off the tourist track. (p190)

PUNTA ALLEN

Prepare yourself for a four-hour, transmission-grinding road trip to this small fishing village, but all is forgiven once you settle into a hotel on the quiet beach here. (p124)

PUNTA HERRERO

At the end of a long, bumpy dirt road, this remote fishing village sits pretty between the Caribbean Sea and the lush Sian Ka'an jungle. It makes for a great day trip from Mahahual. (p129)

DZIBANCHÉ

This archaeological site is out of the way and you'll need a car to get here, but the precious country scenery along the road makes it all worthwhile. Inside, it's usually just you, the ruins and the iguanas. (p136)

CENOTES MIGUEL COLORADO

A 10km potholed road leads to the village of Miguel Colorado, where you can set out on a hike along rocky trails to reach two wonderfully scenic cenotes (limestone sinkholes). Swimming is prohibited but you can take a kayak out. (p215)

Colorful fish, Cancún (p56

Plan Your Trip

Diving & Snorkeling

The Mexican Caribbean is world famous for its wonderful coral reefs and translucent waters full of tropical fish, and without a doubt diving and snorkeling are the area's top activity draw. Add cenote (limestone sinkhole) dives to the mix and you truly have one of the most intriguing dive destinations on the planet.

Best Dives

Isla Cozumel

Hands down Mexico's most popular scuba-diving location, Cozumel gets high praise for its excellent visibility and wide variety of marine life. The amazing sights are sure to keep even the most experienced diver in a constant state of awe.

Banco Chinchorro

The largest coral atoll in the northern hemisphere, Banco Chinchorro boasts a glorious underwater fantasy world of wrecked ships and colorful reefs. Best of all, rarely will you find crowded dive sites at Chinchorro.

Isla Mujeres

With snorkeler-friendly shallow reefs, shark caves and an underwater sculpture museum, Isla Mujeres' sites appeal to both novice and advanced divers. From June to September you can snorkel with 15-ton whale sharks.

Diving

Isla Cozumel

If you can visit only one dive destination in Mexico, the wonderful underwater world of Isla Cozumel is your best bet. Once a pilgrimage site of the Maya and little more than a small fishing community up until the late 1950s, today Cozumel and its astoundingly rich reefs draw divers from far and wide.

Drift diving is the norm in Cozumel – local divers say there's nothing like the sensation of gliding through the water as you're carried by the strong currents. So what can you see? Imposing drop-off wall reefs, sea turtles, moray eels, black grouper, barracuda, rainbow parrotfish, large coral and giant Caribbean anemones.

Although Cozumel was hammered by two hurricanes (Emily and Wilma) in 2005, most of the island's diveable reefs, and all of the deeper ones, remained unharmed. Unsurprisingly, it was the snorkeling sites that were hardest hit; but thanks to the tireless efforts of the local diving community (whose livelihood depends on the health of the reefs) and to the resilience of this amazing ecosystem, things have returned to normal.

If you're a diver heading to this area, Cozumel's Santa Rosa Wall, Punta Sur Reef and Palancar Gardens are well worth visiting. Snorkelers will want to check out Dzul-Há, near the town of San Miguel de Cozumel, and Colombia Shallows on the island's south side.

For more on what Cozumel has to offer, check out Lonely Planet's *Cozumel: Diving & Snorkeling* guide.

Other Diving Spots

Serious divers will be happy to know that there are great dives to be enjoyed all along the eastern coast of the Yucatán Peninsula. Cancún, Isla Mujeres, Puerto Morelos, Playa del Carmen, Mahahual and Xcalak are all prime places to plan a diving vacation.

The Banco Chinchorro (p129), a sprawling coral atoll off the southern Quintana Roo coast, was pounded by Hurricane Dean in 2007, but the government has designated new dive sites so that the hardest-hit areas can recover. Home to more than 90 coral species, the biosphere reserve of Chinchorro gets fewer visitors than the reefs of Cozumel and Isla Mujeres, making it a much more attractive option for serious divers. Here you can see rays, eels, conch and giant sponges.

In the national marine park of Cancún there's an interesting new snorkeling and diving attraction known as the MUSA (p57), an underwater sculpture museum created by British artist and diving aficionado Jason deCaires Taylor. Built to divert divers away from deteriorating coral reefs, this one-of-a-kind aquatic museum features 403 life-size sculptures in the waters of Cancún and Isla Mujeres. The artificial reefs are submerged at a depth of 28ft, making them ideal for snorkelers and first-time divers.

Cenote Dives

When you find yourself yawning at the green morays, eagle rays, dolphins, sea turtles, nurse sharks and multitudinous tropical fish, you're ready to dive a cenote (a deep limestone sinkhole containing water). Hook up with a reputable dive shop and prepare for (in the immortal words of Monty Python) 'something completely different.' The Maya saw cenotes as gateways to the underworld.

You'll be lucky if you see four fish on a typical cenote dive. Trade brilliance for darkness, blue for black, check that your regulator is working flawlessly and enter a world unlike anything you've ever dived before. Soar around stalactites and stalagmites, hover above cake-frosting-like formations and glide around tunnels that will make you think you're in outer space.

Keep in mind that these are fragile environments. Avoid applying sunscreen or insect repellent right before entering. Use care when approaching, entering or exiting, as the rocks are often slippery. Loud noises, such as yelling, disturb bats and other creatures – though most people find themselves subdued by the presence in these caverns. In rare cases, tourists have been seriously injured or killed by climbing on the roots or stalactites.

Coral reef, Isla Cozumel (p84)

Be very careful when cenote diving: it can be an extremely dangerous activity, especially when done in caves. A good rule of thumb is to go with a professional local diver who has knowledge of the cave system. And above all, do not attempt cave diving without proper training.

WHEN TO GO

Generally, you can dive year-round in the Yucatán, but when planning your trip you should take into account a few weather considerations:

- From November through January, the peninsula gets northerly winds and showers known as *nortes*. In Cozumel they can blow so strongly that the harbormaster closes ports – sometimes for days. While this won't affect the ferry between Cozumel and Playa del Carmen, it can wreck diving plans.
- From June to November, keep a watchful eye out for hurricane alerts.

Snorkeling

Many spots on the Yucatán's Caribbean side make for fine snorkeling. The best sites are generally reached by boat, but the areas near Akumal, Isla Mujeres and Cozumel all offer pretty decent beach-accessed spots. In Cozumel, you'll find some of the most popular snorkeling sites along the western shore.

Inland you can snorkel in some of the Yucatán's famed cenotes. Some places rent gear, but when in doubt take your own.

Snorkeling with whale sharks has become very popular in recent years. Just about all of the dive shops in Isla Mujeres and Isla Holbox offer whale-shark tours. Just make sure before signing up that

Green sea turtle

the tour operator abides by responsible practices recommended by the World Wildlife Fund. Only three swimmers (including your guide) are allowed in the water at a time. Also, you are not allowed to touch these gentle giants, and you must wear either a life jacket or wetsuit to ensure you do not dive below the shark.

Responsible Diving & Snorkeling

Remember that coral reefs and other marine ecosystems are particularly fragile environments. Consider the following tips when diving and help preserve the ecology and beauty of the reefs:

➡ Never use anchors on the reef, and take care not to ground boats on coral.

➡ Avoid touching or standing on living marine organisms or dragging equipment across the reef. Polyps can be damaged by even the gentlest contact. If you must hold on to the reef, only touch exposed rock or dead coral.

➡ Be conscious of your fins. Even without contact, the surge from fin strokes near the reef can damage delicate organisms. Take care not to kick up clouds of sand, which can smother them.

➡ Practice and maintain proper buoyancy control and avoid over-weighting. Major damage can be done by divers descending too fast and colliding with the reef.

➡ Take great care in underwater caves. Spend as little time in them as possible as your air bubbles may be caught within the roof and thereby leave organisms high and dry. Take turns to inspect the interior of a small cave.

➡ Resist the temptation to collect or buy corals or shells or to loot marine archaeological sites (mainly shipwrecks).

➡ Ensure that you take home all your rubbish and any litter you may find as well. Plastics in particular are a serious threat to marine life.

➡ Do not feed the fish. In doing so you may be encouraging aggressive behavior or giving them food that may be harmful to their health.

➡ Minimize your disturbance of marine animals. Never ride on the backs of turtles.

KAREN DOODY / STOCKTREK IMAGES / GETTY IMAGES ©

Diver, Yucatán cenote

Safety

Most dive shops expect that you have your own equipment. If you do rent diving gear, check that it's up to standard. Before embarking on a scuba-diving or snorkeling trip, consider the following tips to ensure a safe and enjoyable experience:

➡ If scuba diving, carry a current diving-certification card from a recognized instruction agency.

➡ Regardless of skill level, you should be in good condition and know your physical limitations.

➡ If you don't have your own equipment, ask to see the dive shop's before you commit. Also, make sure you feel comfortable with your dive master.

➡ Obtain reliable information about physical and environmental conditions at the dive site from a reputable local dive operation, and ask how locally trained divers deal with these considerations.

➡ Be aware of local laws, regulations and etiquette about marine life and the environment.

➡ Dive only at sites within your level of experience: if available, engage the services of a competent, professionally trained dive instructor or dive master.

➡ Avoid decompression sickness by diving no less than 18 hours prior to a high-altitude flight.

➡ Know the locations of the nearest decompression chambers and emergency phone numbers.

➡ Find out if your dive shop has up-to-date certification from **PADI** (www.padi.com), **NAUI** (www.naui.org) or the internationally recognized Mexican diving organization **FMAS** (www.fmas.com.mx).

➡ Always put safety above cost considerations – in the spirit of competition, some dive shops offer great deals but as the wise old saying goes, sometimes you get what you pay for.

Casa del Adivino (p159), Uxmal

Plan Your Trip

Exploring Maya Ruins

When you think about it, the Maya accomplished absolutely remarkable feats. Not only did they pull off some pretty sophisticated architecture, but they also made mind-blowing contributions to mathematics, astronomy and art. The cities they left behind remind us of their brilliance and are most certainly a top highlight of the Yucatán.

Planning Your Trip

When to Go

The best time of year to visit archaeological sites is from November to April, when the peninsula has cooler climes and is generally dry. Keep in mind, though, that this is also high season, meaning you'll be dealing with large crowds unless you arrive early in the morning.

Where to Stay

Tulum makes a great base for visiting both the Tulum archaeological site and Cobá. For the ruins of Chichén Itzá and Ek' Balam, consider staying in colonial Valladolid. Many folks who go to Palenque use San Cristóbal de las Casas as a jumping-off point. An overnight in Campeche is convenient for getting an early start at Edzná, and the tranquil town of Santa Elena works as a nice little hub for exploring the Ruta Puuc, Kabah and Uxmal.

What to See

So many interesting sites, so little time. Definite must-sees include Chichén Itzá, Palenque, Tulum, Uxmal and Calakmul.

What to Take

Ensure you have comfortable walking shoes, a hat, sunscreen and plenty of water. Oh, and don't forget that camera.

Amazing Maya

Classic Maya (AD 250–900), seen by many experts as the most glorious civilization of pre-Hispanic America, flourished in three areas:

North The low-lying Yucatán Peninsula.

Central The Petén forest of Guatemala and the adjacent lowlands in Chiapas and Tabasco in Mexico (to the west) and Belize (to the east).

South Highland Guatemala and a small section of Honduras.

It was in the northern and central areas that the Maya blossomed most brilliantly, attaining groundbreaking heights of artistic and architectural expression.

Among the Maya's many accomplishments was the development of a complex writing system, partly pictorial, partly phonetic, with 300 to 500 symbols. They also refined a calendar used by other pre-Hispanic peoples into a tool for the exact recording and forecasting of earthly and heavenly events. Temples were aligned to enhance observation of the heavens, helping the Maya predict solar eclipses and movements of the moon and Venus.

The Maya also believed in predestination and developed a complex astrology. To win the gods' favor they carried out elaborate rituals involving dances, feasts, sacrifices, consumption of the alcoholic drink *balché*, and bloodletting.

They believed the current world to be just one of a succession of worlds, and the cyclical nature of their calendrical system enabled them to predict the future by looking at the past.

Top Museums

The following museums provide interesting background that's often missing from some of the archaeological sites.

➡ **Museo Maya de Cancún** This new museum houses one of Mexico's most important Maya collections. The adjoining San Miguelito archaeological site contains more than a dozen restored Maya structures and an 8m-high pyramid. The entrance fee for the museum includes access to San Miguelito. (p56)

➡ **Gran Museo del Mundo Maya** Adding to Mérida's rich cultural tradition, this shiny new museum showcases more than 500 Maya artifacts. Permanent and temporary exhibits focus on all things Maya, from culture and art to science and Maya cosmovision. There's a free nightly light-and-sound show here too. (p148)

➡ **Museo Arqueológico de Campeche** Set in an old fortress, this museum exhibits pieces from the Maya sites of Calakmul and Edzná. Stunning jade jewelry and exquisite vases, masks and plates are thematically arranged in 10 halls; the star attractions are the jade burial masks from Calakmul. (p200)

➡ **Museo de la Cultura Maya** Chetumal's pride and joy illustrates the Maya's calendrical system, among other intriguing exhibits. It's organized into three levels, mirroring Maya cosmology. The main floor represents this world; the upper floor the heavens; the lower floor Xibalbá, the underworld. Try to visit here before seeing the nearby sites of Kohunlich and Dzibanché. (p134)

Practicalities

- Admission to the Yucatán's archaeological sites ranges from free to M$182; children under 13 often cost a fraction of the adult entrance fee. Nightly light-and-sound shows at Chichén Itzá and Uxmal are included in the cost of admission if you retain your ticket stub.
- Opening hours at most major sites are 8am to 5pm.
- Drink lots of water and bring protection against the sun. Insect repellant keeps the mosquitoes away when visiting jungle sites.
- Explanatory signs may be in Spanish only, or both Spanish and English. Audio translators are available at Chichén Itzá and Uxmal (M$39).
- Multilingual guides offer one- to two-hour tours (from M$400 to M$600). Official tour-guide rates are posted at the entrances of some sites; legit guides carry government-issued badges.
- Seldom-visited sites have no food or water available; pack a lunch or stop off for a meal or supplies along the way.
- Avoid midday visits when the sun is beating down and tourists are out in full force.

CHRIS CHEADLE / GETTY IMAGES ©

Nohoch Mul (p120), Cobá

Resources

The following books and organizations provide a wealth of information on Maya history and culture.

SITES AT A GLANCE

SITE	PERIOD	HIGHLIGHTS
Chichén Itzá	approx AD 100-1400	El Castillo pyramid, Mexico's biggest ball court, El Caracol observatory, Cenote Sagrado
Uxmal	AD 600-900	pyramids, palaces, riotous sculpture featuring masks of rain god Chac
Tulum	AD 1200-1550	temples and towers overlooking the Caribbean Sea
Calakmul	approx AD 1-900	high pyramids with views over rainforest
Cobá	AD 600-1100	towering pyramids in jungle setting
Kabah	AD 750-950	Palace of the Masks with nearly 300 Chac masks
Ruta Puuc	AD 750-950	three sites (Sayil, Xlapak, Labná), palaces with elaborate columns & sculpture, including Chac masks
Edzná	600 BC-AD 1500	five-story pyramid-palace, Temple of the Masks
Becán	550 BC-AD 1000	towered temples
Xpujil	flourished AD 700-800	three-towered ancient 'skyscraper'
Ek' Balam	approx AD 600-800	huge Acrópolis & high pyramid with unusual carving
Dzinbanché	approx 200 BC-AD 1200	semiwild site with palaces & pyramids
Kohunlich	AD 100-600	Temple of the Masks

El Castillo (p177), Chichén Itzá

➡ **Incidents of Travel in Yucatán** A travelogue written by American explorer John Lloyd Stephens documenting the Maya sites he visited with English artist Frederick Catherwood in the mid-19th century.

➡ **Instituto Nacional de Antropología e Historia** (INAH; www.inah.gob.mx) The website of Mexico's National Institute of Anthropology and History offers virtual tours of its sites and museums, practical information for visiting the ruins, and details of the historical significance of each site. Most of it is in Spanish.

➡ **Mesoweb** (www.mesoweb.com) A great, diverse resource that focuses on the ancient cultures of Mexico; specializes in the Maya.

➡ **An Archaeological Guide to Central and Southern Mexico** Joyce Kelly's book was published in 2001 and is still the best of its kind, covering 70 sites.

➡ **Archaeology of Ancient Mexico and Central America: An Encyclopedia** An excellent reference book by Susan Toby Evans and David L Webster incorporating recent discoveries and scholarship.

➡ **Chronicle of the Maya Kings and Queens** Looks at the dynasties and rulers of the most important ancient Maya kingdoms, by Simon Martin and Nikolai Grube.

➡ **Maya Exploration Center** (www.mayaexploration.org) A Maya-specific nonprofit organization offering education programs, tours and study abroad courses.

Behind the Names

➡ **Chichén Itzá** (mouth of the well of the Itzaes) The ancient Maya city was built around a well known today as the 'sacred cenote.'

➡ **Tulum** (wall) Refers to the stone walls that once protected the city. The original Maya name, Zamá, has been translated as 'dawn' or 'sunrise.'

➡ **Calakmul** (adjacent mounds) Dubbed as such by US botanist Cyrus Lundell when he first come across the hidden jungle ruins in the 1930s.

➡ **Palenque** (palisade) The Spanish name has no relation to the city's ancient name, Lakamha, which means 'big water' and probably refers to the area's springs, streams and waterfalls.

➡ **Uxmal** (thrice built) Alludes to how many times the city was built, though it was actually constructed five times.

Stone carving, Palenque (p234)

LIFE AFTER THE APOCALYPSE

We're happy to report all is well in Maya country. As you may have heard, some folks were predicting the end of the world on December 21, 2012, when the Maya long-count calendrical cycle came to an end, yet the date actually signaled the beginning of a new *bak' tun* (about a 400-year period).

Despite all the media hype focusing on doomsday scenarios, some good came out of all the attention: in the year leading up to that December day, federal and state governments were spending some serious pesos on new Maya-themed museums and sites. The 2012 Mundo Maya program, for instance, was a campaign devoted exclusively to promoting all things Maya. Now that the so-called apocalypse event has come and gone, archaeologists can only keep their fingers crossed that all the renewed interest in ancient and modern Maya culture will lead to more funding for ongoing research and excavations.

Tours

If you don't have a car, tours are especially convenient when you're pressed for time or find that a site is difficult to reach by bus. Youth hostels in the Yucatán often provide the most affordable tour services and they usually welcome non-guests. Here are some excellent tour operators:

➡ **Nomadas Hostel** Does day trips from Mérida to Uxmal, Chichén Itzá and Kabah. Tours include transportation and guide, but you'll have to cover entrance fees. (p148)

➡ **Mundo Joven** This Cancún hostel/agency runs day trips to Chichén Itzá and Tulum. Both tours offer guide, transportation, entry and one meal; the Chichén Itzá excursion stops at a cenote (limestone sinkhole) to take a dip. (p58)

➡ **Turitransmérida** This Mérida-based tour operator goes to Ruta Puuc, Dzibilchaltún, Chichén Itzá, Kabah and Uxmal. Tours include transportation, a meal and guide. For Ruta Puuc, a four-person minimum is required. (p149)

➡ **Community Tours Sian Ka'an** This Maya-run ecotourism outfit will take you on a guided walk of the interpretive trail at the Muyil archaeological site, south of Tulum. (p115)

➡ **Ecoturismo Yucatán** One-day excursions to Chichén Itzá and Uxmal include entrance fees, guide and lunch. The owners of this tour operator are passionate about both sharing and protecting the state's natural treasures. (p149)

Plan Your Trip

Travel with Children

Snorkeling in caves, playing on the beach, hiking in the jungle... kids will find plenty of ways to keep busy in the Yucatán. And, as with elsewhere in Mexico, children take center stage – with few exceptions, children are welcome at all kinds of hotels and in virtually every cafe and restaurant.

Best Regions for Kids

Riviera Maya

If you're planning on visiting the Yucatán's famed theme parks, *this* is the region; the parks can burn a hole in your pocket and some have a very Disneyesque quality, but even grown-ups can have a blast at these places.

Cancún

Cancún was made with children in mind. From pirate-ship cruises and hotels with kids' clubs to a wide offering of water-related activities and tours, boredom is not an option (especially if mom and dad are willing spenders).

Isla Mujeres

With its shallow and swimmable beaches, several marine amusement parks and snorkeling opportunities galore, Isla Mujeres is a big hit with kids. Oh yeah, Isla Contoy is nearby, which means yet another fun-filled boating and snorkeling op.

The Yucatán for Kids

Getting Around

Watching scenery go by doesn't go over too well with most kids, so try to do your traveling between towns in smallish chunks of a few hours. Most Mexican buses show nonstop movies on video screens, which diverts kids above toddler age, and most of the movies are pretty family-friendly. Children under 13 pay half-price on many long-distances buses, and if they're small enough to sit on your lap, they usually go for free. If you're traveling with a baby or a toddler, consider investing in deluxe buses for the extra space and comfort.

Car rental is a practical alternative to buses. If you need a child-safety seat, the major international car-rental firms are the most reliable providers. You will probably have to pay a few dollars extra per day. Car seats are compulsory for children under five.

Of course, some forms of traveling are fun – there are boat trips of many kinds to be had, bicycles, ATVs (all terrain vehicles) and horses to be rented for outings.

Health & Safety

Children are more easily affected than adults by heat, disrupted sleeping patterns

PLANNING

➡ Cots for hotel rooms and high chairs for restaurants are available mainly in midrange and top-end establishments.

➡ It's usually not hard to find an inexpensive babysitter – ask at your hotel. Some top-end hotels provide the service at an additional cost.

➡ Diapers (nappies) are widely available, but if you depend on some particular cream, lotion, baby food or medicine, bring it with you.

➡ It's a good idea to book some accommodations for at least the first couple of nights, even if you plan to be flexible once you've arrived.

➡ When booking a room, make sure that the establishment accepts children – some are adults-only.

➡ Lonely Planet's *Travel with Children* has lots of practical advice on the subject, drawn from firsthand experience.

and strange food. Be particularly careful that they don't drink tap water or consume any questionable food or beverage. Take care to avoid sunburn, cover them up against insect bites, and ensure you replace fluids if a child gets diarrhea.

See a doctor about vaccinations at least one month – preferably two – before your trip. Once there, don't hesitate to go to a doctor if you think it may be necessary. In general, privately run hospitals and clinics offer better facilities and care than the public ones. Make sure you have adequate travel insurance that will cover the cost of private medical care.

Child safety provisions in Mexico may be less strict than what you're accustomed to. Check out things like toddler pools, cribs, guardrails and even toys so that you're aware of any potential hazards.

Breast-feeding in public is not common in the Yucatán.

Sleeping

The peninsula has an exciting variety of different places to stay that should please most kids – anything beachside is usually a good start, and rustic *cabañas* (cabins) provide a sense of adventure (but choose one with good mosquito nets).

Many hotels have a rambling layout and a good amount of open-air space – courtyards, pool areas, gardens – allowing for some light exploring by kids. The most family-oriented hotels, with expansive grounds and facilities such as shallow pools, playgrounds and kids clubs, tend to be found in the big resorts.

Family rooms are widely available, and many hotels will put an extra bed or two in a room at little or no extra cost. However, baby cots may not be available in budget accommodations. You can find a room with air-conditioning nearly everywhere, and most midrange and top-end hotels have wi-fi access and child-friendly channels on the TV and/or DVD players for when your kids just need to flop down in front of something entertaining.

Eating

The Yucatán has plenty of eateries serving up international comfort food should Mexican fare not sit well with your children. Along the Riviera Maya you'll find many Italian-owned establishments preparing pizzas and pastas, while in gringo-friendly Cancún, there are so many restaurants doing burgers and the like that it'll seem like you never left home. *Yucateco antojitos* (snacks) such as *sopa de lima* (which tastes like chicken soup with a twist of lime) and *salbutes* (lightly fried tortillas topped with shredded poultry and other fixings) are fairly neutral options for trying local flavors.

The closer you are to tourist centers, the better chance you have of finding more diverse and child-friendly menus. When all else fails, most large cities have familiar fast-food joints. If your child doesn't take to experimenting, consider packing a lunch when visiting small towns where the eating options may be somewhat limited.

The spacious open-air character of many Yucatán eateries conveniently means that children aren't compelled to sit nicely at

UNDER-18 AIR TRAVELERS

To conform with regulations to prevent international child abduction, minors (people aged under 18) traveling to Mexico without one or both of their parents may need to carry a notarized consent form signed by the absent parent or parents, giving permission for the young traveler to make the international journey. Though Mexico does not specifically require this documentation, airlines flying to Mexico may refuse to board passengers without it. In the case of divorced parents, a custody document may be required. If one or both parents are dead, or the traveler has only one legal parent, a death certificate or notarized statement of the situation may be required.

These rules are aimed primarily at visitors from the US and Canada but may also apply to people from elsewhere. Procedures vary from country to country; contact your country's foreign affairs department and/or a Mexican consulate to find out exactly what you need to do. Forms for the purposes required are usually available from these authorities.

the table all the time. Some restaurants even have play areas or small pools to keep kids busy.

Children's Highlights

Apart from the ruins, beaches and swimming pools, you'll find excellent special attractions such as amusement and water parks, zoos, aquariums and other fun places on the peninsula. Kids can also enjoy activities such as snorkeling, riding bicycles and boats, and watching wildlife. Archaeological sites can be fun if your kids are into climbing pyramids and exploring tunnels.

Water Worlds

➡ **Spot crocodiles and whale sharks** Boat tours at Isla Holbox (p73) and Río Lagartos (p190).

➡ **Sail on a pirate ship** A replica Spanish galleon stages nightly swashbuckler battles off the waters of Cancún (p60) and pirate ships sail in Campeche, too (p199).

➡ **Snorkel in the Caribbean** Many beaches on the Yucatán's Caribbean coast provide calm waters and colorful marine life for beginners.

➡ **Swim and explore** Visitors make their way through underground rivers and caves at theme park Xcaret in the Riviera Maya (p102).

➡ **Cruise the jungle** Reach the ancient cities of Yaxchilán by an adventurous river boat trip (p240).

Inland Fun

➡ **Selvática** Award-winning zip-line circuit through jungle near Cancún, with its own cenote (limestone sinkhole) for swimming. (p102)

➡ **Cobá** This jungle-surrounded ancient Maya site near Tulum has pyramids, a zip line and bicycles for pedaling around the network of dirt trails. (p121)

➡ **Aktun Chen** Near Akumal, this park features a 60m-long cave, a 12m-deep cenote, 10 zip lines and a small zoo. (p102)

➡ **Boca del Puma** Zip-lining, horseback riding, wall climbing and a cenote to dip into, near Puerto Morelos. (p99)

➡ **Hidden Worlds** Four-hour adventure tours that combine up to six activities, including snorkeling in a cenote, rapelling into a cave and soaring above the jungle on a zip line. (p112)

Animal Encounters

➡ **Isla Mujeres Turtle Farm** Has hundreds of sea turtles, both big and small, plus an aquarium. The staff is very friendly and will take the time to explain how and why the farm protects the turtles (p77).

➡ **Parque Zoológico del Centenario** Park in Mérida with lions, bears, an aviary, playground, bumper boats and much more. (p147)

➡ **Reserva de la Biosfera Ría Celestún** A boat tour through the mangroves of Ría Celestún, home to flamingos and harpy eagles. (p170)

➡ **Crococun Zoo** Visitors can interact with the animals, such as spider monkeys, at this petting zoo near Puerto Morelos. You can also get an up-close look at the crocs. (p60)

Conchinita pibil (suckling pig)

Plan Your Trip

Eat & Drink Like a Local

The Yucatán is an endless feast of traditional flavors, fresh fish and seafood, and an eclectic mix of international cuisine. The wonderfully unique tastes you'll encounter on the peninsula leave absolutely no doubt: folks in this corner of Mexico are passionate about food.

The Year in Food

March

The Cancún-Riviera Maya Wine & Food Festival (www.crmfest.com) draws celebrity chefs from Mexico and abroad; a good chance to sample Mexican wines and gourmet dishes.

July to March

You can get lobster year-round on the coast but this is the time of year when fisherfolk are bringing in fresh catches daily.

August

The Jats'a Já festival in Mahahual celebrates the town's fishing tradition with culinary exhibits and Maya ceremonies right on the beach.

October to November

Pibipollo (chicken tamales) are cooked underground for Day of the Dead festivities in many cities throughout the peninsula.

November

The Taste of Playa International Food Festival (www.tasteofplaya.com) is held on Playa del Carmen's main plaza on the last Saturday of November with Riviera Maya chefs offering samples of their latest creations.

Food Experiences

Meals of a Lifetime

➡ **La Chaya Maya, Mérida** Extraordinary *yucateco* fare in a precious downtown colonial building. (p152)

➡ **Cetli, Tulum** Sophisticated take on Mexican classics in a homey backstreet restaurant. (p118)

➡ **La Cueva del Chango, Playa del Carmen** Superb and surprisingly affordable Mexican dishes in a jungly setting. (p107)

➡ **El Merkadito, Puerto Morelos** Fish and seafood done right, plus ocean views. (p101)

➡ **La Fuente, Campeche** Waterfront cafe does local faves like *pibipollo* (chicken tamales) cooked underground. (p213)

Cheap Treats

You'll find the best cheap eats at market stalls, street stands, cafes and *cocinas económicas* (affordable eateries). Keep in mind that some budget options have sketchy hygiene standards, so it can be a bit of a crapshoot (no pun intended).

➡ **El Paisano del 23, Cancún** The famous *pierna tortas* (pork sandwiches) have been a local fave for more than 40 years; get there early. (p61)

➡ **La Socorrito, Mérida** This hole-in-the-wall market eatery has been perfecting *cochinita* (slow-cooked pork) for six decades. (p152)

➡ **Los Aguachiles, Playa del Carmen** Artfully prepared *tostadas* (fried tortillas) with fresh fish and seafood in a *cantina*-like setting. (p107)

➡ **Tierradentro, San Cristóbal de las Casas** Run by Zapatista supporters, this cafe keeps it real with affordable and delicious set meals. (p231)

Dare to Try

➡ Pickled pigs feet, snout and ears in Mérida's sprawling Mercado Municipal Lucas de Gálvez (p151).

➡ The four-alarm habanero chili salsas at Tacos de Cochinita Chepe's (p133) in Laguna Bacalar.

➡ Lionfish at Sulumar (p130) in the southern Quintana Roo beach town of Mahahual – hold the venom please!

Local Specialties

Food is a tremendous source of pride on the peninsula and the origins of some of the most popular dishes can easily become a topic of hot debate. We've broken down what's on offer in each state, but you'll definitely find variations of the following dishes across state lines.

Yucatán State

➡ **Cochinita/pollo pibil** Suckling pig or chicken marinated in citrus juices and *achiote* (a spice made from annatto seed). When done properly, *cochinita* is slow-cooked in an underground pit.

➡ **Sopa de lima** Soup with shredded turkey or chicken, lime and tortilla strips.

➡ **Papadzules** Diced hard-boiled eggs wrapped in corn tortilla and topped with pumpkin seed and tomato sauces.

➡ **Queso relleno** A hollowed-out ball of Edam cheese stuffed with ground pork and smothered in tomato sauce and gravy.

➡ **Panuchos** Fried tortilla filled with beans and topped with chicken, lettuce, tomato and pickled red onion.

Quintana Roo

➡ **Lobster** A popular menu item in Cancún and other coastal towns. Some restaurants prepare it in *guajillo* (a type of chili pepper) and tamarind sauces, giving it a very distinct Mexican taste.

➡ **Fish and shrimp tacos** Beer-battered fish and shrimp are topped with shredded cabbage and the salsas of your choice. They're fast, cheap and highly addictive.

➡ **Ceviche** Raw fish or seafood marinated in lime juice and spices and served with *tostadas*. *Ceviche* and *cerveza* (beer) are a winner on a warm day.

➡ **Fusion** With so many Americans, Italians and other transplants living in these parts, you get some interesting blends of international and Mexican cuisine.

Campeche

➡ **Pibipollo** Chicken and pork tamales cooked underground and usually wrapped in banana leaves; a popular Day of the Dead dish.

DABBLE IN THE CULINARY ARTS

Take a cooking course to find out about the ingredients and techniques that go into Mexican cooking. Some recommended schools:

➡ **Los Dos** In Mérida, focuses strictly on *yucateco* cuisine. Take a cooking course with a market tour, attend a tasting class, or go for a multiday, all-inclusive culinary workshop. (p148)

➡ **Little Mexican Cooking School** In Puerto Morelos, gives a general overview of regional Mexican cuisine. You'll learn how to prepare seven to eight dishes, plus some background on the culture and traditions behind the food. (p99)

Maya dish of shrimp, peppers and goat cheese

➡ **Chocolomo** A hearty stew made of beef, kidneys, brain, tongue, liver etc. You get the point – nothing goes to waste.

Chiapas

➡ **Coffee** Optimal growing conditions (high altitude, good climate, rich soil) produce some of the finest coffee in the country.

➡ **Tamales** If you haven't tried a tamale with the aromatic *hoja santa* herb, wrapped in a banana leaf, you're missing something truly special.

How to Eat & Drink

When to Eat

➡ **Desayuno** (breakfast) Usually consists of fresh fruit, *pan dulce* (sweet bread) or egg dishes; served between 8am and 11am in restaurants and cafes.

➡ **Almuerzo** (light lunch) Locals tend to take a light lunch when they've missed breakfast or are just looking for something to hold them over until *la comida*, the big meal of the day.

Street food Cancún-style

➡ **La comida** (heavy lunch) From 2pm to 5pm. Many establishments offer gut-busting four-course meals. Shops can close between these hours, especially in smaller towns.

➡ **La cena** (supper) Some people like to grab a light dinner, between 8pm and 11pm, before hitting the bars and clubs; it's also a popular hour for munching tacos or *pan dulce*.

Where to Eat

➡ **Restaurante** Restaurants offer the widest variety in terms of menu items, price ranges and hours; most are family-friendly establishments and they're usually your best shot at finding vegetarian options.

EATING PRICE INDICATORS

In this guide we define a main dish in a restaurant as:

Budget (**$**)	less than M$80
Midrange (**$$**)	M$80-150
Top End (**$$$**)	above M$150.

➡ **Cocina Económica** These affordable eateries specialize in home-style cooking, plus they're great spots to mingle with locals.

➡ **Taquería** Taco shops are the perfect late-night option and the food is always cheap if you're looking to pinch some pesos.

➡ **Mercado** Many markets have a cluster of food stalls preparing decent and reasonably priced local dishes.

➡ **Cafe** Coffee shops are a good breakfast option when you have an early start.

➡ **Puesto** Street stalls whip up everything from tacos to *ceviche* cocktails. Opening hours vary considerably; some work mornings, others keep night hours.

Menu Decoder

➡ **Menú del día/comida corrida** Affordable set menu with three or four courses.

➡ **Menú degustación** A menu that normally consists of six to eight tasting-size courses.

➡ **Entradas/antojitos** Appetizers or snacks; common in the Yucatán, especially in bars.

Sopa de lima (lime soup)

➡ **Plato fuerte** Main course or main dish.

➡ **Postre** Dessert.

For an explanation of the dishes you'll find on *yucateco* menus, see p259.

Where to Drink

➡ **Cantinas** All *cantinas* sell *cerveza* and some, but not all, have licenses to pour tequila and other spirits. Some may even have *xtabentún*, a regional anise-flavored liqueur made from fermented honey. *Cantinas* usually open at noon and close around 11pm or midnight at the latest. The *cantina* experience varies considerably from one watering hole to the next. Some are festive, family-friendly establishments offering live music and complimentary snacks, others have a down-and-dirty barfly vibe that's best avoided, especially for women traveling alone.

A FEW TIPS

➡ When sharing a table or dining in close quarters with Mexicans , it's customary to wish them '*buen provecho*' (enjoy your meal) before you eat or leave the table.

➡ Waiters will not bring you the check until you ask for it. In Mexico it is considered rude to leave a check on a table before the customers have finished their meal.

➡ The standard tip in Mexico is 10% of the bill. If you liked the service, you can bump it up to 15% or 20%.

➡ **Nightclubs** Some nightclubs in the region charge hefty covers (that means you, Cancún) with open bar included in the price of admission. So of course you're gonna try to get your money's worth – just don't say we didn't warn you about the nasty hangover. The booze fest usually gets started around 11pm and thumps well into the wee hours of the morning.

➡ **Mezcalerías** Essentially small bars that specialize in *mezcal*, a distilled alcoholic drink made from the agave plant. Though *mezcal* is not actually made in the Yucatán, *mezcalerías* have grown very popular in recent years, especially in larger cities such as Cancún, Mérida and Playa del Carmen. *Mezcal* has a higher alcohol content than tequila, so expect the unexpected in these watering holes.

➡ **Juice Bars** Usually found in markets, *juguerías* sell fresh-squeezed juices, *liquados* (fruits blended with milk) and *aguas frescas* (water flavored with local treats like *chia* seed and *chaya* greens). The water used to prepare drinks in juice bars is purified.

➡ **Cafes** There's no shortage of cafes in the Yucatán serving quality organic coffee from Chiapas, Oaxaca and Veracruz, Mexico's top coffee-producing regions. Most cafes open early and close at around 10pm.

Regions at a Glance

Cancún & Around

Beaches
Nature
Water Sports

Beach-Bumming

Millions of people each year head to Cancún and its surrounding areas with just one simple objective: lazing around on sugary white-sand beaches and swimming in the turquoise-blue waters of the Mexican Caribbean. OK, some may also be going to revel in spring-break debauchery.

Wildlife Watching

Swim with the whale sharks at Isla Holbox or bird-watch at national park Isla Contoy. Both islands north of Cancún will appeal to those looking for unique outdoor experiences. Just don't miss the boat back from Isla Contoy or you'll be sleeping under a coconut tree.

Water Sports

Name your water sport and you'll find it here: snorkeling, kayaking, wakeboarding, fishing – there's even a unique underwater sculpture museum for beginner divers. And if you have kids, they'll be splashing themselves silly with all the water-related activities on offer.

p54

Isla Mujeres

Wildlife Conservation
Beaches
Outdoor Activities

Wildlife Conservation

Check out the Isla Mujeres Turtle Farm, where more than 120,000 of these little guys are liberated each year. Watch while eggs are gathered and secured in safe sands during peak nesting season from June to August.

Calm Beaches

Not only does Isla Mujeres have postcard-perfect, bleach-white beaches, the waters on the north shore are shallow, calm and a joy to swim in. At nearby Playa Secreto you'll find a great little swimming and snorkeling spot that's ideal for children.

Great Outdoors

Snorkel with whale sharks, hook big game fish on a sportfishing excursion, or go diving and spot manta rays, barracuda and sea turtles. You also have the option of driving around in a golf cart and visiting various beach clubs on the island's south side.

p75

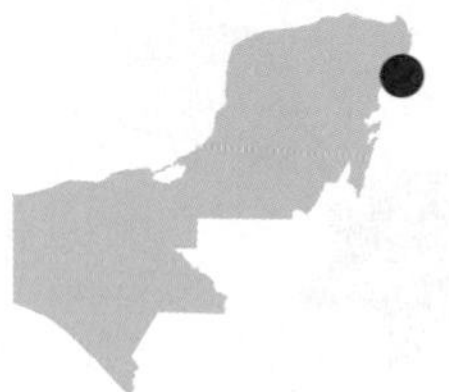

Isla Cozumel

Diving & Snorkeling
Scenery
Food

Divine Diving

Isla Cozumel is widely considered Mexico's top diving destination and some might even say one of the world's best. Why all the fuss? It's all about the year-round visibility, spectacular walls and impressive variety of colorful marine life.

Island Escape

A road trip on a scooter or convertible VW to the island's less-visited sides is a moving picture of uninhabited, windswept beaches and small Maya ruins – plus it's a nice escape from the cruise-ship crowds back in town.

Wining & Dining

Cozumel certainly has no shortage of quality restaurants doing fine local and international cuisine. They dot the oceanfront avenue and surround the pleasant town plaza, so the scenery is pretty much a given.

p84

Riviera Maya

Beaches
Nightlife
Diving

Beach Life

The Riviera Maya has stretches of sublime beach that make advertisers very happy. In Tulum, Maya ruins perched atop a cliff rise high above the beach in dramatic fashion. On a quiet day on the shore of Paamul, it's just you and the sea urchins.

Party Central

Get your fiesta on in Playa del Carmen, where sandy beaches become impromptu stages for fire dancers and beachside clubs rage into the wee hours of the morning. South of Playa, happening Tulum is fast approaching *pueblo*-that-never-sleeps status.

Cenote Diving

Take a plunge into a cenote (limestone sinkhole) and explore amazing caverns and caves. Cenotes also make for great swimming holes for nondivers. The Maya referred to these fascinating underground river systems as gateways to the underworld.

p97

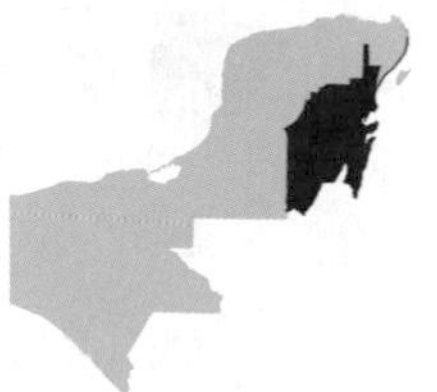

Costa Maya & the Southern Caribbean Coast

Scenery
Diving
Beaches

Shades of Blue

The unparalleled scenery of Laguna Bacalar is something to behold. Called the 'lake of seven colors,' the crystalline water has blues you never even knew existed. While in town, check out the imposing 18th-century colonial fortress.

Take the Plunge

Divers won't want to miss out on the opportunity to explore Banco Chinchorro, the largest coral atoll in the northern hemisphere and a ship graveyard. There's good snorkeling here as well.

Sleepy Beach Towns

Once tiny fishing villages, Mahahual and Xcalak are seeing more and more tourism these days but have managed to retain a tranquil vibe. They're about as far south as you can remove yourself from the mega-resort madness of Cancún.

p126

Yucatán State & the Maya Heartland

Ruins
Nature
Food

Ruins Hopping

Yucatán has so many Maya ruins that you'd probably need a leave of absence to visit them all. The most famous of them all, Chichén Itzá, draws a million visitors a year thanks to its recently acquired status as one of the new seven wonders of the world.

Birdies & Crocs

Nature buffs just can't get enough of Yucatán's two largest biosphere reserves in Celestún and Río Lagartos. Tour boats take you out to watch flamingos, which flock to the wetlands in the winter, and to spot crocodiles at night.

Food, Glorious Food

Ask any foodie and they'll tell you that Yucatán state is one of Mexico's most exciting culinary destinations. Sure, you can try classic *yucateco* fare like *cochinita pibil* (slow-cooked pork) or *poc-chuc* (grilled pork) elsewhere in Mexico, but it won't taste the same.

p140

Campeche & Around

History
Wildlife
Ruins

Pirates Ahoy

Not many cities like Campeche exist, with a pretty historical center surrounded by stone walls to ward off fierce pirate attacks. Today it's a serene destination with few tourists, and a beachside boardwalk creates an atmosphere more romantic than ravaged.

Fins & Flippers

Laguna de Terminos' collection of estuaries and mangroves makes up a rich coastal habitat for many critters. Go on a lookout for migratory birds or spot playful dolphins from a boat.

Lofty Pyramids

Deep in a jungle full of toucans and monkeys lies Calakmul, a significant Maya site. Originally a huge city, it covered 72 sq km and supported over 50,000 people – and it boasts one of the tallest Maya pyramids in Mexico.

p194

Chiapas

Architecture
Ruins
Nature

Colonial Grace

San Cristóbal's cobbled streets and colonial architecture are charming enough, but add a dash of Zapatista history and colorful indigenous people, and you've hit something special. Visit the church in nearby San Juan Chamula – it's almost magical.

Exquisite Temples

Unique in the Maya world is Palenque's four-story stone tower – perhaps an old observatory? And the Templo de las Inscripciones once held the skeleton of Pakal the Great, draped with jewels and a priceless jade mask.

Riverside Adventure

It takes a long bus trip, plus a half-hour boat ride, but a visit to the Maya city of Yaxchilán is unforgettable. Note the hieroglyphics and interesting facades on buildings, and listen for howler monkeys in the jungle. And did we mention the croc-infested waters?

p221

On the Road

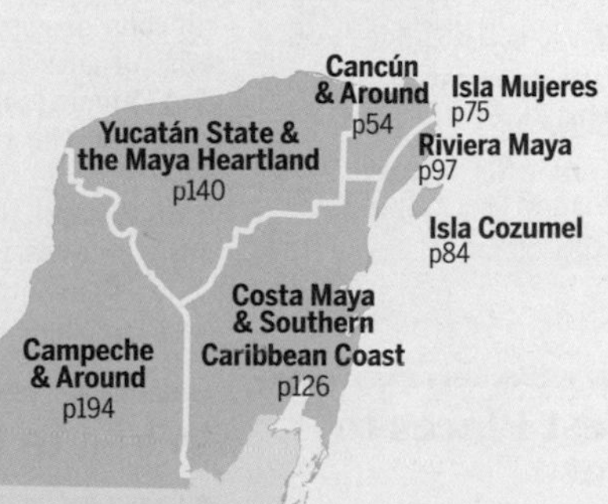

Cancún & Around
p54
Isla Mujeres
p75
Yucatán State & the Maya Heartland
p140
Riviera Maya
p97
Isla Cozumel
p84
Costa Maya & Southern Caribbean Coast
p126
Campeche & Around
p194
Chiapas & Tabasco
p221

Cancún & Around

☎998 / POP 628,300

Includes ➡

Best Places to Eat

- Checándole (p63)
- El Paisano del 23 (p61)
- Lorenzillo's (p65)
- Viva Zapata (p73)
- Los Peleones (p74)

Best Places to Stay

- Hotel El Rey del Caribe (p61)
- Hostel Mundo Joven (p59)
- Le Blanc (p64)
- Casa Takywara (p72)
- Hotel Arena (p72)

Why Go?

Cancún is a tale of two cities. There's the glitzy hotel zone with its famous white-sand beaches, unabashed party scene and sophisticated seafood restaurants. Then there's the actual city itself, which gives you a taste of local flavor at, say, a neighborhood bar or taco joint.

That's what keeps Cancún interesting. Had your fill of raucous discos in the hotel zone? Escape to a downtown salsa or jazz club. Tired of lounging around the pool in Ciudad Cancún? Simply hop on a bus and head for the sapphire waters of the hotel zone. Or even better, venture out and explore more of Quintana Roo state. Just a day trip away from Cancún, the pristine national park of Isla Contoy beckons with a fascinating variety of bird and plant species. And up north awaits low-key Isla Holbox, where swimming with massive whale sharks has become all the rage.

When to Go

- A visit to Cancún in April/May, in the wake of spring break madness, shows you a relatively quiet side of the resort city, plus many accommodations offer great online deals.
- Don't miss the thrilling opportunity to snorkel with whale sharks off the coast of Isla Holbox; the gentle giants congregate around the island from mid-May to September.
- Four species of sea turtles flock to the shores of Parque Nacional Isla Contoy for nesting season from April to October; the uninhabited island is also home to more than 150 bird species.

Cancún & Around Highlights

❶ Dive among life-size sculptures at the one-of-a-kind **Museo Subacuático de Arte** (p57)

❷ Swim with massive whale sharks and enjoy laid-back island living on **Isla Holbox** (p71)

❸ Snorkel and get in some birding at the uninhabited island of **Isla Contoy** (p70), a wildlife refuge that receives only 200 visitors a day

❹ Grab dinner and drinks in **Ciudad Cancún** (p61), then shake your booty to live salsa music

❺ Chill on the soft sands of the **Zona Hotelera** (p56), take a dip in the Caribbean blue, then check out the city's new Maya museum

CANCÚN

History

When you look around you at the giant hotels and supermalls it's hard to imagine that 40 years ago there was nothing here but sand and fishing boats. In the 1970s Mexico's ambitious planners decided to outdo Acapulco with a brand-new, world-class resort located on the Yucatán Peninsula. The place they chose was a deserted sandspit located offshore from the little fishing village of Puerto Juárez, on the peninsula's eastern shore, known as Isla Cancún (Cancún Island). Vast sums were sunk into landscaping and infrastructure, yielding straight, well-paved roads, potable tap water and great swaths of sandy beach. As the Zona Hotelera (Hotel Zone) mushroomed, Ciudad Cancún cropped up on the mainland and became one of the fastest growing cities in Mexico – today it's Quintana Roo's most populated city.

Hurricanes Wilma and Emily whipped into town in 2005, destroying area hotels, flooding much of the city and carrying off tons of Cancún's precious beach sand. The hotels have been rebuilt and the sands have since been replaced. That's right, the sands have been replaced. Much to the ire of environmentalists, this involved a massive undertaking of dredging sand from the ocean floor and then moving it ashore. Those in favor call it 'beach nourishing,' those opposed warn that it causes serious environmental damage to the marine ecosystem. But it's not just the storms that are washing Cancun's sand away. Making matters even more complicated, beaches are eroding because of sea-level rise. It certainly appears that mother nature will have the final say on the future of Cancun's beaches.

Sights & Activities

Most of Cancun's star attractions, namely its beaches, ruins and water-related activities, are in the Zona Hotelera. If you're staying in Ciudad Cancún, any 'R-1' or 'Zona Hotelera' bus will drop you off at any point along the coast.

Maya Ruins

You'll find three Maya archaeological sites in the Zona Hotelera that are worth a look.

Museo Maya de Cancún MUSEUM
(Maya Museum; Map p58; www.inah.gob.mx; Blvd Kukulcán, Km 17.5; admission M$57; 10am-7pm Tue-Sun; R-1) Housing one of the most important collections of Maya artifacts in all of Mexico, this modern, new museum is a welcome sight in a city known more for its party scene than cultural attractions. On display are some 350 pieces found at key sites in and around the peninsula, ranging from jewelry to ceramics and sculptures. One of the three display halls showcases temporary Maya-themed exhibits. Cancún's original anthropology museum, which once stood next to the convention center, shut down in 2006 due to structural damage from hurricanes. This time around, the new museum features hurricane-resistant reinforced glass. The price of admission includes access to the San Miguelito ruins. The museum opened shortly after our last visit.

Zona Arqueológica El Rey ARCHAEOLOGICAL SITE
(Map p58; Blvd Kukulcán, Km 17.5; admission M$42; 8am-5pm; R-1) In the Zona Arqueológica El Rey, on the west side of Blvd Kukulcán between Km 17 and Km 18, there's a small temple and several ceremonial platforms. The site gets its name from a sculpture excavated here of a dignitary, possibly a *rey* (king), wearing an elaborate headdress.

San Miguelito ARCHAEOLOGICAL SITE
(Map p58; 885-3842; Blvd Kukulcán, Km 17; admission M$57; R-1) Cancún's newest archaeological site contains more than a dozen restored Maya structures inhabited between 1250 and 1550, prior to the arrival of the conquistadors. A path from the adjoining Museo Maya leads to remains of houses, a palace with 17 columns, and the 8m-high Gran Piramide (Grand Pyramid). The price of admission includes entry to the shiny new Museo Maya.

Yamil Lu'um ARCHAEOLOGICAL SITE
(Map p58; off Blvd Kukulcán, Km 12.5; R-1) FREE Also known as the Templo de Alácran (Scorpion's Temple), Yamil Lu'um was used between 1200 and 1500, and sits atop a beachside knoll in the parklike grounds between the Park Royal and Westin Lagunamar hotels. The ruin makes for a pleasant venture for its lovely setting more than anything else. Only the outward-sloping remains of the weathered temple's walls still stand. To reach the site visitors must pass through either of the hotels flanking it or approach it from the beach (the easiest way) – there is no direct access from the boulevard.

Beaches

Starting from Ciudad Cancún in the northwest, all of Isla Cancún's beaches are on the left-hand side of the road (the lagoon is on your right). The first beaches are Playas Las Perlas, Juventud, Linda, Langosta, Tortugas and Caracol. With the exception of Playa Caracol, these stand out as Cancún's most swimmable beaches. After you round Punta Cancún, the water gets rougher (though still swimmable) and the beaches become more scenic as white sands meet the turquoise-blue Caribbean, from Playas Gaviota Azul all the way down south to Playa Delfines at Km 17. Delfines is about the only beach with a public parking lot big enough to be useful; unfortunately, its sand is coarser and darker than the exquisite, fine white sand of the more northerly beaches.

Access

Under Mexican law you have the right to walk and` swim on every beach in the country except those within military compounds. In practice, it is difficult to approach many stretches of beach without walking through the lobby of a hotel, particularly in the Zona Hotelera. However, as long as you look like a tourist (this shouldn't be hard, right?), you'll usually be permitted to cross the lobby and proceed to the beach.

Safety

Cancún's ambulance services respond to as many as a dozen near-drownings per week. The most dangerous beaches seem to be Playa Delfines and Playa Chac-Mool. Though rare, accidents with kiteboards, paragliders or jet skis can happen; be aware of other beachgoers at all times.

Though the surf is usually gentle, undertow is a possibility, and sudden storms (called *nortes*) can blacken the sky and sweep in at any time without warning. A system of colored pennants warns beach-goers of any potential danger:

Blue Normal, safe conditions.

Yellow Use caution, changeable conditions.

Red Unsafe conditions; use a swimming pool instead.

Diving & Snorkeling

For decent snorkeling, you need to travel to one of the nearby reefs. Several dive shops now offer diving and snorkeling outings to the MUSA, a unique underwater attraction.

Museo Subacuático de Arte DIVING, SNORKELING

(MUSA Underwater Museum; www.musacancun.com; snorkeling tour M$380, 1-tank dive from M$700) Built to divert divers away from deteriorating coral reefs, this one-of-a-kind aquatic museum features 403 life-size sculptures in the waters of Cancún and Isla Mujeres. The artificial reefs are submerged at a depth of 28ft, making them ideal for snorkelers and first-time divers. Organize dives through diving outfits; Scuba Cancún, which does several tours to the sculpture gardens, is recommended.

The underwater museum is a creation of British-born sculptor Jason deCaires Taylor.

Scuba Cancún DIVING

(Map p58; 849-7508; www.scubacancun.com.mx; Blvd Kukulcán, Km 5.2; 1-/2-tank dives M$702/884, equipment rental extra) A family-owned and PADI-certified dive operation with many years of experience, Scuba Cancún was the first dive shop in Cancún. It offers a variety of snorkeling, fishing and diving options (including cenote and night dives). It also does snorkeling and diving trips to the underwater sculpture museum, aka MUSA.

Other Watersports

Most of the major resorts rent kayaks and the usual water toys; a few make them available to guests free of charge.

Cancún has pretty weak surf. But a core group of locals still heads out to Playa Chac-Mool and Playa Marlin to hit the little rollers. 'Surf season' runs from October to March. There's no place in town to rent boards, but you can buy one at Koko Dog'z.

Koko Dog'z WATER SPORTS

(Map p62; 887-3635; www.kokodogz.com; Av Náder 42-1; noon-8pm Mon-Fri, to 6pm Sat; R-1) Sells all sorts of boards – surf, kite, boogie, skim – and arranges wakeboarding on the lagoon for M$2000 an hour per boat.

Courses

Teatro Xbalamqué THEATER

(Map p62; 147-7322; http://teatroxbalamque.blogspot.com; cnr Jazmines & Av Yaxchilán) Offers yoga and theater courses.

Tours

Most hotels and travel agencies work with companies that offer tours to surrounding attractions. Popular day trips are to Chichén

Cancún

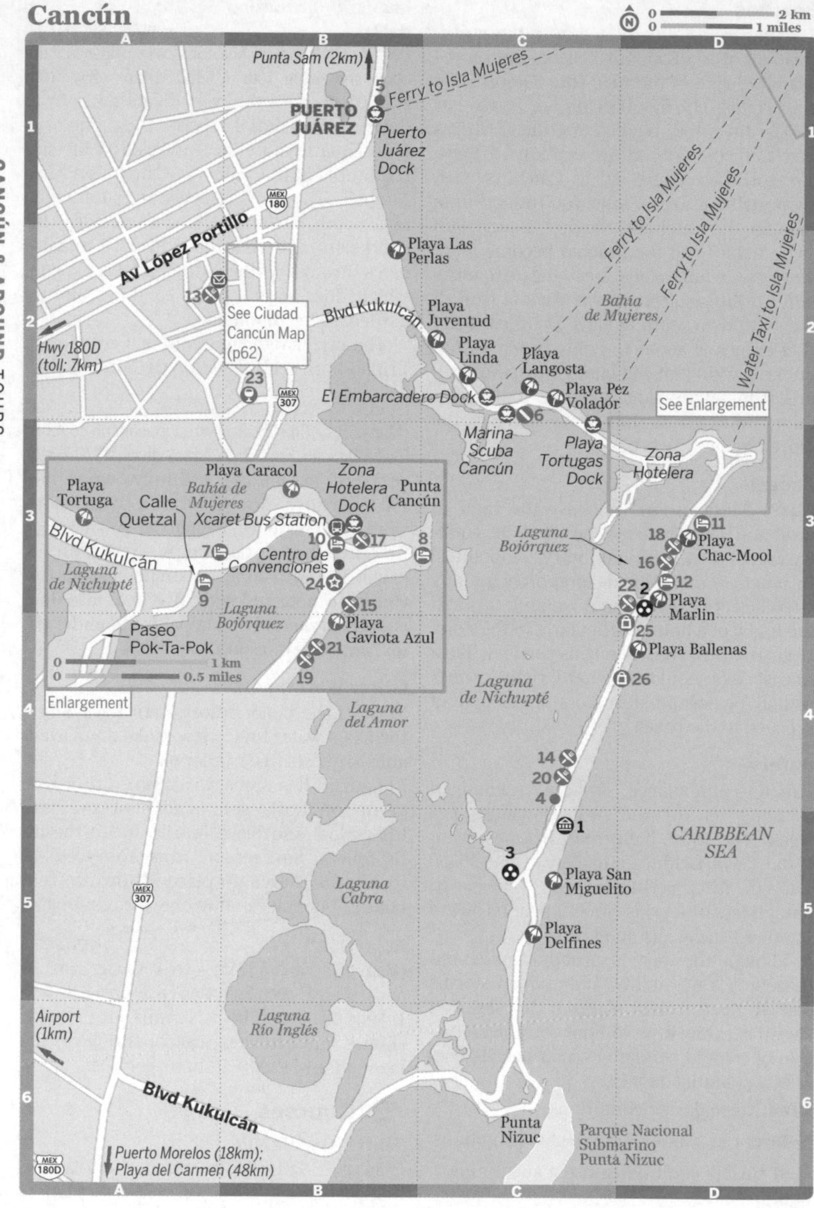

Itzá, Cobá, Tulum, and the theme parks at Xel-Há and Xcaret.

Hostel Mundo Joven TOUR
(Map p62; ☎271-4740; www.mundojovenhostels.com; cnr Av Uxmal 25 & Laurel; ⏰10am-7pm Mon-Fri, 10am-2pm Sat; 🚌R-1) Drop by this excellent downtown travel agency to hook up tours to Tulum and Chichén Itzá. Other options include snorkeling and *temazcal* (sweat-lodge) outings.

Cancún

Sights

1 Museo Maya de Cancún C5
San Miguelito .... (see 1)
2 Yamil Lu'um D3
3 Zona Arqueológica El Rey C5

Activities, Courses & Tours

4 Aqua World C4
Asterix .... (see 6)
5 Captain Hook B1
6 Scuba Cancún C2

Sleeping

7 Beachscape Kin Ha Villas & Suites A3
8 Dreams C3
9 Grand Royal Lagoon A3
10 Hostal Mayapan B3
11 Le Blanc D3
12 Me by Melia D3

Eating

13 Checándole A2
14 Crab House C4
15 Forum Mall B3
16 Lorenzillo's D3
17 Mocambo B3
18 Plaza Flamingo D3
19 Restaurante Natura B4
20 Savio's Bistro C4
21 Surfin' Burrito B4
22 Thai Lounge D3

Drinking & Nightlife

La Cura de Todos los Males .... (see 13)
23 Marakame Café B2

Entertainment

Cinemark .... (see 22)
Coco Bongo .... (see 15)
24 Dady'O B3

Shopping

25 La Europea D4
La Isla Shopping Village .... (see 22)
Mercado 28 .... (see 13)
26 Plaza Kukulcán D4

Sleeping

Almost all hotels offer discounts in the 'low' season, but at many places there are up to five different rates: Christmas and New Year are at a premium you can count on, but there are high rates from late February to early March for US spring break, Easter, and even July and August (when locals have their holidays). Ask if there is a 'promotion,' as many places may be willing to deal. Many Zona Hotelera spots offer internet specials, so it's best to book ahead of time if you want to stay near the beach.

Ciudad Cancún

'Budget' is a relative term; prices in Cancún are higher for what you get than most anywhere else in Mexico. There are many cheap lodging options within a few blocks of the bus terminal, northwest on Av Uxmal. The area around Parque de las Palapas has numerous hostels and budget digs as well.

Midrange in Cancún is a two-tiered category; the Ciudad Cancún area is much cheaper than the Zona Hotelera and only a short R-1 bus ride away from the Zona's beaches.

Hostel Mundo Joven HOSTEL $

(Map p62; ☎898-2104; www.mundojovenhostels.com; Av Uxmal 25; dm/d incl breakfast from M$180/550; ❄@📶; 🚌R-1) One of downtown's best budget deals, common-area offerings at this HI affiliate include a rooftop bar and hot tub. Need we say more? Dorm rooms are tidy and cost slightly more with air-conditioning. If you really feel like splurging, Mundo Joven has a private room with your very own Jacuzzi.

Hostel Ka'beh HOSTEL $

(Map p62; ☎892-7902; www.facebook.com/hostelkabeh; Alcatraces 45; dm incl breakfast from M$150; ❄@📶; 🚌R-1) A good central option just off the buzzing Parque de las Palapas, this small hostel has a lived-in feel (some might say cluttered), which goes hand in hand with the relaxed vibe. Expect many social activities at night, most organized around food and drink.

Las Palmas Hotel HOTEL $

(Map p62; ☎884-2513; Palmera 43; dm/d incl breakfast M$120/360; ❄📶; 🚌R-1) A family-run affair, the Palmas has a tidy downstairs dorm room with much-appreciated air-con. There's a handful of clean, affordable rooms upstairs, some in better shape than others. If you are looking to get away from the backpacker scene for a bit, stay here.

Oasis Smart HOTEL $$

(Map p62; ☎848-8600; www.oasishotels.com; Av Tulum; r incl breakfast M$1060; ❄📶🏊; 🚌R-1) You get a lot of bang for your buck at this self-proclaimed lounge hotel. Rooms are modern and comfortable, the bars are chic

CANCÚN FOR CHILDREN

With such easy access to sand, sea and swimming pools, most kids will have a blast in Cancún. Some hotels offer babysitting or day-care services – be sure to check in advance if these are needed. Remember that the sun, strong enough to scald even the thickest of tourist hides, can be even more damaging for kids or babies.

If the beach gets boring or you want a change of scene, check out the numerous theme parks south of town (p102). For a bit more culture, head over to the Maya ruins at Chichén Itzá, Tulum or Cobá, or check out Cancún's new Maya Museum and the adjoining ruins of San Miguelito.

When all else fails, you can never go wrong with a day at the zoo or perhaps a nighttime swashbuckling adventure.

Aqua World (Map p58; ☎848-8300; www.aquaworld.com.mx; Blvd Kukulcán, Km 15.2; bodyboard/windsurf board per day M$156/468, fishing from M$6500) Aqua World has a little bit of everything to keep kids entertained for hours on end. It offers bodyboard rentals, submarine and boat tours and many other fun-filled water activities.

Crococun Zoo (☎850-3719; www.crococunzoo.com; Carretera Cancún-Tulum, Km 31; admission adult/child 6-12yr M$312/194; ⏰9am-5pm Mon-Sat) About 30km south of Cancún (see Map p98), this former crocodile farm now calls itself a '100% conservationist project' that protects the area's endangered species. The price of admission includes a guided tour in which visitors are allowed to interact with some of the animals, such as spider monkeys. Watch out for jealous crocs!

Captain Hook (Map p58; ☎849-4451; www.capitanhook.com; Av López Portillo; adult/child M$1289/645; ⏰tour 7-10:30pm) Kids dig the sword fights and cannon battles on this 3½-hour tour aboard a replica Spanish galleon, located 100m past the Puerto Juárez ferry dock. It costs a pretty doubloon but it comes with lobster or steak dinner.

and you have access to a gym and a very nice swimming pool. And yes, it has Smart car-package deals (thought it wouldn't?).

Soberanis Hotel HOTEL $$
(Map p62; ☎800-101-0101, 884-4564; www.soberanis.com.mx; Av Cobá 5; dm/d incl breakfast M$200/595; @ 📶; 🚌R-1) It's good value here, with a nice location, and it's a fun place to meet friends. All rooms have very comfortable beds, tiled floors, cable TV and nicely appointed bathrooms. Though primarily a midrange hotel, the Soberanis also has four-bed 'hostel' rooms with the same amenities as the regular rooms.

Mallorca HOTEL $$
(Map p62; ☎884-4285; www.mallorcahotelandsuites.com; cnr Gladiolas 11 & Alcatraces; r/ste M$890/1300; ❄ 📶; 🚌R-1) Fusing modern and colonial styles, the well-appointed rooms and suites in this new hotel are a mighty fine value and you can't beat the location – right off the Parque de las Palapas and conveniently close to downtown's restaurant and bar zone.

Hotel Antillano HOTEL $$
(Map p62; ☎884-1132; www.hotelantillano.com; Claveles 1; s/d incl breakfast M$780/910; ❄ 📶 🏊; 🚌R-1) Just off Av Tulum, this is a very pleasant and quiet place with a relaxing lobby, nice pool, good central air-con and cable TV. Rooms on Av Tulum are noisier than those in the back. Rates drop considerably during low season.

Colonial Cancún HOTEL $$
(Map p62; ☎884-1535; www.economyclasshotels.com; Tulipanes 22; d incl breakfast M$850; ❄ 📶; 🚌R-1) Rooms are anything but colonial, but they're pleasant enough and they overlook a leafy central courtyard with a tinkling fountain. Get a room toward the back to distance yourself from the street noise in this party zone.

Hotel Bonampak HOTEL $$
(Map p62; ☎884-0280; www.hotelbonampak.com; Av Bonampak 225 ; r M$749; P ❄ @ 📶 🏊; 🚌R-27) Good value by Cancún standards, rooms at this business-style hotel got a recent makeover with comfy new mattresses, dark wood furnishings and LCD TVs. Ask for a room overlooking the sunny pool area.

Hotel Plaza Caribe HOTEL $$
(Map p62; ☎800-215-1500, 884-1377; www.hotelplazacaribe.com; Pino; r M$1100; P ❄ 📶 🏊;

R-1) Directly across from the bus terminal between Avs Tulum and Uxmal, this all-business hotel offers 140 comfortable rooms with full amenities, including a pool, a restaurant and gardens with peacocks roaming about. Rooms have white-tile floors, good beds and clean bathrooms.

★Hotel El Rey del Caribe HOTEL $$$
(Map p62; 884-2028; www.elreydelcaribe.com; cnr Avs Uxmal & Náder; s/d M$1170/1400; ; R-1) El Rey is a true ecotel that recycles, employs solar collectors and cisterns, uses gray water on the gardens, and has some rooms with composting toilets. This is a beautiful spot with a swimming pool and Jacuzzi in a jungly courtyard that's home to a small family of *tlacuaches* (opossums). All rooms have a fully equipped kitchenette, comfortable beds and fridges. Look for great deals in low season.

Zona Hotelera

With few exceptions, most hotels lining Blvd Kukulcán are of the top-end variety. Many offer all-inclusive packages, often at reasonable rates if you're willing to forgo eating or entertainment elsewhere. Often the best room rates are available through booking hotel-and-airfare packages, so shop around.

Hostal Mayapan HOSTEL $
(Map p58; 883-3227; www.hostalmayapan.com; Blvd Kukulcán, Km 8.5; dm incl breakfast M$200-240, r M$600; ; R-1) Located in an abandoned mall, this is the only budget spot in the Zona Hotelera. Thanks to its location just 30m from the beach, it's one of our favorite hostels in town. The rooms are superclean and there's a little hangout spot in an atrium upstairs (the old food court?).

Grand Royal Lagoon HOTEL $$
(Map p58; 883-1270; www.grandroyallagoon.jimdo.com; Quetzal 8A; r/ste M$1000/1100; ; R-1) A breezy place and relatively affordable for the hotel zone, the Grand Royal offers cable TV, safes and a small pool. Most rooms have two double beds, while some have kings, lagoon views and balconies. The hotel is 100m off Blvd Kukulcán Km 7.7.

Beachscape Kin Ha Villas & Suites HOTEL $$$
(Map p58; 891-5400; www.beachscape.com.mx; Blvd Kukulcán, Km 8.5; r from M$2480; ; R-1) A good family spot, Beachscape offers babysitting service and a play area for kids. You'll never need to leave the hotel's grounds (though we think you should), as there are 132 big rooms and suites in five buildings in this rolling complex. All rooms feature a balcony and two double beds or one king-sized bed. There are bars, markets, travel and car-rental agencies and more on the premises. Price listed is for European plan, but you can arrange an all-inclusive stay.

Me by Melia LUXURY HOTEL $$$
(Map p58; 881-2500; www.mebymelia.com; Blvd Kukulcán, Km 12; s/d all-inclusive M$4500/6800; ; R-1) 'Enough about you, let's talk about me!' That's the philosophy at this ubermodern, expressionist-inspired hotel. It won't suit everyone, but if you prefer clean lines over your standard Cancún baroque, then Me is the place for you. Only half the rooms have ocean views, and it just ain't worth it to pay this much and not have a view of the Caribbean blue.

Eating

Ciudad Cancún

Eating options in Ciudad Cancún range from your standard-issue taco joints to upscale seafood restaurants. You'll find many restaurants near Parque de las Palapas and along Av Yaxchilán. Mercados 23 and 28 serve up good market food, and there are some **food stands** (Map p62; Parque de las Palapas) right on the Palapas plaza. For groceries, try **Comercial Mexicana** (Map p62; cnr Avs Tulum & Uxmal), close to the bus station, or **Chedraui Supermarket** (Map p62; 7am-11pm; ; R-1).

El Paisano del 23 MEXICAN $
(Map p62; Mercado 23; tacos M$12, tortas M$30; 6am-3pm; R-1) A local favorite for more than 40 years, the *paisano* ('fellow countryman' – it's the owner's nickname) marinates *pierna* (pork leg) in red wine and then slow-cooks it to perfection. The *tortas* (sandwiches) go fast, especially on weekends.

Los de Pescado SEAFOOD $
(Map p62; Av Tulum 32; tacos & tostadas M$24-26, ceviche M$78-117; 9am-6:30pm; R-27) It's easy to order at a place where you have only four choices: *ceviche* (seafood marinated in lemon or lime juice, garlic and seasonings), tacos, *tostadas* (fried tortilla) or burritos.

Ciudad Cancún

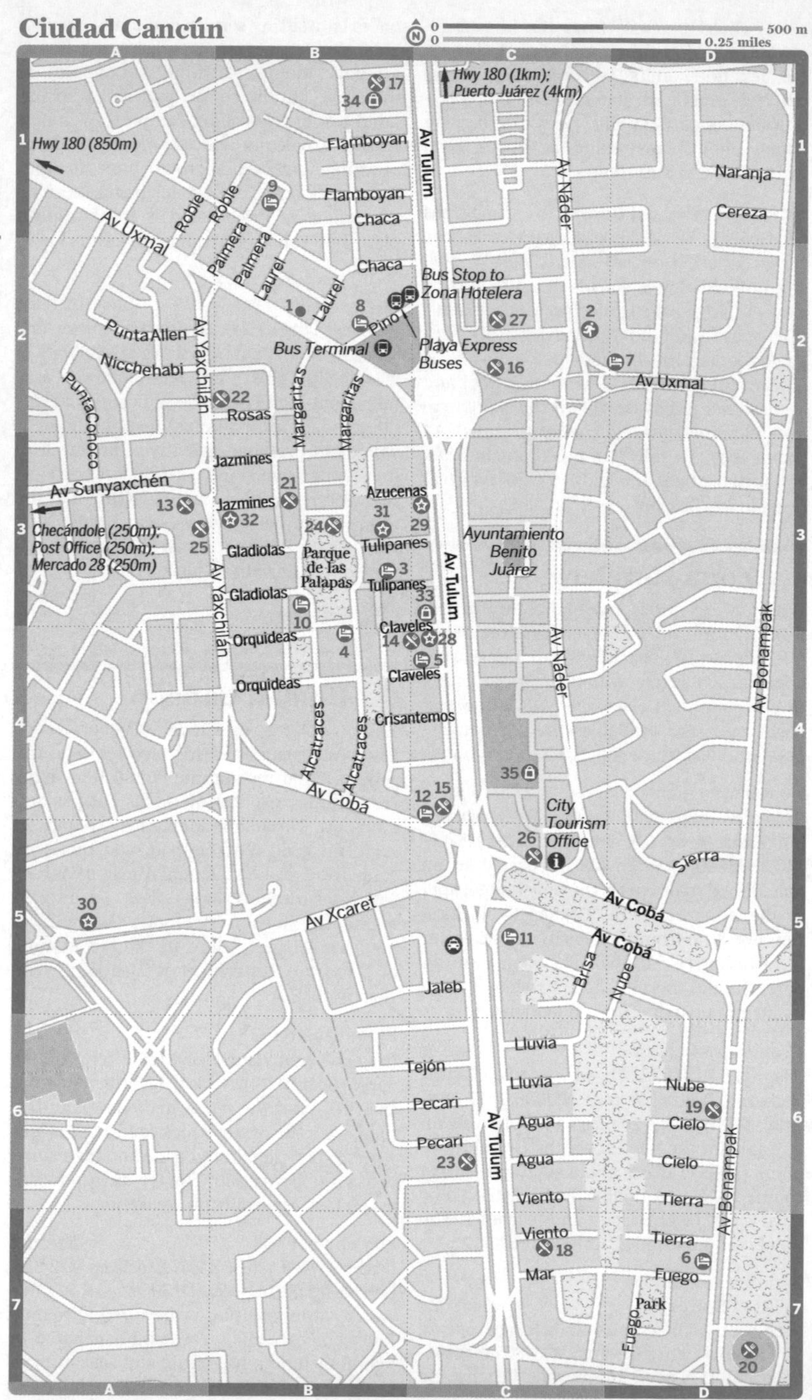

Ciudad Cancún

Activities, Courses & Tours

1 Hostel Mundo Joven ... B2
2 Koko Dog'z ... C2
Teatro Xbalamqué ... (see 32)

Sleeping

3 Colonial Cancún ... B3
4 Hostel Ka'beh ... B4
Hostel Mundo Joven ... (see 1)
5 Hotel Antillano ... C4
6 Hotel Bonampak ... D7
7 Hotel El Rey del Caribe ... D2
8 Hotel Plaza Caribe ... B2
9 Las Palmas Hotel ... B1
10 Mallorca ... B3
11 Oasis Smart ... C5
12 Soberanis Hotel ... C4

Eating

13 100% Natural ... A3
14 Carrillo's Lobster House ... C4
15 Chedraui Supermarket ... C4
16 Comercial Mexicana ... C2
17 El Paisano del 23 ... B1
18 Irori ... C7
19 K Sadillas del Jalisco ... D6
20 La Barbacoa de la Tulum ... D7
21 La Habichuela ... B3
22 La Parrilla ... B2
23 Los de Pescado ... C6
24 Mexican Food Stalls ... B3
25 Pescaditos ... A3
26 Rolandi's Restaurant-Bar ... C5
27 Ty-Coz ... C2

Drinking & Nightlife

Plaza de Toros ... (see 20)

Entertainment

28 11:11 ... C4
29 Karamba ... C3
30 Mambo Café ... A5
31 Roots ... B3
32 Teatro Xbalamqué ... B3

Shopping

33 Colormax ... C3
34 Mercado 23 ... B1
35 Mercado Municipal Ki-Huic ... C4

Try the fish and shrimp tacos and you'll see why this is one of the best budget spots in Ciudad Cancún.

La Barbacoa de la Tulum MEXICAN $
(Map p62; Plaza de Toros; M$15-18; 24hrs; R-27) If you love tacos, head to this 24-hour restaurant/bar, where the specialties are *cochinita* (marinated pork) and *barbacoa* (mutton).

Ty-Coz SANDWICHES $
(Map p62; 884-6060; Av Tulum; sandwiches M$35-70; 8am-10pm Mon-Sat; P; R-1) This bakery-cafe has granite tabletops, a pleasing ambiance, and serves good coffee, baguettes and croissants, as well as sandwiches made with a variety of meats and cheeses.

K Sadillas del Jalisco MEXICAN $
(Map p62; Av Bonampak 193; quesadillas M$18, set meals M$60; 8am-5pm Mon-Sat) For a cheap lunch on this side of town, head over to the small sidewalk restaurant K Sadillas, where the friendly owner Javier serves up affordable lunches and, you guessed it...quesadillas.

★ **Checándole** MEXICAN $$
(Map p58; 884-7147; cnr Av Xpujil 6 & Tankah; mains M$59-128; noon-8pm Mon-Sat; R-2) If you can only eat at one restaurant in Cancún, then you should eat here. Checándole specializes in chilango (Mexico City) cuisine. The *menú del día* (fixed three-course meal) is just M$50 – great value. If it's offering *pollo en mole poblano* (chicken smothered in a handmade chocolate and chili sauce), you should definitely go for it.

Va Q' Va SEAFOOD $$
(Calle 107, btwn Avs Leona Vicario & Niños Héroes; M$80-260; 10am-7pm Mon-Thu, 9am-7pm Fri-Sun) The fish and seafood are pretty good here but the real draw is the festive atmosphere, plus you get to enjoy a meal in a working-class 'hood far away from the tourist center. It's worth it just for the marimba music and *clamato micheladas* (beer with Clamato juice – a tomato and clam cocktail mix – lime and salt). You'll need a taxi to get here.

Pescaditos SEAFOOD $$
(Map p62; Av Yaxchilán 69; M$36-110; 11:30am-midnight;) The namesake *pescaditos* (fried fish sticks served with a mayo-chipotle sauce) are the star attraction here, but the menu features plenty of other fresh fish and seafood dishes well worth trying.

100% Natural MEXICAN $$
(Cien Por Ciento Natural; Map p62; 884-0102; www.100natural.com.mx; Av Sunyaxchén 62; mains

LIVING LARGE IN THE MEXICAN CARIBBEAN

Cancún and its surrounding areas have so many establishments selling the 'resort' experience, but only some are truly worth the splurge. Rest assured that all of the following places occupy prime beachfront property, so it's really just a question of what best suits your needs: some hotels put a premium on over-the-top comfort and elegance, others specialize in the family-friendly getaway with around-the-clock activities. When booking a room, keep in mind that some resorts do not accept children and most, though not all, offer all-inclusive plans with an endless banquet of food and drink. Rates listed here are for double occupancy with meal plans.

Grand Velas (800-831-1165; www.rivieramaya.grandvelas.com; Carretera Cancún-Tulum , Km 62; d from M$9100, all-inclusive, child 4-16yr M$1287;) The mother of all beach resorts, the sprawling Grand Velas boasts one of the best spas on the coast; an azure, free-form infinity pool; marble-floored rooms that put other so-called luxury accommodations to shame; loads of activities for kids and grown-ups; and the list goes on. It's 6km north of Playa del Carmen.

Le Blanc (Map p58; 881-4740; www.leblancsparesort.com; Blvd Kukulcán, Km 10; d all-inclusive M$8962; ; R-1) You can't miss the glaring white exterior of the aptly-named Le Blanc, arguably Cancun's most sophisticated resort. This adults-only retreat comes with all the amenities you'd expect in this category – there's even butler service should life in Cancún become too complicated. Too pricey? A day pass (M$1850) gets you access to sweet infinity pools, free drinks and several meals in the hotel's restaurants.

Dreams (Map p58; 848-7000; www.dreamsresorts.com; Punta Cancún s/n; d all-inclusive from M$5044, child 4-11yr M$520; ; R-1) Dreams sits pretty on Punta Cancún (the easternmost point of the hotel zone), giving you some amazing ocean views. All rooms are luxurious here but not all were created equal – views and level of comfort vary considerably depending on what you spend. Parents itching for alone time will welcome the babysitter service and kids club.

Petit Lafitte (877-4000; www.petitlafitte.com; Carretera Cancún-Chetumal, Km 296, Playa Xcalacoco, 6km north of Playa del Carmen; d/bungalow incl breakfast & dinner from M$2600/3192, child 3-11yr additional M$715;) Occupying a quiet beach far removed from the Playa del Carmen party scene, Petit Lafitte is an excellent family vacation spot. Stay in a room or a 'bungalow' (essentially a wood cabin with tasteful rustic furnishings, some of which sleep up to five guests). Kids stay entertained with the large pool, small zoo, games room and various water activities. See website for directions.

M$64-136; 7am-11pm;) Vegetarians and health-food nuts delight at this health-food chain near Av Yaxchilán, which serves juice blends, a wide selection of yogurt-fruit-vegetable combinations, brown rice, pasta, fish and chicken dishes. The onsite bakery turns out whole-wheat products, and the entire place is very nicely decorated and landscaped.

Rolandi's Restaurant-Bar ITALIAN $$
(Map p62; 884-4047; Av Cobá 12; mains M$128-188; noon-midnight; ; R-1) A Swiss-Italian eatery with a wood-fired pizza oven, between Avs Tulum and Náder just off the southern roundabout, Rolandi's serves elaborate pizzas, spaghetti plates and a range of northern Italian dishes.

Irori JAPANESE $$
(Map p62; 892-3072; Av Tulum 226; M$90-300; 1-11pm Mon-Sat, to 10pm Sun; ; R-27) Enjoy the show as the chef slices and dices the night away at this Japanese-run restaurant serving sushi and many other Japanese favorites in an intimate and nicely decorated setting. There's even a kids' menu and play room if you've got little sushi-scoffers in tow.

La Habichuela FUSION $$$
(Map p62; 884-3158; Margaritas 25; mains M$167-268, cocobichuela M$400; noon-midnight; R-1) An elegant restaurant with a lovely courtyard dining area, just off Parque de las Palapas.

The specialty is the *cocobichuela* (shrimp and lobster in curry sauce served inside a coconut with tropical fruit), but almost anything on the menu is delicious. The seafood ceviche and *tapa al ajillo* (assorted seafood accented with garlic) are mouthwatering.

La Parrilla MEXICAN **$$$**
(Map p62; 884-8193; www.laparrilla.com.mx; Av Yaxchilán 51; mains M$133-295; noon-2am) Any Cancún eatery founded before the saccharine 1980s gets to call itself venerable. And La Parrilla (founded in 1975) should get a capital 'V.' A traditional Mexican restaurant popular with locals and tourists alike, it serves a varied menu from all over Mexico, including the house specialty, enchiladas in *mole* (sauce). There's live mariachi music every night at 8pm.

Carrillo's Lobster House SEAFOOD **$$$**
(Map p62; 884-1227; Claveles 35; shrimp & fish dishes M$110-200, lobster M$400-485; 1pm-10pm; R-1) Try Carrillo's Plato Cozumel if you're looking for something a bit special; the surf & turf is a great option for two people. Just follow the good smells leading to the blue building and you'll be in the right place.

Zona Hotelera

'Pay-per-view' takes on a whole different meaning in the Zona Hotelera. Prices sometimes reflect the location of the restaurant and what's outside the window more than the quality of food. That being said, there are a fair share of excellent seafood restaurants along the strip too.

For budget eats in the Zona Hotelera, you can always hit the food courts at any large mall. La Isla Shopping Village, **Plaza Flamingo** (Map p58) and the **Forum Mall** (Map p58) have other options to get a bite.

Surfin' Burrito FAST FOOD **$**
(Map p58; Blvd Kukulcán, Km 9.8; M$49-75; 24hrs; R-1) A real crowd-pleaser on the strip, where cheap eats come few and far between, this small burrito joint prepares beef, shrimp, fish and vegetarian burritos with your choice of tasty fixings. It's open 24/7, making it a popular after-hours munchies spot.

Restaurante Natura VEGETARIAN **$$**
(Map p58; Blvd Kukulcán, Km 9.8; mains M$79-150; 7:30am-11pm; ; R-1) This little bistro offers up a good mix of natural and vegetarian Mexican cuisine – think giant natural juices, and quesadillas with Chihuahua cheese, spinach, mushrooms and whole-wheat tortillas. There's also a vegan menu.

Lorenzillo's SEAFOOD **$$$**
(Map p58; 883-1254; www.lorenzillos.com.mx; Blvd Kukulcán, Km 10.5; mains M$295-460, lobster M$620-780; 1pm-12:30am; P; R-1) Reputed by locals to be Cancún's best seafood restaurant, Lorenzillo's gives you 20 separate choices for your lobster presentation, including a tastebud-popping chipotle, plum and tamarind sauce. Facing the lagoon, it's a wonderful sunset joint.

Thai Lounge THAI **$$$**
(Map p58; 176-8070; www.thai.com.mx; Blvd Kukulcán, Km 12.5, in Plaza La Isla; M$230-500; 6pm-11:30pm) Tucked away in the rear of La Isla shopping mall, Thai food is served here under your own private, stilted *palapa* (shelter with a thatched, palm-leaf roof and open sides), either with a garden or lagoon view. The Pla de Phuket, a crunchy fish fillet in tamarind chili sauce, is especially good.

Crab House SEAFOOD **$$$**
(Map p58; 193-0370; www.crabhousecancun.com; Blvd Kukulcán, Km 14.8; dishes M$165-450; noon-11:30pm; P; R-1) Offering a lovely view of the lagoon that complements the seafood, the long menu here includes many shrimp and fish-fillet dishes. Crab and lobster are priced by the pound.

Savio's Bistro ITALIAN **$$$**
(Map p58; 885-0161; www.cancunitalianrestaurant.com; Blvd Kukulcán, Km 15; pizzas M$170-190, mains M$195-365; noon-11:30pm; R-1) One of Cancún's smartest Italian restaurants offers great lagoon views. The fish and seafood dishes come highly recommended; try the *boquinete* (Caribbean snapper) or salmon in white-wine sauce. Dine at sunset if you want to sweeten the mood.

Mocambo SEAFOOD **$$$**
(Map p58; 883-0398; Blvd Kukulcán, Km 9.5; mains M$195-260; noon-11pm; P) Definitely one of the best spots in the Zona Hotelera, the *palapa*-covered Mocambo sits right on the ocean and serves up excellent seafood dishes like grouper, grilled conch and a savory seafood paella. There's nightly live music Tuesday through Sunday.

Drinking & Nightlife

Ciudad Cancún

Ciudad Cancún's clubs and bars are generally mellower than those in the rowdy Zona Hotelera. Stroll along Av Yaxchilán down to Parque de las Palapas and you are sure to run into something (or somebody) you like.

Roots JAZZ

(Map p62; ☎884-2437; www.rootsjazzclub.com; Tulipanes 26; ⏰7pm-2am Thu-Sat; 🚌R-1) Pretty much the coolest bar in Ciudad Cancún, Roots features mostly jazz bands and the occasional international act. It's also a pretty decent restaurant, serving pasta, salads, seafood and meat dishes, with main dishes running from M$120 to M$190.

Mambo Café CLUB

(Map p62; ☎884-4536; www.mambocafe.com.mx; cnr Avs Xcaret & Tankah; ⏰10:30pm-6am Wed-Sat; 🚌R-2) The large floor at this happening club in Plaza Hong Kong is perfect to practice those Latin dance steps you've been working on. Live groups play Cuban salsa and other tropical styles.

Marakame Café BAR

(Map p58; ☎887-1087; www.marakamecafe.com; Av Circuito Copán, near Av Nichupte; ⏰8am-1am Mon-Wed, 8am-2am Thu & Fri, 9am-2am Sat, 9am-midnight Sun; 📶) An excellent open-air breakfast and lunch spot by day and popular bar by night, with live music Wednesday through Saturday. The bartenders, or mixologists if you will, prepare interesting concoctions such as kiwi-flavored mojitos and margaritas blended with *chaya* (a leafy Mexican green), cucumber and lime. It's a short taxi ride from downtown.

La Cura de Todos los Males BAR

(Map p58; cnr Av Xel-Ha & Erizo, In Mercado 28; ⏰2pm-1am Mon-Sat, 6pm-1am Sun; 🚌R-2) Paying tribute to Mexican pop culture and all things retro, this hip *mezcal* bar draws a young, mostly local crowd. Knock back *mezcal* (an alcoholic agave drink), beer served in buckets of ice, or try the 'Llamarada Moe,' aka the Flaming Moe.

Karamba GAY

(Map p62; ☎884-0032; www.karambabar.com; Av Tulum 9, cnr Azucenas; ⏰10:30pm-6am Tue-Sun; 🚌R-1) A venerable standby, this nightclub offers a mixed bag of entertainment throughout the week, from gogo-boy dancers to drag-queen shows and various theme parties. Admission ranges from free to M$100.

11:11 GAY

(Once Once; Map p62; cnr Av Tulum & Claveles; ⏰10pm-6am Wed-Sun; 🚌R-1) The main room in this large house stages drag shows, go-go dancers and the like, while DJs in smaller rooms spin electronica and pop tunes till the break of dawn.

Plaza de Toros BAR

(Map p62; Bullring, cnr Avs Bonampak & Sayil) Built into the Plaza de Toros are several bars, some with music, that draw a largely local crowd.

Zona Hotelera

The club scene in the Zona Hotelera is young, loud and booze-oriented – the kind that often has an MC urging women to display body parts to hooting and hollering crowds. The big dance clubs charge around M$600 to M$900 admission, which includes open-bar privileges (ie drink all you want). Most don't get hopping much before midnight.

A number of clubs are clustered along the northwest-bound side of Blvd Kukulcán, all within easy stumbling distance of each other. Be careful crossing the street.

Coco Bongo CLUB

(Map p58; ☎883-5061; www.cocobongo.com.mx; Km 9.5, Forum Mall; ⏰10pm-4am; 🚌R-1) This is the spot where spring breakers go wild, and tends to be a happening spot just about any day of the year. Dancing is interspersed with live acts featuring celebrity impersonators, dancers and circus acts (think clowns, acrobats and the like) throughout the night.

Dady'O CLUB

(Map p58; ☎800-234-9797; Blvd Kukulcán, Km 9.5; ⏰10pm-4am; 🚌R-1) One of Cancún's classic dance clubs. The setting is a five-level, black-walled faux cave with a two-level dance floor and what seems like zillions of laser beams and strobes. The predominant beats are Latin, house, techno and pop, and the crowd is mainly 20-something.

☆ Entertainment

Cinemark CINEMA

(Map p58; ☎883-5603; www.cinemark.com.mx; La Isla Shopping Village; 🚌R-1) In general, Hollywood movies are shown in English with Spanish subtitles; however, English-language children's movies are usually dubbed in Spanish. Tickets cost M$70.

Teatro Xbalamqué THEATER
(Map p62; ☎147-7322; http://teatroxbalamque.blogspot.com; cnr Jazmines & Av Yaxchilán) Has musical comedies, monologues and actors workshops.

Shopping

Shopaholics will enjoy the city's colorful markets, which offer jewelry, handicrafts and souvenirs, as well as a variety of inexpensive Mexican food. Locals head to either **Mercado 28** (Mercado Veintiocho; Map p58; cnr Av Xel-Há & Av Sunyaxchén) or **Mercado 23** (Map p62; Av Tulum s/n; R-1) for clothes, shoes, inexpensive food stalls and so on. Of the two, Mercado 23 is the least frequented by tourists. If you're looking for a place without corny T-shirts, this is the place to go.

Neither Ciudad Cancún nor the Zona Hotelera fits the bill as a bargain-hunter's paradise, but if you're feeling homesick, you can rest easy knowing there's no shortage of modern malls.

La Europea DRINK
(Map p58; www.laeuropea.com.mx; Blvd Kukulcán, Km 12.5; 10am-9pm Mon-Sat, 11am-6pm Sun; R-1) La Europea has reasonable prices, knowledgeable staff and hands down the best liquor selection in town, including top-shelf tequilas and *mezcals*. Most airlines allow you to travel with up to 3L of alcohol, but you might want to double-check. Salud!

La Isla Shopping Village MALL
(Map p58; www.laislacancun.com.mx; Blvd Kukulcán, Km 12.5; ; R-1) Unique among the malls, this is an indoor-outdoor place with canals, an aquarium, a movie theater and enough distractions to keep even the most inveterate hater of shopping amused. For drinkers on your gift list, consider picking up a bottle of *xtabentún*, a *yucateco* anise-flavored liqueur.

Plaza Kukulcán MALL
(Map p58; www.kukulcanplaza.com; Blvd Kukulcán, Km 13; ; R-1) The largest (and definitely among the stuffiest, attitude-wise) of the indoor malls is Plaza Kukulcán. Of note here is the huge art gallery (taking up nearly half of the 2nd floor); the many stores selling silverwork; and La Ruta de las Indias, a shop featuring wooden models of Spanish galleons and replicas of conquistadors' weaponry and body armor.

Mercado Municipal Ki-Huic MARKET
(Map p62; Av Tulum; R-1) This warren of stalls and shops carries a wide variety of souvenirs and handicrafts.

Colormax ACCESSORIES
(Map p62; Av Tulum 22; 9am-9pm Mon-Fri, 10am-5pm Sat; R-1) Just north of Claveles, Colormax sells memory cards for digital cameras and film for you old-school photographers.

Orientation

Cancún consists of two very distinct areas: Ciudad Cancún (downtown) and Isla Cancún (the Zona Hotelera).

The Zona Hotelera is what most people think of when they say 'Cancún': the sandy spit that encloses a scenic lagoon on one side and has the Caribbean's azure-greens on the other. Its main road, Blvd Kukulcán, is a four-lane, divided avenue that leaves Ciudad Cancún and heads eastward for a few kilometers, passing condominium developments, several hotels and shopping complexes, to Punta Cancún (Cancún Point) and the Centro de Convenciones (Convention Center).

From Punta Cancún, the boulevard heads south for about 13km, flanked on both sides for much of the way by huge hotels, shopping centers, dance clubs and many restaurants and bars, to Punta Nizuc (Nizuc Point). Here it turns westward and then rejoins the mainland, cutting through light tropical forest for a few more kilometers to its southern terminus at Cancún's international airport.

Addresses in the Zona Hotelera are refreshingly simple: instead of a street name (usually Blvd Kukulcán anyway), a kilometer distance from the 'Km 0' roadside marker at the boulevard's northern terminus in Ciudad Cancún is given. Each kilometer is similarly marked. Most bus drivers will know the location you're heading but, if in doubt, you can just ask to be dropped off at the appropriate kilometer marker.

Information

DANGERS & ANNOYANCES

The biggest safety danger in Cancún isn't street crime – it's the streets themselves. Traffic speeds by along narrow roads and pedestrians (often drunk) are frequently injured. A night spent clubbing is more likely to lead to a poked eye or twisted ankle than a mugging; however, if anyone *does* demand money, don't argue with them. Most violent incidents have involved fights where tourists or locals have actively put themselves in danger.

Theft of valuables left unattended is a possibility, but no more so than in other parts of the world. Use prudence, keeping vital items with you or leaving them in a hotel safe, and you'll avoid problems. Napping sunbathers may wake up to find cameras or wallets gone; don't leave anything unattended on the beach.

Hawkers can be quite irritating but are not dangerous. The best way to avoid them is to just keep walking. As frustrating as this may be, remember that these vendors are just trying to make a living for themselves and their families.

EMERGENCY

Cruz Roja (Red Cross; ☎884-1616) Red Cross.

Fire (☎066)

Police (☎066; Blvd Kukulcán, Km 13.5; 🚌R-1)

Tourist Police (☎885-2277)

IMMIGRATION

Instituto Nacional de Migración (Immigration Office; ☎881-3560; cnr Av Náder 1 & Av Uxmal; ⏰9am-1pm Mon-Fri) For visa and tourist-permit extensions. Enter the left-hand, southernmost of the two offices.

INTERNET ACCESS

Internet cafes in Cancún *centro* are plentiful, speedy and cheap, costing M$15 per hour or less.

MEDIA

Cancun Tips (www.cancuntips.com.mx) A quarterly print magazine with good info on the area, though the website could use a few tips.

MEDICAL SERVICES

Hospital Playa Med (☎140-5258; cnr Av Náder 13 & Av Uxmal; ⏰24hrs; 🚌R-1) Modern facility with 24-hour assistance.

MONEY

There are several banks with ATMs throughout the Zona Hotelera and downtown on Av Tulum (between Avs Cobá and Uxmal). Cancún's airport also has ATMs and money exchange.

American Express (cnr Av Tulum 208 & Agua)

Banamex ATM (Blvd Kukulcán, Km 8.5; ⏰24hr)

Bancomer (Av Tulum 150) Next to Mercado Municipal Ki-Huic; there is a second branch at Av Tulum 20.

Scotiabank (La Isla Shopping Village, Zona Hotelera; ⏰24hr)

POST

There is no post office in the Zona Hotelera, but most hotels' reception desks sell stamps and will mail letters.

Main Post Office (☎884-1418; cnr Avs Xel-Há & Sunyaxchén; ⏰8am-4pm Mon-Fri, 9am-12:30pm Sat) Downtown at the edge of Mercado 28. You can also post mail in the red postal boxes sprinkled around town.

TOURIST INFORMATION

Cancún Visitors Bureau (www.cancun.travel) An informative website, but no tourist office.

City Tourism Office (☎887-3379; www.cancun.gob.mx; Av Náder s/n, cnr Av Cobá; ⏰8am-4pm Mon-Fri, 9am-12:30pm Sat) The only city tourist office in town; has ample supplies of printed material.

ℹ Getting There & Away

AIR

Cancún's **Aeropuerto Internacional de Cancún** (☎848-7200; www.asur.com.mx; Carretera Cancún-Chetumal, Km 22) is the busiest in southeastern Mexico. It has all the services you would expect from a major international airport: ATMs, money exchange, rental-car agencies.

Cancún is served by many direct international flights and by connecting flights from Mexico City. Low-cost carriers **Viva Aerobus** (www.vivaaerobus.com), **Interjet** (www.interjet.com) and **Volaris** (www.volaris.com) all have service from Mexico City.

The following is just some of the dozens of carriers with flights to Cancún. For a more complete list, see the airport website.

Aeroméxico (☎287-1860; www.aeromexico.com; Av Cobá 80; 🚌R-1) Direct flights from New York. Office just west of Av Bonampak.

American Airlines (☎ in Mexico 800-904-6000, USA 800-433-7300; www.aa.com) Service from Miami, Dallas and New York.

British Airways (☎ in USA 866-835-4133; www.britishairways.com) Nonstop from London.

Cubana (☎887-7210; www.cubana.cu; Av Tulum btwn Mar & Av Sayil; 🚌R-27) To Habana.

Delta Airlines (☎866-0660; www.delta.com) Serves Atlanta.

Magnicharters (☎884-0600; www.magnicharters.com.mx; cnr Av Náder 93 & Av Cobá; 🚌R-1) Does flights with vacation packages from Mexico City.

United Airlines (☎ in Mexico 800-900-5000, USA 800-864-8331; www.united.com) Direct from Chicago and San Francisco.

US Airways (☎886-0373, USA 800-428-4322; www.usairways.com) Nonstop from Philadelphia and Phoenix.

BOAT

There are several points of embarkation to reach Isla Mujeres from Cancún by boat. From **Puerto Juárez** it costs M$70, and leaving from the Zona Hotelera runs about M$135. If you want to transport a vehicle you'll need to head to **Punta Sam**, 8km north of Ciudad Cancún (p83). For

Isla Holbox, ferries leave from Chiquilá, and for Isla Contoy boats depart from the **Marina Scuba Cancún**. For more on hours and departure points to Isla Mujeres, see www.granpuerto.com.mx.

BUS

Cancún's modern **bus terminal** (cnr Avs Uxmal & Tulum) occupies the wedge formed where Avs Uxmal and Tulum meet. It's a safe area and you'll be fine walking around. Across Pino from the bus terminal, a few doors from Av Tulum, is the ticket office and miniterminal of **Playa Express** (Calle Pino), which runs air-con buses down the coast to Playa del Carmen every 10 minutes until early evening, stopping at major towns and points of interest. **ADO** (☎800-009-9090; www.ado.com.mx) covers the same ground and beyond with its 1st-class service.

Boletotal (www.boletotal.mx) is an excellent online source for up-to-date bus schedules. You can buy tickets through the site, too, but they charge a commission.

ADO sets the 1st-class standard, while ADO Platino (p292), ADO GL (p292) and **OCC** (☎800-900-0105; www.occbus.com.mx) provide luxury services. Mayab provides good 'intermediate class' (modern air-con buses, tending to make more stops than 1st class) to many points, while Oriente's 2nd-class air-con buses often depart and arrive late; purchase tickets for these companies at the bus-terminal counter.

CAR

You're better off leaving the rental car parked inside Cancún and walking or catching a bus to most places in town till you're ready to get out of town. Be warned also that Hwy 180D, the 238km *cuota* (toll road) running much of the way between Cancún and Mérida, costs M$381 for the distance and has only two exits before the end. The first, at Valladolid, costs M$241 to reach from Cancún and the second, at Pisté (for Chichén Itzá), is an additional M$59.

Hertz (☎800-709-5000; www.hertz.com)

National (☎881-8760; www.nationalcar.com; Cancún Airport)

Getting Around

If you're staying in Ciudad Cancún, the Zona Hotelera is just a 15-minute ride away. The main north–south thoroughfare, Av Tulum, is the easiest street to catch city buses and taxis.

TO/FROM THE AIRPORT

ADO buses to Ciudad Cancún (M$52) leave the airport every 30 minutes between 8:15am and 11pm. They depart from a parking lot next to the international arrivals terminal. Once in town, the buses travel up Av Tulum and will stop most anywhere you ask. One central stop is across from the Chedraui supermarket on Av Cobá. Going to the airport from Ciudad Cancún, the same ADO airport buses (Aeropuerto Centro) leave regularly from the bus terminal.

BUSES FROM CANCÚN

Some of the major routes serviced daily:

DESTINATION	COST (M$)	DURATION (HR)	FREQUENCY
Chetumal	302-362	5½-6	frequent
Chichén Itzá	119-194	3-4	8 daily
Chiquilá	86	3½	2 daily Mayab 7:50am & 12:40pm
Felipe Carrillo Puerto	126-186	3½-4	frequent
Mérida	180-490	4-7	frequent
Mexico City	1536-1788	24-26	4 daily to Terminal Norte
Mexico City (TAPO)	1518-1788	23-26	6 daily
Palenque	684-816	12-13½	7 daily
Playa del Carmen	34-45	1-1¼	frequent ADO & Playa Express
Puerto Morelos	20-26	½-¾	frequent ADO & Playa Express
Ticul	220	8½	frequent
Tizimín	98	4	5 daily
Tulum	80-104	2½	frequent
Valladolid	150-158	2-3	6 daily
Villahermosa	746-945	12-13½	frequent
Xcaret	42-90	1½	frequent Playa Express & ADO

DAY-TRIPPER: FIVE GREAT EXCURSIONS FROM CANCÚN

What are you waiting for? There's a whole world beyond Cancún. And here's a quick sustainable travel tip: skip the group tour and use that extra dough to hire a local guide and buy some crafts. Staying the night in your destination will bring even more money into the local community.

- **Chichén Itzá** (p177) Rent a car so you can take the old highway through Valladolid. Stop in the small Maya communities along the way for out-of-sight *panuchos* (small corn tortillas stuffed with mashed beans and topped with shredded turkey or chicken).
- **Isla Mujeres** (p75) Take the ferry from Puerto Juárez. Check out the turtle farm in the morning, then swing up north to a sweet little swimming spot near the Avalon Reef Club.
- **Tulum** (p113) Get up early and rent a car to make your way down to Tulum. Along the way you'll want to stop in Akumal's Laguna Yal-Kú for a dip. On the way back, stop at one of the numerous cenotes clearly marked from the highway.
- **Puerto Morelos** (p99) Just a half-hour ride heading south of Cancún, you'll find this quiet beach town with a small plaza, an excellent crafts market and surprisingly good restaurants. Playa Express buses depart frequently from in front of the bus terminal.
- **Nuevo Durango and beyond** Make your own way through the Maya hinterland as you explore small villages such as Nuevo Durango (Map p98), and forgotten cenotes that don't even make it into the guidebooks. Offer a reasonable payment and locals will often put you up in a *palapa* (thatched palm leaf–roofed shelter). Bring your own hammock and a sense of adventure.

Yellow Transfers (www.yellowtransfers.com), with ticket booths in each terminal, runs shuttles to and from Ciudad Cancún and the Zona Hotelera for M$160 per person. Comfortable Gray Line Express *colectivos* (shared vans) depart from the curb in front of the international terminal about every 15 minutes for the Zona Hotelera and Ciudad Cancún; they charge about M$195 per person for Cancún destinations (like Yellow Transfers, they do multiple drop-offs unless you hire a private car). The shuttles also serve nearby Puerto Morelos (M$235) and Playa del Carmen (M$390).

Regular taxis into town or to the Zona Hotelera cost up to M$500 (up to four people) if you catch them right outside the airport. If you follow the access road out of the airport, however, and past the traffic-monitoring booth (a total of about 300m), you can often flag down an empty taxi leaving the airport that will take you for much less (you can try for M$100 to M$150) because the driver is no longer subject to the expensive regulated airport fares.

Colectivos head to the airport from a stand in front of the Hotel Cancún Handall on Av Tulum about a block south of Av Cobá. These usually operate from 2am to 3pm (hours may vary), charge M$40 per person, and they leave when full. The official rate for private taxis from town is M$170.

BUS

To reach the Zona Hotelera from Ciudad Cancún, catch any bus with 'R-1,' 'Hoteles' or 'Zona Hotelera' displayed on the windshield as it travels along Av Tulum toward Av Cobá then eastward on Av Cobá. The one-way fare is M$8.50. Having correct change in advance makes things easier. Air-conditioned white buses running between the Zona Hotelera and downtown charge M$11.

To reach Puerto Juárez and the Isla Mujeres ferries, catch a Ruta 13 bus ('Pto Juárez' or 'Punta Sam'; M$8.50) heading north on Av Tulum. Some R-1 buses make this trip as well.

TAXI

Cancún's taxis do not have meters. Fares are set, but you should always agree on a price before getting in; otherwise you could end up paying for a 'misunderstanding.' From Ciudad Cancún to Punta Cancún it's usually M$120 to M$130, to Puerto Juárez M$40 to M$60. Trips within the Zona Hotelera or downtown zones cost around M$25 to M$50. Hourly and daily rates should run about M$200, and M$1500 to M$2000, respectively.

NORTH OF CANCÚN

Parque Nacional Isla Contoy

Spectacular Isla Contoy is a bird-lover's delight: an uninhabited national park and sanctuary that is an easy day trip from Cancún and from Isla Mujeres. About 800m at its widest point and more than 7km long, it has dense foliage that provides ideal shelter for more than 150 species of bird, including brown pelicans, olive cormorants, turkey birds, brown boobies and frigates, as well as being a good place to see red flamingos, snowy egrets and white herons. Whale sharks are often sighted north of Contoy between May and September.

In an effort to preserve the park's pristine natural areas, only 200 visitors are allowed each day. Most of the trips stop for snorkeling both en route to and just off Contoy. Bring binoculars, mosquito repellent and sunblock.

The trip gives you several hours of free time to explore the island's two interpretive trails, skim through materials in the visitors center and climb the 27m-high observation tower. For more information you can contact **park headquarters** (998-234-9905) in Puerto Juárez or **Amigos de Isla Contoy** (884-7483; www.islacontoy.org), which has a website with detailed information on the island's ecology.

Daily visits to Contoy are offered by **Asterix** (Map p58; 886-4270; www.contoytours.com; Blvd Kukulcán, Km 5.2; adult/child 5-11yr M$1300/750; tours 9am-7pm Tue, Thu & Sat) in Cancún and by the **fisherman's cooperative** (274-0106, 886-4847; cnr Av Rueda Medina & Madero; M$750 per person; tour 8am-4pm) on Isla Mujeres.

Isla Holbox

984 / POP 1500

Isn't life great when it's low-fi and low-rise? That's the attitude on friendly Isla Holbox (hol-bosh) with its sandy streets, colorful Caribbean buildings, and lazing, sun-drunk dogs. Holbox is a welcome refuge for anyone looking to just get away from it all ('all' likely meaning the hubbub of Cancún).

The island is about 30km long and from 500m to 2km wide, with seemingly endless beaches, tranquil waters and a galaxy of shells in various shapes and colors. Lying within the Yum Balam reserve, Holbox is home to more than 150 species of bird, including roseate spoonbills, pelicans, herons, ibis and flamingos. In summer, whale sharks congregate relatively nearby in unheard-of quantities.

Golf carts are big here, but walking to the town square from the dock takes less than 10 minutes and the beach is just a few blocks away from the square. Nobody uses street names, but just so you know, it's Av Tiburón Ballena that connects the town with the ferry dock.

The water is not the translucent turquoise common to Quintana Roo beach sites, because here the Caribbean mingles with the darker Gulf of Mexico. The island's dark-water lagoon on the south side inspired the Maya to name it Holbox or 'black hole.' During the rainy season there are clouds of mosquitoes: bring repellent and be prepared to stay inside for a couple of hours after dusk.

Sights & Activities

Most people come here for the whale sharks and to lounge on the beach. But you can also head out to explore the birds and other wildlife around the island.

Many hotels will book tours of the area's attractions. Posada Mawimbi (below) offers canoe and kayak trips to the other side of the island, as well as motorboat trips toward the central areas of the island.

Punta Coco BEACH

On the western edge of the island, about 2.5km from downtown, Punta Coco is a great sunset beach.

OFF THE MAP – ALTERNATIVE TOURISM ON THE RISE

Many Maya communities are beginning to welcome tourism – it may be the only way to maintain their language and culture as mass migration to boom towns such as Cancún draws away the best and brightest, and children ask to study English rather than Yucatec.

Ecoturísmo Certificado (www.ecoturismocertificado.mx) supports ecotourism in numerous communities throughout Mexico, including two projects that can be found on the road to Chiquilá, in the towns of Solferino and San Ángel. Ecotourism center **El Corchal** (cell 984-879-1001; pepecorcho05@gmail.com; tour M$400), in Solferino, has an orchid garden, jungle camping sites and canopy tours, while at San Ángel you can go kayaking, cycling or learn about medicinal plants.

Punta Mosquito BEACH

On the eastern side of the island, Punta Mosquito is about 2.5km east from the downtown area. It has a large sandbar and is a good spot to sight flamingos.

Abarrotes Addy BICYCLE RENTAL

(Av Damero; per hour/day M$15/100) To get around the island, consider renting a bike here. It's 1½ blocks east of the plaza.

Tours

Willy's Tours

(☎875-2008; holbox@hotmail.com; Av Tiburón Ballena) Willy's Tours offers birding tours (M$1500 per six-person boat), crocodile-spotting (M$2600 per eight-person boat) and fishing (M$3500 per six-person boat).

Villas HM TOUR

(☎875-2062; www.holbox-island.com; Av Plutarco Elías, Zona Hotelera; M$350 per person) Beachfront hotel Villas HM arranges a '*tres islas*' (three islands) tour, which goes to Isla Pájaros and Isla Pasión for bird-watching and to the Yalahau cenote for swimming.

Sleeping

Not surprisingly, *cabañas* (cabins) and bungalows are everywhere along the beach. Some of the most upscale places can be found east of town, out along the island's northern shore in what locals calls the Zona Hotelera. Budget and midrange hotels are clustered around the plaza.

Hostel Tribu HOSTEL $

(☎875-2507; www.tribuhostel.com; Av Pedro Joaquín Coldwell; dm/r M$150/400; ❄📶) With so many activities available here (from salsa lessons to yoga and kayaking), it doesn't take long to settle in with the tribe. Six-room dorms and private rooms are clean, colorful and cheerful. Tribu also has a book exchange and a bar that stages Sunday jam sessions. From the plaza, it's one block north and two blocks west.

Hostel Ida y Vuelta HOSTEL $

(☎875-2358; www.holboxhostel.com; Av Paseo Kuka; campsites & hammocks M$80, dm M$100, bungalows M$390, house with kitchen M$500; 📶) A great spot for modern primitives, the basic dorm room sleeps eight, or you can stay in a bungalow with a private bathroom. There's also a very affordable house – an ideal setup for small groups. From the plaza, head two blocks north, then walk about six blocks east (the hostel is near Hotel Xaloc).

Posada Los Arcos HOTEL $

(☎875-2043; www.hotelarcosholbox.com; Av Tiburón Ballena; r with fan/air-con M$400/500; ❄) Rooms in this budget hotel are nothing to write home about but it's right on the plaza and just a few blocks from the beach so it's a fair-enough deal, especially in low season when a triple room goes for as low as M$350.

Hotel Arena HOTEL $$

(☎875-2169; www.hotelarenaholbox.com; Av Tiburón Ballena; r M$700-1300; ❄📶) A straight shoot from the ferry dock, all of the comfortable rooms here are decked out with minimalist decor and some have balconies overlooking the plaza. There's not much of a lobby but who needs one when you have a rooftop bar and Jacuzzi upstairs.

Casa Lupita HOTEL $$

(☎875-2017; www.casalupitaholbox.com; Calle Palomino; r M$600-800, ste M$1000; ❄📶) A great midrange option on the east side of the plaza, the spacious rooms here catch good breezes and the suites have private balconies overlooking the action on the town square.

★**Casa Takywara** HOTEL $$$

(☎875-2255; www.takywara.com; r incl breakfast M$1690-2340; ❄📶) Out at the quiet western end of town, on the beach, this beautiful hotel stands out for its striking architecture and stylishly decorated rooms with kitchenettes and sea-view balconies. It's built next to a patch of protected wetland, which is home to a pet crocodile. Rates drop considerably in low season.

Posada Mawimbi HOTEL $$$

(☎875-2003; www.mawimbi.net; incl breakfast r M$1170-1625, bungalow M$1495-1885, ste M$2145; ❄📶) Mosquito nets are a welcome luxury in this pleasant two-story place just off the beach and about three blocks east of the plaza. On offer are standard rooms with comfortable beds, bungalows with kitchenettes and ocean-view suites. Conch lamps light the walkways after dark – a beautiful finishing touch.

Hotel La Palapa HOTEL $$$

(☎875-2121; www.xperiencehotelsresorts.com/lapalapa; Calle Morelos; r from M$1500, bungalows M$1200; ❄📶) La Palapa offers cozy beachfront rooms, private patios (complete with hammocks) and a cloistered beach area complete with an outdoor bar that also serves scrumptious Italian food. The staff is efficient and friendly, and it's located right near the restaurants of the town's center, 100m east of Av Tiburón Ballena along the beach.

Villas Delfines BUNGALOW $$$

(875-2196; www.villasdelfines.com; bungalows M$2371-3556;) This ecotel on the beach about 1km east of town composts waste, catches rainwater and uses solar power. Its large beach bungalows are built on stilts and fully screened. It's great for those going green, but the rustic-chic accommodations are not quite as accommodating as other lodgings in this price category.

Eating

Holbox has a surprising number of good restaurants for such a small island. Just remember that some places close early, especially in low season.

Las Panchas MEXICAN $

(Calle Morelos, btwn Avs Damero and Pedro Joaquín Coldwell; anotojitos M$10; 7am-noon & 1pm-5pm) Ask just about anyone in town where to go for good, cheap eats and they'll probably send you to Las Panchas, where you get delicious *yucateco antojitos* (snacks) such as *panuchos* and *salbutes,* which are fried tortillas with toppings, and *chaya* (leafy green) tamales.

Taco Cueto MEXICAN $

(Calle Palomino; tacos M$10-21, burritos M$66-90; 6:30pm-midnight) Tired of seafood? Head to this trailer for good *arrachera* (flank steak) and *al pastor* (marinated pork) tacos and burritos. There's even a few vegetarian options for noncarnivores. It's just north of the plaza.

Edelyn Pizzería & Restaurant PIZZERIA $$

(pizzas M$80-280, mains M$90-190; noon-11pm) You'll see other places on the island trying to cash in on the lobster pizza craze, but these guys claim to be the originals. There are many other items on the menu if you're not sold on the cholesterol-heavy pairing of cheese and shellfish. It's on the east end of the plaza.

La Isla del Colibrí MEXICAN $$

(Av Tiburón Ballena; breakfast M$68-120, mains M$110-180; 7:30am-11pm;) A small restaurant in a gaily painted, Caribbean-style wooden house on the southwest corner of the plaza. It serves huge fruit plates, breakfasts (and coffee), *licuados* (fresh fruit drinks blended with milk or water), juices and a variety of meat and seafood dishes.

★ **Viva Zapata** SEAFOOD $$$

(Av Damero; mains M$80-250; 5-11:30pm) You really shouldn't leave the island without trying the mixed seafood grill here (order for two or ask for a single portion if traveling solo). Prepared by a friendly local fisherman-turned-restaurateur, it's a wonderful feast of lobster tail, crab, fish and any other fresh catch that he may throw onto the grill that evening. Check your bill carefully. It's just off plaza's northwest end.

GAME OF DOMINOES – SWIM WITH THE WHALE SHARKS

Between mid-May and mid-September, massive whale sharks congregate around Isla Holbox to feed on plankton. They are the largest fish in the world, weighing up to 15 tons and extending as long as 15m from gaping mouth to arching tail. Locals call them dominoes because of their speckled skin.

The best time to swim with these gentle giants is in July. During the shoulder seasons, you can get up to a dozen boats rotating around a single whale shark. It's unpleasant for both shark and swimmer, so think twice about taking a tour during this season.

The World Wildlife Fund has been working with the local community since 2003 to develop responsible practices for visiting the whale sharks, trying to balance the economic boon of these tours with the environmental imperatives of protecting a threatened species.

When swimming with the whale shark only three swimmers (including your guide) are allowed in the water at a time. You are not allowed to touch the fish, and are required to wear either a life jacket or wetsuit to ensure you do not dive below the shark.

Turística Moguel (875-2028, cell 984-114-9921; www.holboxislandtours.com; cnr Av Tiburón Ballena & Calle Damero; M$1030 per person), operating out of the minimarket on the plaza, offers whale shark tours. Ask to stop for a quick snorkel on the way back from your trip – the guides will normally agree to this.

Los Peleones FUSION $$$
(Av Tiburón Ballena; mains M$140-250; ⏱4-11:30pm) Mexico meets Argentina at this small, wrestling-themed restaurant overlooking the town square. The fresh-made pasta is something special here – try the portobello raviolis in gorgonzola sauce.

Buena Vista Grill SEAFOOD
(☎875-2102; Av Tiburón Ballena; mains M$100-200; ⏱11am-9pm) This casual eatery one block north of the plaza has plastic chairs, but serves up grilled fish specialties including whole fish or fillets wrapped in banana leaves. The menu varies by day.

Drinking & Nightlife

Nightlife on Holbox is pretty tame but there's just enough action to keep you entertained. Some places close early or don't open at all in low season.

Carioca's BAR
(⏱11am-2pm) Beachside just northeast of 'downtown,' this little *palapa* bar is a great chill-out spot. There's a disco here as well.

Habana Nights CLUB
(Av Damero; ⏱9pm-2am Wed-Sun) One of the few discos on the island. Often closed during low season.

Raices Beach Club & Marina BAR
(⏱till 1am) This *palapa* bar on the beach has good *ceviche* and cheap beer.

Entertainment

Tribango LIVE MUSIC
(Av Pedro Joaquín Coldwell; ⏱7pm-1am) The *palapa* bar at Hostel Tribu hosts Sunday jam sessions and Friday night salsa classes.

El Cine CINEMA
(Av Tiburón Ballena, in Plaza Pueblito; tickets M$27; ⏱8pm Fri, Sat & Sun) Screens mostly second-run Hollywood movies that are dubbed in Spanish and subtitled in English.

Information

Holbox has no banks. Bancomer has an ATM on the second story of the Alcaldía on the plaza. There's also an ATM at Hotel La Palapa. It's a good idea to bring enough cash to float your trip, just in case the machines run out.

Cyber Shark (☎875-2044; Av Damero; per hr M$15; ⏱10am-11pm) About one block east of the plaza, offers internet and VOIP/phone connections.

Emergency (☎066) Police, fire or medical assistance.

Getting There & Around

Barcos (boats) ferry passengers to Holbox from the port town of Chiquilá, usually from 5am to 7pm (M$80 round-trip). It takes about 25 minutes to reach the island. Smaller, faster and wetter *lanchas* (motorboats) make the crossing for M$400 during the day and M$500 after dark.

Buses (all 2nd-class) from the terminal in Cancún (M$86, 3½ hours) leave for Chiquilá at 7:50am and 12:40pm. Alternatively, you have the option of taking a taxi from Cancún for about M$1000.

Buses departing Chiquilá usually wait for the boat to arrive. They leave Chiquilá for Cancún at 7:40am and 1:45pm; for Mérida (M$175, four hours) at 5:40am; and for Tizimín (M$75, 2½ hours) at 4:40pm. Departure times are subject to change; ask for bus schedule information at the ferry-station ticket booth.

If you're driving, your vehicle will be safe in the Chiquilá parking lot for M$50 per day. You definitely won't need a car on the island.

Holbox's sand streets see few autos, but golf carts have become ubiquitous – consider using your walking shoes instead. Golf-cart taxis cost M$30 in town and M$80 out to Punta Coco or to the easternmost point of Av Paseo Kuka. If you need to rent a cart, see **Rentadora El Brother** (☎875-2018; Av Tiburón Ballena, north of plaza; cart per hr/day M$100/700).

Isla Mujeres

☎ 998 / POP 12,600

Includes ➜

Best Places to Eat

- ➜ Mañana (p81)
- ➜ Olivia (p82)
- ➜ Mininos (p81)
- ➜ Angelo (p82)
- ➜ Pita Amore (p81)

Best Places to Stay

- ➜ Poc-Na Hostel (p78)
- ➜ Casa El Pío (p79)
- ➜ Hotel Villa Kiin (p81)
- ➜ Hotel Rocamar (p79)
- ➜ Hotel Na Balam (p81)

Why Go?

Some people plan their vacation around Cancún and pencil in Isla Mujeres for a whirlwind visit. But Isla Mujeres is a destination in its own right, and it's generally quieter and more affordable than what you get across the bay.

Sure, there's quite a few ticky-tack tourist shops, but folks still get around by golf cart and the crushed-coral beaches are even better than those of Cozumel and Holbox. As for the calm, turquoise-blue water of Isla Mujeres, well, you really just have to see it for yourself.

There's just enough here to keep you entertained: snorkel or scuba dive, visit a turtle farm, or just put on the sunglasses and open that book you've been dying to finish. Come sunset, there's plenty of dining options, and the nightlife scene moves at a relaxing island pace.

When to Go

➜ For the experience of a lifetime, go between June and September and you can snorkel with 15-ton whale sharks in nearby waters.

➜ It's quite a sight to watch sea turtles come ashore for nesting season in August and September, and if you want to get a closer look at the little fellas you can always drop by the island's turtle farm.

➜ Hotels tend to get booked up during the winter high season (December to April), so you're better off visiting in November when you'll find vacancies and low-season discounts to boot.

History

A glimpse at the sunbathers on the beach will have you thinking the moniker 'Island of Women' comes from the bikini-clad tourists; however, the name Isla Mujeres goes at least as far back as Spanish buccaneers, who (legend has it) kept their lovers in safe seclusion here while they plundered galleons and pillaged ports on the mainland. An alternate theory suggests that in 1517, when Francisco Hernández de Córdoba sailed from Cuba and arrived here to procure slaves, the expedition discovered a stone temple containing clay figurines of Maya goddesses; it is thought Córdoba named the island after the icons.

Today some archaeologists believe that the island was a stopover for the Maya en route to worship their goddess of fertility, Ixchel, on Isla Cozumel. The clay idols are thought to have represented the goddess. The island may also have figured in the extensive Maya salt trade, which extended for hundreds of kilometers along the coastline.

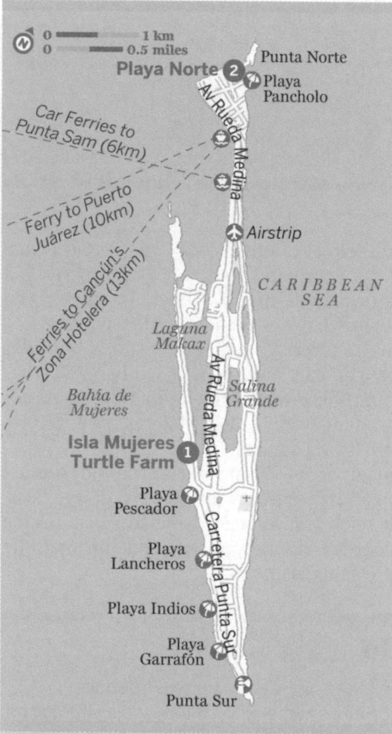

Isla Mujeres Highlights

1. Drop by the **Isla Mujeres Turtle Farm** (p77) and say hello to your new flippered friends
2. Relax on the white sands of **Playa Norte** (p76) and swim in the shallow, crystalline waters
3. Rent a golf cart or scooter and feel the warm ocean wind in your face as you explore other parts of the island
4. Head out on a boat to go snorkeling with **whale sharks** (p77), the largest fish in the world
5. Dive into the deep Caribbean blue and explore an underwater world of sunken ships and shark caves (p77)

Sights

Museo Capitán Dulché MUSEUM
(Map p78; www.capitandulche.com; Carretera a Garrafón, Km 4.5; ⌚10am-7pm) And you thought Isla Mujeres had no culture. Here you not only get a maritime museum detailing the island's naval history but there's also a sculpture garden dotted with dozens of grinding stones. There also happens to be one of the best beach clubs here – and we're not just saying that because of the cool boat bar.

Punta Sur LOOKOUT/GARDEN
(ruins admission M$30) At the southern point you'll find a lighthouse, sculpture garden and the worn remains of a temple dedicated to Ixchel, Maya goddess of the moon and fertility. Various hurricanes have pummeled the ruins over time and there's now little to see other than the sculpture garden, the sea and Cancún in the distance. Taxis from town cost about M$80.

Beaches

Playa Norte BEACH
(Map p80) FREE Once you reach Playa Norte, the island's main beach, you won't want to leave. Its warm shallow waters are the color of blue-raspberry syrup and the beach is crushed coral. Unlike the outer beach, Playa Norte is safe and the water is only chest-deep even far from shore.

Playa Secreto BEACH
(Map p80; 👪) The lagoon separating the Avalon Reef Club from the rest of the island has a shallow swimming spot that's ideal for kids.

Playa Lancheros BEACH
(Map p78) About 5km south of town and the southernmost point served by local buses, this beach is less attractive than Playa

DREAM GREEN BY VISITING ISLA MUJERES TURTLE FARM

Although they are endangered, sea turtles are still killed throughout Latin America for their eggs and meat, which is considered a delicacy. Three species of sea turtle lay eggs in the sand along Isla Mujeres' calm western shore, and they are now being protected – one *tortuguita* (little turtle) at a time.

In the 1980s, efforts by a local fisherman led to the founding of the **Isla Mujeres Turtle Farm** (Isla Mujeres Tortugranja; Map p78; 888-0705; Carretera Sac Bajo, Km 5; admission M$30; 9am-5pm;), 5km south of town, which protects the turtles' breeding grounds and places wire cages around their eggs to protect against predators.

Hatchlings live in three large pools for up to a year, then are tagged for monitoring and released. Because most turtles in the wild die within their first few months, the practice of guarding them through their first year greatly increases their chances of survival. Moreover, the turtles that leave this protected beach return each year, which means their offspring receive the same protection. The sanctuary releases about 125,000 turtles each year.

There are several hundred sea turtles, ranging in weight from 150g to more than 300kg. The turtle farm also has a small but good-quality aquarium, displays on marine life and a gift shop. Tours are conducted in Spanish and English.

If you're driving, cycling or walking from the bus stop, bear right at the 'Y' just beyond Hacienda Mundaca's parking lot (the turn is marked by a tiny sign). The facility is easily reached from town by taxi (M$54).

Norte, but it sometimes has free musical festivities at night. A taxi ride from town costs M$40.

Playa Garrafón Reef Park BEACH, PARK
(Map p78; 877-1100; www.garrafon.com; admission M$767; 10am-5pm daily high season, 10am-5pm Sun-Fri low season) From Playa Lancheros, 1.5km south is Playa Garrafón Reef Park, where the steep admission gets you snorkeling, a buffet, open bar and use of kayaks. The star attraction – an over-the-water zip-line – costs an additional M$130 a pop.

Activities

Diving & Snorkeling

Within a short boat ride of the island there's a handful of lovely dives, such as **La Bandera**, **Arrecife Manchones** and **Ultrafreeze** (El Frío), where you'll see the intact hull of a 60m-long cargo ship – thought to have been deliberately sunk in 30m of water. Expect to see sea turtles, rays and barracuda, along with a wide array of hard and soft corals.

There's good shore-snorkeling near **Playa Garrafón**, along the *malecón* (waterfront; look for sandy spots surrounded by reef) and at the **Yunque Reef**. As always, watch for boat traffic when you head out snorkeling.

Snorkeling with whale sharks (around M$1500) is the latest craze on the island. The season runs from June through September. It can get a bit crazy with several boats circling one whale shark, but they try to limit the number of swimmers in the water to three people (including one guide). All dive shops listed below offer whale-shark trips.

For day trips to Isla Contoy, look for the Fisherman's Cooperative booth near the ferry docks.

Aqua Adventures DIVING
(Map p80; cell 998-236-4516; www.diveislamujeres.com; cnr Av Juárez & Morelos; 1-/2-tank dives M$850/1100, whale-shark tour M$1500; 9am-7pm) Great option for snorkeling with whale sharks and reef dives.

Mundaca Divers DIVING
(Map p80; 999-2071; www.mundacadiversisla.com; Zazil Ha s/n; 1-/2-tank dives M$650/800, snorkeling tours M$455-585) At Avalon Reef Club, this outfit does everything from shark-cave dives to snorkeling trips at a one-of-a-kind underwater sculpture museum known as the MUSA.

Sea Hawk Divers DIVING
(Map p80; 877-1233; seahawkdivers@hotmail.com; Carlos Lazo; 1-/2-tank dives M$700/900, resort course M$1080, PADI M$3850) Offers resort courses and PADI Open Water certification.

Fisherman's Cooperative Booth TOUR
(Map p80; 877-1363; cnr Av Rueda Medina & Madero; snorkeling incl lunch M$330-450;

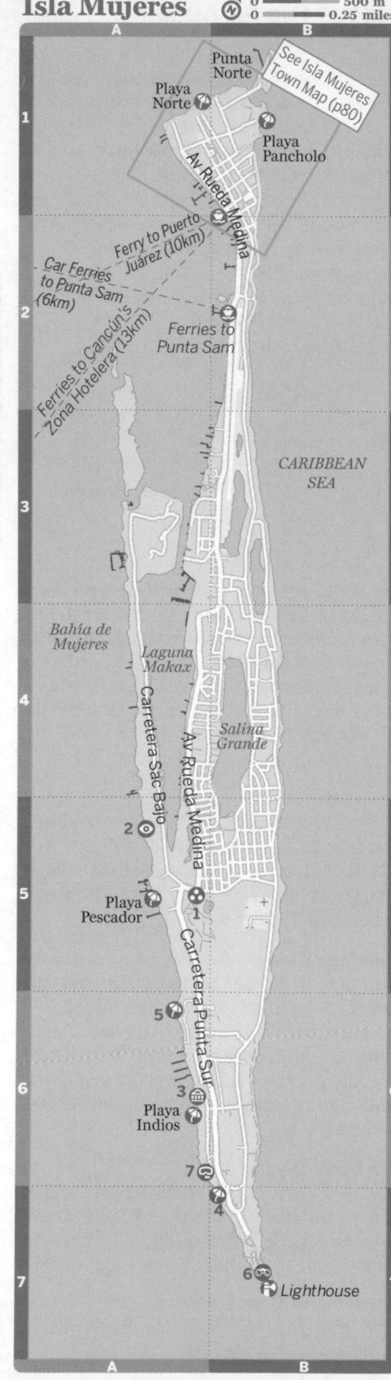

Isla Mujeres

Sights

1 Hacienda Mundaca A5
2 Isla Mujeres Turtle Farm A5
3 Museo Capitán Dulché A6
4 Playa Garrafón Reef Park B7
5 Playa Lancheros A6
6 Punta Sur B7

Activities, Courses & Tours

7 Hotel Garrafón de Castilla A6

8am-5pm) You can get reasonably priced snorkeling trips at the Fisherman's Cooperative booth in a *palapa* near the gas station. Booking here ensures that your money goes to locals. Their boats also go to Isla Contoy (M$750) from 9am to 3pm.

Hotel Garrafón de Castilla SNORKELING
(Map p78; 877-0107; Carretera Punta Sur, Km 6; admission M$50; 9am-5pm) Avoid the overpriced Parque Garrafón Reef Park and visit instead Hotel Garrafón de Castilla's beach club for a day of snorkeling. Gear rental costs an additional M$100.

Boating & Fishing

The fishing cooperative offers trips to catch marlin, swordfish and dorado from M$2000 per half-day, including bait and tackle, soft drinks, snacks and beer.

Felipez Water Sports Center WATER SPORTS
(Map p80; 998-593-3403; nachankan@aol.com; Playa Norte; kayak/paddle boat/catamaran per hour M$250/350/650) Hit the water in a catamaran, kayak or paddle boat. Felipez also does fishing trips (M$6000).

Sleeping

Many hotels on the island are booked solid for high season, roughly from mid-December through April.

★ **Poc-Na Hostel** HOSTEL $
(Map p80; 877-0090; www.pocna.com; Matamoros 15; dm with fan/air-con M$115/175, r with/without bathroom & air-con M$300/400;) This hostel is only moments away from lovely Playa Pancholo and is tastefully decorated with shells and hibiscus flowers. The *palapa*-roofed common area has wood picnic benches, hammocks and good tunes for chilling out. The property extends through 100m of sand and coconut palms to the edge of the Caribbean. You'll never be bored with all the activities offered here.

Apartments Trinchan APARTMENT $
(Map p80; ☎998-166-6967; atrinchan@prodigy.net.mx; Carlos Lazo 46; r M$400-450, apt M$450-500; ❄📶) Since they have no website, you'll have to take our word for it when we say this is one of the best budget deals in town – and the beach is right around the corner. If available, opt for one of the spacious apartments.

Hotel D'Gomar $
(Map p80; ☎877-0541; Av Rueda Medina 150; d from M$500; ❄📶) A friendly, old-school place facing the ferry dock, this has four floors of ample and well-maintained rooms with double beds, minibars and cable TV. The mirror in the stairway gives warped, funhouse-style reflections as you head to your room.

Casa El Pío BOUTIQUE HOTEL $$
(Map p80; ☎229-2799; www.casaelpio.com; Hidalgo 3; M$960-1070; ❄📶🏊) Book a room well in advance if you want to stay at this small – and very popular – boutique hotel. Two of the four rooms have ocean views, and all have well-crafted wood furnishings, fantastic photographs of the island and many other interesting design details.

Hotel Rocamar HOTEL $$
(Map p80; ☎877-0101; www.rocamar-hotel.com; Bravo s/n, cnr Guerrero; r from M$1100; P❄📶🏊) Almost achingly modern rooms (the goldfish-bowl bathrooms may not appeal if you're sharing with a casual acquaintance) featuring private balconies with sea views. The view from the pool ain't too shabby either. Prices drop considerably in the off-season.

Xbulu-Ha Hotel HOTEL $$
(Map p80; ☎877-1783; www.islamujeres.biz; Guerrero 4; d/tr/ste from M$650/770/920; ❄📶) Quite a bargain, especially if you're traveling with a small group or family. Some of the standard and deluxe rooms here can accommodate three to four people, as can the more spacious suites, which come with kitchenettes.

Hotel Bucaneros HOTEL $$
(Map p80; ☎877-1228, USA 800-227-4765; www.bucaneros.com; Hidalgo 11; d M$572-1016; ❄) On the main pedestrian corridor, the nicely decorated rooms here increase in price depending on to what extent you want to supersize your digs. All have air-con, TVs and some come with balconies, tubs and fridges. Rooms air out nicely if the windows are opened.

Hotel Belmar HOTEL $$
(Map p80; ☎877-0430; www.hotelbelmarisla.com; Hidalgo 110; s/d M$878/1000; ❄📶) Above Rolandi's pizzeria and run by the same friendly family, all rooms are comfy and well kept, with tiled floors and (some) balconies. Prices span four distinct seasons.

Hotel Francis Arlene HOTEL $$
(Map p80; ☎877-0310; www.francisarlene.com; Guerrero 7; r with fan/air-con M$812/890; ❄📶) This place offers comfortable, good-sized

HACIENDA MUNDACA

This **hacienda** (Map p78; Av Rueda Medina; admission M$20; ⌚9am-4pm) is at the large bend in Av Rueda Medina, about 4km south of town. Its story is perhaps more intriguing than the ruins that remain. A 19th-century slave trader and reputed pirate, Fermín Antonio Mundaca de Marechaja, fell in love with a local woman known as La Trigueña (Brunette). To win her, Mundaca built a two-story mansion complete with gardens and graceful archways, as well as a small fortification.

But while Mundaca was building the house, La Trigueña married another islander. Brokenhearted, Mundaca died and his house, fortress and garden fell into disrepair. Some documents indicate that Mundaca died during a visit to Mérida and was buried there. Others say he died on the island, and indeed there's a grave in the town cemetery that supposedly contains his remains. Despite the skull and crossbones on his headstone (a common *memento mori*) there's no evidence in history books that Mundaca was ever a pirate. Instead, it is said he accumulated his wealth by transporting slaves from Africa to Cuba, where they were forced to work in mines and sugarcane fields.

Today the mostly ruined complex has some walls and foundations, a large central pond, some rusting cannons and a partially rebuilt house. At the southern end stand a gateway and a small garden. You can still make out the words 'Entrada de La Trigueña' (La Trigueña's Entrance) etched into the impressive stone arch of the gate.

The shady grounds make for pleasant strolling. Hacienda Mundaca is easily reached by bus, bike or taxi.

Isla Mujeres Town

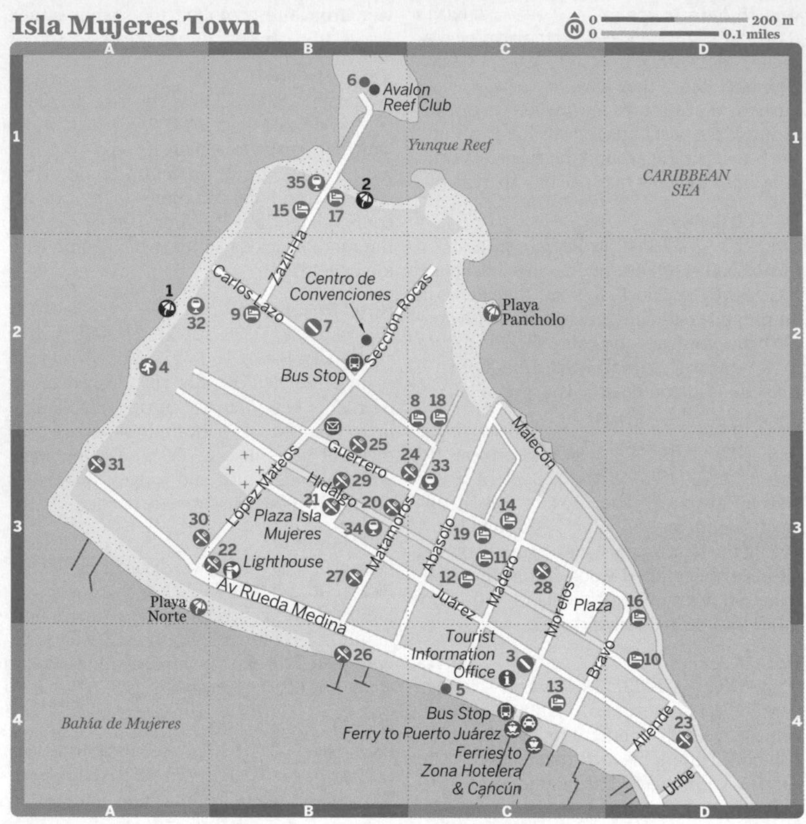

Isla Mujeres Town

Sights
1 Playa Norte A2
2 Playa Secreto B1

Activities, Courses & Tours
3 Aqua Adventures C4
4 Felipez Water Sports Center A2
5 Fisherman's Cooperative Booth C4
6 Mundaca Divers B1
7 Sea Hawk Divers B2

Sleeping
8 Apartments Trinchan C2
9 Cabañas María del Mar B2
10 Casa El Pío D4
11 Hotel Belmar C3
12 Hotel Bucaneros C3
13 Hotel D'Gomar C4
14 Hotel Francis Arlene C3
15 Hotel Na Balam B1
16 Hotel Rocamar D3
17 Hotel Villa Kiin B1
18 Poc-Na Hostel C2
19 Xbulu-Ha Hotel C3

Eating
20 Aluxes Coffee Shop B3
21 Angelo B3
22 Jax Bar & Grill B3
23 La Lomita D4
24 Mañana C3
25 Mercado Municipal B3
26 Mininos B4
27 Olivia B3
28 Pita Amore C3
29 Qubano B3
Rolandi's .... (see 11)
30 Satay A3
31 Sunset Grill A3

Drinking & Nightlife
32 Buho's A2
33 El Patio C3
34 Fayne's B3
35 Fenix Lounge B1
Poc-Na Hostel .... (see 18)

rooms with fan (or air-con) and fridge. Most have a king-sized bed or two doubles, and many have balconies and sea views. The lounging frog sculptures will either seem hokey or cute. Either way they kinda fit right in. Great low-season rates.

Hotel Villa Kiin BUNGALOW **$$$**
(Map p80; ☎877-1024; www.villakiin.com; Zazil Ha 129; r from M$1105, bungalows M$1430-1820, all incl continental breakfast; ❄📶) Location alone makes this a great deal. Rooms are somewhat ordinary so you're better off staying in one of the bungalows right by the beach – they range from pleasant rustic digs with palm-leaf roofs to upscale honeymooner setups with private jacuzzis. Palm-shaded hammocks make it easy to do nothing all afternoon and with one of the island's safest beaches for swimming, it's ideal for kids.

Hotel Na Balam HOTEL **$$$**
(Map p80; ☎881-4770; www.nabalam.com; Calle Zazil-Ha 118; r/ste from M$2275/5330, incl breakfast; ❄📶🏊) Butterflies flit around the beautiful hibiscus and palm garden, and many rooms face Playa Norte. All rooms are decorated with simple elegance and have safes, hammocks, private balconies or patios…and no TVs. The hotel offers yoga and meditation classes as well as massage services, and has a pool and restaurant.

Cabañas María del Mar HOTEL **$$$**
(Map p80; ☎877-0179; www.cabanasdelmar.com; Carlos Lazo 1; d M$1655 incl breakfast; ❄📶🏊) Near Playa Norte, the 73 rooms come with firm beds, balconies or terraces (many with sea or pool views), and lovely tiled bathrooms. A lush courtyard, restaurant and swimming pool top things off.

Eating

Súper Xpress, a supermarket on the plaza, has a solid selection of groceries, baked goods and snacks.

★Mañana CAFE **$**
(Map p80; ☎877-0555; cnr Matamoros & Guerrero; dishes M$40-85; ⏲8am-4pm; 📶🌿) A good-vibe place with colorful hand-painted tables, superfriendly service and some excellent veggie options – the hummus-and-veggie baguette is the restaurant's signature dish – Mañana is perhaps the best lunch spot on the island. It also has coffee, *licuados* (blends of fruit or juice with water or milk, and sugar) and some Middle Eastern dishes. There's a book exchange, too.

Pita Amore MEDITERRANEAN **$**
(Map p80; Guerrero; M$35-45; ⏲12:30-10pm Mon-Sat; 🌿) This unassuming shack does just three varieties of pita sandwiches and does them extremely well. The chicken, beef and vegetarian pitas are the creation of a New York Culinary Institute alum. The secret lies in the homemade sauces and outstanding pita bread, which comes from a Lebanese bakery in Mérida.

Jax Bar & Grill INTERNATIONAL **$**
(Map p80; López Mateos; breakfast M$65-100; ⏲8am-10:30pm) Jax upper deck affords a birds-eye view of the beach scene along the boardwalk, so aside from the hearty breakfasts you get optimal people-watching. And it probably has the biggest TV screens on the island if you need your sports fix.

El Retorno MEXICAN **$**
(Av Rueda Medina; tacos/tortas M$10/20; ⏲7am-11am) Hidden away in the ferry terminal parking lot, this affordable, mornings-only taco stand keeps locals happy with its *lechón* (suckling pig) and *cochinita* (slow-cooked pork) tacos and tortas.

La Lomita MEXICAN **$**
(Map p80; Juárez; mains M$60-220; ⏲9:30am-11pm Mon-Sat) The 'Little Hill' serves good, cheap Mexican food in a small, colorful setting. Seafood and chicken dishes predominate. Try the fantastic bean and avocado soup, or *ceviche*.

Aluxes Coffee Shop CAFE **$**
(Map p80; Matamoros; bagels M$25-43, baguettes M$45-50; ⏲7am-10pm; 📶) Aluxes serves bagels with cream cheese, baguettes, muffins, and hot and iced coffee.

Mercado Municipal MARKET **$**
(Map p80; Town Market; Guerrero; ⏲6am-4pm) Inside the remodeled market are a couple of stalls selling hot food cheap. Other stalls sell a variety of produce, and a juice stand serves up liquid refreshments. Four open-air restaurants out front prepare simple regional fare like *sopa de lima* (lime soup) at decent prices.

Mininos SEAFOOD **$$**
(Map p80; Av Rueda Medina; mains M$70-150; ⏲noon-9pm) A tiny, colorfully painted shack with a sand floor and daily marimba sets, Mininos dishes up tasty garlic shrimp, conch and octopus, as well as delicious seafood soups.

Olivia MEDITERRANEAN **$$**

(Map p80; ☎877-1765; www.olivia-isla-mujeres.com; Matamoros; M$88-180; ⏰5-9:30pm Tue-Sat) This delightful, Israeli-run restaurant makes everything from scratch, from Moroccan-style fish served on a bed of couscous to chicken shawarmas wrapped with fresh-baked pita bread. Ask for a candlelit table out back in the garden.

Angelo ITALIAN **$$**

(Map p80; ☎877-1273; Hidalgo; M$119-219; ⏰4pm-midnight) You can't miss the odd blue lighting at this sidewalk steak house/restaurant. Pretty much everything on the menu is good, especially the black grouper fillet and the baked mussels. When he's around, Italian owner Angelo is a good source of information.

Qubano CUBAN **$$**

(Map p80; Hidalgo; mains M$80-140; ⏰noon-11:30pm Tue-Sun) It competes for decibel levels with neighboring restaurants, but really, we all like Cuban *son* (a type of dance) more than bad disco remixes, don't we? Apart from that, you get a well-deserved break from Mexican fare with *ropa vieja* (slow-cooked shredded beef), Cuban lobster and mojitos.

Sunset Grill INTERNATIONAL **$$**

(Map p80; ☎877-0785; Playa Norte at Av Rueda Medina; mains M$95-240; ⏰10am-10pm; 🖉) This is a romantic spot for sunset cocktails and a beachside meal. While the menu runs the gamut from seafood to pasta, the Caribbean black grouper is especially tasty. There's a smattering of vegetarian options on offer here, too, like crispy tofu with sautéed veggies.

Rolandi's ITALIAN **$$**

(Map p80; ☎877-0430; www.rolandirestaurants.com; Hidalgo; mains M$128-195; ⏰8am-11pm; 📶) Below the Hotel Belmar, Rolandi's bakes very good thin-crust pizzas and calzones in a wood-fired oven. The menu also includes pasta, fresh salads, fish and some Italian specialties – definitely *don't* come here looking for Mexican.

Satay ASIAN **$$$**

(Map p80; ☎848-8484; López Mateos; mains M$150-190; ⏰6-10:30pm) Mix things up a little with the Thai red snapper or toro and papaya salad at this Asian-fusion restaurant. It's not beachfront, but the modern, cool ambiance is pleasant enough.

Drinking & Nightlife

Isla Mujeres' highest concentration of nightlife is along Hidalgo, and hot spots on or near the beach form an arc around the northern edge of town.

Poc-Na Hostel BAR

(Map p80; www.pocna.com; Matamoros 15; ⏰11pm-3am Mon-Sat; 📶) Has a beachfront joint with bonfires and more hippies than all the magic buses in the world. It's a scene, and an entertaining one at that.

Buho's BAR

(Map p80; Playa Norte; ⏰10am-midnight) The quintessential swing-bar experience right on the beach.

El Patio BAR

(Map p80; Hidalgo; ⏰4pm-midnight) This fun spot has a sand floor and an open-air back patio. There's occasional live music and the food's worth checking out.

Fayne's BAR

(Map p80; Hidalgo; ⏰5pm-midnight) This disco-bar-restaurant often features live reggae, salsa and other Caribbean sounds. Near Matamoros.

Fenix Lounge BAR

(Map p80; ☎274-0073; www.fenixisla.com; Zazil-Ha; ⏰11am-midnight Tue-Sun; 📶) Catch DJ sessions or live reggae, salsa and jazz acts here at this waterfront, *palapa*-covered lounge bar.

Orientation

The island is 8km long, 150m to 800m wide. You'll find most restaurants and hotels in the town of Isla Mujeres, with the pedestrian corridor on Hidalgo the focal point. The ferry arrives in the town proper on the island's northern side. On the southern tip are the lighthouse and vestiges of the Maya temple. The two are linked by Av Rueda Medina, a loop road that more or less follows the coast. Between them are a handful of small fishing villages, several saltwater lakes, a string of westward-facing beaches, a large lagoon and a small airstrip.

The eastern shore is washed by the open sea, and the surf there is dangerous. The most popular sand beach (Playa Norte) is at the northern tip of the island.

Information

Several banks are directly across from the Zona Hotelera ferry dock. Most exchange currency, have ATMs and are open 9am to 5pm Monday to

Friday and 9am to 2pm Saturday. The island has an abundance of Telmex card phones.

Hospital Integral Isla Mujeres (877-1792; Guerrero, btwn Madero & Morelos) Doctors available 24/7.

HSBC (Av Rueda Medina)

Hyperbaric Chamber (877-1792; Morelos) Next to Hospital Integral Isla Mujeres. It's often closed; inquire at the hospital.

Internet Café (cnr Matamoros & Guerrero; per hr M$15; 9am-9:30pm Mon-Sat) As yet unnamed.

Police (066)

Post Office (877-0085; cnr Guerrero & López Mateos; 9am-5:30pm Mon-Fri, 9am-1pm Sat)

Tourist Information Office (877-0307; Av Rueda Medina; 9am-4pm Mon-Fri) Between Madero and Morelos, it offers a number of brochures and some members of the staff speak English.

Getting There & Away

There are several points of embarkation from Cancún to reach Isla Mujeres. Punta Sam, 8km north of Ciudad Cancún, is the only one that transports vehicles. From Punta Sam, drivers are included in prices for the following one-way fares: cars (M$256), motorcycles (M$87), bicycles (M$82); additional passengers pay M$35. Get there at least an hour before if you're transporting a vehicle. See www.maritimaisla-mujeres.com for departure times.

The R-1 'Ultramar' city bus in Cancún serves all Zona Hotelera points and Puerto Juárez. To reach Punta Sam you'll need to take a taxi or a northbound 'Ruta 13' bus along Av Tulum. Passenger ferries (www.granpuerto.com.mx) depart from the following docks:

- **Puerto Juárez** (4km north of Ciudad Cancún) Leave every 30 minutes; one way M$70.
- **Playa Linda** (Blvd Kukulcán, Km 4) Six daily departures; one way M$110.
- **Playa Tortugas** (Blvd Kukulcán, Km 6.5) Eight daily departures; one way M$110.
- **Playa Caracol** (Blvd Kukulcán, Km 9.5) Four daily departures; one way M$140.

Getting Around

With all rented transportation it's best to deal directly with the shop supplying it, as opposed to going through a middleperson. Rates are sometimes open to negotiation.

BICYCLE

Cycling is a great way to get around on the island's narrow streets and to explore outlying areas. **Fiesta** (Av Reuda Medina, btwn Morelos & Bravo; per hour/day M$30/100; 8am-5pm) has mountain bikes and beach cruisers.

BUS & TAXI

Local buses depart about every 25 minutes (but don't bank on it) from next to the Centro de Convenciones (near the back of the market) or from the ferry dock, and head along Av Rueda Medina, stopping along the way. You can get to the entrance of Hacienda Mundaca, within 300m of the Turtle Farm (Tortugranja), and as far south as Playa Lancheros (1.5km north of Playa Garrafón).

Get taxis from the stand at the dock or flag one down. Taxi rates are set by the municipal government and posted at the taxi stand just south of the passenger ferry dock. As always, agree on a price before getting in.

MOTORCYCLE & GOLF CART

Inspect all scooters carefully before renting. Costs vary, and are sometimes jacked up in high season, but generally start at about M$100 per hour, with a two-hour minimum, and M$250 all day (9am to 5pm).

Many people find golf carts a good way to get around the island, and caravans of them can be seen tooling down the roads. The average cost is M$180 per hour and M$600 all day (9am to 5pm). A good, no-nonsense place for both scooters and golf carts is **Gomar** (877-1686; Av Rueda Medina, cnr Bravo; golf carts per hour/day M$180/600, scooter M$250 per day).

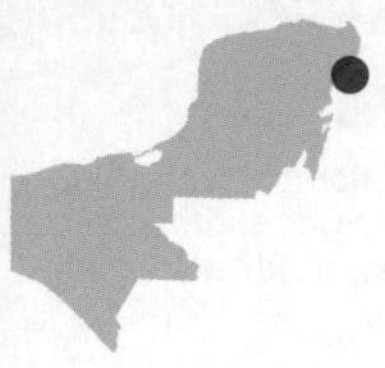

Isla Cozumel

987 / POP 77,200

Includes ➡

Best Places to Stay

➡ Hotel B Cozumel (p92)

➡ Hotel Flamingo (p91)

➡ Casa Mexicana (p92)

➡ Hostelito (p90)

➡ Guido's Boutique Hotel (p92)

Best Places to Eat

➡ Kinta (p93)

➡ La Cocay (p93)

➡ Pepe's Grill (p93)

➡ Restaurant La Choza (p93)

➡ Taquería El Sitio (p93)

Why Go?

Cozumel is too resilient, too proud to let itself become just another cheesy cruise ship destination. Leaving the tourist area – and the gringo-friendly souvenir shops behind – you still see an island of quiet cool and genuine authenticity. Garages still have shrines to the Virgin, there's a spirited Caribbean pathos, and of course there are some tourist things to do – such as diving down to some of the best reefs in the world.

While diving and snorkeling are the main draws, the pleasant town square is a nice place to spend the afternoon, and it's highly gratifying to explore the less-visited parts of the island on a rented scooter or convertible bug. The coastal road leads to small Maya ruins, a marine park and captivating scenery along the unforgettable windswept shore.

When to Go

➡ The festive Carnaval celebration in February brings live music acts and dancers festooned with feathers out into the streets. It's not Rio de Janeiro, but it sure is a hoot.

➡ In late April and early May folks in the town of El Cedral pay tribute to Caste War refugees with a fun-filled fair featuring rides, rodeos and traditional dance, including the time-honored Dance of the Pigs' Heads.

➡ If you're planning a trip around diving and snorkeling you might want to visit in April or May when you don't have to worry about hurricanes or strong winter winds.

History

Maya settlement here dates from AD 300. During the Postclassic period, Cozumel flourished as a trade center and, more importantly, a ceremonial site. Every Maya woman living on the Yucatán Peninsula and beyond was expected to make at least one pilgrimage here to pay tribute to Ixchel, the goddess of fertility and the moon, at a temple erected in her honor. Archaeologists believe this temple was at San Gervasio, a bit north of the island's geographical center.

At the time of the first Spanish contact with Cozumel (in 1518, by Juan de Grijalva and his men), there were at least 32 Maya building groups on the island. According to

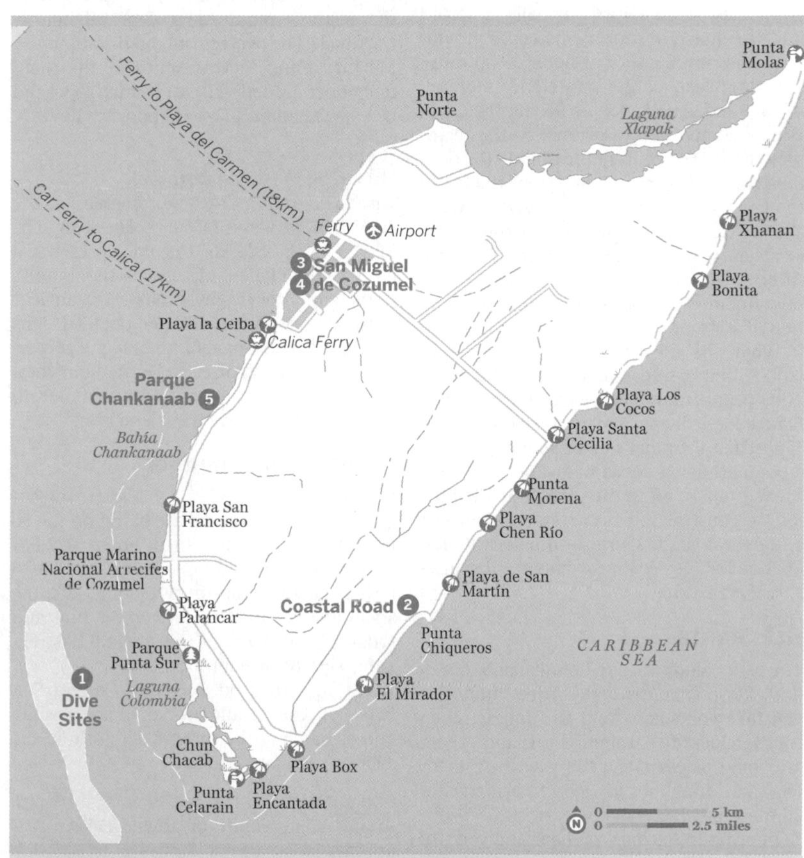

Isla Cozumel Highlights

1 Plunge into the deep blue and explore some of the world's best **dive sites** (p91), offering the likes of drift diving and imposing underwater walls that descend deep into the Caribbean

2 Rent a scooter, bike or car to cruise the coastal road to **Maya ruins** and **beaches** along Cozumel's wild, windswept southeastern side (p89)

3 Spend an evening hanging out at a bar or sidewalk restaurant in the buzzing town plaza of **San Miguel de Cozumel** (p93)

4 Learn all kinds of interesting tidbits about the island's geology and Maya history at the **Museo de la Isla de Cozumel** (p86)

5 Take the kids to see turtles, crocs and sea lions at **Parque Chankanaab** (p89) and while you're there get in some snorkeling or enjoy a relaxing *temazcal* (steam bath)

Spanish chronicler Diego de Landa, a year later Hernán Cortés sacked one of the Maya centers but left the others intact, apparently satisfied with converting the island's population to Christianity. Smallpox introduced by the Spanish wiped out half the 8000 Maya and, of the survivors, only about 200 escaped genocidal attacks by conquistadors in the late 1540s.

The island remained virtually deserted into the late 17th century, its coves providing sanctuary for several notorious pirates, including Jean Lafitte and Henry Morgan. In 1848 indigenous people fleeing the Caste War began to resettle Cozumel. At the beginning of the 20th century the island's (by then mostly *mestizo*) population grew, thanks to the craze for chewing gum. Cozumel was a port of call on the chicle-export route, and locals harvested the gum base on the island. After the demise of chicle, Cozumel's economy remained strong owing to the construction of a US air base here during WWII.

When the US military departed, the island fell into an economic slump, and many of its people moved away. Those who stayed fished for a living and it wasn't until the 1960s that Cozumel started to gain fame as a popular diving destination. Tourism really started taking off in the early 1980s following the construction of a commercial airport and the island's first cruise-ship dock. Today, Cozumel is Mexico's most important cruise-ship destination.

Sights

The route along Parque Chankanaab, El Cedral, Playa Palancar and Parque Punta Sur will take you south from San Miguel, then counterclockwise around the island. There are some places along the way to stop for food and drink, but it's good to bring water all the same.

In order to see most of the island you will need to rent a vehicle or take a taxi (M$700 to M$1000 for a day trip); cyclists will need to brave the regular strong winds.

Access to many of Cozumel's best stretches of beach has become limited. Resorts and residential developments with gated roads create the most difficulties. Pay-for-use beach clubs occupy some other prime spots, but you can park and walk through or around them and enjoy adjacent parts of the beach without obligation. Sitting under their umbrellas or otherwise using the facilities requires you to fork out some money, either a straight fee or a *consumo mínimo* (minimum consumption of food and drink), which can add up in some places. It's not always strictly applied, especially when business is slow.

San Miguel de Cozumel

It's easy to make your way on foot around the island's main town, San Miguel de Cozumel. The waterfront boulevard is Av Melgar; along Melgar south of the main ferry dock (Muelle Fiscal) is a narrow sand beach. The main plaza is opposite the ferry dock.

Museo de la Isla de Cozumel MUSEUM

(Map p88; ☎872-1434; www.cozumelparks.com; Av Melgar; admission M$50; ⏲9am-5pm) The Museo de la Isla de Cozumel presents a clear and detailed picture of the island's flora, fauna, geography, geology and ancient Maya history. Thoughtful and detailed signs in English and Spanish accompany the exhibits. It's a good place to learn about coral before hitting the water, and it's one not to miss before you leave the island.

South of San Miguel

El Cedral ARCHAEOLOGICAL SITE

FREE This Maya ruin is the oldest on the island. It's the size of a small house and has no ornamentation. El Cedr al is thought to have been an important ceremonial site; the small church standing next to the tiny ruin today is evidence that the site still has religious significance for locals.

It's on a road off Carretera Costera Sur, between Kms 17 and 18 (you'll see a white and red arch at the turnoff, across from the Alberto's Restaurant sign).

Playa Palancar BEACH

About 17km south of town, Palancar is another great beach. It has a beach club renting hydro bikes, kayaks, snorkel gear and sailboats, plus a restaurant and a dive operation. Near the beach, Arrecife Palancar (Palancar Reef) has some very good diving (it's known as Palancar Gardens), as well as fine snorkeling (Palancar Shallows).

Parque Punta Sur NATURE RESERVE

(Map p87; ☎872-4014; www.cozumelparks.com; Carretera Costera Sur, Km 27; adult/3-11yr M$156/104; ⏲9am-4pm Mon-Sat) At this eco-

Isla Cozumel

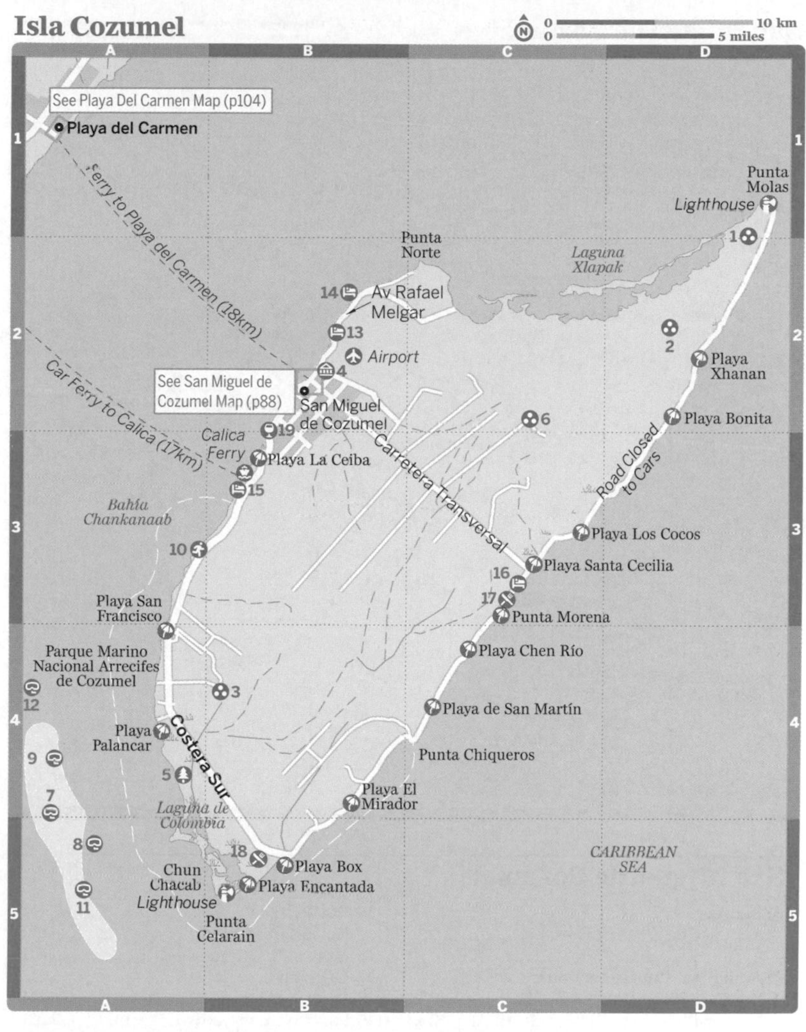

Isla Cozumel

Sights

1 Aguada Grande D1
2 El Castillo Real D2
3 El Cedral B4
4 Museo de la Isla de Cozumel B2
5 Parque Punta Sur A4
6 San Gervasio C2

Activities, Courses & Tours

7 Arrecife Palancar A4
8 Colombia Shallows A5
9 Palancar Gardens A4
10 Parque Chankanaab A3
11 Punta Sur Reef A5
12 Santa Rosa Wall A4

Sleeping

13 Hotel B Cozumel B2
14 Hotel Playa Azul B2
15 Presidente Intercontinental Cozumel .. B3
16 Ventanas al Mar C3

Eating

17 Coconuts Bar & Grill C3
18 Rasta Bar B5

Drinking & Nightlife

19 La Hach B2

San Miguel de Cozumel

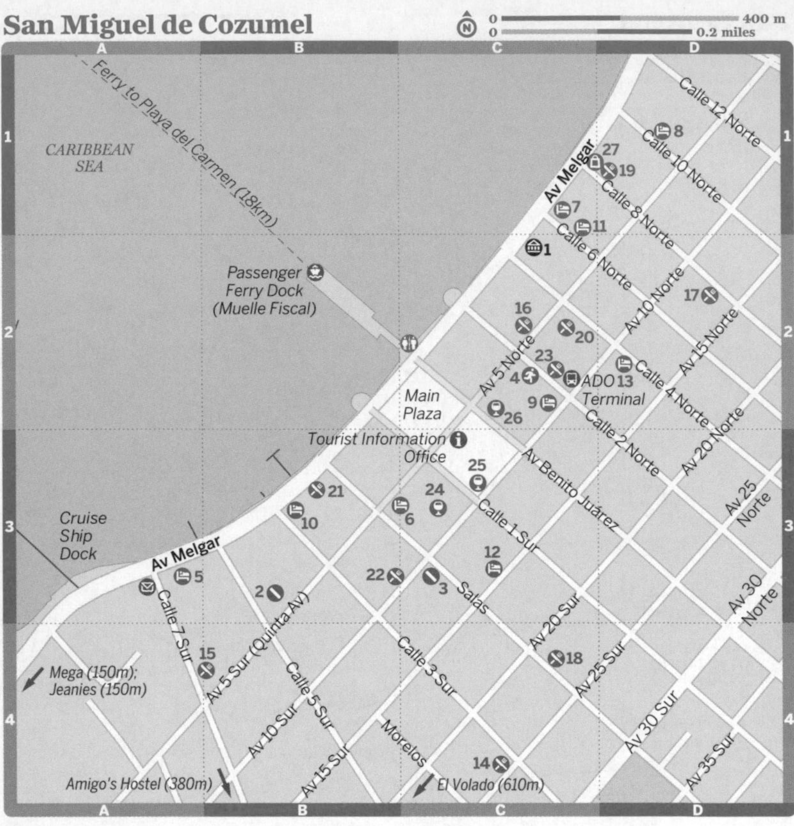

San Miguel de Cozumel

Sights
1 Museo de la Isla de Cozumel C2

Activities, Courses & Tours
2 Aldora Divers B3
3 Deep Blue C3
4 Shark Rider C2

Sleeping
5 Casa Mexicana A3
6 Colonial Hotel & Suites C3
7 Guido's Boutique Hotel C1
8 Hacienda San Miguel D1
9 Hostelito C2
10 Hotel Bahía B3
11 Hotel Flamingo C1
12 Hotel Pepita C3
13 Suites Vima D2

Eating
14 Cocina Económica Las Palmas C4
15 Costa Brava B4
Guido's Restaurant .... (see 7)
16 Kinta C2
17 La Cocay D2
18 Mercado Municipal C4
19 Pancho's Backyard D1
20 Pastelería y Panadería Zermatt C2
21 Pepe's Grill B3
22 Restaurant La Choza B3
23 Taquería El Sitio C2

Drinking & Nightlife
24 Ambar C3
Aqua .... (see 11)
25 La Abuelita C3
La Cocay .... (see 17)
26 Woody's Bar & Grill C2

Shopping
27 Los Cinco Soles C1

touristic park, you can visit a lighthouse and a small nautical museum. About 10 minutes away by car is an observation tower where you can see migratory birds and possibly crocodiles. This park area offers a beach, restaurant and three midday boat tours of **Laguna Colombia**. You'll need a vehicle or taxi (M$300 one-way) to get here.

East Coast

The eastern shoreline is the wildest part of the island and presents some beautiful seascapes and many small blowholes (there's a bunch around Km 30.5). Swimming is dangerous on most of the east coast because of riptides and undertows. With a bit of care you can sometimes swim at Punta Chiqueros, Playa Chen Río and Punta Morena.

As you travel along the coast, consider stopping for lunch or a drink at the **Rasta Bar** (Km 29.5) or **Coconuts Bar & Grill** (Km 43.5). Or just bring a picnic lunch and plan on having the beach to yourself.

Punta Molas

Beyond where the east-coast highway meets the Carretera Transversal, intrepid travelers may take a poorly maintained, infrequently traveled and almost impossible to find track toward Punta Molas, the island's northeast point, accessible only by all-terrain vehicles (ATV) or on foot. At last visit, a sign at the entrance said, 'Enter at your own risk. Irregular path even for 4x4 vehicles.'

If you head up the road, be aware that you can't count on flagging down another motorist for help in the event of a breakdown or accident, and most rental agencies' insurance policies don't cover any mishaps on unpaved roads. About 17km up the road are the Maya ruins known as **El Castillo Real**, and a few kilometers further is **Aguada Grande**. Both sites are quite far gone, their significance lost to time. In the vicinity of Punta Molas are some fairly good beaches and a few more minor ruins.

San Gervasio

San Gervasio ARCHAEOLOGICAL SITE

(Map p87; www.cozumelparks.com; Carretera Transversal, Km 7.5; admission M$104; ⏲8am-4pm) This overpriced Maya complex is Cozumel's only preserved ruins, and a prime example of the local government's efforts to milk dollars out of cruise-ship passengers. San Gervasio is thought to have been the site of the sanctuary of Ixchel, goddess of fertility, and thus an important pilgrimage site at which Maya women – in particular prospective mothers – worshipped.

But its structures are small and crude, and the clay idols of Ixchel were long ago destroyed by the Spaniards.

Activities

Several sites along the island's west coast offer horseback riding (most of the horses look ready to keel over). The asking price is M$200 to M$300 an hour; bargain hard.

Parque Chankanaab AMUSEMENT PARK

(Map p87; ☎872-4014; www.cozumelparks.com; Carretera Costera Sur, Km 9; adult/3-11yr M$273/182; ⏲8am-4pm Mon-Sat; 👪) The price of admission here includes access to a sea lion show, a nice beach and pool, a botanical garden with 400 tropical plant species, a limestone lagoon inhabited by turtles, a crocodile exhibit and a pre-Hispanic tour. Other activities, including snorkeling, diving, snuba and *temazcal* (sweat lodge) steam baths, will cost you extra.

The park has a restaurant and snack shops. A taxi from town costs M$130.

Diving

Cozumel and its 65 surrounding reefs have recovered from the massive hit of Hurricane Wilma in 2005, and they remain among the world's most popular diving spots.

The sites have fantastic year-round visibility (commonly 30m or more) and a jaw-droppingly impressive variety of marine life that includes spotted eagle rays, moray eels, groupers, barracudas, turtles, sharks, brain coral and some huge sponges. The island can have strong currents (sometimes around three knots), making drift dives the standard, especially along the many walls. Even when diving or snorkeling from the beach you should evaluate conditions and plan your route, selecting an exit point down-current beforehand, then staying alert for shifts in currents. Always keep an eye out (and your ears open) for boat traffic as well. It's best not to snorkel alone away from the beach area.

Prices vary, but in general expect to pay about M$1000 to M$1600 for a two-tank dive (equipment included), M$910 for an introductory 'resort' course and M$5500 to M$6000 for PADI open-water certification. Multiple-dive packages and discounts for groups or those paying in cash can bring rates down significantly. For more information, pick up a copy of Lonely Planet's *Diving & Snorkeling Cozumel*, with detailed descriptions of local dive sites.

If you encounter a decompression emergency, head immediately to Cozumel International Clinic (p94) hyperbaric chamber.

There are scores of dive operators on Cozumel. All limit the size of their groups to six or eight divers, and take pains to match up divers of similar skill levels. Some offer snorkeling and deep-sea fishing trips as well as diving instruction.

Deep Blue DIVING
(Map p88; ☎872-5653; www.deepbluecozumel.com; Calle Rosado Salas 200; 2-tank dives M$1000-1200, resort courses M$910) This PADI and National Association of Underwater Instructors (NAUI) operation has knowledgeable staff, very good gear and fast boats that give you a chance to get more dives out of a day.

Aldora Divers DIVING
(Map p88; ☎872-3397, cell 987-876-1529; www.aldora.com; Calle 5 Sur No 37; 1-/2-tank dives M$1050/1600; ⏰7am-8pm) One of the best dive shops in Cozumel. Will take divers to the windward side of the island when weather is bad on the west side.

Snorkeling

The best snorkeling sites are reached by boat. Most snorkeling-only outfits in town go to one of three stretches of reef near town, all accessible from the beach. If you go with a dive outfit instead, you can often get to better spots, such as Palancar Reef or the adjacent Colombia Shallows, near the island's southern end.

You can save on boat fares (and see fewer fish) by walking into the gentle surf north of town. One good spot is Hotel Playa Azul, 4km north of the turnoff to the airport; its *palapas* offer shade, and it has a swimming area with a sheltering wharf and a small artificial reef.

But your best option for snorkeling is heading out on a diving boat with Deep Blue (see above), which will take you to three sites for M$650 per person, plus a M$25 marine park fee. They'll provide the equipment.

Bicycling

A full day's bicycle rental typically costs M$100 to M$130 (depending on the season), and can be a great way to get to the northern and southern beaches on the west side of flat Cozumel. The completely separate bicycle-scooter lane on the Carretera Costera Sur sees a good deal of car traffic from confused tourists and impatient cab drivers, so be careful.

Shark Rider BICYCLE RENTAL
(Map p88; Av 5 Norte, btwn Av Benito Juárez & Calle 2 Norte; mountain/racing bikes per day M$130/195; ⏰8am-7pm) On an alley off Avenida 5, Shark Rider rents beach cruisers, mountain bikes and racing bikes.

Festivals & Events

Carnaval RELIGIOUS
We know, it's not the wild Carnaval of Rio de Janeiro, but don't underestimate a century-old tradition along the waterfront. The five-day celebration in February brings dancers festooned with feathers out into the streets, along with colorful floats, live music acts, food stall and impromptu fiestas just about everywhere you turn.

Feria del Cedral RELIGIOUS
Held in late April and early May in Cozumel's southern town of El Cedral, this annual celebration honors a group of Caste War refugees forced to flee the mainland and settle in Cozumel in 1848. May 3 marks the Day of the Holy Cross (a religious procession paying tribute to a wooden cross carried over by the settlers).

The fair features rides, food stands, rodeos and traditional dance, including the time-honored *Baile de las Cabezas de Cochino* (Dance of the Pigs' Heads).

Sleeping

Hotel rooms come with bathroom and fan, unless otherwise noted. Almost all places raise their rates at Christmas and Easter. 'High season' is mid-December to mid-April, but whatever the season, if business is slow, most places are open to negotiation.

Many budget and midrange places are in San Miguel de Cozumel. Several kilometers north and south of town are a few big luxury resort hotels.

Hostelito HOSTEL $
(Map p88; ☎869-8157; www.hostelcozumel.com; Av 10, btwn Av Benito Juárez & Calle 2 Norte; dm M$150, d/q with air-con from M$450/650; ❄📶) The hostel's tagline says it all: affordable *and* clean. There's one shared dorm room

COZUMEL'S TOP DIVE SITES

Ask any dive operator in Cozumel to name the best dive sites in the area and the following names will come up time and again.

Santa Rosa Wall

This is the biggest of the famous sites. The wall is so large most people are able to see only a third of it on one tank. Regardless of where you're dropped, expect to find enormous overhangs and tunnels covered with corals and sponges. Stoplight parrot fish, black grouper and barracuda hang out here. The average visibility is 30m and minimum depth 10m, with an average closer to 25m. Carry a flashlight with you, even if you're diving at noon, as it will help to bring out the color of coral at depth and illuminate the critters hiding in crevices. Hurricane Wilma left shallower spots with uncovered coral, but for the most part it is unharmed.

Punta Sur Reef

Unforgettable for its coral caverns, each of which is named, this reef is for very experienced divers only. Before you dive be sure to ask your divemaster to point out the Devil's Throat. This cave opens into a cathedral room with four tunnels, all of which make for some pretty hairy exploration. Only certified cave divers should consider entering the Devil's Throat. Butterfly fish, angelfish and whip corals abound at Punta Sur Reef.

Colombia Shallows

Also known as Colombia Gardens, Colombia Shallows lends itself equally well to snorkeling and scuba diving. Because it's a shallow dive (maximum depth 10m, average 2m to 4m), its massive coral buttresses covered with sponges and other resplendent life-forms are well illuminated. The current at Colombia Gardens is generally light to moderate. This and the shallow water allows you to spend hours at the site if you want, and you'll never get bored spying all the elkhorn coral, pillar coral and anemones that live here.

Palancar Gardens

Also known as Palancar Shallows, this dive can be appreciated by snorkelers due to the slight current usually found here and its modest maximum depth (20m). The Gardens consists of a strip reef about 25m wide and very long, riddled with fissures and tunnels. The major features here are enormous stovepipe sponges and vivid yellow tube sponges, and you can always find damselfish, parrot fish and angelfish around you. In the deeper parts of the reef, divers will want to keep an eye out for the lovely black corals.

downstairs for guys and gals, giant lockers and amazingly clean showers. (How's that for truth in advertising?) Upstairs you'll find a great terrace, kitchen and common area, as well as private double rooms or group rooms that sleep four to nine people.

Hotel Pepita HOTEL **$**
(Map p88; ☎872-0098; www.hotelpepitacozumel.com; Av 15 Sur No 120; r M$400; ❄ 📶) The HP's owner, Maria Teresa, takes pride in her work, and it shows. This is the best economical hotel in the city. It's friendly, with well-maintained rooms grouped around a garden. All have two double beds, refrigerators and air-con (many catch a good breeze), and there's free morning coffee.

Amigo's Hostel HOSTEL **$**
(☎872-3868; www.cozumelhostel.com; Calle 7 Sur No 57; dm/r incl breakfast M$156/585; ❄ @ 📶 🏊) Unlike some cramped budget digs, here you get a large garden, an inviting pool and a good lounge area stocked with reading material. Some guests say it's too far removed from the tourist center; others like staying in a quiet residential area. Bike and snorkel gear rentals available.

Hotel Flamingo BOUTIQUE HOTEL **$$**
(Map p88; ☎872-1264; www.hotelflamingo.com; Calle 6 Norte 81; r/ste incl breakfast M$1135/1307;

) The colorful Hotel Flamingo is a nicely decorated place with spacious air-conditioned rooms. Common areas include a leafy courtyard (where you can eat breakfast), a pool table room, a popular bar and a rooftop sundeck with hot tub. The hotel can arrange various activities, such as bicycling, horseback riding, windsurfing and fishing.

Casa Mexicana HOTEL **$$**

(Map p88; 872-9080, in USA 877-228-6747; www.casamexicanacozumel.com; Av Melgar 457; d incl breakfast with/without ocean view from M$1391/910;) The breezy open-air lobby with a swimming pool and ocean view is pretty darn sweet here. Rooms are standard issue for the most part, but all in all Casa Mexicana offers a pretty good deal given its prime location and free breakfast buffet.

Hotel Bahía HOTEL **$$**

(Map p88; 800-227-2639, in USA 877-228-6747; www.suitesbahia.com; cnr Av Melgar & Calle 3 Sur; d incl breakfast M$637-715, ocean-view room M$1053;) Opt for a standard room with a street-facing balcony or a more expensive one with balcony and ocean view. You can pinch some pesos by staying in one of the smaller, enclosed rooms, but it's not worth it.

Colonial Hotel & Suites HOTEL **$$**

(Map p88; 800-227-2639, in USA 877-228-6747; www.suitescolonial.com; Av 5 Sur; r/ste incl breakfast M$715/975;) This place is down a passageway off Av 5 Sur between Calles 1 Sur and Rosado Salas. It has lovely 'studios' (rooms with cable TV, fridge and lots of varnished-wood touches) and nice, spacious one-bedroom suites with kitchenettes.

Suites Vima HOTEL **$$**

(Map p88; 872-5118; http://student.santarosa.edu/~hcannon/html/rooms.html; Av 10 Norte; s/d M$450/550;) Vima has spotless and spacious modern rooms with tile floors, Barney Rubble–hard beds, good air-con and bathrooms, fridges, tables and chairs. A small swimming pool lies in a green area in the back of this family-run hotel.

★ **Hotel B Cozumel** BOUTIQUE HOTEL **$$$**

(Map p87; 872-0300; www.hotelbcozumel.com; Carretera Playa San Juan, Km 2.5; r M$1560-1992, ste M$3000;) The place to B and B seen, this hip hotel on the north shore may not have that sand beach you're after, but just wait till you get a look at the azure infinity pool, saltwater pool and oceanfront hot tub. Done up in contrived simplicity, the rooms are fashioned with recycled objects. Bikes are available to hit the town. It's about 2.5km north of the ferry station.

Guido's Boutique Hotel BOUTIQUE HOTEL **$$$**

(Map p88; 872-0946; www.guidosboutiquehotel.com; Av Melgar 23, btwn Calles 6 & 8 Norte; ste M$1625-1925;) Right on the main strip with an ocean view, Guido's has four chic suites that can accommodate four to eight guests. With full kitchens, large common areas and private balconies, the spacious suites are ideal for families and groups. The same owners run a great Italian restaurant downstairs.

Hacienda San Miguel HOTEL **$$$**

(Map p88; 872-1986; www.haciendasanmiguel.com; Calle 10 Norte; r/ste M$1222/1378, townhouse M$2002;) This quiet place was built and furnished to resemble an old hacienda, and niceties such as bathrobes and kitchenettes in every room make it a very good value. It offers divers' and honeymooners' packages – check the web for deals. Rates include continental breakfast.

Hotel Playa Azul HOTEL **$$$**

(Map p87; 869-5160; www.playa-azul.com; Carretera a San Juan, Km 4; d from M$2500;) This is in the sedate area north of town on a pretty little stretch of beach (it's not deep but it's a gem), and there's good snorkeling. All rooms have a sea view, a balcony or terrace, and one king or two queen beds. The hotel has a gorgeous pool, and guests can play golf free at a nearby course.

Ventanas al Mar HOTEL **$$$**

(Map p87; www.ventanasalmarcozumel.com; Carretera Costera Oriente, Km 43.5; r/ste incl breakfast M$1430/2400;) Notable as it's the only windward hotel on the island, Ventanas al Mar might be right for you if you are looking to get away from it all (*way* away from it all). After dark you'll need to go into town as the windward-side restaurants are closed; that is, if you don't want to eat at the hotel's restaurant every day. The rooms have great ocean views, but beware: the constant wind may drive you batty.

Presidente Intercontinental Cozumel LUXURY HOTEL **$$$**

(Map p87; 872-9500; www.intercontinental.com; Carretera Costera Sur, Km 6.5; r from M$4200;) This is one of the island's oldest and best luxury hotels. It has a lovely beach and 220 posh guestrooms, many with sea views, set amid tropical gardens and swimming pools. Wild (large!) iguanas roam the grounds. Unlike the resorts further south, the Presidente is sufficiently close to town.

Eating

Cozumel pretty much has it all, from cheap market eats and taco joints to candlelit restaurants serving seafood and gourmet fare. In an effort to appease the cruise-ship crowd, international cuisine abounds. The *comida corrida* (a set meal of several courses, usually offered at lunchtime) is always filling and reasonably priced in most places.

Taquería El Sitio MEXICAN **$**
(Map p88; Calle 2 Norte; tacos & tortas M$10-33; 7:30am-12:30pm) For scrump-diddily-umptious tacos and *tortas* (sandwiches), head over to El Sitio. It has fancied up the canopy-covered eating area with a mural of a cruise ship and jumping dolphins.

Cocina Económica Las Palmas MEXICAN **$**
(Map p88; cnr Calle 3 Sur & Av 25 Sur; set meals M$60; 9am-7pm Mon-Sat) This place packs out with locals come lunchtime. And while it gets hotter than Hades, you'll love the *chicharrones* (fried pork rinds) and Maya favorites such as *poc-chuc* (grilled pork) on offer.

Pastelería y Panadería Zermatt BAKERY **$**
(Map p88; cnr Av 5 Norte & Calle 4 Norte; bread M$7-16; 7am-8:30pm Mon-Sat) Zermatt bakes pastries, cakes, pizzas and whole-wheat breads and serves decent coffee. Unlike many Mexican bakeries, it does its cooking in the early morning.

★Kinta MEXICAN **$$**
(Map p88; 869-0544; www.kintacozumel.com; Av 5 Nte; mains M$120-195; 5:30-11pm Tue-Sun) Putting a gourmet twist on Mexican classics, this chic bistro is one of the best restaurants on the island. The grilled scallops and shrimp with tomato-corn salsa and cilantro pesto is delightful, even more so when served in the garden.

Restaurant La Choza MEXICAN **$$**
(Map p88; 872-0958; Av 10 Sur No 216; mains M$120-192; 7am-10pm) An excellent and popular restaurant specializing in regional Mexican cuisine, with classics like chicken in *mole poblano*. All mains come with soup. La Choza sometimes offers a *comida corrida* (M$100) in the afternoon.

Costa Brava MEXICAN **$$**
(Map p88; 869-0093; Calle 7 Sur No 57; mains M$70-190; 6:30am-11pm) Painted in bright, preschool primary colors, this casual place, with its lovely Virgencita shrine, has good prices on lobster dishes, chicken and shrimp.

Los Dorados de Villa MEXICAN **$$**
(872-0196; Calle 1 Sur; mains M$60-150; 8am-11pm;) Near the edge of the plaza, this place specializes in food from the Distrito Federal (Mexico City and surroundings) but has a wide variety of Mexican dishes, including seafood and cuts of meat. There's a vegetarian menu as well. The spinach crêpes are great, as are the complimentary chips.

Jeanie's MEXICAN **$$**
(off Map p88; 878-4647; www.jeaniescozumel.com; cnr Av Melgar & Calle 11 Sur; breakfasts M$70-95, mains M$75-220; 7am-10pm;) The views of the water are great from the outdoor patio. Jeanie's serves waffles, plus hash-brown potatoes, eggs, sandwiches and other tidbits like vegetarian fajitas. Great frozen coffees beat the midday heat.

La Cocay MEDITERRANEAN **$$$**
(Map p88; 872-5533; www.lacocay.com; Calle 8 Nte No 208; mains M$120-262; 5:30-11pm Mon-Sat) Romantic, coconut-scented candlelight and an intimate atmosphere make this snazzy restaurant a lot of fun. Sit at the bar sipping a good single malt or find a quiet table in the corner (or the back garden) to chat with someone special. The menu changes seasonally, but focuses on light, Mediterranean-influenced fare. The welcoming owners, Gary and Kathy Klein, seem to know every guest by name.

Pepe's Grill STEAKHOUSE **$$$**
(Map p88; 872-0213; www.pepesgrillcozumel.com; Av Melgar; set-lunch menus M$180, mains M$165-400; 11am-1am Mon-Sat, 5pm-midnight Sun) This is traditionally considered Cozumel's finest restaurant and the prices reflect its reputation. It's mostly red meat (steaks and prime rib), but there's also charcoal-broiled lobster (available at market prices). The daily set-lunch menu includes three courses with dessert.

Guido's Restaurant ITALIAN **$$$**
(Map p88; www.guidoscozumel.com; Av Melgar 23; mains M$160-250, pizzas M$155-195; 11am-11pm Mon-Sat, 3-9:30pm Sun) Guido's varied

menu ranges from homemade pastas and wood-fired pizzas to stuffed pork chops and prosciutto-wrapped scallops.

Pancho's Backyard MEXICAN **$$$**
(Map p88; ☎872-2141; www.panchosbackyard.com; cnr Av Melgar & Calle 8 Nte; mains M$167-265; ⏰9am-11pm Mon-Sat, 4-11pm Sun) Pancho's is very atmospheric, set in a beautifully decorated inner courtyard. The food's not bad either, focusing on Mexican dishes, international favorites and (drum roll please) seafood.

Mega SUPERMARKET
(off Map p88; cnr Av Melgar & Calle 11 Sur; ⏰7am-11pm) Head to this large supermarket to hook up your picnic lunch.

Mercado Municipal MARKET
(Map p88; Calle Rosado Salas, btwn Avs 20 & 25 Sur; ⏰7am-4pm) Visit this downtown market for your daily supply of fruits and veggies; it's also a good spot to munch on cheap eats.

Drinking & Entertainment

San Miguel de Cozumel's nightlife is quiet and subdued. Most restaurants are open for drinks, but by 11pm things wind down, though several places around the plaza keep later hours.

Ambar BAR
(Map p88; Av 5 Sur; ⏰8am-midnight Mon-Fri, 8am-4am Sat, noon-midnight Sun) There are good tunes, a pool table and a lively beer garden in the back. What more could you ask of a drinking establishment?

Aqua BAR
(Map p88; www.hotelflamingo.com; Calle 6 Nte No 81; 📶) The Hotel Flamingo's lobby bar is a fairly hip spot catering to an older crowd. There's live jazz in the high season.

Woody's Bar & Grill BAR
(Map p88; Av Benito Juárez, btwn Avs 5 & 10; ⏰9am-1am) This easygoing shotgun bar is about as friendly as you can get.

El Volado BAR
(Av 20 Sur & Calle 15 Sur; ⏰7:30pm-2:30am Tue-Sun) Rarely visited by foreigners, this two-story Mexican pub is a good spot to brush up on your Spanish. If you can't muster up the courage to converse, order a beer tower and see how that works for you.

La Cocay BAR
(Map p88; ☎872-5533; Calle 8 Nte No 208; ⏰5:30-11pm Mon-Sat) La Cocay is great place for an after-dinner drink; there's a nice ambiance, with candles and a high ceiling.

La Abuelita BAR
(Map p88; cnr Calle 1 Sur & Av 10 Sur; ⏰9pm-3am) Grab a drink with locals at the 'little grandma.' Turns out granny is quite an enterprising lady: there's an Abuelita Dos *and* Tres in other parts of town.

La Hach LIVE MUSIC
(Map p87; www.lahachcozumel.com; Av Melgar,, Km 2.9; ⏰10am-1am Sun-Tue, 10am-3am Wed-Sat) Cozumel doesn't have much of a live music scene, so the cover bands playing here are about as good as it gets. That being said, the ocean view here rocks and the restaurant whips up decent pub grub in a cantina-like atmosphere. It's a 10-minute cab ride from the town center.

Shopping

Los Cinco Soles ARTS & CRAFTS
(Map p88; www.loscincosoles.com; cnr Av Melgar & Calle 8 Nte; ⏰9am-8pm Mon-Sat, 11am-5pm Sun) Like many shops along the *avenida*, this large store sells a fair share of junk, but there are some keepers on the shelves, such as black ceramics from Oaxaca and Talavera pottery, if you take the time to browse.

Information

EMERGENCY

Police (☎066)

INTERNET ACCESS

Phonet (Av 10 Nte; per hr M$10; ⏰8am-10:30pm) Internet and cheap calls to the US and Europe (M$4 and M$5 per minute, respectively).

MEDICAL SERVICES

Cozumel International Clinic (☎872-1430; Calle 5 Sur, btwn Av Melgar and Av 5 Sur) Medical clinic with hyperbaric chamber.

MONEY

ATMs are the best way to get quick cash. For currency exchange, try any of the banks near the main plaza, such as Banorte or HSBC. Banks are open 9am to 5pm Monday to Friday and most also on Saturday morning. The many *casas de cambio* (currency-exchange offices) around town may charge as much as 3.5% commission (the bank rate is 1%) to cash a traveler's check.

Banorte (Av 5 Nte, btwn Av Benito Juárez & Calle 2 Nte)

HSBC (cnr Av 5 Sur & Calle 1 Sur)

POST

Post Office (cnr Calle 7 Sur & Av Melgar; ⌚9am-4pm Mon-Sat)

TELEPHONE

The **Telecomm Office** (⌚8am-7:30pm Mon-Fri), near the post office, handles faxes and money orders. Telmex card phones are abundant around town and are often cheaper than making calls at internet cafes.

TOURIST INFORMATION

Tourist Information Office (☎869-0211; Plaza del Sol, 2nd fl; ⌚9am-3pm Mon-Fri) Pick up maps and travel brochures here.

ℹ Getting There & Away

AIR

Cozumel's airport is 2km northeast of town; follow the signs along Av Melgar. Some airlines fly direct from the USA; European flights are usually routed via the USA or Mexico City. The following carriers serve Cozumel.

American Airlines (☎800-904-6000, in USA & Canada 800-433-7300; www.aa.com) Direct to Dallas.

Delta Airlines (☎800-123-4710, in USA & Canada 800-241-4141; www.delta.com) Non-stop to Atlanta.

Frontier Airlines (☎in USA 800-432-1359; www.flyfrontier.com) Flies to Denver.

Interjet (☎800-011-2345, USA 866-285-8307; www.interjet.com) Serves Mexico City.

Maya Air (☎872-3609; www.maya-air.com) To Cancún.

United Airlines (☎800-900-5000, in USA & Canada 800-864-8331; www.united.com) Direct to Houston.

BOAT

Passenger ferries operated by **México Waterjets** (www.mexicowaterjets.com) and **Ultramar** (www.granpuerto.com.mx) run to Cozumel from Playa del Carmen (one-way M$155, hourly 6am to 9pm). See websites for schedules.

To transport a vehicle to Cozumel, go to the Calica car ferry terminal (officially known as the Terminal Marítima Punta Venado), about 10km south of Playa del Carmen. There are four daily departures Tuesday to Saturday and two on Sunday. See www.transcaribe.net for the schedule. You'll need to line up at least one hour before departure, two hours beforehand in high season. Fares are M$500 to M$1153, depending on the size of the vehicle.

BUS

You can get long-distance bus tickets in advance at **ADO** (☎869-2553; cnr Av 10 & Calle 2 Nte; ⌚6:30am-9pm). Tickets are for services from the Playa del Carmen Terminal del Centro for all over Yucatán and Mexico.

ℹ Getting Around

TO/FROM THE AIRPORT

The airport is about 2km northeast of town. Frequent, shared shuttle vans run from the airport into town (M$60), to hotels on the island's north end (M$96) and to the south side (M$97 to M$140). To return to the airport in a taxi, expect to pay nearly double that.

CAR

A car is the best way to get to the island's further reaches, and you'll get plenty of offers to rent one. All rental contracts should automatically include third-party insurance *(daños a terceros)*. Check that taxes are included in the price you're quoted: they often are not. Collision insurance is usually about M$150 extra with a M$5000 deductible for the cheapest vehicles.

Rates start at around M$500 all-inclusive, though you'll pay more during late December and January. There are plenty of agencies around the main plaza, but prices are about 50% lower from the dock to the fringes of the tourist zone.

When renting, check with your hotel to see if it has an agreement with any agencies, as you can often get discounts. Some agencies will deduct tire damage (repair or replacement) from your deposit, even if tires are old and worn. Be particularly careful about this if you're renting a 4WD for use on unpaved roads; straighten out the details before you sign. And always check your car's brakes before driving off.

If you rent, observe the law on vehicle occupancy. Usually only five people are allowed in a vehicle. If you carry more, the police will fine you. You'll need to return your vehicle with the amount of gas it had when you signed it out or pay a premium. There's a gas station on Av Benito Juárez, five blocks east of the main square.

Rentadora Isis (☎872-3367; rentadoraisis@prodigy.net.mx; Av 5 Nte; ⌚8am-6:30pm) A fairly no-nonsense place with cars in good shape, Rentadora Isis rents VW Beetles for around M$400, with little seasonal variation in prices.

SCOOTER

Solo touring of the island by scooter is a blast provided you have experience with them and with driving in Mexico. Two people on a bike is asking for trouble, though, as the machines' suspension will be barely adequate for one. Many auto drivers speed and pass aggressively on Cozumel, and the island has its share of *topes* (speed bumps). Riders are injured in solo crashes on a regular basis, so always wear a helmet and stay alert. That said, rental opportunities abound. Collision insurance is not usually available for scooters: you break, you pay. Be sure to carefully inspect the scooter for damages before driving off, or you may get hit with a repair bill.

To rent, you must have a valid driver's license and leave a credit-card slip or put down a deposit (usually M$1000). There is a helmet law, and it is enforced.

Rentadora Isis (p95) and Shark Rider (p90) rent scooters for M$250 per day.

TAXI

As in some other towns on the Yucatán Peninsula, the taxi syndicate on Cozumel wields a good bit of power. Fares are around M$40 (in town), M$90 (to the Zona Hotelera), and M$700 to M$1000 (day trip around the island); luggage may cost extra. Carry exact change, as drivers often 'can't' provide it.

Riviera Maya

Includes ➡

Best Beaches

- Tulum (p113)
- Puerto Morelos (p99)
- Playa del Carmen (p102)
- Punta Allen (p124)
- Xcacel (p111)

Best Places to Eat

- El Merkadito (p101)
- La Cueva del Chango (p107)
- Cetli (p118)
- John Gray's Kitchen (p101)
- Los Aguachiles (p107)

Why Go?

If you like to get out and about, you'll love road-tripping in the Riviera Maya, a tourist corridor of postcard-perfect beaches, scenic ruins and fun-filled cenotes (limestone sinkholes). Yes, the Riviera Maya is growing fast, too fast some might say, but in spite of all the development, you can still find that small fishing town or head inland to catch a glimpse of the Mexico that tourism forgot.

If it's action you're after, you'll find it in boomtowns Playa del Carmen and Tulum. Ultrachic Playa del Carmen still trumps Tulum as the hippest city on the coast, but Playa has nothing on Tulum's spectacular Maya ruins perched high above the beach.

Whether traveling by car or bus, getting from one town to the next is a breeze – after all, the Riviera Maya is basically 135km of coastline that stretches south from Puerto Morelos to Tulum. Everything is so close by that you can easily go diving in Puerto Morelos by day and still have more than enough time to have dinner by candlelight in Tulum.

When to Go

- The Riviera Maya Film Festival in April screens films on beaches and at various venues up and down the coast. Weatherwise, it usually stays dry throughout the month.
- Playa del Carmen hosts a wild Halloween street bash at the end of October, then you can stick around for the first few days of November for colorful Day of the Dead festivities.
- The Riviera Maya Jazz Festival in Playa del Carmen features renowned performers from Mexico and abroad. The annual event is held during low season in November, so good hotel deals can be found.

Riviera Maya Highlights

1 Marvel at Maya ruins dramatically situated on a rugged cliff in **Tulum** (p113), then go for a swim down below

2 Hang out at chic sidewalk restaurants and beachside bars in **Playa del Carmen** (p102), or if you feel inspired, take a Spanish course

3 Dive into the waters of **Puerto Morelos** (p99) and explore a colorful barrier reef

4 Splash around or do some serious diving at impressive **cenotes** (limestone sinkholes; p115) in Tulum's surrounding areas

5 Rent a bike at **Cobá** (p120) and follow trails that lead to amazing Maya ruins, then go for a dip in nearby swimming holes

Puerto Morelos

998 / POP 9200

Halfway between Cancún and Playa del Carmen, Puerto Morelos retains its quiet, small-town feel despite the building boom north and south of town. While it offers enough restaurants and bars to keep you entertained by night, it's really the shallow Caribbean waters that draw visitors here. Brilliantly contrasted stripes of bright green and dark blue separate the shore from the barrier reef – a tantalizing sight for divers and snorkelers – while inland a series of excellent cenotes beckon the adventurous. Unfortunately, Hurricanes Wilma and Emily in 2005 knocked down most of the beach's lovely palms, although they did leave behind the sparkling sand beaches. There's a nice market just a few minutes' walk from the plaza, with a great selection of crafts, hammocks and reasonably priced souvenirs.

Sights & Activities

Jardín Botánico Yaax Che GARDENS

(www.ecosur.mx/jb/YaaxChe; Carretera Chetumal-Cancún, Km 320; adult/child M$100/50; 8am-4pm Mon-Sat;) Two kilometers south of the Puerto Morelos turnoff is a 60-hectare nature reserve with nearly 3km of trails. The garden has sections dedicated to epiphytes (orchids and bromeliads), palms, ferns, succulents (cacti and their relatives) and plants used in traditional Maya medicine. The preserve also holds a large animal population, including the only coastal troops of spider monkeys left in the region.

Boca del Puma SWIMMING

(241-2855; www.bocadelpuma.com; Ruta de los Cenotes, Km 16; adult/child 5-14yr M$120/60; 9am-5pm;) For chilling cenote action, check out the ecopark Boca del Puma, 16km west of Puerto Morelos. Other activities available include horseback riding, bicycling and zip lining.

Siete Bocas SWIMMING

(208-9199; Ruta de los Cenotes, Km 15; admission M$200; 8:30am-7pm;) Seldom-visited Siete Bocas, 15km west of Puerto Morelos, has seven 'mouths,' or openings, in a jungle setting.

Diving & Snorkeling

The barrier reef that runs along most of the coast of Quintana Roo is only 600m offshore here, providing both divers and snorkelers with views of sea turtles, sharks, stingrays, moray eels, lobsters and, of course, loads of colorful tropical fish. Several sunken ships make great wreck diving, and the dive centers have cenote trips as well.

Wet Set DIVING

(206-9204; www.wetset.com; Av Rojo Gómez, at Hotel Ojo de Agua; 1-/2-tank dive incl equipment M$845/1170; 8am-4pm) Operates trips to more than 30 dive sites, including Dos Ojos cenote. Also has two-hour snorkeling outings for M$325.

Dive In Puerto Morelos DIVING

(206-9084, in USA 801-738-0169; www.diveinpuertomorelos.com; Av Rojo Gómez; 1-/2-tank/cenote dives M$780/975/1950; 7:30am-6pm Mon-Sat) Just past the plaza's northwest end, this outfit offers both reef and cenote dives, as well as PADI open water certification for M$5200.

Health & Fitness

Sivananda Center YOGA

(230-5573; www.sivananda.com.mx; Av Niños Héroes 790) A yoga studio and healing center that doubles as a vegetarian restaurant. Yoga instructors here accept donations for classes, so pay what you consider fair. The vegetarian restaurant, called Govinda's, serves an affordable four-course set meal prepared from organic ingredients. From the main square the center is one block west, then four blocks north along Niños Héroes.

Goyo's HEALTH & FITNESS

(221-2679; goyosjungle@gmail.com; temazcal sessions M$250; sessions 7pm Sun & Wed) Goyo, an expert on edible and medicinal jungle plants, offers two-hour *temazcal* (sweat lodge) sessions. The rituals behind *temazcals* date back to pre-Hispanic times – and they're a great way to sweat out those party toxins! Goyo usually holds court at Le Café d'Amancia (off the plaza) between 7am to 11am and 4pm to 8pm, or contact him by phone (cell) or email.

Courses

Little Mexican Cooking School COOKING COURSE

(251-8060; www.thelittlemexicancookingschool.com; Av Rojo Gómez 768, cnr Lázaro Cárdenas; courses M$1400; 10am-3:30pm Tue-Fri) Ever wonder how to cook some of that delicious regional Mexican cuisine that you've been trying? Here's your chance. During this six-hour course you'll learn about ingredients

THE YUCATÁN PENINSULA'S TOP FIVE CENOTES

One look and it's easy to see why the Maya thought cenotes (limestone sinkholes) were sacred: fathomless cerulean pools, dancing shafts of light, a darkened chamber. Even if you don't buy the spiritual aspects, they're still awe-inspiring examples of nature's beauty. Here's our five favourite cenote experiences:

- A two-tank dive at **Dos Ojos** (p111), near Xcacel-Xcacelito.
- Diving or swimming at **Gran Cenote** (p120), northwest of Tulum.
- Splashing around at the lovely cavern pool of **Dzitnup** (p186), near Valladolid.
- Sinking through eerie layers of 'foggy' water in **Angelita** (p115), southwest of Tulum.
- Plunging into the cool triple cenotes of **Cuzamá** (p166) after a bouncy ride in a horse-pulled train cart, southeast of Mérida.

Keep in mind these are fragile environments. Avoid applying sunblock or insect repellent right before entering the cenote. Be aware that the rocks are often slippery. Loud noises disturb bats and other creatures. In rare cases, tourists have been seriously injured or killed by climbing on tree roots or stalactites.

For more information about Yucatán's fascinating cenotes, pick up a copy of Steve Gerrard's *The Cenotes of the Riviera Maya*, a beautiful book with spectacular photos as well as detailed information about each listing.

used in Mexican cooking and how to prepare at least seven dishes. See website for available courses.

Puerto Morelos Language Center LANGUAGE COURSE
(☎871-0162; www.puertomorelosspanishcenter.com; Av Niños Héroes 46; private classes per hour M$300, group classes per week M$1250) In addition to hourly and weekly classes, this language center also offers an immersion program with the option of living with a Mexican host family.

Sleeping

Puerto Morales hotels can be surprisingly full even at off-peak times, so call or book ahead if possible.

Hacienda Morelos HOTEL $$
(☎871-0448; www.haciendamorelos.com; Av Rafael Melgar; d from M$1000;) With a fantastic location right on the beach and just 150m south of the plaza, the large, rather plain rooms here are a good bet. The rooms downstairs have a pool and beach right outside your door.

Posada el Moro HOTEL $$
(☎206-9005; www.posadaelmoro.com; Av Rojo Gómez; r with fan/air-con incl continental breakfast M$760/875; P) This property has cheery geraniums in the halls and courtyard, and white walls with red trim. Some rooms have kitchenettes, all have couches that fold out into futons, and there's a small pool. Prices drop substantially in low season. It's northwest of the plaza.

Hotel Ojo de Agua HOTEL $$
(☎871-0027; www.ojo-de-agua.com; Av Rojo Gómez; r/ste M$1020/1300; P) Ojo de Agua offers 36 rooms on a nice stretch of beach. You can get a standard room for M$800, but it's well worth a few hundred pesos more for the deluxe, which affords an ocean view. The studio suite, which sleeps five, is good value for families. You'll find the hotel about three blocks north of the plaza.

Posada Amor HOTEL $$
(☎871-0033; www.posada-amor.wix.com/puertom; Av Rojo Gómez; s with fan/air-con M$492/550, d with air-con M$660;) About 100m southwest of the plaza, Posada Amor has been in operation for many years. The simple white-walled rooms have some creative touches. There's a shady back area with tables and plenty of plants, the restaurant offers good meals, and there's a friendly expat bar. Prices drop by 15% from May to October.

★ **Abbey del Sol Two** APARTMENT $$$
(☎871-0127; www.abbeydelsol.com; Av Niñoes Héroes; apt from M$1690;) No need to hole up in a stuffy hotel room when you have this spacious option, one of two sister properties. Eight blocks north of town center, these studio and one-bedroom apartments, some with full kitchens and large balconies,

overlook a well-manicured garden and pool area. Some units come with sleeper sofas to accommodate small families and groups. Other perks: free bikes and a DVD library.

Eating

Le Café d'Amancia CAFE $
(sandwiches M$35-55; 7am-2pm & 5-10pm;) In the southwest corner of plaza, this is a spotlessly clean place with pleasing ambiance. It serves bagels, sandwiches, pies, good strong coffee, and fruit and veggie *licuados* (fresh juice drinks blended with milk or water).

★ **El Merkadito** SEAFOOD $$
(www.elmerkadito.mx; Av Rafael Melgar; mains M$45-185; noon-9pm;) You gotta love a place that serves tortilla chips in a '*Hecho en Mexico*' (Made in Mexico) paper bag. North of the lighthouse, this is quite possibly the best seafood in town. The shrimp *aguachile ceviche* is excellent, as are the green mussels in white wine. Top it off with a refreshing ice cream served in a hollowed-out orange peel.

El Pirata MEXICAN $$
(Av Rojo Gómez; mains M$80-150; 7am-11pm) Known for its extensive menu and casual atmosphere, this place north of the plaza does everything from tacos and classic Mexican dishes to gringo comfort food such as burgers.

John Gray's Kitchen INTERNATIONAL $$$
(871-0665; Av Niños Héroes 6; mains M$175-300; 5-10pm Mon-Sat) One block west and two blocks north of the plaza, this 'kitchen' turns out some truly fabulous food. John, the personable owner-chef, has won international acclaim. The eclectic menu changes frequently and may include duck breast with chipotle-tequila-honey sauce, and an array of scrumptious desserts.

Drinking & Entertainment

Puerto Morelos' nightlife scene is pretty chill. You can hop in a taxi or bus for a night of raunchy fun in neighboring Playa del Carmen if you just can't stand the quiet. Some of the restaurants and hotels have bars and live music.

Bara Bara BAR
(Av Rojo Gómez; 8pm-4am Tue-Sun) The party usually spills out onto the street at this popular bar just southwest of the plaza. Bara Bara spins the best tunes in town, prepares martinis that would have made Sinatra proud and has a foosball table!

Que Hora Es BAR
(Av Rojo Gómez; dance class M$50; 9pm Fri) Come here southwest of the plaza for Friday night salsa class, then put those moves into practice with a live salsa band.

Cheers LIVE MUSIC
(www.cheerscaribbean.com; Av Rojo Gómez; 4pm-2am) Definitely not the most original name for a bar and the music isn't all that original either, but Cheers has a live reggae act on Saturday with talent from Jamaica.

Shopping

One of the best reasons to come to Puerto Morelos is to hit the artisans market, one block south of the plaza.

Artisans Market ARTS & CRAFTS
(Av Rojo Gómez; 9am-8pm) Find authentic Tixkokob hammocks, fine jewelry, pottery and clothing at much better prices than you'll see in Playa del Carmen or Cancún. It's refreshingly low-key, and you can often see the craftspeople at work.

Alma Libre BOOKS
(www.almalibrebooks.com; 10:30am-1:30pm & 3-8pm, closed Jun–mid-Nov) Has more than 20,000 new and used books. The friendly owners are a great resource for information about the area, as is the website, which has vacation rental listings, a monthly newsletter and other interesting info. The store also carries gift items and local gourmet food.

Orientation

Puerto Morelos' central plaza is 2km east of Hwy 307 nearly at the end of the main road into town (the main dock is the true end of the road). The town, all of three streets wide from east to west, stretches several blocks to the north of the plaza and about three long blocks south.

Information

The HSBC ATM stands off the northeast corner of the plaza.

Play Net Cafe (Av Rojo Gómez; per hour M$20; 9am-10pm) Just off the town square.

Getting There & Away

Playa Express and ADO buses that travel between Cancún and Playa del Carmen drop you on the highway. Buses from Cancún cost M$20 to M$26; a taxi costs around M$235 to M$300.

THE RIVIERA THEME PARKS

Always a big hit with kids, there are several theme parks between Cancún and Tulum, many of which have absolutely fantastic scenery – truly some of the most beautiful lagoons, cenotes (limestone sinkholes) and natural areas on the coast. Sure, some people will find these places too Disneyesque, but they usually make for a fun day nonetheless. Here are some of the more popular ones:

Aktun Chen (984-806-4962; www.indiana-joes.com; Hwy 307, Km 107; full tour incl hotel pick-up adult/child M$1300/778; 9am-5pm Mon-Sat;) This inland park offers three main activities: swimming in a cenote, a cave expedition and zip lining, or you can combine all three for a full tour.

Xplor (800-212-8951; www.xplor.travel; adult/child 5-12yr M$1677/845; 9am-5pm;) Located 6km south of Playa del Carmen, Xcaret's sister resort has amphibious four-wheelers, underground river raft rides, a zip line and a lagoon.

Xel-Há (998-251-6560, in USA & Canada 888-922-7381; www.xelha.com; Hwy Chetumal-Puerto Juárez, Km 240; adult/child 5-11yr M$1027/514; 8:30am-6pm;) Once a pristine natural lagoon brimming with iridescent tropical fish and ringed on three sides by mangroves, Xel-Há (shell-hah) is now a private park with landscaped grounds, developed cenotes, caves, nature paths and a wide array of water-based activities, such as snorkeling and scuba diving.

Xcaret (998-883-0470; www.xcaret.com; adult/child 5-12yr M$1027/514; 8:30am-9:30pm;) At Xcaret you can swim and snorkel in underground rivers and caves. Some of the cultural attractions can certainly be experienced elsewhere, beyond the confines of Xcaret's gates. Buses for Xcaret leave from the Zona Hotelera in Cancún.

Selvática (998-898-4312; www.selvatica.com.mx; Ruta de los Cenotes, Km 19; canopy tour incl hotel pickup adult/child 5-12yr M$1287/637; tours 9am-1:30pm Mon-Sat;) Inland from Puerto Morelos, this adventure outfit only runs prearranged tours. Come for adrenaline-pumping zip lining, swimming in a cenote and more. Check the website for departure times and age restrictions for each tour.

Taxis are usually waiting at the turnoff to shuttle people into town; cabs parked at the plaza will take you back to the highway. Some drivers will tell you the fare is per person or overcharge in some other manner; strive for M$20 for the 2km ride, for as many people as you can stuff in.

Punta Bete

A rocky, reef-hugged point 65km south of Cancún, Punta Bete is reached by a dirt road that runs past a large new housing development and weaves 2.5km from Hwy 307 (turn at the sign for Xcalacoco) before reaching the sea. North and south of the stubby point there are beautiful and occasionally wide stretches of beach upon which sit a few low-profile hotels, a few restaurants and a super-pricey resort. The hotels and restaurants in Punta Bete are within walking distance of each other, but you're best off getting here by rental car or taxi.

A short walk from the beach, **Coco's Cabanas** (994-133-7598; www.cocoscabanas.com; r/ste from M$1060/1400;) offers six nicely decorated *cabañas* (cabins) with good beds, hammocks, iPod docks, and TVs with DVD players. It also has a bar, a small pool, a pleasant garden and a restaurant.

Playa del Carmen

984 / POP 150,000

Playa del Carmen, now the third-largest city in Quintana Roo, is the trendiest spot on the Yucatán Peninsula. Sitting coolly on the lee side of Cozumel, the town's beaches are jammed with superfit Europeans. The waters aren't as clear as those of Cancún or Cozumel, and the beach sands aren't quite as champagne-powder-perfect as they are further north, but still Playa (as it's locally known) grows and grows.

Strolling down Playa del Carmen's pedestrian corridor, Quinta Avenida (*keen-ta*; 5 Avenida), is a fabulous game of see-and-be-seen. La Nueva Quinta (New Fifth Ave) is also called La Zona Italiana for the number of Italians operating businesses there. It begins on Calle 22 and stretches north for 10 blocks.

The town is ideally located: close to Cancún's international airport, but far enough south to allow easy access to Cozumel, Tulum, Cobá and other worthy destinations. The reefs here are excellent, and offer diving and snorkeling close by. Look for rays, moray eels, sea turtles and a huge variety of corals. The lavender sea fans make for very picturesque vistas.

With daily cruise-ship visitors, Playa is starting to feel like a mass-tourism destination, but it retains its European chic, and you need only head two blocks west of the main strip to catch glimpses of the non-touristic side of things.

Sights & Activities

Beaches

Avid beachgoers won't be disappointed here. Playa's lovely white-sand beaches are much more accessible than Cancún's: just head down to the ocean, stretch out and enjoy. Numerous restaurants front the beach in the tourist zone and many hotels in the area offer an array of water-sport activities.

If crowds aren't your thing, go north of Calle 38, where a few scrawny palms serve for shade. Here the beach extends for uncrowded kilometers, making for good camping, but you need to be extra careful with your belongings, as thefts are a possibility.

Some women go topless in Playa (though it's not a common practice in most of Mexico, and is generally frowned upon by locals – except the young bucks, of course). **Mamita's Beach**, north of Calle 28, is considered the best place to let loose.

Diving & Snorkeling

In addition to great ocean diving, most outfits offer cenote dives. Prices are similar at most shops: resort dives (M$1400), one-/two-tank dives (M$630/900), cenote dives (M$1400), snorkeling (M$450), whale-shark tour (M$2500), and open-water certification (M$5000).

Dive Mike DIVING
(☎803-1228; www.divemike.com; Calle 8; tours M$455) Dive Mike, between Quinta Avenida and the beach, offers snorkeling tours by boat to reefs and a secluded beach including refreshments and all gear. English, German, French, Italian and Spanish are spoken.

Scuba Playa DIVING
(☎803-3123; www.scubaplaya.com; Calle 10) A PADI five-star instructor development dive resort, with technical diving courses available.

Phocea Mexico DIVING
(☎873-1210; www.phoceamexico.com; Calle 10) French, English and Spanish are spoken at Phocea Mexico. The shop does dives with bull sharks from November to March.

Yucatek Divers DIVING
(☎803-2836; www.yucatek-divers.com; 15 Av) Yucatek Divers has pretty good deals that include diving and lodging at the nearby Paraiso Azul hotel.

Bicycling

A bike outing is a great way to discover outlying neighborhoods and beyond.

Arrendadora Turística Noa BICYCLE RENTAL
(☎129-4227; 10 Av; per hour/day M$25/M$130; 8am-8pm) Rent some wheels here to explore the city on your own or go on a five-hour tour (M$300) that includes a stop at a cenote.

Fishing

Playa used to be a fishing village, and you can still go out on small skiffs in search of kingfish, tarpon, barracuda, and maybe even a sailfish. April to July is the best time.

Fisherman's Cooperative FISHING
(☎876-3557; coopturmarcaribe@hotmail.com; Calle 16 Bis; up to 4 people M$2900) Support the locals and head to the fisherman's cooperative at this beachfront kiosk. Options include four-hour fishing and snorkeling trips, or you can combine both activities.

Courses

Playa has a couple of good language schools and you'll find plenty of folks to practice Spanish with, especially if you venture out beyond the tourist center.

International House LANGUAGE COURSE
(☎803-3388; www.ihrivieramaya.com; Calle 14; per week M$2860) Has homestays (the best way to learn a language), a small residence hall and 20 hours of Spanish class. Residence-hall rooms are M$434 per night (you can stay there even if you aren't taking classes). Homestays cost M$631 per night, including two meals.

Playa del Carmen

0 200 m
0 0.1 miles

A B C D

Los Anguachiles (700m)
Hyperbaric Chamber (580m)
Playa Lingua del Caribe (200m); La Fé (390m); El Diez (490m); Piola (900m); La Cueva del Chango (1.5km)
Calle 16 Bis
3
Calle 14 Bis
15 Av
4
Calle 14
Quinta Av (5 Av)
1 Av
1 Av Bis
17
20 Av
Calle 12 Bis
27
10 Av
21
Terminal ADO
20
Calle 12
8
15
Calle 10 Bis
23
24
18
5
Calle 10
6
15 Av
19
10
Calle 8
2
22
12
Calle 6 Norte Bis
1
28
25
30
Calle 6
29
9
13
Calle 4
14
CARIBBEAN SEA
20 Av
15 Av
10 Av
Quinta Av (5 Av)
Colectivos to Tulum & Cancún
7
26
Calle 2
16
11
Playa Express
Parque Turístico Leona Vicario
Terminal del Centro
Av Juárez
Plaza Mayor
To Gas Station (400m); Hwy 307 (450m); Alux (800m); Cozumel (10km)
Quinta Av (5 Av)
Cozumel Ferry Ticket Booth
Calle 1 Sur
Calle 1 Sur
10 Av
Ferries to Cozumel (19km)
20 Av

Playa del Carmen

Activities, Courses & Tours
1 Arrendadora Turística Noa B4
2 Dive Mike C3
3 Fisherman's Cooperative D1
4 International House B1
5 Phocea Mexico D2
6 Scuba Playa C3
7 Yucatek Divers B5

Sleeping
8 Blue Parrot Suites D2
9 Casa de las Flores A4
10 Hostel Playa A3
11 Hostel Quinta Playa C5
12 Hostel Río Playa C3
13 Hotel Barrio Latino B5
14 Hotel Casa Tucán B5
15 Hotel Deseo C2
16 Hotel Hacienda del Caribe C5
17 Hotel Playa del Karma B1
18 Kinbé Hotel C3
19 Mosquito Beach D3
20 Mosquito Blue C2
21 Playa Palms D2
22 Sahara Hotel B3

Eating
23 100% Natural C3
24 Babe's C3
25 Buenos Aires C4
26 Club Náutico Tarraya D5
27 Don Sirloin B2
28 Market B4

Drinking & Nightlife
Blue Parrot Bar .... (see 8)
29 Playa 69 .... C4

Entertainment
30 Fusion D4

Playa Lingua del Caribe LANGUAGE COURSE
(☎873-3876; www.playalingua.com; Calle 20; 1 week with/without homestay M$5200/2925) This offers 20-hour-per-week classes as well as homestays. It also has occasional classes in Maya language, cooking and even salsa dancing.

Tours

Alltournative ADVENTURE TOUR
(☎803-9999, in USA 877-437-4990; www.alltournative.com; Carretera Chetumal-Puerto Juárez, Km 287; ⏰9am-7pm Mon-Sat) Alltournative's packages include zip lining, rappelling and kayaking, as well as custom-designed trips. It also takes you to nearby Maya villages for an 'authentic' experience that could easily be had on your own. The office is out of the way; you're better off calling or reserving online.

Sleeping

Fairly affordable midrange hotels can be found within several blocks of the beach, and a number of hostels offer dorm-style lodging and private rooms. Regular high season runs from January to April, while prices spike by as much as M$1000 for the 'super high season' around Christmas.

Hostel Río Playa HOSTEL $
(☎803-0145; see www.hostelworld.com; Calle 8; dm incl breakfast M$245-270, r without bathroom incl breakfast M$450-500; ❄@📶🏊) A good budget buy, the Río offers easy beach access, a women's-only dorm, two large dorms sleeping 14 and a smaller six-person dorm. It also has a shared kitchen, a cool rooftop bar and hangout area – with a remarkably shallow pool – and air-con in all the rooms. Did we mention it's close to the beach?

Hostel Quinta Playa HOSTEL $
(☎147-0428; www.quintaplaya.com; Calle 2, btwn Quinta Av & beach; dm with/without air-con M$200/170; ❄@📶🏊) It's all about the location here. Just 30m from the beach, one block from the bus station and two blocks from the Playa del Carmen ferry terminal. Now that's convenience. The hostel runs a fairly simple operation: six rooms each with six clean beds, a small pool, a restaurant and a full kitchen for guests.

Hotel Playa del Karma BOUTIQUE HOTEL $$
(☎803-0272; www.hotelplayadelkarma.com; 15 Av, btwn Calles 12 & 14; r from M$845; P❄📶🏊) The closest you're going to get to the jungle in this town, rooms here face a lush courtyard featuring a plunge pool. All rooms have air-con and sweet little porches with hammocks and sitting areas; the more expensive digs have TVs.

Casa de las Flores HOTEL $$
(☎873-2898; www.hotelcasadelasflores.com; 20 Av; r from M$1170; ❄📶🏊) With a good mix of colonial charm and modern comfort, this sizable but intimate family-run hotel offers big, fresh rooms set around a delightful plant-filled patio.

THOSE MYSTERIOUS ALUXES

Aluxes (a-loosh-es) are *yucateco* forest sprites, and many of the Maya still believe they can bring good or bad luck, even death, to those around them. Therefore, when forests are cleared, whether to make a field or build a house, offerings of food, alcohol and even cigarettes are made to placate them.

Hotel Casa Tucán HOTEL **$$**
(☎873-0283; www.casatucan.com.mx; Calle 4; r with fan/air-con M$600/720, ste M$1200; P ❄ 📶 🏊) This German-run hotel is a warren of 30 rooms of several types. Rooms have fans or air-con, a couple have kitchenettes, and some come with a minibar. The Casa has a pleasant tropical garden (that draws in a lot of mosquitoes) and a cafe serving good, affordable food.

Hotel Barrio Latino HOTEL **$$**
(☎873-2384; www.hotelbarriolatino.com; Calle 4; r with fan/air-con incl continental breakfast from M$700/820; ❄ @ 📶) Offers 18 clean, colorful rooms with good ventilation, ceiling fans, tiled floors, bathrooms and hammocks (in addition to beds). The place is often full and the front gate often locked. Discounted rates are available for extended stays, and the prices drop precipitously in low season. Guests get to make free international calls.

Sahara Hotel HOTEL **$$**
(☎873-2236; www.tucasaenplaya.com; 15 Av; r/ste M$785/1390; P 📶) An Italian-owned establishment with 25 comfortable rooms (most with balconies), the centrally located Sahara also has a suite with kitchenette that can accommodate families or small groups. If you're pinching pesos, the hotel has several cheaper, dark interior rooms, but they're not worth it if you like natural light.

Hotel Hacienda del Caribe HOTEL **$$**
(☎873-3132; www.haciendadelcaribe.com; Calle 2 No 130; d M$1026; P ❄ 🏊) This Mexican-run place has quiet, comfortable rooms with bright rustic decor, air-con and cable TV, and many come with balconies. The hacienda-style courtyard's centerpiece is a small pool with hydro-massage. Parking in a nearby lot is free while you stay.

★**Kinbé Hotel** HOTEL **$$$**
(☎873-0441; www.kinbe.com; Calle 10; r M$1500-2600; ❄ 📶 🏊) An Italian-owned and operated hotel, Kinbé has 29 clean, simple but elegant rooms with lovely aesthetic touches and a breezy rooftop terrace with fab views from the 3rd floor. Choose a room in the soothing 'water' section, which has an indoor pool and waterfall, or opt for the 'land' side and surround yourself with lush vegetation.

Playa Palms BOUTIQUE HOTEL **$$$**
(☎803-3908; www.playapalms.com; 1 Av Bis; r M$2489-3013, studio M$3340-4125; ❄ @ 📶 🏊) A rip-roaring deal in low season (get the best price online), Playa Palms is right on the beach. The shell-shaped rooms have balconies that look out to the ocean past the curly-whirly plunge pool. Go with the cheaper studios to get the best views at the best price.

Mosquito Blue BOUTIQUE HOTEL **$$$**
(☎873-1245; www.mosquitoblue.com; Calle 12; r M$1580-2186, ste M$3735; P ❄ @ 📶 🏊) Strives for – and at times achieves – ultrachicness. Its cloistered interior boasts two pools and courtyards, a bar and restaurant, and very nicely decorated rooms and suites furnished in Indonesian mahogany. Art and artistic touches abound throughout the hotel. For the same service and style beachside, head to the sister hotel, **Mosquito Beach** (Calle 8).

Blue Parrot Suites HOTEL **$$$**
(☎206-3350; www.blueparrot.com; Calle 12; r M$2080-2635; ❄ 📶) Many of the charming units have terraces, sea views and full kitchens. But it's a bit pricey to not be right on the ocean. It also has an immensely popular bar, which can make for some late nights.

Hotel Deseo BOUTIQUE HOTEL **$$$**
(☎879-3620; www.hoteldeseo.com; cnr Quinta Av & Calle 12; d M$2500-2900, ste M$4600; ❄ @ 📶 🏊) If you can still afford your rock-and-roll lifestyle, then you're going to love the urbane atmosphere of Deseo. There's a very chill lounge and plunge pool right in front of your blindingly white room (white is evidently the color of desire). Pay a bit more for an upstairs balcony room, and be prepared to stay up late.

✕ Eating

For cheap eats, head away from the tourist center, or try the small **market** (Av 10, btwn Calles 6 & 8; mains M$30-70; ⏲9am-4pm) for some homestyle regional cooking.

Don Sirloin MEXICAN $

(10 Av; tacos M$13; ⌚noon-7am) *Al pastor* (marinated pork) and sirloin beef are sliced right off the spit at this popular all-night taco joint.

★**La Cueva del Chango** MEXICAN $$

(www.lacuevadelchango.com; Calle 38, btwn Quinta Av & beach; breakfast M$60-68, lunch & dinner M$74-158; ⌚8am-11pm) You're in for a real treat when you visit the 'Monkey's Cave.' Grab a table in the stylish rustic dining area or enjoy the verdant garden area out back. The restaurant uses fresh, natural ingredients and is remarkably affordable. Try the *chilaquiles* (lightly fried tortillas with salsa, egg and cheese) with *xcatic* chili for breakfast; for dinner, go for the sesame-encrusted tuna.

Los Aguachiles SEAFOOD $$

(Calle 34, btwn Avs 25 & 30; tostadas M$33, mains M$89-159; ⌚12:30-7:30pm) Done up in typical Mexican *cantina*-style yet with one big difference: the menu – consisting of tacos, *tostadas* (fried tortillas) and the like – was designed by a chef. So yeah, good luck finding artfully prepared fresh tuna *tostadas* in any of the neighborhood watering holes.

Piola PIZZERIA $$

(www.piola.it; Calle 38, btwn Quinta Av & 1 Av Norte; pizzas M$82-190; ⌚1pm-1am; ✎) Boasting it's '*famosi per la pizza*', this Italian chain lives up to its claim. Thin-crust pizzas here are prepared with fresh ingredients like basil, asparagus and artichoke hearts. And with a gurgling stream running below the open-air deck, it's a pleasant spot to relax with a glass of wine.

Babe's FUSION $$

(www.babesnoodlesandbar.com; Calle 10; mains M$95-168; ⌚1-11:30pm Tue-Sun; ✎) Babe's serves some excellent Asian food, including a yummy homestyle *tom kha gai* (chicken and coconut-milk soup) brimming with veggies. Vietnamese shrimp and rice noodles is another good one. Most dishes can be done vegetarian, and to mix things up a bit the Swedish cook has some tasty Korean and Indian items on the menu as well.

Club Náutico Tarraya SEAFOOD $$

(Calle 2; mains M$50-185; ⌚noon-9pm) One of the few restaurants in Playa del Carmen that dates from the 1960s. It continues to offer good seafood at decent prices in a casual place on the beach with a nice view.

100% Natural VEGETARIAN $$

(Cien Por Ciento Natural; www.100natural.com.mx; cnr Quinta Av & Calle 10; mains M$64-136; ⌚7am-11pm; ✎) The trademark offerings of this quickly establishing chain – vegetable- and fruit-juice blends, salads, various vegetable and chicken dishes and other healthy foods – are delicious and filling.

El Diez ARGENTINE $$

(www.eldiez.com.mx; cnr Quinta Av & Calle 30; pizzas M$99-148, mains M$95-169; ⌚1pm-midnight; 📶) In a loving nod to soccer legend Diego Maradona, who wore the number *diez* (10), El Diez serves up pizzas and *parrilladas* (Argentine-style barbecues) just the way the master would have wanted them. The outside seating on La Nueva Quinta makes for some great people-watching.

Alux MEXICAN $$$

(☎206-2589; www.aluxrestaurant.com; Av Juárez; mains M$150-380; ⌚5:30-11pm) About three blocks west of Hwy 307, the Alux is an amazing must-visit. It's a restaurant-lounge situated in a cavern: stalactites, stalagmites, pools and all. Candles and dim electric lights illuminate numerous nooks and crannies converted into sofa-like seating. Wander through, have a bite to eat or a drink, and revel in the atmosphere.

Buenos Aires ARGENTINE $$$

(☎873-2751; Calle 6; mains M$115-280; ⌚noon-11:30pm) In a new location, this Argentine-owned steakhouse is well known for its *parrilla*, an all-you-can-eat smorgasbord (M$155 per person) on Tuesday and Thursday. You can also order rib eye, *empanadas*, (turnovers stuffed with meat or cheese) burgers and other 'lighter' fare off the menu.

Drinking & Entertainment

Venues here come and go, so ask around if you're wondering where the party is (or where it isn't). You'll find everything from mellow, tranced-out lounge bars to classic rock-and-roll places. The party generally starts on Quinta Av then heads down toward the beach on Calle 6.

Blue Parrot Bar DANCE

(☎873-0083; www.blueparrot.com/beach-club; Calle 12; ⌚10am-4am) This is the Blue Parrot Suites' immensely popular open-sided *palapa* (thatched-roof) beachfront bar with swing chairs, a giant outdoor dance stage and lots of sand. The bar also has a nightly fire dancers show on the beach.

La Fé BAR

(cnr Quinta Av & Calle 26; ⏲11am-4am; 📶) This Nueva Quinta bar caters to a younger hipster crowd.

Playa 69 GAY

(www.rivieramayagay.com; Callejón off Quinta Av, btwn Calles 4 & 6; ⏲8pm-2am Tue, 8pm-6am Wed-Sun) This gay dance club proudly features foreign strippers from such far-flung places as Australia and Brazil.

★**Fusion** LIVE MUSIC

(www.fusionhotelmexico.com; Calle 6; ⏲7am-2am) Groove out beachside under that Playa moon at Fusion. There's live music most nights, and the beachside eating is worth checking out.

Information

DANGERS & ANNOYANCES

Playa is generally safe: you are very unlikely to experience street crime or muggings. However, pickpockets do circulate, especially in crowded dance clubs. Never leave valuables unattended on the beach. Run-and-grab thefts while victims are swimming or sleeping, especially on the isolated beaches to the north, are a common occurrence (the jungle has eyes).

EMERGENCY

Tourist Police Kiosk (☎873-2656; ⏲24hr) Guards the north corner of the Plaza Mayor. The police officers sometimes speak English and are good sources of tourist information.

INTERNET ACCESS

There are enough internet cafes in Playa to keep Bill Gates in fancy khakis for the rest of his life.

Lavandería & Internet Estrella (Calle 2 No 402; per hour M$10; ⏲8am-10pm Mon-Sat) Conveniently has an internet cafe in front of the laundry (M$15 per kilo).

MEDICAL SERVICES

Clinic & Hyperbaric Chamber (Playa International Clinic; ☎803-1215; cnr 10 Av & Calle 28; ⏲9am-8:30pm) Excellent medical clinic with onsite hyberbaric chamber.

Hospiten (☎803-1002; www.hospiten.com; Hwy 307; ⏲24hr) South on Hwy 307, just past Sam's Club in front of Centro Maya.

MONEY

These are some of the many banks around town:

Banamex (cnr Calle 12 & 10 Av)

Bancomer (cnr Av Juárez & 25 Av)

Scotiabank (Quinta Av)

POST

Post Office (cnr 20 Av & Calle 2; ⏲9am-3pm Mon-Fri, 9am-12:45pm Sat)

Getting There & Around

BOAT

Ferries depart frequently to Cozumel (M$156 one-way), usually from 7am to 9pm. For schedules of the two ferry operators, see www.granpuerto.com.mx and www.mexicowaterjets.com. The trip takes about half an hour, depending on weather. Ticket booths are on Calle 1 Sur.

BUS

Playa has two bus terminals; each sells tickets and provides information for at least some of the other's departures. The newer one, **Terminal ADO** (20 Av), just northeast of Calle 12, is where most 1st-class bus lines arrive and depart.

The old bus station, **Terminal del Centro** (cnr Av Juárez & Quinta Av), gets all the 2nd-class (called 'intermedio' by such lines as Mayab) services. You can save money by buying a 2nd-class bus ticket, but remember that it's often

BUSES FROM PLAYA DEL CARMEN

DESTINATION	COST (M$)	DURATION (HR)	FREQUENCY
Cancún	32-48	1¼	frequent
Cancún International Airport	120	1	frequent
Chetumal	190-252	4¼-5½	frequent
Chichén Itzá	130	4	7:30am, 2:30pm (2nd-class)
Cobá	72-92	2	11 daily
Mérida	334-404	4¼-5	frequent
Palenque	448-750	11-12	4 daily
San Cristóbal de las Casas	540-796	16½-18	4 daily
Tulum	38-66	1	frequent
Valladolid	106-150	2½-3½	frequent

stop-and-go along the way. A taxi from Terminal ADO to the Plaza Mayor will run about M$25.

Playa Express (Calle 2 Norte) shuttles offer quick service to Puerto Morelos for M$20 and downtown Cancún for M$34.

The table opposite shows prices and travel times for buses.

COLECTIVO

Colectivos (shared vans) are a great option for cheap travel southward to Tulum (M$40, 45 minutes). They depart from Calle 2 near Av 20 as soon as they fill (about every 15 minutes) from 5am to 10pm. They will stop anywhere along the highway between Playa and Tulum, charging a minimum of M$20. Luggage space is somewhat limited, but they're great for day trips. From the same spot, you can grab a *colectivo* to Cancún (M$30).

Punta Venado

A delightful spot for horseback riding and swimming, Punta Venado lies about 5km south of Xcaret and 2km further east of the highway.

Punta Venado Caribbean Eco-Park (☎800-503-0046; www.caribbeanecopark.com; horseback riding M$1100; ⏲8am-5pm), which sits on some 8 sq km of mostly virgin jungle terrain, does guided **horse tours**, during which you're likely to see monkeys, deer and various other mammals, as well as crocodiles, snakes and lots of birds. The trail leads to a **cenote** and a 3km-long stretch of isolated beach, where there's a *palapa* restaurant. The horses are well cared for and the owners are very hospitable. In addition to horseback riding, you can also make arrangements to snorkel or kayak.

Paamul

Paamul, 87km south of Cancún, is a de facto private beach on a sheltered bay. Like many other spots along the Caribbean coast, it has signs prohibiting entry to nonguests, and parking is limited.

The attractions here are great diving and a sandy, palm-fringed beach, which, though lovely, has many small rocks, shells and spiked sea urchins in the shallows offshore; take appropriate measures. A large recreational vehicle (RV) park here is greatly favored by snowbirds; the 'BC' license plates you see are from British Columbia, not Baja California. An attractive alabaster sand beach lies about 2km north.

Giant sea turtles come ashore here at night in July and August to lay their eggs. If you run across one during an evening stroll along the beach, keep your distance and don't turn your flashlight on – or take flash photography – or you might scare it away.

If you come by bus, it's a 500m walk from the highway to the hotel and beach.

Scuba-Mex (☎984-115-7514, in USA 512-697-9580; www.scubamex.com; Carretera Cancún-Tulum, Km 85; 1-tank dive with own/rental gear M$390/520, 1-/2-tank cenote dive M$1040/1820) offers trips to 30 superb sites at very reasonable prices, including cenote dives.

You can choose between gorgeous, modern beachfront rooms or rustic, spacious *cabañas* built on stilts at **Paamul Hotel** (☎984-875-1050; www.paamul.com.mx; Carretera Cancún-Tulum, Km 85; campsites/cabañas M$520/1100, r from M$1300; P ❄ ≋). Each *cabaña* has two beds, a ceiling fan, bathrooms with hot water and a veranda. Gaps in the wooden floors provide additional ventilation. A serene atmosphere prevails in both accommodations. There are also campsites available.

Xpu-Há

Xpu-Há (shpoo-*ha*) is a beach area about 95km south of Cancún that extends for several kilometers. It's reached by numbered access roads (most of them private). They are building all-inclusive resorts here faster than you can say 'cultural degradation,' but it's still worth a trip if you are looking to get away from it all.

Right on the beach, the **Al Cielo Hotel** (☎984-840-9012; www.alcielohotel.com; Carretera Federal Cancún-Tulum, Km 118, Xpu-Há Beach 1.5; r/ste incl breakfast from M$4160/5850; P ☎) stands out in this land of giant all-inclusives for its intimacy. On offer are six upscale bungalows, two recently added suites, a spa and an excellent onsite restaurant. Reservations are recommended for both the hotel and restaurant.

Akumal

☎984 / POP 1400

Famous for its beautiful beach and large, swimmable lagoon, Akumal (Place of the Turtles) does indeed see some sea turtles come ashore to lay their eggs in the summer, although fewer and fewer arrive each year due to resort development. Akumal is one of the

WORTH A TRIP

CRISTALINO CENOTE

On the west side of the highway south of Playa del Carmen is a series of cenotes (limestone sinkholes) that you can visit and swim in for a price. Among these is **Cristalino Cenote** (admission M$40; 6am-5:30pm), just south of the Barceló Maya Resort. It's easily accessible, only about 70m from the entrance gate, which is just off the highway. The well-tended cenote has mangrove on one side and a large open section you can dive into by climbing a ladder up to a ledge above it. The water extends about 20m into an overhung, cavelike portion.

Two more sinkholes, Cenote Azul and El Jardín del Edén, are just south of Cristalino along the highway, but Cristalino is definitely the best of the three.

Yucatán Peninsula's oldest resort areas and consists primarily of pricey hotels, condominiums and residential developments (occupied mostly by North Americans) on nearly 5km of wide beach bordering four consecutive bays. With the exception of Villa Las Brisas, all sights and facilities are reached by taking the first turnoff, Playa Akumal, as you come south on the highway. It's about 500m from the highway to the entrance.

Sights & Activities

Although the increasing population is taking its toll on the reefs that parallel Akumal, diving remains the area's primary attraction. Hurricane Dean also reportedly did some minor damage to the area's reef in 2007, but it has gradually recovered. There are several ecoparks near here, but with such good snorkeling in town they're hardly worth it.

You can also simply find a place to park and snorkel or swim on your own, as the shallow waters are appealing and fun. Close to the shore you will not have problems with currents, though at times the surf can be rough.

Centro Ecológico Akumal MUSEUM
(875-9095; www.ceakumal.org; P) To learn more about the area's ecology, check out the Centro Ecológico Akumal. The center, on the east side of the road at the town's entrance, has a few exhibits on reef and turtle ecology. And, for those aged over 21, it offers six- to 12-week volunteer programs that cost M$2600 to M$19,500 per month, including lodging.

Laguna Yal-Kú SWIMMING
(adult/child 4-12yr M$120/85; 8am-5:30pm;) Laguna Yal-Kú is a beautiful lagoon 2km north of the Playa Akumal entrance. The rocky lagoon, without a doubt one of the region's highlights, runs about 500m from its beginning to the sea. It is home to large schools of brightly colored fish, and the occasional visiting turtle. There is a tasteful sculpture garden along the shore.

Showers, parking and bathrooms are included in the admission price; lockers are an extra M$25, and snorkel gear and life jackets cost M$60 each to rent. Taxis from the Playa Akumal entrance charge about M$80 to the lagoon. In an effort to protect the lagoon's fragile environment, sunblock is prohibited.

Akumal Dive Shop DIVING
(875-9032; www.akumaldiveshop.com; 1-/2-tank dive M$650/960, fishing per boat M$1800-2400) Dive trips and deep-sea fishing excursions are offered by Akumal Dive Shop, at the town entrance. It also does snorkeling trips to the reef and beaches unreachable by car for M$300. You can also rent a catamaran for M$540 to M$1140.

Sleeping & Eating

You'll find a bunch of houses for rent on www.akumalvacations.com, or you can check out one of the area's hotels.

Just outside the entrance to Playa Akumal are two minimarkets that stock a good selection of inexpensive food.

El Ultimo Maya HOTEL $
(802-7202; r M$400;) There's not much joy for budget travelers in Akumal, but across the highway in Akumal Pueblo (about a 10-minute walk or M$15 taxi ride from the beach), this family-run place offers rather sparse but clean rooms.

Villa Las Brisas HOTEL $$
(876-2110; www.aventuras-akumal.com; off Hwy 307; r M$950, condos M$1677-2405) On the beach in Aventuras Akumal, this is an attractive, modern place with two hotel-type rooms, some one- and two-bedroom condos and a studio apartment – all under two roofs.

Room prices vary greatly by category and season. The friendly owners Horacio and Kersten speak five languages! The turnoff is 2.5km south of the turnoff for Playa Akumal.

Vista del Mar HOTEL **$$**
(☎875-9060; www.akumalinfo.com; r from M$1170, apt M$2600; P ❄ ☎) A rare midrange find in Akumal, this hotel has compact but pleasant rooms with beach-view balconies and patios. More spacious two-bedroom condos are good for families and small groups. You can also rent bikes here for M$12 per hour.

Lunchería Akumalito MEXICAN **$**
(sandwiches & mains M$50-110; ⏰7am-9pm) A good spot to pick up some *tortas* (sandwiches) for a picnic on the beach. It's at the town's entrance.

La Cueva del Pescador SEAFOOD **$$**
(mains M$90-180; ⏰noon-9pm) Just north of the town's entrance, this restaurant does good grilled fish dishes and shrimp tacos in a casual atmosphere with outdoor seating and a pool table inside.

Xcacel-Xcacelito

This sanctuary is located at Km 112 of the Cancún–Tulum Hwy (between the Chemuyil and Xel-Há exits), with only a tiny sign on the east side of the highway marking the short dirt road that leads here. Along the two arching bays – Xcacel and Xcacelito – you'll find a cenote, good snorkeling and, most notably, Quintana Roo's most important loggerhead and white sea-turtle nesting site.

About 500m south of the parking area, there's a lovely cenote, while the northern edge of the beach has a protected coastal reef perfect for snorkeling. There's no food or lodging on this protected beach and it's open to the public from 9am to 5pm.

Sign up online or make a phone booking with the **Flora, Fauna y Cultura** (☎984-871-5244; www.florafaunaycultura.org; turtle observation M$390; ⏰9pm-3am Mon-Fri Jul-Sep) office to watch turtles come ashore to lay their eggs. You can also arrange one- to two-month volunteer stays through the organization for a very low fee of M$1000, including room and board at an oceanside campsite.

South of Xcacel-Xcacelito

About 4km south of Xcacel-Xcacelito – and 1km south of Xel-Há – is the turnoff for **Cenote Dos Ojos**, which provides access to the enormous Dos Ojos cave system. You can take guided snorkel (M$300) and dive tours (M$780 to M$1170) of some amazing underwater caverns, floating past illuminated stalactites and stalagmites in an eerie wonderland. With an aggregate length of nearly

RIVIERA BUDGET DIGS

Let's face it: staying on the Riviera Maya can get awfully pricey, but don't worry, the deals are out there if you look. Hostel World (www.hostelworld.com) is always a good source, not only for hostels but also for affordable hotels. Here are three good options in the three biggest cities:

El Jardín de Frida (☎984-871-2816; www.fridastulum.com; Av Tulum, Tulum; dm/r incl breakfast M$200/600; P ☎) Mexican pop art and colorful murals are just about everywhere you turn in the main house, while out back, dorms and private rooms surround a lush garden area. Even if you're not staying here, drop by the hostel's happening open-air restaurant/bar for organic food and live music.

Hostel Playa (☎984-803-3277; www.hostelplaya.com; Calle 8, Playa del Carmen; dm/d/tr incl breakfast M$160/420/630; P ☎) This place was made for mingling with its central common area, a cool garden space and a rooftop terrace. The private rooms are simple but decent enough, and the staff is extremely helpful with great suggestions on what to see and do.

Mexico Plus (☎998 871-0232; Av Niños Héroes, Puerto Morelos; r with/without air-con M$550/450; ❄ ☎) Puerto Morelos has surprisingly few budget options, so this place, one blocl west of the plaza, is probably your best bet. The modern rooms come with mini-fridges and clean tiled floors. You may be kept up by the music from the hotel's adjoining open-air bar, or you could just join the party.

57km, it's the third-largest underwater cave system in the world.

Ox Bel Ha and **Nohoch Nah Chich** (about 97km and 61km total length, respectively) are nearby. Divers have tried for years to find a passage linking Dos Ojos and Nohoch Nah Chich to prove them to be one humongous system. They succeeded in linking Nohoch with one of its outlets to the sea (at Cenote Manatí in Tankah). While that was going on, new kid on the block Ox Bel Ha was found to be really big.

Hidden Worlds (☎984-115-4514; www.hiddenworlds.com; ⏲9am-5pm) is a Costa Rica-based outfit offering four-hour adventure tours for M$1040 (M$780 for children under 12). The tour combines six activities, including snorkeling in a cenote, rapelling into a cave and soaring above the jungle on a zip line. Also available is a diving package (M$1690) with equipment and transport to and from cenotes that form part of a fascinating cavern system.

Another way to see part of the system is through the **Dos Ojos** (www.cenotedosojos.com; admission M$100; ⏲8am-5pm) operation, a short distance north of Hidden Worlds. It's run by the Maya community that owns the land. The entrance fee is M$100 and snorkeling gear is an additional M$30. You can dive here as well, if you have open-water certification. Prices vary, depending on whether you bring your own equipment and how many dives you'd like to do. See the website for details.

Bahías de Punta Solimán

These two beautiful, protected bays are separated by a narrow point, 123km south of Cancún and 11km north of Tulum.

To get here, head east (toward the sound of the ocean) on an unmarked road directly opposite Hwy 307's Oscar y Lalo's Restaurant. When you get to the ocean, you'll need to pass through a guarded gate to gain access to the bays.

You can rent a kayak here and paddle out to the reef that shelters the mouth of the bay. You could probably snorkel out, too, if you are a good swimmer. There's a dense mangrove forest, and the mozzies and sand flies on the powder-white beach can get a bit rough.

Birds of interest here include Yucatán vireos, Yucatán woodpeckers, rose-throated tanagers, black catbirds and orange orioles. If you're very lucky you may spot one of the pumas seen in the area from time to time.

Turning right (south) at the beachfront intersection takes you to **Bahía Solimán** (though some call it Bahía de San Francisco). Currently the only spot to find lodging in the area – they are redeveloping the areas north of here – it has terrific coral heads, tons of colorful fish, plenty of grouper and reef sharks, and the occasional sea turtle and even tuna.

A number of beach houses, some quite luxurious, line the dirt road. Most of them rent by the week, some at well over M$20,000. A good website for house rentals in the area is www.locogringo.com.

Most people get to Punta Solimán by car, or by taking a bus to Tulum and a taxi from there.

Sleeping & Eating

Nah Uxibal APARTMENT **$$$**

(☎USA 707-407-8033; www.nahuxibal.com; studio/villa/ste M$1950/2535/4550) It's rare to find a place in these parts offering nightly (as opposed to weekly) stays, and this one, 500m south of entrance, is relatively affordable for the area. The 'studios' and beachside villas here are spacious spreads with fully equipped kitchens, lovely tilework and private porches with hammocks. The enormous suite upstairs can accommodate a small army, but only six are allowed.

Chamicos SEAFOOD **$$**

(mains M$100-200; P) At the south end of the road, Chamicos is the one-stop spot for all your budget traveler needs. The restaurant prepares reasonably priced fish and seafood dishes, the oceanfront campsite costs M$100 per person, and kayaks are M$50 per hour. The campsite has plenty of shaded palm-covered areas and there's a night watchman. Bring insect repellent.

Tankah

A few kilometers south of the Hwy 307 turnoff for Punta Solimán is the turnoff for Tankah, which also has a picturesque stretch of beach and accommodations that have the sea for a front yard and mangrove out the back.

Besides the attractions of beach and reef, Tankah offers **Cenote Manatí**, named for the gentle 'sea cows' that used to frequent it.

It's actually a series of seven cenotes connected by a channel that winds through the mangrove a short distance before heading back underground briefly to reach the sea. The snorkeling's great, as is the birding, and both are free.

Sleeping

Casa Cenote HOTEL $$$

(☎984-115-6996; www.casacenote.com; ste incl breakfast from M$1800; P ❄ ≋) Across the road from a gorgeous cenote, the seven beachside *casitas* (small houses) are lovingly done up with Maya touches, and each has a screened sliding glass door leading to its own little terrace with hammock. The restaurant serves fresh seafood. To get here, turn east at the 'Casa Cenote' sign and it's about 2km from the highway.

Tankah Inn HOTEL $$$

(☎984-100-0703, in USA 918-582-3743; www.tankah.com; Tankah 3, Lote 16; d incl breakfast M$1690; P ᯤ) Tankah Inn has five comfortable rooms with tiled floors, all with private terraces, good beds and nice cross-ventilation. A large upstairs kitchen, dining room and common area have splendid views. A slew of activities are offered here, including snorkeling, fishing and kayaking. It's less than 2km east of the highway.

Tulum

☎984 / POP 18,200

Tulum's spectacular coastline – with all its powdered-sugar sands, jade-green water, balmy breezes and bright sun – makes it one of the top beaches in Mexico. Where else can you get all that *and* a dramatically situated Maya ruin? There's also excellent diving, fun cenotes, great snorkeling, and a variety of lodgings and restaurants to fit every budget.

Some may be put off by the fact that the town center, where the really cheap eats and sleeps are found, sits right on the highway, making the main drag feel more like a truck stop than a tropical paradise. But rest assured that if Tulum Pueblo isn't to your liking, you can always head to the coast and find that tranquil beachside bungalow.

Exploring Tulum's surrounding areas pays big rewards: there's the massive Reserva de la Biosfera Sian Ka'an and the ruins of Cobá, both doable day trips.

History

Most archaeologists believe that Tulum was occupied during the late post-Classic period (AD 1200–1521) and that it was an important port town during its heyday. The Maya sailed up and down this coast, maintaining trading routes all the way down into Belize. When Juan de Grijalva sailed past in 1518, he was amazed by the sight of the walled city, its buildings painted a gleaming red, blue and yellow and a ceremonial fire flaming atop its seaside watchtower.

The ramparts that surround three sides of Tulum (the fourth side being the sea) leave little question as to its strategic function as a fortress. Several meters thick and 3m to 5m high, the walls protected the city during a period of considerable strife between Maya city-states. Not all of Tulum was situated within the walls. The vast majority of the city's residents lived outside them; the civic-ceremonial buildings and palaces likely housed Tulum's ruling class.

The city was abandoned about 75 years after the Spanish conquest. It was one of the last of the ancient cities to be abandoned; most others had been given back to nature long before the arrival of the Spanish. But Maya pilgrims continued to visit over the years, and indigenous refugees from the Caste War took shelter here from time to time.

'Tulum' is Maya for 'wall,' though its residents called it Zama (Dawn). The name Tulum was apparently bestowed by explorers during the early 20th century.

Present-day Tulum is growing fast: since 2006 the population has more than doubled and there are no signs of it slowing down.

Sights & Activities

Tulum Ruins ARCHAEOLOGICAL SITE

(admission M$57; ⌚8am-5pm; P) The ruins of Tulum preside over a rugged coastline, a strip of brilliant beach and green-and-turquoise waters that'll leave you floored. It's true the extents and structures are of a modest scale and the late post-Classic design is inferior to those of earlier, more grandiose projects – but wow, those Maya occupants must have felt pretty smug each sunrise.

Tulum is a prime destination for large tour groups. To best enjoy the ruins without feeling like part of the herd, you should visit them either early in the morning or late in the afternoon. Parking costs M$60 for cars and M$120 for vans and pickups. A M$20 train takes you to the ticket booth from the entrance, or you can just hoof the 300m; taxis from town charge M$50 and can drop you off at the old entrance road, about an 800m walk from the ticket booth. There's a less-used southern foot entrance from the beach road. See the boxed text for more information on exploring the ruins.

Sian Kite Watersports KITESURFING
(☎cell 984-116-3774, cell 984-127-1125; Carretera Tulum-Boca Paila, Km 4.5, at Papaya Playa Project; surfing/kitesurfing per hour M$520/900) Offers one-hour introductory kitesurfing lessons (if you can round up other people you'll save some pesos by paying a cheaper group rate). You can also take surfing classes here. Papaya Playa Project is 3km southeast of

EXPLORING TULUM RUINS

Visitors are required to follow a prescribed route around the ruins. From the ticket booth, head north along nearly half the length of Tulum's enormous **wall**, which measures approximately 380m south to north and 170m along its sides. The **tower** at the corner, once thought to be a guard post, is now believed by some to have been a type of shrine. Rounding the corner, you enter the site through a breach in the north wall.

Once inside, head east toward the **Casa del Cenote**, named for the small pool at its southern base, where you can sometimes see the glitter of little silvery fish as they turn sideways in the murky water. A small tomb was found in the casa. Walk south toward the bluff holding the **Templo del Dios del Viento** (Temple of the Wind God) – roped off at the time of research – which provides the best views of El Castillo juxtaposed with the sea below.

Below the Wind God's hangout is a lovely little stretch of **beach** (also roped off at last visit). Next, head west to **Estructura 25**, which has some interesting columns on its raised platform and, above the main doorway (on the south side), a beautiful stucco frieze of the Descending God. Also known as the Diving God, this upside-down, part-human figure appears elsewhere at Tulum, as well as at several other east-coast sites and Cobá. It may be related to the Maya's reverence for bees (and honey), perhaps a stylized representation of a bee sipping nectar from a flower.

South of Estructura 25 is **El Palacio**, notable for its X-figure ornamentation. From here, head east back toward the water and skirt the outside edge of the central temple complex (keeping it to your right). Along the back are some good views of the sea. Heading inland again on the south side, you can enter the complex through a corbeled archway past the restored **Templo de la Estela** (Temple of the Stela), also known as the Temple of the Initial Series. Stela 1, now in the British Museum, was found here. It was inscribed with the Maya date corresponding to AD 564 (the 'initial series' of Maya hieroglyphs in an inscription gives its date). At first this confused archaeologists, who believed Tulum had been settled several hundred years later than this date. It's now thought that Stela 1 was brought to Tulum from Tankah, a settlement 4km to the north dating from the Classic period.

At the heart of the complex you can admire Tulum's tallest building, a watchtower appropriately named **El Castillo** (The Castle) by the Spaniards. Note the Descending God in the middle of its facade, and the Toltec-style Kukulcánes (plumed serpents) at the corners, echoing those at Chichén Itzá. To the Castillo's north is the small, lopsided **Templo del Dios Descendente**, named for the relief figure above the door. South of the Castillo you'll find steps leading down to a (usually very crowded) beach, where you can go for a swim.

After some beach time, heading west toward the exit will take you to the two-story **Templo de las Pinturas**, constructed in several stages around AD 1400 to 1450. Its decoration was among the most elaborate at Tulum and included relief masks and colored murals on an inner wall. The murals have been partially restored, but are nearly impossible to make out. This monument might have been the last built by the Maya before the Spanish conquest and, with its columns, carvings and two-story construction, it's probably the most interesting structure at the site.

the Av Tulum-Cobá intersection and about 500m south of the coast road T-junction.

I Bike Tulum BICYCLE RENTAL
(Av Cobá; per day incl gear M$100; ⌚9am-6pm) Rents mountain bikes and beach cruisers.

Diving & Snorkeling

You'll find many shops offering their services for reef dives, as well as cavern and cave dives (a big draw in Tulum's surrounding areas). Keep in mind that cave diving can be very dangerous and should not be attempted without proper certification. Even with certification it's a good idea to dive with professionals who are well familiar with the cave systems.

The spectacular **Cenote Angelita** is most notable to divers for the unique, curious, even eerie layer of hydrogen sulfide that 'fogs' the water about halfway through the descent. Look up and see the sunlight filtering down through ancient submerged tree branches that are wonderfully creepy – like outstretched witches' arms. The dive is deep and should only be done by experienced divers; it's best to make arrangements through a dive center.

Snorkeling or swimming from the beach is possible and fun, but be extra careful of boat traffic (a dive flag is a good idea), as the strip between the beach and reef offshore is traveled by dive and fishing boats. If there's a heavy wind onshore, strong currents can develop on the lee side of the reef. Inexperienced swimmers should stay close to shore.

Xibalba Dive Center DIVING
(☎871-2953; www.xibalbadivecenter.com; Andromeda 7; 1-/2-tank cenote dive M$940/1500, snorkeling M$390-585) Considered one of the best dive shops in Tulum, Xibalba is known for its safety-first approach to diving. The center specializes in cave and cavern diving, but you can also arrange snorkeling trips here. Xibalba doubles as a hotel and offers attractive packages combining lodging, diving and/or technical training if so desired.

Tours

Community Tours Sian Ka'an ECOTOUR
(☎871-2202; www.siankaantours.org; cnr Osiris & Sol; ⌚office 7am-8pm) Community Tours Sian Ka'an runs tours to the magnificent Reserva de la Biosfera Sian Ka'an, stopping at various ancient Maya sites, including the Muyil archaeological site south of Tulum. Community

Tulum Ruins

Tours is a sustainable tourism project run by locals from Maya communities.

Sleeping

The biggest decision, aside from budget, is whether to stay in the town center or out along the beach. Both have their advantages: most of the daytime action is at the beach or the ruins, while at night people tend to hit the restaurants and bars in town.

Tulum Pueblo

Unless you're up for a long walk, you'll have to take a taxi, bike or hitchhike to the beach. If you crave sand and surf, consider staying along the Zona Hotelera.

Weary Traveler HOSTEL $
(☎871-2390; www.wearytravelerhostel.com; Av Tulum; dm/r incl breakfast from M$150/375; ❄@📶) A great place to meet friends, the Weary Traveler is known for a full breakfast and a great central courtyard with hammocks and picnic benches. It even has its own bar. The hostel also has a shuttle to the beach for M$15. Don't worry about the odd electronic check-in...normally somebody is around to help you get situated.

Tulum

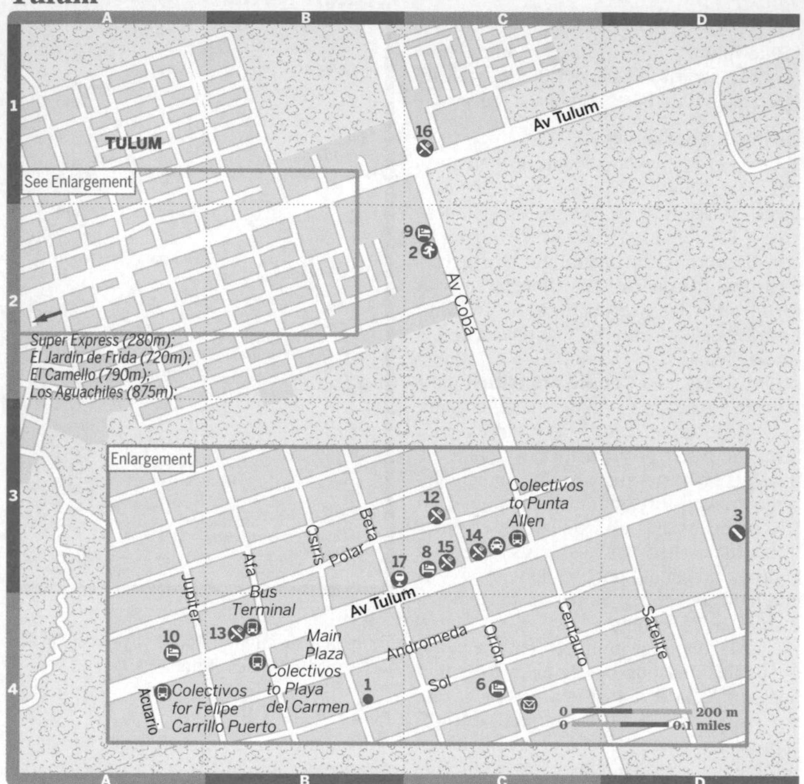

Rancho Tranquilo HOTEL **$**
(☎871-2784; www.ranchotranquilotulum.com; Av Tulum; dm M$150, r incl breakfast with/without bathroom M$600/400, with air-con from M$600; ❄@📶) A nice option for those looking for hostel-type lodging, Rancho Tranquilo offers a mix of *cabañas,* dorms and rooms in a low-key, lushly landscaped garden. It's quite far south on Av Tulum, but there have been a lot of new restaurants cropping up in the area as Tulum just keeps growing and growing.

★**L'Hotelito** HOTEL **$$**
(☎136-1240; www.hotelitotulum.com; Av Tulum; d incl breakfast M$750-840; ❄@📶) Wooden boardwalks pass through a jungle-like side patio to generous, breezy rooms at this character-packed, Italian-run hotel. The attached restaurant does good breakfasts, too.

Kin-Ha Suites HOTEL **$$**
(☎871-2321; www.hotelkinha.com; Orión; d with fan/air-con M$650/750; ❄) While it's a bit overpriced, this Italian-owned joint has pleasant rooms surrounding a small courtyard garden, each with a hammock out front. It's between Sol and Venus.

Teetotum BOUTIQUE HOTEL **$$$**
(☎143-8956; www.teetotumhotel.com; Av Cobá; r incl breakfast M$1885; ❄📶🏊) There's just four minimalist-style rooms in this retro-hip boutique hotel. There are iPod docks, an upstairs lounge and a plunge pool, and the restaurant is excellent. It's a bit overpriced for not being on the beach, but a fun place to stay all the same. It's 200m south of Av Tulum.

Zona Hotelera

Quality and price are so varied here that it's best to look before you decide. Accommodations range from rustic *cabañas* with sand floors to pricey bungalows with pricier restaurants. Some places have no electricity,

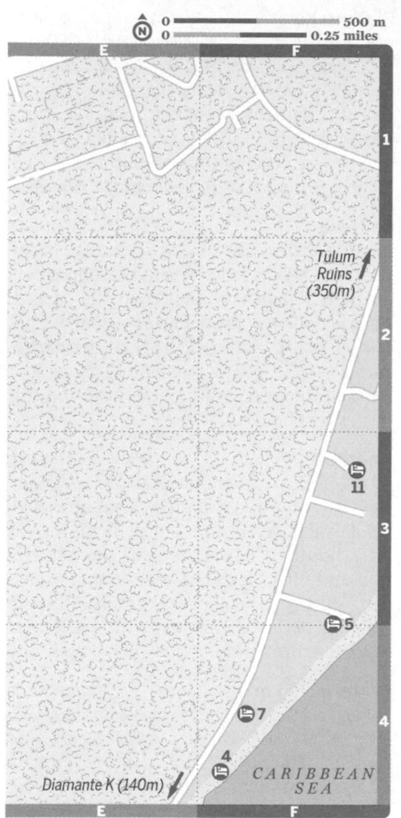

Tulum

Activities, Courses & Tours

1 Community Tours Sian Ka'an B4
2 I Bike Tulum C2
3 Xibalba Dive Center D3

Sleeping

4 Cabañas Playa Condesa F4
5 El Paraíso F3
6 Kin-Ha Suites C4
7 La Vita è Bella F4
8 L'Hotelito C3
9 Teetotum C2
10 Weary Traveler A4
11 Zazil-kin F3

Eating

12 Cetli C3
13 Charlie's B4
14 El Mariachi Loco C3
15 La Nave C3
16 Súper San Francisco de Asis C1

Drinking & Nightlife

17 Curandero B3

or shut their generators off at 9pm or 10pm; some have no phone.

Bedbugs, sand fleas and mosquitoes are all a possibility. Bring repellent or consider burning a noxious mosquito coil near your door. Nights can be cold if there's a breeze blowing.

Places are found along the coastal road, either north or south of the T-junction.

Cabañas Playa Condesa CABINS **$**

(Carretera Tulum-Boca Paila, Km 3; r with/without bathroom M$500/400) About 1km north of the T-junction, this group of thatched *cabañas* is a great budget deal. Along with the basic rooms – which are actually rather clean – you also get mozzie nets (believe us, you'll need them). The coast is rocky here, but there's a sandy beach just 100m away.

Cabañas Xbalamque CABINS **$**

(☎146-6021; xbalamquetulum@hotmail.com; Carretera Tulum-Boca Paila, Km 10; dm M$150, campsite with tent M$150, cabin with shared bathroom M$500;) The cheapest budget buy in the Zona Hotelera, with dorms, private cabins and a campsite. You get a shared kitchen, a large cenote onsite (watch out for the crocs!), plus free use of kayaks, snorkel gear and bikes. All in all, not a bad little spot, and the beach is just 50m away. It's about 6km south of the T-junction.

Diamante K CABINS **$$**

(☎876-2115; www.diamantek.com; Carretera Tulum-Boca Paila, Km 2.5; cabin with/without bathroom M$1200/600;) A great midrange option on the beach, with cabins ranging from budget-rustic to rustic-chic. Those with bathrooms vary hugely in size and design – check out a few if you can.

Zazil-kin CABINS **$$**

(☎124-0082; www.hotelstulum.com/zazilkin; Carretera Tulum-Boca Paila, Km 1; cabañas with/without bathroom M$975/650, r from M$1716;) About a 10-minute walk from the ruins, this popular place resembles a little Smurf village with its dozens of tidy and nicely painted *cabañas*. Zazil-kin also has more expensive air-conditioned, double occupancy rooms, as well as large rooms and rustic *cabañas* that sleep four to five people.

El Paraíso HOTEL $$$

(☎113-7089, in USA 310-295-9491; www.elparaisotulum.com; Carretera Tulum-Boca Paila, Km 1.5; r M$2015; ❄📶) Has 10 rooms in a one-story hotel-style block, each with two good beds, private hot-water bathroom, fine cross-ventilation and 24-hour electricity. The restaurant is very presentable, with decent prices, and the level beach, with its palm trees, *palapa* parasols, swing-chaired bar and soft white sand, is among the nicest you'll find on the Riviera Maya.

La Vita è Bella BUNGALOW $$$

(☎151-4723, in USA 305-831-4970; www.lavitaebella-tulum.com; Carretera Tulum-Boca Paila, Km 1.5; bungalows from M$1300; 📶) A few hundred meters south of El Paraíso, La Vita è Bella offers lovely bungalows with tiled floors, big comfy beds, well-screened sliding doors, good bathrooms with colorful basins and wide verandas with hammocks. All overlook a narrow but nice beach with umbrellas and chairs. It's Italian-run, so the restaurant serves delicious handmade pastas and thin-crust pizza.

Posada Margherita HOTEL $$$

(☎801-8493; www.posadamargherita.com; Carretera Tulum-Boca Paila, Km 7; d from M$1800; 📶) Unlike many so-called 'ecotels,' everything here is totally solar- or wind-powered – even the kitchen, which makes amazing food using mainly organic ingredients. All rooms have tiled floors, good bug screening, 24-hour lights and a terrace or balcony with hammock. The beach here is wide and lovely and the hotel also has something virtually unheard of on the Yucatán Peninsula: wheelchair access. It's 3km south of the T-junction.

Eating

Tulum Pueblo

To escape the tourist traffic, consider putting the guidebook down for a second, leaving the main drag and finding a nice, quiet, friendly *taquería* (taco place) on a side street.

Los Aguachiles SEAFOOD $$

(☎802-5482; cnr Av Tulum & Palenque; tostadas M$33, mains M$89-159; ⏱noon-7pm Tue-Sun; P) If you skipped this place while in Playa del Carmen, here's another chance. Fish tacos and tuna *tostadas* go down oh-so-nicely with a *michelada* (beer, lime juice and clamato juice) in this airy cantina-style restaurant at the south end of town.

El Camello SEAFOOD $$

(cnr Avs Tulum & Kukulcán; mains M$90-150; ⏱10:30am-9pm Mon, Tue & Thu-Sat, 10:30am-6pm Sun) Founded by a local fishermen's cooperative, this immensely popular roadside eatery guarantees fresh fish and seafood. Locals don't even need to look at the menu – it's all about the fish or mixed seafood *ceviches*.

La Nave ITALIAN $$

(☎871-2592; Av Tulum; mains M$95-170; ⏱7am-11pm Mon-Sat) Perched over Av Tulum, this open-air Italian joint is perpetually packed. There's delicious pasta dishes – who doesn't love a bit of authentic spaghetti *amatriciana*? – plus crispy stone-fired pizzas and an assortment of continental meat and fish dishes on offer.

Charlie's MEXICAN $$

(☎871-2573; Av Tulum mains M$85-160; ⏱7:30am-11pm Tue-Sun) An old standby with attractive conch-shell decor and a wall made of old glass bottles, Charlie's is near the bus station and offers a choice of indoor or courtyard dining. The food is largely Mexican (such as *mole enchiladas*) with a selection of salads thrown in.

El Mariachi Loco MEXICAN $$

(Av Tulum, btwn Orión and Centauro; mains M$90-150; ⏱7am-3am) Popular with locals and tourists alike, this spot delivers yummy slow-cooked pork *enchiladas*, fresh grilled fish and about every cut of meat you could imagine.

★Cetli MEXICAN $$$

(☎108-0861; Polar; mains M$190-250; ⏱5-10pm Thu-Tue) Mexico City–born chef Claudia Perez Rivas performs wonders in this homey restaurant on a quiet Tulum backstreet. Her gourmet creations (try the exquisite *moles*) are inspired by traditional dishes and prepared with a fine-tuned eye for detail.

Zona Hotelera

Many hotel restaurants also welcome nonguests.

Hartwood FUSION $$$

(www.hartwoodtulum.com; Carretera Tulum-Boca Paila, Km 7.6; mains M$220-260; ⏱6-10pm Wed-Sun) Take a break from all that Italian at this sweet 'n' simple nouveau cuisine eatery down on the beach road. Ingredients are fresh and local, flavors and techniques are international. The menu is small and changes daily, and the open kitchen and simple decor serve to accentuate the delicious dishes. It's 3.5km south of the T-junction.

Posada Margherita ITALIAN **$$$**
(☎801-8493; Carretera Tulum-Boca Paila, Km 7; mains M$80-250) This hotel's restaurant is candlelit at night, making it a beautiful, romantic place to dine. The fantastic food, including pasta, is made fresh daily and consists mostly of organic ingredients. The wines and *mezcals* (alcoholic agave drinks) here are excellent. It's 3km south of the T-junction.

Self-Catering

You'll find a large supermarket at the intersection of Avenidas Tulum and Cobá and a smaller grocery store at the south end of town.

Súper San Francisco de Asis SUPERMARKET
(cnr Av Tulum & Av Cobá; ⊙7am-10pm) This large supermarket is just east of the town center.

Súper Express SUPERMARKET
(cnr Av Tulum 81 & Luna; ⊙7am-10pm) Another option for self-caterers just west of the center.

Drinking & Nightlife

Curandero BAR
(www.facebook.com/curandero.tulum; cnr Av Tulum & Beta; ⊙7am-3pm Mon-Sat) This cool space fashioned almost entirely from recycled objects has bands playing four nights a week, as well as DJ sets and the occassional film screening. At last visit, electronica and afro-funk sounds were in the air.

Papaya Playa Project BAR
(www.facebook.com/papayaplayaproject; Carretera Tulum-Boca Paila, Km 4.5) Design hotel Papaya Playa Project regularly hosts festive parties and music events at its beachside venue Tribal Room. Those in the know say it's the place to be. It's 500m south of the T-junction.

Shopping

Av Tulum is lined with shops offering many items (hammocks, blankets, handicrafts) that you'll see everywhere. Prices drop drastically the farther you go from the bus station – up to 50%.

Orientation

Tulum lies some 135km south of Cancún and is spread out over quite a large area. Approaching from the north on Hwy 307, the first thing you reach is Crucero Ruinas, where the old access road (closed to vehicle traffic about 100m in from the highway) heads in a straight line about 800m to the ruins' ticket booth. About 400m further south on Hwy 307 (past the gas station) is the new entrance for vehicles going to the ruins; it leads to a parking lot. Another 1.5km south on the highway brings you to the Cobá junction; turning right (west) takes you to Cobá, and turning east leads about 3km to the north–south road (or T-junction) servicing the Zona Hotelera, the string of waterfront lodgings extending for more than 10km south from the ruins. This road eventually enters the Reserva de la Biosfera Sian Ka'an, continuing some 50km past Boca Paila to Punta Allen.

The town center, sometimes referred to as Tulum Pueblo, straddles the highway (called Av Tulum through town) south of the Cobá junction.

Information

Tulum has Telmex pay phones, numerous currency-exchange booths and a **HSBC bank** (Av Tulum; ⊙8am-5pm Mon-Sat;) offering good exchange rates and an ATM. There's also an ATM in the bus station.

There are numerous internet cafes (M$10 per hour) on Av Tulum.

Emergency (☎066)

DANGERS & ANNOYANCES

Tulum is generally safe and locals welcome tourists. However, if you nod off on the beach, your valuables (and even nonvaluables) may disappear. And bring your own lock if you plan on staying in the cheap, no-frills beachfront *cabañas*.

Getting There & Away

The bus terminal (just a waiting room, really) is toward the southern end of town.

If you're headed for Valladolid, be sure your bus is traveling the short route through Chemax, not via Cancún. *Colectivos* leave from Avenida Tulum for Playa del Carmen (M$35, 45 minutes) and Punta Allen (2pm; M$240, four hours). Colectivos for Felipe Carrillo Puerto (M$50, one hour) leave from just south of the Weary Traveler hostel. For buses from Tulum see p120.

Getting Around

Except for the shuttles operated from the youth hostels, there are no *colectivos* out to the beach. You either hitch, grab a taxi, rent a bike or scooter, or walk. And it's a long walk.

Bicycles can be a good way to get around. Many hotels have them free for guests. I Bike Tulum (p115) has a good selection of mountain bike rentals and **Krasivo** (☎807-0524; cnr Av Cobá & Sol Oriente; scooter per day M$400; ⊙9am-6pm) rents scooters.

Taxi fares are fixed; from either of the two taxi stands in Tulum Pueblo (one south of the bus terminal, which has fares posted; the other, four blocks north on the opposite side of the street) to the ruins is M$50. Fares from town to the Zona Hotelera are M$80 to M$130.

Around Tulum

There's much to be explored around Tulum. Head inland to visit cenotes, the ruins at Cobá and the grass-roots tourism project at Punta Laguna. Or cruise down the coast to Punta Allen and the wild Reserva de la Biosfera Sian Ka'an.

Gran Cenote

A little over 3km from Tulum on the road to Cobá is Gran (Grand) Cenote, a worthwhile stop on your way between Tulum and the Cobá ruins, especially if it's a hot day. You can snorkel (M$100) among small fish and see underwater formations in the caverns here if you bring your own gear. A cab from downtown Tulum costs around M$60 one-way, or it's an easy bike ride. About 2km west of Gran Cenote are the smaller cenotes **Zacil-Ha** (M$50) and **Aktún-Ha** (M$50).

Cobá

984 / POP 1300

Though not as large as some of the more famous ruins, Cobá is 'cool' because you feel like you're in an Indiana Jones flick. It's set deep in the jungle and many of the ruins are yet to be excavated. Walk along ancient *sacbes* (stone-paved avenues), climb vine-covered mounds, and ascend to the top of Nohoch Mul for a spectacular view of the surrounding jungle.

From a sustainable-tourism perspective, it's great to stay the night in small communities such as Cobá, but truthfully it has pretty slim pickings in the way of hotel offerings. Other ways to help are by hiring local guides, buying local crafts and simply stopping here for lunch.

History

Cobá was settled earlier than Chichén Itzá or Tulum, and construction reached its peak between AD 800 and 1100. Archaeologists believe that this city once covered 50 sq km and held 40,000 Maya.

Cobá's architecture is a mystery: its towering pyramids and stelae resemble the architecture of Tikal, which is several hundred kilometers away, rather than the much nearer sites of Chichén Itzá and the northern Yucatán Peninsula.

Archaeologists say they now know that between AD 200 and 600, when Cobá had control over a vast territory of the peninsula, alliances with Tikal were made through military and marriage arrangements in order to facilitate trade between the Guatemalan and Yucatecan Maya. Stelae appear to depict female rulers from Tikal holding ceremonial bars and flaunting their power by standing on captives. These Tikal royal females, when married to Cobá's royalty, may have brought architects and artisans with them.

Archaeologists are still baffled by the extensive network of *sacbes* in this region, with Cobá as the hub. The longest runs nearly 100km from the base of Cobá's great Nohoch Mul pyramid to the Maya settlement of Yaxuna. In all, some 40 *sacbes* passed through Cobá, parts of the huge astronomical 'time machine' that was evident in every Maya city.

BUSES FROM TULUM

DESTINATION	COST (M$)	DURATION (HR)	FREQUENCY
Cancún	98	2	frequent
Chetumal	142-194	3½-4	14 daily
Chichén Itzá	92-148	3½	5 daily
Cobá	44	45min	2 daily
Felipe Carrillo Puerto	54	1½	frequent, consider taking a *colectivo*
Mérida	228	4 (2nd-class buses take much longer)	7 daily
Playa del Carmen	62	1	frequent
Valladolid	84	2	7 daily

The first excavation was led by Austrian archaeologist Teobert Maler in 1891. There was little subsequent investigation until 1926, when the Carnegie Institute financed the first of two expeditions led by Sir J Eric S Thompson and Harry Pollock. After their 1930 expedition, not much happened until 1973, when the Mexican government began to finance excavation. Archaeologists now estimate that Cobá contains some 6500 structures, of which just a few have been excavated and restored, though work is ongoing.

Sights

Cobá Ruins ARCHAEOLOGICAL SITE

(www.inah.gob.mx; admission M$57, guides M$500-750; 8am-5pm; P) The archaeological site entrance, at the end of the road on the southeast corner of Laguna Cobá, has a parking lot that charges M$40 per car. Be prepared to walk several kilometers on paths, depending on how much you want to see. If you arrive after 11am you'll feel a bit like a sheep in a flock.

Bring insect repellent and water (although the shop next to the ticket booth sells both at reasonable prices). There is a drink stand within the site near the Nohoch Mul pyramid.

A short distance inside, at the Grupo Cobá, there is a concession renting bicycles at M$35 per day. These can only be ridden within the site, and are useful if you really want to get around the further reaches; they're also a great way to catch a breeze and cool off. If the site is crowded, however, it's probably best to walk. Pedicabs (two people and driver cost M$170 for two hours) are another popular option for those who are tired or have limited mobility.

➡ Grupo Cobá

Walk just under 100m along the main path from the entrance and turn right to get to **La Iglesia** (The Church), the most prominent structure in the Grupo Cobá. It's an enormous pyramid; if you were allowed to climb it, you could see the surrounding lakes (which look lovely from above on a clear day) and the Nohoch Mul pyramid.

Take the time to explore Grupo Cobá; it has a couple of corbeled-vault passages you can walk through. Near its northern edge, on the way back to the main path and the bicycle concession, is a very well-restored *juego de pelota* (ball court).

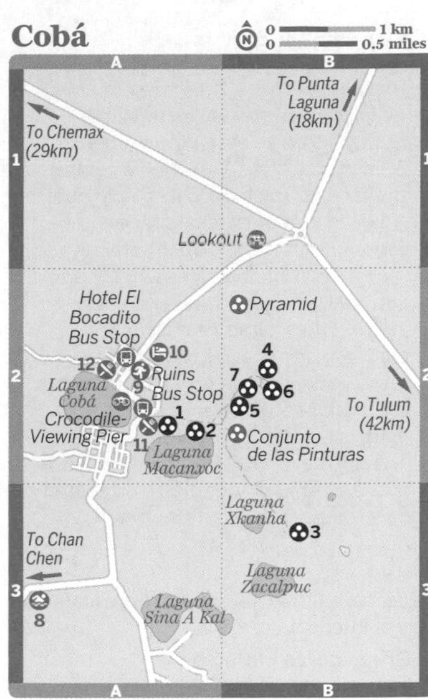

Cobá

Sights

1	Grupo Cobá	A2
2	Grupo de las Pinturas	A2
3	Grupo Macanxoc	B3
4	Grupo Nohoch Mul	B2
5	Juego de Pelota	B2
6	Templo 10	B2
7	Xaibé	B2

Activities, Courses & Tours

8	Cenotes Choo-Ha, Tamcach-Ha & Multún-Ha	A3
9	Cob-Ja	A2

Sleeping

	Hotel El Bocadito	(see 9)
10	Hotel Sac-bé	A2

Eating

11	Restaurant Ki-Jamal	A2
12	Restaurant La Pirámide	A2

➡ Grupo Macanxoc

About 200m beyond the *juego de pelota*, the path forks. Going straight gets you to the Grupo Macanxoc, a group of recently restored stelae that bore reliefs of royal women who are thought to have come from

TINY TRAILBLAZERS

The small trails you'll see crisscrossing the cleared areas in many of the Cobá ruins baffle observant visitors. What made them? A rodent? To get the answer right you have to think tiny: ants.

Leaf-cutter ants, to be specific. Sometimes marching up to several kilometers from their colony, leaf-cutter ants walk in single file along predetermined routes, often wearing down a pathway over a period of months or years. Patient observers can often see the tiny landscapers at work, carrying fingernail-sized clippings back home. Though they can bite if disturbed, these ants are generally harmless and should be left in peace to do their work.

Tikal. It's a 1km walk, but the flora along the way is interesting.

➡ **Grupo de las Pinturas**

Heading back in the same direction you came from, you can reach the Grupo de las Pinturas (Paintings Group) by walking about 1km, then turning right. If you're on a bike, you'll have to park it here and return to it (this is the case at a few other spots as well). The temple here bears traces of glyphs and frescoes above its door and remnants of richly colored plaster inside.

You approach the temple from the southeast. Leave by the trail at the northwest (opposite the temple steps) to see two stelae. The first of these is 20m along, beneath a *palapa*. Here, a regal figure stands over two others, one of them kneeling with his hands bound behind him. Sacrificial captives lie beneath the feet of a ruler at the base. You'll need to use your imagination, as this and most of the other stelae here are quite worn. Continue along the path past another badly weathered stela and a small temple to rejoin the Nohoch Mul path and turn right (or, if you rented a bike, turn around or go left to retrieve it).

➡ **Grupo Nohoch Mul**

Continuing northeast you will reach another **juego de pelota** on the right side of the path. Look at the ground in the center of the court to spot a carved stone skull (the winner or the loser of the ball game?) and the carved relief of a jaguar.

More weathered stelae lie at the north end. After the ball court, the track bends between piles of stones – a ruined temple – and you reach a junction of sorts. Turn right (east) and head to the structure called **Xaibé**. This is a tidy, semicircular stepped building, almost fully restored. Its name means 'the crossroads,' as it marks the juncture of four separate *sacbes*.

Going north from here takes you past **Templo 10** and **Stela 20**. The exquisitely carved stela – worn, but not nearly so badly as the others – bears the date AD 730 and a familiar theme: a ruler standing imperiously over two captives. In front of it is a modern line drawing depicting the original details.

By this time you will have noticed **Nohoch Mul** (Big Mound) just to the north. Also known as the Great Pyramid, which sounds a lot better than Big Mound, Nohoch Mul reaches a height of 42m, making it the second-tallest Maya structure on the Yucatán Peninsula. Calakmul's Estructura II, at 45m, is the tallest. Climbing the old steps can be scary for some.

Two diving gods are carved over the doorway of the temple at the top (built in the post-Classic period, AD 1100–1450), similar to the sculptures at Tulum. The view from up top is over many square kilometers of flat scrubby forest, with peeks of lake, and Xaibé as the sole visible Maya structure. Still, it's inspiring.

After descending, walk past Templo 10 and turn right to make a loop back to the ruined-temple junction. In all it's a 1.4km, half-hour walk back to the site entrance.

Activities

In the archaeological site's parking lot there's a **zip line** that soars above the lake (don't fall…there are crocs in them there waters). It costs M$130 per zip.

About 6km south of town on the road to Chan Chen you'll find a series of three locally administered cenotes: **Choo-Ha**, **Tamcach-Ha** and **Multún-Ha**. These cavernlike cenotes are nice spots to cool off with a snorkel or swim. It costs M$45/70/100 (one/two/three cenotes).

Cob-Ja BICYCLE RENTAL

(per 4hr M$50) Rent a bike here and go for a spin around the lake or pedal to the series of cenotes south of town if you're up for a longer ride.

Sleeping & Eating

Cobá has limited sleeping options. Most people use Tulum or Valladolid as bases for day trips here. Several small restaurants by the site's parking lot serve inexpensive meals.

Hotel Sac-bé HOTEL $
(☎144-3006; r with fan/air-con M$350/450; ❄) The best digs in town. Clean and friendly, the Sac-bé is on the main strip heading into Cobá. The chickens are a bit noisy in the morning, but it has a restaurant, nice hot showers and so-so beds.

Hotel El Bocadito HOTEL $
(☎807-2071; r with fan/air-con M$200/450; ❄) Just north of Laguna Cobá, at the entrance to town, this place has very basic rooms and is only worth staying in if the other hotel in town is full. El Bocadito also serves as Cobá's bus terminal.

Restaurant Ki-Jamal MEXICAN $$
(mains M$70-160; ⏲8am-5pm; P) Owned by the local Maya community, Ki-Jamal (which means 'tasty food' in Maya) actually does some tasty traditional dishes. Head upstairs for a lake view and possibly a quiet meal – that is if no tour groups drop in. It's right off the ruins' parking lot.

Restaurant La Pirámide MEXICAN $$
(mains M$100-150) At the end of the town's main drag, by the lake, this restaurant does decent *yucateco* fare like *cochinita* and *pollo pibil*. The open-air setup allows for nice views.

Information

You may want to buy a book on Cobá before coming. Onsite signage and maps are minimal and cryptic. Tours in English generally run about M$500 to M$750. The Nohoch Mul pyramid is the only structure the public is allowed to climb.

Be careful not to picnic beside the lake outside the entrance, as it has large crocodiles.

Getting There & Away

Most buses serving Cobá swing down to the ruins to drop off passengers at a small bus station; some only go as far as Hotel El Bocadito, which also serves as a bus station. Buses run six to eight times daily between Tulum and Cobá (M$36 to M$44); six of these also serve Playa del Carmen (M$66 to M$86, one to 1¾ hours). Buses also run to Valladolid (M$40 to M$62, 45 minutes) and Chichén Itzá (M$68 to M$90, 1½ hours).

Day-trippers from Tulum can reach Cobá by forming a group to split the cost of a taxi, which costs about M$700 round-trip, including two hours at the site.

The road from Cobá to Chemax is arrow-straight and in good shape. If you're driving to Valladolid or Chichén Itzá this is the way to go.

Punta Laguna

Punta Laguna is a fair-sized lake with a small Maya community nearby, 20km northeast of Cobá on the road to Nuevo Xcan. The forest around the lake supports populations of spider and howler monkeys, as well as a variety of birds, and contains small, unexcavated ruins and a cenote. A surprising jaguar population was recently discovered, though chances of seeing one are very slim. Toucans sometimes flit across the road.

A **tourist cooperative** (Najil Tucha; ☎985-107-9182; www.puntalaguna.com.mx; ⏲6am-5pm) charges M$60 for entrance to the lake area, and about M$250 per hour for a guided visit, which is your best chance of spotting monkeys. Arrive at dusk or dawn to further increase your chances. The local community is increasing its tourist offerings in an effort to keep the town's youth from fleeing to work in the big cities. The new activities include a zip-line tour, a rappel into a nearly pitch-black cenote and a shamanic ceremony for M$300 at a 'traditional' altar that's been erected fortuitously right on the trail to the lake. While these are fun, the best activity is renting a canoe (M$100 per hour) to explore the lake, an eerily beautiful sight when shrouded in morning mist.

Intrepid travelers can call ahead and reserve a *palapa* for the night. Or bring your own tent and camp out near the lake. Camping or a *palapa* costs around M$150 per night. It's best to bring your own hammock and a mosquito net. There's a restaurant near the cenote, but it rarely opens, so consider bringing your own food.

Also consider stopping for a hike on a new nature trail in the town of **Campamento Hidalgo** (5km south of Punta Laguna) or checking out the caverns in **Nuevo Durango** (10km north of here).

Public transportation is so sparse as to be nonexistent. In a car, you can reach Punta Laguna by turning south off Hwy 180 at Nuevo Xcan and driving 26km, or by heading 18km north from the Cobá junction.

Tulum to Punta Allen

Punta Allen sits at the end of a narrow spit of land that stretches south nearly 40km from its start below Tulum. There are some charming beaches along the way, with plenty of privacy, and most of the spit is within the protected, wildlife-rich Reserva de la Biosfera Sian Ka'an. Hurricane Dean whipped the region pretty good in 2007, but the mangrove forest was not substantially damaged.

The road can be a real muffler-buster between gradings, especially when holes are filled with water from recent rains, making it impossible to gauge their depth. The southern half, south of the bridge at Boca Paila, is the worst stretch – some spots require experienced off-road handling or you'll sink into a meter of sand. It is doable even in a non-4WD vehicle, but bring along a shovel and boards just in case – you can always stuff palm fronds under the wheels to gain traction – and plan on returning that rental with a lot more play in the steering wheel.

There's an **entrance gate** to the reserve about 10km south of Tulum. At the gate, there's a short nature trail taking you to a rather nondescript cenote (Ben Ha). The trail's short, so go ahead and take a second to have a look.

This is where intrepid adventuring really takes off. Bring a couple of hammocks, lots of water, a sixer of *cerveza,* and mosquito nets for remote coastal camping. Around 30km from the entrance gate is an excellent camping spot with the lagoon on one side and glorious blue ocean on the other.

One *colectivo* makes the four-hour trip daily, leaving Tulum center at 2pm and arriving in Punta Allen about 6pm. It returns to Tulum the next day, departing from Punta Allen at 5am. You may also be able to come on a motorboat via the mainland, though it's very expensive and less frequent.

RESERVA DE LA BIOSFERA SIAN KA'AN

More than 5000 sq km of tropical jungle, marsh, mangroves and islands on Quintana Roo's coast have been set aside by the Mexican government as a large biosphere reserve. In 1987 the UN classified it as a World Heritage Site – an irreplaceable natural treasure.

Sian Ka'an (Where the Sky Begins) is home to howler monkeys, anteaters, foxes, ocelots, pumas, crocodiles, eagles, raccoons, tapirs, peccaries, giant land crabs, jaguars and hundreds of bird species, including *chocolateras* (roseate spoonbills) and some flamingos.

Entering the reserve by land on the road to Punta Allen, you pass **Boca Paila Camps** (Cesiak; ☎984-871-2499; www.cesiak.org; Carretera Tulum-Boca Paila; r from M$1470; P). Stay the night in the hotel's pimped-out wall tents – it's like camping at the Hyatt. The ecological center also takes online reservations for guided tours, such as kayaking (M$650), birding (M$1000) and fly-fishing (M$5000).

About 1km south of here is the **Centro de Visitantes Reserva de la Biosfera Sian Ka'an**, where you'll find a watchtower that provides tremendous bird's-eye views of the lagoon.

There are no hiking trails through the reserve; it's best explored with a professional guide.

Community Tours Sian Ka'an (p115) runs tours out of Tulum that include pick-up in the Zona Hotelera. Tours include a guided walk of the interpretive trail at the Muyil archaeological site south of Tulum, and a boat trip or float trip (M$1287) through Lagunas Muyil, Chunyaxché and Boca Paila via an ancient Maya trade route along a natural channel. On the way you can see abundant birdlife and visit little-known Maya temples. It also offers snorkeling (M$975), birding, and fly-fishing trips (M$7150) further into the reserve. If you're with young ones, ask about discounts for children under 12.

Community Tours Sian Ka'an is a sustainable tourism project run by locals from Maya communities.

Punta Allen

☎984

The town of Javier Rojo Gómez is more commonly called by the name of the point 2km south, Punta Allen. Hurricane Gilbert nearly destroyed the town in 1988, and there was some damage and a lot of wind-scrubbed palms, after Hurricane Dean. But Punta Allen is still walking tall. This is truly the end of the road; the 400-odd residents mostly work as fishers, although some residents work in restaurants popular with day-trippers. The village exudes a laid-back ambience reminiscent of the Belizean cays. There's also a healthy reef 400m from shore that offers snorkelers and divers wonderful sights.

The area is known primarily for its catch-and-release bonefishing; tarpon and snook are very popular sportfish as well. Guides in Sian Ka'an, as well as cooperatives in town (enquire at Galletanes or Vigía Grande eateries), do fishing trips for about M$3500 for a full day.

An hour's tour of the lagoon costs about M$700 to M$800 per boat. You'll be offered trips by one of the three co-ops. Encourage your captain not to get so close to birdlife that he scares it away. Though very rare, manatee spottings are possible.

There are no ATMs or internet cafes in town. Electricity generally works between 10am and 2pm, and 7pm and midnight.

Sleeping & Eating

Vigía Grande and Galletanes are among several of the town's dining choices, both close to the water and both owned by co-ops. They serve Mexican dishes and seafood, naturally including lobster. Neither has a phone and opening hours vary based on whether any customers are there.

Hotel Costa del Sol BUNGALOW **$$**
(☎113-2639; reservaciones@bungaloscostadelsol.com; campsites M$200, r M$1100) At the entrance to town, this beachfront spot has quaint fan-cooled bungalows and a laid-back feel. The restaurant is pretty decent, and it has karaoke on weekend nights. Significant low-season discounts available.

Cuzán BUNGALOW **$$**
(☎139-4349; www.flyfishmx.com; r M$1000) Just south of the town's center along the main road, Cuzán has oceanfront *cabañas* – one set on the remains of an old boat. It also offers fishing and snorkeling trips.

Casa Sirena BUNGALOW **$$**
(www.casasirena.com; d M$500-975) Offers fully furnished *cabañas* with kitchens and hot-water showers. The rooms are simple and very big; some sport sitting areas and hammocks. You'll need to request maid service.

Grand Slam Flyfishing Lodge HOTEL **$$$**
(☎139-2930, 998-800-1047; www.grandslam-flyfishinglodge.com; r M$4550; P❄📶≋) If you've got money to burn this place is for you. The upscale lodge boasts 12 oceanfront rooms with Jacuzzis, iPod docks, large balconies and around-the-clock electricity (a true luxury in Punta Allen). Fly-fishing enthusiasts can request bundled lodging and fishing packages.

Kai INTERNATIONAL **$$$**
(breakfast M$195-260, lunch & dinner M$325-585; ⏰6am-10pm) The chic *palapa* restaurant at the Grand Slam Flyfishing Lodge, at the town's entrance, prepares hearty breakfasts fit for early-rising fisherfolk; lunch and dinner menus change regularly, but they usually feature gourmet fish, seafood and steak dishes.

Getting There & Away

The best way to reach Punta Allen by public transportation is by *colectivo* out of Tulum: one leaves daily from Tulum center at 2pm and arrives about four hours later (M$240 one way). Driving in a rental car is another option, but prepare for 5km/h to 10km/h speeds and more than a few transmission-grinding bumps.

Costa Maya & Southern Caribbean Coast

Includes ➡

Off the Beaten Track

- ➡ Xcalak (p131)
- ➡ Corozal (p138)
- ➡ Dzibanché (p136)
- ➡ Kohunlich (p138)
- ➡ Kinich-Ná (p138)

Best Places to Eat

- ➡ Leaky Palapa (p131)
- ➡ Los Aluxes (p133)
- ➡ Fernando's 100% Agave (p130)
- ➡ Tacos de Cochinita Chepe's (p133)
- ➡ Sulumar (p130)

Why Go?

The Southern Caribbean Coast, or the Costa Maya if you will, is the latest region to get hit by the development boom. But if you're looking for a quiet escape on the Mexican Caribbean, it's still the best place to be.

For those looking to get away from it all, Laguna Bacalar, aka the 'lake of seven colors,' provides mesmerizing scenery thanks to the water's intense shades of blue and aqua-green. East of Bacalar, the tranquil fishing towns of Mahahual and Xcalak offer great beach-bumming, birding and diving opportunities along a relatively pristine stretch of coast.

In the interior, the seldom-visited ruins of Dzibanché and Kohunlich seem all the more mysterious without the tour vans. For both the ruins and trips down south to Belize, Quintana Roo's state capital Chetumal is a great jumping-off point.

When to Go

➡ Don't miss the Caribbean-flavored Carnaval (p134) street festival in February in the Quintana Roo state capital, Chetumal. It's definitely one of the best fiestas of the year on the southern coast.

➡ Featuring pre-Hispanic music, dance and culinary events, the Jats'a Já (p130) has emerged as one of the region's most interesting annual festivals; it's held on the third weekend of August in the fishing town of Mahahual.

➡ A visit between mid-November and mid-December has several advantages: hurricane season has passed, the weather has cooled considerably and many great hotel deals can be found ahead of the holiday season.

Costa Maya & Southern Caribbean Coast Highlights

1. Dive at **Banco Chinchorro** (p129), the largest coral atoll in the northern hemisphere and a fascinating ship graveyard

2. Take a refreshing dip in the 90m-deep Cenote Azul, then bask on **Laguna Bacalar** (p132), one of the most beautiful lakes that you'll ever set your eyes on

3. Go snorkeling, fishing or birding in **Mahahual** (p129), or simply chill at a boardwalk bar or restaurant in this laid-back coastal town

4. Escape to the remote beach village of **Xcalak** (p131) for quality beach-bumming, diving and fishing

5. Beat your own path to the remote ruins at **Dzibanché** (p136) and **Kohunlich** (p138), west of Chetumal.

Felipe Carrillo Puerto

983 / POP 25,700

Now named for a progressive governor of Yucatán, this crossroads town 95km south of Tulum was once known as Chan Santa Cruz, the rebel headquarters during the Caste War. Besides its historical and cultural significance, Carrillo Puerto has few attractions other than the only gas station, bank and hotels for some distance around. There's a main square with a clock tower, church and cultural center; the plaza is center stage in late April and early May when the town celebrates its patron saint, Santa Cruz.

History

In 1849, when the Caste War turned against them, the Maya of the northern Yucatán Peninsula made their way here. They were ready to sally forth again in 1850 when a 'miracle' occurred. A wooden cross erected at a cenote (limestone sinkhole) on the western edge of the town began to 'talk,' telling the Maya they were the chosen people, to continue the struggle against the Spanish and promising victory. The talking was actually done by a ventriloquist who used sound chambers, but the people looked upon it as the authentic voice of their aspirations.

The 'oracle' guided the Maya in battle for more than eight years, until their great victory conquering the fortress at Bacalar. For the latter part of the 19th century, the Maya in and around Chan Santa Cruz were virtually independent of governments in Mexico City and Mérida.

A military campaign by the Mexican government retook the city and the surrounding area at the beginning of the 20th century, and the talking-cross shrine was desecrated. Many of the Maya fled to small villages in the jungle and kept up the fight into the 1930s; some resisted even into the 1950s.

Carrillo Puerto today remains a center of Maya pride. The talking cross, hidden away in the jungle for many years following the Mexican takeover, has been returned to its shrine, and Maya from around the region still come to visit it, especially on May 3, the day of the Holy Cross.

Sights

Centro Cultural Chan Santa Cruz ARTS CENTER
(8am-9:30pm Mon-Fri, 8am-1pm & 6-8pm Sat & Sun) FREE On the plaza, the cultural center has art exhibitions, workshops and the occasional exhibit on the Caste War. Be sure to check out the mural outside, which highlights accomplishments of Maya culture.

Santuario de la Cruz Parlante SHRINE
(4am-8pm) Folks come from all over to pray before this shrine dedicated to the talking cross, a symbol of the Maya people's struggle against inequality and injustice. You'll find the thatch-roof sanctuary next to a dried-up cenote in a small park about five blocks west of the town's gas station. No one may enter wearing hats or shoes.

Sleeping & Eating

Hotel Chan Santa Cruz HOTEL $
(834-0021; www.hotelchansantacruz.com.mx; cnr Calles 67 & 68; d M$360; P ❄ ☎) The rooms are just a bit too pink, giving them the feel of Martha Stewart's jail cell. But they are clean, and there's a mighty fine central courtyard complete with gaudy statuary.

Hotel Esquivel HOTEL $
(834-0313; www.hotelesquivel.blogspot.com; cnr Calles 63 & 68; d with fan/air-con M$500/670, ste M$670; P ❄ ☎) Around the corner from the plaza and bus terminal, the Esquivel has air-con rooms that are a good deal, with very clean bathrooms and tiled floors. The fan rooms have good beds and showers, but are dark, windowless and overperfumed. Across the way, the hotel has two larger suites with kitchenettes and fridges.

Mercado Público MARKET $
(cnr Calles 70 & 71) A decent spot to fuel up and do a bit of people-watching.

Hotel El Faisán y El Venado MEXICAN $$
(834-0702; cnr Av Juárez & Calle 69; mains M$75-135, r M$430; 6am-10pm) Come here for the best eats in town. The house specialty (not listed on the menu) is grilled *venado* (deer) steaks prepared *poc-chuc* style (marinated and grilled). There are other *yucateco* dishes as well. This is also one of the best hotels in town, with clean, comfy rooms.

Information

HSBC (cnr Calles 69 & 70) Has an ATM.

Post Office (Calle 69; 9am-12:30pm Mon-Fri)

Getting There & Away

Most buses serving Carrillo Puerto are *de paso* (they don't originate there). The table shows some of the routes.

Frequent *colectivos* (shared vans) leave for Playa del Carmen (M$75, two hours) and Tulum (M$50, one hour) from Hwy 307 just south of Calle 73.

At Calles 66 and 63 you'll find *colectivos* for Chetumal (M$60, two hours).

Mahahual

983 / POP 900

Some locals weren't exactly crying the blues after Hurricane Dean rolled into town in 2007 and badly damaged the town's new cruise-ship dock. But the dock has been rebuilt and despite ongoing concerns about encroaching development, Mahahual has managed to retain a pretty laid-back Caribbean vibe.

Sure, cruise-ship tourism has brought quite a few tacky shops and gringo-friendly bars to the north side of town, but head south in the direction of Xcalak and you'll have no problem finding your own private beach with sugary white sand.

What's more, there's great diving and snorkeling here, and there's just enough nightlife along the beachfront *malecón* (waterfront promenade) to keep you howling at the moon.

Sights & Activities

Malecón BEACH

The beach right off Mahahual's beautiful *malecón* has great sand, plus water so shallow you can swim out a good 100m.

Banco Chinchorro DIVE SITE

Divers won't want to miss the reefs and underwater fantasy worlds of the Banco Chinchorro, the largest coral atoll in the northern hemisphere. Some 45km long and up to 14km wide, Chinchorro's western edge lies about 30km off the coast, and dozens of ships have fallen victim to its barely submerged ring of coral.

The atoll and its surrounding waters were made a biosphere reserve (Reserva de la Bio-sfera Banco Chinchorro) to protect them from depredation. But the reserve lacks the personnel and equipment needed to patrol such a large area, and many abuses go undetected.

Most dives here go to a maximum of 30m, as there are no decompression chambers for miles. With a ban on wreck dives recently lifted, there are plenty of shipwreck sites worth exploring. Along the way you'll also spot coral walls and canyons, rays, turtles, giant sponges, grouper, eels and, in some spots, reef, tiger and hammerhead sharks.

There's good snorkeling as well, including **40 Cannons**, a wooden ship in 5m to 6m of water. Looters have taken all but about 25 of the cannons, and it can only be visited in ideal conditions.

Local tour operators arrange fishing trips (M$700 per hour for up to four people) and hour-long snorkeling tours (M$250 per person). Look for them beachside along the *malecón.*

Dreamtime Dive Center DIVING

(124-0235, in USA 904-730-4337; www.dreamtimediving.com; Av Mahahual, Km 2.5; 1-tank/2-tank dives M$650/975, snorkeling M$450) South of town, this dive shop runs trips to stretches of the barrier reef and offers PADI open-water certification (M$5460).

Doctor Dive DIVING

(136-9069, 103-6013; www.doctordive.com; Av Mahahual; 2-tank dives M$1000, birding M$500; 8am-9pm) More than just a dive shop, the Doctor does birding, kayaking and snorkeling trips to the remote fishing town of Punta Herrero.

Las Cabañas del Doctor CANOEING

(832-2102; www.lascabanasdeldoctor.com; Av Mahahual, Km 2) You can rent a canoe here for M$100 an hour.

BUSES FROM FELIPE CARRILLO PUERTO

DESTINATION	COST (M$)	DURATION (HR)	FREQUENCY
Cancún	126-202	3½-4	frequent
Chetumal	70-128	2-3	frequent
Mahahual	78	2	2 daily
Mérida	164-206	5-6	3 daily
Playa del Carmen	75-126	2½	frequent
Ticul (for Uxmal)	112	4½	11 daily

Festivals & Events

Jats'a Já Festival FESTIVAL
Held on the third weekend of August, this festival is a prayer offering of sorts to the hurricane gods. Activities include pre-Hispanic dancing, art exhibitions and culinary events.

Sleeping

Addresses here are given with distances from the military checkpoint at the north entrance to town.

Macho's Hostel HOSTEL $
(☎903-106-0840; Av Mahahual, Km 1.5; dm/r M$120/500) Located about 100m south of the *malecón*, this simple beachfront joint has the cheapest rooms in town. They're bare bones, and the vibe here is just a bit odd, but you have beach views and use of the owner's kitchen. The dorm sleeps up to eight people.

★**Posada Pachamama** HOTEL $$
(☎834-5762; www.posadapachamama.net; Calle Huachinango, Km 1; r M$700-1000; P ❄ ☎) Breakfast is brought to your room in this small, recently remodeled hotel. The place has nice Mexican design touches throughout, such as Talavera tilework, and the staff is extremely helpful.

Las Cabañas del Doctor HOTEL $$
(☎102-5676, 832-2102; www.lascabanasdeldoctor.com; Av Mahahual 6, Km 2; cabañas s/d M$400/550, r with/without air-con M$900/550; P ❄) Across the street from the beach and about 200m south of the end of the *malecón*, this spot offers several simple *palapa* (shelter with a thatched, palm-leaf roof) bungalows, as well as more-upscale hotel-style rooms. There's also the option of camping (M$80 per person) right on the beach with use of the hotel's shared bathroom.

Hotel Matan Ka'an HOTEL $$
(☎834-5679; www.matankaan.it; Calle Huachinango; r/ste M$800/1789; P ☎ ☒) On the south side of the soccer field, this large whitewashed hotel has a relaxed resort feel, plenty of common areas and large, clean rooms. We only wish 'the gift from the heavens' – that's what Matan Ka'an means in Maya – included beach access, but hey, the ocean is only 100m away.

Posada de los 40 Cañones HOTEL $$
(☎834-5730; www.40canones.com; Calle Huachinango, Km 1.5; r M$1100-1350, ste M$2300-2400; ❄ ☎) This stylish Italian-owned hotel on the *malecón* is clean and comfortable. Only a few of the rooms have ocean views, but you're right on the boardwalk, so you can always get your fix. The restaurant is definitely worth checking out.

Quinto Sole BOUTIQUE HOTEL $$$
(☎834-5942; www.hotelquintosole.com; Carretera Mahahual-Xcalak, Km 0.35; r M$1440-1800, ste M$3000-3240; P ❄ ☎) One of the fanciest hotels in town, the Quinto Sole has spacious rooms with heavenly beds and private balconies (some with Jacuzzi). It's on a quiet beach north of the boardwalk and 350m south of the lighthouse at town's entrance.

Eating

There are about a dozen restaurants along the *malecón*, each offering the standard assortment of seafood, Mexican favorites and pub grub.

★**Fernando's 100% Agave** MEXICAN $$
(Calle Huachinango; M$70-115; ⏰noon-10pm) Located just north of the soccer field one block inland from the *malecón*, this restaurant-bar offers up *yucateco* fish and seafood dishes and pours tasty margaritas, too.

Sulumar SEAFOOD $$
(Mahahual beach; mains M$100-130; ⏰9am-7pm) Lobster, lionfish, octopus, you name it: this fishermen's cooperative cooks up the fresh catch of the day and serves it to you right on the beach, at the south end of the *malecón*. Locals love Sulumar.

Maya Bar SEAFOOD $$
(mains M$60-130; ⏰9am-10pm) On the northern end of the *malecón*, this friendly family place specializes in *ceviche* (seafood marinated in lemon or lime juice, garlic and seasonings) and seafood cocktails. There's also a swing bar for the swinger in all of us.

Getting There & Around

Mahahual is 127km south of Felipe Carrillo Puerto, and approximately 100km northeast of Bacalar. A new ADO bus terminal, located next to the Hotel Mahahual, a block inland from the *malecón*, has made getting here easier than ever, though buses are infrequent.

Buses depart here for Cancún (M$368, five hours, 8:30am), Chetumal (M$106, 2½ hours, 9am and 6:30pm), Felipe Carrillo Puerto (M$99, two hours, 8:30am), Laguna Bacalar (M$72, two hours, 9am and 6:30pm) and Tulum (M$176, four hours, 8:30am).

There's a Pemex gas station if you need to fill your tank.

Xcalak

☎983 / POP 400

The rickety wooden houses, beached fishing launches and lazy gliding pelicans make this tiny town plopped in the middle of nowhere a perfect escape. And by virtue of its remoteness and the Chinchorro atoll, Xcalak may yet escape the development boom.

If diving isn't your thing, there's still plenty to do. Come here to walk along dusty streets and sip frozen drinks while frigate birds soar above translucent green lagoons. Explore a mangrove swamp by kayak, or just doze in a hammock and soak up some sun. And, though tiny, Xcalak has a few nice restaurants and an easygoing mix of foreigners and local fishers.

The mangrove swamps stretching inland from the coastal road hide some large lagoons and form tunnels that invite kayakers to explore. These swamps and the drier forest teem with wildlife; in addition to the usual herons, egrets and other waterfowl, you can see agoutis, jabirus (storks), iguanas, javelinas (peccaries), parakeets, kingfishers, alligators and more. Unfortunately, the mangrove also breeds mosquitoes and some vicious *jejenes* (sand flies).

Xcalak was an important port during the Caste War, and the town even had a cinema until a series of hurricanes wiped everything away. Today, the town shows no signs of getting a bank, grocery store or gas station anytime soon, so stock up before you come.

Activities

XTC Dive Center DIVING
(www.xtcdivecenter.com; Coast road, Km 0.3; 2-tank dives to Banco Chinchorro M$2580, snorkeling trips M$325) Offers dive and snorkel trips to the wondrous barrier reef just offshore, and to Banco Chinchorro. It also rents diving equipment and offers PADI open-water certification for M$6500 and NAUI instruction, as well as fishing and birding tours. You can get your biosphere reserve wristband to visit Chinchorro here – XTC is 300m north of town – or at the park office in town.

XTC also rents rooms, and very nice and affordable ones at that.

Sleeping

There are bargain-basement cabins at the entrance to town, but they are pretty dirty, so we'd suggest going to one of the following on the old coastal road leading north from town. All have purified drinking water, ceiling fan, hot-water bathroom, 24-hour electricity (from solar or wind with gener-ator backup), and bikes and/or sea kayaks for guest use.

Most places don't accept credit cards without prior arrangement, and are best contacted through their websites or via email. Addresses here are given in kilometers north along the coast from town.

Costa de Cocos RESORT **$$**
(www.costadecocos.com; Coast road, Km 1; r incl breakfast M$900; P 📶) Most guests stay here for the fly-fishing and scuba-diving tours available. It doesn't have a very good beach for swimming, but the *palapa* rooms are a good deal.

Hotel Tierra Maya HOTEL **$$$**
(☎839-8012, in USA 800-216-1902; www.tierramaya.net; Coast road Km 2; r M$1320-1470) A modern beachfront hotel with six lovely rooms (three quite large), each tastefully appointed and with many architectural details. Each of the rooms has mahogany furniture and a balcony facing the sea; the bigger rooms even have small refrigerators.

Casa Carolina HOTEL **$$$**
(www.casacarolina.net; Coast road Km 2.5; r incl continental breakfast M$1480; 📶) A bright, cheery yellow, the Casa has four guest rooms with large, hammock-equipped balconies facing the sea. Each room has a kitchen with fridge, and the bathrooms try to outdo one another with their beautiful Talavera tilework. All levels of scuba instruction (NAUI) are offered here, as are dives at the barrier reef.

Eating & Drinking

Food in Xcalak tends to be tourist-grade seafood or Mexican; the Leaky Palapa is a delectable exception.

Leaky Palapa INTERNATIONAL **$$**
(www.leakypalaparestaurant.com; mains M$80-200; ⏲5-10pm Thu-Sun Nov-May, Fri & Sat only Jun-Oct) Chef Marla and owner Linda have turned an old standby into a new sensation, serving wonderful meals, such as lobster in caramel ginger sauce. Opinion is unanimous that this is the best place to go to treat your taste buds. It's two blocks north past the lighthouse and one block inland. Online reservations required.

Toby's SEAFOOD $$
(mains M$79-149; ⏲11am-8pm) The friendly chitchat and well-prepared fish and seafood dishes here make this a popular expat spot, Try the coconut shrimp and you'll know why. It's on the main drag in town.

Lonchería Silvia's SEAFOOD $$
(mains M$90-100; ⏲9am-10pm) About three blocks south of the plaza and a block in from the coast, Silvia's serves mostly fish fillets and *ceviche* and keeps pretty regular hours. The long menu doesn't mean that everything is available. You'll likely end up having the fish.

Xcalak Caribe BAR
About three blocks north of the plaza along the beach, this is your best bet for nightlife in town. Hours are erratic, but when it's open, it's open till late.

Getting There & Around

Buses to Chetumal (and Limones) leave at 5am and 2pm and cost M$90. The bus stops by the lighthouse.

Cabs from Limones, on Hwy 307, cost about M$600 (including to the northern hotels). Driving from Limones, turn right (south) after 55km and follow the signs to Xcalak (another 60km). Keep an eye out for the diverse wildlife that frequents the forest and mangrove; a lot of it runs out onto the road.

You can take a coastal road from Xcalak to Mahahual, but don't be surprised if it's closed during the rainy season.

You can hire a boat at XTC Dive Center for M$780 per person (minimum four people) to San Pedro, Belize.

Laguna Bacalar

☎983 / POP 11,000

Laguna Bacalar comes as a surprise in this region of tortured limestone and scrubby jungle. More than 60km long with a bottom of sparkling white sand, this crystal-clear lake offers opportunities for camping, swimming, kayaking and simply lazing around.

The small, sleepy, lakeside town of Bacalar lies east of the highway, 125km south of Felipe Carrillo Puerto. It's noted mostly for its old Spanish fortress and popular *balneario* (swimming facility). There's not a lot else going on, but that's why people like it here. On the town plaza, you'll find an ATM, a small grocery store and a tourist office.

Sights & Activities

Fortress FORT
(admission M$57; ⏲9am-7pm Tue-Sun) The fortress above the lagoon was built to protect citizens from raids by pirates and the local indigenous population. It also served as an important outpost for the Spanish in the Caste War. In 1859 it was seized by Maya rebels, who held the fort until Quintana Roo was finally conquered by Mexican troops in 1901. Today, with formidable cannons still on its ramparts, the fortress remains an imposing sight. It houses a museum exhibiting colonial armaments and uniforms from the 17th and 18th centuries.

Balneario SWIMMING
(admission M$10; ⏲7am-7pm) This swimming spot lies a few hundred meters north along the *costera* below the fort. There are some small restaurants along the avenue and near the *balneario,* which is very busy on weekends.

Cenote Azul SWIMMING
(www.cenoteazul.com; Hwy 307; life vests M$35; ⏲8am-6pm; P) FREE Just shy of the south end of the *costera* (coast highway) is this cenote, a 90m-deep natural pool with an onsite bar and restaurant (mains M$80 to M$250). It's 200m east of Hwy 307, so many buses will drop you nearby.

Sleeping

Bacalar

All places are along the *costera* and right on the lagoon.

Casita Carolina GUESTHOUSE $
(☎834-2334; www.casitacarolina.com; d M$300-600, palapa M$700; P wi-fi) A delightful place about 1½ blocks south of the fort, the Casita has a large lawn leading down to the lake, five fan-cooled rooms and a deluxe *palapa* that sleeps up to four. For tight budgets, there's a camping site (M$200) and two small funky trailers (M$250) parked on the lawn. Guests can explore the lake in kayaks.

Amigos B&B Laguna Bacalar B&B **$$**
(www.bacalar.net; d M$700; P ❄ @ ☎) Right on the lake and about 500m south of the fort, this ideally located property has five spacious guest rooms with hammocks, terraces and a comfy shared common area. Breakfast will cost you an additional M$100. No phone; accepts walk-ins and online reservations only.

Hotel Laguna HOTEL **$$**
(☎834-2205; www.hotellagunabacalar.com; Av Costera 479; d with fan/air-con M$944/1180, bungalow from M$1580; P ☎ ≋) This breezy place boasts a small swimming pool, a restaurant and excellent views of the lagoon, which you can explore by way of kayak or boat tours offered by the hotel. It's 2km south of Bacalar town and only 150m east of Hwy 307, so if you're traveling by bus you can ask the driver to stop at the turnoff.

Villas Bakalar APARTMENT **$$$**
(☎835-1400; www.villasbakalar.com; Av 3 No 981, btwn Calles 28 & 30; d M$1580; P ❄ ☎ ≋) Villas Bakalar offers a little of everything: a pool area with an excellent lake view, lush gardens, large apartments with full kitchens and activities such as kayaking and sailing.

Around Bacalar

Laguna Azul CABIN **$**
(☎999-159-5200, 984-103-9154; www.hotellagunaazul.com; off Hwy 307, Km 59; cabañas M$500, campsites and RV sites per person M$75; P) Want to really get away from it all? Head to the lagoon's north end and stay in one of three shoreside solar-powered *cabañas* with tile floors, good beds and hammocks. There are also camping and RV sites. You'll find the road to Laguna Azul off Hwy 307, about 200m south of the town of Pedro A Santos. It's about a half-hour drive to get here.

You can ask to be let off 2nd-class buses at the entrance (and walk the 3.2km in) or in Pedro A Santos itself, where you can take a taxi for M$80.

★ **Rancho Encantado** CABIN **$$$**
(☎998-884-2071, 983-839-7900; www.encantado.com; Hwy 307, Km 24; d/ste incl breakfast from $1525/2066; P ☎) Laguna Bacalar is absolutely beautiful in and of itself, so imagine what it's like to stay at one of the most striking locations along the shore. A typical day on the ranch goes something like this: wake up in comfy thatch-roof cabin, have breakfast with lagoon view, snorkel in crystalline waters. The ranch is 3km north of Bacalar.

EATING

Tacos de Cochinita Chepe's MEXICAN **$**
(cnr Av 7 & Calle 22; tacos/tortas M$9/18; ⌚6am-noon) There's no sign outside this mornings-only taco joint, so just follow your nose to the sweet smell of *cochinita* (slow-cooked pork).

Orizaba MEXICAN **$**
(Av 7, btwn Calles 24 & 26; mains M$35-48; ⌚8am-4:30pm) Highly recommended by locals and expats alike, this place prepares home-style Mexican favorites in a casual setting.

Los Aluxes MEXICAN **$$**
(Av Costera; mains M$100-130; ⌚1-9pm Thu-Tue) An open-air *palapa* restaurant specializing in *yucateco* fare, this waterfront place prepares wonderful creations like flambéed shrimp in an *achiote* (annatto spice) reduction. It's 150m south of Amigos B&B.

Getting There & Away

Southbound 2nd-class buses go through Bacalar town on Calle 7, passing a block uphill from the central square *(el parque)*, which is just above the fort and has a taxi stand.

Northbound 2nd-class buses run along Calle 5, a block downhill from Calle 7. Most 1st-class buses don't enter town, but many will drop you along Hwy 307 at the turnoffs to Hotel Laguna and Cenote Azul; check before you buy your ticket.

If you're driving from the north and want to reach the town and fort, take the first Bacalar exit and continue several blocks before turning left (east) down the hill. From Chetumal, head west to catch Hwy 307 north; after 25km on the highway you'll reach the signed right turn for Cenote Azul and the *costera*.

Chetumal

☎983 / POP 151,200

The capital city of Quintana Roo, Chetumal is a relatively quiet capital going about its daily paces. The bayside esplanade hosts carnivals and events, and the modern Maya museum is impressive (though a bit short on artifacts). Impressive Maya ruins, amazing jungle and the border to neighboring Belize are all close by. Though sightings are infrequent (there are no tours), manatees can sometimes be seen in the rather muddy bay or nearby mangrove shores.

History

Before the Spanish conquest, Chetumal was a Maya port for shipping gold, feathers, cacao and copper to the northern Yucatán Peninsula. After the conquest, the town was not actually settled until 1898, when it was founded by the Mexican government to put a stop to the arms and lumber trade carried on by descendants of the Maya who fought in the Caste War. Dubbed Payo Obispo, the town changed its name to Chetumal in 1936. In 1955, Hurricane Janet virtually obliterated it; 2007's Hurricane Dean did a bit of damage to the rebuilt town's infrastructure.

Sights & Activities

Museo de la Cultura Maya MUSEUM

(☎832-6838; Av de los Héroes 68, cnr Av Gandhi; admission M$62; ⊙9am-7pm Tue-Sat, to 5pm Sun) The Museo de la Cultura Maya is the city's claim to cultural fame – a bold showpiece beautifully conceived and executed. It's organized into three levels, mirroring Maya cosmology. The main floor represents this world; the upper floor the heavens; and the lower floor Xibalbá, the underworld. The various exhibits cover all of the Mayab (lands of the Maya).

Scale models show the great Maya buildings as they may have appeared, including a temple complex set below Plexiglas you can walk over. Though artifacts are in short supply, there are replicas of stelae and a burial chamber from Honduras' Copán, reproductions of the murals found in Room 1 at Bonampak, and much more. Ingenious mechanical and computer displays illustrate the Maya's complex calendrical, numerical and writing systems.

The museum's courtyard, which you can enter for free, has salons for temporary exhibitions of modern artists. In the middle of the courtyard is a *na* (thatched hut) with implements of daily Maya life on display: gourds and grinding stones.

Look for a bronze bust in the middle of Av de los Héroes, just east of the museum's entrance. It depicts Jacinto Pat, one of the Maya leaders who planned the insurrection that became the Caste War.

Museo de la Ciudad MUSEUM

(Local History Museum; cnr Héroes de Chapultepec & cnr Av de los Héroes; admission M$13; ⊙9am-7pm Tue-Sat, to 2pm Sun) The Museo de la Ciudad is small but neatly done, displaying historic photos, military artifacts and old-time household items (even some vintage telephones and a TV). All labels are in Spanish, but even if you don't read the language, it's worth visiting for 15 minutes of entertainment.

Cocomoco BICYCLE RENTAL

(cnr Blvd Bahía & Emiliano Zapata; bike/inline skates per hour M$20/15; ⊙4pm-11pm) Rent a bike or inline skates here and go for a bayside spin.

Festivals & Events

Carnaval RELIGIOUS

Carnaval in late February/early March is particularly lively in Chetumal. Colorful nightly parades bring locals into the streets to watch floats and plumed dancers pass by.

Sleeping

Hotel Xcalak HOTEL $

(☎129-1708; www.hotelxcalak.com.mx; cnr Av Gandhi & 16 de Septiembre; r M$400; ❄📶) That rare Chetumal budget hotel that doesn't look like it's trapped in the '70s. It's near the city's best museum, as well as transport to Laguna Bacalar, and there's a good restaurant downstairs.

Villa Fontana Hotel HOTEL $

(☎129-2004; Av de los Héroes 181, btwn Efraín Aguilar & Av Gandhi; d M$520; ❄📶) No surprises at this middle-of-the-road hotel. Rooms could be a bit bigger, but they've got touches of style and are a fair deal overall.

★**Noor Hotel** HOTEL $$

(☎835-1300; www.hotelnoor.com.mx; Blvd Bahía 3, cnr Av José María Morelos; r M$1020; P❄📶🏊) Right on the bay, the Noor will appeal to those looking to get away from the bustling *centro*. Rooms are done up in modern, dark-wood furnishings, and some afford bay views. There's a nice pool and a restaurant that prepares international cuisine, and the boardwalk across the way is sweet for afternoon strolls.

Hotel Grand Marlon HOTEL $$

(☎285-3279; www.hotelesmarlon.com; Av Juárez 88, btwn Zaragoza & Plutarco Elías Calles; r/ste from M$750/875; P❄📶🏊) With modern clean lines, a rather funky pool area (complete with Astroturf and a lukewarm Jacuzzi), the 'Grand' almost achieves 'hip boutique' status. The simple, stylish rooms are an excellent deal for the price. Or, you can save a few hundred pesos by heading across the street to the plain ol' Marlon, its sister hotel (doubles M$570).

BODY ARTISTS: CRANIAL DEFORMATION, PIERCING & TATTOOS

Take a second to imagine what Maya at the height of the Classic period must have looked like. Their heads were sloped back; their ears, noses, cheeks and sometimes even genitals were pierced; and their bodies were tattooed. These were, indeed, some of the first body artists.

Cranial deformation was one of the Maya's most unusual forms of body art, and was most often performed to indicate social status. Mothers would bind the head of their infant (male or female) tightly to a board while the skull was still soft. By positioning the board either on top of or behind the head, the mother could shape the skull in many ways – either long and pointy (known as 'elongated') or long and narrow, extending back rather than up (known as 'oblique'). As the infant grew older and the bones calcified, the headboard was no longer needed: the skull would retain its modified shape for life. Apparently, compressing the skull did not affect the intelligence or capabilities of the child. Both practices became less and less common after the Spanish arrived.

Hotel Los Cocos HOTEL **$$**
(☎835-0430; www.hotelloscocos.com.mx; Av de los Héroes 134, cnr Héroes de Chapultepec; d/ste with air-con from M$912/1824; P ❄ @ ᯤ ≋) Has a great location and a seriously mirrored lobby that gets your inner disco dancer rising. There's also a nice swimming pool, a Jacuzzi, gym and a popular sidewalk restaurant. All rooms have small fridges and cable TV service.

Holiday Inn Chetumal-Puerta Maya HOTEL **$$$**
(☎835-0400; www.holiday-inn.com/chetumalmex; Av de los Héroes 171, cnr Av Gandhi; d M$1644, ste M$2125-4200; P ❄ @ ᯤ ≋) The fanciest in town, with comfortable rooms that overlook a small courtyard, a swimming pool set amid tropical gardens, and a restaurant and bar. The Maya sun mirror in the lobby adds interesting flair.

Eating & Drinking

Across from the Holiday Inn is the Mercado Ignacio Manuel Altamirano and its row of small, simple eateries serving inexpensive meals.

Los de Pescado SEAFOOD **$**
(cnr Blvd Bahía & Emiliano Zapata; tacos/tostadas M$24/26; ⏲9am-6pm Wed-Mon) Tasty fish tacos and *ceviche tostadas* with a bayside view. You might even have a rare croc or manatee sighting.

El Taquito de Don Julio MEXICAN **$**
(Plutarco Elías Calles 220, btwn Avs de los Héroes & Juárez; tacos M$13-17, mains M$35-130; ⏲6:30pm-1am Mon-Sat) This is an airy, simple dining room and a good spot for night owls. The small tacos cost slightly more with cheese; other menu offerings include cheap snacks, *tortas* (sandwiches) and vegetarian brochettes (M$70).

Café-Restaurant Los Milagros CAFE **$**
(☎832-4433; cnr Zaragoza & Av 5 de Mayo; mains M$25-65; ⏲7:30am-9pm Mon-Sat, to 1pm Sun) Serves great espresso and food outdoors. A favorite with Chetumal's student and intellectual set, it's a good spot to chat it up with locals or while away the time with a game of dominoes.

Restaurant Pantoja MEXICAN **$**
(☎832-3957; cnr Avs Gandhi & 16 de Septiembre; mains M$40-70; ⏲7am-6pm Mon-Sat) A popular family-run restaurant serving breakfasts, *enchiladas* (tortillas with spicy meat) and a variety of meat dishes. It offers a M$60 set meal *(menu del día)*. Although fan-cooled, it gets a bit warm in the afternoon.

El Fenicio MEXICAN **$$**
(Av de los Héroes 74, cnr Zaragoza; mains M$60-145; ⏲24hr) Come here at 11pm and you'll feel like you've stepped into a Hopper painting: the yellow light and the few solitary diners hunched over a meal. The food, a selection of mainly Mexican fare, is tasty and served promptly. Flan and decent US-style coffee are a tasty way to finish the day.

La Choza MEXICAN **$$**
(☎117-6168; Zaragoza 166, btwn Avs 5 de Mayo & 16 de Septiembre; mains M$60-180; ⏲11am-9pm Tue-Sun) A popular *palapa*-topped bar-restaurant with a fun Caribbean-Chetumalan vibe, the Choza is a good spot to sample regional *antojitos* (little snacks). It has live music on weekends.

Sergio's Pizzas INTERNATIONAL **$$**

(☎832-2991; Av Obregón 182, cnr Av 5 de Mayo; pizzas M$67-155, mains M$76-193; ⏰7am-midnight; ❄) This cool air-conditioned place serves pizzas and cold beer in frosted mugs, plus Mexican dishes, steaks and seafood.

Orientation

Chetumal is laid out on a grand plan with a grid of wide boulevards. The southern edge is bordered by the water. The main street, Av de los Héroes, divides the city into east and west sides, ending at the waterfront. Av Obregón parallels the bay and leads, heading westward, first to a *glorieta* (traffic circle), then to the airport and nearby immigration office, then to the turn for Belize.

Information

There are numerous banks and ATMs around town, including an ATM inside the bus terminal.

Arba (☎832-2581; Efraín Aguilar; per hr M$10; ⏰7am-11:30pm) Internet cafe with several similar cafes nearby.

Banorte (Av de los Héroes, btwn Plutarco Elías Calles & Lázaro Cárdenas) For ATM and bank services.

Cambalache (Av de los Héroes, btwn Plutarco Elías Calles & Zaragoza; ⏰10am-6pm Mon-Sat) Currency exchange office.

Cruz Roja (Red Cross; ☎832-0571; cnr Avs Independencia & Héroes de Chapultepec; ⏰24hr) For medical emergencies.

Emergency (☎066)

Instituto Nacional de Migración (Immigration Office; www.inm.gob.mx; Carretera Chetumal; ⏰9am-1pm) Head to this office, across from the airport, to replace lost tourist permits.

Post Office (☎832-2281; cnr Plutarco Elías Calles & Av 5 de Mayo; ⏰9am-5pm Mon-Fri, 9am-noon Sat)

Getting There & Away

Gibson's Tours & Transfers (☎501-423-8006; www.gibsonstoursandtransfers.com) provides transport from Mexico to Belize and facilitates border crossings for rental cars. Santa Elena to Corozal border transport is M$290.

AIR

Chetumal's small airport is roughly 2km northwest of the city center along Av Obregón. It's served by **Interjet** (☎800-011-2345; www.interjet.com) for Mexico City flights.

BOAT

Catch boats bound for San Pedro, Belize, at the Muelle Fiscal (dock) on Blvd Bahía. See www.sanpedrowatertaxi.com for schedule and rates.

BUS

The **main bus terminal** is about 2km north of the center, near the intersection of Avs Insurgentes and Belice. Services are provided by ADO and OCC (1st class) and Mayab (2nd class), among other bus lines.

The **ADO 2nd-class terminal** (Av Belice; ⏰6am-10pm), just west of the Museo de la Cultura Maya, is a good place to get info. TRT, Sur and Mayab (a cut above) buses leave from here.

Many local buses, and those bound for Belize, begin their runs from the **Nuevo Mercado Lázaro Cárdenas**, on Calzada Veracruz at Confederación Nacional Campesina Campeche (also called Segundo Circuito), about 10 blocks north of Av Primo de Verdad. From this market, most 1st-class Belize-bound buses continue to the main bus terminal and depart from there 15 minutes later. Tickets can be purchased on board the buses or (1st-class only) at the main terminal.

The **minibus terminal** (cnr Avs Primo de Verdad & Hidalgo) has services to Bacalar (M$25) and other nearby destinations.

Check your bus details before departure because buses leave from multiple locations and this information is subject to change. Departures listed in the table opposite leave from the main terminal, unless noted otherwise.

TAXI

City cabs charge about M$20 for short trips. White-and-blue taxis on the corner of Av Juárez and Efraín Aguilar charge M$30 for Laguna Bacalar.

Getting Around

From the traffic circle at Av de los Héroes, you can get a *combi* (van) to the town center on the Santa María or Calderitas lines. To reach the main bus terminal from the center, catch a *colectivo* from Av Belice behind the Museo de la Cultura Maya. Ask to be left at the *glorieta* at Av Insurgentes. Head left (west) to reach the terminal.

Corredor Arqueológico

The Corredor Arqueológico comprises the archaeological sites of Dzibanché and Kohunlich, two intriguing and seldom-visited Maya ruins that can be visited on a day trip from Chetumal.

Sights

Dzibanché ARCHAEOLOGICAL SITE

(admission M$46; ⏰8am-5pm) Though it's a chore to get to, this site is definitely worth a visit for its secluded, semi-wild nature.

Dzibanché (meaning 'writing on wood') was a major city extending more than 40 sq km, and on the road to it, you'll pass huge mounds covered in trees. There are a number of excavated palaces and pyramids, but the site itself is not completely excavated.

The first restored structure you come to is Edificio 6, the **Palacio de los Dinteles** (Palace of the Lintels), which gave the site its name. This is a perfect spot to orient yourself for the rest of the site: facing Edificio 6's steps, you are looking east. It's a pyramid topped by a temple with two vaulted galleries; the base dates from the early Classic period (AD 300–600), while the temple is from the late Classic period (AD 600–900). Climb the steps and stand directly under the original lintel on the right (south) side of the temple. Looking up you can see a Maya calendrical inscription with the date working out to AD 733. This is some old wood.

On descending, head to your left (south) and thread between a mound on the right and a low, mostly restored, stepped structure on the left. This structure is Edificio 16, **Palacio de los Tucanes**; in the center from the side you first approach on are the visible remains of posts that bore a mask. The path then brings you into **Plaza Gann**. Circling it counterclockwise takes you past Edificio 14 (stuck onto the north side of a larger building), decorated at the base with *tamborcillos* (little drums), in late Classic Río Bec style – look up the dirt hill to see them. The larger building to the south is Edificio 13, **Templo de los Cautivos**, so named for the carvings in its steps of captives submitting to whatever captives submitted to in those days. This seems to be the dominant (if you'll pardon the pun) theme in most Maya stelae.

On the east side of the plaza is Dzibanché's highest structure, the **Templo de los Cormoranes** (Temple of the Cormorants; Edificio 2), whose upper structure has been restored.

Exit the plaza by climbing the stone steps to the north of Edificio 2. At the top of the stairs is **Plaza del Xibalbá** (Plaza of the Underworld), though it's higher than Plaza Gann.

Opposite Palacio Norte is, of course, Palacio Sur, and from here you can see more of Edificio 2, but the most notable building is across the plaza: Edificio 1, the recently restored **Templo del Buho** (Temple of

BUSES FROM CHETUMAL

DESTINATION	COST (M$)	DURATION (HR)	FREQUENCY
Bacalar	25-36	¾	frequent (A)
Belize City, Belize	150	3-4	frequent (N)
Campeche	344	6	12pm
Cancún	205-302	5½-6	frequent
Corozal, Belize	35-40	1	frequent (N)
Escárcega	222	4	7 daily
Felipe Carrillo Puerto	78-128	2½-3	frequent
Flores, Guatemala (for Tikal)	400	8	7am
Mahahual	80-100	4	3 daily (A)
Mérida	246-336	5½-7	5 daily
Orange Walk, Belize	35-50	2¼	frequent (N)
Palenque	394-414	6½-7½	5 daily
Tulum	179-204	3¼-4	frequent
Valladolid	183	5½	3 daily
Veracruz	698	16	2 daily (A)
Villahermosa	458	8¼-9	6 daily
Xcalak	80	5	2 daily (A)
Xpujil	68-100	2-3	8 daily

(A) = ADO 2nd-Class Terminal, (N) = Nuevo Mercado Lázaro Cárdenas

the Owl). It had an inner chamber with a stairway leading down to another chamber, in which were found the remains of a Very Important Personage (VIP) and burial offerings. The nearly 360-degree views from the very top of the temple (it's a bit dicey, so be careful) are quite impressive. You can see Grupo Lamay to the west and you may spot Kinich-Ná, more than 2km to the northwest.

Part of Dzibanché but well removed from the main site, **Kinich-Ná** consists of one building. But what a building: the megalithic **Acrópolis** held at least five temples on three levels, and a couple more dead VIPs with offerings. The site's name derives from the frieze of the Maya sun god once found at the top of the structure. It's an easy drive of 2km along a narrow but good road leading north from near Dzibanché's visitors center.

Kohunlich ARCHAEOLOGICAL SITE

(admission M$55; ⌚8am-5pm) This archaeological site sits on a carpeted green. The ruins, dating from both the late pre-Classic (AD 100–200) and the early Classic (AD 300–600) periods, are famous for the great **Templo de los Mascarones** (Temple of the Masks), a pyramid-like structure with a central stairway flanked by huge, 3m-high stucco masks of the sun god.

The thick lips and prominent features are reminiscent of Olmec sculpture. Of the eight original masks, only two are relatively intact following the ravages of archaeological looters.

The masks themselves are impressive, but you can only see them from close up because the large thatch coverings that have been erected to protect them from further weathering obscure the view. Try to imagine what the pyramid and its red masks must have looked like in the old days as the Maya approached them across the sunken courtyard at the front.

A few hundred meters southwest of Plaza Merwin are the 27 Escalones (27 Steps), the remains of an extensive residential area.

The hydraulic engineering used at Kohunlich was a great achievement: 90,000 of the site's 210,000 sq meters were cut to channel rainwater into Kohunlich's once-enormous reservoir.

Getting There & Away

The turnoff for Dzibanché from Hwy 186 is about 44km west of Chetumal, on the right just after the Zona Arqueológica sign. From there it's another 24km north and east along a narrow road. Just after the tiny town of Morocoy you'll need to turn right again. It's easy to miss the sign unless you're looking for it.

Kohunlich's turnoff is 3km west along Hwy 186 from the Dzibanché turnoff, and the site lies at the end of a potholed 8.5km road. It's a straight shot from the highway.

At the time of writing, there was no public transportation running directly to either of the sites. They're best visited by car, though Kohunlich could conceivably be reached by taking an early bus to the village of Francisco Villa near the turnoff, then either hitchhiking or walking the 8.5km to the site. To return by bus to Chetumal or head west to Xpujil or Escárcega you must hope to flag down a bus on the highway; not all buses will stop.

Taxis can be rented per hour in Chetumal for as little as M$200 per hour; to visit both sites you'd need at least five hours, or roughly M$1000. A group could pile in and split the cost.

South to Belize & Guatemala

Corozal

☎501 / POP 9900

This fairly laid-back town, 18km south of the Mexico-Belize border, is an appropriate introduction to English-speaking Belize. There's a simple plaza in the center, a waterfront, some nearby ruins and a lot of chickens running around. A Belize Bank with an ATM is at the plaza.

Sights

Santa Rita ARCHAEOLOGICAL SITE

(www.nichbelize.org; ⌚dawn-dusk) FREE Santa Rita was an ancient Maya coastal town that once occupied the same strategic trading position as present-day Corozal Town, namely the spot between two rivers – the Río Hondo (which now forms the Belize-Mexico border) and the New River (which enters Corozal Bay south of town). Much of Santa Rita remains unexcavated, but it's worth a visit.

To reach the Maya site, head out of town on Santa Rita Rd. Continuing north on the main highway toward Mexico, turn left at the Super Santa Rita store. Some 300m past the store you'll find a wooded area on the right and in its midst a partially restored pyramid offering an amazing view of the surrounding town and bay.

NO-MAN'S-LAND

'No-Man's-Land' is the strip of territory after the Mexican exit but before you've crossed into Belize. Many tourists head to Chetumal expecting to make a quick zip across the border and back to renew their tourist permit. While most tourists cross without problem, the occasional unscrupulous official will invent an excuse to not let you through even though it is perfectly legitimate.

They may say there's a 'minimum 72-hour stay in Belize.' (There isn't.) Or they'll claim that you need a Mexican re-entry stamp for them to let you through. (You don't.) Sometimes they'll say that Belize doesn't welcome day trips, as 'tourists don't spend enough money in their country.' (The Belizean consulate says trips, even day trips, across the border are perfectly fine, as do the Mexican officials.)

If a guard decides to single you out, there's not a lot you can do other than pay up or beg your way back into Mexico and try again. The following should help:

- Group up with other foreign travelers.
- Don't disclose that you're intending a day trip.
- Crossing back into Mexico, be sure to check that your Belize exit stamp is clear and easy to read, with the official's signature and the date written inside.

Sleeping & Eating

Maya World Guest House GUESTHOUSE **$**
(627-2511; byronchuster@gmail.com; 2nd St North; r BZ$27.50) An offbeat and artistically done guesthouse, Maya World consists of two houses and an enclosed garden-filled courtyard. The front house is a restored colonial building with a wraparound veranda complete with hammock. The two-story out back has simple but functional rooms.

Patty's Bistro BELIZEAN **$**
(402-0174; 13 4th Ave, cnr 2nd St; mains BZ$8-18; 7am-9pm Mon-Sat) A Corozal favorite, Patty's is best known for its conch soup, a thick potato based chowder with vegetables and chunks of conch meat that's a meal in itself. Patty's also has good Belizean dishes.

Al's Cafe BELIZEAN **$**
(5th Ave; mains BZ$5-8; 7am-4pm Mon-Fri, 6-10pm Sat) Locals love Al's for its affordable, home-style Belizean cooking. You'll find it two blocks south of the plaza.

Getting There & Away

Belize-bound buses (M$35 to M$40) depart from Chetumal's Nuevo Mercado Lázaro Cárdenas, on Calzada Veracruz (near Confederación Nacional Campesina). See p291 for more on crossing the border. The same buses return to Chetumal, departing from the Corozal bus station. From Corozal, you can head to Belize City or to Melchor de Mencos, Guatemala, which will take you to Flores and the Maya supersite of Tikal.

Yucatán State & the Maya Heartland

POP 1,955,600

Includes ➡

Best Places to Eat

- Kinich (p176)
- La Chaya Maya (p152)
- Manjar Blanco (p152)
- Casa Peon (p171)

Best Places to Stay

- Luz en Yucatán (p150)
- Nómadas Hostel (p150)
- Pickled Onion (p162)
- Hotel Celeste Vida (p171)

Why Go?

Sitting regally on the northern tip of the peninsula, Yucatán state sees less mass tourism than its flashy neighbor, Quintana Roo. It is sophisticated and savvy, and the perfect spot for travelers more interested in cultural exploration than beach life. Sure, there are a few nice beaches in Celestún and Progreso, but most people come to this area to explore the ancient Maya sites peppered throughout the region, like the Ruta Puuc, which will take you to four or five ruins in just a day.

Visitors also come to experience the past and present in the cloistered corners of colonial cities, to visit *henequén* haciendas (vast estates that produced agave plant fibers, used to make rope) lost to time or restored by caring hands to old glory, and to discover the energy, spirit and subtle contrasts of this authentic corner of southeastern Mexico.

When to Go

- Every vernal and autumnal equinox, visitors at Chichén Itzá can witness the appearance of a shadow serpent figure on the stairs of the site's iconic pyramid, El Castillo.
- Nature lovers flock to the estuary of the Celestún biosphere reserve during migration season to check out the colonies of flamingos and other bird species that congregate there; August and September are ideal.
- Beat the heat from November to March, especially if you're planning on visiting inland cities such as Mérida; northerly winds, known as *nortes*, keep the coast nice and cool in the afternoon.

MÉRIDA

999 / POP 830,700

Since the Spanish conquest, Mérida has been the cultural capital of the entire peninsula. At times provincial, at others '*muy cosmopolitano*,' it is a town steeped in colonial history, with narrow streets, broad central plazas and the region's best museums. It's also a perfect place from which to kick off your adventure into the rest of Yucatán state. There are cheap eats, good hostels and hotels, thriving markets and other goings-on just about every night somewhere in the downtown area.

Long popular with European travelers looking to go beyond the hubbub of Quintana Roo's resort towns, Mérida is not an 'undiscovered Mexican gem' like some of the tourist brochures claim. Simply put, it's a tourist town, but a tourist town too big to feel like a tourist trap. And as the capital of Yucatán state, Mérida is also the cultural crossroads of the region, and there's something just a smidge elitist about it: the people who live here have a beautiful town, and they know it.

History

Francisco de Montejo (the Younger) founded a Spanish colony at Campeche, about 160km to the southwest, in 1540. From this base he took advantage of political dissension among the Maya, conquering T'ho (now Mérida) in 1542. By decade's end, Yucatán was mostly under Spanish colonial rule.

When Montejo's conquistadors entered T'ho, they found a major Maya settlement of lime-mortared stone that reminded them of the Roman architecture in Mérida, Spain. They promptly renamed the city and proceeded to build it into the regional capital, dismantling the Maya structures and using the materials to construct a cathedral and other stately buildings. Mérida took its colonial orders directly from Spain, not from Mexico City, and Yucatán has had a distinct cultural and political identity ever since.

During the Caste War, only Mérida and Campeche were able to hold out against the rebel forces. On the brink of surrender, the ruling class in Mérida was saved by reinforcements sent from central Mexico in exchange for Mérida's agreement to take orders from Mexico City.

Mérida today is the peninsula's center of commerce, a bustling city that has been growing rapidly ever since *maquiladoras* (low-paying, for-export factories) started cropping up in the 1980s and '90s, and as the tourism industry picked up during those decades as well. The growth has drawn migrant workers from all around Mexico and there's a large Lebanese community in town.

Sights

Plaza Grande & Around

Plaza Grande is one of the nicest plazas in Mexico, and huge laurel trees shade the park's benches and wide sidewalks. It was the religious and social center of ancient T'ho; under the Spanish it was the Plaza de Armas, the parade ground, laid out by Montejo. There's a crafts market on Sunday, and dance or live music nearly every night.

A ceremony is held daily marking the raising and lowering of the Mexican flag.

Catedral de San Ildefonso CATHEDRAL
(Calle 60 s/n; 6am-1pm & 4-7pm) On the site of a former Maya temple is Mérida's hulking, severe cathedral, begun in 1561 and completed in 1598. Some of the stone from the Maya temple was used in its construction. The massive crucifix behind the altar is **Cristo de la Unidad** (Christ of Unity), a symbol of reconciliation between those of Spanish and Maya heritage.

To the right over the south door is a painting of Tutul Xiu, *cacique* (indigenous chief) of the town of Maní paying his respects to his ally Francisco de Montejo at T'ho. (Montejo and Xiu jointly defeated the Cocomes; Xiu converted to Christianity, and his descendants still live in Mérida.)

In the small chapel to the left of the altar is Mérida's most famous religious artifact, a statue called **Cristo de las Ampollas** (Christ of the Blisters). Local legend says the statue was carved from a tree that was hit by lightning and burned for an entire night without charring. It is also said to be the only object to have survived the fiery destruction of the church in the town of Ichmul (though it was blackened and blistered from the heat). The statue was moved to the Mérida cathedral in 1645.

Other than these items, the cathedral's interior is largely plain, its rich decoration having been stripped away by angry peasants at the height of anticlerical fervor during the Mexican Revolution.

Yucatán State & the Maya Heartland Highlights

1. Marvel at colonial architecture or enjoy a free concert in the cultural capital of **Mérida** (p141)

2. Find out why they named **Chichén Itzá** (p177) one of the 'new seven wonders of the world,' and why **Ek' Balam** (p188) should have made the short list

3. Scan the salty horizon for flamingos at the **Reserva de la Biosfera Ría Celestún** (p170) or **Reserva de la Biosfera Ría Lagartos** (p190)

4. Bump your way through the countryside on a horse-drawn rail cart, stopping to dive into the azure **Cenotes de Cuzamá** (p166)

5. Spin off the tourist track to the less-visited areas around **Valladolid** (p184) and the archaeological sites of the **Ruta Puuc** (p163)

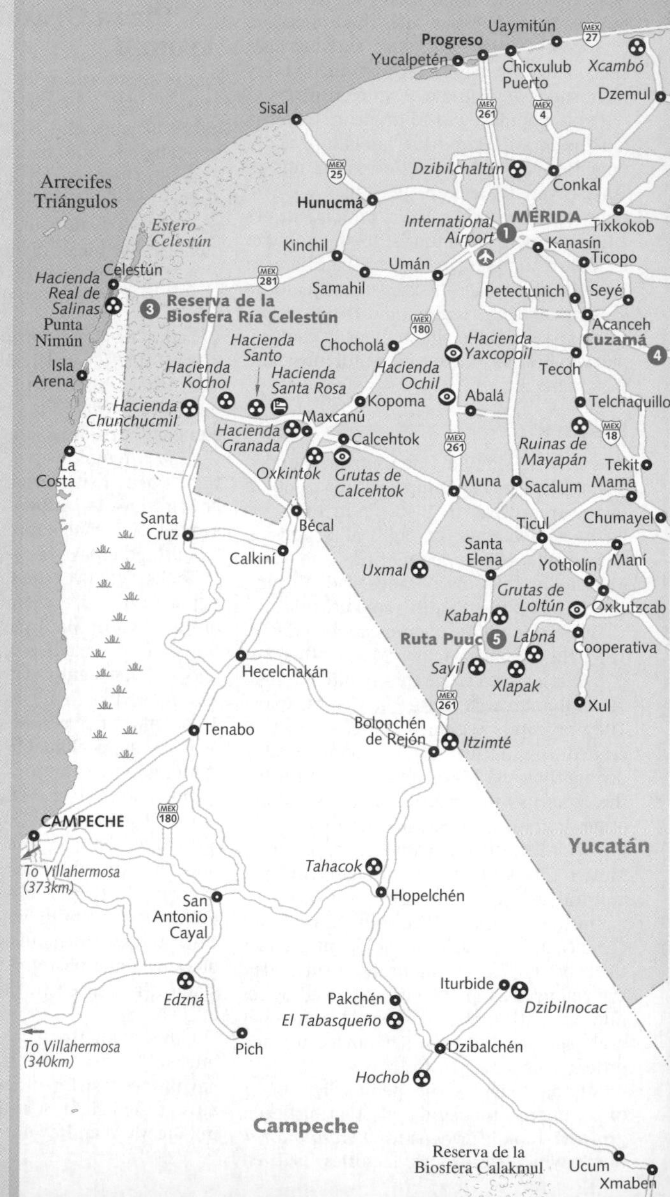

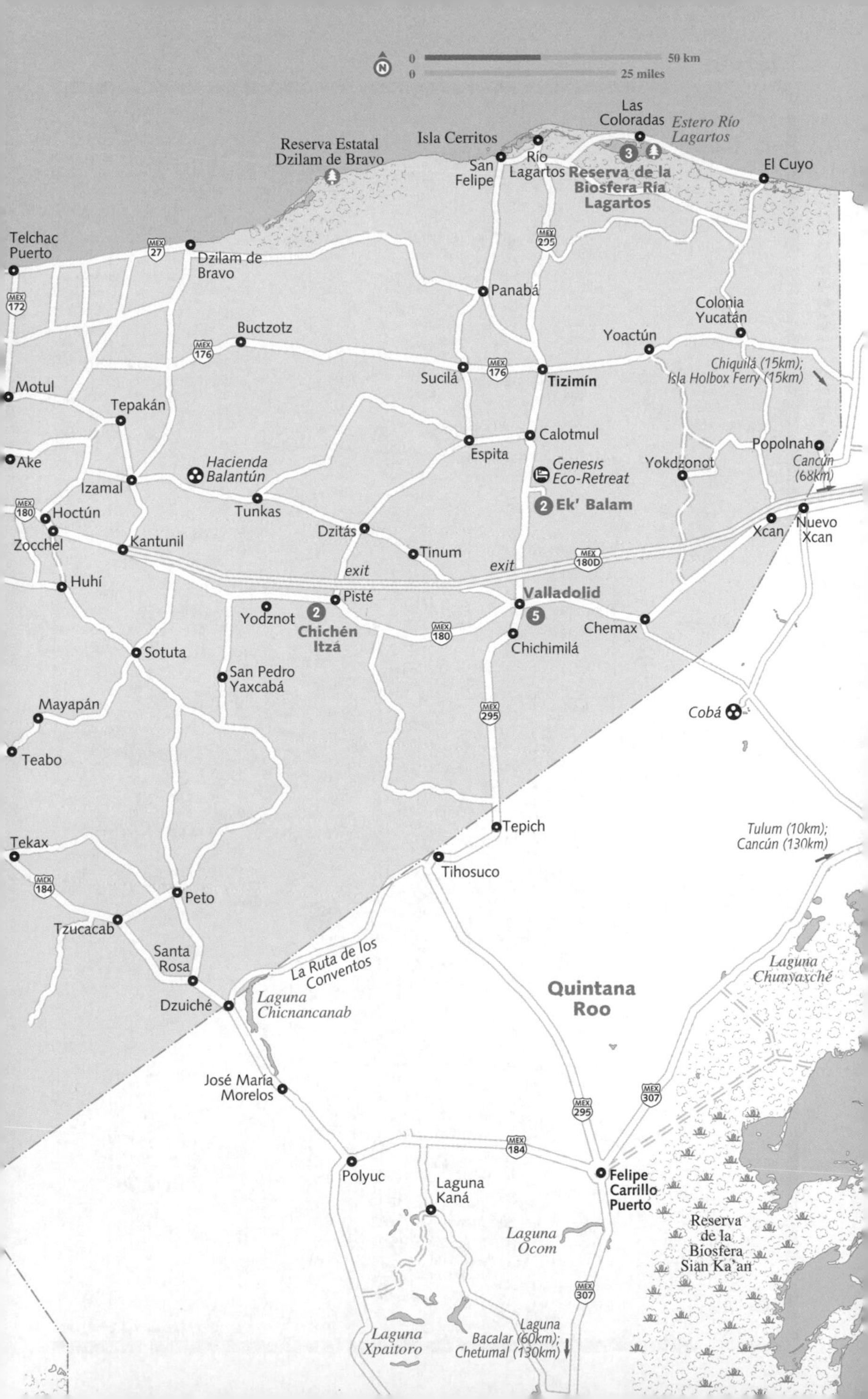

0 50 km
0 25 miles

Las Coloradas
Estero Río Lagartos
Reserva Estatal Dzilam de Bravo
Isla Cerritos
San Felipe
Río Lagartos
Reserva de la Biosfera Ría Lagartos
El Cuyo
Telchac Puerto
MEX 27
Dzilam de Bravo
MEX 295
MEX 172
Panabá
Colonia Yucatán
Buctzotz
Yoactún
MEX 176
Sucilá
Tizimín
Chiquilá (15km); Isla Holbox Ferry (15km)
Motul
Tepakán
Calotmul
Espita
Popolnah
Ake
Hacienda Balantún
Genesis Eco-Retreat
Yokdzonot
Cancún (68km)
Izamal
Ek' Balam
MEX 180
Hoctún
Tunkas
Xcan
Nuevo Xcan
Zocchel
Kantunil
Dzitás
Tinum
exit
MEX 180D
Huhí
Pisté
Valladolid
Yodznot
Chichén Itzá
Chemax
Chichimilá
Sotuta
San Pedro Yaxcabá
Mayapán
Cobá
Teabo
Tepich
Tulum (10km); Cancún (130km)
Tekax
Tihosuco
MEX 184
Peto
Tzucacab
Santa Rosa
La Ruta de los Conventos
Laguna Chunyaxché
Quintana Roo
Dzuiché
Laguna Chicnancanab
José María Morelos
MEX 307
Polyuc
Felipe Carrillo Puerto
Laguna Kaná
Reserva de la Biosfera Sian Ka'an
Laguna Ocom
Laguna Xpaitoro
Laguna Bacalar (60km); Chetumal (130km)

Mérida

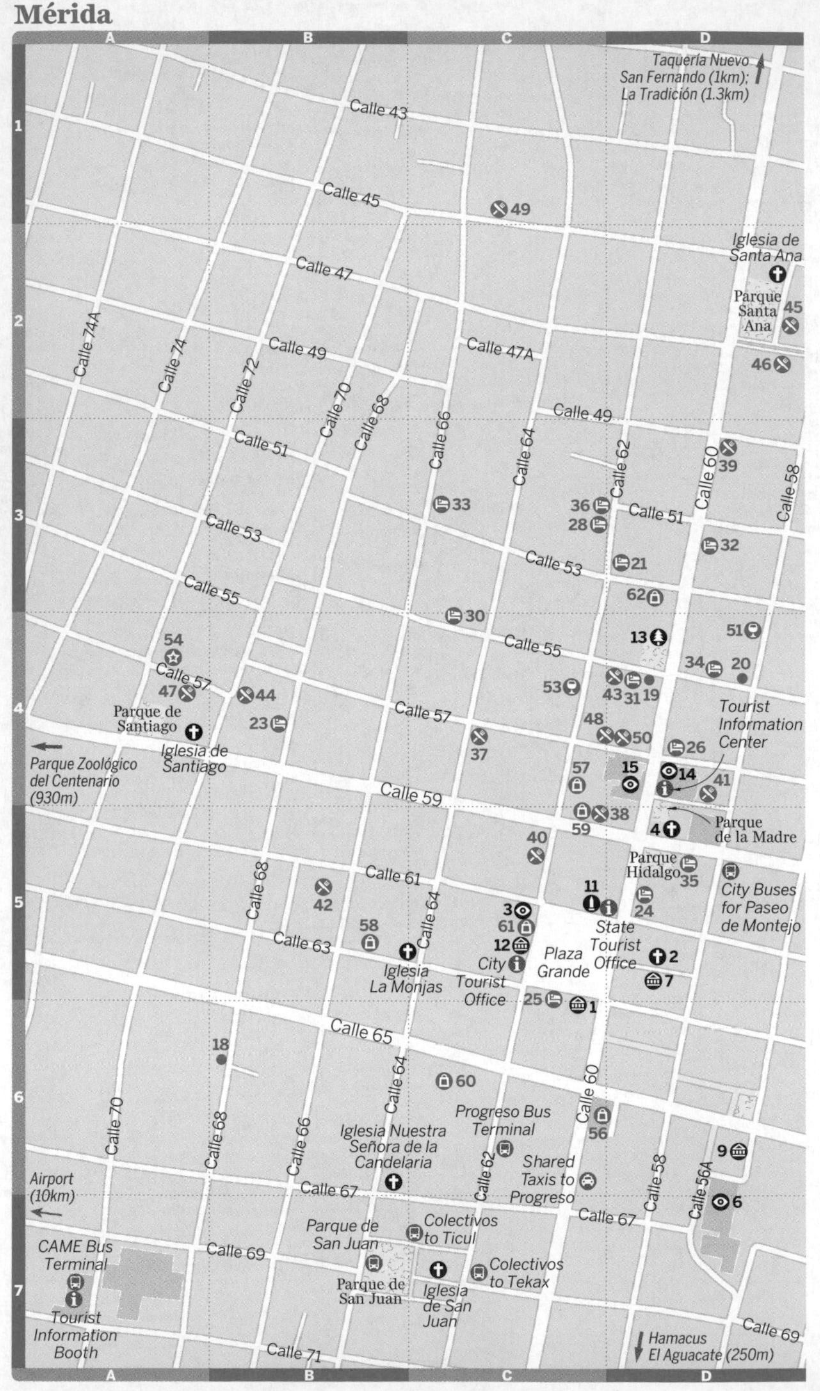

Taquería Nuevo San Fernando (1km); La Tradición (1.3km)
Calle 43
Calle 45
Calle 47
Calle 47A
Calle 49
Calle 51
Calle 53
Calle 55
Calle 57
Calle 59
Calle 61
Calle 63
Calle 65
Calle 67
Calle 69
Calle 71
Calle 74A
Calle 74
Calle 72
Calle 70
Calle 68
Calle 66
Calle 64
Calle 62
Calle 60
Calle 58
Calle 56A
Iglesia de Santa Ana
Parque Santa Ana
Parque de Santiago
Iglesia de Santiago
Parque Zoológico del Centenario (930m)
Tourist Information Center
Parque de la Madre
Parque Hidalgo
City Buses for Paseo de Montejo
State Tourist Office
Plaza Grande
City Tourist Office
Iglesia La Monjas
Progreso Bus Terminal
Iglesia Nuestra Señora de la Candelaria
Shared Taxis to Progreso
Airport (10km)
Parque de San Juan
Colectivos to Ticul
Colectivos to Tekax
Iglesia de San Juan
CAME Bus Terminal
Tourist Information Booth
Hamacus El Aguacate (250m)

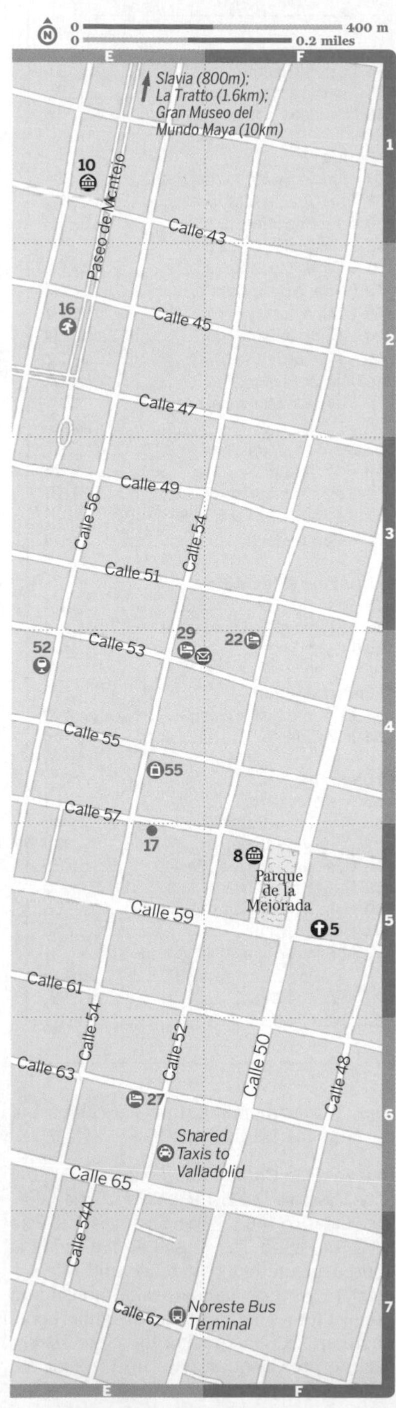

Museo de Arte Contemporáneo MUSEUM
(Macay; ☎928-3236; www.macay.org; Pasaje de la Revolución, btwn Calles 58 & 60; ⊙10am-6pm Wed-Mon) FREE Housed in the former archbishop's palace, the attractive Museo de Arte Contemporáneo holds permanent exhibitions of Yucatán's most famous painters and sculptors, as well as revolving exhibitions by local craftspeople.

Casa de Montejo MUSEUM
(Museo Casa Montejo; www.casasdeculturabanamex.com/museocasamontejo; Calle 63 No 506, Palacio de Montejo; ⊙10am-7pm Tue-Sat, 10am-2pm Sun) FREE Casa de Montejo is on the south side of the Plaza Grande and dates from 1549. It originally housed soldiers but was soon converted into a mansion that served members of the Montejo family until 1970. Today it houses a bank and museum with a permanent exhibition of renovated Victorian, neo-rococo and neo-renaissance furnishings of the historic building.

Outside, take a close look at the facade, where triumphant conquistadors with halberds hold their feet on the necks of generic barbarians (though they're not Maya, the association is inescapable). Typical of the symbolism in colonial statuary, the vanquished are rendered much smaller than the victors; works on various churches throughout the region feature big priests towering over or in front of small indigenous people. Also gazing across the plaza from the facade are busts of Montejo the Elder, his wife and his daughter.

Palacio Municipal HISTORIC BUILDING
(City Hall) Originally built in 1542, Mérida's Palacio Municipal was twice refurbished, in the 1730s and the 1850s.

Centro Cultural Olimpo CULTURAL BUILDING
(☎942-0000, ext 80125; www.merida.gob.mx/capitalcultural; cnr Calles 61 & 62) Adjoining the Palacio Municipal is the Centro Cultural Olimpo, Mérida's municipal cultural center. Attempts to create a modern exterior for the building were halted by government order to preserve the colonial character of the plaza. The ultramodern interior serves as a venue for music and dance performances, as well as other exhibitions. Schedules for performances are posted outside.

Palacio de Gobierno PUBLIC ART
(Calle 61; ⊙8am-9.30pm) FREE Built in 1892, the Palacio de Gobierno houses the state of Yucatán's executive government offices (and

Mérida

Sights

1 Casa de Montejo ... C6
2 Catedral de San Ildefonso ... D5
3 Centro Cultural Olimpo ... C5
4 Iglesia de Jesús ... D5
5 Iglesia La Mejorada ... F5
6 Mercado Municipal Lucas de Gálvez ... D7
7 Museo de Arte Contemporáneo ... D5
8 Museo de Arte Popular de Yucatán ... F5
9 Museo de la Ciudad ... D6
10 Museo Regional de Antropología ... E1
11 Palacio de Gobierno ... C5
12 Palacio Municipal ... C5
13 Parque Santa Lucía ... D4
14 Teatro Peón Contreras ... D4
15 Universidad Autónoma de Yucatán ... D4

Activities, Courses & Tours

16 Bici Mérida ... E2
City Tourist Office ... (see 12)
17 Instituto Benjamín Franklin ... E5
18 Los Dos ... B6
Nómadas Hostel ... (see 36)
19 Transportadora Turística Carnaval ... D4
20 Turitransmérida ... D4

Sleeping

21 Álvarez Family Guest House ... D3
22 Casa Ana B&B ... F4
23 Casa Mexilio ... B4
24 Gran Hotel ... D5
25 Hostel Zocalo ... C5
26 Hotel Casa del Balam ... D4
27 Hotel Dolores Alba ... E6
28 Hotel Hacienda Mérida ... C3
29 Hotel Julamis ... E4
30 Hotel Medio Mundo ... C4
31 Hotel Santa Lucía ... D4
32 Hotel Trinidad Galería ... D3
33 Los Arcos Bed & Breakfast ... C3
34 Luz en Yucatán ... D4
35 Mansión Mérida ... D5
36 Nómadas Hostel ... C3

Eating

37 Alberto's Continental Patio ... C4
38 Amaro ... C5
39 Café Chocolate ... D3
40 El Trapiche ... C5
41 Il Caffé Italiano ... D4
42 La Casa de Frida ... B5
43 La Chaya Maya ... D4
44 La Flor de Santiago ... B4
45 La Socorrito ... D2
46 Manjar Blanco ... D2
Mercado Municipal Lucas de Gálvez ... (see 6)
47 Mercado Municipal No 2 ... A4
48 Pop Cafetería ... C4
49 Restaurante Kantún ... C1
50 Restaurante Pórtico del Peregrino ... D4

Drinking & Nightlife

51 Casa Pompidou ... D4
52 La Fundación Mezcalería ... E4
53 Mayan Pub ... C4

Entertainment

Centro Cultural Olimpo ... (see 3)
54 MM Cinemas ... A4

Shopping

55 Alma Mexicana ... E4
56 Artesanías Bazar García Rejón ... C6
57 Camisería Canul ... C4
58 Casa de las Artesanías ... B5
59 Guayaberas Jack ... C5
60 Hamacas Mérida ... C6
61 Librería Dante ... C5
Mercado Municipal Lucas de Gálvez ... (see 6)
Miniaturas ... (see 59)
62 Tejon Rojo ... D3

a tourist office). Have a look inside at the murals painted by local artist Fernando Castro Pacheco. Completed in 1978, they were 25 years in the making and portray a symbolic history of the Maya and their interaction with the Spaniards.

Mercado Municipal Lucas de Gálvez
(Market; cnr Calles 56A & 67) Mérida's main market is an ever-evolving mass of commerce, with stalls selling everything from *panuchos* (fried tortillas stuffed with beans and topped with meat and veggies) to ponchos. The surrounding streets are all part of the large market district.

Museo de la Ciudad MUSEUM
(City Museum; ☎923-4273; Calle 56 No 529A, btwn Calles 65 & 67; ⏲9am-6pm Tue-Fri, to 2pm Sat & Sun) FREE The Museo de la Ciudad is housed in the old post office and offers a great reprieve from the hustle, honks and exhaust fumes of this market neighborhood. There are exhibits tracing the city's history back to pre-Conquest days up through the belle epoque period, when *henequén* (sisal)

brought riches to the region, and into the 20th century.

Parque Zoológico del Centenario ZOO
(www.merida.gob/centenario; cnr Av Itzáes & Calle 59; 6am-6pm Tue-Sun) FREE The large, verdant Parque Centenario, bordered by Av Itzáes, features lions, bears, an aviary, a playground and bumper boats. It's about 12 blocks west of Plaza Grande; to get here take a bus west along Calle 61 or 65.

Calle 60

Lined with many of the city's most emblematic sights, Calle 60 cuts through the heart of the Centro and farther north it runs parallel to Paseo de Montejo, a wide main avenue known for its elegant mansions.

Iglesia de Jesús CHURCH
(Calle 60) Just beyond shady Parque Hidalgo rises the 17th-century Iglesia de Jesús, also called Iglesia de la Tercera Orden. Built by Jesuits in 1618, this is the sole surviving edifice from a complex of buildings that once filled the entire city block. The church was built from the stones of a destroyed Maya temple that once occupied the same site. On the west wall facing Parque Hidalgo, look closely and you can see two stones still bearing Maya carvings.

Teatro Peón Contreras THEATER
(cnr Calles 60 & 57; 9am-6pm Tue-Sat) In front of the university building stands the enormous Teatro Peón Contreras, built between 1900 and 1908, during Mérida's *henequén* heyday. It boasts a main staircase of Carrara marble, a dome with faded frescoes by Italian artists, and various paintings and murals throughout the building. The **Yucatán Symphony Orchestra** performs here Friday evening and Sunday at noon.

Universidad Autónoma de Yucatán UNIVERSITY
(Calle 60) The modern Universidad de Yucatán was established in the 19th century by Governor Felipe Carrillo Puerto and General Manuel Cepeda Peraza. Inside you'll find the university cultural center, which stages dance, music and theater performances.

Parque Santa Lucía PARK
(cnr Calles 60 & 55) The pretty little Parque Santa Lucía has arcades on the north and west sides: when Mérida was a lot smaller, this was where travelers would get on or off the stagecoaches that linked towns and villages with the provincial capital.

The Bazar de Artesanías, the local handicrafts market, is held here at 11am on Sunday. At last visit, the park was getting revamped to make way for several new restaurants and shops.

Parque de la Mejorada

Head six blocks east of Calle 60 and you'll find this pleasant square flanked by a pretty colonial-era monastery and a small pop-art museum.

Iglesia La Mejorada CHURCH
Near Parque de la Mejorada stands Iglesia La Mejorada, a large 17th-century church. The building just north of it was a monastery (El Convento de La Mejorada) until the late 19th century. It now houses an architectural school, but visitors are sometimes allowed to view the grounds.

Museo de Arte Popular de Yucatán MUSEUM
(Yucatecan Museum of Popular Art; Calle 50A No 487; 10am-5pm Tue-Sat, to 3pm Sun) FREE In a 1906 building, the Museo de Arte Popular de Yucatán has a small rotating exhibition downstairs that features pop art from around Mexico. The upstairs exhibitions don't have any explanatory signs yet, but they give you an idea of how locals embroider *huipiles* (long, woven, white sleeveless tunics with intricate, colorful embroidery), carve ceremonial masks and weave hammocks.

Paseo de Montejo

Paseo de Montejo, which runs parallel to Calles 56 and 58, was an attempt by Mérida's 19th-century city planners to create a wide boulevard similar to the Paseo de la Reforma in Mexico City or the Champs-Élysées in Paris. Though more modest than its predecessors, the Paseo de Montejo is still a beautiful swath of green, relatively open space in an urban conglomeration of stone and concrete. There are occasional sculpture exhibits along the *paseo* (promenade).

Europe's architectural and social influence can be seen along the *paseo* in the fine mansions built by wealthy families around the end of the 19th century. The greatest concentrations of surviving mansions are north of Calle 37, and on the first block of Av Colón west of Paseo de Montejo.

Museo Regional de Antropología MUSEUM
(Regional Anthropology Museum of the Yucatán; ☎923-0557; www.palaciocanton.inah.gob.mx; Paseo de Montejo No 485; admission M$46; ⏰8am-5pm Tue-Sun) The massive Palacio Cantón houses the Museo Regional de Antropología. The museum covers the peninsula's history from the age of mastodons. If you plan to visit archaeological sites near Mérida, you can study the exhibits here covering the great Maya cities of Mayapán, Uxmal and Chichén Itzá, as well as lesser-known sites such as Ek' Balam.

Exhibits on Maya culture include explanations of such cosmetic practices as forehead-flattening (done to beautify babies), which caused eyes to cross, and sharpening teeth and implanting them with tiny jewels.

Construction of the mansion lasted from 1909 to 1911, and its owner, General Francisco Cantón Rosado (1833–1917), lived here for only six years before his death. The Palacio's splendor and pretension make it a fitting symbol of the grand aspirations of Mérida's elite during the last years of the Porfiriato – the period from 1876 to 1911 when Porfirio Díaz held despotic sway over Mexico.

Gran Museo del Mundo Maya MUSEUM
(www.granmuseodelmundomaya.com; Calle 60 Nte No 299E; adult/child under 12yr M$150/50; ⏰8am-5pm Wed-Mon) Considered an important addition to Mérida's rich cultural tradition, this new Maya-themed museum showcases a permanent exhibit of 500 artifacts ranging from stone sculptures and jewelry to ceramics and etchings. Opened in 2012, the museum is divided into six sections: ancient Maya, modern Maya, culture and nature, art and science, society, and world view.

Additionally, the museum offers a free light-and-sound show nightly at 9pm with images projected on a wall outside. There's also a 'Mayamax' movie theater here that screens mostly Hollywood movies in 2D and 3D. You'll find the museum about 12km north of downtown along the road to Progreso. Public transportation departing from Calle 58, between Calles 57 and 59, heads to the Gran Plaza mall, which is a short walk away from the museum.

Activities

Bicycling

In an effort to make the city more bike-friendly, Mérida closes down stretches of Paseo de Montejo and Calle 60 to traffic on Sunday morning. For night tours, the bicycle activist group **Cicloturixes** (www.cicloturixes.blogspot.mx) gathers at Parque Santa Ana, usually on Wednesdays at around 8pm. See their blog for times.

Bici Mérida BICYCLE RENTAL
(☎287-3538; Paseo de Montejo, btwn Calles 45 & 47; per hourM$20; ⏰4-11pm Mon-Sat, 7am-1pm Sun) Has mountain bikes, tandems, bicycles for kids and many other cool rides.

Courses

Instituto Benjamín Franklin LANGUAGE COURSE
(☎928-0097; www.benjaminfranklin.com.mx; Calle 57 No 474; per hour/4-week course M$155/9360) This nonprofit offers intensive Spanish-language courses and content courses on Mexican history for advanced students.

Los Dos COOKING COURSE
(www.los-dos.com; Calle 68 No 517; one-day course M$1625-2535) Run by US-educated chef David Sterling, this cooking school offers a wide variety of courses with a focus on flavors of the Yucatán. If you're sticking around for a while, look into its three-day or week-long culinary workshops.

Tours

City

City Tourist Office WALKING TOUR
(☎942-0000, ext 80119; www.merida.gob.mx/turismo; Calle 62, Plaza Grande; ⏰8am-8pm) The city tourist office runs free guided walking tours of the historic center departing daily from the Palacio Municipal at 9.30am. You can also rent audio guides here for M$80 if you prefer to go it alone.

Transportadora Turística Carnaval BUS TOUR
(☎927-6119; carnavalito@turitransmerida.com.mx; Calle 55, btwn Calles 60 & 62; tours M$90) Conducts two-hour guided tours of Mérida in English and Spanish on its Paseo Turístico bus departing from Parque Santa Lucía (on the corner of Calles 55 and 60) at 10am, 1pm, 4pm and 7pm Monday to Saturday, and 1pm and 3pm Sunday.

Regional

Nómadas Hostel TOUR
(☎924-5223; www.nomadastravel.com; Calle 62, No 433; tours to Celestún/Chichén Itzá M$575/330) Nómadas arranges a variety of tours, such as day trips with transportation and guide to the ecological reserve of Celestún and outings to the Maya ruins of Chichén Itzá. They're also more than happy to offer recommendations

DAY TRIPS FROM MÉRIDA

Mérida makes a great base for day trips to all kinds of interesting destinations in the countryside, from quiet coastal towns and fun-filled swimming holes to Maya ruins and excellent birding locations. Here are some worthwhile trips:

Cuzamá Three amazing cenotes (limestone sinkholes) can be accessed by horse-drawn cart (p166).

Ruta Puuc Ruin yourself by visiting all five sites (including megadraw Uxmal) in one day. Extend your trip by visiting Mayapán (p165) and the Loltún Caverns (p164).

Celestún Head out early to catch a mangrove birding boat tour (p170). For a bit more dough, you can visit the ruined haciendas along the way.

Dzibilchaltún & Progreso Visit the ruins and cenote (p172) or extend your trip for an afternoon of beach time in Progreso (p173).

Sisal This Gulf-coast town, about 60km northwest of Mérida, doesn't see much tourist traffic. There's a foggy-bottomed reef here, as well as a little shipwreck that you can snorkel out to. Plus, they release sea turtles during the month of August.

Bird-watching Yucatán state has 465 distinct bird species. To head out on a birding adventure, check out www.yucatanbirds.org.mx.

for DIY trips with written instructions detailing costs and transportation tips for more than a dozen destinations in the region.

Turitransmérida TOUR
(☎928-1871; www.turitransmerida.com.mx; cnr Calles 55 & 58; tours M$400-500) Turitransmérida is one of the largest of the many agencies offering group tours to sites around Mérida, including Celestún, Chichén Itzá, the Ruta Puuc and Izamal.

Oriente BUS TOUR
(tours M$178; ⏰Sun) Bus line Oriente runs a day tour to Uxmal, Kabah and the Ruta Puuc sites, departing from the Terminal de Segunda Clase (2nd-class terminal) in Mérida at 8am and returning to the city at 4pm.

Ecoturismo Yucatán ECOTOUR
(☎920-2772; www.ecoyuc.com.mx; Calle 3 No 235) The owners of reputable Ecoturismo Yucatán are passionate about both sharing and protecting the state's natural treasures. Trips focus on archaeology, birding, natural history, biking and kayaking. One-day excursions to Chichén Itzá or Uxmal cost M$700 and include entrance fees.

Festivals & Events

Mérida Fest CULTURAL
(www.merida.gob.mx/capitalcultural) This cultural event held throughout most of January celebrates the founding of the city with art exhibits, concerts, theater and book presentations at various venues.

Anniversary of the Universidad Autónoma de Yucatán CULTURAL
For most of February the Universidad de Yucatán celebrates its anniversary with free performances by the Ballet Folklórico, concerts of Afro-Cuban music and *son* (Mexican folk music that blends elements of indigenous, Spanish and African musical styles), and other manifestations of Yucatán's cultural roots.

Carnaval RELIGIOUS
Prior to Lent, in February or March, Carnaval features colorful costumes and nonstop festivities. It's celebrated with greater vigor in Mérida than anywhere else in Yucatán state.

Semana Santa RELIGIOUS
(Holy Week) A major celebration in Mérida over Easter week. The main feature of the celebrations is the city's Passion Plays.

Primavera Cultural MUSIC
A month-long festival in May celebrates *trova* (Latin American protest music and ballads) and just about any other music genre you can imagine.

Exposición de Altares de los Muertos RELIGIOUS
A big religious tradition. Throughout Mexico families prepare shrines to welcome the spirits of loved ones back to earth for Day of the Dead. Many Maya prepare elaborate dinners outside their homes, and Mérida observes the occasion with festivities and

displays in the town center from 11am on November 1 until 11am the next day.

Sleeping

Budget rooms generally have fans; spending the extra money for air-con is well worth it in the hotter months.

★Nómadas Hostel HOSTEL $
(924-5223; www.nomadastravel.com; Calle 62 No 433; dm incl breakfast M$129, d incl breakfast with/without bathroom M$420/320;) This is hands down Mérida's best hostel. There are mixed and women's dorms, as well as private rooms. Guests have use of a fully equipped kitchen with fridge, showers and hand-laundry facilities. It even has free salsa classes and an amazing pool out back. Luggage lockers are free during your stay and M$15 a day while you travel.

Álvarez Family Guest House GUESTHOUSE $
(924-3060; www.casaalvarezguesthouse.com; Calle 62 No 448, btwn Calles 51 & 53; d with fan/air-con M$500/600, ste M$700;) Impeccably clean and in a family's home, this guesthouse offers a friendly, one-of-the-family ambience, along with nice showers, spotless bathrooms and in-room fridges. The house is full of beautiful antiques, including an old cylinder-style gramophone player. Guests have use of a kitchen and a new plunge pool out back.

Casa Ana B&B B&B $
(934-0005; www.casaana.com; Calle 52 No 469; r incl breakfast from M$520;) Though out of the way, Casa Ana is an intimate escape and one of the best deals in town. It has a small natural-bottom pool and a cozy overgrown garden complete with Cuban tobacco plants (memories of home for the Cuban owners, no doubt). The rooms are spotless and have Mexican hammocks and (whew) mosquito screens.

Hostel Zocalo HOSTEL $
(930-9562; hostal_zocalo@yahoo.com.mx; Calle 63 No 508; dm incl breakfast M$100, r with/without bathroom incl breakfast M$330/280;) Great location and a beautiful old colonial building make this hostel unique. It has firm beds and a big buffet breakfast. The service can be a bit gruff, though, and you may have problems getting hot water.

Hotel Santa Lucía HOTEL $
(928-2672; www.hotelsantalucia.com.mx; Calle 55 No 508; s/d/tr M$410/490/550;) Across from the park of the same name, this centrally located hotel is clean, secure and popular, and has an attractive lobby. The pool is small but clean, and the rooms have TV, phone and just so-so mattresses. Someone here really likes potted plants.

Hotel Trinidad Galería HOTEL $
(923-2463; www.hotelestrinidad.com; Calle 60 No 456; r with fan/air-con M$395/475;) It's like walking into the 'General's Labyrinth' or a Salvador Dalí dream: odd – even freakish – artwork and statuary gather dust in every corner of this rambling hotel. You will either love this wacky place or find it disquieting. The rooms vary considerably: some are dark and musty, while others offer well-vented bathrooms with good mosquito screens. All rooms have original artwork and interesting posted rules, which include: 'All deaths will be reported to the authorities.' The art is the main reason to come here, a refreshing change from the usual framed poster. Even if you don't stay, it's worth popping your head in. For more rooms check out sister property **Hotel Trinidad** (Calle 62, btwn Calles 55 & 57).

★Luz en Yucatán BOUTIQUE HOTEL $$
(924-0035; www.luzenyucatan.com; Calle 55 No 499; r M$700-850, house M$1800;) While many much blander hotels are loudly claiming to be 'boutique,' this one is quietly ticking all the boxes – individually decorated rooms, fabulous common areas and a wonderful pool/patio area out back. The house it offers for rent across the road, which sleeps seven people and has a hot tub, is just as good, if not better.

Hotel Julamis BOUTIQUE HOTEL $$
(924-1818, in USA 305-677-9560; www.hoteljulamis.com; Calle 53 No 475; r/ste incl breakfast from M$560/1090;) Reserve well in advance if you expect to stay at this highly popular boutique hotel. Each room is different but all offer wonderful details: some have original hardwood floors, while others have tasteful murals. All rooms come with fridges that are stocked daily with free beverages.

Hotel Medio Mundo HOTEL $$
(924-5472; www.hotelmediomundo.com; Calle 55 No 533; d incl breakfast M$910-1105;) This former private residence has been completely remodeled and painted in lovely colors. Its ample, simply furnished rooms have supercomfortable beds, beautiful tiled

sinks and plenty of natural light. One of the two courtyards has a small swimming pool, the other a fountain. The well-traveled, charming hosts make their guests feel at home.

Gran Hotel HOTEL **$$**
(☎923-6963; www.granhoteldemerida.com; Calle 60 No 496; s/d M$585/795; P ❄ ✆) This was indeed a grand hotel when built in 1901. Some rooms in this old-timer got a recent makeover; others have the same old period furnishings and faded carpets. Despite the wear, they retain many elegant and delightful decorative flourishes.

Hotel Dolores Alba HOTEL **$$**
(☎928-5650; www.doloresalba.com; Calle 63, btwn Calles 52 & 54; d incl breakfast M$550-750; P ❄ ✆ ≋) Rooms here are on three floors (with an elevator) around two large courtyards. Those in the pricier, modern wing have shiny new tile floors and flat-screen TVs, and they face the lovely pool. The hotel has secure parking and is quiet, well managed and friendly.

Los Arcos Bed & Breakfast B&B **$$$**
(☎928-0214; www.losarcosmerida.com; Calle 66 No 448B; d incl breakfast M$1235; ✆ ≋) Certainly not for minimalists – there's art on every wall – Los Arcos is a lovely, gay-friendly B&B with two guestrooms at the end of a drop-dead-gorgeous garden and pool area. Rooms have an eclectic assortment of art and antiques, excellent beds and bathrooms.

Hotel Casa del Balam HOTEL **$$$**
(☎924 2150; www.hotelcasadelbalam.com; Calle 60 No 488; d/ste incl breakfast from M$1200/1500; ❄ ✆ ≋) This place is centrally located, with a great pool and large, quiet colonial-style rooms with firm beds. It often offers hefty discounts during quiet times.

Casa Mexilio GUESTHOUSE **$$$**
(☎928-2505; www.casamexilio.com; Calle 68 No 495; r incl breakfast M$1235; P ❄ ✆ ≋) It occupies a well-preserved, historic house with a maze of quiet, beautifully appointed rooms (all with air-con), and a small pool with Jacuzzi. A full breakfast in the period dining room is included, and the tapas bar on the roof is always a hit. Children under 14 not allowed.

Hotel Hacienda Mérida BOUTIQUE HOTEL **$$$**
(☎924-4363; www.hotelhaciendamerida.com; Calle 62, btwn Calles 51 & 53; r/ste from M$2030/2810; P ❄ ✆ ≋) A newish entrant in the upscale boutique category, the Hacienda is lovely by night, with illuminated columns leading you past the pool to your classically styled chambers. For all-out luxury consider upgrading to a 'VIP' room.

Mansión Mérida LUXURY HOTEL **$$$**
(☎924 4642; www.mansionmerida.mx; Calle 59 No 498; r incl breakfast M$4290-7800) Even if you can't afford to stay in this French-style colonial 'palace,' it's worth taking a peek inside. Rooms and common areas in the restored 19th-century building are elegant, spacious and fit for a king, as the price reflects.

Eating

Don't miss 'Mérida en Domingo,' an all-day food and crafts market on the main plaza every Sunday. It's a great place to try a wide array of regional dishes, and the food is cheap, too!

Mercado Municipal Lucas de Gálvez MARKET **$**
(cnr Calles 56A & 67; mains & ceviche M$60; ⏲6am-5pm) Some of Mérida's least expensive eateries. Upstairs joints have tables and chairs and more diverse menus offering main courses of beef, fish or chicken; look for *recados* (spice pastes). Downstairs at the north end are some cheap *taquerías* (taco stalls), while near the south end are *coctelerías* – seafood shacks specializing in shellfish cocktails as well as *ceviche* (seafood marinated in lemon or lime juice, garlic and seasonings).

Café Chocolate CAFE **$**
(www.cafe-chocolate.com.mx; Calle 60 No 442; breakfast buffets M$69, mains M$69-89; ⏲7am-midnight Mon-Sat; ✆ ✎) The food is excellent at this colonial cafe – and vegetarian-friendly to boot. Sandwiches and paninis are made with homemade bread; there's a sandwich with baked ham marinated in white *recado* (try finding that one at the coffee shop back home). There's also an art gallery here.

El Trapiche MEXICAN **$**
(☎928-1231; Calle 62 No 491; mains M$26-90; ⏲8am-midnight; ✎) A great place close to the Centro, El Trapiche has cheap Mexican eats in a casual environment. It bills itself as the best pizza joint in town, but it's actually the *yucateco* dishes that stand out. The menu has a fair share of vegetarian options.

THE COCHINITA QUEST

It seems like just about everyone in Mérida has an opinion on where you can get the best *cochinita pibil* (slow-cooked pork marinated in citrus juice and annatto spice). *Cochinita* is prepared in tacos, *tortas* (sandwiches) or as a main dish. Here are some of our picks.

La Socorrito (Calle 47, btwn Calles 58 & 60; tortas M$17; ⏲6am-2pm) These old pros started slow-cooking *cochinita* in underground pits more than six decades ago. You'll find this delightful hole-in-the-wall on the plaza side of the Mercado de Santa Ana.

Taquería Nuevo San Fernando (Av Cupules, btwn Calles 60 & 62; tortas M$20; ⏲7am-1pm) Out-of-towners staying in the nearby business-class hotels have been known to buy kilos of this stuff to take back home with them. The freshmade bread, roasted habanero salsa and tender *cochinita* is *that* good.

La Tradición (www.latradicionmerida.com; cnr Calles 60 & 25; mains M$105-180; ⏲11am-6pm) For a more upscale take on *cochinita*, cloth napkin and all, this popular restaurant serves a generous portion accompanied with pickled red onion and handmade tortillas..

La Flor de Santiago CAFE **$**
(☎928-5591; Calle 70, btwn Calles 57 & 59; mains M$45-89; ⏲7am-11pm) Chiapas coffee is served in incongruous Willow-ware cups in this cafeteria-style eatery. There is a wide selection of *yucateco* comfort foods, such as *poc-chuc* (grilled pork) and lime soup. A breakfast buffet on Saturday and Sunday costs M$90.

Mercado Municipal No 2 MARKET **$**
(Calle 70; mains M$40-60; ⏲8am-4pm) Numero Dos is less crowded than Mercado Municipal Lucas de Gálvez, but the market is still cheap and good. On the north side of Parque de Santiago, it's packed with juice stalls, *loncherías* (simple restaurants only open for lunch) and even a cheap ice-cream place.

★La Chaya Maya MEXICAN **$$**
(Calle 55 No 510; mains M$57-175; ⏲7am-11pm) Popular with locals and tourists alike, this restaurant recently opened a new location in a lovely downtown colonial building. Consider La Chaya Maya your introduction to classic *yucateco* fare like *relleno negro* (black turkey stew) or *cochinita pibil* (slow-cooked pork). The original location is at the corner of Calles 62 and 57.

★Manjar Blanco MEXICAN **$$**
(Calle 47, btwn Calles 58 & 60; mains M$70-110; ⏲8am-6pm) This family-run restaurant puts a gourmet twist on regional favorites. The *tortillitas tropicales* (fried plantains topped with smoked pork) are delicious, and sweet tooths will love the namesake *manjar blanco* (a coconut-cream dessert).

Amaro INTERNATIONAL **$$**
(☎928-2451; www.restauranteamaro.com; Calle 59 No 507; mains M$90-175; ⏲11am-2am; 🌶) This romantic dining spot (especially at night, when there's performing *trova* acts) is in the courtyard of the house where Andrés Quintana Roo – poet, statesman and drafter of Mexico's Declaration of Independence – was born in 1787. The menu includes *yucateco* dishes and a variety of vegetarian plates, as well as some continental dishes.

La Casa de Frida MEXICAN **$$**
(www.lacasadefrida.com.mx; Calle 61 No 526; mains M$120-175; ⏲6-10pm Mon-Sat) Go here for delicious duck in *mole* sauce or another well-prepared Mexican classic, *chile en nogada* (stuffed poblano chili). Don't be surprised if pet bunny Coco hops into the dining area to greet you. No rabbit on the menu here.

Restaurante Kantún SEAFOOD **$$**
(☎286-4318; reskantun@hotmail.com; Calle 45 No 525C; mains M$62-125; ⏲noon-7pm Mon-Sat, to 6pm Sun) The Kantún serves some of the best seafood in town, but be patient because all dishes are prepared to order. Try the *filete Normanda*, a fillet stuffed with smoked oysters and topped with anchovies. There are a few meat offerings for nonfishy types. The service is friendly and attentive, if almost formal at times.

Pop Cafetería CAFE **$$**
(☎928-6163; Calle 57, btwn Calles 60 & 62; breakfasts M$45-70, lunches M$65-100; ⏲7am-midnight Mon-Sat, from 8am Sun) There's an art deco bebop feel to this little cafeteria-style restau-

rant, which serves cheap breakfast combinations and a good variety of Mexican dishes; try the chicken in dark, rich *mole* sauce.

Restaurante Pórtico del Peregrino MEXICAN **$$**
(☎928-6163; Calle 57, btwn Calles 60 & 62; mains M$80-150; ⊙noon midnight) There are several pleasant, traditional-style dining rooms surrounding a small courtyard in this upscale eatery. *Yucateco* dishes such as *pollo pibil* (chicken flavored with *achiote* – annatto spice – sauce and wrapped in banana leaves) are its forte, but you'll find many international dishes and a broad range of seafood and steaks, too. *Mole poblano,* a chocolate and chili sauce, is a house specialty.

La Tratto ITALIAN **$$**
(☎927-0434; www.trottersmerida.com; Av Prolongación Montejo 479C; mains M$115-149; ⊙6pm-3am) A sidewalk bistro known for its gourmet pizzas, handmade pastas and excellent wine list. It's about three blocks north of Monumento a la Bandera. To get here, catch a 'San Lucas' bus from Calles 59 and 56 in downtown.

Il Caffé Italiano CAFE **$$**
(☎928-0093; Calle 57A, btwn Calles 58 & 60; mains M$100-160; ⊙3.30-11pm Mon-Thu, 3.30pm-2am Fri & Sat) An Italian-style cafe with piping-hot espressos, good mains and tasty desserts like *panna cotta* topped with raspberry sauce.

Alberto's Continental Patio MIDDLE EASTERN **$$$**
(☎928-5367; cnr Calles 64 & 57; mains M$150-215, set dinners M$225-275; ⊙1-11pm Mon-Sat, 6-11pm Sun;) The colonial-courtyard setting here is extremely atmospheric, chock-full of religious artifacts, Maya ceramic figures and greenery. Middle Eastern dishes such as hummus, baba ghanoush and tabbouleh can be a welcome change from Mexican food. The steaks, poultry and seafood are also good, as is the service.

Drinking & Nightlife

You need not look far to find a friendly neighborhood bar.

★La Fundación Mezcalería BAR
(Calle 56 No 465; ⊙8pm-3am Wed-Sat) A popular bicyclists' hangout, especially on Wednesdays, this retro-styled bar has an excellent selection of organic *mezcals* (an alcoholic agave drink) and an atmosphere conducive to knocking 'em back. Careful though: the stuff packs a mean punch.

Casa Pompidou BAR
(Calle 58, btwn Calles 53 & 55; ⊙10am-3pm Thu-Sat) Part bar, part art gallery, Casa Pompidou packs them in on weekends with live DJ sets in an open-air patio with colorful murals. The *casa* also has a pebbly restaurant area where you can order wood-fired pizza, and the art gallery's small exhibitions are usually worth checking out.

Mayan Pub BAR
(www.mayanpub.com; Calle 62, btwn Calles 55 & 57; ⊙7pm-3am Wed-Sun) Popular with backpackers and *meridiano* (local) would-be backpackers, this place keeps it real with a pool table, a big beer garden and live music.

Slavia BAR
(cnr Paseo de Montejo & Calle 29; ⊙7pm-2am) Jam-packed with Asian knickknacks and serving up fusion food in a casual environment, Slavia hosts DJ sessions from Thursday to Saturday.

Entertainment

Mérida offers many folkloric and musical events in parks and historic buildings, put on by local performers of considerable skill. Admission is mostly free. The website www.yucatantoday.com offers monthly news and often highlights seasonal events.

Movies are often dubbed in Spanish; check beforehand.

Centro Cultural Olimpo CONCERT VENUE
(☎924-0000, ext 80152; cnr Calles 62 & 61) Offers something nearly every night: films, concerts, art installations, you name it.

MM Cinemas CINEMA
(www.cinemex.com; Calle 57, btwn Calles 70 & 72; matinee/general tickets M$15/35) Screens first-run Hollywood movies, either dubbed in Spanish or in English with Spanish subtitles.

Shopping

Guayaberas Jack CLOTHING
(www.guayaberasjack.com.mx; Calle 59 No 507A; ⊙10am-8.30pm Mon-Sat, to 2.30pm Sun) The *guayabera* (embroidered men's dress shirt) is the classic Mérida shirt, but in buying the wrong one you run the risk of looking like a waiter. Drop into this famous shop to avoid getting asked for the bill.

CRAFTS & TRADITIONAL WEAR

The Yucatán is a fine place for buying handicrafts and traditional clothes. Purchases to consider include *guayaberas*, colorfully embroidered *huipiles* and, of course, wonderfully comfortable hammocks.

Women throughout the Yucatán Peninsula traditionally wear straight, white cotton dresses called *huipiles*, the bodices of which are always embroidered. You'll come across these loose-fitting garments in many markets across the peninsula.

Men commonly wear *guayaberas* (light, elegant shirts, usually with four square pockets). They can be worn in both casual and formal settings, and the cotton and linen materials keep the body cool on warm, humid days.

You'll also find craft shops and street stalls selling wooden handicrafts of Spanish galleons and carvings of Maya deities. Campeche is the state most associated with such items, but they are made by accomplished artisans in the states of Yucatán and Quintana Roo as well.

For more on handicrafts, pick up a copy of *The Crafts of Mexico*, by Margarita de Orellana and Alberto Ruy Sánchez.

Alma Mexicana ARTS & CRAFTS
(www.casaesperanza.com; Calle 54, btwn Calles 55 & 57; ⏲9.30am-6pm Mon-Sat, 11am-3pm Sun) Sells Mexican folk art and crafts as well as other interesting gift items.

Mercado Municipal Lucas de Gálvez MARKET
(cnr Calles 56A & 67) Mérida's main market is a great spot to pick up that perfect piece of kitsch.

Tejon Rojo SOUVENIRS
(tejonrojomex@hotmail.com; Calle 53 No 503; ⏲1-9.30pm Mon-Sat) Sells trendy graphic T-shirts and an assortment of Mexican pop culture souvenirs.

Casa de las Artesanías HANDICRAFTS
(☎928-6676; Calle 63, btwn Calles 64 & 66; ⏲9.30am-10pm Mon-Sat) One place to start looking for handicrafts is this government-supported market for local artisans selling just about everything. Prices are fixed.

Artesanías Bazar García Rejón HANDICRAFTS
(cnr Calles 60 & 65) A wide variety of products concentrated into one area of shops.

Miniaturas HANDICRAFTS
(☎928-6503; Calle 59, btwn Calles 60 & 62; ⏲10am-8pm) Here you'll find lots of small Día de Muertos (Day of the Dead) tableaux, tinwork and figurines of every sort, from ceramics to toy soldiers. They all have two things in common: they're easy to pack and have nothing to do with yucateno artisan traditions!

Camisería Canul CLOTHING
(☎923-5661; www.camiseriacanul.com.mx; Calle 62 No 484; ⏲9am-8pm Mon-Sat, 10am-2pm Sun) A good place for *guayaberas* and *huipiles*. It has been in business for years, offers fixed prices and does custom tailoring.

Librería Dante BOOKS
(www.editorialdante.com; cnr Calles 61 & 62, Plaza Grande; ⏲8am-10.30pm Mon-Sat, to 9.30pm Sun) Has a small selection of paperbacks in English, as well as some guidebooks, and a large selection of archaeology books in English, French, German and Spanish. There are other branches throughout the city.

Orientation

The Plaza Grande has been the city's heart since the time of the Maya. Though Mérida now sprawls several kilometers in all directions, most of the services and attractions for visitors are within 10 blocks of the Plaza Grande. Following the classic colonial plan, the square is ringed by several barrios (neighborhoods), each with its own park and church.

Odd-numbered streets run east–west; even-numbered streets run north–south. House numbers may increase very slowly, and addresses are usually given in this form: 'Calle 57 No 481 x 46 y 48' (between streets 46 and 48).

Information

EMERGENCY

Emergency (☎066)
Fire (☎924-9242)
Red Cross (☎924-9813)
Tourist Police (☎924-0060)

INTERNET ACCESS

Most internet places around town charge M$10 per hour. The Plaza Grande and several other downtown plazas are wi-fi hot spots.

Chandler's Internet (Calle 61, btwn Calles 60 & 62; per hr M$15; ⏲9am-11pm) Inside the commercial plaza.

MEDIA

Yucatán Today (www.yucatantoday.com) A free Spanish/English magazine devoted to tourism in Yucatán. Pick up a copy of the magazine or visit the website for great tips.

MEDICAL SERVICES

The website for the US consulate in Mérida (http://merida.usconsulate.gov) has a good list of doctors and hospitals.

Hospital O'Horán (☎930-3320; cnr Av de los Itzáes & Av Jacinto Canek) A centrally located public hospital for emergencies. For less urgent matters, such as prescriptions and consultations, consider going to a private clinic.

MONEY

Banks and ATMs are scattered throughout the city. There is a cluster of both along Calle 65 between Calles 60 and 62, one block south of the Plaza Grande. *Casas de cambio* (money-exchange offices) have faster service and longer opening hours than banks, but often with poorer rates.

POST

Main Post Office (☎928-5404; Calle 53 No 469, btwn Calles 52 & 54; ⏲9am-4pm Mon-Fri, 9am-noon Sat)

TELEPHONE

Card phones can be found throughout the city. Internet cafes also offer VOIP-based phone services.

TOURIST INFORMATION

The tourist-information booths at the airport and the CAME bus terminal have coupons for lodging discounts and hotel suggestions. Three tourist offices downtown have more current information, brochures, bus schedules and maps.

City Tourist Office (☎942-0000; Calle 62, Plaza Grande; ⏲8am-8pm Mon-Sat, to 2pm Sun) Just south of the main entrance to the Palacio Municipal, it is staffed with helpful English speakers. It offers free walking tours of the city at 9.30am, as well as audio guides for M$80.

State Tourist Office (☎930-3101; Calle 61, Plaza Grande; ⏲8am-9pm Mon-Sat, 8am-8pm Sun) In the entrance to the Palacio de Gobierno. There's usually an English speaker on hand.

Tourist Information Center (☎924-9290; cnr Calles 60 & 57A; ⏲8am-9pm Mon-Sat, to 8pm Sun) On the southwest edge of the Teatro Peón Contreras, this office always has an English-speaker on hand.

Getting There & Away

AIR

Mérida's tiny airport is a 10km, 20-minute ride southwest of the Plaza Grande off Hwy 180 (Av

YUCATECO HAMMOCKS: THE ONLY WAY TO SLEEP

Yucateco hammocks are normally woven from strong nylon or cotton string and dyed in various colors. There are also natural, undyed cotton versions. Some sellers will try to fob these off as *henequén* or jute, telling you it's much more durable (and valuable) than cotton, and even that it repels mosquitoes. Don't be taken in; real *henequén* hammocks are very rough and not something you'd want near your skin. Silk hammocks are no longer made, but a silk-rayon blend has a similar feel.

Hammocks come in several widths, and though much is made of the quantity of pairs of end strings they possess, a better gauge of a hammock's size and quality is its weight. The heavier the better. A *sencilla* (for one person) should be about 500g and cost around M$250. The queen, at 1100g, runs about M$350, and a 1500g-king usually starts at M$400. *De croché* (very tightly woven) hammocks can take several weeks to produce and cost double or triple the prices given here.

Some good spots for buying a hammock:

Hamacas El Aguacate (☎289-5789; www.hamacaselaguacate.com.mx; cnr Calles 58 & 73; ⏲8.30am-7.30pm Mon-Fri, 9am-5pm Sat) Hamacas El Aguacate has quality hammocks and decent prices, and there's absolutely no hard sell.

Hamacas Mérida (☎924-0440; www.hamacasmerida.com.mx; Calle 65, btwn Calles 62 & 64; ⏲9am-7pm Mon-Fri, to 2pm Sat) Has a large catalogue with all kinds of sizes, shapes and colors, plus worldwide shipping.

Tixkokob This weaving town about 20km east of Mérida on Hwy 80 is famous for it quality hammocks. Frequent buses (M$14) to Tixkokob depart from Calle 65, between Calles 48 and 50.

de los Itzáes). It has car rental desks, an ATM, a currency-exchange office and a tourist information booth.

Most international flights to Mérida are connections through Mexico City. Nonstop international services are provided by Aeroméxico and United Airlines.

Low-cost airlines Interjet and Vivaaerobus serve Mexico City. MayaAir runs prop planes to Cancún.

Aeroméxico (☎800-021-4000; www.aeromexico.com) Flies direct from Miami.

Interjet (☎800-011-2345, in USA 866-285-9525; www.interjet.com)

MayaAir (☎987-872-3609; www.maya-air.com)

United Airlines (☎926-3100, in USA 800-900-50-00; www.united.com; Paseo Montejo No 437, at Calle 29) Flies nonstop from Houston.

Vivaaerobus (☎in Mexico City 554-777-5050, in USA 888-935-9848; www.vivaaerobus.com)

BUS

Mérida is the bus transportation hub of the Yucatán Peninsula. Take care with your bags on night buses and those serving popular tourist destinations (especially 2nd-class buses); there have been reports of theft on some routes.

There are a number of bus terminals, and some lines operate from (and stop at) more than one terminal. Tickets for departure from one terminal can often be bought at another, and destinations overlap greatly among bus lines. Some lines offer round-trip tickets to nearby towns that reduce the fare quite a bit. Check out www.boletotal.mx for good ticket info. Following are some of the terminals, the bus lines operating from them and the areas served.

CAME Bus Terminal (☎reservations 920-4444; Calle 70, btwn Calles 69 & 71) Sometimes referred to as the Terminal de Primera Clase, Mérida's main bus terminal has (mostly 1st-class) buses – including ADO, OCC and ADO GL – to points around the Yucatán Peninsula and faraway places such as Mexico City.

Fiesta Americana Bus Terminal (☎920-5523; Av Colón, near Calle 56A) A small 1st-class terminal on the west side of the hotel complex servicing guests of the luxury hotels on Av Colón, north of the city center. The ADO buses run between here and Cancún, Villahermosa and Ciudad del Carmen.

Noreste Bus Terminal (Calle 67, btwn Calles 50 & 52) Noreste, Sur and Oriente bus lines use this terminal. Destinations served from here include many small towns in the northeast part of the peninsula, including Tizimín and Río Lagartos; Cancún and points along the way; and small towns south and west of Mérida, including Celestún (served by Occidente), Ticul, Ruinas de Mayapán and Oxkutzcab.

Some Oriente buses depart from Terminal de Segunda Clase and stop here; others depart from here (eg those to Izamal and Tizimín).

Parque de San Juan (Calle 69, btwn Calles 62 & 64) From all around the square and church, vans and *combis* (vans or minibuses) depart for Dzibilchaltún, Muna, Oxkutzcab, Tekax, Ticul and other points.

Progreso Bus Terminal (Calle 62 No 524) There's a separate terminal with buses leaving for Progreso (one-way M$16, every 10 minutes).

Terminal de Segunda Clase (Calle 69) Also known as Terminal 69 (Sesenta y Nueve) or simply Terminal de Autobuses, this terminal is just around the corner from the CAME bus terminal. ADO, Mayab, Oriente and Sur run mostly 2nd-class buses to points in the state and around the peninsula.

CAR

The most flexible way to tour the many archaeological sites around Mérida is to travel with a rental car. Assume you will pay M$600 to M$700 per day (tax, insurance and gas included) for short-term rental of a cheap car. Getting around Mérida's sprawling tangle of one-way streets and careening buses is better done on foot or on a careening bus.

Several agencies have branches at the airport as well as on Calle 60 between Calles 55 and 57. You'll get the best deal by booking online.

There is an expensive toll highway between Mérida and Cancún (M$397).

Easy Way (☎930-9500; www.easywayrentacar-yucatan.com; Calle 60 No 484, btwn Calles 55 & 57; ⏲7am-11pm)

National (☎923-2493; www.nationalcar.com; Calle 60 No 486F, btwn Calles 55 & 57; ⏲7am-10pm)

ℹ Getting Around

TO/FROM THE AIRPORT

Transporte Terrestre (☎946-1529) provides speedy service between the airport and downtown, charging M$180 per carload (same price for hotel pick-up). A street taxi from the city center to the airport should cost about M$80 to M$100. If you want to get this same price *from* the airport, you'll need to walk out to the main street and flag down a city cab.

A city bus labeled 'Aviación' travels between the main road of the airport entrance (the bus does not enter the airport) and the city center every 15 to 30 minutes until 9pm, with occasional service until 11pm. The half-hour trip (M$8) is via a roundabout route; the best place to catch the bus to the airport is on Calle 70, south of Calle 69, near the CAME bus terminal.

BUS

Most parts of Mérida that you'll want to visit are within five or six blocks of the Plaza Grande. Given the slow speed of city traffic, particularly in the market areas, travel on foot is also the fastest way to get around.

City buses are cheap at M$8, but routes can be confusing. Most start in suburban neighborhoods, skirt the city center and terminate in another distant suburban neighborhood.

To travel between the Plaza Grande and the upscale neighborhoods to the north along Paseo de Montejo, catch the Ruta 164 on the corners of Calles 59 and 58, a block north of the Parque Hidalgo, or catch a 'Tecnológico', 'Hyatt' or 'Montejo' bus on Calle 60 and get off at Av Colón. To return to the city center, catch any bus heading south on Paseo de Montejo displaying the same signs and/or 'Centro.'

TAXI

More and more taxis in town are using meters these days. If you get one with no meter, be sure to agree on a price before getting in; M$30 to M$40 is fair for getting around downtown and to the bus terminals. Taxi stands can be found at most of the barrio parks, or dial ☎928-3035 for a radio taxi (dispatch fees may cost an additional M$10 to M$20).

SOUTH OF MÉRIDA

There's a lot to do and see south of Mérida. The major draws are the old *henequén* plantations, some still used for cultivating leaves, and the well-preserved Maya ruins like Uxmal and the lesser-known sites along the Ruta Puuc. Beyond these tourist draws you'll find seldom-visited cenotes and caves, and traditional villages where life moves at an agrarian pace: women wear *huipiles* and speak Yucatec Maya, and men still bike out to cut firewood or shoot a pheasant for dinner. The smell of tortillas mixes with the citrus-like smell of the semiarid plants. It's a rough-and-tumble landscape, and one of the few spots on the peninsula where you'll actually find some hills.

BUSES FROM MÉRIDA

DESTINATION	FARE (M$)	DURATION (HR)	FREQUENCY
Campeche	122-180	2½-3	frequent
Cancún	180-290	4½-6½	frequent
Celestún	49	2½	frequent; Noreste terminal
Chetumal	246-366	6-8	8 daily
Chichén Itzá	68-114	1½	frequent; CAME and Noreste terminal
Escárcega	213-284	5-5½	10 daily
Felipe Carrillo Puerto	192	6½	9 daily
Izamal	23	1½	frequent; Noreste terminal
Mayapán Ruinas & Oxkutzcab	30	1½	hourly; Noreste terminal
Mexico City	1322-1558	21	5 daily
Palenque	446	8	4 daily
Playa del Carmen	195-376	5-7½	frequent
Progreso	16	1	frequent; Progreso bus terminal
Río Lagartos	155	3½	5.30am; Noreste terminal
Ruta Puuc (round-trip; 30min at each site)	187	8	8am; Terminal de Segunda Clase
Ticul	42	1¾	frequent
Tizimín	85-114	2½-4	frequent; Noreste terminal
Tulum	152-220	5-8	frequent
Uxmal	47	1½	4 daily; Terminal de Segunda Clase
Valladolid	90-150	2½-3½	frequent

THE LOST HENEQUÉN HACIENDAS OF YUCATÁN

Yucatán state would have been little more than a provincial backwater if it weren't for a spiky son-of-a-bitch plant named *Agave fourcroydes*. Some call it *henequén*, others call it sisal; call it what you will, the lanced-leaved plant used to create strong maritime rope and twine was 'green gold' from the late 19th century to the end of WWII. It was during this time that the 'sisal barons' of Yucatán built their elaborate haciendas for the booming business. But the industry bottomed out post-WWII with the advent of synthetic fibers.

Not only did the demise of *henequén* force the region's haciendas to shutter operations, but it had a devastating economic impact on the town of Sisal, the main seaport for *henequén* exports back in the heyday.

Most of the area's *henequén* haciendas are now in ruins, while others have been restored to past glory and now make for amazing upscale retreats.

One of the finest, no doubt, you'll find off Hwy 261, heading north to Progreso. Originally built in the 18th century for agricultural activities and later converted into a *henequén* plant, **Hacienda Xcanatun** (☎800-202-2566; www.xcanatun.com; Calle 20 s/n, Carretera Mérida-Progreso, Km 12; r from M$4230, mains M$165-270) now houses a luxury hotel. Even a standard room here gets you an elegant setup, with marble floors, high ceilings with wood beams, and tasteful rustic furnishings. Even if you don't stay, you can drop by the hacienda's award-winning Casa de Piedra restaurant.

In the opposite direction, south of Mérida off Hwy 261, are two former haciendas. **Hacienda Yaxcopoil** (☎999-900-1193; www.yaxcopoil.com; Hwy 261, Km 186; admission M$75, r M$1040; ⊙8am-6pm Mon-Sat, 9am-5pm Sun; P) is a vast estate that grew and processed *henequén*. Many of its French Renaissance–style buildings have undergone picturesque restorations, and a small museum offers glimpses at the (now defunct) giant rasping machines that turned the leaves into fiber. You can stay in one of two restored rooms, which have high ceilings and antique furniture (they're fairly affordable for hacienda accommodations). Frequent Mérida–Ticul buses pass Yaxcopoil, 33km southwest of Mérida, but it's easiest to drive.

About 10km south you'll reach **Hacienda Ochil** (☎999-924-7465; www.haciendaochil.com; Hwy 261, Km 176; admission M$30, mains M$92-125; ⊙10am-6pm; P ♿), which has no lodging but provides a fascinating look at how *henequén* was grown and processed. From the parking lot, folllow the tracks once used by small-wheeled carts to haul materials to and from the processing plant. You'll pass workshops and a small museum with exhibits illustrating the cultivating, harvesting and processing of the plant. The *casa de maquinas* (machine house) and smokestack still stand. Ochil also has a restaurant, bar and small cenote.

Starwood Resorts also operates three converted haciendas in Yucatán state – Hacienda Temozón, Hacienda San José and Hacienda Santa Rosa (p172).

Oxkintok

Archaeologists have been excited about the ruins of **Oxkintok** (adult/child under 13yr M$42/free, guides M$400; ⊙8am-5pm; P) for several years. Inscriptions found at the site contain some of the oldest known dates in the Yucatán, and indicate the city was inhabited from the Preclassic to the Postclassic period (300 BC to AD 1500), reaching its greatest importance between AD 475 and 860.

Three main groups of the approximately 8-sq-km site have been restored thus far, all near the site entrance. Though much of the rebuilding work looks like it was done with rubble, you can see examples of Oxkintok, Proto-Puuc and Puuc architecture. The highest structure (15m) is Ma-1, **La Pirámide**, in the Ah-May group, which provides good views of the area. Probably the most interesting structure is **Palacio Chich** (Estructura Ca-7), in the Ah-Canul group, for its original stonework and the two columns in front carved with human figures in elaborate dress. Recently researchers discovered a labyrinth beneath La Pirámide, which unfortunately is closed to the public.

The ruins are reached via a west-leading fork off the road to the Grutas de Calcehtok, which is 75km southwest of Mérida off Hwy 184, a few kilometers south of the town of Calcehtok.

Grutas de Calcehtok

The **Calcehtok caves** (999-276-8122; 1hr 4-person tour M$200; 9.30am-3.30pm Mon-Fri, 8am-5pm Sat & Sun;) are said to comprise the longest dry-cave system on the Yucatán Peninsula. More than 4km have been explored so far, and two of the caves' 25 vaults exceed 100m in diameter (one has a 30m-high 'cupola'). The caves hold abundant and impressive natural formations, human and animal remains, and plenty of artifacts, including cisternlike *haltunes*.

Archaeologists have found and removed ceramic arrowheads, quartz hammers and other tools, and you can still see low fortifications built by the Maya who sheltered here during the Caste War.

The opening of the main entrance is an impressive 30m in diameter and 40m deep, ringed by vegetation often buzzing with bees. It's about 1m deep in bat guano at the bottom (some visitors wear dust masks to avoid infection from a fungus on the guano). There's nothing to stop you from exploring on your own (and possibly getting lost), but you'd be wise to employ one of the six guides, all members of the Cuy family, whose great-grandfather rediscovered the caves in 1840. They carry lanterns and flashlights.

You can opt for a basic tour or an adventure package – one that involves belly-crawling, rope descents to see human skeletons and possibly the 7m long by 20cm wide 'Pass of Death,' or 'El Parto' (The Birth: you figure it out). Tours last one to six hours.

The caves are 75km southwest of Mérida off Hwy 184, a few kilometers south of the town of Calcehtok. They are best reached by car.

Uxmal

Pronounced oosh-mahl, **Uxmal** (Hwy 261, Km 78; admission M$182, parking M$22, guides M$550; 8am-5pm;) is one impressive set of ruins, easily ranking among the top (and unfortunately most crowded) Maya archaeological sites. It is a large site with some fascinating structures in good condition and bearing a riot of ornamentation. Adding to its appeal is its setting in the hilly Puuc region, which lent its name to the architectural patterns in this area. *Puuc* means 'hills,' and these, rising up to about 100m, are the first relief from the flatness of the northern and western portions of the peninsula.

The site is entered through the modern Unidad Uxmal building, which has an air-conditioned restaurant, a small museum, shops selling souvenirs and crafts, a bookstore and an ATM. The price of admission includes entrance to a nightly sound-and-light show (8pm April to September, 7pm October to March). It's in Spanish but there are audio translators available for M$39.

History

Uxmal was an important city in a region that encompassed the satellite towns of Sayil, Kabah, Xlapak and Labná. Although Uxmal means 'Thrice Built' in Maya, it was actually constructed five times.

That a sizable population flourished in this dry area is yet more testimony to the engineering skills of the Maya, who built a series of reservoirs and *chultunes* (cisterns) lined with lime mortar to catch and hold water during the dry season. First settled about AD 600, Uxmal was influenced by highland Mexico in its architecture, most likely through contact fostered by trade. This influence is reflected in the town's serpent imagery, phallic symbols and columns. The well-proportioned Puuc architecture, with its intricate, geometric mosaics sweeping across the upper parts of elongated facades, was strongly influenced by the slightly earlier Río Bec and Chenes styles.

The scarcity of water in the region meant that Chac, the rain god or sky serpent, carried a lot of weight here. His image is ubiquitous at the site in the form of stucco masks protruding from facades and cornices. There is much speculation as to why Uxmal was abandoned in about AD 900; a severe drought may have forced the inhabitants to relocate.

Rediscovered by archaeologists in the 19th century, Uxmal was first excavated in 1929 by Frans Blom. Although much has been restored, there is still a good deal to discover.

Sights

Casa del Adivino ARCHAEOLOGICAL SITE

As you climb the slope to the ruins, the Casa del Adivino comes into view. This tall temple (the name translates as 'Magician's House'), 39m high, was built in an unusual oval

Uxmal

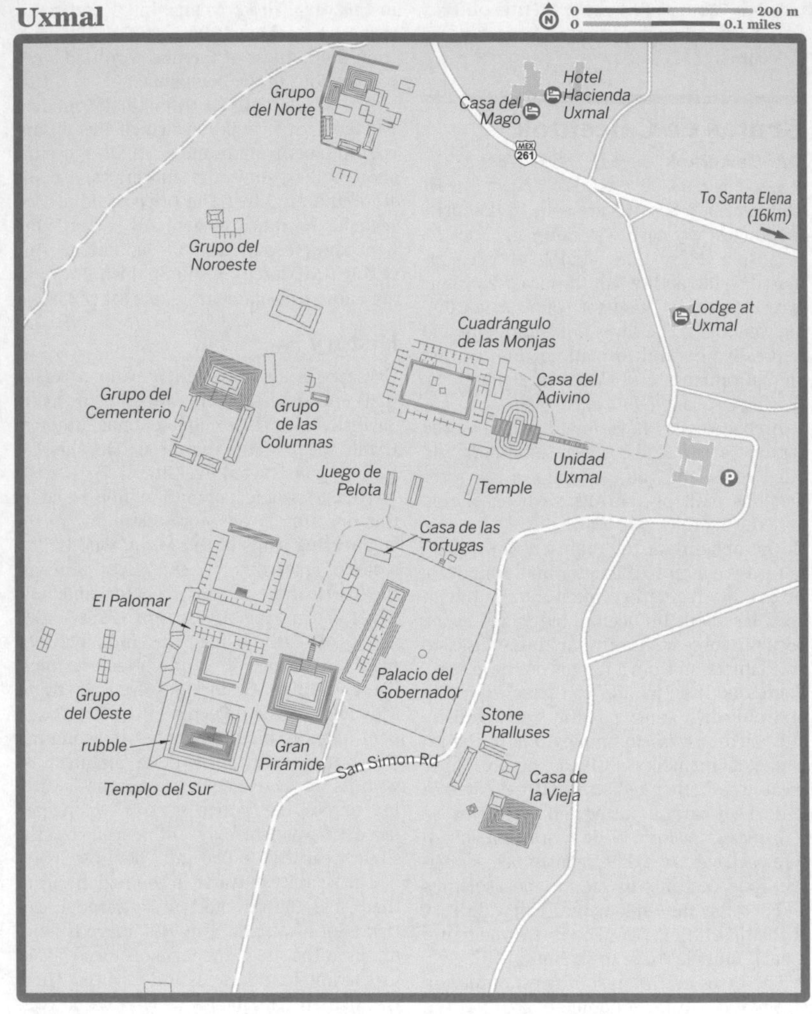

shape. It gives a rather bad first impression of Uxmal to the visitor, consisting of round stones held rudely together with lots of cement. What you see is a restored version of the temple's fifth incarnation. Four earlier temples were completely covered in the final rebuilding by the Maya, except for the high doorway on the west side, which remains from the fourth temple. Decorated in elaborate Chenes style (a style that originated further south), the doorway proper forms the mouth of a gigantic Chac mask.

Cuadrángulo de las Monjas ARCHAEOLOGICAL SITE

The 74-room, sprawling Nuns' Quadrangle is directly west of the Casa del Adivino. Archaeologists guess variously that it was a military academy, royal school or palace complex. The long-nosed face of Chac appears everywhere on the facades of the four separate temples that form the quadrangle. The northern temple, the grandest of the four, was built first, followed by the southern, then the eastern and finally the western.

Several decorative elements on the exuberant facades show signs of Mexican, perhaps Totonac, influence. The feathered-serpent (Quetzalcóatl, or in Maya, Kukulcán) motif along the top of the west temple's facade is one of these. Note also the stylized depictions of the *na* (traditional Maya thatched hut) over some of the doorways in the northern and southern buildings.

Passing through the corbeled arch in the middle of the south building of the quadrangle and continuing down the slope takes you through the **Juego de Pelota** (Ball Court). From here you can turn left and head up the steep slope and stairs to the large terrace. If you've got time, you could instead turn right to explore the western **Grupo del Cementerio** (which, though largely unrestored, holds some interesting square blocks carved with skulls in the center of its plaza), then head for the stairs and terrace.

Casa de las Tortugas ARCHAEOLOGICAL SITE

To the right at the top of the stairs is the House of the Turtles, which takes its name from the turtles carved on the cornice. The Maya associated turtles with the rain god, Chac. According to Maya myth, when the people suffered from drought, so did the turtles, and both prayed to Chac to send rain.

The frieze of short columns, or 'rolled mats,' that runs around the temple below the turtles is characteristic of the Puuc style. On the west side of the building a vault has collapsed, affording a good view of the corbeled arch that supported it.

Palacio del Gobernador ARCHAEOLOGICAL SITE

The Governor's Palace, with its magnificent facade nearly 100m long, has been called 'the finest structure at Uxmal and the culmination of the Puuc style' by Mayanist Michael D Coe. The buildings have walls filled with rubble, faced with cement and then covered in a thin veneer of limestone squares; the lower part of the facade is plain, the upper part festooned with stylized Chac faces and geometric designs, often latticelike or fretted.

Other elements of Puuc style are decorated cornices, rows of half-columns (as in the House of the Turtles) and round columns in doorways (as in the palace at Sayil).

Gran Pirámide ARCHAEOLOGICAL SITE

The 32m-high pyramid has been restored only on its northern side. Archaeologists theorize that the quadrangle at its summit was largely destroyed in order to construct another pyramid above it. That work, for reasons unknown, was never completed. At the top are some stucco carvings of Chac, birds and flowers.

El Palomar ARCHAEOLOGICAL SITE

West of the Gran Pirámide sits a structure whose roofcomb is latticed with a pattern reminiscent of the Moorish pigeon houses built into walls in Spain and northern Africa – hence the building's name, which means the Dovecote or Pigeon House. The nine honeycombed triangular 'belfries' sit on top of a building that was once part of a quadrangle.

Casa de la Vieja ARCHAEOLOGICAL SITE

Off the southeast corner of the Palacio del Gobernador's platform is a small complex, now largely rubble, known as the Casa de la Vieja (Old Woman's House). In front of it is a small *palapa* (thatch-roof shelter) that covers several large phalluses carved from stone.

Sleeping & Eating

There is no town at Uxmal, only several hotels. Cheaper lodgings can be found in Santa Elena, 16km away, or in Ticul, 30km to the east.

Casa del Mago HOTEL **$$**

(997-976-2012; www.casadelmago.com; Hwy 261, Km 78; r incl breakfast M$780; P) The only midrange option in Uxmal, Casa del Mago consists of four basic rooms with red-tile floors and ceiling fans. Guests have use of the adjoining sister property's pool. These are the cheapest rooms in town so book ahead.

Lodge at Uxmal LUXURY HOTEL **$$$**

(998-887-2495, in USA 877-240-5864; www.mayaland.com; Hwy 261, Km 78; r from M$1700; P) This Mayaland Resort is Uxmal's newest luxury hotel. Its rooms could be nicer for the price, but you can't beat the easy access to the ruins and the pool certainly adds value. Some of the more expensive rooms have Jacuzzis. Don't suppose Stephens and Catherwood enjoyed such luxury when they passed through the area in the late 1830s.

Hotel Hacienda Uxmal HISTORIC HOTEL **$$$**

(997-976-2012, in USA 877-240-5864; www.mayaland.com; Hwy 261, Km 78; r from M$2112; P) This Mayaland Resort is 500m from the ruins. It housed the archaeologists who explored and restored Uxmal. Wide, tiled verandas, high ceilings, great bathrooms and a beautiful swimming pool make this a very comfortable place to stay. There are even rocking chairs to help you kick back after a hard day of exploring.

Getting There & Away

Uxmal is 80km from Mérida. Departures on the Sur bus line (M$47, 1½ hours, four daily) are from Mérida's 2nd-class terminal. But going back to Mérida, passing buses may be full. If you get stuck, a taxi to nearby Santa Elena costs M$150 to M$200.

Tours offered by Nómadas Hostel (p148) in Mérida are always a good option, or you can rent a car and visit other ruins in the area.

Santa Elena

The nearest town to Uxmal is Santa Elena. It was originally called Nohcacab, and was virtually razed in 1847 in the Caste War. '*Elena*' means burnt houses in Maya. The Mexican government changed the name to Santa Elena in a bold PR stunt. There's a small **museum** (admission M$10; 9am-6:30pm Mon-Fri, to 7pm Sat & Sun) dedicated to a gruesome find – 18th-century child mummies found buried beneath the adjoining cathedral – and some *henequén*-related exhibits. Go for a little DIY adventure by heading 4km outside of town to the Mulchic pyramid; locals can tell you how to get there. If time permits, try asking if you can take in the view from the roof of the cathedral.

Santa Elena is 16km southeast of Uxmal and 8km north of Kabah.

Sleeping & Eating

★Pickled Onion B&B $
(997-111-7922; www.thepickledonionyucatan.com; cabins incl breakfast from M$500, mains M$90-100; P) The Pickled Onion offers the chance to stay in a modern adobe-walled hut with lovely tiled floors and bathrooms. The recently renovated rooms keep you cool with *palupa* roofs, and all come with coffee makers and mosquito netting. We love the pool and its surrounding gardens, and the excellent restaurant does food to go if you want to picnic while visiting nearby ruins. Room rates include continental breakfast.

Bungalows Sacbé BUNGALOW $
(997-978-5158; www.sacbebungalows.com.mx; d/tr/q from M$400/500/550; P) At Bungalows Sacbé there's a verdant garden and a new pool, and all the rooms have fans, good screens and decent beds. Each room has an excellent book with information about local activities, flora and fauna. The friendly Mexican and French owners serve a good, cheap breakfast (M$65). It's about 200m south of the town's southern entrance.

Flycatcher Inn B&B $$
(997-978-5350; www.flycatcherinn.com; off Hwy 261; d incl breakfast M$750, ste & cottage incl breakfast from M$1000; P) Flycatcher Inn features six squeaky-clean rooms, an enormous master suite and a separate cottage. All have great porches, supercomfy imported beds, plus hammocks, excellent screenage and spiffy bathrooms. The inn's driveway is less than 100m north of Santa Elena's southern entrance, near Restaurant El Chac-Mool.

The owners, a local Maya and his North American wife, have kept most of the land around the inn undeveloped, and a number of bird and animal species can be seen here, including the flycatchers that gave their name to the place. The Flycatcher closes from mid-September to mid-October.

Restaurant El Chac-Mool MEXICAN $$
(997-978-5117; www.facebook.com/chacmooluxmal; mains M$60-110; 9am-10pm) On Hwy 261 at the southern entrance to Santa Elena, Restaurant El Chac-Mool is a friendly place serving *yucateco* food that includes a hearty vegetarian plate of rice, beans and fried bananas. It has a hotel, too.

Kabah

These **ruins** (Hwy 261; admission M$42; 10am-5pm), 23km southeast of Uxmal, are right astride Hwy 261. The guard shack/souvenir shop/office sells snacks and cold drinks. The bulk of the restored ruins are on the east side of the highway.

On entering, head to your right to climb the stairs of the structure closest to the highway, **El Palacio de los Mascarones** (Palace of the Masks). Standing in front of it is the Altar de los Glifos, whose immediate area is littered with many stones carved with glyphs. The palace's facade is an amazing sight, covered in nearly 300 masks of Chac, the rain god or sky serpent. Most of their huge curling noses are broken off; the best intact beaks are at the building's southern end. These noses may have given the palace its modern Maya name, Codz Poop (Rolled Mat; it's pronounced more like 'Codes Pope' than some Elizabethan curse).

When you've had your fill of noses, head north and around to the back of the Poop to check out the two restored **atlantes** (an atlas – plural 'atlantes' – is a male figure used as a supporting column). These are especially interesting, as they're some of the very few 3D human figures you'll see at the main Maya sites. One is headless and the other wears a jaguar mask atop his head.

Descend the steps near the *atlantes* and turn left, passing the small **Pirámide de los Mascarones**, to reach the plaza containing **El Palacio**. The palace's broad facade has several doorways, two of which have a column in the center. These columned doorways and the groups of decorative *columnillas* (little columns) on the upper part of the facade are characteristic of the Puuc architectural style.

Steps on the north side of El Palacio's plaza put you on a path leading about 200m through the jungle to the **Templo de las Columnas**. This building has more rows of decorative columns on the upper part of its facade.

West of El Palacio, across the highway, a path leads up the slope and passes to the south of a high mound of stones that was once the **Gran Pirámide** (Great Pyramid). The path curves to the right and comes to a large restored **monumental arch**. It's said that the *sacbé* (cobbled and elevated ceremonial road), leading from here goes through the jungle all the way to Uxmal, terminating at a smaller arch; in the other direction it goes to Labná. Once, all of the Yucatán Peninsula was connected by these marvelous 'white roads' of rough limestone.

At present nothing of the *sacbé* is visible, and the rest of the area west of the highway is a maze of unmarked, overgrown paths leading off into the jungle.

Nómadas Hostel (p148) in Mérida runs tours to Kabah. For good lodging, head to Santa Elena, about 8km north.

Getting There & Away

Kabah is 104km from Mérida. Campeche-bound Linea Sur buses (M$47) departing from Mérida's Terminal de Segunda Clase (2nd-class terminal) will drop you off at the site.

Ruta Puuc

The Ruta Puuc (Puuc Route) meanders through rolling hills dotted with seldom-visited Maya ruins sitting pretty in dense forests. A road branches off to the east (5km south of Kabah) and winds past the ruins of Sayil, Xlapak and Labná, eventually leading to the Grutas de Loltún. The sites offer some marvelous architectural detail and a deeper acquaintance with the Puuc Maya civilization.

> **PYRAMID SCHEME**
>
> It's tempting to skirt the (often unpoliced) signs that prohibit climbing, but please climb only where it's allowed – a million bootsteps can certainly take their toll. Be careful, and if you're worried about heights, give this surefire technique a try: zigzag up or down the steps, making diagonal passes to either side of the stairway. Once you master this style, you'll never descend again using the embarrassing sit-and-bump-down-on-your-butt method, or the painful trip-and-fall-to-your-near-death method, which is why most of the pyramids are closed to climbing in the first place.

Sights

Sayil ARCHAEOLOGICAL SITE

(admission M$42; ⏲8am-5pm) Sayil is best known for **El Palacio**, the huge three-tiered building that has an 85m-long facade and is reminiscent of the Minoan palace on Crete. The distinctive columns of Puuc architecture are used here often, either as supports for the lintels, as decoration between doorways or as a frieze above them, alternating with stylized Chac masks and 'descending gods.'

Taking the path south from the palace for about 400m and bearing left, you come to the temple named **El Mirador**, whose roosterlike roofcomb was once painted a bright red. About 100m beyond El Mirador, beneath a protective *palapa*, is a stela bearing the relief of a fertility god with an enormous phallus, now sadly weathered.

Grupo Sur is a bit further, and offers beautiful jungle-covered ruins with tree roots twisting through the walls.

The ruins of Sayil are 4.5km from the junction of the Ruta Puuc with Hwy 261.

Xlapak ARCHAEOLOGICAL SITE

(⏲8am-5pm) FREE The ornate *palacio* at Xlapak (shla-pak) is quite a bit smaller than those at nearby Kabah and Sayil, measuring only about 20m in length. It's decorated with the inevitable Chac masks, columns and colonnettes and fretted geometric latticework of the Puuc style. The building is interesting and on a bit of a lean.

Plenty of motmots brighten up the surrounding forests. From the entrance gate at Sayil, it's 6km east to the entrance gate at Xlapak. The name means 'Old Walls' in Maya and was a general term among local people for ancient ruins.

Labná ARCHAEOLOGICAL SITE

(admission M$42; 8am-5pm) This is *the* site not to miss. Archaeologists believe that, at one point in the 9th century, some 3000 Maya lived at Labná. To support such numbers in these arid hills, water was collected in *chultunes*. At Labná's peak there were some 60 *chultunes* in and around the city; several are still visible.

El Palacio, the first building you come to at Labná, is one of the longest in the Puuc region, and much of its interesting decorative carving is in good shape, thanks in part to a massive renovation project completed in 2006. On the west corner of the main structure's facade, straight in from the big tree near the center of the complex, is a serpent's head with a human face peering out from between its jaws, the symbol of the planet Venus. Toward the hill from this is an impressive Chac mask, and nearby is the lower half of a human figure (possibly a ballplayer) in loincloth and leggings.

The lower level has several more well-preserved Chac masks, and the upper level contains a large *chultun* that still holds water. The view of the site and the hills beyond from there is impressive.

Labná is best known for **El Arco**, a magnificent arch once part of a building that separated two quadrangular courtyards. It now appears to be a gate joining two small plazas. The corbeled structure, 3m wide and 6m high, is well preserved, and the reliefs decorating its upper facade are exuberantly Puuc in style.

Flanking the west side of the arch are carved *na* with multitiered roofs. Also on these walls, the remains of the building that adjoined the arch, are lattice patterns atop a serpentine design. Archaeologists believe a high roofcomb once sat over the fine arch and its flanking rooms.

Standing on the opposite side of the arch and separated from it by the *sacbé* is a pyramid known as **El Mirador**, topped by a temple. The pyramid itself is largely stone rubble. The temple, with its 5m-high roofcomb, is well positioned to be a lookout, thus its name.

From the entrance gate at Xlapak, it's 3.5km east to the gate at Labná.

Sleeping

Uma Sabacche CABIN $

(997-105-9821; robcar-08@hotmail.com; Carretera Zona Puuc, Km 15; cabins M$250-350, camping M$100; P) In the heart of the forested Puuc region, this grassy 'ecolodge' offers basic rustic cabins and camping about 3km north of Labná. The owners rescue wild animals from poaching (at last visit they were trying to find a home for an ocelot and puma). You can also see wild turkeys and white-tailed deer here. Horseback riding can be arranged and the hosts will prepare meals upon request.

Getting There & Away

To visit the Ruta Puuc sites, you can take a weekly Oriente bus (M$178, Sunday at 8am) that makes stops at all three ruins, plus Kabah and Uxmal. The bus leaves from the Terminal de Segunda Clase in Mérida.

Turitransmérida (p149) does Ruta Puuc tours on a more regular basis.

Grutas de Loltún

The **Grutas de Loltún** (Loltún Caverns; adult/child under 13yr M$105/6, parking M$22; 9am-4pm;), one of the largest dry-cave systems on the Yucatán Peninsula, provided a treasure trove of data for archaeologists studying the Maya. Carbon dating of artifacts found here reveals that the caves were used by humans 2200 years ago. Chest-high murals of hands, faces, animals and geometric motifs were apparent as recently as 20 years ago, but so many people have touched them that scarcely a trace remains, though some handprints have been restored. A few pots are displayed in a niche, and an impressive bas-relief, El Guerrero, guards the entrance. Other than that, you'll mostly see floodlit limestone formations, or the poorly aimed floodlights shining into your eyes.

To explore the labyrinth, you must take a scheduled guided tour at 9.30am, 11am, 12.30pm, 2pm, 3pm or 4pm, but it may depart earlier if enough people are waiting, or switch to English if the group warrants it (tours are usually in Spanish). The services of the guides are included in the admission price, though they expect a tip

THE RISE OF MAYAPÁN & THE DEATH WARRANT OF MAYA INDEPENDENCE

The rise of Mayapán played an integral role in the ultimate demise of Maya rule in the region. The city was supposedly founded by Kukulcán (Quetzalcóatl) in 1007, shortly after the former ruler of Tula arrived in Yucatán. His dynasty, the Cocom, organized a confederation of city-states that included Uxmal, Chichén Itzá and many other notable cities. Despite their alliance, animosity arose between the Cocomes of Mayapán and the Itzáes of Chichén Itzá during the late 12th century, and the Cocomes stormed Chichén Itzá, forcing the Itzáe rulers into exile. The Cocom dynasty emerged supreme in all of northern Yucatán.

Cocom supremacy lasted for almost 250 years, until the ruler of Uxmal, Ah Xupán Xiú, led a rebellion of the oppressed city-states and overthrew Cocom hegemony. The capital of Mayapán was utterly destroyed and remained uninhabited ever after.

But struggles for power continued in the region until 1542, when Francisco de Montejo (the Younger) conquered T'ho and established Mérida. At that point the current lord of Maní and ruler of the Xiú people, Ah Kukum Tutul Xiú, proposed to Montejo a military alliance against the Cocomes, his ancient rivals. Montejo accepted, and Xiú was baptized as a Christian, taking the name Francisco de Montejo Xiú (original, no?). The Cocomes were defeated and – too late – the Xiú rulers realized that they had signed the death warrant of Maya independence.

afterward (M$100 per person is fair). Tours last about one hour and 20 minutes, with lots of lengthy stops. Some guides' presentations are long on legends (and jokes about disappearing mothers-in-law) and short on geological and historical information.

Getting There & Away

About 15km north and east of Labná, a sign points left to the Grutas de Loltún, 5km further northeast. The road passes through lush orchards and some banana and palm groves, an agreeable sight in this dry region.

Buses to Oxkutzcab (osh-kootz-kahb; M$38, 1½ hours), depart at 8.30am and 4pm from the Noreste bus terminal in Mérida. Loltún is 7km southwest of Oxkutzcab, and there is usually some transportation along the road. *Camionetas* (pickup trucks) charge about M$15 for a ride. A taxi from Oxkutzcab costs M$120 or so one-way.

Renting a car is the best option for reaching the caves, though; once you're out of Mérida it's easy going on pretty good roads.

Ruinas de Mayapán

Though far less impressive than many Maya sites, **Mayapán** (admission M$35; ⌚8am-5pm) is historically significant – it was one of the last major dynasties in the region. The site's main attractions are clustered in a compact core, and it is one of few sites where you can ascend to the top of the pyramid. Visitors usually have the place to themselves.

The city of Mayapán was large, with a population estimated to be around 12,000; it covered 4 sq km, all surrounded by a great defensive wall. More than 3500 buildings, 20 cenotes and traces of the city wall were mapped by archaeologists working in the 1950s and in 1962. The late-Postclassic workmanship is inferior to that of the great age of Maya art.

Among the structures that have been restored is the **Castillo de Kukulcán**, a climbable pyramid with fresco fragments around its base and, at its rear side, friezes depicting decapitated warriors. The reddish color is still faintly visible. The **Templo Redondo** (Round Temple) is vaguely reminiscent of El Caracol at Chichén Itzá. Close by is Itzmal Chen, a cenote that was a major Maya religious sanctuary.

These ruins are some 50km southeast of Mérida. Don't confuse the ruins of Mayapán with the Maya village of the same name, which is some 40km southeast of the ruins, past the town of Teabo.

Getting There & Away

The Ruinas de Mayapán are just off Hwy 18, a few kilometers southwest of the town of Telchaquillo. LUS runs 2nd-class buses to Telchaquillo (M$15 each way, 1½ hours, hourly 5.30am to 8pm) from the Noreste bus terminal in Mérida. They'll let you off near the entrance to the ruins and pick you up on your way back.

Again, you may want to consider renting a car to get here.

Cenotes de Cuzamá

Three kilometers east of the town of Cuzamá, accessed from the small village of Chunkanan, are the **Cenotes de Cuzamá** (999-142-8772; horse, driver & 1-4 people M$250; 8am-4pm), a series of three amazing limestone sinkholes accessed by horse-drawn railcart in an old *henequén* hacienda.

The fun, horse-drawn ride will jar your fillings loose while showing you attractive scenes of the surrounding, overgrown agave fields. Iguana sightings are a sure bet here, but keen eyes can also see vultures or caracaras, as well as other birds, lizards and the occasional rabbit or two.

One of the cenotes is featured in much of Yucatán's tourist literature, and all three are spectacular, with ropelike roots descending along with ethereal shafts of light to the crystal-clear, deep blue water. Though you may find yourself sharing a dip with other bathers, it's more likely that the drivers will time the trip so you have most of the swimming to yourself. Several cenotes have steep stairways or ladders that are often slippery, so use caution at all times.

To get here by car, take Hwy 180 toward Cancún until you get to a turnoff for Ticopo on the right; after Akankeh (there's a small pyramid here), bear to the left to reach Cuzamá. From there, head east at the cathedral for 3km to the cenotes. Signs will lead the way; keep your eyes peeled for kids, dogs, livestock and sun-drunk iguanas – all will be on the road at some point. Follow the road all the way to the hacienda (some competitors along the way will try to offer their services, telling you the hacienda no longer exists – not true).

Shared vans leave for Cuzamá (M$40 round-trip, two hours) from Calle 67 (between Calles 50 & 52) in Mérida. If you use the vans, you'll need to take a pedicab from the van stop to Chunkanan, an additional M$40.

Ticul

997 / POP 37,700

Ticul, 30km east of Uxmal, is the largest town in this ruin-rich region. It's dusty and quiet, with few signs of nightlife other than perhaps a few watering holes. But it has hotels, restaurants and transportation, so it's a good base for day trips to nearby ruins. (It's not as attractive a jumping-off point as nearby Santa Elena, though). Ticul is also a center for fine *huipil* weaving, and ceramics made here from the local red clay are renowned throughout the Yucatán.

Ticul's main street is Calle 23, sometimes called Calle Principal, starting from the highway and going past the *mercado* (market) to the main plaza, Plaza Mayor.

Sights

Iglesia de San Antonio de Padua CHURCH
(Calles 25 & 26) Because of the number of Maya ruins in the vicinity, from which to steal building blocks, and the number of Maya in the area 'needing' conversion to Christianity, Franciscan friars built many churches in the region, including this 16th-century. Although looted on several occasions, the church has some original touches. Among them are the stone statues of friars in primitive style flanking the side entrances and a Black Christ altarpiece ringed by crude medallions.

Plaza de la Cultura PLAZA
It's all cement and stone but nevertheless the Plaza de la Cultura is an agreeable place to take in the evening breeze, enjoy the view of the church and greet passing townspeople.

Sleeping

Hotel Villa Real HOTEL $
(972-2828; restaurantevillareal@hotmail.com; Calle 23, btwn Calles 26A & 28; r M$400-480; P) Considered one of the nicest places in town, which isn't saying much for Ticul's hotel offerings. But at least the rooms here have balconies so you can get some fresh air, and there's a restaurant as well.

Hotel Plaza HOTEL $
(972-0484; www.hotelplazayucatan.com; Calle 23 No 202, btwn Calles 26 & 26A; d/ste M$380/480; P) Spacious rooms with white-tiled floors and small but fun balconies make this a pretty good choice. The old building adds character, though the street-facing rooms are sometimes noisy. Laundry service, phone and pick-up/drop-off in Mérida are additional reasons to consider staying here.

Hotel San Antonio HOTEL $
(972-1893; hotelsan-antonio@hotmail.com; Calle 25, btwn Calles 26 & 26A; d M$380-390; P) Some rooms have great views of the Plaza de la Cultura. The hotel lacks

character, but here in Ticul that's kind of reassuring. All rooms have TV and phone; there's also a small parking lot and a pleasant restaurant.

Eating & Drinking

Mercado MARKET $
(Calle 28A, btwn Calles 21 & 23; mains M$30-40, ⌚7am-2pm) Ticul's lively *mercado* provides all the ingredients for picnics and snacks, and offers nice photo ops, too. It also has lots of those wonderful eateries where the food is good, the portions generous and the prices low.

Bazar de Comidas MEXICAN $
(cnr Calles 25 & 22; mains M$25-50; ⌚7am-5pm) The friendly stalls here serve inexpensive regional food, such as *poc-chuc* (grilled pork) and *queso relleno* (stuffed cheese).

El Buen Samaritano BAKERY $
(Calle 23; breads M$6-16; ⌚7am-10.30pm) Fresh bread and sweet rolls.

Pizzería La Góndola PIZZERIA $$
(☎972-0112; Calle 23 No 208; pizzas M$85-130, sandwiches M$30; ⌚8am-1pm & 5pm-2am) Open late, this clean place on the corner of Calle 26 has sandwiches and pizzas with the usual toppings. 'Order by number' options make it easy for non-Spanish-speakers to get exactly what they want.

Super Willy's SUPERMARKET
(Calle 23, btwn Calles 28 & 30; ⌚7am-10pm) Across from the market, Super Willy's is a small supermarket with a big variety of groceries and household items.

Flor del Campo JUICE BAR
(☎972-1875; Calle 28, btwn Calles 23 & 25; juices M$8-12; ⌚7am-7pm Mon-Sat, to 1pm Sun) Juice up for the day at this tiny place, which just has chilled juices (no smoothies). It's near the market.

Information

You'll find banks with ATMs on the main plaza. Several internet cafes are in the area as well.

Post Office (Plaza Mayor, Calle 23; ⌚8am-2.30pm Mon-Fri)

Getting There & Away

BUS

Bus Terminal (Calle 24, btwn Calles 25 & 25A) Ticul's 24-hour bus terminal is behind the massive church.

CAR

The quickest way to Uxmal, Kabah and the Ruta Puuc sites is via Santa Elena. From central Ticul, go west to Calle 34 and turn south; it heads straight to Santa Elena.

Those headed east to Quintana Roo and the Caribbean coast can take Hwy 184 from Ticul through Oxkutzcab to Tzucacab and José María Morelos (which has a gas station). At Polyuc, 130km from Ticul, a road turns left (east), ending after 80km in Felipe Carrillo Puerto. The right fork of the road goes south to Laguna Bacalar. Between Oxkutzcab and Felipe Carrillo Puerto or Bacalar there are few restaurants or gas stations.

COLECTIVO

Colectivos (shared vans) go direct to Mérida's Parque de San Juan (M$40, 1½ hours, 6am to 7.30pm) from the shiny new *colectivo* terminal as soon as they're full. You can also catch a *colectivo* to Tekax (M$22, one hour) here.

Combis (minibuses) for Oxkutzcab (M$14, 30 minutes, 7am to 8pm) leave from Calle 25A on the south side of the church.

Colectivos to Santa Elena (M$10, 6.50am to 8pm), between Uxmal and Kabah, depart from Calle 30. In Santa Elena, catch another bus northwest to Uxmal (15km) or south to Kabah (3.5km).

TAXI

Taxis in front of the *colectivo* terminal, on the corner of Calles 24 and 25, charge M$800 for a full day touring the Ruta Puuc ruins. You can ask to make stops at Grutas de Loltún, Labná, Sayil, Xlapak, Kabah and Uxmal if time permits.

BUSES FROM TICUL

DESTINATION	FARE (M$)	DURATION (HR)	FREQUENCY
Cancún	224	8	frequent
Chetumal	180	6	5 daily
Mérida	42	1½	frequent
Oxkutzcab	12	½	frequent
Playa del Carmen	204	7	frequent
Tulum	176	6½	frequent

Ticul to Tihosuco

The route from Ticul to Tihosuco, in Quintana Roo, is seldom traveled by tourists. Some might say there's nothing to see. But others will welcome the opportunity to travel through farmland and jungle and see glimpses of Maya life that have remained the same for centuries. Part of the route is called La Ruta de los Conventos (The Route of the Convents), as each of these tiny villages has a cathedral or church, many in beautiful disrepair. Prepare to hear mainly Yucatec Maya, though many people speak Spanish as well.

The towns of Oxkutzcab, Tekax and Tihosuco offer budget accommodations. Beyond Oxkutzcab, the towns along this route are linked by *combis* and, less frequently, local buses; they may be hailed from the roadside.

Oxkutzcab

Oxkutzcab is renowned for its daily produce market and colonial church. Markets were the principal means of trade for the ancient Maya, and the peninsula's indigenous people still travel from the countryside to central communities to exchange produce at stalls beside a main square. Oxkutzcab is such a community.

Here, alongside Hwy 184, which becomes a slow-moving, two-lane road as it passes through the town center, you can't miss seeing the magnificent **Franciscan mission**; in front is the sprawling produce market.

The church is remarkable mostly for its ornamental facade, at the center of which is a stone statue of St Francis, the mission patron. The church, which was constructed at a snail's pace from 1640 to 1693, is also remarkable for its magnificent altarpiece. Indeed, it's one of only a few baroque altarpieces in the Yucatán to survive the revolts that have occurred since its construction.

A mural in the plaza across from the market depicts inquisitor Friar Diego de Landa's auto-da-fé in Maní, when he burnt thousands of idols.

Oxkutzcab, or 'osh,' as locals call it, makes for a good stopover if you want to visit the Grutas de Loltún or visit nearby towns.

Sleeping & Eating

Hotel Puuc HOTEL **$**
(997-975-0103; www.hotelpuuc.com.mx; cnr Calles 55 & 44; d with fan/air-con M$400/450, ste M$550;) Offers a great deal for the price, with your choice of air-con or fan in every business-hotel-style room. The beds are Flintstone firm, there's a good restaurant downstairs, and the rear garden has a nice pool.

El Príncipe Tutul-Xiu MEXICAN **$$**
(www.restaurantestutulxiu.com; Calle 45 No 102, btwn Calles 50 & 52; mains M$80-85; 11am-7pm;) Famous for its *poc-chuc*, El Príncipe Tutu-Xiu has several other classic *yucateco* dishes and yummy desserts as well.

Getting There & Away

Oxkutzcab is 16km southeast of Ticul. Buses depart frequently to Oxkutzcab from the Ticul terminal.

Tekax

The church in Tekax has been looted a couple of times, initially during the Caste War and later during the Mexican Revolution.

The Tekax area is increasingly prosperous (due to a successful crop switch from corn to sugarcane and citrus), and its residents recently replaced the church's damaged floor with a beautiful tiled floor and added a lovely new stone altar. According to *Maya Missions: Exploring the Spanish Colonial Churches of Yucatán,* a fabulous book by Richard and Rosalind Perry, during construction of the church one of the church's belfries collapsed, burying (and presumably crushing) the many indigenous laborers under tons of rubble. Miraculously, as local legend has it, no one died in the collapse.

Also noteworthy is the shape of the church, which undoubtedly was constructed of materials taken from nearby Maya temples. The general form of the church is that of a three-tiered pyramid. Possibly the architecture was based on the Maya structure from which the blocks were taken.

There are some very interesting caves nearby, including a beautiful crystalline number called **La Boca del Diablo**. **Mario Alberto Novelo Dorantes** (997-997-7963; topaso_25@hotmail.com; cnr Calles 50A & 57; tours M$300-500) is a knowledgeable local guide with equipment. Drop by his house (it's pink), or give him a ring to arrange a by-the-seat-of-your-pants adventure.

On the main square, the **Hotel Sultán de la Sierra** (997-974-2169; hector_pduarte@hotmail.com; Calle 50 No 211A, btwn Calles 55 & 57;

THE MODERN MAYA

The area between Ticul and Tihosuco is truly the Maya heartland. Indeed, the Maya in these parts continue to honor the gods of rain, wind and agriculture, just as their ancestors did before them.

Yucatán state has the second-highest percentage of indigenous-language speakers in all of Mexico, after Oaxaca. But the number of Yucatec Maya speakers is rapidly declining. In 2005, about 34% of *yucalecos* claimed to speak Yucatec Maya; in 2010 only 28% said they spoke any type of indigenous language at all.

So where have all the Maya gone? Many have moved to big tourist cities like Cancún, while others have moved all the way to the US. Many small Maya communities are beginning to welcome tourists in an effort to keep young folks from fleeing to the cities. It's ironic, but inviting foreigners in may prove the best way to maintain traditions.

The homes of today's rural Maya are still rectangular wood-framed huts with lean-to roofs of palm. The walls are made of bamboo poles or branches, and the spaces between the poles are often filled with mud to keep pests out. The Maya tend to prefer hammocks to beds.

Anywhere from a stone's throw to an hour's walk from a Maya hut is a *milpa* (cornfield). Corn tortillas remain a staple of the Maya diet, but the Maya also raise pigs and turkeys and produce honey, squash and other crops, which they sell at town markets. Many of the younger generation, particularly men, hitchhike out to work for a week in the larger towns such as Playa del Carmen or Cancún, returning for a day or two, or for long weekends or holidays. A *small* family will have about five children.

The *yucateco* Maya are said to prefer baseball to soccer. And on any given Sunday, you are likely to witness a down-home game played on the town square. It's a serious endeavor with hired hitters, uniforms and plenty of spectators.

d M$250; P ❄ ☎ ≋) is a decent budget option with rooms that stay fairly cool during the day and a swimming pool just off the lobby.

Shared vans run here from Ticul's *colectivo* terminal (M$22, 1½ hours).

Tihosuco

Located inside the state of Quintana Roo, Tihosuco was a major military outpost for the Spanish during the late 16th century and for 300 years thereafter. During this time the town came under numerous Maya assaults, and in 1686 it was attacked, though not sacked, by pirates led by legendary Dutch buccaneer Lorencillo.

During many of those attacks, the Spaniards retreated to the heavily fortified 17th-century church at the town center, which for much of its life served as a house of God, an arsenal and a stronghold. But the town and church fell to rebel hands in 1866 following a long siege, and much of the magnificent building was gutted. What remains of the once-great church is worth investigating. Services are still held inside, as in many other roofless churches in the region.

Housed in an 18th-century building, the **Museo de la Guerra de Castas** (Caste War Museum; cnr Calles 17 & 26; admission M$60; ⊙10am-6pm Tue-Sun) does a good job of detailing the more than four centuries of oppression suffered by the Maya on the peninsula, but only a couple of explanations are translated into English. There's a small botanical garden here, as well, and there are cotton-weaving and traditional medicine workshops offered.

About 30 minutes outside of town by car is a ruined 16th-century **Franciscan church** worth visiting. The area is known locally as Lal-Ka or La Capilla Poza. And while many consider it a sacred – and possibly haunted – site, you can usually get a taxi to take you here (you won't find it on your own).

If you've got your own wheels, it's worth taking a drive through the nearby Maya villages of Ixcabil, Saban, Sacalaca and Huay-Max. Every town has a unique church, and many even have a nearby cenote or two that the locals can point out.

From Tihosuco, it's a fast ride up Hwy 295 to Valladolid. Going the other way, Hwy 295 goes south to Felipe Carrillo Puerto.

WEST & NORTH OF MÉRIDA

Celestún

988 / POP 6800

West of Mérida, Celestún is a sleepy sun-scorched fishing village that moves at a turtle's pace – and that's the way locals like it. There's a pretty little square in the center of the town and some nice beaches, but the real draw here is the Reserva de la Biosfera Ría Celestún, a wildlife sanctuary abounding in waterfowl, with flamingos as the star attraction.

Celestún makes a good beach-and-bird day trip from Mérida, and it's also a great place to kick back and do nothing for a few days, especially if you've become road-weary. Fishing boats dot the appealing white-sand beach that stretches to the north for kilometers, and afternoon breezes cool the town on most days. Celestún is sheltered by the peninsula's southward curve, resulting in an abundance of marine life and less violent seas during the season of *nortes* (winds and rains arriving from the north).

Calle 11 is the road into town (it comes due west from Mérida), ending at Calle 12, the road paralleling the beach.

Sights

Reserva de la Biosfera Ría Celestún WILDLIFE RESERVE

The 591-sq-km Reserva de la Biosfera Ría Celestún is home to a huge variety of animals and birdlife, including a large flamingo colony. The best months to see the flamingos (via a boat tour) are from March or April to about September, outside the season of the *nortes*. Morning is the best time of day, though from 4pm onward the birds tend to concentrate in one area after the day's feeding, which can make for good viewing.

Hacienda Real de Salinas HISTORIC BUILDING

This abandoned hacienda a few kilometers south and east of town once produced dyewood and salt, and served as a summer home for a Campeche family. It's 5km in from the mouth of the *ría* (estuary). Out in the *ría* you can see a cairn marking an *ojo de agua dulce* (freshwater spring) that once supplied the hacienda.

The buildings are decaying in a most scenic way; you can still see shells in the wall mixed into the building material, as well as pieces of French roof tiles that served as ballast in ships on the way from Europe. Many intact tiles with the brickworks' name and location (Marseille) are still visible in what's left of the roofs.

The hacienda makes a good bicycle excursion from town. Coming south, go left at the Y junction, or turn right to reach El Lastre (The Ballast), a peninsula between the estuary and its western arm. Flamingos, white pelicans and other birds are sometimes seen here. If the water is high enough, it's possible to ask your flamingo tour captain to try stopping here on the way back from the birds.

Activities

Inland from the stretches of beach north of town lies a large section of scrub stretching east to the estuary that also provides good **birding** opportunities.

South and east of town, toward the abandoned Hacienda Real de Salinas, is another good area for nature observation. Flamingos, white pelicans, cormorants, anhingas and many other species frequent the shores and waters of the *ría*.

Tours

In Celestún, you can hire a motorboat for bird-watching either from the bridge on the highway into town (about 1.5km inland) or from the beach itself. Boats depart from outside Restaurant Celestún, at the foot of Calle 11.

Hiring a boat can be frustrating. Operators tend to try to collect as many people as possible, and might tell one customer, 'Sure, the tour will leave at 8.30am,' and another customer, 'We'll wait for you until 9am.' Prices are often quoted based on six to eight passengers, but if fewer people show up, the quoted price rises. You can avoid this problem by coming up with a group of six or eight on your own. Expect to pay M$200 per passenger.

Trips from the beach last 2½ to three hours and begin with a ride along the coast for several kilometers, during which you can expect to see egrets, herons, cormorants, sandpipers and many other bird species. The boat then turns into the mouth of the *ría* and passes through a 'petrified forest,' where tall coastal trees once belonging to a freshwater ecosystem were killed by saltwater intrusion long ago and remain standing, hard as rock.

Continuing up the *ría* takes you under the highway bridge where the other tours begin and beyond which lie the flamingos. Depending on the tide, the hour and the season, you may see hundreds or thousands of the colorful birds. Don't encourage your captain to approach them too closely; a startled flock taking wing can result in injuries and deaths (for the birds). In addition to taking you to the flamingos, the captain will wend through a 200m mangrove tunnel and visit one or both (as time and inclination allow) of the freshwater cenote-springs welling into the saltwater of the estuary, where you can take a refreshing dip.

Tours from the bridge – where there is a parking lot, ticket booth and a place to wait for fellow passengers – last about two hours. For M$250 per passenger (maximum six passengers), you get to see the flamingos, mangrove tunnel and spring. There's also a small park-entrance fee for each passenger.

With either the bridge or beach option, your captain may or may not speak English. An English-speaking guide can be hired at the bridge for about M$300 per hour (if one is available).

Also offering tours in town is **Manglares de Dzinitún** (☎999-232-5915; tours M$300), an ecotour outfit that does kayak, canoe and mountain-bike tours. The canoe tour runs through a mangrove tunnel and good birding spots, made all the better by the lack of engine noise. To get here from the beach, turn right on the street after the second transmission tower. It's about 300m ahead.

Sleeping

Celestún's hotels are all on Calle 12, within a short walk of one another. Book ahead for a sea view, especially on weekends.

Hotel Gutiérrez HOTEL **$**
(☎999-173-2118, 916-2648; Calle 12 No 107, cnr Calle 13; r with/without air con M$500/400; 📶) A nice remodeled budget option right on the beach. Rooms recently got a fresh coat of paint, new bathroom tiling, and there's a restaurant.

Hotel María del Carmen HOTEL **$**
(☎916-2170; hotelmariadelcarmen@hotmail.com; cnr Calles 12 & 15; d with fan/air-con M$450/550; P ❄ 📶) This place has 14 bare-bones beachfront rooms; ones on the upper floors have balconies facing the sea. Prices drop when business is slow.

★**Hotel Celeste Vida** HOTEL **$$**
(☎916-2536; www.hotelcelestevida.com; Calle 12; r/apt M$1100/1500; P 📶) This friendly little Canadian-run place offers comfortably decked-out rooms with full kitchen and an apartment that sleeps four – all with water views and the beach at your doorstep. Kayak and bike use are free for guests. The hotel is 1.5km north of Calle 11.

Topper Hotel HOTEL **$$**
(☎916-2000; topperhotel@hotmail.com; Calle 12; s/d M$700/1000; P ❄ 📶) Sitting on a quiet beach just north of town, 1km north of Calle 11, the Topper has clean modern rooms with satellite TV and wi-fi. Some of the larger units, which can accommodate up to four people, come with kitchenettes and pull-out sofa beds. Rates drop considerably during low season.

Hotel Manglares HOTEL **$$**
(☎916-2156; www.hotelmanglares.com.mx; Calle 12; d/cabañas M$1100/1600; P ❄ 📶 🏊) Although the architecture doesn't blend perfectly with the laid-back town, this is a nice midrange choice. The rooms all have sea views and private balconies. The well-appointed *cabañas* have minikitchens, Jacuzzis and a small common area. It's 1km north of Calle 11.

Xixim RESORT **$$$**
(☎916-2100; www.hotelxixim.com; ste incl breakfast M$2600-4160; P 📶 🏊) About 10km north of town, this quietly luxurious resort offers beachfront bungalows (the view blocked only by the foredune). They have no air-con but all are designed to get nice cross breezes. The restaurant serves reasonably priced meals, and the open-air bar upstairs is a good spot to while away the hours.

Eating

Celestún's specialties are crab, octopus, small shrimp from the lagoon and, of course, fresh fish. Many restaurants close around 7pm.

★**Casa Peon** INTERNATIONAL **$$**
(☎916-2628; www.facebook.com/casapeon; Calle 12 No 120B; breakfasts M$55-95, dinners M$70-150; ⏲8am-3am; 📶) Casa Peon's restaurant does the best breakfast in town, it has a great dinner menu, and the bar has become party central since it's the only spot in Celestún where you can drink after hours. The Casa doubles as a small hotel, with two comfortable rooms (M$400-500), and a campground (per person M$100).

La Playita SEAFOOD **$$**
(Calle 12; mains M$80-150; ⏲10am-6pm) Of all the sandy-floored beachfront joints here, this one gets the thumbs-up from the locals. Fresh seafood and *ceviche* are its main draw.

La Palapa SEAFOOD **$$**
(Calle 12; mains M$80-150; ⏲11am-7pm) A cut above the other seaside joints, La Palapa has an expansive dining area looking down to the sea, attentive staff and savory seafood dishes, including coconut-coated shrimp served in a coconut shell.

Restaurant Los Pampanos SEAFOOD **$$**
(Calle 12; mains M$60-140; ⏲11am-7pm) A tranquil joint on the beach, north of Calle 11, this is a great spot for afternoon drinks on the sand. Try the octopus *ceviche* or a fish fillet stuffed to the brim with shellfish.

Restaurante Chivirico SEAFOOD **$$**
(cnr Calles 11 & 12; mains M$70-140; ⏲10am-7.30pm) A large place with wicker chairs and a TV that gives you a daily dose of Spanish soaps, the Chivirico has excellent seafood and is well worth the visit. The *ensalada de jaiba* (crab salad) is delicious.

ℹ Information

There are no banks in town. You'll find an ATM on the plaza and another one inside Super Willy's, also located on the plaza. Don't plan on using high-speed internet here.

ℹ Getting There & Away

Frequent buses head for Celestún (M$49, 2½ hours) from Mérida's Noreste bus terminal. The route terminates at Celestún's plaza, a block inland from Calle 12.

There are also *colectivos* (shared vans) on the plaza that will take you to downtown Mérida for M$35.

By car from Mérida, the best route to Celestún is via the new road out of Umán.

Ruined Haciendas Route

Still very much under the radar, this fascinating route allows you to appreciate some impressive old haciendas in rural Maya communities. If you're driving out of Celestún, turn south off Hwy 281 and head toward Chunchucmil, the name of both a ruined *henequén* hacienda and a nearby Maya archaeological site. A caretaker there will gladly show you around – just make sure to pay him a tip.

After Chunchucmil (look for the covered Maya mounds as you drive away), about every 5km you'll pass another ruined hacienda all the way to Hacienda Granada, shortly before the road hits old Hwy 180. Several of the buildings are hard to see from the road, so you'll need to stop frequently to really give them their due.

There are two **talleres de arte popular** (pop-art workshops) near the church in Granada. Stop by from 10am to 6pm Monday to Friday and 10am to 2pm Saturday to watch local women create *jipijapa* (palm frond) hats and baskets as well as *henequén* crafts. They make a living doing this, so it's a nice gesture to buy something from them.

Hacienda Santa Rosa (☎999-923-1923; www.thehaciendas.com; Carretera Merida-Campeche, Km 129; r/ste from M$7096/8418; P❄📶🏊) is the only hacienda in the area that has been converted into a hotel, and it has a lovely botanical garden. The luxury rooms and suites show amazing variety; some have private walled gardens with bathtubs or plunge pools. The hacienda has a gourmet restaurant serving regional cuisine (mains M$160 to M$360); nonguests welcome.

Dzibilchaltún

The longest continuously utilized Maya administrative and ceremonial city, **Dzibilchaltún** (Place of Inscribed Flat Stones; adult/child under 13yr M$118/6, parking M$20; ⏲8am-5pm; P) served the Maya from around 1500 BC until the European conquest in the 1540s. At the height of its greatness, Dzibilchaltún covered 15 sq km. Some 8400 structures were mapped by archaeologists in the 1960s; few of these have been excavated.

In some ways it's unimpressive if you've already seen larger places, such as Chichén Itzá or Uxmal, but twice a year humble Dzibilchaltún shines. At sunrise on the equinoxes (approximately March 21 and September 23), the sun aligns directly with the main door of the **Templo de las Siete Muñecas** (Temple of the Seven Dolls), which got its name from seven grotesque dolls discovered here during excavations. As the sun rises, the temple doors glow, then 'light up' as the sun passes behind. It also casts a cool square beam on the crumbled wall behind. Many who have seen both feel the sunrise here is more spectacular than Chichén Itzá's

OFF THE BEATEN TRACK

DIY ADVENTURE IN YUCATÁN

There are so many great adventures to be had in this region. Here are some ideas to get you started as you leave the guidebook behind for a few days of DIY adventure.

- Just off the road to Mayapán, **Tekit** has a cenote worth visiting.
- Friar Diego de Landa burned 5000 idols, 13 altars, 27 religious and historic codices and 197 ceremonial vases in an auto-da-fé in 1562 in the town of **Maní**. The town has a nice cathedral, and the Príncipe de Tutul-Xiu restaurant's *poc-chuc* (grilled pork) is so popular that families drive here from afar to delight in the famed dish.
- The rarely visited tourist route **La Ruta de los Conventos** takes you to colonial-era convents in the towns of Maní, Oxkutzcab, Teabo, Mama, Chumayel, Tekax and Yotholín.
- The seldom-visited town of **Yodznot**, west of Chichén Itzá on the old highway, is developing grassroots tourism.

famous snake, and is well worth getting up at the crack of dawn to witness.

Enter the site along a nature trail that terminates at the modern, air-conditioned **Museo del Pueblo Maya** (8am-4pm Tue-Sun). It has artifacts from throughout the Maya regions of Mexico, including some superb colonial-era religious carvings and other pieces. Exhibits explaining both ancient and modern Maya daily life are labeled in Spanish and English. Beyond the museum, a path leads to the central plaza, where you'll find an open chapel that dates from early Spanish times (1590 to 1600).

The **Cenote Xlacah** is more than 40m deep. In 1958 a National Geographic Society diving expedition recovered more than 30,000 Maya artifacts, many of ritual significance, from the cenote. The most interesting of these are now on display in the site's museum. South of the cenote is **Estructura 44** – at 130m it's one of the longest Maya structures in existence.

Dzibilchaltún is about 17km due north of central Mérida. Minibuses and *colectivos* depart frequently from Mérida's Parque de San Juan for the village of Dzibilchaltún Ruinas (M$11, 30 minutes), a little over 1km from the museum. Taxis cost around M$200 round-trip.

Progreso

969 / POP 37,400

If Mérida's heat has you dying for a quick beach fix, or if you want to see the longest wharf (7km) in Mexico, head to Progreso (also known as Puerto Progreso). The beach is fine, well groomed and long. However, except for the small *palapas* erected by restaurants, it's nearly shadeless and is dominated by the view of the wharf, giving it a rather industrial feel. Winds can hit here full force off the Gulf in the afternoon and can blow well into the night, which makes for good kitesurfing. As with other Gulf beaches, the water is murky; visibility even on calm days rarely exceeds 5m. None of this stops *meridanos* from coming in droves on weekends, especially in summer. Even on spring weekdays it can be difficult to find a room with a view. Once or twice a week the streets flood with cruise-ship tourists, but the place can feel empty on off nights, which makes a refreshing change.

Activities

Kite Beach KITESURFING

(999-910-8721; www.kitebeachyucatan.com; Calle 21, btwn Calles 34 & 36; kitesurfing classes per hr M$900, bicycle rental per hr M$50) The best – and only – kitesurfing operation in town, run by friendly Canadian and British expats. Also rents out bikes and offers sleeping accomodations.

Sleeping & Eating

The majority of hotels and restaurants in Progreso are no more than 11 blocks north and east of the bus terminal. Head inland to get cheaper, more authentic eats.

Playa Linda Hotel HOTEL $

(985-858-0519, 999-220-8318; www.playalindahotel.com.mx; Calle 76, btwn Calles 19 & 21; r/ste from M$500/800;) Rooms go fast at this new budget hotel on the boardwalk, so book ahead. Comfy standard rooms are decked out with contemporary dark-wood furnishings, while suites come with kitchenettes and beachfront balconies.

Hotel Colonial HOTEL $

(935-2021; are@multired.net.mx; Calle 33 No 151, btwn Calles 82 & 84; r M$390;) It's a five-minute walk to the beach, but it's so much more comfortable here than at some of the run-down, boardwalk budget hotels. Rooms have two good beds and cable TV, and there's a small pool if you want to take a dip.

Hotel Yakunah HOTEL $$

(935-5600; www.hotelyakunah.com.mx; Calle 21, btwn Calles 48 & 50; r/apt M$850/1500; P) About 1.5km east of downtown, this fantastic hotel is set in an old rancher's mansion. Rooms are spacious and atmospheric, with good fittings and excellent beds. The beach is a short walk away and the on-site restaurant-bar is hugely inviting.

Condhotel HOTEL $$

(935-5079; info@condhotelprogreso.com; Calle 21, btwn Calles 66 & 68; d/ste from M$650/800;) Just a block from the beach, street-facing rooms here catch a nice ocean breeze, and the open-air lobby has a small swimming pool with lounge chairs and an adjoining bar. The larger apartments and suites are good for families.

El Naranjo MEXICAN $

(Calle 27, btwn Calles 78 & 80; tacos/tortas M$7/14; 6am-2pm) One of the best options in the market for *cochinita* – and it's spiffy clean.

Restaurant El Cordobes MEXICAN $

(935-2621; cnr Calles 80 & 31; breakfast mains M$42-75, lunch & dinner mains M$66-110; 6am-midnight) This locals' joint is on the north side of the plaza in a 100-year-old building. Weak 'American' coffee is served quickly, with a warm smile, and it's a perfect place to relax for a bit, sluice down a *cerveza* (beer) and look out on the main plaza.

La Casa del Malecón SEAFOOD $$

(Calle 19, btwn Calles 62 & 64; mains M$85-140; 9am-7pm Sun, Mon & Wed, 10am-8pm Thu, 10am-2am Fri & Sat) Right on the boardwalk, this pleasant beach house serves excellent fresh fish and seafood in a palm-shaded garden with a small swimming pool. It's also a nice spot to knock back a few cold ones.

Eladio's SEAFOOD $$

(www.eladios.com.mx; cnr Calles 19 & 80; mains M$75-155; 10am-9pm;) The local's choice is this casual beachfront eatery under the *palapa* roof. Five complimentary sampler plates of seafood and salads comes to your table before your main dish arrives, so you better be good and hungry.

Buddy's INTERNATIONAL $$

(999-233-3171; Calle 19 No 150; mains M$85-145; 9am-midnight;) Popular with snowbirds, this casual beachfront joint prepares fresh fish and seafood along with a fair share of American comfort food. The bar warms up after dark.

Orientation

Progreso's even-numbered streets run north–south; odd ones, east–west. The bus terminal, on Calle 29, is west of Calle 82, a block north (toward the water) from the main plaza. From the plaza on Calle 80, it's six short blocks to the *malecón* (waterfront promenade; Calle 19) and *muelle* (wharf).

Information

There are two Banamex banks, one with an ATM, on Calle 80. Internet cafes offering so-so access are sprinkled everywhere, especially around the bus terminal. Some stay open until 9pm, others as late as 1am, charging about M$10 per hour.

Getting There & Away

Progreso is 33km north of Mérida along a fast four-lane highway that's basically a continuation of the Paseo de Montejo.

The **bus station** (Calle 27, btwn Calles 80 & 82) has frequent Mérida-bound buses (M$16). There are also *colectivos* to Mérida departing from the corner of Calles 80 & 29. To get to Progreso from Mérida, go to the Progreso Bus Terminal (p156).

East of Progreso

Heading east from Progreso, Hwy 27 parallels the coast for 70km, to Dzilam de Bravo, before turning inland. It's a beautiful drive, and you'll pass miles of mixed mangrove clumps and notice that on the right (south) the mud takes on a pink color. Unsurprisingly, this area is named the Laguna Rosada (Pink Lagoon).

On the seaward (north) side of the Pink Lagoon, things are less pristine, with a lot of new timeshares, condo-mondos and hotels. Local fishing communities are taking a big hit as land prices rise with the tourism and second-home boom. But things are still pretty laid-back here. It might even be a good spot to do a little guerrilla camping on the beach. Remember, the beach is public property in Mexico.

From a tall wooden observation tower at the edge of the lagoon at **Uaymitún**, you can watch flamingos, as well as ibis, herons, spoonbills and other waterfowl.

The buildings thin out beyond Uaymitún, and about 16km east of it, a road heads south from the coast some 3km across the bird-riddled lagoon to the turnoff for the ruins of **Xcambó**, a Maya salt-distribution center with a few rebuilt structures. While it's technically free to visit the ruins, the caretaker may ask for a small donation. Following the road south beyond the ruins turnoff takes you into grassy marshland with cattails and scatterings of palm trees, a beautiful landscape providing ample opportunities for bird-spotting without even getting out of the car.

Back on Hwy 27 heading east, the next town you'll reach is **Telchac Puerto**, which has the most eating and sleeping options in the region. If you're up for roughing it, you'll find several *cabañas* (cabins) on a quiet palm-flanked beach in the sleepy fishing town of **San Crisanto**, east of Telchac, and further east, just before reaching Dzilam de Bravo, you'll come across more cabins at the **Perla Escondida** (☎991-107-9321; cabins M$500).

Telchac Puerto

There really isn't much to do in Telchac Puerto but sit on the brown-sand beach, suck the briny air and wait for the earth to turn another rotation. There are no ATMs or banks here, and it's best to arrive by car. The town, a few kilometers east of the turnoff to Xcambó on the road to Dzilam, is a good place to base yourself for adventures along this forgotten-but-not-totally-lost coast.

Sleeping & Eating

Hotel Libros y Sueños HOTEL **$**

(☎991-917-4125; Calle 23 No 200; s/d M$250/350; 📶) The simple Hotel Libros y Sueños offers a big English-language library and clean rooms, and it's just a block away from the beach.

Hotel Reef Yucatán HOTEL **$$$**

(☎991-917-5000, reservations 999-941-9494; www.reefyucatan.com; Zona Hotelera Telchac Puerto; s/d M$975/1900; P ❄ 🏊) The monstro all-inclusive Hotel Reef Yucatán has 150 rooms and family-friendly facilities such as a large swimming pool, a miniature golf course and a kids club.

La Picuda SEAFOOD **$$**

(Calle 20; mains M$60-150; ⏲10.30am-6pm) Locals highly recommend this eatery just off the square near the pier. The *filete al mojo de ajo* (fish sautéed with garlic) is really good, as are the free *botanas* (snacks) that come to the table before the main dish.

EASTERN YUCATÁN STATE

Scrub jungle, intact colonial cities, cenotes aplenty and Yucatán's largest coastal estuary are but a few of the attractions in the eastern portion of this state. Oh, and then there's one of the new wonders of the world, Chichén Itzá, as well as a smattering of less-visited (but nonetheless impressive) Maya ruins.

Izamal

☎988 / POP 16,200

In ancient times Izamal was a center for the worship of the supreme Maya god, Itzamná, and the sun god, Kinich-Kakmó. A dozen temple pyramids were devoted to these or other gods. No doubt these bold expressions of Maya religiosity are why the Spanish colonists chose Izamal as the site for an enormous and impressive Franciscan monastery, which still stands at the heart of this town, located about 70km east of Mérida.

The Izamal of today is a quiet provincial town, nicknamed La Ciudad Amarilla (The Yellow City) for the traditional yellow buildings that spiral out from the center like a budding daisy. It's easily explored on foot, and horse-drawn carriages add to the city's charm.

Sights

It's worth taking the time to visit the **talleres de arte** (artisan workshops) found throughout the city. Most hotels and some restaurants have free tourist maps with the workshops' locations labeled.

Convento de San Antonio de Padua MONASTERY

(admission free, sound-and-light show admission M$87, museum M$5; ⏲6am-8pm, sound-and-light show 8.30pm Tue, Thu & Sat, museum 10am-1pm & 3-6pm Mon-Sat, 9am-5pm Sun) When the

Spaniards conquered Izamal, they destroyed the major Maya temple, the Ppapp-Hol-Chac pyramid, and in 1533 began to build from its stones one of the first monasteries in the western hemisphere. Work on Convento de San Antonio de Padua was finished in 1561. Under the monastery's arcades, look for building stones with an unmistakable maze-like design; these were clearly taken from the earlier Maya temple.

The monastery's principal church is the **Santuario de la Virgen de Izamal**, approached by a ramp from the main square. The ramp leads into the **Atrium**, a huge arcaded courtyard in which the **fiesta of the Virgin of Izamal** takes place each August 15. There's a **sound-and-light show** here three nights a week.

At some point the 16th-century **frescoes** beside the entrance of the sanctuary were completely painted over. For years they lay concealed under a thin layer of whitewash until a maintenance worker who was cleaning the walls discovered them.

The church's original altarpiece was destroyed by a fire believed to have been started by a fallen candle. Its replacement, impressively gilded, was built in the 1940s. In the niches at the stations of the cross are some superb small figures.

In the small courtyard to the left of the church, look up and toward the Atrium to see the original sundial projecting from the roof's edge. A small **museum** at the back commemorates Pope John Paul II's 1993 visit to the monastery. He brought with him a silver crown for the statue of the patron saint of Yucatán, the Virgin of Izamal.

The monastery's front entrance faces west; it's flanked by Calles 31 and 33 on the north and south, respectively, and Calles 28 and 30 on the east and west. The best time to visit is in the morning, as the church is occasionally closed during the afternoon siesta.

Centro Cultural y Artesanal MUSEUM
(www.centroculturalizamal.org.mx; Calle 31 No 201; admission M$25; ⏲9am-9pm Mon-Sat, to 5pm Sun) Southeast of the convent, this cultural center and museum showcases pop art from around Mexico. The center also rents bicycles (M$25 per hour) and has an excellent shop selling fair trade–certified crafts made by artisans from 12 indigenous communities. Any purchase you make is a direct source of income for rural indigenous families.

Kinich-Kakmó ARCHAEOLOGICAL SITE
(⏲8am-5pm) Three of the town's original 12 Maya pyramids have been partially restored. The largest (and the third-largest in Yucatán) is the enormous Kinich-Kakmó, three blocks north of the monastery. You can climb it for free.

Sleeping & Eating

Several *loncherías* occupy spaces in the market on the monastery's southwest side.

Posada Flory INN $
(☎954-0070; cnr Calles 30 & 27; s M$200, d with air-con M$250; ❄) There's a nice little center patio in this small, uberclean budget hotel – probably the best low-end deal in town. The family that runs it is quite friendly.

★**Romantic Hotel Santo Domingo** HOTEL $$
(☎967-6136; www.izamalhotel.com; Calle 18, btwn Calles 33 & 35; campsites M$120-210, cabaña with shared bathroom M$590, r M$790-1190, ste M$1390-1890; P 📶 🏊) Don't let the name fool you. Sure, you can snuggle up with your cutie-pie here, but it's not *that* kind of place. It's actually a really cool spot with lovely gardens, a nice pool and accommodations for all budgets, from affordable camping to large family suites that sleep up to five people.

Macan Ché B&B $$
(☎954-0287; www.macanche.com; Calle 22 No 305, btwn Calles 33 & 35; r/ste incl breakfast M$700/850; P ❄ 📶 🏊) It's about three long (yes, long!) blocks east of the monastery (take Calle 31 toward Cancún and turn right on Calle 22) to this very Zen hotel, which has a cluster of cottages and a small 'cenote' pool in a woodsy setting. The most expensive of the rooms has air-con and a kitchenette.

San Miguel Arcangel HOTEL $$
(☎954-0109; www.sanmiguelhotel.com.mx; Calle 31A No 308; r incl breakfast from M$600; ❄ 📶) You have the main square right at the doorstep of this hotel, while in the rear there's a quiet garden area. Rooms are done up colonial style with a few modern creature comforts like cable TV and air-con.

★**Kinich** MEXICAN $$
(www.kinichizamal.com; Calle 27 No 299, btwn Calles 28 & 30; mains M$70-95; ⏲noon-9pm) This is fresh, handmade *yucateco* cuisine at its best. The *papadzules kinich* – rolled tortillas stuffed with diced egg and topped with

pumpkin seed sauce and smoky sausage – is a delightful house specialty.

El Toro MEXICAN **$$**
(Calle 33 No 303; mains M$85-100; ⌚8am-midnight) At the southeast corner of the roundabout in front of the monastery, this small family-run establishment specializes in *yucateco* fare (with a few international favorites thrown in to keep the tourists happy). Try traditional classics like *queso relleno* and *relleno negro*.

Information

Most restaurants and hotels here have a copy of the excellent free tourist map. The map is available in several languages and describes various walking tours and locations for handicraft demonstrations.

Getting There & Around

Oriente operates frequent buses to Mérida (M$23, 1½ hours) from Izamal's **bus terminal** (☎954-0107), two blocks west of the monastery. There are buses to Valladolid (M$50, two hours, three daily) as well. Going to Chichén Itzá (M$57, 1½ hours, hourly), you must change buses at Hoctún. There are also departures to Tizimín (M$78, 2½ hours, two daily) and Cancún (M$130, six hours, three daily).

Taxis around town charge M$15, and horse carriage rides cost M$200 per hour.

OFF THE BEATEN TRACK

PUEBLOS & PLACES OFF THE MAP

There's a ton of good off-the-map adventures to be had in and around Izamal. Here are a few of our favorites:

Cuauhtémoc A small community 6km south of Izamal on an extension of Calle 24, with a 17th-century chapel.

Kimbilá Located 8km west of Izamal on an extension of Calle 31, this town is famous for its embroidery.

Iztamatul, Habuk, Chaltún Há & beyond Some 80 pre-Hispanic structures have been discovered within Izamal's city limits. Habuk, Itzamatul and Chaltún Há are just a few. They are all free to the public, and you can hire a guide at the tourist center.

Chichén Itzá

☎985 / POP 5500

The most famous and best restored of the Yucatán Maya sites, **Chichén Itzá** (Mouth of the Well of the Itzáes; off Hwy 180, Pisté; admission M$182, parking M$22, sound & light show M$75, guide M$600; ⌚8am-6pm Apr-Sep, to 5:30pm Oct-Mar), while tremendously overcrowded – every gaper and his grandmother is trying to check off the new seven wonders of the world – will still impress even the most jaded visitor. Many mysteries of the Maya astronomical calendar are made clear when one understands the design of the 'time temples' here. Other than a few minor passageways, climbing on the structures is not allowed.

At the **vernal and autumnal equinoxes** (around March 21 and September 23), the morning and afternoon sun produces a light-and-shadow illusion of the serpent ascending or descending the side of El Castillo's staircase. The site is mobbed on these dates, however, making it difficult to see, and after the spectacle, parts of the site are sometimes closed to the public. The illusion is almost as good in the week preceding and following each equinox (and draws much smaller crowds), and is recreated nightly in the light-and-sound show year-round. Some find the spectacle fascinating, others think it's overrated. Either way, if you're in the area around the equinox and you've got your own car, it's easy to wake up early for Dzibilchaltún's fiery sunrise and then make it to Chichén Itzá by midafternoon, catching both spectacles on the same day.

The heat, humidity and crowds can be fierce; try to explore the site (especially around El Castillo) either early in the morning or late in the afternoon.

Hold on to your wristband ticket; it gives you in-and-out privileges and admission to that evening's sound-and-light show. The 45-minute show in Spanish begins each evening at 8pm in summer and 7pm in winter. It costs M$75 if you don't already have a ruins wristband, and it counts toward the admission price the following day. Devices for listening to English, French, German or Italian translations (beamed via infrared) rent for M$39. Specify the language you need or it may not be broadcast.

History

Most archaeologists agree that the first major settlement at Chichén Itzá, during the late Classic period, was pure Maya. In about the 9th century, the city was largely abandoned for reasons unknown.

Chichén Itzá

It doesn't take long to realize why the Maya site of Chichén Itzá is one of Mexico's most popular tourist draws. Approaching the grounds from the main entrance, the striking castle pyramid **El Castillo** 1 jumps right out at you – and the wow factor never lets up.

It's easy to tackle Chichén Itzá in one day. Within a stone's throw of the castle, you'll find the Maya world's largest **ball court** 2 alongside eerie carvings of skulls and heart-devouring eagles at the Temple of Jaguars and the Platform of Skulls. On the other (eastern) side are the highly adorned **Group of a Thousand Columns** 3 and the **Temple of Warriors** 4. A short walk north of the castle leads to the gaping **Sacred Cenote** 5, an important pilgrimage site. On the other side of El Castillo, you'll find giant stone serpents watching over the High Priest's Grave, aka El Osario. Further south, marvel at the spiral-domed **Observatory** 6, the imposing Nunnery and Akab-Dzib, one of the oldest ruins.

Roaming the 47-hectare site, it's fun to consider that at its height Chichén Itzá was home to an estimated 90,000 inhabitants and spanned approximately 30 sq km. So essentially you're looking at just a small part of a once-great city.

THE LOWDOWN

» **Arrive** at 8am and you'll have a good three hours or so before the tour-bus madness begins. Early birds escape the merchants, too.

» **Remember** that Chichén Itzá is the name of the site; the actual town where it's located is called Pisté.

El Caracol
Observatory
Today they'd probably just use a website, but back in the day priests would stand from the dome of the circular observatory to announce the latest rituals and celebrations.

Grupo de las Mil Columnas
Group of a Thousand Columns
Not unlike a hall of fame exhibit, the pillars surrounding the temple reveal carvings of gods, dignitaries and celebrated warriors.

LONELY PLANET/GETTY IMAGES ©

El Castillo

The Castle

Even this mighty pyramid can't bear the stress of a million visitors ascending its stairs each year. No climbing allowed, but the ground-level view doesn't disappoint.

AFP/GETTY IMAGES ©

Gran Juego de Pelota

Great Ball Court

How is it possible to hear someone talk from one end of this long, open-air court to the other? To this day, the acoustics remain a mystery.

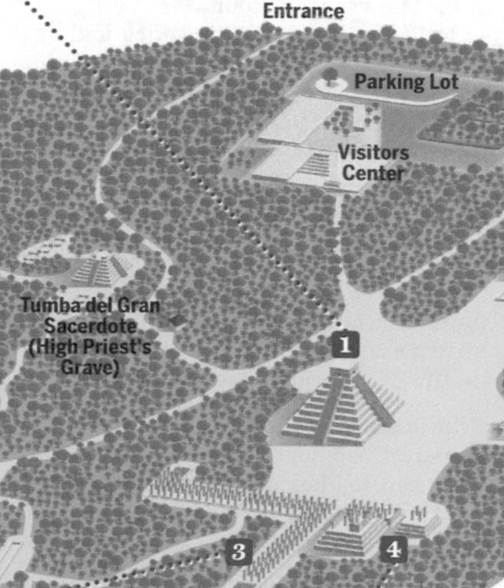

Cenote Sagrado

Sacred Cenote

Diving expeditions have turned up hundreds of valuable artifacts dredged from the cenote (limestone sinkhole), not to mention human bones of sacrificial victims who were forced to jump into the eternal underworld.

Templo de los Guerreros

Temple of Warriors

The Maya associated warriors with eagles and jaguars, as depicted in the temple's friezes. The revered jaguar, in particular, was a symbol of strength and agility.

EDUCATION IMAGES/UIG/GETTY IMAGES ©

JUAN CARLOS MUNOZ/GETTY IMAGES ©

It was resettled around the late 10th century, and shortly thereafter it is believed to have been invaded by the Toltecs, who had migrated from their central highlands capital of Tula, north of Mexico City. The bellicose Toltec culture was fused with that of the Maya, incorporating the cult of Quetzalcóatl (Kukulcán, in Maya). You will see images of both Chac, the Maya rain god, and Quetzalcóatl, the plumed serpent, throughout the city.

The substantial fusion of highland central Mexican and Puuc architectural styles makes Chichén unique among the Yucatán Peninsula's ruins. The fabulous El Castillo and the Plataforma de Venus are outstanding architectural works built during the height of Toltec cultural input.

The sanguinary Toltecs contributed more than their architectural skills to the Maya: they elevated human sacrifice to a near obsession, and there are numerous carvings of the bloody ritual in Chichén demonstrating this.

After a Maya leader moved his political capital to Mayapán while keeping Chichén as his religious capital, Chichén Itzá fell into decline. Why it was subsequently abandoned in the 14th century is a mystery, but the once great city remained the site of Maya pilgrimages for many years.

Sights

Exploring the Site

Visitors Center Museum MUSEUM

(8am-5pm) The visitors center has a small museum, with sculptures, reliefs, artifacts and explanations in Spanish, English and French.

Chilam Balam Auditorio GALLERY

The Chilam Balam Auditorio, next to the museum, sometimes has video shows about Chichén and other Mexican sites. The picture quality can be truly abominable, but the air-con is great. In the central space of the visitors center stands a scale model of the archaeological site, and off toward the toilets is an exhibit on Edward Thompson's excavations of the Cenote Sagrado.

El Castillo ARCHAEOLOGICAL SITE

Entering the grounds, El Castillo (aka the Pyramid of Kukulcán) rises before you in all its grandeur. The first temple here was pre-Toltec, built around AD 800, but the present 25m-high structure, built over the old one, has the plumed serpent sculpted along the stairways and Toltec warriors represented in the doorway carvings at the top of the temple.

You won't get to see these temple-top carvings, however, as ascending the pyramid is not allowed.

The structure is actually a massive Maya calendar formed in stone. Each of El Castillo's nine levels is divided in two by a staircase, making 18 separate terraces that commemorate the 18 20-day months of the Maya Vague Year. The four stairways have 91 steps each; add the top platform and the total is 365, the number of days in the year. On each facade of the pyramid are 52 flat panels, which are reminders of the 52 years in the Maya calendar round.

To top it off, during the spring and autumn equinoxes, light and shadow form a series of triangles on the side of the north staircase that mimic the creep of a serpent (note the carved serpent's heads flanking the bottom of the staircase).

The older pyramid inside El Castillo has a red jaguar throne with inlaid eyes and spots of jade; also lying behind the screen is a *chacmool* (Maya sacrificial stone sculpture). The entrance to **El Túnel**, the passage up to the throne, is at the base of El Castillo's north side. You can't go in, though.

Gran Juego de Pelota ARCHAEOLOGICAL SITE

The great ball court, the largest and most impressive in Mexico, is only one of the city's eight courts, indicative of the importance of the games held here. The court, to the left of the visitors center, is flanked by temples at either end and is bounded by towering parallel walls with stone rings cemented up high.

There is evidence that the ball game may have changed over the years. Some carvings show players with padding on their elbows and knees, and it is thought that they played a soccer-like game with a hard rubber ball, with the use of hands forbidden. Other carvings show players wielding bats; it appears that if a player hit the ball through one of the stone hoops, his team was declared the winner. It may be that during the Toltec period, the losing captain, and perhaps his teammates as well, were sacrificed (and you thought your dad was hard on you in Little League).

Along the walls of the ball court are stone reliefs, including scenes of decapitations of players. The court exhibits some interesting acoustics: a conversation at one end can be

DREDGING CHICHÉN'S SACRED CENOTE

Around 1900, Edward Thompson, a Harvard professor and US consul to Yucatán, bought the hacienda that included Chichén Itzá for M$750. No doubt intrigued by local stories of female virgins being sacrificed to the Maya deities by being thrown into the site's cenote, Thompson resolved to have the cenote dredged.

He imported dredging equipment and set to work. Gold and jade jewelry from all parts of Mexico and as far away as Colombia was recovered, along with other artifacts and a variety of human bones. Many of the artifacts were shipped to Harvard's Peabody Museum, but some have since been returned to Mexico.

Subsequent diving expeditions in the 1920s and 1960s turned up hundreds of other valuable artifacts. It appears that all sorts of people – children and old people, the diseased and the injured, and the young and the vigorous – were forcibly obliged to take an eternal swim in Chichén's Cenote Sagrado.

The cenote is reached by walking about 200m north from the Plataforma de Venus.

heard 135m away at the other, and a clap produces multiple loud echoes.

Templo del Barbado & Templo de los Jaguares y Escudos TEMPLE

The structure at the northern end of the ball court, called the Temple of the Bearded Man after a carving inside it, has some finely sculpted pillars and reliefs of flowers, birds and trees. The Temple of the Jaguars and Shields, built atop the southeast corner of the ball court's wall, has some columns with carved rattlesnakes and tablets with etched jaguars. Inside are faded mural fragments depicting a battle.

Plataforma de los Cráneos ARCHAEOLOGICAL SITE

The Platform of Skulls (Tzompantli in Náhuatl, a Maya dialect) is between the Templo de los Jaguares and El Castillo. You can't mistake it, because the T-shaped platform is festooned with carved skulls and eagles tearing open the chests of men to eat their hearts. In ancient days this platform was used to display the heads of sacrificial victims.

Plataforma de las Águilas y los Jaguares TEMPLE

Adjacent to the Tzompantli, the carvings on the Platform of the Eagles and Jaguars depict those animals gruesomely grabbing human hearts in their claws. It is thought that this platform was part of a temple dedicated to the military legions responsible for capturing sacrificial victims.

Cenote Sagrado ARCHAEOLOGICAL SITE

From the Tzompantli, a 300m rough stone *sacbé* runs north (a five-minute walk) to the huge sunken well that gave the city its name. The Sacred Cenote is an awesome natural well, some 60m in diameter and 35m deep. The walls between the summit and the water's surface are ensnared in tangled vines and other vegetation. There are ruins of a small steam bath next to the cenote, as well as a concession stand with toilets.

Grupo de las Mil Columnas ARCHAEOLOGICAL SITE

This group to the east of El Castillo takes its name – which means 'Group of the Thousand Columns' – from the forest of pillars stretching south and east. The star attraction here is the **Templo de los Guerreros** (Temple of the Warriors), adorned with stucco and stone-carved animal deities.

At the top of its steps is a classic reclining *chacmool* figure, but ascending to it is no longer allowed.

Many of the columns in front of the temple are carved with figures of warriors. Archaeologists working in 1926 discovered a Temple of Chacmool lying beneath the Temple of the Warriors.

You can walk through the columns on its south side to reach the **Columnata Noreste**, notable for the 'big-nosed god' masks on its facade. Some have been reassembled on the ground around the statue. Just to the south are the remains of the **Baño de Vapor** (Steam Bath or Sweat House) with an underground oven and drains for the water. The sweat houses (there are two onsite) were regularly used for ritual purification.

El Osario ARCHAEOLOGICAL SITE

The Ossuary, otherwise known as the Bonehouse or the **Tumba del Gran Sacerdote**

(High Priest's Grave), is a ruined pyramid to the southwest of El Castillo. As with most of the buildings in this southern section, the architecture is more Puuc than Toltec. It's notable for the beautiful serpent heads at the base of its staircases.

A square shaft at the top of the structure leads into a cave beneath that was used as a burial chamber; seven tombs with human remains were discovered inside. These days a snack bar with telephone and toilets stands nearby.

El Caracol ARCHAEOLOGICAL SITE

Called El Caracol (The Snail) by the Spaniards for its interior spiral staircase, this **observatory**, to the south of the Ossuary, is one of the most fascinating and important of all Chichén Itzá's buildings (but, alas, you can't enter it). Its circular design resembles some central highlands structures, although, surprisingly, not those of Toltec Tula.

In a fusion of architectural styles and religious imagery, there are Maya Chac rain-god masks over four external doors facing the cardinal points. The windows in the observatory's dome are aligned with the appearance of certain stars at specific dates. From the dome the priests decreed the times for rituals, celebrations, corn-planting and harvests.

Edificio de las Monjas & La Iglesia PALACE

Thought by archaeologists to have been a palace for Maya royalty, the so-called Edificio de las Monjas (Nunnery), with its myriad rooms, resembled a European convent to the conquistadors, hence their name for the building. The building's dimensions are imposing: its base is 60m long, 30m wide and 20m high.

The construction is Maya rather than Toltec, although a Toltec sacrificial stone stands in front. A smaller adjoining building to the east, known as La Iglesia (The Church), is covered almost entirely with carvings. On the far side at the back there are some passageways that are still open, leading a short way into the labyrinth inside. They are dank and slippery, they smell of bat urine, and it's easy to twist an ankle as you go, but Indiana Jones wannabes will think it's totally cool.

Akab-Dzib ARCHAEOLOGICAL SITE

East of the Nunnery, the Puuc-style Akab-Dzib is thought by some archaeologists to be the most ancient structure excavated here. The central chambers date from the 2nd century. The name means 'Obscure Writing' in Maya and refers to the south-side annex door, whose lintel depicts a priest with a vase etched with hieroglyphics that have yet to be successfully translated.

Cenote

Ik Kil Parque Eco-Arqueológico SWIMMING

(☎858-1525; cenote_ikkil@hotmail.com; Hwy 180, Km 122; adult/child M$70/35; ⏲8am-5pm; 👪) About 3km east of the western entrance to the ruins, the cenote here has been developed into a divine swimming spot. Cascades of water plunge from the high limestone roof, which is ringed by greenery. Arrive no later than 1pm to beat the tour groups.

The on-site restaurant has a good lunch buffet (M$150), and there are also well-appointed, spacious *cabañas* (some sleep up to eight). The large doubles go for M$1250, while the huge family-friendly duplex with kitchen costs M$3000.

Caverns

Grutas de Balankanché CAVES

(Hwy 180; adult/child 7-12yr M$105/6; ⏲9am-4pm) In 1959 a guide to the Chichén ruins was exploring a cave on his day off when he came upon a narrow passageway. He followed the passageway for 300m, meandering through a series of caverns. In each, perched on mounds amid scores of glistening stalactites, were hundreds of ceremonial treasures the Maya had placed there 800 years earlier.

Among the discovered objects were ritual *metates* and *manos* (grinding stones), incense burners and pots. In the years following the discovery, the ancient ceremonial objects were removed and studied. Eventually most of them were returned to the caves, and placed exactly where they were found.

Outside the caves, you'll find a good botanical garden (displaying native flora with information on the medicinal and other uses of the trees and plants) and a small museum. The museum features large photographs taken during the exploration of the caves, and descriptions (in English, Spanish and French) of the Maya religion and the offerings found in the caves. Also on display are photographs of modern-day Maya ceremonies called Ch'a Chaac, which continue to be held in all the villages on the Yucatán Peninsula during times of drought and consist mostly of praying and making numerous offerings of food to Chac.

Compulsory 45-minute tours (minimum six people, maximum 30) have melodramatic, not-very-informative recorded narration that is nearly impossible to make out, but if you'd like it in a particular language, English is at 11am, 1pm and 3pm; Spanish is at 9am, noon, 2pm and 4pm; and French is at 10am.

Be warned that the cave is unusually hot, and ventilation is poor in its further reaches. The lack of oxygen (especially after a few groups have already passed through) makes it difficult to draw a full breath until you're outside again.

The turnoff for the caverns is 6km east of Chichén Itzá on the highway to Valladolid. Second-class buses heading east from Pisté toward Valladolid will drop you at the Balankanché road. The entrance to the caves is 350m north of the highway.

Sleeping

Most of Chichén Itzá's lodgings, restaurants and services are arranged along 1km of highway in the town of Pisté, to the western (Mérida) side of the ruins. It's 1.5km from the ruins' main (west) entrance to the nearest hotel (Pirámide Inn) in Pisté, and 2.5km from the ruins to Pisté's town plaza.

On the eastern (Valladolid) side, it's 1.5km from the highway along the access road to the eastern entrance to the ruins; top-end hotels line the road, the closest being only about 100m from the entrance.

Don't hesitate to haggle for a bed in the low season (May, June, September and October), when prices drop. Hwy 180 is known as Calle 15 on its way through Pisté. There are two top-end hotels close to the archaeological zone's eastern entrance.

Pirámide Inn HOTEL $

(851-0115; www.chichen.com; Calle 15A No 30; campsites per person M$50, hammocks/r M$100/500; P) Campers can pitch a tent or hang a hammock under a *palapa*, enjoy the inn's pool, have use of tepid showers and watch satellite TV in the lobby. Campers also have use of clean shared toilet facilities and a safe place to stow gear. Spacious rooms have good bathrooms and two spring-me-to-the-moon double beds.

The hotel also has a book exchange and a Maya-style sweat lodge. Located on the main drag in Pisté, this place is as close as you can get to the ruins for cheap, though it's still a hike of about 3km. Animals are welcome.

Posada Olalde INN $

(851-0086; cnr Calles 6 & 17; s/d M$250/300;) Two blocks south of the highway by Artesanías Guayacán, this is the best of Pisté's several *posadas* (inns). It has clean, quiet rooms, a few twiddling parakeets and four decent-sized bungalows. Some toilets are missing seats. All accommodations are fan-cooled, and the friendly manager speaks Spanish and English, as well as some Maya.

Hotel Dolores Alba HOTEL $$

(858-1555; www.doloresalba.com; Hwy 180, Km 122; r incl breakfast M$700; P) About 2.5km east of the site's eastern entrance, this is a good midrange option. Kids dig the hotel's two pools (one is an 'ecological' pool with a rock bottom). Rooms here won't wow you, but the price is right. The hotel offers transport to the ruins, but you're on your own getting back.

Hotel Chichén Itzá HOTEL $$

(Best Western; 851-0022, in USA 800-235-4079; www.mayaland.com; Calle 15 No 45; r/ste M$860/1365; P) On the west side of Pisté, this hotel has 42 pleasant rooms with tiled floors and old-style brick-tiled ceilings. Rooms in the upper range face the pool and the landscaped grounds, and all have firm beds and minibars. Parents may bring two kids under 13 years for free.

Hacienda Chichén RESORT $$$

(999-920-8407, in USA 877-631-4005; www.haciendachichen.com; Zona Hotelera, Km 120; d from M$2350; P) About 300m from the ruins' entrance, this resort is on the grounds of a 16th-century estate. The hacienda's elegant main house and ruined walls make a great setting, and huge ceiba trees offer welcome shade. The archaeologists who excavated Chichén during the 1920s lived here in bungalows, which have been refurbished and augmented with new ones.

Hotel Mayaland HOTEL $$$

(985-851-0100, in USA 800-235-4079; www.mayaland.com; d/ste M$3029/4485; P) The Mayaland is less than 100m from the site's eastern entrance: from the lobby and front rooms you can look out at El Caracol. The rooms, pools and garden bungalows are nice and all, but when you're at El Caracol you'll wish the hotel hadn't cut an ugly swath through the jungle just so patrons could have a better view.

Eating

The highway (Calle 15) through Pisté is lined with more than 20 eateries, large and small. The cheapest are clustered in a roadside market, known as Los Portales, on the west end of town.

Las Mestizas MEXICAN **$$**
(Calle 15 s/n; mains M$40-100; 8am-10pm) The place to go in town if you're craving decent *yucateco* fare. There's indoor and outdoor seating – depending on the time of day, an outdoor table may mean you'll be getting some tour-bus fumes to go along with that *cochinita*.

Mr Chaak CAFE **$**
(Calle 15 No 45; coffees M$26-40, mains M$45-80; 7am-10pm; P) The best cup of joe on the strip, and the shady outdoor deck makes for a nice little breakfast stop before hitting the ruins.

Restaurant Sayil MEXICAN **$**
(851-0033; Calle 15; mains M$30-80; 8am-10pm) An old standby, with a pleasant garden and simple but tasty regional fare. It's attached to the Felix Inn.

Restaurant Hacienda Xaybe'h d'Camara MEXICAN **$$**
(851-0039; buffet lunches M$150; 8am-5pm;) Set a block back from the highway opposite Hotel Chichén Itzá, this is a large place with well-manicured grounds. It's popular with tours and the food is a bit overpriced, but the selection of salads makes it a good option for vegetarians. Diners can use the swimming pool free of charge.

Information

The ruin's western entrance has a large parking lot and a big visitors center with an ATM and restaurant serving somewhat pricey food.

Getting There & Away

Oriente has ticket offices near the east and west sides of Pisté, and 2nd-class buses passing through town stop almost anywhere along the way. Many 1st-class buses only hit the ruins and the west side of town, close to the toll highway.

Oriente's 2nd-class buses pass through Pisté on their way to Mérida (M$64, 2½ hours), Valladolid (M$22, 50 minutes, nine daily), Cancún (M$115, 4½ hours, seven daily), Tulum (M$85, three hours, one daily), Playa del Carmen ($123, four hours, one daily) and Cobá (M$58, two hours, one daily).

First-class buses serve Mérida (M$120, 1¾ hours, 5.15pm), Cancún (M$202, three hours, 4.30pm) and Tulum (M$148, 2½ hours, 8.25am and 4.30pm).

Shared vans to Valladolid (M$20, 40 minutes) pass through town regularly.

Getting Around

Buses to Pisté generally stop at the plaza; you can make the hot walk to and from the ruins in 20 to 30 minutes. There is a taxi stand near the west end of town; the price to the ruins is M$30.

During Chichén Itzá's opening hours, 1st- and 2nd-class buses serve the ruins (check with the driver), and they will take passengers from town for about M$8 when there's room. For a bit more, 2nd-class buses will also take you to the Cenote Ik Kil and the Grutas de Balankanché (be sure to specify your destination when buying your ticket). If you plan to see the ruins and then head directly to another city by 1st-class bus, buy your bus ticket at the visitors center before hitting the ruins, for a better chance of getting a seat.

Valladolid

985 / POP 49,000

Also known as the Sultaness of the East, Yucatán's third-largest city is known for its quiet streets and sun-splashed pastel walls. It's worth staying here for a few days or even a week, as the provincial town makes a great hub for visits to Río Lagartos, Chichén Itzá, Ek' Balam and a number of nearby cenotes. The city resides at that magic point where there's plenty to do, yet it still feels small, manageable and affordable.

History

Valladolid has seen its fair share of turmoil and revolt. The city was first founded in 1543 near the Chouac-Ha lagoon some 50km from the coast, but it was too hot and there were way too many mosquitoes for Francisco de Montejo, nephew of Montejo the Elder, and his merry band of conquerors. So they upped and moved the city to the Maya ceremonial center of Zací (sah-*see*), where they faced heavy resistance from the local Maya. Eventually the Elder's son – Montejo the Younger – took the town. The Spanish conquerors, in typical fashion, ripped down the town and laid out a new city following the classic colonial plan.

During much of the colonial era, Valladolid's physical isolation from Mérida kept it relatively autonomous from royal

Valladolid

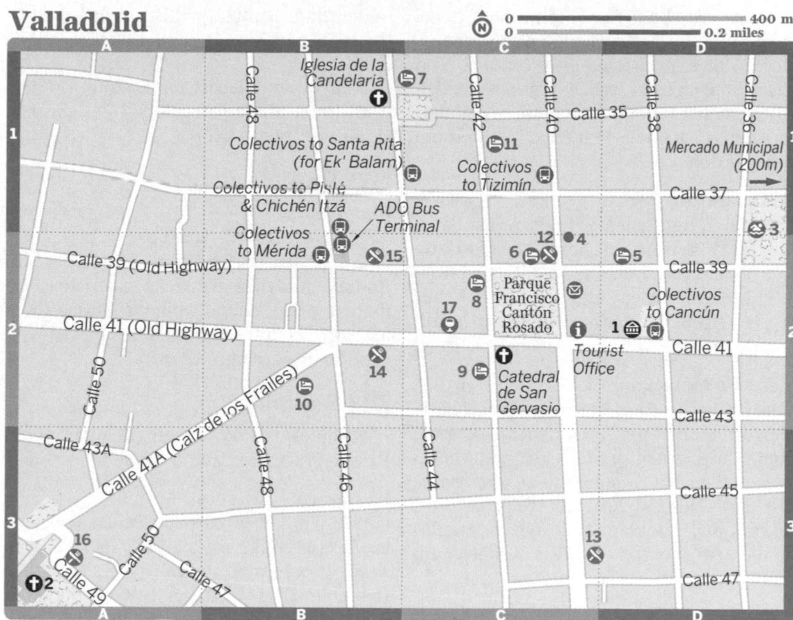

rule, and the Maya of the area suffered brutal exploitation, which continued after Mexican independence. Barred from entering many areas of the city, the Maya made Valladolid one of their first points of attack following the 1847 outbreak of the Caste War in Tepich. After a two-month siege, the city's occupiers were finally overcome. Many fled to the safety of Mérida; the rest were slaughtered.

Today Valladolid is a prosperous seat of agricultural commerce, augmented by some light industry and a growing tourist trade. Many *vallisetanos* speak Spanish with the soft and clear Maya accent.

Sights & Activities

Templo de San Bernardino & Convento de Sisal CHURCH

(Church of San Bernardino; cnr Calles 49 & 51; convent admission M$30; 9am-6pm Mon-Fri, to 3pm Sat) The Templo de San Bernardino and the Convento de Sisal are about 700m southwest of the plaza. They were constructed between 1552 and 1560 to serve the dual functions of fortress and church. The church's charming decoration includes beautiful rose-colored walls, arches, some recently uncovered 16th-century frescoes, and a small image of the Virgin on the altar.

Valladolid

Sights
1 Museo de San Roque ... D2
2 Templo de San Bernardino & Convento de Sisal ... A3

Activities, Courses & Tours
3 Cenote Zací ... D1
4 Rudy Tours ... C2

Sleeping
5 Casa Tía Micha ... D2
6 El Mesón del Marqués ... C2
7 Hostel La Candelaria ... C1
8 Hotel María de la Luz ... C2
9 Hotel San Clemente ... C2
10 Hotel Tunich-Beh ... B2
11 La Aurora ... C1

Eating
12 Bazar Municipal ... C2
13 Conato 1910 ... C3
Hostería del Marqués ... (see 6)
14 Panificadora El Cielo ... B2
15 Squimz ... B2
16 Taberna de los Frailes ... A3

Drinking & Nightlife
17 La Chispa de 1910 ... C2

These are about the only original items remaining; the grand wooden *retablo* (altarpiece) dates from the 19th century. The adjacent convent's walled grounds hold a cenote with a vaulted dome built over it and a system of channels that once irrigated the large garden.

Museo de San Roque MUSEUM
(Calle 41; 8am-8pm Mon-Fri, 9am-6pm Sat & Sun) FREE Previously a church, the Museo de San Roque has models and exhibits relating the history of the city and the region. Other displays focus on various aspects of traditional Maya life.

Mercado Municipal MARKET
(Calle 32) Locals come to this good, authentic Mexican market to shop for cheap clothing, homewares, meat, produce and what-have-you, and to eat at inexpensive *taquerías*. The east side is the most colorful, with flowers and stacks of fruit and vegetables on offer. Most of the activity is between 6am and 2pm.

Cenote Zací SWIMMING
(www.cenotezaci.com.mx; Calle 36; admission M$15; 7am-6pm) Among the region's several underground cenotes is Cenote Zací, set in a park that also holds traditional stone-walled thatched houses and a small zoo (under renovation at last visit). People swim in this open-air swimming hole, and while it's pleasant enough, don't expect crystalline waters. Look in the water for catfish or overhead for a colony of bats. Enter the cenote from Calle 39.

Cenote Dzitnup SWIMMING
(Xkekén & Samulá; admission M$56; 8am-5pm) About 7km west of town, Dzitnup is essentially two cenotes. Xkekén, a massive limestone formation with stalactites hanging from its ceiling, is artificially lit and very swimmable. Across the road about 100m is Cenote Samulá, a lovely cavern pool with *álamo* roots stretching down many meters.

Pedaling a rented bicycle to the cenotes takes about 20 minutes. By bike from the town center take Calle 41A (Calzada de los Frailes), a street lined with colonial architecture. Go one block past the Templo de San Bernardino park and turn left on Calle 54, then make a right on Calle 49, which becomes Av de los Frailes and hits the old highway. Follow the *ciclopista* (bike path) paralleling the road to Mérida, then turn left at the sign for Dzitnup and continue for just under 2km; Samulá will be off this road to the right and Xkekén a little further on the left.

Shared vans depart for Dzitnup (M$20) from Hotel María Guadalupe (on Calle 44). Otherwise, take a taxi.

Tours

Rudy Tours BICYCLE TOUR
(856-2026, 985-113-1565; Calle 40, btwn Calles 37 & 39; tours M$250, bike rental per hr M$20) Rodolfo 'Rudy' Escalante, an experienced bilingual guide, offers two-hour bicycle tours to nearby cenotes. He also rents bikes if you want to explore on your own.

Sleeping

Most hotels are on or near the main plaza, Parque Francisco Cantón Rosado.

La Aurora HOTEL $
(856-1219; www.hotelcoloniallaaurora.blogspot.mx; Calle 42 No 192; s/d/tr M$420/490/570; P) If only more budget hotels were like the colonial-style Aurora. Well-appointed rooms overlook a pretty courtyard with a pool and potted plants, and at last visit the hotel was installing a rooftop hot tub and bar. If possible, avoid the noisier street-facing rooms.

Hostel La Candelaria HOSTEL $
(856-2267; www.hostelvalladolidyucatan.com; Calle 35 No 201F; dm/r incl breakfast M$120/330; @) A friendly place right on a quiet little square, this hostel can get a little cramped and hot, but there are two kitchens, a cozy garden area complete with hammocks, a gals-only dorm, and plenty of hangout space, making it the best hostel in town. The hostel also rents bikes for M$15 per hour.

Hotel San Clemente HOTEL $
(856-3161; www.hotelsanclemente.com.mx; Calle 42 No 206; d with fan/air-con M$467/490; P) One of the best budget options in town. The rather basic rooms surround a large, sun-filled courtyard with a swimming pool and lots of greenery.

Casa Tía Micha BOUTIQUE HOTEL $$
(856-2957; www.casatiamicha.com; Calle 39 No 197; r/ste incl breakfast from M$1000/1550; P) The corridor and rear garden are beautifully lit at night in this family-run boutique hotel just off the plaza. Some of the tastefully adorned colonial-style rooms have king-size beds, and the upstairs suite comes with a Jacuzzi.

Casa Quetzal BOUTIQUE HOTEL **$$**
(☎856-4796; www.casa-quetzal.com; Calle 51 No 218; r M$900; P❄📶🏊) The spacious rooms here offer a good mix of modern comfort and colonial style. They're set around a lush patio with a decent-sized pool. Get a room upstairs for better ventilation and a private balcony. It's about 200m south of the Convento de Sisal.

Hotel Tunich-Beh HOTEL **$$**
(☎856-2222; www.tunichbeh.com; Calle 41A, btwn Calles 46 & 48; d M$700; P❄📶🏊) At this great old house lovingly converted into a hotel, rooms with king-size beds surround a swimming pool and there are some nice *palapa*-shaded common areas for kicking back.

Hotel María de la Luz HOTEL **$$**
(☎856-1181; www.mariadelaluzhotel.com; Calle 42 No 193C; d/tr incl breakfast M$580/750; P❄📶🏊) Rooms here got a recent makeover, with new beds and upgraded furnishings. (Not all rooms had been renovated at last visit, though, so check what you're getting beforehand). Rates include a breakfast buffet served in the hotel's airy restaurant overlooking the plaza. There's a pool, too.

El Mesón del Marqués HOTEL **$$**
(☎856-2073; www.mesondelmarques.com; Calle 39 No 203; r M$885-1095, ste M$1680-1830; P❄📶🏊) It's only worth staying in this hotel if you're willing to up the ante for the superior rooms, with their crispy-clean bedspreads, quaint blue-and-yellow tilework and firm mattresses. There's also a charming old courtyard and the fine Hostería del Marqués restaurant.

Eating & Drinking

★**Conato 1910** MEXICAN **$**
(Calle 40 No 226; mains M$50-80; ⏲5pm-midnight Wed-Mon; 🌿) A meeting spot for revolutionaries in the early 20th century, this historic building now houses one of the best restaurants in town in an atmospheric muraled setting. The vegetarian-friendly menu features a wide variety of options, such as salads and pastas, and there are also excellent chicken and beef dishes.

Bazar Municipal MARKET **$**
(cnr Calles 39 & 40; mains M$30-50; ⏲6am-10pm) A collection of market-style eateries that are popular for their big, cheap breakfasts. At lunch and dinner some offer *comidas corridas* (set meals of several courses). **El Amigo Casiano**, on the left side nearly at the back, is good and always crowded; it closes by 2pm. **Lonchería Canul**, at the back, stays open later.

Squimz MEXICAN **$**
(☎856-4156; Calle 39 No 219; mains M$43-99; ⏲7am-11pm Mon-Sat, 8am-4pm Sun) A delightful little shop just a few doors east of the ADO bus terminal, Squimz offers cakes, pastries and good espresso drinks, and has a nice rear courtyard. Its rich, creamy flan is one of Valladolid's best.

Taberna de los Frailes MEXICAN **$$**
(www.tabernadelosfrailes.com; Calle 49, cnr Calle 41A; mains M$90-190; ⏲noon-11pm) The New Age music has gotta go, but the verdant garden and wonderfully prepared *yucateco* food make up for it. Try the Tikin Xic, a grilled *pibil*-style red snapper (marinated in citrus juice and annatto spice).

Hostería del Marqués MEXICAN **$$**
(☎856-2073; www.mesondelmarques.com; El Mesón del Marqués, Calle 39 No 203; mains M$70-220; ⏲7am-11pm; P❄) Dine in a tranquil colonial courtyard with a bubbling fountain, or the air-con salon looking onto it. The restaurant specializes in *yucateco* fare – ie *longaniza* Valladolid (Valladolid-style sausage), *cochinita pibil* (marinated pork) – and there are also international dishes such as Angus beef cuts.

Panificadora El Cielo BAKERY **$**
(Calle 41, btwn Calles 44 & 46; breads M$5-10; ⏲8am-9pm) Valladolid has several good bakeries, and this is one of the best.

La Chispa de 1910 KARAOKE
(☎856-2668; Calle 41 No 201, btwn Calles 42 & 44; ⏲5pm-3am) Sparks fly at this bar-restaurant that often features live music. Test your liquid courage at nightly karaoke sessions.

Entertainment

Following a centuries-old tradition, dances are held in the main plaza from 8pm to 9pm Sunday, with music by the municipal band or other local groups.

La Solana LIVE MUSIC
(Calle 39 No 241A, cnr Calle 58; ⏲8pm-3am) This pleasant open-air bar stages live *trova* on Sunday, and on Friday and Saturday DJs spin electronica, reggae and reggaeton tracks. It's about eight blocks west of the plaza.

Information

Various banks (most with ATMs) near the town center are generally open 9am to 5pm Monday to Friday and to 1pm Saturday.

High-speed internet is available at numerous small cafes in and around the town center; all charge around M$10 per hour and are open 9am-ish to as late as midnight.

Grupo Médico del Centro (☎100-5287, 856-5106; Calle 40 No 178B, btwn Calles 33 & 35) A centrally located private medical clinic.

Main Post Office (cnr Calles 39 & 40; ⊙8am-4.30pm Mon-Fri, 8am-1pm Sat)

Tourist Office (☎856-2529, ext 114; cnr Calles 40 & 41; ⊙8am-9pm Mon-Sat, 9am-2pm Sun) On the east side of the plaza, it provides mediocre information.

Getting There & Away

BUS

Valladolid's main bus terminal is the convenient **ADO bus terminal** (cnr Calles 39 & 46). The main 1st-class services are ADO, ADO GL and OCC; Oriente and Mayab run 2nd-class buses.

Buses to Chichén Itzá/Pisté stop near the ruins during opening hours.

COLECTIVO

Often faster, more reliable and more comfortable than 2nd-class buses are the *colectivos* that depart as soon as their seats are filled. Most operate from 7am or 8am to about 7pm.

Direct services run to Mérida (near the ADO bus terminal; M$100, two hours) and Cancún (one block east of the plaza; M$140, two hours); confirm they're nonstop. *Colectivos* for Pisté and Chichén Itzá (M$23, 40 minutes) leave north of the ADO bus terminal; for Tizimín (M$30, 40 minutes) from Calle 40 between Calles 35 and 37; and for Ek' Balam (M$40) take a 'Santa Rita' *colectivo* from Calle 44, between Calles 35 and 37.

Getting Around

The old highway passes through the town center, though most signs urge motorists toward the toll road north of town. To follow the old highway eastbound, take Calle 41; westbound, Calle 39.

Bicycles are a great way to see the town and get out to the cenotes. You can rent them at Hostel La Candelaria (p186) or Rudy Tours (p186) for M$15 to M$20 per hour.

Ek' Balam

The town of Ek' Balam itself is worth a visit to see what a traditional Maya village looks like. There are two nice hotels, as well as a handful of artisan stands along the main plaza, which also serves as the town's soccer field.

Sights

Ek' Balam ARCHAEOLOGICAL SITE

(adult/child 7-12yr M$98/6, guides M$600; ⊙8am-5pm; P) Vegetation still covers much of this intriguing archaeological site, but excavations and restoration continue to add to the sights, including an interesting ziggurat-like structure near the entrance, as well as a fine arch and a ball court.

Ek' Balam's most fascinating structure is the gargantuan **Acrópolis**, whose well-restored base is 160m long and holds a 'gallery' – actually a series of separate chambers. Built atop the base is a massive main pyramid, reaching a height of 32m and featuring a huge jaguar mouth with 360-degree dentition.

Below the mouth are stucco skulls, while above and to the right sits an amazingly expressive figure. On the right side stand unusual winged human figures (some call them

BUSES FROM VALLADOLID

DESTINATION	FARE (M$)	DURATION (HR)	FREQUENCY
Cancún	90-150	2-3½	frequent
Chichén Itzá/Pisté	23-62	¾	frequent
Chiquilá (for Isla Holbox)	90	3½	2.30am
Cobá	33	1	4 daily
Izamal	50	2	12.50pm
Mérida	90-150	2-3	frequent
Playa del Carmen	100-150	2½-3½	frequent
Tizimín	22	1	frequent
Tulum	66-88	2	frequent

Maya angels), whose hands are poised in gestures looking for all the world like Hindu or Buddhist mudras. It's enough to make you wonder, either about connections between ancient civilizations or the artistic license taken by the restoration crew (though much of the plaster is supposed to be original). The view from the top of the pyramid is fantastic as well. Across the flat terrain you can make out the pyramids of Chichén Itzá and Cobá.

On your way out, just before reaching the exit, you'll find a local cooperative offering visits to the **X-Canché Cenote** (985-107-4774; admission M$30; 8am-5pm), a refreshing swimming spot where you can cool off after a day at the ruins. It's a 1.5km walk or pedicabs will take you there for M$100 round-trip. The admission costs M$30 or you can opt for a guided tour (M$300) of the area that includes bicycling, rappeling and zip lining.

The turnoff for Ek' Balam is 17km north of Valladolid, from where the archaeological site is a further 6km east.

Sleeping & Eating

★Genesis Eco-Retreat GUESTHOUSE $$
(985-100-4805; www.genesisretreat.com; Ek' Balam pueblo; d with/without bathroom from M$705/570;) Genesis Eco-Retreat offers B&B intimacy in a quiet, ecofriendly setting. This is a true ecotel: gray water is used for landscaping, some rooms are naturally cooled and there's even an entire wall made out of plastic bottles. The place is postcard-beautiful – there's a chilling plunge pool and a *temazcal* (steam bath) onsite – and it offers delicious veggie meals.

The hotel is sometimes closed between September and early October.

Dolcemente Ek' Balam HOTEL $$
(986-106-8086; Ek' Balam pueblo; d M$700;) This Italian-run property has a fine collection of 15 superclean fan-cooled and air-conditioned rooms. The yummy restaurant specializes in (you guessed it) Italian fare.

Getting There & Away

You can catch a *colectivo* from Calle 44 between Calles 35 and 37 in Valladolid for Ek' Balam (M$40). A taxi from the ruins' parking lot to Valladolid costs M$150.

Tizimín

986 / POP 47,000

You won't find much in Tizimín that's designed with the tourist in mind; in fact, for most folks it serves as a mere stopover point en route to the coast. That said, some travelers may find the town a refreshing change if they've just come from Playa del Carmen or Cancún.

Two great colonial structures – **Parroquia Los Santos Reyes de Tizimín** (Church of the Three Wise Kings) and its former **Franciscan monastery** (the ex-*convento*) – are worth a look. They're on opposite sides of Calle 51, reached by walking two blocks south on Calle 48, which itself is a block west of the bus terminals.

The city fills with people from outlying ranches during its annual fair to celebrate **Día de los Reyes Magos** (Three Kings' Day; January 1 to 15).

The church fronts Tizimín's main plaza, the Parque Principal, which has an HSBC bank with ATM and currency exchange on its southwest side.

Sleeping & Eating

Hotel San Carlos HOTEL $
(863-2094; hotelsancarlos@hotmail.com; Calle 54 No 407, btwn Calles 51 & 53; r with fan/air-con M$350/420;) Two blocks west of the plaza, this is one of the nicest hotels in town. All the air-con rooms have private patios looking onto the shared garden area.

Posada María Antonia HOTEL $
(863-2857; Calle 50 No 408; r with air-con M$325;) Just south of the church, it has 12 bare-bones rooms, each holding up to four people.

Market MARKET $
(cnr Calles 47 & 48) The market, half a block west of the Noreste bus terminal, has the usual cheap eateries (mains M$30 to M$70).

Pizzería César's PIZZERIA $
(Calle 50; mains M$49-167; 8am-1am) A popular joint near the Posada María Antonia, it serves inexpensive pasta dishes, sandwiches and burgers in addition to pizza and steak.

Getting There & Away

Buses offering 2nd-class services share a **bus terminal** (Calle 47, btwn Calles 46 & 48) just east of the market. You'll find Mérida-bound *colectivos* (M$100) here too. The **Noreste bus terminal** (Calle 46), with 1st- and 2nd-class services, is just around the corner.

Río Lagartos

986 / POP 2200

On the windy northern shore of the peninsula, sleepy Río Lagartos (Alligator River) is a fishing village that also boasts the densest concentration of flamingos in Mexico - supposedly two or three flamingos per Mexican, if one believes the provided math. Lying within the **Reserva de la Biosfera Ría Lagartos**, this mangrove-lined estuary also shelters 334 other species of resident and migratory birds, including snowy egrets, red egrets, tiger herons and snowy white ibis, as well as a small number of once-numerous crocodiles that gave the town its name. It's a beautiful area. At the right time of year you can see numerous species of birds without even getting out of your vehicle.

The Maya knew the place as Holkobén and used it as a rest stop on their way to Las Coloradas, a shallow part of the vast estuary that stretches east almost to the border of Quintana Roo. There they extracted precious salt from the waters, a process that continues on a much vaster scale today. Spanish explorers mistook the narrowing of the *ría* (estuary) for a *río* (river) and the crocs for alligators, and the rest is history.

Less than 1km east of town, on the edge of the estuary, an *ojo de agua dulce* (natural spring) has been developed into a swimming hole. A sometimes-empty tourist kiosk sits at the end of Calle 10 by the waterfront.

Most residents aren't sure of the town's street names, and signs are few. The road into town is the north–south Calle 10, which ends at the *malecón*.

There's no bank or ATM in town, so bring lots of cash.

Sights & Activities

Isla Cerritos ISLAND

Just 5km from the nearby fishing village of San Felipe, tiny Isla Cerritos was an important Maya port city back in the day. And while the entire island was covered with buildings during this era – archaeological expeditions have turned up nearly 50,000 artifacts – it's virtually deserted today, and none of the buildings have been restored. The only way to get here is with a tour.

Río Lagartos Ecotours SNORKELING

(862-0000; www.riolagartosecotours.net16.net; Calle 19 No 134; per 6-person group M$1560) Operating out of Restaurante-Bar Isla Contoy, this tour outfit does four-hour snorkeling trips to Isla Cerritos.

Tours

The brilliant orange-red flamingos can turn the horizon fiery when they take wing. Depending on your luck, you'll see either hundreds or thousands of them. The best months for viewing them are June to August. The four primary haunts, in increasing distance from town, are Punta Garza, Yoluk, Necopal and Nahochín (all flamingo feeding spots named for nearby mangrove patches).

To see the flamingos, you'll need to rent a boat and driver. You'll see more birdlife if you head out at sunrise or around 4pm. Prices vary by boat, group size (maximum six) and destination. A three-hour trip costs around M$900. In addition, the reserve charges visitors a M$27 admission fee. Plan on packing something to eat the night before, as most restaurants open long after you'll be on the water. Ask to stop at the *arcilla* (mud bath) on the way back.

You can negotiate with one of the eager men in the waterfront kiosks. They speak English and will connect you with a captain (who usually doesn't).

BUSES FROM TIZIMÍN

DESTINATION	FARE (M$)	DURATION (HR)	FREQUENCY
Cancún	98	3½	6 daily
Izamal	60-74	2½	4 daily
Mérida	90-120	2½-4	6 daily; Noreste
Río Lagartos/San Felipe	30-36	1	10 daily; Noreste
Valladolid	23	1	frequent

CELEBRATING LA FERIA DE SANTIAGO & DÍA DE LA MARINA

Río Lagartos knows how to party, and two festivals, La Feria de Santiago and Día de la Marina, are well worth checking out. **La Feria de Santiago**, the patron-saint festival of Río Lagartos, is held mid-July. A bullfight (really bullplay) ring is erected in the middle of town during the weeklong event, and every afternoon anyone who wishes is able to enter it and play matador with a young bull. The animal is not killed or even injured, just made a little angry at times. Don't turn your back to it or it will knock you down. Call a hotel in town to find out when the festival is being held.

Another big annual event in Río Lagartos is **Día de la Marina** (Day of the Marine Force), which is always on June 1. On this day, following 9am Mass, a crown of flowers is dedicated to the Virgin and carried from the church to a boat, where it is then taken 4km out to sea and placed in the water as an offering to all the fishermen who have perished at sea. The boats, not incidentally, are heavily decorated on this day, and tourists are welcome to ride to the site for free. Just ask if you can go, and be friendly and respectful. A tip for their kindness, following the service, is always appreciated (M$50 to M$100 per visitor).

The best guides are to be found at **Restaurante-Bar Isla Contoy** (☎862-0000; www.riolagartosecotours.net16.net; Calle 19 No 134); driving into town, turn left on Calle 19 at the sign for the restaurant. From the bus terminal, head to the water and turn left (west). Ask for **Ismael Navarro** (☎866-5216, 862-0000; riolaga@hotmail.com), a licensed guide with formal training as a naturalist. Another knowledgeable guide, **Diego Núñez Martínez** (☎100-8390; www.birdingyucatan.com), is based out of the waterfront La Torreja restaurant. Both speak English and are up to date on the fauna and flora in the area, including the staggering number of bird species.

Besides the flamingo expeditions, Ismael takes four-hour shorebird tours along the mudflats in winter, and Diego offers catch-and-release fly-fishing trips for tarpon and snook (half-day tour M$1800) and birding excursions (M$1080 per boat). Both also offer night rides looking for crocodiles (M$900) and, from May to September, sea turtles.

Sleeping & Eating

Punta Ponto Hotel HOTEL $
(☎862-0509; www.hotelpuntaponto.com; Calle 9 Diagonal # 140, cnr Calle 19; r incl breakfast M$450-600, ste M$700; P ❄ wi-fi) Aside from having a fun name to say, Punta Ponto offers one of the best deals in town. Some of the rooms have balconies with river views, and the breezy, open-air common spaces seal the deal.

Posada Inn INN $
(☎100-8390; diego.rio@hotmail.com; Calle 9; palapa M$300, r M$450-600; wi-fi) A nice little family-run setup next to the lighthouse, the Posada houses three superclean rooms with TVs and mini-fridges. Or opt for the open-air rooftop *palapa* with a hammock and panoramic view of the river. You also can rent bikes here for M$10 per hour.

Hotel Villas de Pescadores HOTEL $$
(☎862-0020; www.hotelriolagartos.com.mx; cnr Calles 14 & 9; d M$700-800; P ❄ wi-fi) Near the water's edge, this nice hotel offers nine very clean rooms, each with good ventilation (all face the estuary), two beds and a fan. Upstairs rooms have balconies, and there's a rickety spiral staircase leading up to a rooftop lookout tower where guests can watch the sun set or sip a relaxing beverage.

La Torreja SEAFOOD $$
(mains M$50-140; ⌚8am-9pm) Fresh seafood, a nice waterfront view and sand floors at this restaurant next to Hotel Villa de Pescadores. What's not to like?

Restaurante-Bar Isla Contoy SEAFOOD $$
(Calle 19; mains M$70-120; ⌚8am-9pm) A popular eatery at the waterfront, this is a good place to meet other travelers and form groups for the boat tours. Lobster, at market price, is a delicious specialty.

Getting There & Away

Several Noreste buses run daily between Tizimín (M$30, one hour), Mérida (M$156, three to four hours) and San Felipe (M$7, 20 minutes).

FLAMINGO ETIQUETTE

Although the sight of flamingos taking to the wing is impressive, for the well-being of the birds, please ask your boat captain not to frighten the birds into flight. You can generally get to within 100m of the birds before they walk or fly away.

Noreste serves Cancún (M$156, four hours), but you'll have to transfer in Tizimín.

East of Río Lagartos

The road between Río Lagartos and El Cuyo is truly a birder's delight. It's best to take the trip early in the morning, when you are likely to see egrets, blue heron, osprey and gaggles of pink flamingos. If you do stop to observe wildlife, be as quiet as possible and remember that there are crocodiles in the shallows, as well as venomous snakes: don't let that great-roseate-spoonbill photo opportunity send you to the hospital.

Start your trip by turning east at the junction about 2km south of Río Lagartos. About 8km from the junction, on the south side of the road, is the beginning of a 1km **interpretive trail** to Petén Tucha (a *petén* is a hummock or rise often forming around a spring).

Continuing east on the road 4km beyond the trailhead you'll reach a bridge over a very narrow part of the estuary. Fishers cast nets here, and you can sometimes see crocs lurking in the water (look for dead horseshoe crabs on the bridge). Another 6km beyond this is **Las Coloradas**, a small town housing workers who extract salt from the vast shallow lagoons of the same name; they stretch eastward for kilometers on the south side of the road. The salt is piled in gleaming mounds that look like icebergs, up to 15m high, and from a distance it appears oddly incongruous, as if you've arrived in the Arctic despite the blistering heat.

The road turns to sand after Las Coloradas, but you can still make it to El Cuyo most times of year. You may consider spending a few Robinson Crusoe days on the beach here, but the brown sands are pretty littered with trash. The unique vegetation includes the century plant, an agave species that lives quietly for decades before sending up a tall stalk that blossoms, in turn triggering the final demise of the plant. These are different from the *henequén* agaves that you see further south.

The road often washes out in rainy season, but it's normally passable in dry season (even with a non-4WD vehicle). Ask locally before you take the trip (you'll need your own wheels).

El Cuyo

At the end of the road, El Cuyo has a clear white-sand beach and muddy waters, and, curiously, smells a bit like old socks. The town sees a few local tourists looking for a short beach vacation, but not many foreigners pass through. Maybe this is the off-the-beaten-track spot you were looking for all this time.

At El Cuyo the road passes through broad expanses of grassy savanna with palms and some huge-trunked trees, passing the site of the original founding of Valladolid, in 1543. At Colonia Yucatán, a little over 30km south of El Cuyo, you can head east to pick up the road to Chiquilá and Isla Holbox (or in the opposite direction to Hwy 180) or west to Tizimín.

Sleeping

Posada El Faro HOTEL $

(☎986-853-4015; Calle 40; d M$500; P ❄) The rooms here are about as modern as you get in El Cuyo. It's just south of the plaza.

Hotel Aida Luz HOTEL $

(☎986-105-3293, 986-853-4088; www.hotelaidaluzelcuyo.com; Calle 40 No 3A; r M$500; P ❄) You can't miss this big orange-and-white building just off the plaza. Rooms are nothing spectacular, but they're clean enough and the hotel is just a block from the water.

Getting There & Away

The Noreste bus line has eight daily departures to El Cuyo (M$50) from Tizimín; going the other way, buses head to Tizimín seven times daily from the town plaza. Hitchhiking may be possible, but a rental car is by far the better way to go.

San Felipe

☎986 / POP 1800

About 12km west of Río Lagartos, San Felipe is a fishing village seldom visited by travelers. It's notable for its orderly streets, cheery Caribbean feel and painted wooden houses. With its laid-back air, this is a good alternative to staying in Río Lagartos. Getting there you'll pass primarily swampy mangrove-dotted lagoons, and perhaps surprise a turtle or two crossing the road. Its beach lies across the mouth of the estuary, at Punta Holohit, and the mangroves there and on the western edge of town are a birdwatcher's paradise. Just looking out the windows of the town's main hotel you can see white and brown pelicans, terns, cormorants, great blue herons, magnificent frigatebirds and jabirus (storks).

The beach, though not great, usually has *palapas* providing shade. *Lancheros* (boatowners) charge M$100 per boatload (roundtrip) to take passengers across, or M$800 for a half-day fishing excursion; a birding expedition to Isla Cerritos runs M$450.

The **Hotel San Felipe de Jesús** (☎862-2027; hotelsfjesus@hotmail.com; Calle 9A, btwn Calles 14 & 16; d M$560-610, ste M$640) is a friendly, clean and cleverly constructed hotel at the edge of San Felipe's harbor. It's definitely worth a few extra pesos to get a room with private balconies and water views. The restaurant offers good seafood at low prices. To get here, turn left at the water and proceed about 200m.

Buses from Tizimín pass through Río Lagartos and continue to San Felipe (M$35, one hour, 10 daily). The bus ride from Río Lagartos (M$10) takes 20 minutes. San Felipe-bound *colectivos* (M$30, four daily) depart from the *mercado* in Tizimín.

You can take a taxi from Tizimín to San Felipe for M$250, but you will possibly need to arrange return pick-up in advance or pay the driver an hourly rate to wait until you're ready to return.

Campeche & Around

Includes ➡

Best Places to Eat

- Río Bec Dreams Restaurant (p218)
- Luz de Luna (p203)
- La Fuente (p213)

Best Places to Stay

- Hotel López (p202)
- Río Bec Dreams (p218)
- Hacienda Puerta Campeche (p202)

Why Go?

Tucked into the southwestern corner of the Yucatán Peninsula, Campeche state is home to serene villages, vast stretches of tangled jungle, bird-dotted mangroves and lagoons, and some of the region's most imposing Maya ruins – many of which you might have all to yourself. On deserted beaches endangered turtles lay their eggs, while offshore playful dolphins frolic in the surf. The walled capital city of Campeche is the region's cultural epicenter, providing a great jumping-off point for your adventures into this offbeat hinterland.

Campeche is the least visited of the Yucatán's states, laced through with lonely back roads, friendly people, quiet coastlines and a provincial, lost-land charm. It makes a welcome break from the tourist hordes that descend around the peninsula's more popular destinations; here you'll find peace and surprising attractions.

When to Go

- Visit Campeche city any time of year, though high season is from mid-December to Easter. Hotel prices are at their peak during this time, but there are also some merry festivities – especially Carnaval (late February to early March).
- The dry months of November through March are most pleasant for visiting Calakmul and its nearby sites. Also, during the rainy season access is often limited because of muddy roads.
- To set turtle hatchlings free in Sabancuy, be there from April to October (peak June to August).

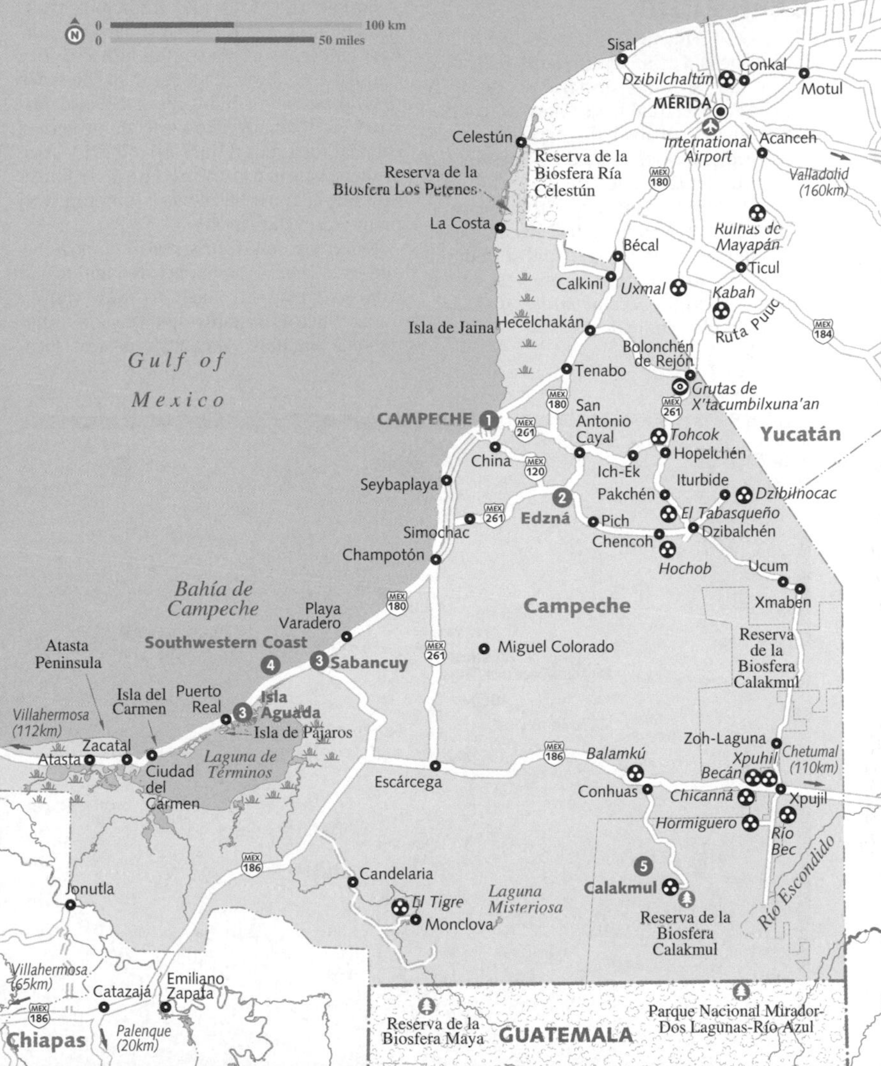

Campeche Highlights

1 Stroll through history along the colonial streets of **Campeche** (p196), lined with pastel-hued buildings and edged by stone ramparts

2 Explore the large and impressive complexes of **Edzná** (p209), the most significant Maya ruins near Campeche

3 Spot dolphins and seabirds from **Isla Aguada** (p212), or set turtle hatchlings free at **Sabancuy** (p211)

4 Eat some fresh seafood or find yourself a little patch of deserted beach along the **southwestern coast** (p210)

5 Haul yourself up the massive pyramids of **Calakmul** (p215) while the calls of howler monkeys reverberate in surrounding jungle

CAMPECHE

☎981 / POP 259,000

Campeche is a colonial fairyland, its walled city center a tight enclave of perfectly restored pastel buildings, narrow cobblestone streets, fortified ramparts and well-preserved mansions. Added to Unesco's list of World Heritage sites in 1999, the state capital has been so painstakingly restored it almost doesn't seem like a real city. But leave the inner walls and you'll find a genuine Mexican provincial capital complete with a frenetic market, peaceful *malecón* (boardwalk) and old fishing docks.

Besides the walls and numerous mansions built by wealthy Spanish families during Campeche's heyday in the 18th and 19th centuries, no fewer than seven of the *baluartes* (bastions or bulwarks) have also survived. Additionally, two perfectly preserved colonial forts guard the city's outskirts, one of them housing the Museo de la Arquitectura Maya, an archaeological museum with many world-class pieces.

Relatively few tourists visit Campeche, and its citizens - the big-hearted and proud *campechanos* - are likely to show you an unobtrusive hospitality not seen in other regional capitals. The city's central loca-

Campeche

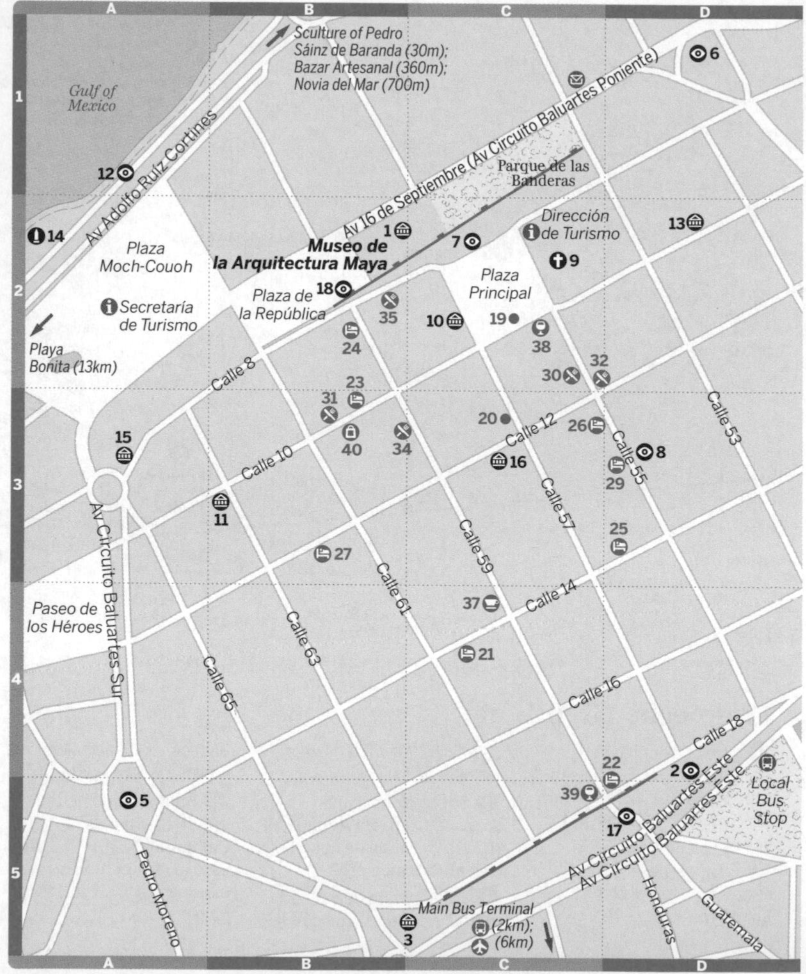

tion on the Gulf of Mexico also makes it the perfect base for day trips to Edzná, the Chenes sites and neighboring beaches. And at night, the gauzy lights on the illuminated church and other central landmarks add an almost magical atmosphere to this gem of a destination.

History

Once a Maya trading village called Ah Kim Pech (Lord Sun Sheep-Tick), Campeche was first briefly approached by the Spaniards in 1517. Resistance by the Maya prevented the Spaniards from fully conquering the region for nearly a quarter-century. Colonial Campeche was founded in 1531, but later abandoned due to Maya hostility. By 1540, however, the conquistadors had gained sufficient control, under the leadership of Francisco de Montejo (the Younger), to found a permanent settlement. They named the settlement Villa de San Francisco de Campeche.

The settlement soon flourished as the major port of the Yucatán Peninsula, but this made it subject to pirate attacks. After a particularly appalling attack in 1663 left the city in ruins, the king of Spain ordered construction of Campeche's famous bastions, putting an end to the periodic carnage.

Today the economy of the city is largely driven by fishing and, increasingly, tourism, which has helped fund the downtown area's renovation.

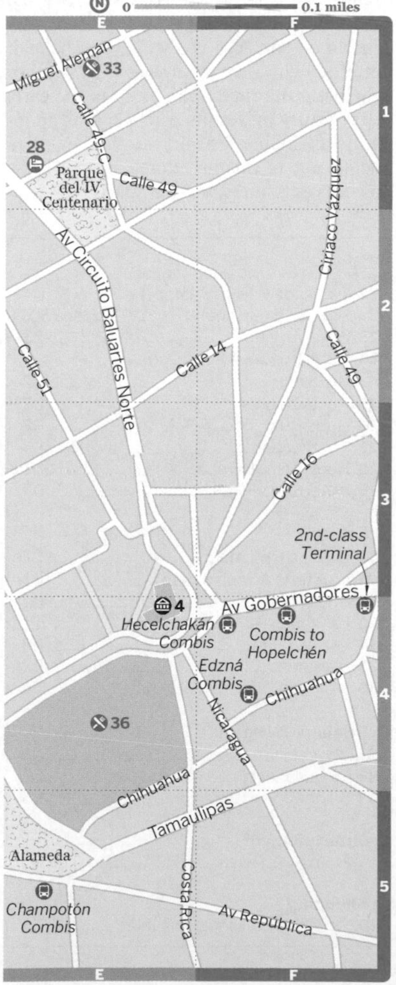

Sights & Activities

Plaza Principal & Around

Shaded by carob trees and ringed by tiled benches and broad footpaths radiating from a belle-epoque kiosk, Campeche's appealingly modest central square started life in 1531 as a military camp. Over the years it became the focus of the town's civic, political and religious activities and remains the core of public life. *Campechanos* come here to chat, smooch, have their shoes shined or cool off with an ice cream. The plaza is at its best on weekend evenings, when it's closed to traffic and concerts are staged.

Catedral de Nuestra Señora de la Purísima Concepción CATHEDRAL

(6:30am-9pm) Dominating Plaza Principal's east side is this two-towered cathedral. The limestone structure has stood on this spot for more than three centuries, and it still fills beyond capacity most Sundays. Statues of Sts Peter and Paul occupy niches in the baroque facade; the sober, single-nave interior is lined with colonial-era paintings.

Centro Cultural Casa Número 6 HISTORIC BUILDING

(816-1782; Calle 57 No 6; admission M$10, audio guide M$15; 8am-9pm Mon-Fri, 9am-9pm Sat & Sun) During the prerevolutionary era, when this mansion was occupied by an upper-class *campechano* family, Número 6 was a prestigious plaza address. Wandering the premises, you'll get an idea of how the city's high society lived back then. The front sitting room is furnished with Cuban-style pieces of the period. Inside are exhibition spaces, a pleasant back patio and a gift shop.

Biblioteca de Campeche LIBRARY
(State Library; ⌚9am-8pm Mon-Fri, 9am-1pm Sat) On the northern (seaward) side stands a replica of the old government center, now housing the modern Biblioteca de Campeche. The impressive porticoed building on the opposite side housed an earlier version of the city hall; it is now occupied by shops and restaurants.

Mansión Carvajal HISTORIC BUILDING
(Calle 10 btwn Calles 51 & 53; ⌚8am-2:45pm Mon-Fri) FREE Once the mansion of wealthy landowner Fernando Carvajal, this beautiful building now houses state offices. Visitors are welcome to take a peek inside, however. Black-and-white tiled floors, Doric columns, elaborate archways and a dramatic marble and ironwork staircase are highlights. Note the historical plaque.

Museo del Archivo General de Estado MUSEUM
(☎816-0939; Calle 12 No 159; ⌚8am-3pm Mon-Fri) FREE Learn how Campeche came to be, at this small museum. It's free and air-conditioned, and you get to check out old documents and maps, and watch a video (in Spanish or English) that recounts the history of the state.

Casa del Arte ARTS CENTER
(Calle 55 btwn Calles 12 & 14; ⌚8am-3pm & 6-9pm Mon-Fri, 10am-3pm Sat) FREE Come here to see rotating art, photography and painting exhibits by local artists.

Ex-Templo de San José HISTORIC BUILDING
(Former San José Church; cnr Calles 10 & 63) Faced with blue-and-yellow tiles, the Ex-Templo de San José is a wonder to behold; note the lighthouse, complete with weather vane, atop the right spire. Built in the early 18th century by Jesuits who ran it as an institute of higher learning until they were booted out of Spanish domains in 1767, it now serves as an exhibition space.

Campeche

Top Sights
1 Museo de la Arquitectura Maya B2

Sights
2 Baluarte de San Francisco D4
3 Baluarte de San Juan C5
4 Baluarte de San Pedro E4
5 Baluarte de Santa Rosa A5
6 Baluarte de Santiago D1
7 Biblioteca de Campeche C2
8 Casa del Arte D3
9 Catedral de Nuestra Señora de la Purísima Concepción C2
10 Centro Cultural Casa Número 6 .... C2
11 Ex-Templo de San José B3
12 Malecón A1
13 Mansión Carvajal D2
14 Monument to the City Gates A2
15 Museo de la Ciudad A3
16 Museo del Archivo General de Estado C3
17 Puerta de Tierra D5
18 Puerta del Mar B2

Activities, Courses & Tours
19 Tranvía de la Ciudad C2
20 Xtampak Tours C3

Sleeping
21 H177 Hotel C4
22 Hacienda Puerta Campeche D4
Hostal La Parroquia .... (see 30)
23 Hotel América B3
24 Hotel Boutique Casa Don Gustavo B2
25 Hotel Colonial D3
26 Hotel Guarandocha Inn C3
27 Hotel López B3
28 Hotel Plaza Campeche E1
29 Hotel Socaires D3

Eating
30 Café La Parroquia C2
31 Cafetería Atrapa Sueño B3
32 Chef Color C2
33 La Pigua E1
34 Luz de Luna B3
35 Marganzo B2
36 Mercado Principal E4

Drinking & Nightlife
37 Chocol-Ha C4
38 La Casa Vieja C2
39 Salón Rincón Colonial C5

Entertainment
Puerta de Tierra .... (see 17)

Shopping
40 Casa de Artesanías Tukulna B3

RIBALD TALES: THE MARAUDING PIRATES OF CAMPECHE

Where there's wealth, there are pirates – this was truer in the 1500s than it is today. And Campeche, which was a thriving timber, *chicle* (gum) and logwood (a natural source of dye) port in the mid-16th century, was the wealthiest place around.

Pirates (or 'privateers', as some preferred to be called) terrorized Campeche for two centuries. Time and time again the port was invaded, ships sacked, citizens robbed and buildings burned – typical pirate stuff. The buccaneers' hall of shame included the infamous John Hawkins, Francis Drake, Henry Morgan and the notorious 'Peg-Leg' himself. In their most gruesome assault, in early 1663, the various pirate hordes set aside rivalries to converge as a single flotilla upon the city, massacring Campeche's citizens.

This tragedy finally spurred the Spanish monarchy to take preventive action, but it was another five years before work on the 3.5m-thick ramparts began. By 1686 a 2.5km hexagon incorporating eight strategically placed bastions surrounded the city. A segment of the ramparts extended out to sea so that ships literally sailed into a fortress to gain access to the city. With Campeche nearly impregnable, pirates turned to other ports and ships at sea. In 1717, brilliant naval strategist Felipe de Aranda began a campaign against the buccaneers, and eventually made this area of the Gulf safe from piracy. Of course, all that wealth from *chicle* and timber was being created using indigenous slaves, leading one to question: who were the real bad guys, anyway?

For a taste of the pirate life, take a 50-minute cruise on the **Lorencillo** (☎816-1990; barcopiratalorencillo@hotmail.com; Av Resurgimiento No 120; adult/child M$110/50), 4km south of town, near restaurant El Faro del Morro. This 'pirate ship' heads out Tuesday through Sunday at noon and 5pm (or noon and 6pm in warmer seasons). Get information at a kiosk near the *tranvía* kiosk, in the Plaza Principal.

Baluartes

After a particularly blistering pirate assault in 1663, the remaining inhabitants of Campeche set about erecting protective walls around their city. Built largely by indigenous labor with limestone extracted from nearby caves, the barrier took more than 50 years to complete. Stretching more than 2.5km around the urban core and rising to a height of 8m, the hexagonal wall was linked by eight bulwarks. The seven that remain display a treasure trove of historical paraphernalia, artifacts and indigenous handicrafts. You can climb atop the bulwarks and stroll sections of the wall for sweeping views of the port.

Two main entrances connected the walled compound with the outside world. The **Puerta del Mar** (Sea Gate; cnr Calles 8 & 59) provided access from the sea, opening onto a wharf where small craft delivered goods from ships anchored further out. (The shallow waters were later reclaimed so the gate is now several blocks from the waterfront.) The **Puerta de Tierra** (Land Gate; Calle 18; admission M$10; ⌚9am-6pm), on the opposite side, was opened in 1732 as the principal ingress from the suburbs. It is now the venue for a sound-and-light show (p204).

★Museo de la Arquitectura Maya MUSEUM, RAMPART
(Calle 8; admission M$35; ⌚9am-5:30pm Tue-Sun) The **Baluarte de Nuestra Señora de la Soledad**, designed to protect the Puerta del Mar, contains the fascinating Museo de la Arquitectura Maya, the one must-see museum in Campeche. It provides an excellent overview of the sites around Campeche state and the key architectural styles associated with them. Five halls display stelae taken from various sites, accompanied by graphic representations of their carved inscriptions with brief commentaries in flawless English.

Baluarte de Santiago GARDEN, RAMPART
(cnr Calles 8 & 49; adult/3-12yr M$10/5; ⌚8am-9pm) Completed in 1704 – the last of the bulwarks to be built – the Baluarte de Santiago houses the **Jardín Botánico Xmuch Haltún**, a botanical garden with numerous endemic and some non-native plants. It's not a huge place, but provides a green and peaceful place to rest up for a bit.

Museo de la Ciudad MUSEUM, RAMPART
(Calle 8; admission M$30; ⌚8am-8pm) Named after Spain's King Carlos II, the **Baluarte de San Carlos** houses the Museo de la Ciudad. This small but worthwhile museum chronologically illustrates the city's tempestuous

history via well-displayed objects: specimens of dyewood, muskets, a figurehead from a ship's prow and the like. The dungeon downstairs alludes to the building's use as a military prison during the 1700s.

Baluarte de San Pedro RAMPART, MUSEUM
(cnr Avs Circuito Baluartes Este & Circuito Baluartes Nte; 9am-9pm) FREE Directly behind Iglesia de San Juan de Dios, the Baluarte de San Pedro served a postpiracy defensive function when it repelled a punitive raid from Mérida in 1824. Carved in stone above the entry is the symbol of San Pedro: two keys to heaven and the papal tiara. Climb the steep ramp to the roof and look between the battlements to see San Juan's cupola. Downstairs, the **Galería y Museo de Arte Popular** displays beautiful indigenous handicrafts.

Baluarte de San Francisco RAMPART
(Calle 18) Once the primary defensive bastion for the adjacent Puerta de la Tierra, the Baluarte de San Francisco houses a small arms museum, but was closed at the time of research.

Baluarte de San Juan RAMPART, MUSEUM
(Calle 18; admission free with San Francisco ticket; 8am-7:30pm Tue-Sun) Closed at research time, Baluarte de San Juan is the smallest of the seven bulwarks.

Baluarte de Santa Rosa RAMPART
(cnr Calles 14 & Circuito Baluartes Sur; admission free; 9am-3pm) FREE The Baluarte de Santa Rosa has some pirate-themed woodcuts and information on the city's forts.

Malecón

A popular path for joggers, cyclists, strolling friends and cooing sweethearts, the **malecón**, Campeche's 7km-long waterfront promenade, makes for a breezy sunrise ramble or sunset bike ride.

A series of monuments along a 2.5km stretch of the *malecón* allude to various personages and events in the city's history. Southwest of the Plaza Moch-Couoh stands a statue of Campeche native **Justo Sierra Méndez**, a key player in the modernization of Mexico's educational system. Next to the plaza is a **monument** of the walled city's four gates. Three blocks up is a monumental sculpture of native son **Pedro Sáinz de Baranda**, who played a key role in defeating the Spanish at their last stronghold in Veracruz, thus ending the War of Independence.

Just beyond the Centro de Convenciones Campeche XXI, the girl gazing out to sea is the **Novia del Mar**. According to a poignant local legend, the *campechana* fell in love with a foreign pirate and awaits his return. About 1km further north, the **Plaza Cuatro de Octubre** (October 4 Plaza) commemorates the date of the city's 'founding,' depicting the fateful meeting of a Maya *cacique* (chief, who was evidently lost, since it took Montejo to found the city), the conquistador Francisco de Montejo and a priest.

At the *malecón*'s northern tip, 4.5km northeast from downtown, lies a cluster of seafood restaurants called Parador Gastrónomico de Cocteleros. It's a good place for lunch, despite the waiters touting for customers.

Outside the City Center

Museo Arqueológico de Campeche & Fuerte de San Miguel MUSEUM, FORT
(Campeche Archaeological Museum; admission M$42; 8:30am-5:30pm; P) Campeche's largest colonial fort, facing the Gulf of Mexico some 4km southwest of the city center, is now home to the excellent Museo Arqueológico de Campeche. Here you can admire findings from the sites of Calakmul and Edzná, and from Isla de Jaina, an island north of town once used as a burial site for Maya aristocracy.

Stunning jade jewelry and exquisite vases, masks and plates are thematically arranged in 10 exhibit halls. The star attractions are the jade burial masks from Calakmul. Also displayed are stelae, seashell necklaces and clay figurines.

Equipped with a dry moat and working drawbridge, the fort itself is a thing of beauty. The roof deck, ringed by 20 cannons, affords wonderful harbor views.

To get here take a bus or *combi* (minibus; marked 'Lerma') from the market. Ask the driver to let you off at the access road (just say 'Fuerte de San Miguel'), then hike 300m up the hill. Taxis cost M$40.

Fuerte Museo San José del Alto FORT
(Av Francisco Morazán; admission M$35; 8:30am-5pm Tue-Sun; P) Built in the late 18th century, this neatly restored fort sits atop the Cerro de Bellavista. Cross a drawbridge over a moat to enter. Inside, a **museum** illustrates

the port's maritime history through ship models, weaponry and other paraphernalia, including a beautiful ebony rudder carved in the shape of a hound. From the parapets you can see where the town ends and the mangroves begin.

To get here, catch a 'Bellavista Josefa' or 'Morelos' bus from the market; some might also be marked 'San Jose del Alto'. You might have to walk a few hundred meters from where the bus lets you off. Taxis cost M$40 to M$45.

Playa Bonita BEACH
(pedestrians free, cars M$5; 8am-5pm; P) About 13km south of downtown – just past the port village of Lerma – is Playa Bonita, the closest real beach to Campeche. Don't expect an isolated paradise with swaying palm trees; rather expect a gated, developed resort with gritty sand and sandbagged swimming areas (to keep sand from washing away). Still, it's not unpleasant – plenty of *palapas* (thatched palm leaf-roofed structures) provide shade (M$20) and you can also rent tables and chairs. There's also a restaurant and *fútbol* pitch. Come on weekdays to avoid the crowds.

To get here, take one of the frequent *combis* from the market (M$5.50, 20 minutes) and ask to be dropped at the beach entrance. Taxis cost M$80.

Tours

Tranvía de la Ciudad TOUR
(tours adult/under 11yr M$80/20; hourly 9am-noon & 5-8pm) Daily bilingual tours by motorized *tranvía* (trolley) depart from Calle 10 beside the Plaza Principal and last 45 minutes. They cover Campeche's historical center, some traditional neighborhoods and part of the *malecón*. Occasionally, another trolley called *El Guapo* goes to the Fuerte de San Miguel and Fuerte de San José (though these tours don't leave enough time to visit the forts' museums). Check schedules at the ticket kiosk in the Plaza Principal.

Xtampak Tours TOUR
(811-6473; www.toursencampeche.com; Calle 57 No 14; 8am-8pm Mon-Sat, to 2pm Sun) Offers comprehensive city tours at 9am and 2pm daily (per person M$300, four hours), as well as archaeological tours to Edzná (M$250), the Chenes sites (M$950) and eastern Campeche. Overnight packages are available to Calakmul and Río Bec.

Festivals & Events

Carnaval CULTURAL
Campeche pulls out all the stops for Carnaval in February (date varies), with at least a week of festivities leading up to 'Sábado de Bando' (Carnaval Saturday), when everyone dresses up in outrageous costumes and parades down the *malecón*. The official conclusion is a week later, when a pirate effigy is torched and hurled into the sea.

Feria de San Román RELIGIOUS
This festival on September 14 honors the beloved Cristo Negro (Black Christ) of the Iglesia de San Román. Fireworks and ferris wheels take over the zone just southwest of the center, along with beauty contests, boxing matches and a music-and-dance competition that brings in traditional ensembles from around the peninsula.

Día de Nuestra Señora de Guadalupe RELIGIOUS
On December 12 pilgrims from throughout the peninsula travel to the Iglesia de Guadalupe, 1.5km east of the Plaza Principal, Mexico's second-most-visited shrine (after the Virgin of Guadalupe).

Sleeping

Campeche has some nice hotels but doesn't generally offer great-value accommodations. Note that during Christmas and Easter prices can skyrocket.

Hotel Guarandocha Inn HOTEL $
(811-6658; rool_2111@hotmail.com; Calle 55 btwn Calles 12 & 14; d M$350-450, tr M$600;) One of the better room values in town is at this modest but pleasant hotel. Rooms are nice and spacious, and the newer ones upstairs come brighter and more open (and cost a bit more). A very simple breakfast is included.

Hotel Colonial HOTEL $
(816-2222; Calle 14 No 122; s M$273, d M$340-380, t M$459;) Time stands still at this stubbornly low-tech establishment. The 29 decent rooms (rustic bathrooms have open showers) are spacious, though the small windows are very high up – lending an institutional feel. All surround a covered patio with tables and chairs, and there's also an upstairs hallway and rooftop area for hanging out. Only one room has air-conditioning (M$530); basic breakfast offered.

Hostal La Parroquia HOSTEL $
(☎816-2530; www.hostalparroquia.com; Calle 55 No 8; dm M$95, d/q without bathroom M$250/400; 📶) Conveniently located half a block from the Plaza Principal, this basic hostel resides in a crumbling late-1500s mansion. Windowless rooms with original stone walls and exposed wood beams flank a large hallway that opens onto a patio with a 'camping style' cooking area and a small nearby lawn. Huge dorms have 10 to 14 bunks, except for the six-bed women's dorm. Overall it's hardly cozy and the hangout areas desperately need help, but at least there's breakfast and bike rental.

★Hotel López HOTEL $$
(☎816-3344; www.hotellopezcampeche.com.mx; Calle 12 No 189; d/tr/q/ste M$620/670/720/900; ❄📶🏊) This elegant hotel is one of Campeche's best midrange options. Small but modern and comfortably appointed rooms open onto curvy art-deco balconies around oval courtyards and pleasant greenery. Bring your swimsuit for the lovely pool out back.

H177 Hotel HOTEL $$
(☎816-4463; www.⊙177hotel.com.mx; Calle 14 No 177; s/d/t M$780/890/960; ❄📶) With its slick and trendy lines, this hotel is different from anything else in traditional Campeche. It boasts 24 spacious and modern rooms decked out in strong natural colors, and the bathrooms have glass-walled showers. There's also a Jacuzzi, and breakfast is included. Ask for a discount in low season.

Hotel América HOTEL $$
(☎816-45-76; www.hotelamericacampeche.com; Calle 10 No 252; s/d M$500/620; P❄@📶) A large central hotel, the América is a good midrange choice. The highlight here is a pretty courtyard restaurant with tables and umbrellas – don't worry, the music dies down at night. Nearly 50 large, clean rooms are located in the surrounding arcaded corridors and can vary widely, so check out a few if you don't like what you first see.

Hotel Socaires HOTEL $$
(☎811-21-30; www.hotelsocaire.com.mx; Calle 55 No 22; d M$840; P❄📶🏊) This pleasant new hotel only has seven rooms, all very spacious, clean and comfortable (though the lighting could be a little less fluorescent). All rooms surround an open courtyard-hallway, so stay here in dry weather – the best time to enjoy the backyard pool anyway. Complimentary breakfast is served in the small diner.

★Hacienda Puerta Campeche BOUTIQUE HOTEL $$$
(☎1-800-837-1970; www.luxurycollection.com; Calle 59 No 71; r M$7039-9331; P❄@📶🏊) This beautiful boutique hotel has 15 suites with high ceilings and separate lounges – just right for that afternoon massage. Perfectly manicured gardens and grassy lawns offer peace, while the partly covered pool has nearby hammocks that are fit for a Maya king. It also runs a restored luxury hacienda 26km outside the city, on the way to the Edzná ruins.

Hotel Boutique Casa Don Gustavo BOUTIQUE HOTEL $$$
(☎816-8090; www.casadongustavo.com; Calle 59 No 4; r from M$2500; P❄📶🏊) This beautiful boutique hotel offers 10 rooms decorated with antique furniture (and huge modern bathrooms), though everything is so perfectly museumlike it's almost hard to relax. Give it a shot at the small pool with hammocks nearby, or try the rooftop Jacuzzi. Colorful tiled hallways line an outdoor courtyard, and there's a restaurant. Call ahead or check the website for promotions.

Hotel Plaza Campeche HOTEL $$$
(☎811-9900; www.hotelplazacampeche.com; cnr Calle 10 & Av Circuito Baluartes; r M$1290-3510; P❄@📶🏊) Just outside the historic center, on somewhat scruffy Parque del IV Centenario, the Plaza caters to business travelers and tour groups. It's elegant enough, with a sumptuous dining room, pleasant patio, fancy bar and attentive bellhops. The 82 rooms come in four categories; all are comfortable and have flat TVs and safes, though they're not superluxurious.

Eating

Café La Parroquia MEXICAN $
(☎816-2530; Calle 55 No 8; mains M$45-150, lunch specials M$70-80; ⊙24hr) This casual restaurant appeals to both locals and foreigners with its wide-ranging menu and attentive staff. Order everything from fried chicken to grilled pork to turkey soup, plus regional specialties and seafood dishes like *ceviche.* (seafood marinated in lemon or lime juice, garlic and seasonings). Tons of drinks make it all go down easy, and don't miss the creamy flan for dessert.

DIG INTO TRADITIONAL CAMPECHANO CUISINE

On weekends look for *campechano* cuisine at Plaza Principal. Before sundown, stalls set up and offer a few regional specialties such as *pibipollo* (chicken tamales traditionally cooked underground) and *brazo de reina* (tamales with chopped *chaya* – a spinachlike vegetable – mixed into the dough), plus various desserts and cold drinks. *Pan de Cazón* is another regional specialty, mostly available in restaurants, but note that these *tostadas* (fried tortillas) are made from small or baby shark meat and that sharks are becoming an endangered species worldwide.

Campeche's bustling **Mercado Principal** offers some good snacks – if you can handle the 'rustic hygiene.' At the Calle 53 entrance, regional-style tamales are dispensed from big pots in the morning. Inside, take a battered stool at Taquería El Amigo Carlos Ruelas and order a *tranca* – a baguette stuffed with *lechón asada* (roast pork) – and an ice-cold glass of *agua de lima* (sweet lemon drink). Nearby, a number of *cocina económicas* (basic eateries) cook up very affordable meals.

★**Parador Gastrónomico de Cocteleros** (Av Costera; mains M$100-130; ⏲9am-6:30pm), 4.5km from Plaza Principal at the northend end of the *malecón* (taxis from center M$30), is a great place to sample the area's bountiful seafood. Over a dozen thatched-roofed restaurants all serve pretty much the same thing: shrimp cocktails, fried fish and other seafood dishes. Competition between restaurants is lively and you'll no doubt be confronted by waiters trying to convince you to eat at their place. Just pick a spot that looks appealing, have a seat and enjoy the sea views.

Cafetería Atrapa Sueño VEGETARIAN **$**
(☎816-5000; Calle 10 No 269; mains M$30-80; ⏲8am-8pm Mon-Sat, plus Sunday Dec-Mar; 🌶) This German-run, new-age eatery – complete with plant-filled patio out back – features a good selection of vegetarian fare, from sandwiches to soups to lasagne. Breakfast is also served, and there are meditation and yoga classes as well as massage services.

Chef Color MEXICAN **$**
(☎811-4455; cnr Calles 55 & 12; half/full lunch platters M$30/50; ⏲12:30-5:30pm Mon-Sat) This cafeteria-style eatery serves up large portions of tasty Central American–influenced Mexican dishes from behind a glass counter; just point at what you want. The menu changes daily but it's always good, cheap and filling.

★**Luz de Luna** INTERNATIONAL **$$**
(☎811-0624; Calle 59 No 6; mains M$75-110; ⏲8am-10pm Mon-Sat) Carved, painted tables and folksy decor add a creative atmosphere to this popular restaurant on a pedestrian street. The menu choices are equally interesting – try the shrimp salad, chicken fajitas, flank steak or vegetarian burritos. There are plenty of breakfast options as well, especially omelettes.

Marganzo MEXICAN **$$**
(☎811-3898; Calle 8 No 267; mains M$82-140; ⏲7am-11pm) Marganzo is popular with tourists, for good reason – the food is great, the portions are large and the complimentary appetizers numerous. An extensive menu offers everything from international fare to regional treats like *chochinita pibil* (roasted suckling pig). Service is attentive, and wandering musicians provide entertainment.

La Pigua SEAFOOD **$$$**
(☎811-3365; Miguel Alemán 179A; mains M$160-195; ⏲1-9pm) Some of Campeche's finest meals are served at this upscale restaurant in a strangely downscale neighborhood. But never mind the location – just enjoy the attentive service and seafood dishes like *camarones al coco* (coconut shrimp), whole fish in cilantro sauce and grilled squid with ground almonds and paprika.

Drinking & Entertainment

There's invariably someone performing on the Plaza Principal every Saturday and Sunday evening from around 6:30pm, be it a rock-and-roll band, pop-star impersonator, traditional dance troupe or a folk trio. On Sunday, the Banda del Estado (State Band) kicks off the program, performing Campeche classics, show music, marches and other rousing fare. The tourist office puts out a weekly events booklet.

For Campeche's hottest nightlife, head 1km south from the center along the *malecón* past the Torres de Cristal, where you'll find a cluster of bars, cafes and discos.

Chocol-Ha CAFE

(☎811-7893; Calle 59 No 30; drinks M$18-39, snacks M$47-55; ⏰5:30-11pm Mon-Thu, to 12:30am Fri & Sat) When that chocolate craving hits, head on over to this cute little cafe with a patio in front and grassy yard in back. Drinks include bittersweet hot chocolate with green tea or chili (try it!), and a chocolate frappé. Sweet treats such as chocolate cake, chocolate crepes and even chocolate tamales are also available.

La Casa Vieja BAR-RESTAURANT

(Calle 10 No 319A; ⏰8:30am-12:30am) There's no better setting for an evening cocktail than La Casa Vieja's colonnaded balcony overlooking the Plaza Principal. Look for the stairs next to the McDonald's ice-cream counter.

Salón Rincón Colonial BAR

(Calle 59 No 60; ⏰10am-6pm) With ceiling fans high over an airy hall and a solid wood bar amply stocked with rum, this Cuban-style drinking establishment appropriately served as a location for *Original Sin,* a 2001 movie with Antonio Banderas that was set in Havana. The *botanas* (appetizers) are exceptionally fine, and check out the little covered patio in back.

Puerta de Tierra LIGHT SHOW

(adult/4-10 yr M$50/25; ⏰8pm Thu-Sun) Incidents from Campeche's pirate past are re-enacted several nights a week at the Puerta de Tierra. It's a Disneyesque extravaganza with lots of cannon blasts and flashing lights; audio guides come in four languages.

Shopping

Bazar Artesanal HANDICRAFTS

(Plaza Ah Kim Pech; ⏰10am-8pm) The state-run Folk Art Bazaar, down by the *malecón* near the Centro de Convenciones Campeche XXI, offers one-stop shopping for regional crafts. One section of the market is reserved for demonstrations of traditional craft techniques.

Casa de Artesanías Tukulna HANDICRAFTS

(☎816-2188; Calle 10 No 33; ⏰8:30am-8pm Mon-Sat) A central shop selling textiles, clothing, hats, hammocks, wood chairs, sweets and so on – all made in Campeche state.

Information

Campeche has numerous banks with ATMs. For internet, there are several 'cibers' in the city center.

Central Post Office (cnr Av 16 de Septiembre & Calle 53; ⏰8:30am-4pm Mon-Fri, 8-11:30am Sat)

Cruz Roja (Red Cross; ☎815-2411; cnr Av Las Palmas & Ah Kim Pech) Medical services; some 3km northeast of downtown.

Dirección de Turismo (☎811-3989; Calle 55 No 3; ⏰8am-9pm Mon-Fri, 9am-9pm Sat & Sun) Basic information on Campeche city.

Emergency (☎066)

Hospital Dr Manuel Campos (☎811-1709; Av Circuito Baluartes Nte) Between Calles 14 and 16.

HSBC Bank (Calle 10 btwn Calles 53 & 55; ⏰9am-5pm Mon-Fri, 9am-3pm Sat) Campeche's only bank that is open Saturday.

Internet Cafe (Calle 10 btwn Calles 59 & 61; ⏰8:30am-9pm Mon-Sat)

Secretaría de Turismo (☎127-33-00; www.campeche.travel; Plaza Moch-Couoh; ⏰8am-9pm Mon-Fri, to 8pm Sat & Sun) Good information on the city and Campeche state.

Getting There & Away

AIR

Campeche's small but modern airport is 6km southeast of the center; it has a tourist office, car-rental offices and a tiny coffeeshop/snack bar. **Aeroméxico** (☎800-021-4010) provides services.

BUS

Campeche's **main bus terminal** (☎811-9910; Av Patricio Trueba 237), usually called the ADO or 1st-class terminal, is about 2.5km south of Plaza Principal via Av Central. Buses provide 1st-class services to destinations around the country, along with 2nd-class services to Sabancuy (M$75), Hecelchakán (M$50) and Candelaria (M$160).

The **2nd-class terminal** (☎811-9910; Av Gobernadores 289), often referred to as the 'old ADO' station, is 600m east of the Mercado Principal. Second-class destinations include Bolonchén de Rejón (M$70), Hopelchén (M$50), Bolonchén (M$69), Xpujil (M$166) and Bécal (M$47).

To get to the new terminal, catch any 'Las Flores,' 'Solidaridad' or 'Casa de Justicia' bus by the post office. To the 2nd-class terminal, catch a 'Terminal Sur' bus from the same point.

CAR

If you're arriving in Campeche from the south, via the *cuota* (toll road), turn left at the roundabout signed for the *universidad* and follow that road straight to the coast, then go north.

If you're heading to either Edzná, the long route to Mérida or the fast toll road going south, take Calle 61 to Av Central and follow signs for the airport and either Edzná or the *cuota*. For the nontoll route south, just head down the *malecón*. For the short route to Mérida go north on the *malecón*.

In addition to some outlets at the airport, several car-rental agencies can be found downtown including **Easy Way** (☎811-2236; www.campechecarrental.com; Calle 59 btwn Calles 8 & 10; ⊙8:30am-9:30pm Mon-Sat). Rates run from M$600 per day.

Getting Around

Taxis from the airport to the center cost M$120 (shared taxis M$50 per person); buy tickets at the taxi booth inside the terminal. Going *to* the airport, some street taxis (ie not called from your hotel, which are more expensive) charge 'only' M$100; penny-pinchers can try taking the hourly bus to Chiná (a village outside Campeche; M$10) from the market, and getting off at the airport entrance, then walking 500m to the airport doors.

Within Campeche city, taxis charge M$25 to M$45; prices are 10% more after 10pm, and 20% more from midnight to 5am.

Most local buses (M$5.50) have a **stop** at or near the market.

Consider pedaling along the *malecón*; get bike rentals at **Buenaventura** (☎144-3388; www.viajesbuenaventura.com.mx; Av 16 de Septiembre 122 Local 3; bike rentals M$30 for the first hour, then M$20 per hour thereafter; M$150 per day; ⊙9am-3pm & 5-8pm Mon-Sat). Rates include helmet and lock.

Drivers should note that even-numbered streets in the *centro histórico* (historic center) take priority, as indicated by the red (stop) or black (go) arrows at every intersection.

NORTH OF CAMPECHE

Along with a quaint town, there are plenty of archeological destinations in this region. The Chenes sites are best done with a private vehicle, though Edzná is easily reached by *combi*.

Hecelchakán

☎996 / POP 10,000

Bicycle taxis with canvas canopies noiselessly navigate the tranquil central plazas of Hecelchakán, a pleasant town 60km northeast of Campeche known for its culinary pleasures and an excellent small museum. Hecelchakán's inhabitants, who include a Mennonite community, are primarily devoted to agriculture.

For tourist information there's the **Dirección de Turismo** (⊙8am-3pm), in a building across from the ADO/ATS bus office and near the plaza. Head up the stairs just left of the Telecomm office and it's the first door on your left.

Sights

Iglesia de San Francisco de Asis CHURCH

Dating from the 16th century, the Iglesia de San Francisco de Asis (on the main plaza) is a former Franciscan monastery with woodbeam ceiling and striking altar; note the flaming hearts flanking a crucifix.

BUSES FROM CAMPECHE

DESTINATION	FARE (M$)	DURATION (HR)	FREQUENCY
Cancún	450-550	7	7 daily
Chetumal	240-345	6½hr	1-2 daily
Ciudad del Carmen	165-230	3	hourly
Mérida	160-200	2½	hourly
Mérida (via Uxmal)	94-105	4½	5 daily from 2nd-class terminal
Mexico City	1175-1400	18	3 daily
Palenque	300	6	4 daily
San Cristóbal de las Casas	435	10	9:45pm
Villahermosa	280-420	6	every 2 hrs
Xpujil	230	5	2pm

LA LOTERÍA

'Twenty-three, *melónes*' (melons)...'47, *volcán*' (volcano)...'41, *mecedora*' (rocking chair)...'78, *rosa*' (rose)...'two, *paloma*' (dove).

It's Saturday night in Campeche, and the tables in front of the cathedral are already full for the ritual game of *la lotería*, held every Saturday and Sunday evening from 6pm to 11pm. The litany of icons is chanted through a microphone by a woman in a *huipil* (colorfully embroidered tunic), as she picks up numbered balls from the spinner cage and places them on a panel of 90 pictures.

A bingolike game of European origin that uses numbered images, *la lotería* has been played on the peninsula since the 19th century. John L Stephens' *Incidents of Travel in Yucatan* has a good description of the game as he observed it at a fiesta in Mérida in 1841. The action now may not be as heated as he describes, but some folks can get pretty excited when they finish a row.

At a peso per card, most anyone can afford to play. Players usually mark the images on their cards with bottle caps. A variation on bingo is that markers can be placed in a variety of patterns: in addition to the usual rows, players can arrange their five markers in the form of a 'V,' a pair of scissors, or several kinds of crosses. The first person to form one of these patterns takes the pot – and the bragging rights that come with it.

Museo Arqueológico del Camino Real MUSEUM
(admission M$34) This museum, on the north corner of the plaza, contains a small but compelling collection of ceramic art excavated from Isla de Jaina, a tiny island due west of Hecelchakán that flourished as a commercial center during the 7th century. Portraying ballplayers, weavers, warriors and priests, the extraordinary figurines on display here paint a vivid portrait of ancient Maya life. There's also a collection of stelae in the courtyard. Look for the entrance to the left of the church and at the end of the yellow building.

Sleeping & Eating

Campechanos sometimes visit Hecelchakán just for its famous snacks. From 6am to 10am (!), outside the church, little pavilions serve up *cochinita pibil* (barbecued suckling pig wrapped in banana leaves) and *relleno negro* (turkey stuffed with chopped pork and laced with a rich, dark chili sauce) in tacos or baguettes, along with *horchata* (a rice-based drink) and *agua de cebada* (a barley beverage served with a spoon).

Hotel Margarita HOTEL $
(☎827-0472; Calle 20 No 80; s/d with fan M$150-190, s/d with air-con M$250-290; ❄📶) On the main drag about 200m from the plaza (look for the green building) is Hotel Margarita, a very basic place with budget rooms that are good enough for a night.

Chujuc Haa MEXICAN $
(☎827-0707; mains M$55-70; ⏰7am-midnight Mon-Sat, 11am-midnight Sun) This popular restaurant serves regional cuisine like *poc-chuc*, a flat but flavorful steak that comes with rice, beans and salad. A half order is plenty! Located four doors left of the ADO/ATS bus office.

Getting There & Away

The ADO/ATS bus office is across from the post office and just south of the plaza on Calle Principal. ATS buses from Campeche's 2nd-class terminal stop here en route to Mérida every half-hour till around 10pm (M$32 to M$50, one hour). In addition, frequent *combis* (M$24, one hour) shuttle passengers between Campeche's market (look for the 'El Cubano' sign; see Map p196) and Hecelchakán's plaza.

Bécal

☎996 / POP 8000

Bécal, about 90km north of Campeche just before you enter the state of Yucatán, is a center of the Yucatán panama-hat trade. Some inhabitants here make their living weaving *jipijapas*, as the soft, pliable hats are known locally. The finest hats are destined for export to connoisseurs in foreign cities. The tranquil town clearly identifies with its stock-in-trade, as is made obvious by the centerpiece of its plaza.

To find out where *jipijapas* are crafted and sold in town, hail a bicycle taxi (M$10) on Bécal's plaza and ask the rider for his recommendation. You'll likely be approached by a young guide (perhaps on a bicycle) – some who work on donation. A half-block from the plaza, on the road into town, is **Artesania Becaleña** (☎431-4046; Calle 30 No 210; ⏰8am-10pm), one of several shops where you can check out some hats.

In April the **Fiesta de Flor del Jipi** is celebrated with dancing and bullfights.

From Campeche's 2nd-class terminal, ATS buses bound for Mérida stop in Bécal's main plaza every half-hour (M$49, two hours).

EAST OF CAMPECHE

Along with a quaint town, there are plenty of archeological destinations in this region. The Chenes sites are best done with a private vehicle, though Edzná is easily reached by *combi*.

Hopelchén

☎996 / POP 7500

The municipal center for the Chenes region, Hopelchén (Maya for 'Place of the Five Wells') makes a pleasant base for visiting the various archaeological sites in the vicinity while also providing a glimpse of everyday life in a small Campeche town.

The **tourist information office** (Calle 20; ⏰8am-3pm) is in the Casa de Cultura, two blocks north of the main plaza.

On a typical morning here, Maya *campesinos* (agricultural workers) and Mennonites congregate under box-shaped laurels as bicycle taxis glide past. Opposite the central plaza, the church **Parroquia de San Antonio de Padua**, dating from the 16th century, features an intricate *retablo* (altarpiece), with a gallery of saints and angels amid lavishly carved pillars.

Herbalists, midwives and shamans practice traditional Maya medicine at the **Consejo Local de Médicos Indígenas** (Colmich, Calle 8; ⏰8am-5pm Tue & Thu), five blocks east of the plaza.

Hotel Los Arcos (☎100-8782; Calle 23 s/n; s/d/tr M$160/210/250; ❄), at the plaza, is a convenient, no-frills option with attached restaurant. The rooms are clean (though TV is an extra M$100) and have hammock hooks for sleeping extra people or just general hanging around.

For a good *caldo de pollo* (chicken soup), try the stalls on Plaza Chica, open from 7am to 3pm and 5pm to midnight.

ℹ Getting There & Away

Combis (located on the main road a half block toward the center from Campeche's 2nd-class bus terminal) run every half-hour from Campeche (M$50, 1½ hours) to Hopelchén's plaza, stopping at villages along the way.

Hopelchén's bus terminal is at the market on Calle 16 between Calles 17 and 19, behind the church. Get tickets at the first *'antojitos regionales'* counter you see. There are buses to Campeche (M$56, 1½ hours, hourly), Mérida (M$96, two hours, six services), and Xpujil (M$105, three hours, one service at 8pm).

DISCOVER THE ROOTS OF THE JIPIJAPA HAT

While on the surface Bécal may look like a somnolent *campechano* town, under ground are people laboring away at the traditional craft of hat making. Called *jipijapas* (or *jipis* for short), these soft, pliable hats have been woven by townsfolk from the fibers of the *huano* palm tree since the mid-19th century, when the plants were imported from Guatemala by a Catholic priest.

The stalk of the plant is cut into strands to make the fibers; the quality of the hat depends on the fineness of the cut. The work is done in humid limestone caves that provide just the right atmosphere for shaping the fibers, keeping them moist and pliable. These caves – often no bigger than a bedroom – are reached by a hole in the ground in someone's backyard. Once exposed to the relatively dry air outside, the panama hat is surprisingly resilient and resistant to crushing.

Today, Bécal's hat-making art is a dying industry due to cheap global competition. So if you want to shade your head in style while supporting a worthy cause, buy a handmade *jipi*. Prices range from around M$200 for coarsely woven hats made in a couple days, to nearly M$3000 for the finest hats that can take months to complete.

Around Hopelchén

Tohcok (spelled Tacob on signs) is 3.5km northwest of Hopelchén. Of the 40-odd structures found at this Maya **site** (8am-5pm) FREE, the only one that has been significantly excavated displays features of the Puuc and Chenes styles. The talkative custodian, Pepe, can point out a *chultún* (Maya underground cistern), one of around 45 in the zone. You can walk to Tohcok from Hopelchén along the main 'highway', but there are also half-hourly white vans (marked 'Transporte Escolares'; M$5) that leave from the plaza and take kids to a nearby school; from here it's only a few hundred meters to the ruins.

Some of the most significant caves in the peninsula are found 31km north of Hopelchén, shortly before you reach the town of Bolonchén de Rejón. The local Maya have long known of the existence of the **Grutas de X'tacumbilxuna'an** (816-1782; admission M$50; 10am-5pm Tue-Sun;), a series of underground cenotes in this water-scarce region. In 1844 the caves were 'discovered' by the intrepid John L Stephens and Frederick Catherwood, who depicted the Maya descending an incredibly high rope-and-log staircase to replenish their water supply. Today the cenote is dry but X'tacumbilxuna'an (*shtaa*-koom-beel-shoo-*nahn*) is open for exploration and admiration of the vast caverns and incredible limestone formations within. A light-and-sound extravaganza accompanies the tour, and you can hear the sounds of motmots echoing off the walls as you descend.

Buses traveling between Hopelchén and Mérida will drop you at the cave entrance before Bolonchén (M$20, 25 minutes). In addition, *combis* depart for Bolonchén from Hopelchén's plaza, passing near the caves. Check with the driver for return times.

Chenes Sites

Northeastern Campeche state is dotted with more than 30 sites in the distinct Chenes style, recognizable by the monster motifs around doorways in the center of long, low buildings of three sections, and temples atop pyramidal bases. Most of the year you'll have these sites to yourself. The three small sites of El Tabasqueño, Hochob and Dzibilnocac make for an interesting single-day trip from Campeche if you have your own vehicle (or you can take a tour from Campeche with Xtampak Tours (p201)).

El Tabasqueño ARCHAEOLOGICAL SITE

(8am-5pm) FREE Supposedly named after a local landowner from Tabasco, El Tabasqueño boasts a temple-palace (Estructura 1) with a striking monster-mouth doorway, flanked by stacks of eight Chac masks with hooked snouts. Estructura 2 is a solid free-standing tower, an oddity in Maya architecture. To reach El Tabasqueño, go 30km south from Hopelchén. Just beyond the village of Pakchén, there's an easy-to-miss sign at a turnoff on the right; follow this rock-and-gravel road 2km to the site.

Hochob ARCHAEOLOGICAL SITE

(admission M$35; 8am-5pm) About 60km south of Hopelchén near the village of Chencoh, Hochob, 'the place where corn is harvested,' is among the most beautiful and terrifying of the Chenes-style sites. Considered a classic example of the Chenes style, the Palacio Principal (Estructura 2, though signposted as 'Estructura 1') is on the north side of the main plaza. It's faced with an elaborate doorway representing Itzamná, the lord creator of the ancient Maya, as a rattlesnake with its jaws open. Facing Estructura 2 across the plaza, Estructura 5 has a pair of raised temples on either end of a long series of rooms; the better preserved temple on the east side retains part of its perforated roofcomb.

To reach Hochob, go 5km south from El Tabasqueño, then turn right just before the Pemex station at Dzilbalchén. Now go 7.5km to the Chencoh sign, turn left, then after 400m go left again. Drive another 3.5km to Hochob.

Dzibilnocac ARCHAEOLOGICAL SITE

(8am-5pm) FREE Though it only has one significant structure, Dzibilnocac possesses an eerie grandeur that merits a visit. Unlike the many hilltop sites chosen for Chenes structures, Dzibilnocac ('big painted turtle' is one translation) is on a flat plain, like a large open park. As Stephens and Catherwood observed back in 1842, the many scattered hillocks in the zone, still unexcavated today, attest to the presence of a large city. The single, clearly discernible structure is A1, a palatial complex upon a 76m platform with a trio of raised temples atop rounded pyramidal bases. The best preserved of the three, on the east end, has fantastically elaborate monster-mask reliefs on each of its four sides and the typically piled-up Chac masks on three of the four corners.

Dzibilnocac is located beside the village of Iturbide (also called Vicente Guerrero), 20km northeast of Dzibalchén. From Campeche's 2nd-class bus terminal there are several buses daily to Iturbide via Hopelchén (M$86, three hours). There's no place to stay here so you'll need to make it back to Hopelchén by nightfall.

Edzná

If you only have the time or inclination to visit one archaeological site in northern Campeche, **Edzná** (admission M$46; ⏲8am-5pm) should be your top pick. It's located about 60km southeast of Campeche.

Edzná's massive complexes were built by a highly stratified society that flourished from about 600 BC to the dawn of the colonial era. During that period the people of Edzná built more than 20 complexes in a mélange of architectural styles, installing an ingenious network of water-collection and irrigation systems.

After its demise in the 15th century, the site remained unknown until its rediscovery by *campesinos* in 1906.

Edzná means 'House of the Itzáes,' in reference to a predominant governing clan of Chontal Maya origin. Edzná's rulers recorded significant events on stone stelae. Around 30 stelae have been discovered adorning the site's principal temples; a handful are on display underneath a *palapa* just beyond the ticket office.

A path from the *palapa* leads about 400m through vegetation; follow the 'Gran Acropolis' sign. Soon, to your left, you'll come upon the **Plataforma de los Cuchillos** (Platform of the Knives), a residential complex highlighted by Puuc architectural features. The name derives from an

Edzná

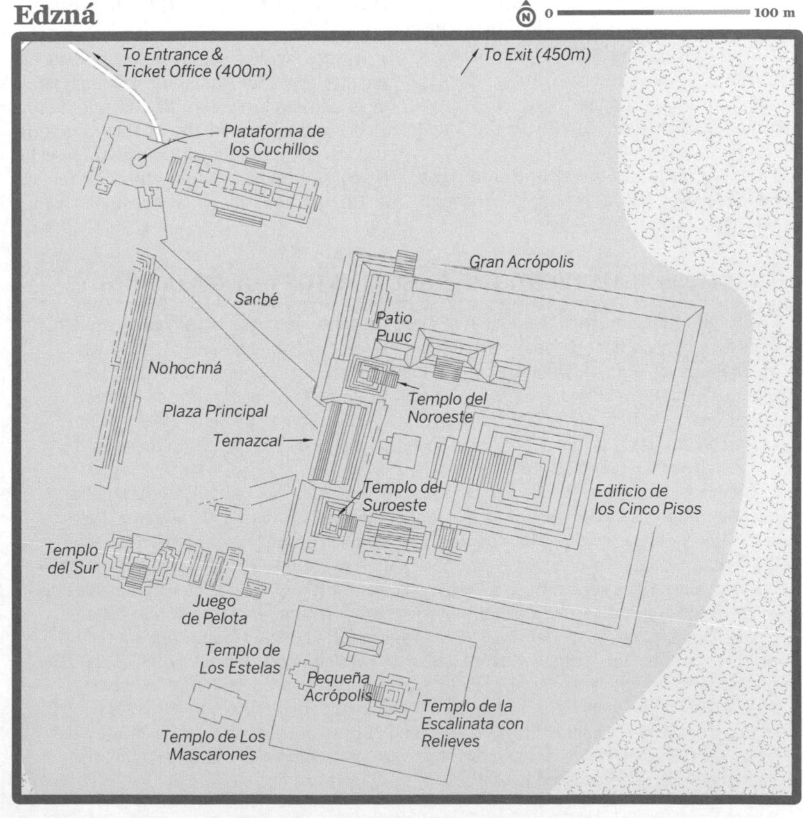

offering of silica knives that had been found within.

Crossing a *sacbé* (stone-lined, grass walkway), you arrive at the main attraction, the **Plaza Principal**. Measuring 160m long and 100m wide, the Plaza Principal is surrounded by temples. On your right is the **Nohochná** (Big House), a massive, elongated structure topped by four long halls likely used for administrative tasks, such as the collection of tributes and the dispensation of justice.

Across the plaza is the Gran Acrópolis, a raised platform holding several structures, including Edzná's major temple, the 31m-high **Edificio de los Cinco Pisos** (Five-Story Building). The current structure is the last of four remodels and was done primarily in the Puuc style. It rises five levels from its base to the roofcomb and contains many vaulted rooms. Note the well-preserved glyphs along the base of the central staircase.

South of Plaza Principal is the **Templo de los Mascarones** (Temple of the Masks), with a pair of reddish stucco masks underneath a protective *palapa*. Personifying the gods of the rising and setting sun, these extraordinarily well-preserved faces display dental mutilation, crossed eyes and huge earrings, features associated with the Maya aristocracy.

There's a fairly tasteful **sound-and-light show** (admission M$121) Thursday through Sunday nights at 8pm from April to October, and 7pm from November to March. Get here a half-hour early (cancelled in heavy rain). Shows are daily during popular times like Mexican holidays; contact Campeche's tourist office for details.

There are minimal services near Edzná, which is an easy day trip from Campeche. If you have the pesos, check out Hacienda Uayamon (www.luxurycollection.com).

Getting There & Away

Combis (M$35, one hour) leave when full from Calle Chihuahua near Campeche's market. Most drop you 200m from the site entrance unless the driver is feeling generous. The last *combi* back is around 4pm, but ask the driver to make sure!

Xtampak Tours (p201) in Campeche provides guided tours of Edzná (including transport) for M$750 per person.

SOUTHWESTERN COAST

This sparsely developed stretch of seafront is fringed with usually deserted beaches that are ideal for watching pelicans, going on shell-searching expeditions and taking an occasional dip in the shallow aquamarine waters. Heading south from Campeche, the coastal highway passes through the city of Champotón, along with small fishing

TRADITIONAL HARVEST: THE SWEET HISTORY OF MAYA HONEY

The Yucatán's flowers yield a sweet, mellifluous harvest, and bees have held an exalted place throughout its honeyed history. Records show that at the time of the conquest, the Maya produced vast amounts of honey and Yucatecan villages paid tribute to the Spanish in honey, which was valued more for its curative properties than as a sweetener. Bees were important in the Maya pantheon: bee motifs appear in the surviving Maya codices, and the image of Ah Mucenkab, god of bees, is carved into the friezes of Chichén Itzá, Tulum and Sayil.

Mexico remains the world's number-four producer of honey, and the nectar of the Yucatán is especially coveted for its blend of flavors and aromas, a result of the diversity of the region's flowers. Many *campesinos* (agricultural workers) keep bees to supplement their agricultural output. However, the stingless variety known to the ancient Maya has long since been supplanted by European bees, which in turn are being pushed aside by the more aggressive African bees, notorious among handlers for their nasty sting.

One Maya women's cooperative in the village of Ich-Ek, near Hopelchén, wants to preserve the ancient heritage. **Koolel Kab** (Women Who Work with Bees; ☎996-822-0073) produces honey with indigenous *melipona* bees, which take up residence in hollow trees. Using techniques much like those of their ancestors, the women place sections of tree trunk under a shelter, capping each end of the trunk with mud. An average trunk yields 12L of honey, which is marketed chiefly for its medicinal properties as throat lozenges, eye drops, soaps and skin creams.

towns and spots like Playa Varadero, where you can stop for a cold beer and hang your hammock in a thatched shelter. Then you'll hit Laguna de Términos, a vast mangrove-fringed lagoon home to riots of migratory birds and a prime sea-turtle nesting spot. After all this the noise and bustle of Ciudad del Carmen will seem like a culture shock.

Champotón

POP 31,000

Champotón, at the mouth of the river of the same name, has great historical significance as the landing place of the first Spanish exploratory expedition from Cuba, led by Francisco Hernández de Córdoba, in 1517. Probably seeking a source of water along the river, the Spaniards were assailed by warriors under the command of the *cacique* Moch Couoh, forcing them to retreat. Hernández de Córdoba died shortly after his return to Cuba from wounds he received at Champotón, which from then on was known as the 'Bahía de la Mala Pelea' (Bay of the Bad Fight).

Now a pleasant enough city between Ciudad del Carmen and Campeche, Champotón sustains itself mainly on fishing, and perhaps the best reason to stop is to sample its abundant seafood. Try **Pelicano's** (982-828-1418; Av Carlos Sansores Pérez, btwn Calles 11 & 13; mains M$80-140; 7:30am-7pm), a clean, modern and family-friendly restaurant on the coastal road about 2km south of the colorful market (which also has cheap seafood eateries). There are also several *coctelerías* (seafood shacks, specializing in shellfish cocktails) under thatched roofs about 4.5km north of town, along the beach. If you want to stay overnight, head to **Snook Inn** (982-828-0018; snookinnchampoton@hotmail.com; Calle 30 No 1; r M$700-800;), a good hotel with spacious rooms and a pool; staff also organize bird- and crocodile-watching river trips to a nearby mangrove.

The bus terminal is easy to find - it's on the coastal road into town, next to the market at the mouth of the river. Destinations include Campeche (M$37 to M$71, one hour), Sabancuy (M$68, one hour), Ciudad del Carmen (M$145, two hours) and Xpujil (M$130, four hours). From Campeche, frequent *combis* (M$30, 45 minutes) leave for Champotón from Av República near the market. If you're driving, note that two roads head south from Campeche to Champotón: a meandering coastal route (free) and a direct toll road (M$60).

Sabancuy

POP 7500

Sabancuy is a picturesque fishing town on the lower side of an estuary that branches off the northeastern end of Laguna de Términos. It's located 2km inland, connected via land bridge to the coast highway, where there's a **state tourist office** (9am-4pm Mon-Sat).

The beaches around Sabancuy are major nesting grounds for hawksbill and green sea turtles. Workers from a local university program called **Campamento Tortuguero La Escollera** (www.unacar.mx/psabancuy/campamento/tortuguero.html) gather up eggs from nests during the season, moving them to protected areas until they hatch. If you're here from April to October (peak season June to August), you can take part in liberating baby sea turtles; over 100,000 hatchlings are set free annually. To find out more about this free program, check out the website and contact **Alfonso Díaz Molina** (938-152-2883; amolina@delfin.unacar.mx), the program director who works at Escuela Preparatoria, which is at the edge of town.

If you're really into crumbly buildings, you can visit the **ex-Hacienda de Tixchel**, 15km from town. This old cattle ranch and sugar plantation is from the late colonial period, constructed by the Spanish from nearby Maya ruins. The easiest way to get here is by boat (M$1200 for up to six people); ask for Marcos at a beach *palapa* just north of the state tourist office. **Dr José de Jesús Ambrosio Reyes** (982-825-0128), who works at the Farmacia de Jesús, one block up from the plaza on the right side of the church, might also have information.

There's a cheap hotel next to the bus terminal, but for more comfort walk to **Hotel Sabancuy Plaza** (982-825-0081; hotelsabancuyplaza@hotmail.com; Calle Hidalgo s/n; r with fan M$200, with air-con M$300, ste M$600; P), just a block west of the plaza. For good seafood with a seaside setting, head to **Viaducto Playa** (982-731-5574; Km 77.5; mains M$95-130; 8am-8pm), on the beach about 500m south of the land bridge (mototaxi M$30).

The bus terminal is right on the village's cute little waterfront plaza, and there are a couple of ATMs nearby. Bus destinations include Campeche (M$75 to M$121, two hours), Champotón (M$68, one hour), Isla Aguada

(M$22, 30 minutes) and Ciudad del Carmen (M$52 to M$79, 1¼ hours). Folks get around via mototaxis; rides around town cost M$7.

Isla Aguada

Isla Aguada is a large fishing town and not quite an island, as its name implies. It's known for its pretty lighthouse, over 100 years old and recently restored into a museum. But you can also take a boat excursion to **Isla de Pájaros**, where thousands of herons, gulls and magnificent frigate birds converge at sunset. Another highlight is spotting dolphins, which are commonly seen, and a visit to a small sandy island, Cayo Arena. Morning and dusk are the best times to take these trips, most of which run from April to July. One boat operator is **El Rey de Los Delfines** (938-146-1866, 938-134-8249), which leaves from the *muelle turístico* (tourist dock); you can also inquire at the **Comisaría** (Administrative Offices; 938-1122-8109), near Parque Benito Juárez. A two-hour excursion for up to eight people costs around M$1000.

If you want to stick around, **Hotel Playa Punta Perla** (938-106-4955; r M$400;) has plain rooms and could use a little upkeep – but at least it has a pool and is right at the beach.

Relatively frequent *combis* and buses connect Isla Aguada with nearby Sabancuy (M$22, 30 minutes) and Ciudad del Carmen (M$25, 40 minutes). If you're driving, the 3.2km Puente La Unidad (M$58 toll) spans the strait toward Ciudad del Carmen, 46km further west.

Laguna de Términos

The largest lagoon in the Gulf of Mexico area, the Laguna de Términos comprises a network of estuaries, swamps and ponds that together form a uniquely important coastal habitat.

Red, white and black mangroves fringe the lagoon, and the area is an important nesting ground for several species of marine turtle and numerous migratory birds. Encompassing not only wildlife habitat but also the state's second-largest city and Mexico's principal oil-production center, the lagoon's ecosystem remains threatened by various environmental dangers – including oil spills and overfishing – despite being designated a Flora and Fauna Protected Area in 1994.

Hemmed in by a narrow strip of land that is traversed by Hwy 180, the lagoon can be explored from various points along the way.

Ciudad del Carmen

938 / POP 170,000

Campeche state's second-biggest city occupies the western end of a 40km-long, narrow island between the Gulf of Mexico and the Laguna de Términos. Ciudad del Carmen was once dependent on jumbo shrimp, dyewood and *chicle* (gum) for its livelihood, but in the late 1970s oil was discovered. Investment poured in, the population swelled and the 3.8km-long Puente Zacatal (Zacatal Bridge) was completed in 1994, linking the city with the rest of Mexico. Unfortunately most of the city's streets remained narrow, and horrific traffic jams are now a daily part of life.

Though Ciudad del Carmen rarely sees foreign tourists, it does have a renowned and colorful **Carnaval** celebration, with locals wearing elaborate costumes and dancing in the streets for four days. Another exciting event is the **Fiesta de la Virgen del Carmen**, which kicks off for two weeks on July 16 when the port's patron saint is taken on a cruise around the harbor; there are also many exhibits of art, culture and local industries.

Sights & Activities

Parque Zaragoza SQUARE, PLAZA

(Central Plaza) Parque Zaragoza has a handsome 19th-century kiosk and is one the city's most pleasant area to hang out, especially in the evenings. On its north side is the 1856 **Santuario de la Virgen del Carmen**, which pays homage to the patron saint of sailors. Vestiges of Carmen's earlier prosperity remain in the *centro histórico,* where *chicle* barons' 19th-century mansions run along Calles 22 and 24, south of the plaza.

Museo Victoriano Nieves MUSEUM

(cnr Calles 22 & 41; admission M$5; 9am-8pm Mon-Fri, 10am-1pm Sat & Sun) The city's decent history museum is located in an interesting old hospital building. Inside are archaeological relics (including stelae from Xpujil), a petroleum exhibition and information on the region's pirate history – plus a kids' pirate ship, complete with plank.

THE MENNONITES OF CAMPECHE

Campeche is in the midst of a quiet invasion by an unlikely community – the Mennonites. Seeing them waiting in bus stations, hanging about the main plazas of villages or crowding a pickup, you may wonder if you've somehow stumbled onto the set of *Little House on the Prairie*. Clad in black coveralls and long-sleeved flannel shirts in the midday heat, the men tower over their Maya neighbors. The women wear dark floral-print dresses and straw hats with broad ribbons.

Tracing their origins to 16th-century Reformist Germany, the Mennonites have inhabited some northern Mexican states since the 1920s. Drawn by cheap land, they first migrated down to Hopelchén, Campeche, in 1983 and since then have established agricultural communities around Dzibalchén, Hecelchakán and Edzná. Once they've settled in, the Mennonites work relentlessly, growing corn, melons and other crops, raising cattle and producing cheese for the domestic market. They live in *campos* (self-contained communities with their own schools and churches), and speak among themselves in a form of Low German.

Mennonite men customarily fraternize and conduct business with the Mexicans and many converse fluently in colloquial Spanish (the women speak only with their own). Though they are generally accepted by the local community, some *campechanos* (residents of Campeche) have expressed resentment at the Mennonite invasion, complaining that the 'Menonas' buy *ejido* (communal) lands for less than they're worth and have the capital to purchase expensive farm machinery while *campechanos* have to scrape by with lesser means.

The film *Luz Silenciosa* (Silent Light) by Mexican director Carlos Reygadas looks at life in Mexico's Mennonite communities. It won the coveted Jury Prize at Cannes in 2007.

Playa Norte BEACH

Playa Norte, on the Gulf of Mexico, is Carmen's beach area. It's rather bleak-looking, with wide expanses of coarse sand, murky green water, parking areas and the occasional *palapa* restaurant. Development is coming fast, however, in the form of shiny new hotels, restaurants and other services. To get here, take a bus from center marked 'Playa Norte' or 'zoológico'.

Sleeping

Because of the oil industry, there aren't any real bargains in town.

Hotel Zacarías HOTEL $

(☎382-0121; Calle 24 No 58; d/t with fan M$280/340, with air-con M$340/425; ❄) Just off the plaza is this mazelike budget hotel with 58 rooms. It's best for penny-pinchers – rooms are sizeable but very basic, and even a bit depressing. Balcony rooms are brighter but much noisier.

Hotel Las Villas HOTEL $$

(☎382-9916; Calle 28 No 116; s/d M$536/607; ❄ wi-fi) The center's best hotel, with just 10 spacious, modern and tasteful rooms surrounding a leafy patio area. It's a peaceful little paradise in a bustling city; room 10 has its own spiral staircase. Look for it just behind the plaza's church.

City Express Hotel HOTEL $$$

(☎800-248-9397; www.cityexpress.com.mx; Av Juárez No 1; r Fri-Sun M$929, Mon-Thu M$1300; P ❄ wi-fi pool) Located across from Playa Norte, this modern business hotel caters to oil-industry businessmen. However, if you have your own car and want to avoid the center, it's a good upscale choice. There's a nice pool, and breakfast is included. If the price is too steep there are several budget cheapies nearby on Av Paseo del Mar.

Eating

★**La Fuente** MEXICAN $

(☎286-0216; Calle 20 No 203; snacks M$30-45, mains M$60-135; ⏰7am-midnight; family-friendly) This classic, open-fronted waterfront cafe is a busy gathering place for families and friends. It's an excellent spot to sample treats such as *pibipollo* (chicken tamales traditionally cooked under ground) and *arrachera encebollado* (marinated flank steak with onions and chilis). There are some play structures nearby for the kids.

El Último Recurso MEXICAN $
(☎384-1275; Calle 28 No 118; set lunch M$40; ⊙7am-9pm) Near the central plaza, this no-frills lunch hall has daily stick-to-your-ribs specials, such as chicken in green sauce (Mondays) and pork in adobo (Thursdays). It's located behind the plaza's church.

Restaurante El Marino SEAFOOD $$
(☎384-1583; Calle 20 No 2; mains M$80-140; ⊙10am-7pm, shorter hours in winter) This large, open-air restaurant overlooks the water and affords terrific views of the Zacatal Bridge and local birdlife – there's even occasional faraway dolphin-spotting. Choose from seafood cocktails, fried fish, *ceviche*, shrimp cooked 15 ways, and seafood paella (weekends only). A small beach is nearby; it's a 15-minute walk south of the plaza.

ℹ Information

There are banks with ATM near the plaza.

Internet Cafe (Calle 31 btwn Calles 28 & 30) Note the concrete 'step over' barrier at the door, for flood control!

Municipal Tourism Office (☎286-0954; Calle 20 s/n, cnr Calle 31; ⊙8am-4pm) Small module inside the city hall with a few brochures.

ℹ Getting There & Away

Interjet (☎866-285-9525; www.interjet.com.mx) has daily flights to/from Mexico City.

Both 1st-class ADO and 2nd-class Sur buses use Ciudad del Carmen's modern **terminal** (Av Periférico s/n), a 15-minute *colectivo* (shared taxi) ride (M$25, after 10pm M$30) east of the main plaza. You can check schedules and buy tickets at the **ADO Ticket Office** (Calle 24) located next to the Hotel Zacarías. Some key destinations: Campeche (M$190, three hours, hourly buses), Mérida (M$358, five hours, hourly buses) and Villahermosa (M$250, three hours, every 45 minutes).

Combis run to/from Isla Aguada (M$25, 40 minutes); the stop is three blocks northeast of the plaza at the corner of Calles 32 and 35.

Atasta Peninsula

West of Ciudad del Carmen across the Puente Zacatal is this lushly tropical peninsula. A scarcely visited ecological wonderland, it stretches along a thin strip between the gulf and a network of small mangrove-fringed lagoons that feed into the Laguna de Términos. Various waterfront seafood shacks prepare crab and shrimp pulled out of the lagoon. **Atasta Mangle Tours** (☎938-286-7026; 2hr boat tours M$1700; ⊙1-5pm Sat & Sun), in the village of Atasta, offers boat excursions for up to eight people. Howler monkeys, manatees and river turtles may be spotted along the journey through the estuarine waterway. They also rent two-person kayaks for M$100 per hour.

ESCÁRCEGA TO XPUJIL

This southern peninsular region – now bordering modern-day Guatemala – was the earliest established, longest inhabited and most densely populated region in the Maya world. Here you'll also find the most elaborate archaeological sites on the Yucatán peninsula.

Hwy 186 heads east across Campeche state, climbing gradually from the unappealing town of Escárcega to a broad, jungle plateau and then down to Chetumal, in Quintana Roo. The highway passes near several fascinating Maya sites including historically significant Calakmul and through the ecologically diverse Reserva de la Biosfera Calakmul. The largest settlement between Escárcega and Chetumal is the town of Xpujil, near where there are three gas stations.

Calakmul and most of the other sites in this area are best visited by private vehicle. If you're on public transport, plan on hiring taxis or taking tours from companies in either Xpujil or Campeche (reserve these ahead of time).

Among the region's archaeological sites, the Río Bec architectural style predominates. It is actually a hybrid of styles fusing elements from the Chenes region to the north and Petén to the south. Río Bec structures are characterized by long, low buildings divided into three sections, with a huge 'monster' mouth glaring from a central doorway. The facades are decorated with smaller masks and geometric designs. At each end are tall, smoothly rounded towers with banded tiers supporting small false temples flanked by extremely steep, non-functional steps.

Balamkú

'Discovered' only in 1990, **Balamkú** (Temple of the Jaguar; ☎555-150-2081; admission M$35; ⊙8am-5pm) boasts a remarkably ornate, stuccoed frieze that bears little resemblance to any of the known decorative elements in the Chenes or Río Bec styles. Well pre-

OFF THE BEATEN TRACK

EL TIGRE & CENOTES MIGUEL COLORADO

Off Hwy 186, heading southwest from Escárcega, is one of Campeche's most recently uncovered Maya sites, **El Tigre** (admission M$35; ⌚8am-5pm). Archaeologists are almost certain it is none other than Itzamkanac, the legendary capital of the Itzáes. This is supposedly the place where Hernan Córtes executed Cuauhtémoc, the last Aztec ruler of Tenochtitlán.

Unlike other Campeche sites, El Tigre occupies a wetlands environment crisscrossed by rivers, with two excavated pyramids amid swaying palms and diverse birdlife. From Candelaria take the road towards Monclova; a short distance beyond the village of Estado de México is the turnoff to the site.

Another interesting place to visit is **Cenotes Miguel Colorado** (☎982-108-5669; village of Miguel Colorado; admission M$120; ⌚7am-5pm). There are two scenic, large cenotes (limestone sinkholes) here, and the price of admission includes kayak rental and a couple of very high ziplines that go over one of them. You can hike on hilly, rocky trails to each cenote, keeping an eye out for spider or howler monkeys. Swimming is currently not allowed but might be in the future; there could be rappelling opportunities as well. It's also possible to visit a bat cave in the area and a lake called Laguna de Mokú (home to crocodiles), but you'll need a guide (M$20 extra for each).

To get to these cenotes, drive 60km south of Champotón on Hwy 261, then take a 10km potholed side road to the village of Miguel Colorado. Turn left at the village and go 3km more.

served with traces of its original red paint, the frieze is a richly symbolic tableau that has been interpreted as showing the complementary relationship between our world and the underworld. Along the base of the scene, stylized seated jaguars (referred to in the temple's Maya name) represent the earth's abundance. These figures alternate with several grotesque fanged masks, upon which stand amphibianlike creatures (toads or crocodiles?) that in turn support some royal personages with fantastically elaborate headdresses. Readers of Spanish can find more details in the explanatory diagrams that front the frieze.

The solid stone that hid the frieze for centuries has been replaced with a protective canopy with slit windows that let in a little light. The door is kept locked, but the site custodian will usually appear to open it and give you a tour (no flash photography allowed).

Balamkú is 91km east of Escárcega and 60km west of Xpujil (2km past the Calakmul turnoff), then about 3km north of the highway along a fissured road.

Calakmul

Possibly the largest city during Maya times, **Calakmul** (☎555-150-2073; admission M$46; road maintenance fee per car M$56 plus per person M$28; Biosphere Reserve entrance fee per person M$54; ⌚8am-5pm) was 'discovered' in 1931 by American botanist Cyrus Lundell. The site bears comparison in size and historical significance to Tikal in Guatemala, its chief rival for hegemony over the southern lowlands during the Classic Maya era. It boasts the largest and tallest known pyramid in Yucatán, and was once home to over 50,000 people.

A central chunk of the 72-sq-km expanse has been restored, but most of the city's approximately 7000 structures lie covered in jungle. Exploration and restoration are ongoing, however, and occasionally something very special comes along. In 2004, amazingly well-preserved painted murals were discovered at the Chiik Naab acropolis of Estructura I. They depicted something never before seen in Maya murals – the typical daily activities of ordinary Mayans (as opposed to the usual political, ceremonial or religious themes). And a few years before that, a significant 20m-long, 4m-high stucco frieze was uncovered at Estructura II, whose features seemed to mark a transition between Olmec and Maya architecture.

The murals and frieze were still not open for public viewing during our research, but hopefully will be in the years to come. For now, their reproductions can be seen at Calakmul's modern **Museo de Naturaleza y Arqueología** (⌚7am-3pm) FREE, at Km 20 on the 60km side road to Calakmul. This worthwhile museum also has geological, archeological and natural-history exhibits.

Visiting Calakmul is also an ecological experience. Lying at the heart of the vast, untrammeled **Reserva de la Biosfera Calakmul** (which covers close to 15% of the state's total territory), the ruins are surrounded by rainforest, with cedar, mahogany and rubber trees dotting a seemingly endless canopy of vegetation. While wandering amid the ruins, you may glimpse ocellated turkeys, parrots and toucans among the over 350 bird species that reside or fly through here. It's also possible to see or hear spider and howler monkeys, but you're much less likely to spot a jaguar – one of five kinds of wildcat in the area. There are also many other mammal, reptile and amphibian species that call this biosphere home. Animals are most active during mornings and evenings.

Calakmul is 60km south of Hwy 186 at the end of a good paved road (the turnoff is 56km west of Xpujil). Near the museum you pay the relevant entry fees. Give yourself at least a full day (or two) not only to get to Calakmul, but to see the extensive ruins – both driving and walking distances are long. Just the 60km side road in from Hwy 186 to the ruins takes an hour. For an online map of the ruins, see http://mayaruins.com/calakmul/calakmul_map.html.

History

From about AD 250 to 695, Calakmul was the leading city in a vast region known as the Kingdom of the Serpent's Head. Its decline began with the power struggles and internal conflicts that followed the defeat by Tikal of Calakmul's King Garra de Jaguar (Jaguar Claw). Calakmul flourished again in the late Classic period by forming alliances with the Río Bec powers to the north.

As at Tikal, there are indications that construction occurred over a period of more than a millennium. Beneath Edificio VII, archaeologists discovered a burial crypt with some 2000 pieces of jade, and tombs continue to yield spectacular jade burial masks; some of these objects are on display in Campeche city's Fuerte de San Miguel. The cleared area of Calakmul holds at least 120 carved stelae, the oldest dating from 435 BC, registering key events such as the ascent to power of kings and the outcome of conflicts with rival states.

 Sights

From the ticket booth at the end of the road to the ruins is about a 1km walk through the woods. Arrows point out three suggested walks – a long, medium and short route. The short route leads straight to the Gran Plaza; the long route directs you through the Gran Acrópolis before sending you to the main attractions.

The **Gran Plaza**, with loads of stelae in front of its buildings (Estructura V has the best ones), makes a good first stop, and climbing the enormous **Estructura II**, at the south side of the plaza, is a must. Each of this pyramid's sides is 140m long, giving it a footprint of just under 2 hectares – the largest and tallest known Maya structure. After a good climb you'll come to what appears to be the top of the building, but go around to the left to reach the real apex. From here, 45m above the forest floor, are magnificent views of Estructura I to the southeast and Estructura VII to the north – as well as jungle canopy as far as you can see. Facing southwest, you'll be looking toward the Maya city El Mirador, in neighboring Guatemala, and with the aid of binoculars you may be able to spot that site's towering El Tigre pyramid.

A path on the left (east) side of Estructura II leads past the palatial **Estructura III**, with a dozen rooms atop a raised platform. Archaeologists found a tomb inside the 5th-century structure that contained the body of a male ruler of Calakmul surrounded by offerings of jade, ceramics and shell beads, and wearing not one but three jade mosaic masks (one each on his face, chest and belt). Walking south you come to **Estructura I**, Calakmul's second great pyramid, which is nearly as big as Estructura II. (Lundell named the site Calakmul, Maya for 'two adjacent mounds,' in reference to the pair of then-unexcavated pyramids that dominated the site.) The steep climb pays off handsomely with more top-of-the-world views.

A trail leading west from Estructura I around the back of Estructura II takes you to the **Gran Acrópolis**, a labyrinthine residential zone with a ceremonial sector containing a ball court. From the northern perimeter of this zone, you head east and follow the path back to the entrance.

Tours

Ka'an Expediciones and Campeche's Xtampak Tours (p201) run tours to Calakmul. Río

Bec Dreams (p218) offers tours by native English speakers, but to their guests only. You can also hire a taxi from Escárgeca or Xpujil (M$850 to M$900 with a three-hour wait).

Ka'an Expediciones TOUR
(☎983-119-6512; www.kaanexpeditions.com; tours 2½/4½hours M$250/350 per person) Good tours by nature specialists. Book two days in advance for an English guide. Three people minimum; must have private vehicle. Tours leave from Calakmul's museum. If you don't have a private vehicle, eight-hour tours from Xpujil are available (M$990 per person); these include transport, food and entrance fees. It also does multiday tours of the region.

Sleeping & Eating

Bring food and drinks while visiting Calakmul – there are sandwiches and snacks sold at the museum, but no services at the site itself.

Hotel Puerta Calakmul HOTEL $$$
(☎998-892-2624; www.puertacalakmul.com.mx; Hwy 186, Km 98; cabañas M$2000, March 17-31 M$2300; P 📶 ❄) This upscale jungle lodge is 700m from the highway turnoff. The 15 spacious bungalows are quite nice though not luxurious, and all come with mosquito nets and overhead fans. There's a decent, screened-in restaurant where you can dine from 7am to 9:30pm (mains M$100 to M$270), plus a small pool. Wi-fi in main building only.

Comedor & Cabañas La Selva CABIN $
(☎private phone of Demetria Ramírez 983-733-8706; Hwy 186, Km 95; complete meals M$80; ⊙6am-10pm) Simple, friendly open *palapa* restaurant with nearby grassy campsites (M$50). Ask about the very basic and rustic *cabañas* (cabins), within the nearby village of Conhuás (M$250 to M$550). Look for the restaurant near the entrance to Balamkú ruins.

Chicanná & Becán

Chicanná

Aptly named 'House of the Snake's Jaws,' this Maya **site** (Chicaná; admission M$42; ⊙8am-5pm) is best known for one remarkably well-preserved doorway with a hideous fanged visage. Located 11km west of Xpujil and 400m south of Hwy 186, Chicanná is a mixture of Chenes and Río Bec architectural styles buried in the jungle. The city attained its peak during the late Classic period, from AD 550 to 700, as a sort of elite suburb of Becán.

Beyond the admission pavilion, follow the rock paths through the jungle to **Estructura XX**, which boasts not one but two monster-mouth doorways, one above the other. The top structure is impressively flanked by rounded stacks of crook-nosed Chac masks.

A five-minute walk along the jungle path brings you to **Estructura XI**, with what remains of some of the earliest buildings. Continue along the main path about 120m northeast to reach the main plaza. Standing on the east side is Chicanná's famous **Estructura II**, with its gigantic Chenes-style monster-mouth doorway, believed to depict the jaws of the god Itzamná – lord of the heavens and creator of all things. Note the painted glyphs to the right of the mask. A path leads from the right corner of Estructura II to reach **Estructura VI**, which has a well-preserved roofcomb and some beautiful profile masks on its facade. Circle around back, noting the faded red-painted blocks of the west wing, then turn right to hike back to the main entrance.

Becán

Located 8km west of Xpujil and 500m north of the highway, this must-visit **site** (admission M$46; ⊙8am-5pm) contains three separate architectural complexes. The Maya word for 'canyon' or 'moat' is *becán,* and indeed a 2km moat snakes its way around this major site, with seven causeways providing access to the 12-hectare complex. The elaborate defense suggests the militaristic nature of the city which, from around AD 600 to 1000, was a regional capital encompassing Xpujil and Chicanná. A strategic crossroads between the Petenes civilization to the south and Chenes to the north, Becán displays architectural elements of both, with the resulting composite known as the Río Bec style.

You enter the complex via the western causeway, skirting Plaza del Este on your left. Proceed through a 66m-long arched passageway and you will emerge onto the Plaza Central, ringed by three monumental structures. The formidable **Estructura IX**, on the plaza's north side, is Becán's tallest building at 32m; though the sign says not to climb it, a rope is provided! **Estructura**

VIII is the huge temple on your right, with a pair of towers flanking a colonnaded facade at the top. It's a great vantage point for the area; with binoculars, you can make out Xpujil's ruins to the east. Across the plaza from VIII is **Estructura X**, with fragments of an Earth Monster mask still visible around the central doorway. The other side of X opens onto the west plaza, with a ritual ball court. As you loop around Estructura X to the south, check out the encased stucco mask on display.

Follow around the right side of the mask to another massive edifice, **Estructura I**, which takes up one side of the eastern plaza. Its splendid south wall is flanked by a pair of amazing Río Bec towers rising 15m. Ascend the structure on the right side and follow the terrace alongside a series of vaulted rooms back to the other end, where a passage leads you into the Plaza del Este. The most significant structure here is **Estructura IV**, on the opposite side of the plaza; experts surmise it was a residence for Becán's aristocrats. A stairway leads to an upstairs courtyard ringed by seven rooms with cross motifs on either side of the doorways. Finally, go around Estructura IV to complete the circle.

Sleeping & Eating

★Río Bec Dreams CABIN **$$**

(www.riobecdreams.com; Hwy 186, Km 142 (marked 145); cabañas for 2 people M$550-1150; per extra person M$150; P Wi-Fi) This Canadian-run jungle lodge is a little paradise. Though it's located just off noisy Hwy 186, once you get here you'll be welcomed by tropical grounds, a lovely restaurant and a few pet dogs. Reception's at the bar. There are seven thatched-roofed *cabañas,* some small and simple and others with two bedrooms and a screened porch. Two have shared bathrooms. Rick and Diane, the friendly owners, also do good tours of area ruins. Breakfast is extra; cash payment only.

The wonderful, open-air **restaurant** (mains M$85-150; 7:30am-9pm), set amid tropical plants, has the best homemade food in the area. The wide variety of main dishes includes roasted pork loin, Mediterranean pasta, Indian curry and chile con carne. Ingredients are high quality and fresh; note IVA and service taxes are added to the bill.

Río Bec Dreams is located 9km west of Xpujil and 2km west of Chicanná; look for the bus stop and flags.

Chicanná Ecovillage Resort HOTEL **$$$**

(981-811-9192; www.chicannaecovillageresort.com; Hwy 186, Km 144; r from M$1300; P Wi-Fi pool) Across from Chicanná ruins, this is the most upscale accommodations in the area – but despite the name, it's not really eco. Two-story, pastel-colored buildings are set on expansive groomed grounds. The 42 rooms are comfortable, modern and very spacious, with king-sized beds, and all have a small front patio on which to hang out. Breakfast is included and there are a couple of pleasant pools – one a kiddie version – for hot days. There's an upscale **restaurant** (mains M$95-230; 7:30am-10:30pm) on the premises. The resort is located 7km west of Xpujil, across from the entrance to Chicanná ruins.

Xpujil

983 / POP 4000

The unremarkable town of Xpujil (shpu-*heel*) is a good base for exploring the area's many ruins, and offers a few hotels, some unexceptional eateries, two ATMs (one at supermarket Willy's), an exchange house (Elektra Dinero on Calle Chicanna near Xnantun), an internet cafe and a bus terminal. Most services are along the seven-block main drag, Av Calakmul (aka Hwy 186). There are three gas stations in the area.

You can also stay in the village of **Zoh-Laguna** (population 1500), 9.5km north along the Hopelchén road. It's much more peaceful than Xpujil, but has only two simple places to stay and hardly any services; it's best reached with your own vehicle (taxis from Xpujil are M$40 to M$50). There's a small **museum** (983-125-0888; cnr Calle Caoba & Zapote; 5-10pm Mon-Fri) FREE on the same block as Cabañas El Viajero; look for the lime-green building. Strangely enough, it's also a pizzeria with internet service but erratic hours.

Sights

On the western edge of town, the ruins of **Xpuhil** (admission M$42; 8am-5pm) are a striking example of the Río Bec style. The three towers (rather than the usual two) of Estructura I rise above a dozen vaulted rooms. The central tower, 53m, is the best preserved. With its banded tiers and impractically steep stairways leading up to a temple that displays traces of a zoomorphic mask, it gives a good idea of what the other two must have looked like in Xpuhil's 8th-century heyday. Go around back to see a fierce jaguar mask embedded in the wall below the temple.

Sleeping & Eating

All of Xpujil's sleeping options are along the main highway, which can be noisy. Around the bus terminal, at the eastern end of town, are cheap hotels and restaurants; the nicer hotels (with nicer restaurants) are at the western end of town.

Xpujil

Mirador Maya HOTEL $
(983-871-6005; www.hotelmiradormaya.com; Av Calakmul No 94; cabañas M$350, d/q M$450/650; P) Look for the large *palapa* roof at the top of the hill on the western end of town. That's the restaurant of this hotel, which has nine simple but decent *cabañas* in a grassy back area with palm trees and perhaps a few chickens. Two basic, modern rooms are also available, as is a **restaurant** (mains M$75-125; 7am-midnight).

Hotel Calakmul HOTEL $
(983-871-6029; www.hotelcalakmul.com.mx; Av Calakmul No 70; cabañas M$250, r from M$500; P) At the western end of town, about 350m west of the stoplight, is this large hotel. It has 27 small, tiled roms with tiny bathrooms and little sitting areas out front. The six so-called *'cabañas,'* near the parking lot, are tiny shacks set too close together and sharing outside bathrooms – a very odd combination with the more modern hotel. With luck they'll just tear them down to make more room around the new pool. There's a good **restaurant** (mains M$40-90; 6am-midnight).

Zoh-Laguna

Cabañas El Viajero HOTEL $
(983-163-9613; Calle Caobas s/n; cabañas M$200, d M$260-300; P) Travelers can choose from two very basic *cabañas* with fan, or six more modern, air-conditioned rooms across the street. All meals are prepared in a simple **restaurant** (meals M$50).

Cabañas Mercedes CABIN $
(983-114-9933; Calle Zapote s/n; cabañas M$200-250) Fifteen very basic bungalows with mosquito nets, ceiling fans and open-shower bathrooms can be found at this rustic place. Decent meals are served in the thatched-roofed **restaurant** (mains M$70 to M$80). Don Antonio is the well-informed host who knows about the area's ruins.

THE ROAD TO RUINS

Maya sites around Xpujil are most conveniently reached by private vehicle. If you're on public transport, either book a tour (p216) or hire taxis. The taxi stop is at the Xpujil junction (stoplight); call 983-871-6101 for a taxi. Here are some typical round-trip fares:

- Balamkú & Calakmul: M$1000 with a three- to four-hour wait
- Becán & Chicanná: M$300 with one hour wait at each
- Hormiguero: M$350 with one hour wait

Getting There & Away

No buses originate in Xpujil, so you must hope to luck into a vacant seat on one passing through. This usually isn't a problem outside holiday times. The **bus terminal** (983-871-6511) is just east of the Xpujil stoplight next to the Victoria Hotel.

There are also *colectivos* to Chetumal (M$100 per person, 1½ hours).

Campeche M$155-232, four to five hours, three to four daily

Cancún M$256, eight hours, one daily at 7:30pm)

Chetumal M$70-100, two hours, three daily

Escárcega M$82-122, two hours, eight daily

Hopelchén M$104, three hours, Sur at 4am

Palenque M$350, six hours, one at 1am or go via Escárcega

SOUTH OF XPUJIL

Río Bec

A collection of small but significant structures in 74 groupings, Río Bec covers a 100-sq-km area southeast of Xpujil. The remoteness of this site and ongoing excavations give it a certain mystique that's lacking in more established sites. Couple this with the fact it's only accessible from February to mid-May (the dry season) and you have the makings of a real adventure.

Grupo B has some of the best-restored buildings, particularly the magnificent **Estructura I** (AD 700). Discovered in 1907 by French archaeologist Maurice de Périgny, this palatial structure features a pair of typical tiered towers crowned by matching temples with cross motifs on their sides. The main structure at Grupo A is a 15m-long **palace** with intact towers and unusual bas-relief glyphs on the lower panels.

Getting here without a guide is nearly impossible – the very rough dirt road is accessible only via 4WD vehicle and it's unsigned, with many twists and turns that can change from year to year. It's best to go with either Ka'an Expediciones (p217), with tours at M$990 per person, or Río Bec Dreams (p218), if you're a guest with them, with tours at M$1800 for up to four people. Reserve at least two to three days in advance for both.

Hormiguero

Though not easy to reach, **Hormiguero** (⌚8am-5pm) FREE has two impressive and unique buildings that are worth the trek. Buildings date as far back as AD 50; the city (whose name is Spanish for 'anthill') flourished during the late Classic period.

As you enter you'll see the 50m-long **Estructura II**. The facade's chief feature is a very menacing Chenes-style monster-mouth doorway, jaws open wide, set back between a pair of Classic Río Bec tiered towers. Around the back is intact Maya stonework and the remains of several columns. Follow the arrows 60m north to reach **Estructura V**, with a much smaller but equally ornate open-jawed temple atop a pyramidal base. Climb the right side for a closer look at the incredibly detailed stonework, especially along the corner columns that flank the doorway.

This site is reached by heading 14km south from Xpujil's stoplight, then turning right and going 8km west on a very rough but (hopefully) improving dirt-sand road, passable except following heavy rains.

Chiapas

Includes ➡

Best Places to Eat

- ➡ Don Mucho's (p239)
- ➡ Trattoria Italiana (p231)
- ➡ Tierradentro (p231)

Best Places to Stay

- ➡ Boutique Hotel Quinta Chanabnal (p238)
- ➡ Casa Felipe Flores (p230)
- ➡ B¨o Hotel (p230)

Why Go?

Chilly pine-forest highlands, wildlife-rich rainforest jungles and well-preserved colonial cities exist side by side within Mexico's southernmost state, a region awash with the legacy of Spanish rule and some fabulous remnants of ancient Maya civilization.

The state has the second-largest indigenous population in the country, and the modern Maya of Chiapas form a direct link to the past, with a traditional culture that persists to this day. The fine city of San Cristóbal de las Casas is at the heart of this region and was once the central bastion for the rebel group Zapatistas, now much less influential than in the 1990s.

Chiapas contains swathes of wild green landscape that have nourished its inhabitants for centuries. And nature lovers willing to venture off the beaten path will be rewarded with frothy cascades, exotic biosphere reserves and adventurous geological destinations.

When to Go

- ➡ The rainy season is between May and October, with the heaviest rainfall mostly in June, September and early October. Some of the less visited, more out-of-the-way Maya ruins are located on dirt roads which are impassable during the rainy season.
- ➡ The dry season is between November and April, when warm sunny days are the norm.
- ➡ Temperatures don't vary much with the changing seasons – altitude is a much more influential factor. Lowland areas (such as Palenque and Villahermosa) are hot and sticky year-round, with punishing humidity and daily highs above 30°C. In more elevated places (like San Cristóbal), however, the climate is fresher and nights get fairly cold in winter (November to March).

Chiapas Highlights

1. Explore the extraordinary ruins of **Palenque** (p234), where jade masks and priceless jewels were found inside a ruler's sarcophagus, and the architecture boasts unique features

2. Wander around high-altitude **San Crístobal de las Casas** (p223), home to charming cobblestone streets, pretty colonial buildings and colorful indigenous peoples

3. Ponder the mysterious sculptural art of the ancient Olmecs while wandering around the junglelike grounds of Villahermosa's **Parque-Museo La Venta** – a paradise within the bustling city (p228)

4. Visit the ancient cities of **Yaxchilán** (p240), reachable via an adventurous river-boat trip, and **Bonampak** (p240), which offers amazingly preserved painted murals

History

Low-lying, jungle-covered eastern Chiapas gave rise to some of the most splendid and powerful city-states of the Maya during the Classic period (about AD 250 to 900), such as Palenque and Yaxchilán. But as Maya culture reached its peak of artistic and intellectual achievement, dozens of lesser powers also prospered here. After the Classic Maya collapse around AD 900, the ancestors of many distinctive indigenous groups of Chiapas appear to have migrated to the highlands.

Central Chiapas was brought under Spanish control by the 1528 expedition of Diego de Mazariegos, and most outlying areas were subdued in the 1530s and '40s. New diseases arrived with the Spaniards, and an epidemic in 1544 killed about half of Chiapas' indigenous population. Chiapas was ineffectively administered from Guatemala for most of the colonial era, with little check on the colonists' excesses against its indigenous people, though some church figures, particularly Bartolomé de las Casas (1474–1566), the first bishop of Chiapas, did fight for indigenous rights.

In 1824 Chiapas opted to join Mexico, rather than the United Provinces of Central America. From then on, a succession of governors appointed by Mexico City maintained control over Chiapas. Periodic uprisings bore witness to bad government, but the world took little notice until January 1, 1994, when Zapatista rebels suddenly and briefly occupied San Cristóbal de las Casas and nearby towns by military force. ('Zapatista' comes from the Mexican revolutionary Emiliano Zapata, whose followers (during the Mexican Revolution in 1910) were known as Zapatistas.)

The rebel movement, with a firm and committed support base among disenchanted indigenous settlers, used remote jungle bases to campaign for democratic change and indigenous rights. The Zapatistas have failed to win any significant concessions at the national level, although increased government funding resulted in improvements in the state's infrastructure, the development of tourist facilities and a growing urban middle class.

San Cristóbal de las Casas

☎967 / POP 200,000

Set in a gorgeous highland valley surrounded by pine forest, the colonial city of San Cristóbal (cris-*toh*-bal) has been a popular travelers' destination for decades. It's a pleasure to explore the cobbled streets and markets, soaking up the unique ambience and wonderfully clear highland light. This medium-sized city also boasts a comfortable blend of city and countryside, with restored century-old houses giving way to grazing animals and fields of corn.

Surrounded by dozens of traditional Tzotzil and Tzeltal villages, San Cristóbal is at the heart of one of the most deeply rooted indigenous areas in Mexico. A great base for local and regional exploration, it's a place where ancient customs coexist with modern luxuries.

Bring a jacket in the cooler months of November to March – the altitude here is 2120m and nights can get downright chilly. Note that street names change at Real de Guadalupe.

Sights

The leafy main **Plaza 31 de Marzo** is a fine place to take in San Cristóbal's highland atmosphere. Its pretty bandstand has occasional live music. For the best views in town, head to **Cerro de Guadalupe** (off Real de Guadalope), just east of town, and **Cerro de San Cristóbal** (off Hermanos Dominguez), southwest of center. You'll have to work for it, because at this altitude the stairs up these hills can be punishing. Churches crown both lookouts, and the Iglesia de Guadalupe becomes a hot spot for religious devotees around the Día de la Virgen de Guadalupe (December 12). Cerro de San Cristóbal has a better view but should be avoided after dark (there have been muggings in the past).

Cathedral CATHEDRAL

(Plaza 31 de Marzo) On the north side of the plaza, the cathedral was begun in 1528 but wasn't finally completed till 1815 because of several natural disasters. Sure enough, new earthquakes struck in 1816 and 1847, causing considerable damage, but it was restored again in 1920-22. The gold-leaf interior has five gilded altarpieces featuring 18th-century paintings by Miguel Cabrera.

Templo & Ex-Convento de Santo Domingo CHURCH

(⏲6:30am-2pm & 4-8pm) Located just north of the center, the 16th-century Templo de Santo Domingo is San Cristóbal's most beautiful church, especially when its facade catches the late-afternoon sun. The baroque

San Cristóbal de las Casas

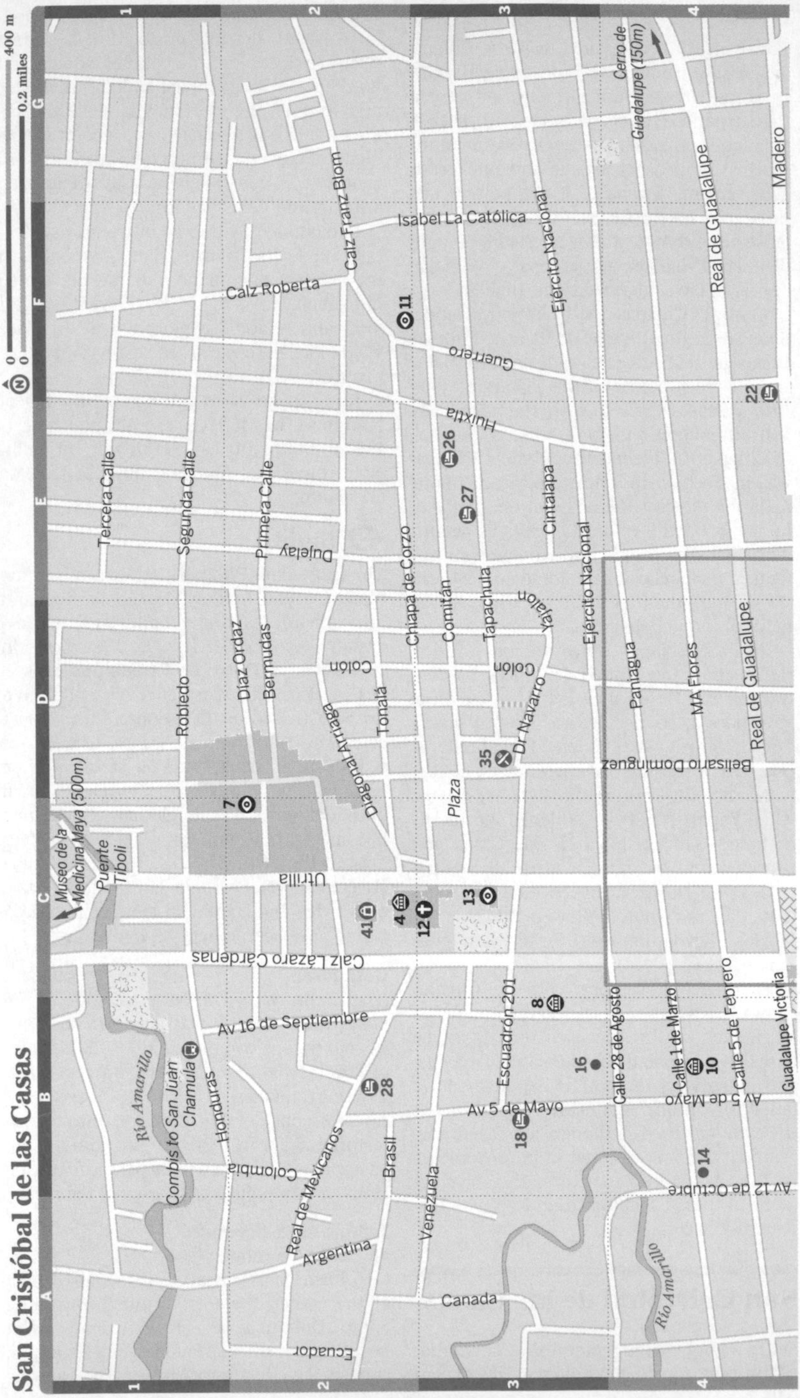

0 — 400 m
0 — 0.2 miles

Museo de la Medicina Maya (500m)
Puente Tiboli
Cerro de Guadalupe (150m)
Combis to San Juan Chamula
Río Amarillo
Tercera Calle
Segunda Calle
Primera Calle
Robledo
Díaz Ordaz
Bermudas
Diagonal Arriaga
Tonalá
Chiapa de Corzo
Comitán
Tapachula
Cintalapa
Ejército Nacional
Calz Franz Blom
Calz Roberta
Isabel La Católica
Guerrero
Huixtla
Dujelay
Colón
Yajalon
Dr Navarro
Plaza
Utrilla
Calz Lázaro Cárdenas
Av 16 de Septiembre
Escuadrón 201
Paniagua
MA Flores
Real de Guadalupe
Madero
Belisario Domínguez
Honduras
Colombia
Real de Mexicanos
Brasil
Venezuela
Argentina
Canada
Ecuador
Av 5 de Mayo
Calle 28 de Agosto
Calle 1 de Marzo
Calle 5 de Febrero
Guadalupe Victoria
Av 12 de Octubre
1 2 3 4 4 7 8 10 11 12 13 14 16 18 22 26 27 28 35 41
A B C D E F G

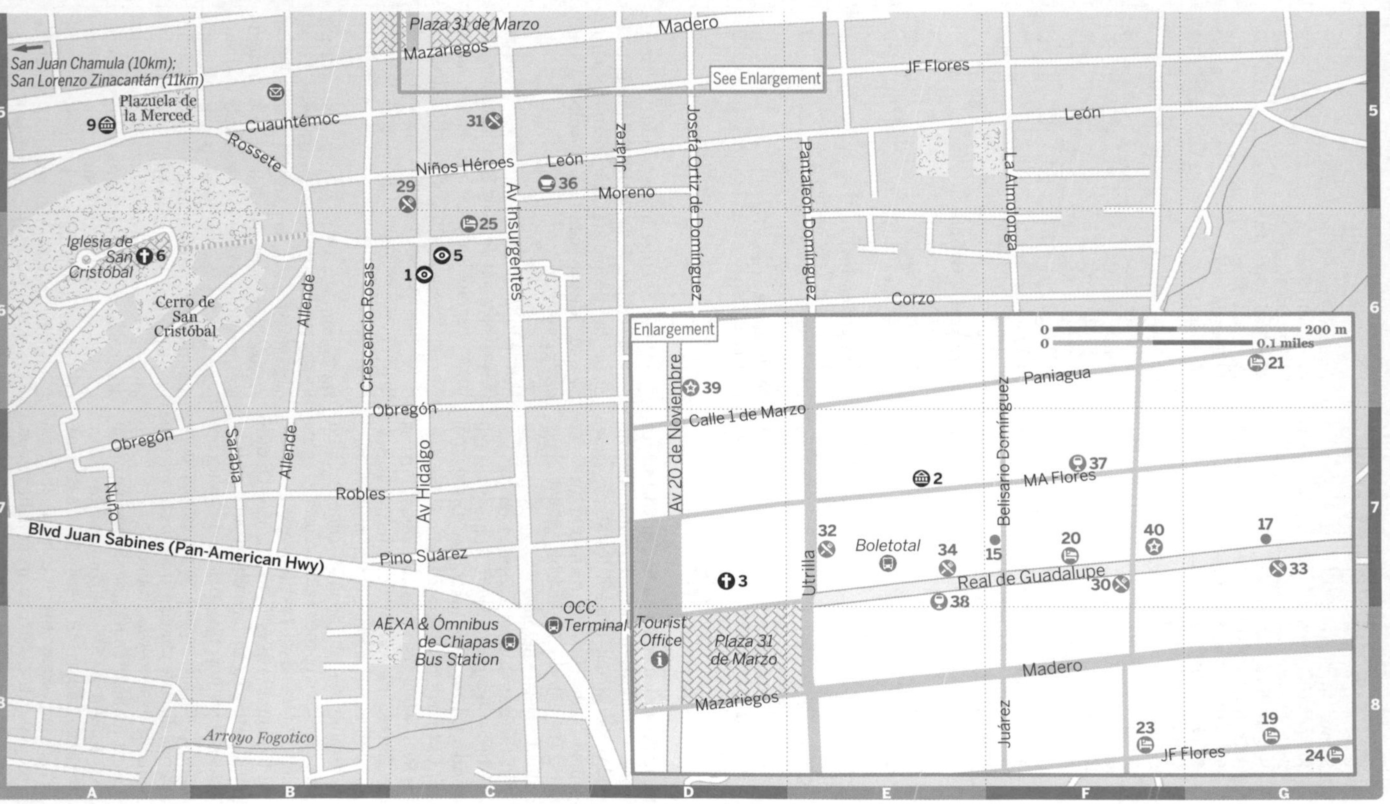

San Juan Chamula (10km); San Lorenzo Zinacantán (11km)
Plazuela de la Merced
Plaza 31 de Marzo
Mazariegos
Madero
See Enlargement
JF Flores
León
Cuauhtémoc
Rossete
Niños Héroes
Juárez
Josefa Ortiz de Domínguez
Pantaleón Domínguez
La Almolonga
Moreno
Av Insurgentes
Iglesia de San Cristóbal
Cerro de San Cristóbal
Allende
Crescencio Rosas
Corzo
Obregón
Sarabia
Robles
Av Hidalgo
Nuño
Blvd Juan Sabines (Pan-American Hwy)
Pino Suárez
AEXA & Ómnibus de Chiapas Bus Station
OCC Terminal
Arroyo Fogotico
Enlargement
0 200 m
0 0.1 miles
Av 20 de Noviembre
Calle 1 de Marzo
Paniagua
Belisario Domínguez
MA Flores
Boletotal
Utrilla
Real de Guadalupe
Tourist Office
Plaza 31 de Marzo
Madero
Mazariegos
Juárez
JF Flores

San Cristóbal de las Casas

Sights

1 Arco del Carmen C6
2 Café Museo Café E7
3 Cathedral D7
4 Centro Cultural de los Altos C2
5 Centro Cultural El Carmen C6
6 Cerro de San Cristóbal A6
7 Mercado Municipal C2
8 Museo Bichos e Insectos B3
9 Museo del Ámbar de Chiapas A5
10 Museo del Cacao B4
11 Na Bolom F2
12 Templo & Ex-Convento de Santo Domingo C3
13 Templo de la Caridad C3

Activities, Courses & Tours

El Puente Spanish Language School .... (see 33)
14 Explora B4
15 Jaguar Adventours F7
16 Posada Ganesha B3
17 SendaSur G7

Sleeping

18 Bô Hotel B3
19 Casa Felipe Flores G8
20 Casa Margarita F7
21 Hotel Posada Jovel G6
Le Gite del Sol F4
23 México Hostel F8
24 Parador Margarita G8
25 Posada La Media Luna C6
26 Posada Moguel E3
27 Posada San Cris E3
28 Rossco Backpackers B2

Eating

29 Anabanana C5
30 El Argentino F7
31 El Caldero C5
32 El Horno Mágico E7
33 La Casa del Pan Papalotl G7
34 Tierradentro E7
35 Trattoria Italiana D3

Drinking & Nightlife

36 Kakao Natura C5
37 La Sandunga F7
38 La Viña de Bacco E7

Entertainment

39 Cafe Bar Revolución D6
40 Cocoliche F7

Shopping

41 Sna Jolobil C2

frontage, with its outstanding filigree stucco work, was added in the 17th century and includes the double-headed Habsburg eagle, symbol of the Spanish monarchy in those days. The interior is lavishly gilded, especially the ornate pulpit.

In the ex-monastery, located on the left side of the Templo de Santo Domingo, is the **Centro Cultural de los Altos** (☎678-1609; Calz Cárdenas s/n; admission M$46; ⏰9am-6pm Tue-Sun), which has two museums. First is the **Museo de los Altos**, which has several impressive archaeological relics as well as exhibits on the Spanish conquest and evangelization of the region. Upstairs is the excellent **Museo de Textile Maya**, showcasing beautiful textiles from Chiapas, Oaxaca and Guatemala throughout several rooms. Videos show how materials and clothes are created, and there are some explanations in English. Free guides (in Spanish) may be available to show you around.

Next to the church is the showroom of the **Sna Jolobil** (☎678-2646; www.snajolobil.com; Calz Lázaro Cárdenas 42; ⏰9am-2pm & 4-6pm Tue-Sat) artisan cooperative. It exhibits and sells high-quality textiles from around the region.

Around Santo Domingo and the neighboring **Templo de la Caridad** (built in 1712), Chamulan people and bohemian types from around Mexico conduct a colorful daily **crafts market**.

Mercado Municipal — MARKET

(⏰6am-6pm outside shops, 8am-3pm inside stalls) For a closer look at local life – and an assault on the senses – visit San Cristóbal's busy municipal market, eight blocks north of the main plaza between Utrilla and Belisario Domínguez.

Na Bolom — HISTORIC HOUSE

(☎678-1418; www.nabolom.org; Guerrero 33; admission M$40, with tour M$50; ⏰7am-7pm) An atmospheric spot, Na Bolom is a museum and research center for the study and support of Chiapas' indigenous cultures and natural environment, and a center for community and environmental programs in indigenous areas. The library of more than 9000 books and documents here is a major resource on the Maya. Tours are 45 minutes long and happen daily at 4:30pm; they're in English or Spanish. You can also stay and/or eat here; see the website for details.

Museo del Ámbar de Chiapas MUSEUM
(☎678-9716; www.museodelambar.com.mx; Plazuela de la Merced; admission M$20; ⏰10am-2pm & 4 8pm Tue-Sun) This museum explains all things amber (with information sheets in English and other languages) and displays and sells some exquisitely carved items and insect-embedded pieces. It also tells you how to spot fake amber, so come here before you go shopping!

Museo de la Medicina Maya MUSEUM
(☎678-5438; Av Salomón González Blanco 10; admission M$20; ⏰9am-5pm Mon-Fri, to 4pm Sat & Sun; P) This interesting museum introduces the system of traditional medicine used by many indigenous people in the Chiapas highlands. Signage is in Spanish but there are English, French and German booklets for translations. Check out the herbal pharmacy in the back yard. The museum is a 20-minute walk north from the main plaza.

Arco del Carmen GATE
The Arco del Carmen, at the southern end of the Andador Turístico on Hidalgo, dates from the late 17th century and was once the city's gateway. The former convent just east is a colonial building with a large, peaceful garden. It's now the **Centro Cultural El Carmen** (Hermanos Domínguez s/n; ⏰9am-6pm Tue-Sun) FREE, occasionally hosting art and photography exhibitions and musical events.

Museo del Cacao MUSEUM
(☎631-7995; 1ro de Marzo 16; admission M$30; ⏰11am-9pm Mon-Sat, to 6pm Sun) This chocolate museum runs along an open upstairs balcony of a cafe. Learn about the history of chocolate and how it was used by the Maya. Also on display are modern chocolate drinking vessels and utensils, and details of the process to create the delicious substance. Includes a free sample.

Café Museo Café MUSEUM
(☎678-7876; MA Flores 10; admission M$30; ⏰7am-10pm) This combined café and coffee museum is a venture of Coopcafé – a grouping of more than 17,000 small-scale, mainly indigenous, Chiapas coffee growers. Only hard-core coffee historians need apply.

Museo Bichos e Insectos MUSEUM
(☎128-7370; Calle 16 de Septiembre No 23; admission adults/1-12yrs M$25/20; ⏰10am-2pm & 4-8pm Mon-Sat, 11am-6pm Sun; 👪) Small museum but still home to over 2000 insects (only a few of them live). Check out old wasp nests, huge beetles, leaf insects, spiders, crickets, butterflies and dragonflies. Live insects and other creepy crawlies include scorpions and centipedes; you can even hold a tarantula.

Courses

El Puente Spanish Language School LANGUAGE
(☎678-3723; www.elpuenteweb.com; Real de Guadalupe 55) For language courses; homestays available.

Posada Ganesha YOGA
(☎678-0212; ganeshaservicios@yahoo.com; Calle 28 de Agosto 23) Hatha and Kundali yoga classes several times weekly.

Tours

Jaguar Adventours BICYCLE RENTAL
(☎631-5062; www.adventours.mx; Av Belisario Domínguez 8A; bicycle rentals per hour M$40, per day M$200; ⏰9am-2:30pm & 3:30-8pm Mon-Sat, 9am-2:30pm Sun) Bicycle tours to Chamula (20km) and Zincantán (32km), plus longer expeditions of up to 80km. Prices start at M$400 per person. Also rents out quality mountain bikes with helmet and lock.

Explora ADVENTURE TOURS
(☎674-6660; www.ecochiapas.com; Calle 1 de Marzo 30; ⏰9:30am-2pm & 4-8pm Mon-Fri, 9:30am-2pm Sat) Specializes in three- to six-day adventures to the Lacandón Jungle communities, including river kayaking and rafting. Also does excursions to Lagos de Montebello and Palenque. Multiday tours start at M$3250 per person.

Festivals & Events

Feria de la Primavera y de la Paz RELIGIOUS
(Spring & Peace Fair) Easter Sunday is the start of the week-long town fair, with parades, musical events, bullfights and so on.

Festival Cervantino Barroco CULTURAL
(Cervantes Festival) A fair with art, music, dance and theater in October or November.

Semana Santa RELIGIOUS
The crucifixion is acted out on Good Friday in the Barrio de Mexicanos, northwest of town.

Festival de las Culturas CULTURAL
(www.conecultachiapas.gob.mx) In mid- to late October, this free, week-long cultural program keeps hopping with music, dance and theater.

TABASCO

They say that Tabasco has more water than land, and if you look at the lagoons, rivers and wetlands on a map you can see why – especially during the rainy season. It's always hot and sweaty, marginally less so when you catch a breeze along the Gulf of Mexico or if you venture into the southern hills. Few travelers linger in Tabasco longer than it takes to see the outstanding Olmec stone sculpture in Villahermosa's Parque-Museo La Venta, but it can be an interesting slice of Mexico, with some intriguing pre-Hispanic sites (both the Olmecs and the Maya flourished here), a large capital city, a beautiful natural environment and a relaxed populace.

Villahermosa

This sprawling, flat, hot and humid city (☎993; pop 650,000), home to more than a quarter of Tabasco's population, was never the 'beautiful town' its name implies. Settled on the winding Río Grijalva, the city's most attractive attribute became its worst enemy when the river burst its banks in 2007. Villahermosa still struggles to control its surging waterway.

The **tourist office** (☎310-9700; www.visitetabasco.com; Parque-Museo La Venta) has erratic hours and is often closed.

Villahermosa's main visitor attraction is the open-air **Parque-Museo La Venta** (☎314-1652; Av Ruíz Cortines; admission M$40; ⏰8am-5pm, last admission 4pm; P 👪), a combined Olmec archaeological museum and zoo in an attractive lakeside park. It was created in 1958, when petroleum exploration threatened the highly important ancient Olmec settlement of La Venta in western Tabasco. Archaeologists moved the site's most significant finds, including three colossal stone heads, to Villahermosa. There's an informative display in English and Spanish on Olmec archaeology as you pass through to the **sculpture trail**, whose start is marked by a giant *ceiba* (the sacred tree of the Olmec and Maya). This 1.2km walk is lined with finds from La Venta. The **zoo** is decent, with mostly open enclosures (except for the big cats and aviaries). Regional critters are highlighted, and you're likely to see coatimundis running wild on the grounds and on the nearby river walk, which is worth exploring in itself (take it to the free 'elevated museum', a 15-minute stroll away). Parque-Museo La Venta is 2.5km from the Zona Luz; a-*colectivo* (shared taxi) between them costs M$20. Bring mosquito repellent.

Just outside the park entrance, the **Museo de Historia Natural** (☎314-2175; Av Ruíz Cortines; admission M$20; ⏰8am-5pm Tue-Sun, last admission 4pm; P) has good displays on dinosaurs, space, early humanity and Tabascan ecosystems (all in Spanish). Villahermosa's shiny, newly rebuilt **Museo Regional de Antropología** (☎312-6344; Periférico Carlos Pellicer; admission M$45; ⏰9am-4:30pm Tue-Sun; P) holds some excellent exhibits on Olmec, Maya, Nahua and Zoque cultures in Tabasco – including Tortuguero #6, the infamous tablet solely responsible for the dire 'end of world' predictions that had been forecast for December 21, 2012. It's a 15-minute walk from Zona Luz and just south of the Paseo Tabasco bridge, in the CICOM complex; look for the statue out front.

A couple of central hotels include the excellent-value **Hotel Provincia Express** (☎314-5378; provinciaexpress09@hotmail.com; Lerdo de Tejada 303; r M$460-530; P ❄ 📶), which has small but tidy and pleasant rooms. It's on a pedestrian street, so get a window if possible; avoid the windowless rooms. There's a cafe in the lobby and breakfast is included. **Hotel Oriente** (☎312-0121; hotel-oriente@hotmailcom; Madero 425; d with fan M$250-330, d with air-con M$350-440, tr with fan/air-con M$420/540; ❄ 📶) is well run, sporting simple budget rooms, all with TV. Rooms overlooking the main street are bright but can be noisy.

Rock & Roll Cocktelería (Reforma 307; mains M$100-150; ⏰10am-10pm) is popular for its seafood cocktails (though it also has good *ceviche* and seafood stew) and cheap beer. It's on a pedestrian street across from the Miraflores Hotel. Pleasant little **Antigua Café** (Lerdo de Tejado 608; breakfast M$40-70, mains M$80-100; ⏰8am-11pm Mon-Sat) offers a bohemian vibe as it serves breakfasts (fruit plate, yogurt, hot cakes) and other meals (chef salad, sandwiches and pastas). It's good for drinks, too - sip a tea, frappé or smoothie.

Villahermosa's **airport** (☎356-00-22) is 13km east of the center, off Hwy 186. It's serviced by Aeroméxico and United Airlines. A taxi from the airport to the center costs M$200 and takes about 20 minutes. You can also walk 600m to the suburb of Dos Montes, where *colectivo* cost M$20 per person and leave you at a market about 1km north of Zona Luz (on Amado Nervo between Piño Suárez and Constitución). Taxis from the center to the airport cost from M$150, or you can take the Dos Montes *colectivo* taxi from that same market.

The first-class **ADO bus station** (ADO; ☎312-8422; Mina 297) is 750m north of the Zona Luz. It's a busy place and long lines can form, so get here early if you're on a schedule. Second-class bus terminals include **Cardesa** (cnr Hermanos Bastar Zozaya & Castillo) and the **Central de Autobuses de Tabasco** (CAT; ☎312-2977; cnr Av Ruíz Cortines & Mina); these terminals are within walking distance of the ADO station. Destinations from Villahermosa include Campeche (M$280 to M$550, six to seven hours, 15 daily), Cancún (M$365 to M$1260, 12 to 16 hours, 14 daily), Mérida (M$382 to M$960, nine to 10 hours, 21 daily), Palenque (M$122, 2½ hours, hourly 7am to 9pm), San Cristóbal de las Casas (M$310, six hours, 11:40pm only) and Ciudad del Carmen (M$180, three hours, half-hourly 4:50am to 11:30pm).

Most taxis in town are *colectivo*, and most of these shared rides within the center cost M$20. Just flag down a taxi and the driver will ask which direction you're going.

Comalcalco

Comalcalco, 51km northwest of Villahermosa, is typical of the medium-sized towns of western Tabasco – hot, bustling, quite prosperous and spread around a broad, open central plaza (Parque Juárez).

What makes it especially worth visiting are the impressive ruins of **ancient Comalcalco** (admission M$46; ⌚8am-5pm), 2km north of the city limits. This Maya site is unique because many of its buildings are constructed of bricks and/or mortar made from oyster shells. The museum at the entrance has a fine array of sculptures and engravings of human heads, deities, glyphs and animals such as crocodiles and pelicans. There is also an interesting exhibit of how Comalcalco's dead were buried under giant jugs. Bring mosquito repellent for your visit.

The site is about 1km (signposted) off the main road. *Combis* (minibuses) to the turnoff run north along López Mateos, two blocks east of the Comalli bus depot (M$7, 10 minutes). A taxi to the site costs M$40; either negotiate a round trip with waiting time or take a *combi* back, which requires walking 1km to the main road, going under the overpass and flagging one down.

In Villahermosa, the Comalli bus depot is near the corner of Gil y Saénz and Aberlardo Reyes, a block northwest of the ADO terminal. Buses to Comalcalco leave every 15 minutes from 5am to 10:30pm (M$28, one hour).

Explore More of Tabasco

The following only scratches the surface of the other adventures to be had in Tabasco.

Cacao haciendas Discover the past at Hacienda La Luz, just west of Comalcalco's central plaza.

Gulf beaches Explore around Puerto Ceiba, where you can take boat rides into Laguna Mecoacán. Or cruise the lost roads along the Barra de Tupilco.

La Venta While most of the cool artifacts have been moved to the museum in Villahermosa, this site, 128km west of Villahermosa, is still worth a visit.

Malpasito Up in Tabasco's beautiful and mountainous far southwestern corner, tiny Malpasito is the site of mysterious ancient Zoque ruins.

Reserva de la Biosfera Pantanos de Centla A massive biosphere reserve with lakes, marshes, rivers and more.

Southern Tabasco Explore riverside swimming holes and caves, using the town of Teapa, 50km south of Villahermosa, as your base.

Sleeping

High season is mid-December through March, with peak times (and prices) around Christmas and Easter. Prices below are for high season; in low season prices drop by 20% or more.

Posada La Media Luna HOTEL **$**
(631-5590; www.hotel-lamedialuna.com; Hermanos Domínguez 5; s/d/tr/q M$400/500/600/700, apt M$1300; @) This friendly, Italian-owned place is a great budget choice. It's well maintained and offers comfortable and pretty rooms with cable TV, all set around a covered patio with potted plants. The one apartment has two rooms and a kitchen. But beware nearby church bells – especially on Sunday morning!

Le Gite del Sol HOTEL **$**
(631-6012; www.legitedelsol.com; Madero 82; s/d/tr without bathroom M$180/220/330, with bathroom M$250/320/420; @) Run by a Quebecois-Mexican couple, this safety-conscious budget choice offers simple yet comfortable rooms with private bathroom (those with shared bathrooms are across the street). Facilities include a front patio, rooftop area and small kitchen; bus tickets are also sold for the same price as at the terminal. Breakfast included.

Rossco Backpackers HOSTEL **$**
(674-0525; www.rosscohostel.com; Real de Mexicanos 16; dm M$165-185, d/tr/q M$500/700/800; P@) Wonderful hostel in an old building with rooms surrounding a lovely garden. Dorms are good though tight, ranging from four to 14 beds. Spacious privates are hotel-quality and come with rustic furniture and towel animals, and some have skylights. Perks include a pool table, movie lounge, nightly bonfires and continental breakfast. Internet and long-stay discounts occasionally available.

México Hostel HOSTEL **$**
(678-0014; www.himexico.com; Josefa Ortiz de Domínguez 12; dm M$160, r with without/with bathroom M$400/440; P@) Located in an old colonial compound with partial mountain views, this HI hostel has a courtyard garden (great for hanging out), several smaller patios, a bright kitchen, a pool table and even a little bar. Dorms and privates are bright, but the dorms all have 10 to 14 beds. HI discount; breakfast included.

Posada San Cris HOTEL **$**
(678-3412; Tapachula 14; d/q M$450/750; P) Good, friendly hotel offering just 10 rooms, all simple but clean, and decorated with rustic furnishings. Two front patios were being renovated at research time, and in the future should be pleasant places to hang out. Breakfast included.

Hotel Posada Jovel HOTEL **$**
(678-1734; www.hoteljovel.com; Paniagua 28; s M$350-890, d M$400-900, tr M$450-1030; P) Most rooms in the economical 'posada' building are basic and OK; those below can be musty and some share bathrooms. For more comfort, head to the 'hotel' section across the street. Here, rooms surrounding a pretty garden are larger and more brightly decorated, come with cable TV and access a wonderful terrace with views. Restaurant available.

Parador Margarita HOTEL **$$**
(116-0164; www.tourshotel.com.mx; JF Flores 39; d M$950-1050, tr/q M$1200/1340; P) The 27 spacious and gorgeous rooms along covered hallways here are well decorated with lovely furniture, and some include fireplace and bathroom skylight. The best ones are near the back patio, which has a burbling fountain and is a little paradise.

Casa Margarita HOTEL **$$**
(631-3349; www.tourshotel.com.mx; Real de Guadalupe 34; s/d/tr/q M$680/820/900/1040; P@) Located right in the middle of things, on a pedestrian street, is this very nice courtyard hotel. The 35 decent-sized rooms are good and offer some style, and come with cable TV and safe boxes. Close by are many restaurants and bars.

★ **Casa Felipe Flores** BOUTIQUE HOTEL **$$$**
(678-3996; www.felipeflores.com; JF Flores 36; r M$1200-1560; P) This amazing colonial guesthouse is decorated with so many outstanding regional handicrafts it's practically a museum. The six rooms are different in size and furnishings, but they're all beautiful and come with stunning tiled bathrooms. There are several flowery courtyards, a gorgeous back patio and even a sun terrace. Breakfast (included) is served in an elegant common room.

★ **B¨o Hotel** HOTEL **$$$**
(678-1515; www.hotelbo.mx; Av 5 de Mayo 38; r M$2900-6500;) San Cristóbal's newest and fanciest boutique hotel breaks the

traditional colonial-architecture barrier with supermodern, trendy lines and unique, artsy touches. The large rooms and suites are very elegant and boast glass-tile bathrooms with ceiling showers, while the flowery gardens host fine water features. The restaurant is a calm oasis serving regional cuisine; check out the outside patio tables lined with water.

Posada Moguel APARTMENTS **$$$**
(☎116-0957; posadamoguel@hotmail.com; Comitán 41B; apt M$1200-2000; P) Six tasteful apartments sleeping two to six people are available here, some set around a tiled patio with potted plants. All have kitchen, fireplace, and living and dining rooms; some have three bedrooms and two floors. Weekly discount.

Eating

San Cristóbal has become a magnet for international immigrants, and with them comes a delicious variety of cuisines. You can find felafel, sushi, Thai, Indian, Italian, Argentine and even Lebanese restaurants in town.

★**Tierradentro** MEXICAN **$**
(☎674-6766; Real de Guadalupe 24; set menu M$40-70; 8:15am-10:30pm;) A popular gathering center for political progressives, laptop-toting locals and international travelers, this large, indoor courtyard restaurant and cafe is run by Zapatista supporters who hold cultural events and conferences on local issues. A delicious *menú del día* (set lunch; M$65 to M$100) rotates daily, but there's also breakfast, pizzas, sandwiches, vegetarian meals and a dozen house specialties.

El Caldero MEXICAN **$**
(Insurgentes 5; soups M$49; 11am-10pm) Simple, friendly little El Caldero specializes in delicious, filling Mexican soups like *pozole* (shredded pork in broth) and *mondongo* (tripe and beef) – all with sides of tortillas, onions and spices. There's a vegetarian soup as well, plus salads.

Anabanana MEXICAN **$**
(Hidalgo 9; mains M$30-70; 10am-6pm Mon-Sat) This long-time *tortas* (sandwiches) and juice joint on a pedestrian street is a cute and cozy choice for typical Mexican food and no-frills international options. Great for people-watching, plus good breakfasts.

El Horno Mágico BAKERY **$**
(Utrilla 7; bread and pastries under M$25; 8:30am-8:30pm) Some of the best French bread in town. Also bakes delicious pastries; come early before they run out.

La Casa del Pan Papalotl MEXICAN **$**
(☎678-7215; Real de Guadalupe 55; mains M$50-100; 8am-10pm Mon-Sat;) This excellent courtyard vegetarian restaurant does a particularly filling buffet lunch from 1:30pm to 4:30pm (M$100). Fresh bread and locally grown organic ingredients are staples here. Choose from soups, salads, pastas, *chiles rellenos* (stuffed chilis) wth vegetables and tofu fajitas.

★**Trattoria Italiana** ITALIAN **$$**
(☎678-5895; Dr Navarro 10; mains M$120-145; 2-10pm Mon & Thu-Sat, 2-5:30pm Sun) This mother and daughter–run Italian eatery specializes in ravioli, handmade fresh every day. Depending on what's in season, expect fillings of sea bass with eggplant; four cheese with walnut and arugula; or rabbit with rosemary and green olive. The sauces are divine – don't miss the mango, chipotle and gorgonzola if it's around.

El Argentino ARGENTINE **$$$**
(☎631-7150; Real de Guadalupe 13D; steaks M$215-289; 1-11pm) Even in Buenos Aires this would be an excellent restaurant. Don't be deceived – prices are high, but the steaks are enormous (up to 400gm) and include sides like fries and salad. In other words, enough for two. Don't miss the *chimichurri* (oil, parsley and garlic) steak sauce. If you're not into beef, there's also fish and pasta – and the flan with *dulce de leche* (milk caramel) is a must.

Drinking & Entertainment

La Viña de Bacco WINE BAR
(☎119-1985; Real de Guadalupe 7; 2pm-midnight Mon-Sat) San Cristóbal's most popular wine bar, with just a handful of tables inside – it gets very crowded. International wines, plus beers, tequila and coffees, are served with free *botanas* (appetizers). On warm nights, the sidewalk tables are hot spots.

Kakao Natura CAFE
(Moreno 2A; 8am-10pm Mon-Sat) For something different, melt into a hot chocolate at this *chocolatería*. Order a classic, semibitter or bitter, and add cardomom, vanilla or even chilis for a few pesos. There's even a lactose-free choice. Pastries, sandwiches and artisanal chocolates also available.

La Sandunga BAR

(MA Flores 16; ⌚7pm-3am Thu-Sat) This low-key hangout is a good intimate place to chill out, offering three sofas and a few tables. The loungy music stays conversation-friendly, and the fruit cocktails are divine – and made sweeter by the *botanas* accompanying them. Live Jazz on Friday and Saturday nights.

Cafe Bar Revolución LIVE MUSIC

(1 de Marzo 11; ⌚noon-3am) There's always something fun going on here, with live music daily from 8:30pm. Every day is different – Monday is blues and electronica, Tuesday salsa and Cubano, Wednesday reggae and jazz etc. Cocktails like mojitos and caipirinhas add joy.

Cocoliche LIVE MUSIC

(Colón 3; ⌚noon-midnight) By day it's a funky bohemian restaurant, but at 9:30pm the live music starts up – expect Mexican bands with the occasional international guest musician. On Saturday evenings, theater and plays take center stage.

Information

There are many internet cafes around town, including a couple on Real de Guadalupe.

Banamex (Insurgentes 9; ⌚9am-4pm Mon-Sat) Has an ATM.

Hospital de la Mujer (☎678-0770; Insurgentes) General hospital with emergency facilities.

Post Office (Allende 3; ⌚8am-4pm Mon-Fri, to noon Sat)

INDIGENOUS PEOPLES OF CHIAPAS

Of the nearly five million people in Chiapas, approximately a quarter are indigenous, with language being the key ethnic identifier. Each of the eight principal groups has its own language, beliefs and customs, a cultural variety that makes Chiapas one of the most interesting states in Mexico.

Travelers to the area around San Cristóbal are most likely to encounter the Tzotziles and the Tzeltales. Their traditional religious belief is nominally Catholic, but integrates pre-Hispanic elements. Most people live in the hills outside the villages, which are primarily market and ceremonial centers.

Tzotzil and Tzeltal clothing is among the most varied, colorful and elaborately worked in Mexico. It not only identifies wearers' villages but also continues ancient Maya traditions. Many of the seemingly abstract designs on these costumes are in fact stylized snakes, frogs, butterflies, birds, saints and other beings. Some motifs have religious-magical functions: scorpions, for example, can be a symbolic request for rain, since they are believed to attract lightning.

The Lacandones dwelled deep in the Lacandón Jungle and largely avoided contact with the outside world until the 1950s. Today they number less than 1000 and mostly live in three main settlements in that same region, with low-key tourism being one of their major means of support. Lacandones are readily recognizable in their white tunics and long black hair cut in a fringe. Most have now abandoned their traditional animist religion in favor of Presbyterian or evangelical forms of Christianity.

Traditionally treated as second-class citizens, indigenous groups mostly live on the least productive land in the state, with the least amount of government services or infrastructure. Many indigenous communities rely on subsistence farming and have no running water or electricity, and it was frustration over lack of political power and their historical mistreatment that fueled the Zapatista rebellion, putting a spotlight on the region's distinct inequities.

Today the Zapatista movement isn't nearly as strong as it once was, but its original tenets of rejecting traditional leadership hierarchies remain, and it continues to raise the rights and profile of indigenous peoples – especially women.

Despite all obstacles, the identities and self-respect of Chiapas' indigenous peoples survive. These people may be suspicious of outsiders, and may resent interference in their religious observances or other aspects of their life, but if treated with due respect they are likely to respond in kind.

Tourist Office (☎678-0665; Plaza 31 de Marzo, Palacio Municipal; ⏰8am-9pm)

Getting There & Away

AIR

San Cristóbal's airport, about 15km from town on the Palenque road, has no regular passenger flights; the main airport serving town is at Tuxtla Gutiérrez. Five daily direct OCC minibuses (M$170, 1¼ hours) run between Tuxtla's airport and San Cristóbal's main bus terminal; book in advance.

BUS, COLECTIVO & VAN

Most of the road between San Cristóbal and Palenque is long and very curvy; take medicine if you're prone to motion sickness.

The main bus terminal is the 1st-class **OCC terminal** (☎678-0291; cnr Pan-American Hwy & Insurgentes). Bus tickets are also sold in the center of town at **Boletotal** (☎678-0291; www.boletotal.mx; Real de Guadalupe 16; ⏰7:30am-10:30pm).

First-class **AEXA** (☎678-6178) and 2nd-class Ómnibus de Chiapas share a **terminal** on the south side of the highway. Also, various *combi* and *colectivo* companies to Ocosingo, Tuxtla and Comitán have depots on the highway in the same area (it's a frenzied madhouse with shouting operators competing for passengers).

For Guatemala, most agencies offer daily van service to Quetzaltenango (M$350, eight hours), Panajachel (M$350, nine hours) and Antigua (M$450, 11 hours).

CAR

A fast toll *autopista* (M$45) zips towards Chiapa de Corzo.

San Cristóbal's only car-rental company, **Optima** (☎674-5409; optimacar1@hotmail.com; Mazariegos 39; ⏰9am-2pm & 4-7pm Mon-Sat, 9am-1pm Sun), rents out VW Beetles for M$500 per day and M$3000 per week, but has other car makes too. It's located inside a hotel; ask for discount if paying with cash.

Getting Around

Combis (M$5) go up Crescencio Rosas from the Pan-American Hwy to the town center. Taxis cost M$25 to M$30 within town and M$30 to M$35 at night.

Croozy Scooters (☎683-2223; croozyscooters@live.com.mx; Belisario Domínguez 7; scooters per 3hr/day M$250/400; ⏰10am-6pm; later by appointment) rents well-maintained Italika CS 125cc scooters, plus 150cc motorcycles and bicycles. Jaguar Adventours (p227) also rents bicycles.

> **BUS TRAVEL WARNING**
>
> Be careful on overnight buses to or from San Cristóbal, especially to Palenque. Use a lock on baggage stored in the hold below, and keep your personal hand luggage close by – even sleeping on it at night. Thefts have occurred in the past.

Around San Cristóbal

The inhabitants of the beautiful Chiapas highlands are descended from the ancient Maya and maintain some unique customs, costumes and beliefs, and some of their villages are worth visiting. In addition to San Juan Chamula, there's San Lorenzo Zinacantán (notable for its old church) and Amatenango del Valle (famous for pottery). Those into natural wonders should head to Las Grutas de Rancho Nuevo (a long cavern).

If you'd like a guide to the villages, contact **Alex y Raúl Tours** (☎967-678-3741, 678-9141; www.alexyraultours.wordpress.com; per person tours M$200) in San Cristóbal. It conducts tours to Chamula and Zinacantán daily including transport, bilingual guide and entry fees; simply meet your guide at 9:30am at the cross in front of San Cristóbal's cathedral. Trips to other surrounding villages can also be arranged.

San Juan Chamula

POP 3330

The Chamulans are a fiercely independent Tzotzil group, more than 80,000 strong. Their principal village is San Juan Chamula, located 10km northwest of San Cristóbal. There's a weekly market on Sunday, when people from the hills stream into the village to shop, trade and visit the main church. Many tour buses also visit on Sunday, so expect crowds then.

The white **Templo de San Juan**, Chamula's pretty main church, is vividly accented in green and blue. Step inside and you'll instantly notice hundreds of flickering candles, clouds of copal incense and worshippers kneeling with their faces to the pine needle-carpeted floor. Chanting medicine men or women may be rubbing patients' bodies with eggs or bones, and you might even see a chicken or two being sacrificed. As you can imagine, it all makes for a powerful impression.

As on outsider, you're allowed to enter the church – but you must obtain a ticket (M$20) first. There's usually someone at the church door selling them, or you can get one at the **tourist office** (⏲7am-7pm) in the orange building in front of (and to the side of) the church's front courtyard.

Be warned: absolutely NO photography is allowed inside the church. However tempting, *do not* ignore this restriction as the community takes it very seriously.

Three blocks back up the hill from the church, toward San Cristóbal (and off a side street), is the town's **graveyard**. Black crosses are for people who died old, white for young, and blue for others.

To get to Chamula, take a *combi* from Calle Honduras in San Cristóbal. They leave frequently from 4am to 6:30pm (M$12, 30 minutes).

Palenque

☎916 / POP 45,000

Deservedly one of the top destinations of Chiapas, the soaring jungle-swathed temples of ancient Palenque are a national treasure and one of the best examples of Maya architecture in Mexico. Modern Palenque town, 8km to the east, is a sweaty place with little appeal except as a hub for many services, and as a jumping-off point for the ruins.

History

The name Palenque (Palisade) is Spanish and has no relation to the city's ancient name, which may have been Lakamha (Big Water). Palenque was first occupied around 100 BC, and flourished from around AD 630 to around 740. The city rose to prominence under the ruler Pakal, who reigned from AD 615 to 683. Archaeologists have determined that Pakal is represented by hieroglyphics of sun and shield, and he is also referred to as Sun Shield (Escudo Solar). He lived to the then-incredible age of 80.

Pakal's son Kan B'alam II (684–702), who is represented in hieroglyphics by the jaguar and the serpent (and is also called Jaguar Serpent II), continued Palenque's expansion and artistic development. During Kan B'alam II's reign, Palenque extended its zone of control to the Rio Usumacinta, but was challenged by the rival Maya city of Toniná, 65km south. Kan B'alam's brother and successor, K'an Joy Chitam II (Precious Peccary), was captured by forces from Toniná in 711, and probably executed there. Palenque enjoyed a resurgence between 722 and 736, however, under Ahkal Mo' Nahb' III (Turtle Macaw Lake), who added many substantial buildings.

After AD 900, Palenque was largely abandoned.

Sights

Palenque Ruins

Just 8km from Palenque city, the ruins of ancient **Palenque** (guides 2hr tour for up to 7 people in English/Spanish/French/Italian $650/450/700/700; ⏲8am-5pm, last entry 4:30pm) stand at the precise point where the first hills rise out of the Gulf Coast plain. The dense jungle covering these hills forms an evocative backdrop to Palenque's exquisite and unique Maya architecture. Hundreds of ruined buildings are spread over 15 sq km, but only a fairly compact central area has been excavated. The forest around these temples is still home to howler monkeys, toucans and ocelots.

The ruins and surrounding forests form a national park, the **Parque Nacional Palenque**, for which you must pay a separate M$27 admission fee at Km 4.5 on the road to the ruins. Plan on staying at the ruins at least three hours.

BUSES FROM SAN CRISTÓBAL DE LAS CASAS

DESTINATION	FARE (M$)	DURATION (HR)	FREQUENCY
Campeche	415	11	1 daily at 6:20pm
Cancún	795-950	18	3 daily
Ciudad Cuauhtémoc (Guatemalan border)	95	3½	1 daily at 11:30am
Mérida	590	14	1 daily at 6:20pm
Palenque	90-160	5	10 daily
Villahermosa	310	6	1 daily at 10am

Palenque Ruins

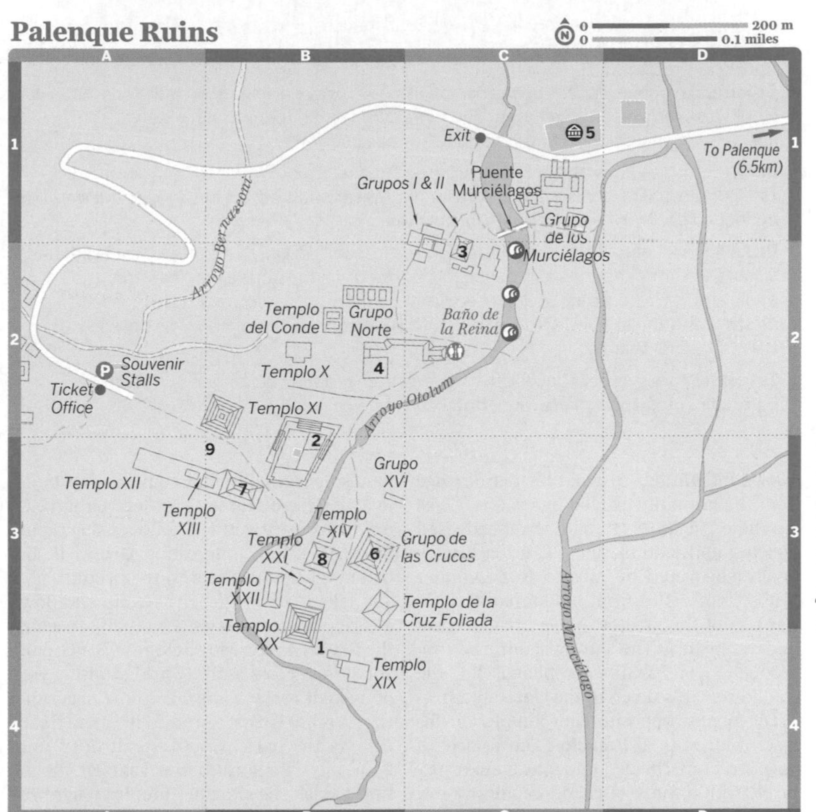

Don't miss Palenque's extraordinary **Museo de Sitio** (Carretera Palenque-Ruinas, Km 6.5; admission free with ruins ticket; 9am-4:30pm Tue-Sun), which displays finds from the site and interprets, in English and Spanish, Palenque's history. The highlight here is the life-size reproduction of Pakal's (Palenque's greatest leader) carved stone sarcophagus lid.

Official site **guides** (2hr tour for up to 7 people in English M$960) hang out near the entrance and can be identified by their neck badges. Unofficial guides are also around and charge less. Food and beverages are available, and there are plenty of souvenir vendors both inside and outside the site.

Transporte Chambalú (345-2849; Allende btwn Hidalgo & Av Juárez) and **Transportes Palenque** (cnr Allende & Av 20 de Noviembre) run *combis* to and from the ruins about every 15 minutes from 6am to 6pm daily (M$10 each way). They will pick up or drop off anywhere along the town-to-ruins road.

Palenque Ruins

Sights

1 Acrópolis Sur B4
2 El Palacio B3
3 Grupos II C2
4 Juego de Pelota B2
5 Museo de Sitio C1
6 Templo de la Cruz B3
7 Templo de las Inscripciones B3
8 Templo del Sol B3
9 Tomb of Alberto Ruz Lhuillier A3

Exploring the Site

As you enter the site, a line of temples rises in front of the jungle on your right, culminating about 100m ahead at the **Templo de las Inscripciones** (Temple of the Inscriptions), the tallest and most stately of Palenque's buildings. From the top, interior stairs lead down into the tomb of Pakal

DRINKS OF CHIAPAS

Comiteco A unique variant of *mezcal* (an alcoholic agave drink) made with *piloncillo* (cooked sugarcane). It's smoother and more syrupy than tequila, with a clear appearance or a greenish tint. Traditionally made in Comitán.

Pox Inexpensive grain alcohol made from sugarcane; it's pronounced (and sometimes spelled) 'posh'. The undisputed choice for those who want to pass out cold on the street, but not so deadly when mixed with lots of fruit juice.

Pozol A thick heavy mixture of *masa* (cornmeal dough) in water, it's often mixed with sugar and sometimes has chili or chocolate added. It's the equivalent of an energy drink, and you can see indigenous people everywhere carrying it around in reused plastic liter bottles. Travelers often take a ball of the *masa* and make some up when there's water available.

Tascalate A cold sweet concoction prepared from ground cacao, pine nuts, toasted corn, cinnamon and *achiote* (annatto). Very interesting and superdelicious!

(closed indefinitely to avoid further damage from the humidity exuded by visitors). This is where, in 1952, Pakal's jewel-bedecked skeleton and jade mosaic death mask were finally uncovered by Alberto Ruz Lhuillier (whose tomb is in front of Templo XIII). It was one of the greatest Maya archeological finds in history. The site museum has a reproduction of Pakal's sarcophagus lid; the real lid remains down in the closed tomb.

Diagonally opposite the Templo de las Inscripciones is **El Palacio** (The Palace), a large structure divided into four main courtyards, with a maze of corridors and rooms. Keep following the path over a bridge and up some stairs; go left at the 'Y' and you'll soon reach the **Grupo de las Cruces** (Group of the Crosses). Soon after the death of his father, Pakal's son Kan B'alam II (684–702) started designing the temples here. The **Templo del Sol** (Temple of the Sun), to the west, has the best-preserved roofcomb at Palenque. Nearby, steep steps climb to the **Templo de la Cruz** (Temple of the Cross), the largest and most impressive in this group.

South of the Grupo de las Cruces is the **Acrópolis Sur**, where archaeologists have recovered some terrific finds in recent excavations. It appears to have been constructed as an extension of the Grupo de las Cruces, but this area was closed at research time and unfortunately will probably remain closed for a few more years.

Follow the path north and back down to the river; you'll eventually reach the **Juego de Pelota** (Ball Court) and, behind it, the handsome and blissfully souvenir-free buildings of **Grupo Norte** (Northern Group). After a visit here you can follow a steep path down to mildly interesting **Grupo II**, but better yet double back to the original path and take it across the river again and down a series of steep stairs, eventually reaching the **Grupo de los Murciélagos** (Bat Group). You'll then cross a pretty bridge with a view of a small rocky waterfall – now head up a short way to Grupo 2 if you'd like, and finally exit via the back way (this exit open until 4pm only). Be sure to give yourself enough time to visit the site museum; from here you can easily flag a transport van back to the entrance, or to Palenque city.

Sleeping

It's very convenient to stay in Palenque town, where most services are located. However, if you'd rather have jungly peace, and especially if you have your own wheels, consider sleeping at one of several accommodations along the 8km road to Palenque ruins. Frequent *combis* (M$10) run between town and the ruins, so getting back and forth is easy.

The hippie-bohemian jungle enclave of El Panchán is a good middle ground (if you can handle 'backpacker rustic'). It's located halfway between town and the ruins, and offers a few accommodation choices, a couple of restaurants and a tour agency.

Palenque town has its own version of a 'jungle' neighborhood, called La Cañada. It's very leafy and more peaceful than staying in the center, which is only a few blocks away.

Prices below are for high season, which is around Christmas, Easter, July and August. Rates drop 20% to 50% outside these times.

In Town

Yaxkin HOSTEL $

(☎345-0102; www.hostalyaxkin.com; Prolongación Hidalgo s/n; hammock/dm M$60/150, d without/with bathroom M$300, d with air-con & private bathroom M$450-600;) In the La Cañada neighborhood, this former discotheque has been amazingly revamped into a luxury hostel with a great living room, multiple hangout spots and a swank restaurant and bar. There are all kinds of rooms (that accommodate up to seven), from simple to luxurious, or you can sleep in a hammock. A nice garden with sweat lodge lies in back. Some private rooms are in a nearby annex.

Hotel Canek HOTEL $

(☎345-0150; www.hotelcanek.com; 20 de Noviembre 43; r with fan/air-con M$450/550;) Good, well-maintained budget choice with simple, good-sized rooms, though some are dark - get one facing the street if you can. Nice rooftop terrace with *palapa* (shelter with thatched roof) and hammocks.

Hotel Maya Rue HOTEL $$

(☎345-0743; maya_rue@hotmail.com; Calle Aldama btwn Juarez & 5 de Mayo; r M$600-800;) Tree-trunk beams and dramatic lighting add unexpected style to this 12-room offering that combines traditional materials and industrial chic. Some rooms have shaded private balconies, but all are spacious and come with cable TV. There are a few imperfections, but overall it's a welcome addition to untrendy Palenque. Cafe on premises.

Hotel Xibalba HOTEL $$

(☎345-0411; www.hotelxibalba.com; Merle Green 9; d/tr/q M$750/850/950; P) Located in the tranquil neighborhood of La Cañada, this midrange hotel offers 35 pleasant, clean and tiled rooms with cable TV. Definite Maya theme here, with rock-accented architectural details, pastel colors and a replica of the lid from Pakal's sarcophagus on display. Restaurant on premises.

Hotel Lacandonia HOTEL $$

(☎345-0057; Allende 77; s/d/tr/q M$500/600/700/800; P) This modern, central hotel has a subtle splash of style, and the tasteful, clean and spacious rooms boast wrought-iron beds with good mattresses, reading lights and cable TV. Balcony rooms are brightest but have traffic noise, though the internal and open restaurant below is also noisy (at least until 11pm).

Outside Town

Margarita & Ed Cabañas HOTEL $

(☎111-9112; Carreterra Palenque-Ruinas, Km 4.5, El Panchán; 2-/3-person cabaña M$270/300, d/tr with fan M$350/400, d with air-con M$450; P) Full of local information, Margarita has welcomed travelers to her homey place in El Panchán for nearly 20 years. A variety of clean and cheerful rooms have good mosquito netting, and the more rustic screened *cabañas* (cabins) are well kept. It's in a humid tropical jungle setting with a creek and cobbled paths.

TRAVELING SAFELY IN CHIAPAS

In general, Chiapas is a safe place to travel. Many people associate the state with the Zapatistas, but this revolutionary organization has become less influential in the last decade and their main significant uprising occurred in 1994. In any case, tourists are not targeted by the Zapatistas.

Drug trafficking and illicit immigration are concerns along the border regions with Guatemala, and military checkpoints are frequent on the Carretera Fronteriza along the Guatemalan border from Palenque to the Lagos de Montebello. These checkpoints generally increase security for travelers, though it's best to be off the Carretera Fronteriza before dark. For similar reasons all border crossings with Guatemala are places you should aim to get through early in the day.

Indigenous villages are often extremely close-knit, and their people can be suspicious of outsiders and particularly sensitive about having their photos taken. In some villages cameras are, at best, tolerated – and sometimes not even that. You may put yourself in physical danger by taking photos without permission. Always ask first.

Travelers to Villahermosa should note the region is subject to seasonal floods.

EXPLORE MORE OF CHIAPAS

For more information on Chiapas, check out our comprehensive coverage in the *Mexico* guidebook or download a PDF copy at www.shop.lonelyplanet.com. Here are some of our DIY adventures:

➡ A respite from both the steamy lowland jungle and the chilly highlands, the bustling market town of **Ocosingo** sits in a gorgeous and broad temperate valley midway between San Cristóbal and Palenque. The impressive Maya ruins of **Toniná** are just a few kilometers away.

➡ Two spectacular water attractions – the thundering cascades of **Agua Azul** and the 35m jungle waterfall of **Misol-Ha** – are both short detours off the Ocosingo–Palenque road.

➡ The largest Lacandón Maya village, **Lacanjá Chansayab**, is 12km from Bonampak. Its family compounds are scattered around a wide area, many of them with creeks or even the Río Lacanjá flowing past their grassy grounds. Check www.ecochiapas.com/lacanja for details on visiting the region.

➡ The temperate pine and oak forest along the Guatemalan border east of Chinkultic is dotted with over 50 small lakes of varied hues, called the **Lagos de Montebello**. The nearby **Chinkultic ruins** add to the mystery.

➡ Ringed by rainforest 140km southeast of Ocosingo in the Reserva de la Biosfera Montes Azules, **Laguna Miramar** is one of Mexico's most remote and exquisite lakes. Rock ledges on small islands make blissful wading spots, and petroglyphs and a sea-turtle cave are reachable by canoe.

➡ The luxuriant cloud forests of **Reserva de la Biosfera El Triunfo**, high in the remote Sierra Madre de Chiapas, are a bird-lover's paradise.

➡ The large **Reserva de la Biosfera La Encrucijada** protects a 1448-sq-km strip of coastal lagoons, sand bars and wetlands.

➡ Set 12km east of Tuxtla Gutiérrez on the way to San Cristóbal, **Chiapa de Corzo** is a small and attractive colonial town with an easygoing, provincial air. Set on the north bank of the broad Río Grijalva, it's the main starting point for trips into the **Cañón del Sumidero**.

➡ The dramatic sinkhole **Sima de Las Cotorras** punches 160m wide and 140m deep into the earth. It's about 1½ hours from Tuxtla Gutiérrez.

Hotel La Aldea HOTEL **$$**
(☎345-1693; www.hotellaaldea.net; Carretera Palenque-Ruinas, Km 2.8; r M$1100-1200; P ❄ 📶 🏊) Nearly 3km from town, the four-star Aldea has 33 large, beautiful and bright *palapa*-roofed rooms set amid lovely grounds. Each room has an outside terrace with hammock. It's a stylish place, with a peaceful hilltop restaurant and a wonderful pool area. There are no TVs, making it an ideal place to get away from it all.

Mayabell HOTEL, CAMPGROUND **$$**
(☎341-6977; www.mayabell.com.mx; Carretera Palenque-Ruinas, Km 6; hammock rental M$20, campsites per person M$60 (plus per car M$30), vehicle site with hookups M$180, r with fan/air-con M$750/950, treehouse M$120-150; P ❄ 📶 🏊) There's something for everyone at this spacious, grassy complex: camping, hammocks, a trailer park, regular hotel rooms and even a rustic 'treehouse.' Rooms with air-con are nice and tastefully decorated; those with fan are more basic. There's a good restaurant, a large pool and even a *temazcal* (sweat lodge) on premises, and it's located just 400m from the Palenque site museum.

★ **Boutique Hotel Quinta Chanabnal** BOUTIQUE HOTEL **$$$**
(☎345-5320; www.quintachanabnal.com; Carretera Palenque-Ruinas, Km 2.2; suites from M$2100; P ❄ 📶 🏊) The Maya-inspired architecture and impeccable service at this decadent boutique hotel will leave you swooning. Enter heavy wood doors carved by local artisans, where spacious stone-floor suites contain majestically draped four-poster beds and

cavernous bathrooms. Water features on the premises include a creek, a small lagoon and a multitiered swimming pool. Massages, a *temazcal* and a fine restaurant are available. The Italian owner, a Maya expert, also speaks German, French, English and Spanish.

Eating

★**Don Mucho's** MEXICAN, INTERNATIONAL $
(☎112-8338; Carretera Palenque-Ruinas, Km 4.5, El Panchán; mains M$40-120; ⏰7am-11pm) The hot spot of El Panchán, popular Don Mucho's provides good-value meals in a jungly setting, with candlelit atmosphere and live music at night. There's wide menu variety – breakfast, light snacks, meats, seafood, Mexican specialties, home-made pastas and wood-fired pizzas.

Café de Yara CAFE $
(☎345-0269; Hidalgo 66; breakfasts M$38-70, tourist menus M$65-100; ⏰7am-11pm;) A sunny start to the day, this modern and beautiful corner cafe has great breakfasts and excellent organic Chiapan coffee. There are also soups, salads, pastas, meat dishes and many kinds of beverages.

El Huachinango Feliz SEAFOOD $
(☎345-4642; Hidalgo s/n; mains M$70-120; ⏰9am-11pm) Popular, atmospheric restaurant in the leafy La Cañada neighborhood. It has an attractive front patio with tables and umbrellas, and there's also an upstairs covered terrace. Seafood is the specialty here – order seafood soup, seafood cocktails, grilled fish or shrimp served 10 different ways. A downside is the rather loud (rather than romantic) music.

Restaurant Las Tinajas MEXICAN $
(☎345-4970; cnr Av 20 de Noviembre & Abasolo; mains M$50-100; ⏰7am-11pm) It doesn't take long to figure out why this open-sided corner restaurant is always busy. It slings large portions of excellent home-style food, and the menu has something for everyone – really. Efficient service.

La Selva MEXICAN $$
(☎345-0363; Hwy 199; mains M$70-175; ⏰11:30am-11:30pm; P) La Selva is Palenque's most upscale restaurant and serves well-prepared traditional and specialty dishes under an enormous *palapa* roof. There's a Sunday afternoon buffet (M$155) and nice back patio. It's about 150m south of the Maya head statue, on the road to the ruins.

Information

There are several internet cafes and banks with ATMs in the center.

Clínica Palenque (☎345-0273; Velasco Suárez 33; ⏰8:30am-1:30pm & 5-9pm)

Post Office (Independencia; ⏰8am-4pm Mon-Fri, 9am-noon Sat & Sun)

Tourist Information Kiosk (cnr Hidalgo & Jiménez, El Parque; ⏰8am-9pm Mon-Fri, 1-9pm Sat & Sun)

Tourist Office (☎345-0356; cnr Av Juárez & Abasolo; ⏰9am-9pm Mon-Sat, to 1pm Sun) Open 9am to 9pm daily during high seasons.

Getting There & Away

Highway holdups are more a thing of the past, but it's still best not to travel Hwy 199 between Palenque and San Cristóbal at night.

Palenque's airport has no commercial flights. The closest major airport is in Villahermosa.

ADO (☎345-1344; Av Juárez) has the main bus terminal, with deluxe and 1st-class services, an ATM and left-luggage facilities; it's also used by OCC (1st-class) and TRT (2nd-class). **AEXA** (☎345-2630; Av Juárez 159), with 1st-class buses, and Cardesa (2nd-class) are 1½ blocks east. Transportes Palenque (p235) runs vans to Tenosique, which has onward connections to Guatemala.

Getting Around

Taxis charge M$50 (M$70 at night) to El Panchán and M$60 to the ruins. *Combis* (M$10) head to the ruins from 6am to 6pm. You can also get picked up along the west half of Av Juarez as the *combis* drive their way out of town.

BUSES FROM PALENQUE

DESTINATION	FARE (M$)	DURATION (HR)	FREQUENCY
Campeche	285-300	5	4 daily
Cancún	470-685	13	5 daily
Mérida	425-450	8	3 daily
San Cristóbal de las Casas	90-160	5	10 daily
Villahermosa	120	2½	hourly

Bonampak & Yaxchilán

The ancient Maya cities of Bonampak and Yaxchilán, southeast of Palenque, are easily accessible thanks to the Carretera Fronteriza. This good, paved road runs parallel to the Mexico–Guatemala border all the way from Palenque to the Lagos de Montebello, and goes around the fringe of the Lacandón Jungle.

Bonampak, famous for its frescoes, is 152km by road from Palenque. The bigger and more important Yaxchilán, with a peerless jungle setting beside the broad and swift Río Usumacinta, is 173km by road, then about 22km by boat. Both can be visited in one long day.

The **Mesoamerican Ecotourism Alliance** (www.travelwithmea.org) and San Cristóbal-based **SendaSur** (☎967-678-3909; www.sendasur.com.mx; Real de Guadalupe 46B) organize multiday excursions to the region, including several Lacandón villages.

Bonampak

The site of **Bonampak** (admission M$46; ⏲8am-4:30pm) spreads over 2.4 sq km, but all the main ruins stand around the rectangular Gran Plaza. Never a major city, Bonampak spent most of the Classic period in Yaxchilán's sphere of influence. The most impressive surviving monuments were built under Chan Muwan II, a nephew of the Yaxchilán's Itzamnaaj B'alam II, who acceded to Bonampak's throne in AD 776. The 6m-high **Stele 1** in the **Gran Plaza** depicts Chan Muwan holding a ceremonial staff at the height of his reign. He also features in **Stele 2** and **Stele 3** on the **Acrópolis**, which rises from the south end of the plaza.

However, it's the vivid frescoes inside the modest-looking **Templo de las Pinturas** (Edificio 1) that have given Bonampak its fame – and its name, which means 'Painted Walls' in Yucatec Maya. The Bonampak site abuts the Reserva de la Biosfera Montes Azules, and is rich in wildlife.

Yaxchilán

Jungle-shrouded **Yaxchilán** (admission M$55; ⏲8am-3:30pm) has a terrific setting above a horseshoe loop in the Río Usumacinta. The control this location gave it over river commerce, plus a series of successful alliances and conquests, made Yaxchilán one of the most important Classic Maya cities in the Usumacinta region. Archaeologically, Yaxchilán is famed for its ornamented facades and roofcombs, and its impressive stone lintels carved with conquest and ceremonial scenes. A flashlight (and repellent) are helpful for exploring some parts of the site.

Yaxchilán peaked in power and splendor between AD 681 and 800 under the rulers Itzamnaaj B'alam II (Shield Jaguar II, 681–742), Pájaro Jaguar IV (Bird Jaguar IV, 752–68) and Itzamnaaj B'alam III (Shield Jaguar III, 769–800). The city was abandoned around AD 810. Inscriptions here tell more about its 'Jaguar' dynasty than is known of almost any other Maya ruling clan. The shield-and-jaguar symbol appears on many buildings and steles; Pájaro Jaguar IV's hieroglyph is a small jungle cat with feathers on its back and a bird superimposed on its head.

As you walk toward the ruins, a signed path to the right leads up to the **Pequeña Acrópolis**, a group of ruins on a small hilltop – to save sweat, visit this later. Staying on the main path, you soon reach the mazy passages of **El Laberinto** (Edificio 19), built between AD 742 and 752, during the interregnum between Itzamnaaj B'alam II and Pájaro Jaguar IV. A few bats shelter under the structure's roof today. From this complicated two-level building you emerge at the northwest end of the extensive **Gran Plaza**.

Though it's difficult to imagine anyone here ever wanting to be any hotter than they already were, **Edificio 17** was apparently a sweat house. About halfway along the plaza, **Stele 1**, under a tarp and flanked by weathered sculptures of a crocodile and a jaguar, shows Pájaro Jaguar IV in a ceremony that took place in AD 761.

The four-ton **Stele 11**, under a *palapa* at the northeastern corner of the Gran Plaza, was originally found in front of Edificio 40. The bigger of the two figures visible on it is Pájaro Jaguar IV. Up the hill, **Edificio 20**, from the time of Itzamnaaj B'alam III, was the last significant structure built at Yaxchilán; its lintels are now in Mexico City.

An imposing stairway climbs from Stele 1 to **Edificio 33**, the best-preserved temple at Yaxchilán, with about half of its roofcomb intact. The final step in front of the building is carved with ball-game scenes, and relief carvings embellish the undersides of the lintels. Inside is a statue of Pájaro Jaguar IV, minus his head, which is nearby (looters sought treasure inside his body).

From the clearing behind Edificio 33, a path leads into the trees. About 20m along this, fork left uphill (signed); go left at another fork after about 80m, and in some 10 to 15 minutes, mostly going uphill, you'll reach three buildings on a hilltop: **Edificio 39**, **Edificio 40** and **Edificio 41**.

Go back down the same way, then left at the sign to Pequeño Acropolis; after a few minutes you'll arrive there, then finally exit down the main stairs you passed on your way in.

Saraguates (howler monkeys) inhabit the tall trees at Yaxchilán, and are an evocative highlight. You'll almost certainly hear their visceral roars, and you stand a good chance of seeing some. Spider monkeys, and occasionally red macaws, are also spotted here at times.

Drinks and snacks are available at the *embarcadero* (wharf; where you'll pay the entry fee). On your boat ride in, keep your eyes peeled for crocodiles sunning on the river banks. Also note that the land on the other side of the river is Guatemala.

Getting There & Away

TOUR & PRIVATE VEHICLE

If you don't have a private vehicle, the easiest way to see both Bonampak and Yaxchilán is by taking a tour from Palenque. This is much more time efficient, less stressful and actually cheaper than dealing with public transport – and gives enough time at each site for most people. Various tour agencies in Palenque organize this tour, and each charges the same: M$550 to M$650 per person, depending on the season.

THE LACANDÓN JUNGLE

The Selva Lacandona (Lacandón Jungle), in eastern Chiapas, occupies just one-quarter of 1% of Mexico. Yet it contains more than 4300 plant species (about 17% of Mexico's total), 450 butterfly species (42% of the total), at least 340 bird species (32% of the total) and 163 mammal species (30% of the total). Among these are such emblematic creatures as the jaguar, red macaw, white turtle, tapir and harpy eagle.

This great fund of natural resources and genetic diversity is the southwestern end of the Selva Maya, a 30,000-sq-km corridor of tropical rainforest stretching from Chiapas across northern Guatemala into Belize and the southern Yucatán. But the Lacandón Jungle is shrinking fast, under pressure from ranchers, loggers, oil prospectors, and farmers desperate for land. From around 15,000 sq km in the 1950s, an estimated 3000 to 4500 sq km of jungle remains today. Waves of land-hungry settlers deforested the northern third of the Lacandón Jungle by about 1960. Also badly deforested are the far eastern Marqués de Comillas area (settled since the 1970s) and Las Cañadas, between Ocosingo and Montes Azules. Most of what's left is in the Reserva de la Biosfera Montes Azules and the neighboring Reserva de la Biosfera Lacantun.

Not surprisingly, property rights within the region have been incredibly contested. In 1971, the Mexican government deeded a large section of land to 66 Lacandón 'guardian' families, ostensibly to protect the forest from over-exploitation. This, however, created tensions with other indigenous communities who were forced off their lands and whose own claims were put aside. It also helped create the Zapatista movement, since they saw the Lacandón Jungle as land that belonged to various indigenous communities – and not just the Lacandones.

The Lacandones argued that they were defending their property against invasive settlers, and have used it wisely for ecotourism projects. Other communities within the reserve, however, viewed it as an obfuscated land grab and pretext for eviction under the guise of environmental protection. They claim that new settlers were also using the forests in sustainable ways and that research companies were seeking to utilize the forests for bioprospecting (patenting) traditional plants, thus benefiting everyone.

Because of ongoing and sometimes violent conflicts since that fateful land deed over 40 years ago, the Mexican government has not been able to clearly demarcate land borders to this day . A new carbon-sequestration program, along with economic development projects for the area, is the newest strategy for 'saving' this region, but only time will tell whether this is likely to make life any better for those living there.

A documentary film called *Keepers of the Earth* chronicles the environmental fight in the Lacandón Jungle.

Entry fees, two meals and all transportation (except a M$15 dock fee at Yaxchilán) are included, but there's no tour guide (these can be hired at each site).

Be aware that a cooperative requires ALL travelers to take a Lacandón van through their jungle to Bonampak. This happens about 3km into the side road toward the ruins; all travelers must stop at a checkpoint (whether they're in private vehicles or tour vans) and switch into a Lacandón van. The charge is high – M$70 per person for essentially a 19km round-trip ride. This charge is *already included* in the price for travelers taking the day tour from Palenque.

Private vehicles: on the Carretera Fronteriza, there's a Pemex gas station at Chancalá and another at Benemerito. Because of its location near Guatemala, expect a few military checkpoints looking for illegal immigrants or drugs; it's best not to drive this road at night.

PUBLIC TRANSPORT

To reach Bonampak from Palenque via public transport, take an hourly *combi* bound for either Frontera Corozal or Benemerito and ask to be let out at San Javier (M$60, two hours). This is the 12km turnoff for Bonampak; from here you'll have to take a Lacandón vehicle to the ruins (M$70 to M$80 per person round trip with two hours' waiting time).

The *combis* that drop you at San Javier leave from a small van depot just south of the Maya Head statue at the entrance to Palenque; look for the black grate fence next to the 'Carne Suprema' sign. They also leave from the Transportes Montebello bus terminal, which is a few blocks northwest of Palenque's center, on Velasco Suárez near the corner of Calle 4a Poniente Norte.

To reach Yaxchilán from Palenque, take an hourly *combi* bound for Frontera Corozal (M$100, 2¾ hours), where you'll have to pay a M$15-per-person charge to enter the *embarcadero* area. From here it's a 40-minute *lancha* (motorboat) ride to the ruins. All boat operators charge the same (return journey with 2½ hours' waiting time: one to three people M$700, four people M$800, five to seven people $950, eight to 10 people M$1300). *Lanchas* normally leave relatively frequently from 7am until 1:30pm or so, and it's sometimes possible to hook up with other travelers or a tour group to share costs.

It's possible to take a *combi* between the two ruins. Visit Yaxchilán first, then wait for a *combi* heading back to Palenque and ask to be let off at San Javier.

Always check when the last *combi* back to Palenque is; usually it's at 4pm or 5pm, depending on the season.

Understand Cancún, Cozumel & the Yucatán

The Yucatán Peninsula Today

Tourism is one of the driving forces behind life in the Yucatán, Mexico's most visited destination. For better or worse, the industry helps shape politics, economics and many of the region's important social issues. And because the peninsula is hands down one of the safest places in all of Mexico, the tourism economy is thriving like never before.

Best on Film

Alamar (To the Sea; 2009) Moving docudrama shot in Quintana Roo about a Maya father-and-son reunion.
Toro Negro (Black Bull; 2005) Shot in various Yucatán Maya communities, this award-winning documentary gives a disturbing portrait of a self-destructive amateur bullfighter.
Che! El Argentino (2009) The colonial city of Campeche stood in as Santa Clara, Cuba, for Steven Soderbergh's biopic about revolutionary Ernesto 'Che' Guevara.
Before Night Falls (2000) Scenes were filmed in Mérida for this Academy Award–nominated biography about Cuban poet Reinaldo Arenas.

Best in Print

Time Among the Maya (Ronald Wright; 1989) A travel memoir that explores past and present-day Maya culture and identity.
Incidents of Travel in Yucatán (John Lloyd Stephens; 1848) American writer Stephens recounts his adventures with English artist Frederick Catherwood in this classic travel book.
The Art of Mexican Cooking (Diana Kennedy; 1989) Culinary expert Diana Kennedy's definitive cookbook features mouthwatering recipes from the Yucatán.

The Return of the PRI

The beginning of the new millennium signaled a new era of Mexican politics when Vicente Fox and his Partido Acción Nacional (PAN) ended 70 years of hegemonic rule by the Partido Revolucionario Institucional (PRI). Or did it?

Even in the Yucatán, hardly known as a PAN stronghold, voters in two states elected the charismatic, probusiness Fox. In 2006 Fox handed the reins to the PAN's Felipe Calderón after he narrowly defeated the left-leaning Andres Manuel López Obrador (albeit, amid fraud allegations).

During his term, Calderón launched a 'Mundo Maya' promotional program ahead of December 21, 2012, when the Maya long-count calendrical cycle was nearing completion. With all eyes on Mexico as the media hyped the cyclical event as a 'countdown to the apocalypse,' the government seized the opportunity to plug the Yucatan's Maya ruins and to build shiny new anthropology museums.

But Calderón will be remembered instead as the president who waged war against Mexico's drug cartels. By the end of 2012, when his term ended, more than 60,000 people had died in the drug war (most of the victims were drug gang members and law enforcement officers). Fortunately the Yucatán suffered minimal drug-related violence over the years and it remains a safe haven to this day.

Calderón's unpopular drug war left the door wide open in 2012 for telegenic PRI candidate Enrique Peña Nieto. In an election allegedly rife with irregularities, Peña Nieto edged out López Obrador and the PRI was back in power. The PRI had not only made its big comeback on a federal level – all three peninsular states (Quintana Roo, Campeche and Yucatán) had PRI governors at the time that Peña Nieto took office.

Tale of Two Economies

Mexico has enjoyed three consecutive years of economic growth following the 2009 recession, and the peninsula's two busiest gateway cities, Cancún and Mérida, saw international arrivals increase by about 5% last year. In other words, tourism is alive and well in the Yucatán and that's great news for the many hotels, restaurants and tour operators who depend on a steady flow of dollars and euros pouring in each year.

Yet despite the rosy economic outlook for the tourism sector, poverty remains a pressing concern. An estimated 51% of the population in Mexico lives below the poverty line and the poorest of the poor are usually indigenous people who live in rural communities, where food, medical services and work are hard to come by. Income inequality is especially a hot-button topic in the state of Yucatán, home to one of the largest indigenous populations in the nation.

Progress at a Cost

There's no denying that the tourism boom has generated many jobs across the peninsula, as has the manufacturing industry in and around Mérida. Having said that, locals worry that rapid development is causing serious environmental and cultural degradation. Yes, the peninsula has some of the largest protected areas in Mexico, such as the Calakmul, Sian Ka'an and Ría Celestún biosphere reserves, but many citizens insist that the government needs to shift its strategy with a stronger emphasis on sustainable development in fast-growing towns and cities.

Of concern, too, is the trend for indigenous languages to be spoken less and less on the peninsula. Due to the growing demand for English speakers in the tourism industry, Maya is losing ground to English as a second language. In Quintana Roo, for instance, only 16% of state residents speak an indigenous language, while in Yucatán, which has the largest Maya population in Mexico, the number of indigenous-language speakers has dwindled to 30%.

POPULATION: **4.1 MILLION**

AREA: **148,961 SQ KM**

PENINSULA COASTLINE: **1764KM**

YUCATÁN PENINSULA REMITTANCES FROM THE US: **US$271 MILLION**

if Mexico were 100 people

60 would be mixed ancestry (mestizo)
31 would be predominantly indigenous ancestry
9 would be predominantly European ancestry

belief systems

(% of population)

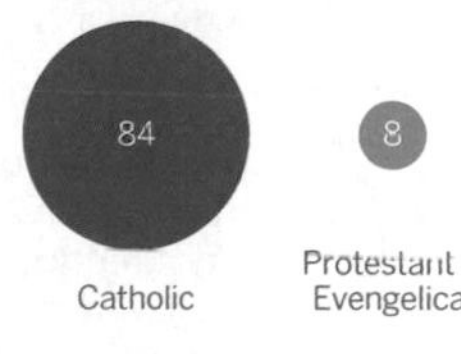

Other

population per sq km

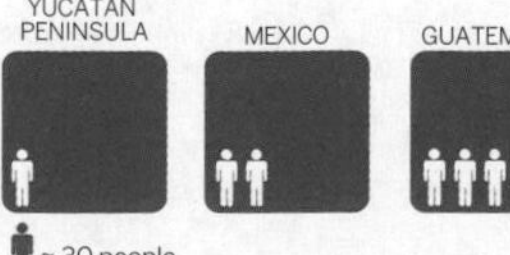

History

Reminders of the Yucatán's storied past are just about everywhere you turn on the peninsula: from extraordinary ancient Maya ruins and old-world colonial cities to Caste War battleground sites and crumbling *henequén* (sisal) haciendas. Even the relatively new kid on the block, the glitzy resort city of Cancún, has left an indelible mark on history as the region's cradle of mass tourism.

For a concise but complete account of the ancient cultures of southern Mexico and Guatemala, read *The Maya*, by Michael D Coe.

The Olmec Influence

Mexico's ancestral civilization arose near the Gulf coast, in the lowlands of southern Veracruz and neighboring Tabasco. These were the Olmecs, who invented a hieroglyphic writing system and erected ceremonial centers for the practice of religious rituals. Best known for the colossal heads they carved from basalt slabs, the Olmecs developed an artistic style, highlighted by jaguar motifs.

Even after their demise, aspects of Olmec culture lived on among their neighbors, paving the way for the later accomplishments of Maya art, architecture and science. Borrowing significantly from the Olmecs, the Zapotec culture arose in the highlands of Oaxaca at Monte Albán, and subsequent civilizations at Teotihuacán (near current-day Mexico City) and at El Tajín in Veracruz also show Olmec influence.

The Maya

Archaeologists believe Maya-speaking people first appeared in the highlands of Guatemala as early as 2500 BC, and in the following century groups of Maya relocated to the lowlands of the Yucatán Peninsula.

Agriculture played an important role in Maya life. Watching the skies and noting the movements of the planets and stars, the Maya were able to correlate their astronomical observations with the rains and agricultural cycles. As the Maya improved their agricultural skills, their society stratified into various classes. Villages sprang up beneath the jungle canopy and temples were constructed from the abundant limestone. An easily carved substance, limestone allowed the builders to demonstrate a

TIMELINE

up to 10,000BC

The first humans arrive in the Yucatán region. Numbers of grassland animals dwindle as temperatures increase over the next 2000 years, leading indigenous populations to begin larger-scale agriculture.

3114 BC

Our current universe is created – at least according to Maya mythology. Archaeologists have even been able to pin down a specific date for the creation: August 13, 3114 BC.

ROBERT FRERCK

Olmec carved head

high degree of artistic expression. The material could also be made into plaster, upon which artists painted murals to chronicle events.

Local potentates were buried beneath elaborate temple-pyramids decorated with huge stylized masks. More and more pyramids were built around large plazas, much as the common people clustered their thatched houses facing a common open space. This heralded the flourishing of the Classic Maya civilization.

The Golden Age

Over the near-seven centuries of the Classic Maya period (AD 250 to 925), the Maya made spectacular intellectual and artistic strides. The great ceremonial centers at Copán, Tikal, Yaxchilán, Palenque, and especially Kaminaljuyú (near present-day Guatemala City), flourished during the early phase of this period. Around AD 400 armies from Teotihuacán invaded the Maya highlands, imposing their rule and their culture for a time, though they were eventually absorbed into the daily life of the Maya.

After AD 600, at the height of the late Classic period, the Maya lands were ruled not as an empire but as a collection of independent – but also interdependent – city-states. Each of these had its noble house, headed by a king who was the social, political and religious focus of the city's life. This ruler propitiated the gods by shedding his blood in ceremonies where he pierced his tongue or penis with a sharp instrument, and led his soldiers into battle against rival cities, capturing prisoners for use in human sacrifices.

Toward the end of the Classic period, the focus of Maya civilization shifted northward to Yucatán, where new nuclei developed at what is now called Chichén Itzá, Uxmal and Calakmul, giving us the artistic styles known as Puuc, Chenes and Río Bec.

MUNDO MAYA

Mundo Maya online (www.mayadiscovery.com) features articles on Maya cosmology, navigation and agriculture, among other aspects of this incredible ancient civilization.

YUCATÁN'S DINOSAUR-KILLING METEORITE

For the past two decades there has been growing scientific agreement that a meteorite slammed into the Yucatán 65 million years ago, kicking up enough debris to block out the sun for a decade, which either triggered a global freeze or made the air so unbreathable that two-thirds of the earth's species became extinct.

In 1980 scientists theorized that the extinction of the dinosaurs had been caused by an 'impact event,' such as a meteor crash. Using seismic monitoring equipment, scientists found evidence for the existence of such an enormous crater off the northern coast of the Yucatán near the port of Chicxulub.

2400 BC	1000 BC–AD 250	AD 250–925	925–1530
Maya-speaking farmers arrive in the Yucatán Peninsula. The Olmec culture creates a system of writing. Olmec culture later influences the Zapotec culture.	Pre-Classic period. Maya villages appear in Yucatán, Chiapas and Guatemala. The Maya become adept farmers and astronomers. The Izapan civilization creates a calendar and writing system, and massive pyramids are built.	Classic period. It's a time of high society, marked by the invasion of Teotihuacán, the rise of the Puuc, and the eventual collapse of the Classic Maya and the ascendancy of the Toltec.	Post-Classic period. The Toltecs of central Mexico establish their domain at Chichén Itzá, then the Itzáes form the League of Mayapán, which dominates politics in northern Yucatán for 200 years.

Post-Classic Period

The Toltecs

The collapse of Classic Maya civilization is as surprising as it was sudden. It seems as though the upper classes demanded ever more servants, acolytes and laborers, and though the Maya population was expanding rapidly, it did not produce enough farmers to feed everyone in the region. Thus weakened, the Maya were effectively prey to the next wave of invaders from central Mexico.

The elite of the Classic Maya often received enemas of a sweet mead name *balché*. They also thought being cross-eyed was particularly beautiful.

In the wake of Teotihuacán's demise, the Toltec people emerged as Mexico's new boss, establishing their capital at Tula (north of present-day Mexico City). According to most historians, a Toltec faction, led by a fair-haired king named Topiltzin – the self-proclaimed heir to the title of Quetzalcóatl (Plumed Serpent) – was forced to leave its native land by hostile warrior clans. Quetzalcóatl and his followers retreated to the Gulf coast and sailed eastward to Yucatán, establishing their new base at Uucil-abnal – which would later be renamed Chichén Itzá. The culture at this Toltec-dominated center flourished after the late 10th century, when all of the great buildings were constructed, but by 1200 the city was abandoned. Many Mexicans believed, however, that the Plumed Serpent king would some day return from the direction of the rising sun to reclaim his domain at Tula.

The Itzáes

Forced by invaders to leave their traditional homeland on the Yucatán's Gulf coast, a group called the Itzáes headed southeast into northeastern Guatemala. Some continued to Belize, later making their way north along the coast and into northern Yucatán, where they settled at the abandoned Uucil-abnal around AD 1220. The Itzá leader proclaimed himself Kukulcán (the Maya name for Quetzalcóatl), as had the city's Toltec founder, and recycled lots of other Toltec lore as well. The Itzáes strengthened the belief in the sacred nature of cenotes (limestone sinkholes that provided the Maya with its water supply), and they even named their new home Chichén Itzá (Mouth of the Well of the Itzáes).

Chronicle of the Maya Kings and Queens, by Simon Martin and Nikolai Grube, tells in superbly illustrated detail the histories of 11 of the most important Maya city-states and their rulers.

From Chichén Itzá, the ruling Itzáes traveled westward and founded a new capital city at Mayapán, which dominated the political life of northern Yucatán for several centuries. From Mayapán, the Cocom lineage of the Itzáes ruled a fractious collection of *yucateco* (of the Yucatán Peninsula) city-states until the mid-15th century, when a subject people from Uxmal, the Xiú, overthrew Cocom power. Mayapán was pillaged, ruined and never repopulated. For the next century, until the coming of the conquistadors, northern Yucatán was alive with battles among its city-states.

late 1400s

Beginning of the end of the post-Classic period. Maya decline hits full tilt, as fractious city-states replace Mayapán rule. Until the coming of the conquistadors, northern Yucatán is riddled with battles and power struggles.

1492

Spanish arrive in the Caribbean, settling momentarily on Hispañola and Cuba, but it will be several hundred years before they truly 'conquer' the region. European diseases will eventually kill 90% of indigenous inhabitants.

1519–21

Hernán Cortés, first landing on Isla Cozumel, begins making his way along the Gulf coast toward central Mexico, home of the Aztec empire. He captures Aztec ruler Moctezuma II and conquers Tenochtitlán.

1527

Francisco de Montejo and his son (the Younger) land in Cozumel and then in Xel-Há with the idea of conquering the region. Eventually they return to Mexico City in defeat.

The New World Order

Led by Christopher Columbus, the Spanish arrived in the Caribbean in 1492 and proceeded to seek a westward passage to Asia. They staged exploratory expeditions to the Yucatán in 1517 and 1518, but hostile locals fiercely resisted their attempts to penetrate Mexico's Gulf coast.

Then Diego Velázquez, the Spanish governor of Cuba, asked his young personal secretary, Hernán Cortés, to lead a new expedition westward. Even though Velázquez subsequently tried to cancel the voyage, Cortés set sail on February 15, 1519, with 11 ships, 550 men and 16 horses.

Landing first at the isle of Cozumel off the Yucatán, the Spaniards were joined by Jerónimo de Aguilar, a Spanish priest who had been shipwrecked there several years earlier. With Aguilar acting as translator and guide, Cortés' force moved around the coastline to Tabasco. After defeating the inhabitants there, the expedition headed inland toward central Mexico.

Central Mexico was then dominated by the Aztec empire from its capital of Tenochtitlán (now Mexico City). The Aztecs, like many other cultures in the area, believed that Quetzalcóatl would one day return from the east, according to most historians, and (conveniently for him) Cortés' arrival coincided with their prophecies of the Plumed Serpent's return. The Aztecs allowed the small Spanish force into the capital, perhaps fearful of angering these strangers who might be gods.

By this time thousands of members of the Aztecs' subject peoples had allied with Cortés, eager to throw off the harsh rule imposed by their overlords. Many Aztecs died of smallpox introduced by the Spanish, and by the time they resolved to make war against Cortés and their subjects, they found themselves outnumbered, though they put up a tremendous fight.

Cortés would later turn his attentions to the Yucatán.

SACRED TEXTS

Check www.sacred-texts.com for good translations of two sacred Maya books, the *Popol Vuh* and *Chilam Balam of Chumayel*.

When the indigenous Xiú leader was baptized, he was made to take a Christian name, so he chose what must have appeared to him to be the most popular name of the entire 16th century – and became Francisco de Montejo Xiú.

Conquest & the Colonial Period

Despite political infighting among the *yucateco* Maya, conquest by the Spaniards was not easy. The Spanish monarch commissioned Francisco de Montejo (El Adelantado, or the Pioneer) with the task, and he set out from Spain in 1527 accompanied by his son, also named Francisco de Montejo (El Mozo, or the Lad) and a band of men. Landing first at Cozumel, then at Xel-Há on the mainland, the Montejos discovered that the local people wanted nothing to do with them.

The father-and-son team then sailed around the peninsula, quelled unrest in Tabasco in 1530 and established their base near Campeche. They pushed inland to conquer, but after four long, difficult years they were forced to return to Mexico City in defeat.

The younger Montejo took up the cause again, with his father's support, and in 1540 returned to Campeche with his cousin named...

1530–1821

The *encomienda* system basically enslaves the indigenous populations, and friars begin to convert the population in earnest. The Maya blend Christian teachings with their own beliefs, creating a unique belief system.

1542

Francisco de Montejo (the Younger) and his cousin (also Francisco de Montejo) avenges his father's legacy, establishing the colonial capital at Mérida upon the ruins of the Maya city of T'ho.

1562

Franciscan Friar Diego de Landa orders the destruction of 27 codices and more than 5000 idols in Maní, essentially cutting the historic record of the Maya at the root.

1810–21

Beginning of the War of Independence from Spain. Yucatán state joins the newly independent Mexican republic. Yucatán will declare independence from Mexico in 1841.

Francisco de Montejo. The two Montejos pressed inland with speed and success, allying themselves with the Xiú against the Cocomes, defeating the Cocomes and converting the Xiú to Christianity.

The Montejos founded Mérida in 1542 and within four years subjugated almost all of Yucatán to Spanish rule. The once proud and independent Maya became peons working for Spanish masters.

Independence for Some

Back in the 1500s traveling Maya merchants would burn incense nightly on their journeys as an offering for safe passage to the god Ek-chuah.

During the colonial period, Spain's New World was a highly stratified society, and nowhere was that more evident than on the peninsula, which operated under a repressive caste system. Native Spaniards were making the big decisions at the very top; next were the *criollos* (people born in the New World of Spanish stock); below them were the *mestizos* or *ladinos* (people of mixed Spanish and indigenous blood); and at the bottom were the pure-race indigenous people and black people. Only the native Spaniards had real power – a fact deeply resented by the *criollos*.

The harshness of Spanish rule resulted in frequent revolts, none of them successful for long, or at least not until the War of Independence. After Mexico proclaimed its independence from Spain in 1821, the state

FRIAR DIEGO DE LANDA

The Maya recorded information about their history, customs and ceremonies in beautifully painted picture books made of beaten-bark paper coated with fine lime plaster. These codices, as they are known, must have numbered in the hundreds when the conquistadors and missionary friars first arrived in the Maya lands. But because the ancient rites of the Maya were seen as a threat to the adoption and retention of Christianity, the priceless books were set aflame upon the orders of the Franciscans. Only four of the painted books survive today, but these provide much insight into ancient Maya life.

Among those Franciscans directly responsible for the burning of the Maya books was inquisitor Friar Diego de Landa, who, in July of 1562 in Maní (near present-day Ticul), ordered the destruction of 27 'hieroglyphic rolls' and 5000 idols. He also had a few Maya burned to death for good measure.

Though despised by the Maya for destroying their cultural records, it was Friar de Landa who wrote the most important existing book on Maya customs and practices – the source for much of what we know about the Maya. Recalled to Spain for displaying a degree of zeal that even the clerical authorities found unwarranted, he was put on trial for his excesses. He was ordered to jot down everything he knew about the Maya. These scribblings resulted in a book, *Relación de las Cosas de Yucatán* (An Account of the Things of Yucatán), which covers virtually every aspect of Maya life in the 1560s, from Maya houses and funeral customs to the calendar and counting system.

1847–48

The Caste War erupts. The Maya are whipped solidly at first, retreating to Quintana Roo. They continue to revolt for another 100 years, though an official surrender is signed in 1936.

1850–93

An independent Maya republic is established with its capital at Chan Santa Cruz. The war wages on, with the Maya (getting arms from the British) winning key victories. Britain stops arming the Maya in 1893.

1876–1911

The Porfiriato – the name given to the era of Porfirio Díaz' 35-year rule as president-dictator, preceding the Mexican Revolution. Under Díaz, the country is brought into the industrial age.

1901

The Mexican army, under Porfirio Díaz, recaptures the Maya-controlled territory, executing many Maya leaders and destroying the shrine of the talking cross in Chan Santa Cruz.

of Yucatán, which at that time encompassed the entire peninsula, joined the Mexican federation as a semi-autonomous entity called the Federated Republic of Yucatán.

Though independence brought new prosperity to the *criollos* of the Yucatán, it worsened the lot of the Maya. The end of Spanish rule meant that the Crown's few liberal safeguards, which had afforded the Maya minimal protection from extreme forms of exploitation, were abandoned. The new powers that be stole the Maya's land and forced them to work under miserable conditions. Eventually, everything would come to a head in the Caste War.

Of the illustrated Maya books called codices, only four survive to the present day: *Dresden Codex*, *Madrid Codex*, *Paris Codex* and *Grolier Codex*.

The Caste War

Just 20 years after independence from Spain, Yucatán's local government voted to break away from the Mexican federation in order to establish a fully sovereign republic that would guarantee individual rights and freedom of religion. Mexican president Antonio López de Santa Anna sent in troops in 1843 but Yucatán's forces managed to stave them off. Economic isolation proved to be a more powerful incentive to return to the fold, however, and a treaty was signed with Mexico that same year. But Yucatán again declared independence in 1846.

For the *yucateco* Maya, independence from Mexico made little difference – they remained subordinate to a white elite. In January 1847 indigenous rebels attacked Valladolid, rampaging through the city, killing and looting. Now alerted, federal authorities caught a Maya *batab* (community leader) with a letter detailing a plot to attack the town of Tihosuco (in present-day Quintana Roo). He was shot at Valladolid. Undaunted, the plotters attacked the town of Tepich, south of Tihosuco, and killed a number of *criollo* families. Thus began the Caste War, which spread relentlessly across the Yucatán region and raged on in some parts until the turn of the 20th century.

The website of the Foundation for the Advancement of Mesoamerican Studies (www.famsi.org) contains numerous resources for broadening your understanding of Maya history.

In little more than a year after the Valladolid uprising, the Maya revolutionaries had driven their oppressors from every part of the Yucatán except Mérida and Campeche. But then the rebels suddenly abandoned the attack and went home to plant the corn they would need to carry on the fight. This gave the *criollos* and *mestizos* a chance to regroup. Yucatán's governor appealed to England, Spain and the US for protection from the indigenous rebels, in exchange for annexation to any of those countries, but all three nations refused to help. Finally, in a desperate move to strengthen its military and economic position, Yucatán rejoined the Mexican federation in 1848, receiving aid from its former adversary and effectively regaining the upper hand against most of the insurgent forces.

But the Maya continued the fight in southern Quintana Roo, where they overwhelmed the Mexican garrison in Bacalar's San Felipe fortress

1910–20

Almost two million people die and the economy is shattered during the Mexican Revolution. Eventual agrarian reform gives much of the Yucatán back to local cooperatives called *ejidos*.

1940s

The Yucatán's once-booming *henequén* (sisal) industry collapses due to the advent of cheaper synthetic fibers.

1970s

Mexico's oil boom: widespread extraction and exploration begins in the Gulf; environmental problems go widely unchecked. In Quintana Roo another boom is taking hold, with the development of Cancún.

1976

Yucatán state elects Francisco Luna Kan, its first governor of pure Maya descent. After his term ends in 1982, it becomes more common to see high-ranking Maya politicians in Yucatán.

in 1858. By about 1866 the governments in Mexico City and Mérida gave up on the area and the British in Belize recognized an independent Maya republic, which remained virtually sovereign for the latter half of the 19th century.

Revolution, Rope & Reform

Porfirio Díaz, who definitively reclaimed current-day Quintana Roo for Mexico, ruled the country from 1876 to 1911 as a dictator, banning political opposition and free press. During this period, Díaz brought the country into the industrial age, and passed laws that created an even larger class of landless peasants and concentrated wealth in the hands of an ever-smaller elite.

The Caste War of Yucatán, by Nelson Reed, is a page-turning account of the modern Maya's insurrection against the *criollo* elite and the establishment of an independent state.

In the Yucatán, enormous fortunes were made by the owners of haciendas producing *henequén*, then a lucrative plant for making into rope and other products.

Díaz was brought down by the Mexican Revolution, a major war that erupted in 1910 and plunged the country into chaos for the next 10 years. The revolution pitted Díaz's military against the forces of revolutionary leaders such as Francisco Madero, Emiliano Zapata and Pancho Villa. In the decades following the revolution, agrarian reforms redistributed much of the peninsula's agricultural land, including many of the haciendas, into the hands of peasant cooperatives called *ejidos*.

Oil Production & Rising Tourism

In the 1970s an Organization of Petroleum Exporting Countries (OPEC) embargo sent world oil prices soaring, around the same time that vast oil reserves were discovered in the Gulf of Mexico. Mexico became the

THE TALKING CROSS

Tucked away off a quiet backstreet in the small town of Felipe Carrillo Puerto, about 95km south of Tulum, you'll find one of the most important Maya shrines at the Santuario de la Cruz Parlante (p128). The history behind the shrine is legendary, to say the least. During the Caste War, some Maya combatants sought refuge in the jungles of what is now southern Quintana Roo. There, they were inspired to continue fighting by a religious leader working with a ventriloquist, who, in 1850 at Chan Santa Cruz (present-day Felipe Carrillo Puerto), made a sacred cross 'talk.' The talking cross convinced the Maya that their gods had made them invincible, and it guided them in a decades-long struggle to maintain their independence. Even after the federal government had captured and executed the last of the rebel chiefs in 1901, local Maya kept alive a guerrilla-style resistance movement until they officially surrendered in 1936. To this day, the cross remains a tremendous source of pride for the Maya people.

1989

To the delight of nature conservationists, the federal government establishes Calakmul (in Campeche) as a biosphere reserve, making it one of the largest protected areas in Mexico.

1994

The North American Free Trade Agreement comes into effect and, lured by jobs in *maquiladoras* (for-export factories) and tourist towns like Cancún, peasants begin an exodus from the countryside.

1994

The Zapatista uprising starts in Chiapas when rebels take over San Cristóbal de las Casas. They later retreat, but continue to fight to overturn the oligarchy's centuries-old hold on land, resources and power.

2000–1

Vicente Fox of Partido Acción Nacional (PAN) elected president of Mexico, ending seven decades of autocratic rule by Partido Revolucionario Institucional (PRI). Yucatán elects PAN governor Patricio Patrón.

darling of international investors who loaned the country billions. With its newly borrowed wealth, the country invested heavily in infrastructure, including the installation of the Cantarell complex in the Bay of Campeche, which, by 1981, was producing over a million barrels of crude oil a day.

But, just as suddenly, a world oil glut caused prices to drop in 1982, leading to a serious debt crisis. As a result, the government restructured the legal framework of the *ejido* system to allow outside investment as well as privatization and sales of cooperative land.

During the 1970s window of prosperity, investment also poured into Quintana Roo for the development of Cancún, igniting the peninsula's tourism industry and radically transforming the economic panorama. As tourism grew, many of the region's Maya left their villages to find work in Cancún, Cozumel, Playa del Carmen and other tourist haunts. The rise of tourism is thought by many scholars to be the single greatest threat to the culture and language of the Maya.

But tourism also represents a very important source of income for many locals – and any issues that affect it have a serious impact on the economy. Hurricane Wilma, for instance, left behind billions of dollars in damages to hotels and restaurants after it ripped through Quintana Roo, plus the economy suffered a significant loss of tourist dollars as visitors stayed away from the area in the aftermath. On the flipside, in 2012, as the Maya long-count calendar was nearing completion, the peninsula benefited from a spike in tourism as the mass media hyped it as the coming of the apocalypse.

LOST TIME

One of the forgotten victims of the Caste War is the Maya calendar: shamans were too busy with war to keep track of the days, thus losing count. Luckily, Maya priests in the Guatemalan highlands still maintain an accurate Maya calendar.

2005

Hurricane Wilma, the largest Atlantic hurricane on record, does wide-scale damage to the tourist centers of Cancún, Cozumel, Isla Mujeres and Isla Holbox, with billions of dollars in damage to Cancún alone.

2006–07

The PAN party's Felipe Calderón holds off leftist Andres Manuel López Obrador in the 2006 election. The next year, Hurricane Dean rolls over the peninsula, leveling the Quintana Roo town of Mahahual.

2009

The misperceived dangers of swine flu and the drug war, plus the global economic crisis, trigger a 30% drop in tourist visitation.

2012

On December 21, 2012, the Maya long count reached completion, signaling the dawn of a new cycle – and not the end of the world as some media outlets were suggesting.

Yucatán Way of Life

Drawing from a blend of ancient Maya and Spanish colonial-era influences, many aspects of domestic and social life on the Yucatán Peninsula remain very much steeped in tradition. Whether you find yourself in a Maya village, a small fishing town or a bustling colonial city, folks in these parts will gladly share with you their passion for song, dance, art and all things uniquely *yucateco* (of the Yucatán Peninsula).

The Everyday Reality

Mesoweb (www.mesoweb.com), Maya Exploration Center (www.mayaexploration.org) and goMaya (www.gomaya.com) are all fabulous resources on the Maya, past and present.

Travelers often comment on the open, gentle and gregarious nature of the people of the Yucatán, especially the Maya. Here, more than elsewhere in Mexico, it seems, you find a willingness to converse and a genuine interest in outsiders. This openness is all the more remarkable when you consider that the people of the Yucatán Peninsula have fended off domination by outsiders for so long. The situation persists today – much of the land is foreign-owned and the Maya generally aren't making the big infrastructure decisions.

Maya culture is facing some difficult challenges moving forward in the 21st century as more and more young Maya people gradually abandon their language and traditions (highly rooted in an agrarian way of life) and head to Cancún or Playa del Carmen to work as busboys, waiters, maids and construction workers. But survival has always been at a premium here, and the Maya (and the region's poor) are finding ways to survive, be it by working in the service and manufacturing industries in big cities or moving to the US to work. Others are staying home and turning to community-based tourism as a means to bring in income – artisans' workshops, Maya-owned tour operators and local cooperatives all have had varying degrees of success.

Despite the winds of progress and modernization, many of the age-old traditions remain. *Yucatecos* highly value family bonds, and are only truly themselves within the context of the family – and though they are hard working, the people of the region still like to enjoy leisure pursuits to the fullest. They are also deeply religious; their faith is a mélange of

SPELLING OUT OUR STYLE

While Lonely Planet tries its darndest to keep up with linguistic trends, we've decided (purposely) to skip the latest trend in Maya orthography: adding an apostrophe to indicate a glottal stop. The apostrophe was adopted by Maya linguists and historians in 1989 as a vehicle to standardize and legitimize the language. The Maya glottal stop (most often used between two vowels) closely resembles the cockney double 't,' as used in the cockney English pronunciation of 'bottle'. Thus, if we were following the new system, Tikal would be spelled Tik'al, and Chichén Itzá would be spelled Chich'en Itza. It was a tough decision, but in the end we decided to balance out the needs of travelers (signs have yet to be converted to the new orthography) with the need to accurately document language.

pre-Hispanic beliefs and Catholicism. As with elsewhere in Mexico, the traditional gender roles may seem exaggerated to the outsider, though the level of machismo on the peninsula is somewhat less pronounced.

Life in Rural Yucatán

Perhaps more than elsewhere in Mexico, ancient rhythms and customs form part of everyday life in the Yucatán. In rural areas this is apparent on the surface level. Women wear colorfully embroidered, loose-fitting *huipiles* (long, woven, white sleeveless tunics, from the Maya regions, with intricate, colorful embroidery) as they slap out tortillas in the yard; families live in traditional oval thatched houses, rest in hammocks after a day's work, and consume a diet of corn, beans and chilies.

Various forms of Maya are widely spoken, pre-Hispanic religious rituals are still observed, and forms of social organization are followed. In some parts of the region, Maya languages prevail over Spanish, or Spanish may not be spoken at all. More than 30 Maya dialects exist, spoken by up to three million people in southern Mexico and northern Central America. Yucatec Maya is the dialect spoken on the Yucatán Peninsula. Eight Maya languages are spoken in Chiapas; Tzeltal, Tzotzil and Chol are the most widely used; the latter is believed to most closely resemble the one spoken by the Classic Maya.

Many youngsters are now choosing to leave their rural roots, heading to the *maquiladoras* (factories) of Mérida, to the megaresorts of Quintana Roo or even to the US. Rather than study Yucatec, many prefer to learn English. But still, there remains a broad, ubiquitous undercurrent of pride in Maya culture: a hopeful sign that the culture will abide.

In *The Modern Maya: A Culture In Transition*, Macduff Everton documents this period among the *yucateco* Maya with superb black-and-white photos, while reflecting on the impact of modern influences on this resilient culture.

Population at a Glance

For more than a millennium the Maya of the Yucatán have intermarried with neighboring and invading peoples. Most of Mexico's population is *mestizo* (mixture of indigenous and Spanish blood), but the Yucatán has an especially high proportion of pure-blooded Maya, about four times the national average. There are around 1.5 million Maya in southern Mexico, with about 800,000 Maya speakers. Yucatán state is second only to Oaxaca state in the number of indigenous-language speakers – about 30% of the Yucatán's population speaks Maya, while in Quintana Roo and Campeche it's about 17% and 12%, respectively.

There are 4.1 million people living in the peninsula states. Quintana Roo is the fastest growing of the three, with a 4.1% growth rate. Campeche and Yucatán ring in with about 1.6% growth each.

Mexico Online (www.mexonline.com) has good history and culture links, and lots of other information.

Passion for Sports

As with elsewhere in Mexico, *fútbol* (soccer) dominates schoolyards and playing fields around the peninsula – though baseball is the traditional Sunday afternoon sport of the rural *yucateco* Maya. Fans are customarily glued to their TV sets to watch televised matches of the region's two professional teams: Cancún's Atlante and Chiapas' Jaguares. The season is divided into two big tournaments: Torneo de Apertura (August to December) and Torneo de Clausura (January to May). Games are played over the weekend; check newspapers for details.

Béisbol (baseball) is popular in Mexico. The level of professional play is quite high, equivalent at least to AAA ball in the US. The Mexican League season runs from March to August; among its teams are the Piratas de Campeche (Campeche Pirates), Olmecas de Tabasco (Tabasco Olmecs), Leones de Yucatán (Mérida Lions) and Tigres de Quintana Roo (Quintana Roo Tigers), which won the national championship in 2011.

Fernando Venezuela, one of the most popular Mexican baseball players ever, was pitching for the Leones de Yucatán before he was signed by the Los Angeles Dodgers.

Yucatecos are also passionate about *charreadas* (rodeos). These events are staples of *ferias* (fairs) around the peninsula.

Hybrid Religion

Among the region's indigenous populations, ancient Maya beliefs blend and mix nearly seamlessly with contemporary Christian traditions – the values and rituals of the two religions are remarkably similar. Today's Maya identify themselves as Catholic but they practice a Catholicism that is a fusion of shamanist-animist and Christian ritual. The traditional religious ways are so important that often a Maya will try to recover from a malady by seeking the advice of a religious shaman rather than a medical doctor. Use of folk remedies linked with animist tradition is widespread in Maya areas.

In a visit to the church at the Tzotzil village of San Juan Chamula, you may see chanting *curanderos* (healers) carrying out shamanic rites.

Mestizos and *criollos* (Creoles; born in Latin America of Spanish parentage) are more likely to follow strict Catholic doctrine, although here, like nearly everywhere else in Latin America, Catholicism is fast losing ground to evangelical sects.

Roman Catholicism accounts for the religious orientation of around 80% of contemporary *yucatecos,* while 11% of the Yucatán's population identify themselves as Protestants or evangelicals. Congregations affiliated with churches such as the Assemblies of God, the Seventh Day Adventists, the Church of Jesus Christ of Latter-day Saints and Jehovah's Witnesses can also be found in the Yucatán.

Arts & Traditional Dress

The Yucatán's arts and crafts scene is enormously rich and varied. The influence of the Maya or Spanish cultures (or both) appears in almost every facet of *yucateco* art, from dance to music to fashion.

Literature

One of Yucatán's earliest-known literary works is the *Chilam Balam of Chumayel.* Written in Maya after the conquest, it is a compendium of Maya history, prophecy and mythology collected by priests from the northern Yucatán town of Chuyamel. It has been translated into English.

Tulum, Chichén Itzá and Isla Cozumel provided backdrops for the 1984 romantic thriller *Against All Odds,* starring Jeff Bridges and Rachel Ward.

Diego de Landa, the Spanish friar, could be said to have produced the first literary work from the Yucatán in Spanish, *Relación de las Cosas de Yucatán* (An Account of the Things of Yucatán), in which he relates his biased perception of the Maya's ceremonial festivals, daily life and traditions, even as he engineered their eradication.

Aside from (unsuccessfully) seeking US intervention against the Maya during the Caste War, Justo Sierra O'Reilly is credited with writing what is possibly the first Mexican novel, *La Hija del Judio* (The Jew's Daugh-

GAME OF DEATH

Probably all pre-Hispanic Mexican cultures played some version of a Mesoamerican ritual ball game, the world's first-ever team sport. The game varied from place to place and era to era, but had certain lasting features. Over 500 ball courts have survived at archaeological sites around Mexico and Central America. The game seems to have been played between two teams, and its essence was to keep a rubber ball off the ground by flicking it with hips, thighs, knees or elbows. The vertical or sloping walls alongside the courts were most likely part of the playing area. The game had (at least sometimes) deep religious significance, serving as an oracle, with the result indicating which of two courses of action should be taken. Games could be followed by the sacrifice of one or more of the players – whether winners or losers, no one is sure.

ter), about the ill-fated romance of a Jewish merchant's daughter in colonial Mexico.

In more recent times, *yucateco* author Ermilio Abreu Gómez synthesized the peninsula's Maya heritage in fictional works such as the novel *Canek: History and Legend of a Maya Hero*, the story of an indigenous laborer's struggle against injustice.

Novelist, playwright and art critic Juan García Ponce, who died in 2003, is perhaps the Yucatán's best-known modern literary figure. *Imagen Primera* (First Image) and *La Noche* (The Night), collections of his short stories, make good starting points for exploring his work.

Music

Two styles of music are traditionally associated with the Yucatán: the *jarana* and *trova yucateca.*

A type of festive dance music, a *jarana* is generally performed by a large ensemble consisting of two trumpets, two clarinets, one trombone, a tenor sax, timbales and a guiro (percussion instrument made from a grooved gourd). The music pauses for the singers to deliver *bombas* – ad-libbed verses, usually with a humorous double meaning, that are aimed at the object of their affections. A *jarana* orchestra always ends its performances with the traditional *torito,* a vivacious song that evokes the fervor of a bullfight.

A hybrid of Cuban, Spanish, Colombian and homegrown influences, the *trova yucateca* is a catchall term for romantic ballads, Cuban claves, tangos, boleros, *yucateco* folk songs and other tunes that can be strummed on a guitar by a *trovador* (troubador). The style is often played by the guitar trios who roam the squares of Mérida seeking an audience to serenade. In a *trova,* as with *jaranas,* the subject matter is usually a suitor's paean of love to an unattainable sweetheart.

A more contemporary figure of *yucateco* song is Armando Manzanero, the singer and composer from Mérida. Though Manzanero speaks to an older generation, his songs are still being covered by contemporary pop stars like Luis Miguel and Alejandro Sanz.

On the Caribbean coast, local DJs spin electronic music, and Cuban-style salsa is popular as well.

Music festivals abound on the peninsula, particularly in Mérida, Playa del Carmen and Campeche. The fests stage traditional and contemporary acts from Mexico and abroad. The Mérida government's website (www.merida.gob.mx/cultura) is a great source for music festivals and live events.

Lively Dance

The Spanish influence on Maya culture is abundantly evident in the *jarana,* a dance *yucatecos* have been performing for centuries. The dance bears more than a passing resemblance to the *jota,* performed in Spain's Alto Aragón region. The movements of the dancers, with their torsos held rigid and a formal distance separating men from women, are nearly identical; however, whereas the Spanish punctuate elegant turns of their wrists with clicks of their castanets, Maya women snap their fingers.

The best place to see dancers perform to the accompaniment of *jarana* is at *vaquerías* – homegrown fiestas held in the atriums of town halls or on haciendas. The women wear their best embroidered *huipiles,* flowers in their hair and white heels; men wear a simple, white cotton outfit with a red bandanna tucked into the waist. In Mérida, you can catch traditional dance performances at Plaza Grande on Sunday afternoon and Monday night.

APOCALYPTO

Mel Gibson's Oscar-nominated *Apocalypto* (2006) was the first major Yucatec Maya–language film. Shot in Veracruz, it drew wide criticism for its portrayal of the Maya; Gibson insisted it was a fictional account.

Guty Cárdenas, un Siglo del Ruiseñor, produced by prestigious Mexican record label Discos Corasón (www.corason.com), includes a CD and DVD covering the musical career of this seminal *yucateco* composer/performer.

MIND YOUR MANNERS

Some indigenous people adopt a cool attitude toward visitors: they have come to mistrust outsiders after five centuries of rough treatment. They don't like being gawked at by tourists and can be very sensitive about cameras. Ask for permission before taking a photo.

Tales from the Yucatan Jungle: Life in a Mayan Village, by Kristine Ellingson, is the story of an American expat who discovers a new world while living in a Maya community.

Traditional Attire

Women throughout the Yucatán Peninsula traditionally wear *huipiles,* the bodices of which are always embroidered. The tunic generally falls to just below the knee; on formal occasions it is worn with a lacy white underskirt that reaches the ankle. The *huipil* never has a belt, which would defeat its airy, cool design. Light and loose fitting, these garments are ideally suited for the tropics. Maya women have been wearing *huipiles* for centuries.

Men commonly wear *guayaberas* (light, elegant shirts, usually with four square pockets). They can be worn in both casual and formal settings, and the cotton and linen materials keep a body cool on warm, humid days.

Yucatán Cuisine

We hope you're hungry because on the Yucatán Peninsula you are in for a real feast. *Yucatecos* (of the Yucatán Peninsula), are enormously proud of their history and cultural background, and they love sharing it with you at the table. Relative geographic isolation from the rest of the country, together with a strong Maya influence, have made *la cocina yucateca* the Mexican regional cuisine with the most distinctive personality, and as you travel around the region you'll find a cuisine based on ingredients and techniques unheard of anywhere else in Mexico.

On the Table

The staples of Mexican food – corn, and an array of dry and fresh chilies and beans – are also basic ingredients in the Yucatán. *Achiote* (the seeds from the annatto flower), *epazote* (a herb called pigweed or Jerusalem oak in the US), *chaya* (a shrub also known as tree spinach), *cat* (a variety of cucumber) and the habanero chili are some of the regional ingredients that are building blocks of *la cocina yucateca.*

Mauricio Velázquez de León was born in Mexico City, where he was given boiled chicken feet and toasted corn tortillas to sooth his teething pains. He is the author of *My Foodie ABC: A Little Gourmet's Guide* (Duo Press, 2010) and lives in Maryland with his wife and twin sons, whose teething pains were soothed with toasted corn tortillas.

Getting Started

On the Yucatán Peninsula you will find an array of typical *antojitos* using corn as the base. The word *antojitos* translates as 'little whims, a sudden craving.' But as any Mexican will quickly point out, it is not just a snack. You can have an entire meal of *antojitos*, or have a couple as appetizers. A classic *yucateco antojito* is *panuchos* – lightly fried, thin-layered tortillas topped with meat, shredded poultry or *cazón* (dogfish). In Maya, *kots'* refer to small stuffed tacos, and that is exactly what minced pork *codzitos* are. *Papadzules* are tortillas filled with hard-boiled egg and bathed in pumpkin-seed sauce, along with a few drops of pumpkin-seed oil.

The peninsula is also distinguished for its variety of tamales. Tamales are made with *masa* (dough) mixed with lard; they are stuffed with stewed meat, fish or vegetables, then wrapped and steamed. Tamale comes from the Nahuatl word *tamalli* and refers to anything wrapped up. *Tamalitos al vapor* are small tamales filled with pork and a sauce made from tomatoes, *epazote* and *achiote*, and wrapped in banana leaves. The *muc bil pollo* is a tamale prepared traditionally on Día de Muertos (Day of the Dead). *El brazo de indio* (Indian Arm) is a large tamale that can be 28cm long and 10cm wide. It is made by rolling layers of *masa* and *chaya* leaves.

TIPPING & TAXES

A mandatory *impuesto de valor agregado* (IVA, or value-added tax; 16%) is added to restaurant checks in Mexico, but the *propina* (gratuity) is not. The average tip is 10% to 15%, or 20% for excellent service.

LOVE STORY

According to legend, *balché* (an alcoholic Maya spirit) was created as an act of love between a beautiful Maya girl Sak-Nicté (White Flower) and a brave young warrior. As the story goes, the young couple fled their tribe when a powerful *cacique* (indigenous chief) also declared his love to Sak-Nicté. After days of wandering in the forest, the lovebirds found a honeycomb. Sak-Nicté and the warrior had a feast with the sweet honey, and decided to save some inside the trunk of a *balché* tree. That night brought rain and thunder, and the water blended with the honey inside the tree creating a luscious beverage.

When the *cacique* found them, he ordered Sak-Nicté to return to her tribe. The young warrior was devastated and in a desperate attempt to keep his lover at his side, he offered to cook a fantastic meal for the *cacique*. The *cacique* accepted and the couple served him a banquet, crowned with the sweet drink they had discovered. The *cacique* was so impressed with the *balché* that he let the two lovers go, under the condition that they share with him how to prepare it.

The Main Attraction

Some *yucateco* dishes take the name of the cities and towns from where they were created. Motul is the birthplace of *huevos motuleños,* fried eggs and beans on a tortilla topped with tomato sauce, cheese, ham, and green peas. *Longaniza de Valladolid* is a chorizo sausage that has been smoked for up to 12 hours, and *pollo ticuleño* (chicken rubbed with *recado rojo* – red marinade) hails from Ticul.

Cochinita pibil is the region's most famous dish. In Maya 'pib' means a hole in the ground, and *'al pibil'* is a centuries-old regional technique for cooking all kinds of meats. Originally *pibil keh* (venison) was all the rage. Today *lechón* (piglet) is the meat of choice, hence the name *cochinita,* meaning little pig, although many places use meat from adult pigs. It's prepared by rubbing the meat with *recado rojo,* which is thinned using the juice of sour oranges. The meat is then wrapped in banana leaves and cooked underground or in an oven for up to eight hours. It is usually served shredded and topped with pickled red onions. You can make *tacos de cochinita pibil* with corn tortillas or use it for *tortas* (sandwiches).

Another popular dish is *pavo en escabeche,* where turkey is marinated in *recado rojo*, then simmered in water and roasted *xcatic* chili (a mild local chili similar to Hungarian wax pepper), and then grilled before serving. *Caldo de pavo* (turkey soup) is also popular, but *sopa de lima* is the favorite *yucateco* soup. This is a local version of chicken soup using tomatoes, *chile dulce* (sweet chili), chopped onion, lightly fried tortilla strips and lime.

With the Caribbean Sea to the east and the Gulf of Mexico to the north and west, you can expect an incredible array of fish and seafood dishes on the Yucatán Peninsula. *Mariscos* (shellfish) and *pescado* (fish) are prepared *al ajillo* (in garlic and *guajillo* chili sauce), *a la plancha* (grilled) or *a la diabla* (with garlic, tomato and *cascabel* chili). *Achiote* is used in dishes like *tikin-xit*, fish wrapped in banana leaves and then grilled. Crab is famous in the coastal lagoons of the Gulf, such as Celestún and Laguna de Términos, and is served in many forms, especially in *chilpachole* (crab soup with *epazote*, tomatoes and smoky chili chipotle).

Salud!

Alcoholic Drinks

Like elsewhere in Mexico, on the peninsula you will find the popular tequila and its cousin *mezcal.* Both spirits are distilled from the agave plant; one difference is that tequila comes from blue agave in the central state of Jalisco, and is protected with Denomination of Origin status.

Cerveza (beer) is also widely available, and although you can find all national brands, such as Corona and Dos Equis, two local beers stand out: the lager Montejo and the darker León.

Balché is a Maya spirit that was offered to the gods during special ceremonies. It is fermented inside the hollow trunk of the *balché* tree with water and honey. In Valladolid, during indigenous weddings, the bride is sprayed with *balché* as a sign of abundance. *Balché* is not commercially available, but another Maya spirit, *xtabentún,* is easy to find in the region. *Xtabentún* is an anise-flavored liqueur that, when authentic, is made by fermenting honey.

Nonalcoholic Drinks

The great variety of fruits, plants and herbs that grow in the Yucatán Peninsula are a perfect fit for the kind of nonalcoholic drinks Mexicans love. *Juguerías* (small establishments selling fresh-squeezed juices) are widely available. In some cases they will serve local fruits, like mangos, *cayumito* (a purple plumlike fruit), *zapote negro* (black fruit with a pearlike consistency) and *marañón* (cashew fruit). *Juguerías* also sell *licuados,* a Mexican version of a milkshake that normally includes banana, milk, honey and fruit.

Aguas frescas (fresh drinks made with fruit, herbs or flowers) are standard Mexican refreshments. Some of them resemble iced teas. In *agua de tamarindo* the tamarind pods are boiled and then mixed with sugar before being chilled, and the *agua de jamaica* is made with dried hibiscus leaves. Others like *horchata* are made with melon seeds and/or rice. Two local favorites are *agua de chia* (a plant from the salvia family), which is typical during Holy Week celebrations in Chiapas and, on the rest of the peninsula, the leaves from the native shrub *chaya* are mixed with lime, honey and pineapple to create *agua de chaya.*

Fiestas

Food and fiestas go hand-in-hand. During the spring *ch'a chaak* ceremony, which takes place in agricultural villages around the peninsula, tortillas and turkey are traditionally offered up to the rain gods and then eaten. The tortillas are made into 'layered cakes,' with ground squash seeds, beans and other vegetables, wrapped in banana leaves and buried to be cooked over charcoals. Turkey and other wild game is cooked in *kol,* a broth thickened with masa. Men drink *balché.*

During Día de Muertos (Day of the Dead) on November 2 it is traditional in many areas of the peninsula to eat a special tamale called *muc*

ANCIENT CHOCOLATE

Archaeologists in the Yucatán recently detected chocolate residue on plate fragments believed to be about 2500 years old, meaning the ancient Maya may have used it as a spice or cacao sauce similar to *mole.*

SAVOR THE RECADO FLAVOR

Recado is the generic name used for the local rubs or marinades that combine dry chilies, spices, herbs and vinegar, and are applied to meats and poultry. The Maya called the *recados 'kuux,'* and they are essential to preparing an array of dishes on the peninsula. Not so long ago you could find *recauderías* (spice stores) in most towns and cities. Today this name is only used to designate some market stalls dedicated to selling spices and dry chilies. Some popular *recados* are *recado blanco* (white), which contains oregano, garlic, cloves, cinnamon, salt, pepper and sour oranges. It's also known as *recado de puchero* because it is used for cooking *puchero,* a hearty beef and vegetable stew. *Recado negro* (black) consists of corn tortillas and local chilies that are charred (hence the color) with an array of spices. It's the foundation of one the region's classic dishes: *relleno negro* - turkey stuffed with minced pork, dried fruits, tomatoes and *epazote* (a herb). But the most famous of all is *recado rojo* (red), which contains black and red pepper, oregano, cloves, cinnamon, salt, water and the *achiote* (annatto) seeds that infuse an intense red color and flavor to *cochinita pibil* and other regional favorites. *Recado rojo* is sometimes simply called *achiote,* but this refers to the prepared paste and not to the *achiote* flower.

H IS FOR HOT, HABANERO & HELP!

That's right, the habanero, among the hottest chilies grown on our planet, finds its home in Yucatán, and it's a foundation of its cuisine. Does this mean that everything you're going to eat will burn your mouth? No. Despite the fierce reputation of the habanero chili, *yucateco* food is not spicy. The habanero is most commonly found in table salsas, and it is up to you how much to add to the dish. The habanero grown in Yucatán has an international reputation for being a high-quality pepper with a bright-orange color, and one of the highest numbers of Scoville Heat Units found in any pepper.

This method, developed by American scientist Wilbur Scoville to measure the piquancy in chilies, quantifies the amount of the chemical compound capsaicin found in chilies. The habanero can have between 100,000 and 500,000 units. In comparison, a jalapeño chili has between 5000 and 15,000 units.

The heat of the habanero is relentless and will spread quickly throughout your mouth. No matter what your instincts tell you, don't drink water, and don't even think about reaching for that beer. Any liquid will spread the flames deeper into your mouth. Instead, eat something that will neutralize the capsaicin: bread, beans or rice are good options. Chocolate is by far the best antidote to cut the burning sensation caused by a hot pepper.

bil pollo. In Maya *mukbil* means buried and that is how this tamale is made. Corn *masa* is mixed with beef broth and placed inside a container covered with banana leaves. The *masa* is stuffed with chicken and pork meat that has been cooked with *achiote, chile dulce, epazote,* onion and habanero chili, and it's wrapped with more banana leaves and tied. The tamale is buried and covered with charcoal and sand.

When & Where

Meal times in Mexico are different from other countries, and if you're outside one of the major tourist destinations, like Cancún, restaurants close early. *Desayuno* (breakfast) is usually served in restaurants and cafeterias from 8am to 11am. Those who have a light breakfast or skip it altogether can have an *almuerzo* (a type of brunch) or an *antojito* or another type of quick bite. *Loncherías* (places that serve light meals) are good options for an *almuerzo*.

The strongest demand for habanero chili grown in Yucatán comes from Japan. Japanese companies normally buy the chili in its powder form and add it to a wide variety of snacks.

The main meal is the *comida*. It's usually served from 2pm to 5pm. Places called *fondas* are small, family-run eateries that serve *comida corrida,* an inexpensive set menu that includes three or four courses and a beverage. *La cena* (dinner) is served anytime after 7pm, and restaurants in small towns rarely open beyond 9pm. Many restaurants close on Monday.

Cantinas are the traditional Mexican watering holes. Beer, tequila and *cubas* (rum and cola) are served at square tables where patrons play dominoes and watch soccer games on large TV screens. Many cantinas often serve *botanas* (appetizers).

Vegetarians & Vegans

Mexicans think of a vegetarian as a person who doesn't eat red meat. Many have never heard the word *veganista* (Spanish term for vegan). The good news is that almost every city, large or small, has real vegetarian restaurants, and their popularity is increasing. Also, many traditional Mexican and *yucateco* dishes are vegetarian. Be warned, however, that many dishes are prepared using chicken or beef broth, or some kind of animal fat, such as *manteca* (lard). Most waiters would be happy to help you in choosing vegetarians or vegan dishes, but you have to make your requirements clear.

Keep in mind that if you have a delicate constitution, only eat unpeeled fruit and uncooked veggies in higher-end restaurants.

Food & Drink Glossary

MEAT & POULTRY

a la parilla	a la pa·*ree*·ya	grilled
a la plancha	a la *plan*·cha	pan-broiled
albóndigas	al·*bon*·dee·gas	meatballs
aves	*a*·ves	poultry
bistec	*bis*·tek	steak
borrego	bo·*re*·ga	sheep
carne (asada)	*kar*·ne (a·*sa*·da)	meat (grilled beef)
carne de puerco	*kar*·ne de *pwer*·ko	pork
carne de res	*kar*·ne de res	beef
chicharrones	chee·cha·*ro*·nes	deep-fried pork skin
chorizo	cho·*ree*·so	Mexican-style sausage made with chili and vinegar
frijol con puerco	fri·*khol* kon *pwer*·ko	*Yucateco*-style pork and beans, topped with a sauce made with grilled tomatoes, and decorated with garnishes; served with rice
jamón	kha·*mon*	ham
lechón	le·*chon*	suckling pig
milanesa	mee·la·*ne*·sa	breaded beef cutlet
pavo	*pa*·vo	turkey
pibil	pee·*beel*	meat wrapped in banana leaves, flavored with *achiote*, garlic, sour orange, salt and pepper, and baked in a pit oven; the two main varieties are *cochinita pibil* (suckling pig) and *pollo pibil* (chicken)
picadillo	pee·ka·*dee*·yo	a ground beef filling that often includes fruit and nuts
poc-chuc	pok·chook	tender pork strips marinated in sour orange juice, grilled and served topped with a spicy onion relish
pollo	*po*·yo	chicken
puchero	pu·*che*·ro	a stew of pork, chicken, carrots, squash, potatoes, plantains and *chayote* (vegetable pear), spiced with radish, fresh cilantro and sour orange
tocino	to·*see*·no	bacon
venado	ve·*na*·do	venison, a popular traditional dish

SEAFOOD

calamar	ka·la·*mar*	squid
camarones	ka·ma·*ro*·nes	shrimp
cangrejo	kan·*gre*·kho	large crab
ceviche	se·*vee*·che	raw fish, marinated in lime juice
filete	fee·*le*·te	fillet
langosta	lan·*gos*·ta	lobster
mariscos	ma·*rees*·kos	shellfish
ostiones	os·*tyo*·nes	oysters
pescado	pes·*ka*·do	fish as food
pulpo	*pool*·po	octopus

EGGS		
(huevos) estrellados	*(hwe*·vos) es·tre·*ya*·dos	fried (eggs)
huevos motuleños	*hwe*·vos mo·too·*le*·nyos	'eggs in the style of Motul'; fried eggs atop a tortilla, garnished with beans, peas, chopped ham, sausage, grated cheese and a certain amount of spicy chili
huevos rancheros	*hwe*·vos ran·*che*·ros	fried eggs served on a corn tortilla, topped with a sauce of tomato, chilies and onions
huevos revueltos	*hwe*·vos re·*vwel*·tos	scrambled eggs
SOUP		
caldo	*kal*·do	broth or soup
consomé	con·so·*may*	broth made from chicken or mutton base
sopa	*so*-pa	soup, either 'wet' or 'dry' as in rice and pasta
sopa de lima	*so*·pa de *lee*·ma	'lime soup'; chicken broth with bits of shredded chicken, tortilla strips, lime juice and chopped lime
SNACKS		
antojitos	an·to·*khee*·tos	'little whims,' corn- and tortilla-based snacks, such as tacos and *gorditas*
empanada	em·pa·*na*·da	pastry turnover filled with meat, cheese or fruits
enchiladas	en·chee·*la*·das	corn tortillas dipped in chili sauce, wrapped around meat or poultry and garnished with cheese
gordita	gor·*dee*·ta	thick, fried tortilla, sliced open and stuffed with eggs, sausage etc, and topped with lettuce and cheese
panuchos	pa·*noo*·chos	Yucatán's favorite snack: a handmade tortilla stuffed with mashed black beans, fried till it puffs up, then topped with shredded turkey or chicken, onion and slices of avocado
papadzules	pa·pad·*zoo*·les	tortillas stuffed with chopped hard-boiled eggs and topped with a sauce of marrow squash (zucchini) or cucumber seeds
papas fritas	*pa*·pas *free*·tas	french fries
quesadilla	ke·sa·*dee*·ya	cheese and other items folded inside a tortilla and fried or grilled
relleno negro	re·*ye*·no *ne*·gro	turkey stuffed with chopped, spiced pork and served in a rich, dark sauce
(queso) relleno	(*ke*·so) re·*le*·no	stuffed (cheese), Dutch edam filled with minced meat and spices
salbutes	sal·*boo*·tes	same as *panuchos* but without the bean stuffing
sope	*so*·pe	thick corn-dough patty lightly grilled, served with salsa, beans, onions and cheese
torta	*tor*·ta	sandwich in a roll, often spread with beans and garnished with avocado slices
DESSERTS		
helado	e·*la*·do	ice cream
nieve	*nye*·ve	sorbet
paleta	pa·*le*·ta	popsicle
pastel	pas·*tel*	cake
postre	*pos*·tre	dessert

FRUIT & VEGETABLES

aceituna	a·say·*too*·na	olive
calabacita	ka·la·ba·*see*·ta	squash
cebolla	se·*bo*·lya	onion
champiñones	sham·pee·*nyo*·nes	mushrooms
coco	*ko*·ko	coconut
elote	e·*lo*·te	corn on the cob
ensalada	en·sa·*la*·da	salad
fresa	*fre*·sa	strawberry
frijoles	fri·*kho*·les	beans
guayaba	gwa·*ya*·ba	guava
jícama	*khee*·ka·ma	turniplike tuber, often sliced and garnished with chili and lime; sweet, crunchy and refreshing
jitomate	khee·to·*ma*·te	tomato
lechuga	le·*choo*·ga	lettuce
limón	lee·*mon*	lemon
maíz	mai·*ees*	corn
papas	*pa*·pas	potatoes
piña	*pee*·nya	pineapple
plátano macho	*pla*·ta·no *ma*·cho	plantain
plátano	*pla*·ta·no	banana
toronja	to·*ron*·kha	grapefruit
verduras	ver·*doo*·ras	vegetables

CONDIMENTS & OTHER FOODS

achiote	a·*cho*·te	reddish paste obtained from annatto seeds
arroz	a·*roz*	rice
azúcar	a·soo·*kar*	sugar
mantequilla	man·te·*kee*·ya	butter
mole	*mo*·le	a handmade chocolate and chili sauce
pan	pan	bread
sal	sal	salt

DRINKS

agua mineral	*a*·gwa mee·ne·*ral*	mineral water or club soda
agua purificada	*a*·gwa poo·ree·fee·*ka*·da	bottled uncarbonated water
atole	a·*to*·le	corn-based hot drink flavored with cinnamon or fruit
café (con leche/ lechero)	ka·*fe* (kon *le*·che/le·*che*·ro)	coffee (with hot milk)
café americano	ka·*fe* a·me·ree·*ka*·no	black coffee
caguama	ka·*gwa*·ma	liter bottle of beer
horchata	hor·*cha*·ta	rice drink
jamaica	kha·*may*·ka	hibiscus flower, chief ingredient of *agua de jamaica*, a cold tangy tea
jugo de naranja	*khoo*·go de na·*ran*·kha	orange juice
leche	*le*·che	milk
té negro	te *ne*·gro	black tea

The Ancient Maya

Not only did the ancient Maya leave behind absolutely stunning architectural monuments, but their vision of the world and beyond remains a source of mystery and intrigue to this day. In fact, all across the peninsula ancient Maya culture and knowledge live on today – most certainly a testament to a wondrous past.

Maya pyramids were painted in brilliant red, green, yellow and white colors, and the people of the region often painted their bodies red.

Religion & Spirituality

The Sacred World-Tree & Xibalbá

For the Maya, the world, the heavens and the mysterious 'unseen world' or underworld, called Xibalbá (shi-bahl-*bah*), were all one great, unified structure that operated according to laws of astrology and ancestor worship. The towering ceiba tree was considered sacred. It symbolized the Wakah-Chan (*Yaxché*, or World-Tree), which united the 13 heavens, the surface of the earth and the nine levels of the underworld of Xibalbá.

Compass Cosmology

In Maya cosmology, each point of the compass had special religious significance. East was most important, as it was where the sun was reborn each day; its color was red. West was black because it was where the sun disappeared. North was white and was the direction from which the all-important rains came, beginning in May. South was yellow because it was the sunniest point of the compass.

Everything in the Maya world was seen in relation to these cardinal points (eg the direction in which a building faced), with the World-Tree at the center, and they were the base for the all-important astronomical and astrological observations that determined fate.

Bloodletting & Piercings

Just as the great cosmic dragon (or the upperworld, if you will) shed its blood, which fell to the earth as rain, so humans had to shed blood to link themselves with the underworld of Xibalbá.

As illustrated in various Maya stone carvings and painted pottery, the nobility customarily drew their own blood on special occasions, such as royal births or deaths, crop plantings, victories on the battlefield or accession to the throne. Blood represented royal lineage (as it does in other societies), and so the blood of kings granted legitimacy to these events. Often using the spine of a manta ray as a lancet, a noble would pierce his cheek, lower lip, tongue or genitalia and pull a piece of rope or straw through the resulting orifice to extract the sacred substance. Performed for lower-ranking members of the nobility or occasionally before dumbstruck commoners, the excruciating ritual served not only to sanctify the event but to appease the gods, as well as to communicate with them through the hallucinogenic visions that often resulted from such self-mutilation.

Ah Tz'ib (scribes) wrote the sacred texts of the Maya, including the *Chilam Balam of Chumayel*. *H-menob* (shamans) and *Ah Tz'ib* still practice their craft throughout the peninsula.

Sacred Places

Maya ceremonies were performed in natural sacred places as well as in their artificial equivalents. Mountains, caves, lakes, cenotes (limestone sinkholes), rivers and fields were all sacred. Pyramids and temples were thought of as stylized mountains; sometimes they had secret chambers within them, like the caves in a mountain. A cave was the mouth of the creature that represented Xibalbá, and to enter it was to enter the spirit of the secret world. This is why you'll see that some Maya temples have doorways surrounded by huge masks: as you enter the door of this 'cave,' you are entering the mouth of Xibalbá.

The plazas around which the pyramids were placed symbolized the open fields or the flat land of the tropical forest. What we call stelae were to the Maya 'tree-stones'; that is, tree-effigies echoing the sacredness of the World-Tree. These tree-stones were often carved with the figures of great Maya kings, for the king was the World-Tree of Maya society.

As these places were sacred, it made sense for succeeding Maya kings to build new and ever grander temples directly over older temples, enhancing the sacred character of a spot. The temple being covered over was preserved, as it remained a sacred artifact. Certain features of these older temples, such as the large masks on the facades, were carefully padded and protected before the new construction was placed over them.

Ancestor worship and genealogy were very important to the Maya, and when they buried a king beneath a pyramid, or a commoner beneath the floor or courtyard of his or her *na* (thatched Maya hut), the sacredness of the location was increased.

Similarities with Christianity

The World-Tree had a sort of cruciform shape and when, in the 16th century, Franciscan friars required the indigenous population to venerate the cross, this Christian symbolism meshed easily with established Maya beliefs.

The ceiba tree's cruciform shape was not the only correspondence the Maya found between their animist beliefs and Christianity. Both traditional Maya animism and Catholicism have rites of baptism and confession, days of fasting and other forms of abstinence, religious partaking of alcoholic beverages, burning of incense and the use of altars.

The *Popol Vuh* legends include some elements that made it easier for the Maya to understand certain aspects of Christian belief, such as

MAYA 'BIBLE': UNRAVELING THE SECRETS OF POPOL VUH

The history, prophesies, legends and religious rites of the Maya were preserved on painted codices and through oral traditions. Nearly all of these codices were destroyed during the time of the conquest (only four survive today), effectively cutting the historic record of the Maya. Lucky for Mayanologists, the *Popol Vuh,* known to many as the Maya Bible, recaptured these myths and sacred stories.

The *Popol Vuh* is said to be written by the Quiché Maya of Guatemala, who had learned Spanish and the Latin alphabet from the Dominican friars – the text was written in Latin characters rather than hieroglyphics. The authors showed their book to Francisco Ximénez, a Dominican who lived and worked in Chichicastenango, in Guatemala, from 1701 to 1703. Friar Ximénez copied the Maya book word for word and then translated it into Spanish. Both his copy and the Spanish translation survive, but the original has been lost.

According to the *Popol Vuh,* the great god K'ucumatz created humankind first from mud. But these 'earthlings' were weak and dissolved in water, so K'ucumatz tried again using wood. The wood people had no hearts or minds and could not praise their creator, so they were destroyed, all except the monkeys who lived in the forest, who are the descendants of the wood people. The creator tried once again, this time successfully, using substances recommended by four animals – the gray fox, the coyote, the parrot and the crow. White and yellow corn were ground into meal to form the flesh, and stirred into water to make the blood.

SWEATING OUT EVIL SPIRITS IN A MAYA TEMAZCAL

The *temazcal* (sweat lodge) has always been a cornerstone of indigenous American spiritual life. The Maya, like their brothers to the north, were no different, using the *temazcal* for both ceremonial and curative purposes.

The word *temazcal* derives from the Aztec word *teme* (to bathe) and *calli* (house). The Maya people used these bathhouses not just to keep clean, but also to heal any number of ailments. Most scholars say they were most likely used during childbirth as well. Large bath complexes have been discovered at several Maya archaeological sites. Ironically, the hygienically suspect conquistadors considered the *temazcales* dirty places and strongholds of sin. To this day, they are used by the Maya (and tourists) for bathing and to keep those evil spirits away.

the virgin birth. As the story goes, a virgin underworld princess named Xquic was impregnated with the seed of a calabash fruit and she gave birth to a pair of Maya hero twins.

Amazing Architecture

Maya architecture is famous for its exquisitely beautiful temples and stone sculptures. Some of the most stunning structures were built during the early and late Classic periods, many of which stand remarkably well preserved today.

Back-Breaking Work

The achievements in Maya architecture are astounding in and of themselves – and even more so when one stops to think about how the architects and laborers went about their work.

Ixchel, the moon goddess, was the principal female deity of the Maya pantheon. Today she is linked with the Virgin Mary.

For starters, Maya architects never seem to have used the true arch (a rounded arch with a keystone). The arch used in most Maya buildings is the corbeled arch (or, when used for an entire room rather than a doorway, corbeled vault). In this technique, large flat stones on either side of the opening are set progressively inward as they rise. The two sides nearly meet at the top, and this 'arch' is then topped by capstones. Though they served the purpose, the corbeled arches severely limited the amount of open space beneath them. In effect, Maya architects were limited to long, narrow vaulted rooms.

Then consider this: boxes used to move around tons of construction did not have wheels. The Maya also lacked draft animals (horses, donkeys, mules or oxen). All the work had to be done by humans, on their feet, with their arms and backs.

What's more, they had no metal tools, yet could build breathtaking temple complexes and align them so precisely that windows and doors were used as celestial observatories with great accuracy.

Lavishly illustrated with sections of friezes, sculpted figurines, painted pottery and other fine specimens of Maya art, *The Blood of Kings*, by Linda Schele and Mary Ellen Miller, deciphers glyphs and pictographs to elicit recurring themes of Classic Maya civilization.

The Styles

Maya architecture's 1500-year history saw a fascinating progression of styles. Styles changed not just with the times, but with the particular geographic area of Mesoamerica in which the architects worked. The Classic Maya, at their cultural height from about AD 250 to 900, were perhaps ancient Mexico's most artistic people. They left countless beautiful stone sculptures, of complicated design and meaning but possessing an easily appreciated touch of delicacy – a talent expressed in their unique architecture. Typical styles in the Yucatán include Esperanza, Puuc, Chenes and Río Bec.

Early Classic (AD 300–600)

The Esperanza culture typifies this phase. In Esperanza-style temples, the king was buried in a wooden chamber beneath the main staircase of the temple; successive kings were buried in similar positions in pyramids built on top of the original.

A good example of the early classic style is La Pirámide at the Oxkintok site (south of Mérida), where a labyrinth inside the structure leads to a burial chamber.

Late Classic (AD 600–900)

The most important Classic sites flourished during the latter part of the period. By this time the Maya temple pyramid had a stone building on top, replacing the *na* of wooden poles and thatch. Numbers of pyramids were built close together, sometimes forming contiguous or even continuous structures. Near them, different structures, now called palaces, were built; they sat on lower platforms and held many more rooms, perhaps a dozen or more.

The Art of Mesoamerica by Mary Ellen Miller is an excellent overview of pre-Hispanic art and architecture.

In addition to pyramids and palaces, Classic sites have carved stelae and round 'altar-stones' set in the plaza in front of the pyramids. Another feature of the Classic and later periods is the ball court, with the sloping playing surfaces of stone covered in stucco.

Of all the Classic sites, one of the most impressive is Uxmal, which stands out for its fascinating blend of Puuc, Chenes and Río Bec architectural styles. Equally impressive is Palenque, especially the towering Templo de las Inscripciones.

Puuc, Chenes & Río Bec (AD 600–800)

Among the most distinctive of the late Classic Maya architectural styles are those that flourished in the western and southern regions of the Yucatán Peninsula. These styles valued exuberant display and architectural bravado more than they did proportion and harmony – think of it as Maya baroque.

THE CELESTIAL PLAN

Every major work of Maya architecture had a celestial plan. Temples were aligned so as to enhance celestial observation of the sun, moon, certain stars or planets, especially Venus. The alignment might not be apparent except at certain conjunctions of the celestial bodies (eg an eclipse), but the Maya knew each building was properly 'placed' and that this enhanced its sacred character.

Temples usually had other features that linked them to the stars. The doors and windows might frame a celestial body at an exact point in its course on a certain day of a certain year. This is the case with the Palacio del Gobernador (Governor's Palace) at Uxmal, which is aligned in such a way that, from the main doorway, Venus would have been visible exactly on top of a small mound some 3.5km away, in the year AD 750. At Chichén Itzá, the observatory building El Caracol was aligned in order to sight Venus exactly in the year AD 1000.

Furthermore, the main door to a temple might be decorated to resemble a huge mouth, signifying entry to Xibalbá (the secret world or underworld). Other features might relate to the numbers of the calendar round, as at Chichén Itzá's El Castillo. This pyramid has 364 stairs to the top; with the top platform, this makes 365, the number of days in the Maya vague year. (The vague year corresponds to our 365-day solar year, with the difference that it is not adjusted every four years by adding an additional day. Therefore, the seasons do not occur at the same time each year but vary slightly from year to year. For that reason, the Maya solar year is characterized as 'vague.') On the sides of the pyramid are 52 panels, signifying the 52-year cycle of the calendar round. The terraces on each side of each stairway total 18 (nine on either side), signifying the 18 'months' of the solar vague year. The alignment of El Castillo catches the sun and makes a shadow of the sacred sky-serpent ascending or descending the side of El Castillo's staircase on the vernal and autumnal equinoxes (March 20 to 21 and September 21 to 22) each year.

The Puuc style, named for the hills surrounding Uxmal, used facings of thin limestone 'tiles' to cover the rough stone walls of buildings. The tiles were worked into geometric designs and stylized figures of monsters and serpents. Minoan-style columns and rows of engaged columns (half-round cylinders partly embedded in a wall) were also a feature of the style; they were used to good effect on facades of buildings at Uxmal and at the Puuc sites of Kabah, Sayil, Xlapak and Labná. Puuc architects were crazy about Chac, the rain god, and stuck his grotesque face on every temple. At Kabah, the facade of the Palacio de los Mascarones (Palace of the Masks) is covered in Chac masks.

The Chenes style, prevalent in areas of Campeche south of the Puuc region, is similar to the Puuc style, but Chenes architects seem to have enjoyed putting huge masks, as well as smaller ones, on their facades.

The Río Bec style, epitomized in the richly decorated temples at the archaeological sites between Escárcega and Chetumal, used lavish decoration, as in the Puuc and Chenes styles, but added huge towers to the corners of its low buildings, just for show. Adorned with stylized Chac faces, the Governor's Palace of Uxmal is a fine example of a Río Bec building.

Early Post-Classic (AD 1000–1250)

The collapse of Classic Maya civilization around AD 1000 created a power vacuum that was filled by the invasion of the Toltecs from central Mexico. The Toltecs brought with them their own architectural ideas, and in the process of conquest these ideas were assimilated and merged with those of the Puuc style.

The foremost example of what might be called the Toltec-Maya style is Chichén Itzá. Elements of Puuc style – the large masks and decorative friezes – coexist with Toltec warrior atlantes (male figures used as supporting columns) and *chac-mools*, which are odd reclining statues that are purely Toltec and have nothing to do with Maya art.

ARCHAEOLOGY GUIDE

Joyce Kelly's *An Archaeological Guide to Mexico's Yucatán Peninsula* gives visitors both practical and background information on 91 sites.

Platform pyramids with broad bases and spacious top platforms, such as Chichén Itzá's Templo de los Guerreros (Temple of the Warriors), look as though they might have been imported from the ancient Toltec capital of Tula (near Mexico City) or by way of Teotihuacán (the Aztec capital, just outside present-day Mexico City), with its broad-based pyramids of the sun and moon. Because Quetzalcóatl (a feathered serpent deity) was so important to the Toltecs, feathered serpents are used extensively as architectural decoration.

Late Post-Classic (AD 1250–1519)

After the Toltecs came the Cocomes, who established their capital at Mayapán, south of Mérida, and ruled a confederation of *yucateco* (Yucatán Peninsula) states during this period. After the golden age of Palenque, even after the martial architecture of Chichén Itzá, the architecture of Mayapán is a disappointment. The pyramids and temples are small and crude compared with the glorious Classic structures. Mayapán's only architectural distinction comes from its vast defensive city wall, one of the few such walls ever discovered in a Maya city. The fact that the wall exists testifies to the weakness of the Cocom rulers and the unhappiness of their subjects.

Tulum, another walled city, is also a product of this time. The columns of the Puuc style are used here, and the painted decoration on the temples must have been colorful. But there is nothing here to rival Classic architecture.

Cobá has the finest architecture of this decadent period, when the building of monumental constructions had ceased. The stately pyramids here had new little temples built atop them in the style of Tulum's two-story Templo de las Pinturas.

Land & Wildlife

Sitting pretty between two seas in Mexico's easternmost corner, the Yucatán Peninsula has an insular character, in both its physical isolation from the Mexican interior and its distinct topography and wildlife. Around 6000 cenotes (limestone sinkholes – natural underground pools) dot the Yucatán Peninsula.

Land & Geology

Separated from the bulk of Mexico by the Gulf of Mexico, and from the Greater Antilles by the Caribbean Sea, the Yucatán Peninsula is a vast, low, limestone shelf extending under the sea for more than 100km to the north and west. The eastern (Caribbean) side drops off much more precipitously. This underwater shelf keeps Yucatán's coastline waters warm and the marine life abundant.

Planeta.com (p279) brims with information and links for those wanting to delve deeper into Mexico and the Yucatán's flora, fauna and environment.

Approaching by air, you can easily make out the barrier reef that runs parallel to the Caribbean coastline at a distance of a few hundred meters to about 1.5km. Known variously as the Great Maya, Mesoamerican or Belize Barrier Reef, it's the longest of its kind in the northern hemisphere – and the second largest in the world – extending from southern Belize to Isla Mujeres off the northern coast of Quintana Roo. On the landward side of the reef, the water is usually no more than 5m to 10m deep; on the seaward side it plummets to depths of more than 2000m in the Yucatán Channel that runs between the peninsula and Cuba.

The peninsula is divided into three states in a 'Y' shape, with the state of Yucatán occupying the upper portion, flanked to the west by the state of Campeche and to the east by Quintana Roo. Note that Tabasco and Chiapas are not actually part of the Yucatán Peninsula.

Unlike much of Mexico, the Yucatán remains unobstructed by mountains. It rises no more than a dozen meters above sea level in its northern section and, at its steepest, in the southern interior of Campeche state, only reaches about 300m. About 60km south of Mérida, near Ticul, the Yucatán plain gives way to the rolling hills of the Puuc ('hill' in Maya) region. South of the peninsula, in Chiapas, it's one extreme to the other – from steamy lowlands to chilly pine-covered highlands. To the east, in southern Quintana Roo, swathes of jungle meet the Caribbean coast.

Capped by a razor-thin crust of soil, the peninsula is less productive agriculturally than elsewhere in Mexico. Formed by cretaceous-era sediments, its porous limestone bedrock does not allow rivers to flow on its surface, except in short stretches near the sea where their roofs have collapsed and in the southernmost reaches of the region where the peninsula joins the rest of Mexico (and Guatemala). Some underground streams don't release their water until well offshore, while others empty their water into lagoons near the sea, such as the lovely Laguna Bacalar, in southern Quintana Roo.

A uniquely Yucatecan geological feature, cenotes (seh-*noh*-tays) – from the Maya word *d'zonot,* meaning 'water-filled cavern' – are limestone sinkholes formed by the erosive effects of rainwater drilling down through the porous limestone. An estimated 6000 cenotes dot

HURRICANE ALLEY

Hurricanes have always walloped the Yucatán, and the peninsula has certainly experienced some big ones. Blame global warming, blame regularly shifting climate patterns: whatever you decide to blame, the real loser has been the people, plants and animals of the Yucatán.

For a while there, *yucatecos* (people of the Yucatán Peninsula) just couldn't catch a break. In 2005, Hurricane Wilma (a category 5) pounded the Yucatán's northeast coast for more than 30 hours, causing well over M$20 billion in damages and leaving many visitors stranded in shelters. Two years later Dean struck with so much force that it leveled the beach town of Mahahual and mowed down thousands of trees in southern Quintana Roo.

Fortunately, recent hurricane seasons have shown some mercy. In 2011, Hurricane Rina was bearing down on the peninsula, prompting mass evacuations of tourists staying in Cancún and along the Riviera Maya. But before making landfall, Rina was downgraded to a tropical storm, and, most importantly, no deaths or major damages were reported. A similar situation occurred in 2012 when Hurricane Ernesto had many people running for cover, but it weakened before hitting land. Once again, *yucatecos* and visitors skirted a potential catastrophe.

Hurricane season runs from June to November. Every time a storm pounds the Caribbean coast, it causes massive erosion of the white-sand beaches. Much to the chagrin of area environmentalists, the quick-fix solution is to restore the beaches by bringing in sands from other areas, such as the channel between Cancún and Isla Mujeres.

the peninsular landscape. *Yucatecos* have traditionally gotten their fresh water from these natural cisterns, while modern visitors favor their crystalline waters for swimming and snorkeling. South of the Puuc region, the inhabitants draw water from the *chenes* (limestone pools), more than 100m below ground.

Into the Wild

The isolation of the Yucatán Peninsula and its range of ecosystems results in an extraordinary variety of plant and animal life, including a number of species that are unique to the region. Whether you like watching exotic birds, following the progress of sea turtles as they nest on the beach, swimming next to manta rays and schools of iridescent fish, or spying wildcats through your binoculars, you'll have plenty to do here.

Animals

The Winged Ones

Birders should carry *Mexican Birds* by Roger Tory Peterson and Edward L Chalif, or *Birds of Mexico & Adjacent Areas* by Ernest Preston Edwards.

For bird-watchers, the Yucatán is indeed a banquet. Over 500 bird species – about half of those found in all of Mexico – inhabit or regularly visit the peninsula. These include dozens of regional endemics; the island of Cozumel alone boasts three unique species.

Most of the peninsula's birds are represented in the various parks and biosphere reserves, and serious birders should make for at least a few of these. Numerous coastal species can be spotted at the Reserva de la Biosfera Ría Celestún and Reserva de la Biosfera Ría Lagartos, on the western and eastern ends, respectively, of Yucatán state's coast. The varied panorama is due to a highly productive ecosystem where substantial freshwater sources empty into the Gulf of Mexico. A similarly diverse coastal habitat can be found at the Laguna de Términos in western Campeche. Parque Nacional Isla Contoy, off the northern coast of Quintana Roo, is a haven for olive cormorants, brown boobies and many other seabirds. It's home to 173 bird species!

Moving inland, the panorama shifts. The low, dry forests of the Puuc region contain two species of motmot, which nest in ruined temples. In the denser forests of the Reserva de la Biosfera Calakmul, train your binoculars on harpy eagles, ocellated turkeys and king vultures.

The Yucatán Peninsula is along the central migratory flyway, and between November and February hundreds of thousands of birds migrate here from harsher northern climes. The region's proximity to the Caribbean Sea also means there are island species not seen elsewhere in Mexico.

In late November environmental group **Ecoturismo Yucatán** (☎999-920-2772; www.ecoyuc.com) holds the Toh Festival, an annual event that attracts bird enthusiasts from far and wide. This bird-a-thon, the name of which is Maya for the locally seen turquoise-browed motmot, is based in Mérida and closes in the archaeological zone of Chichén Itzá.

The Spanish-language monthly magazine México Desconocido (www.mexicodesconocido.com.mx) points out off-the-beaten-track destinations and wildlife-watching spots with copious color photos and maps. Check its website for details.

Forest & Mangrove Dwellers

Around a quarter of the mammal species that exist in Mexico roam the Yucatán Peninsula. Some are the last of their breed.

There are jaguars in the forests, although, despite the Maya's traditional fascination with the New World's largest cat, poaching has all but wiped them out in southeastern Mexico. Of Mexico's estimated jaguar population of 3500, half are found on the peninsula. Your best chances of spotting one in the wild are probably in the Reserva de la Biosfera Calakmul in Campeche state. The peninsula's other native wildcat, the jaguarundi, is also at risk, as are the margay, ocelot and puma, though sightings of the latter aren't all that unusual in southern Yucatán.

The agile spider monkey also inhabits some forested areas of the region. It looks something like a smaller, long-tailed version of the gibbon (an ape native to southwest Asia). Another elusive primate, the howler monkey, frequents forest around the ruins of Calakmul and isolated pockets elsewhere. Howlers are more often heard than seen, but you have a fair chance of seeing both them and spider monkeys at Punta Laguna.

Hiking around the forest, you may run into tapirs and piglike peccaries (javelinas), as well as armor-plated armadillos. There are several species of anteater, all with very long, flexible snouts and sharp-clawed, shovel-like front paws – the two tools needed to seek out and enjoy feeding on ants and other insects. The animal's slow gait and poor eyesight make it a common roadkill victim. Besides the *tepezcuintle* (paca) and *sereque* (agouti) – large, tailless rodents – a few species of deer can be found as well, including the smallest variety in North America.

Crocodiles still ply the mangroves near the towns of Río Lagartos and Celestún in Yucatán state. Although their numbers are fast diminishing, plenty of the beady-eyed amphibious reptiles inhabit the Reserva de la Biosfera Sian Ka'an, while smaller numbers lurk up and down the Caribbean coast, including at Laguna Nichupté, which backs onto Cancún's Zona Hotelera.

PRONATURA

To see recently snapped photos of jaguars, pumas and other Yucatán fauna in their habitat, go to the website of environmental group Pronatura (p274).

Sea Creatures

The Great Maya Barrier Reef, which parallels the length of Quintana Roo's coast, is home to a tremendous variety of colorful marine life. The coney grouper, for example, stands out for its bright-yellow suit (it varies in color from reddish brown to sun yellow). The redband parrot fish is easy to recognize by the striking red circle around its eyes and the red band that runs from the eyes to the gills. Butterfly fish are as flamboyant as their name suggests (there are six species in the area), and the yellow stingray has spots that closely resemble the rosettes of a golden jaguar.

Providing an extraordinary backdrop to these brilliant stars of the sea is a vast array of coral. It comes in two varieties: hard coral, such as the great star coral, the boulder coral and numerous types of brain coral; and soft coral, such as sea fans and sea plumes, which are particularly delicate and sway with the current. Successive generations of coral form a skin of living organisms over the limestone reef.

But there's trouble in the waters of the Mexican Caribbean – invasive lionfish are reproducing at an alarming rate and that's bad news for other fish. Protected by venomous spines and with few known predators, lionfish have a fierce appetite, which is posing a threat to the balance of reef ecosystems. In an effort to control the population explosion, fishermen are being encouraged to catch lionfish for human consumption.

Endangered Species

Pollution, poaching, illegal traffic of rare species and the filling in of coastal areas for yet more resorts are taking an enormous toll on the Yucatán's wildlife. Deforestation is also a major threat – more than five million hectares of forest have been felled in the Yucatán since the 1960s.

Some of the species on the peninsula that are threatened with extinction or are protected include five species of cat (jaguar, puma, ocelot, *margay* and jaguarundi), four species of sea turtle, the manatee, the tapir and hundreds of bird species, including the harpy eagle, the red flamingo and the jabiru stork.

The Selva Maya, which spans northern Guatemala and Belize and the southern part of the Yucatán Peninsula (including the Reserva de la Biosfera Calakmul), is the world's second-largest tropical forest after the Amazon.

Efforts are being made to save these and other endangered creatures from extinction, chiefly by environmental NGOs such as the **Nature Conservancy** (☎USA 703-841-5400; www.nature.org) and its local partner **Pronatura** (☎999-988-4436; www.pronatura-ppy.org.mx; Calle 32 No 269, Col Pinzón). This group focuses on preservation of wildlife habitats, particularly in the Ría Celestún, Ría Lagartos and Calakmul biosphere reserves, as well as the promotion of ecotourism. Pronatura is working to recover jaguar habitat in the area between the Reserva de la Biosfera Ría Lagartos and Isla Holbox, where 120 to 200 of these cats roam.

Camps at Ría Lagartos, Laguna de Términos, Xcacel-Xcacelito, Akumal, Sisal and Isla Holbox have been established to promote the survival of the six species of marine turtle that nest on the Yucatán's beaches. Volunteers collect turtle eggs and release hatchlings into the sea, and patrols prevent poachers from snatching eggs that are laid on the beaches. In Punta Laguna, environmental groups are working with local *campesinos* (agricultural workers) to establish protection zones for endangered spider monkeys, which are closely monitored by researchers. The nutrient-rich waters around Isla Holbox attract whale sharks, which are threatened by commercial fishing, and environmentalists have succeeded in getting this area categorized as a protected zone.

Plants

Vegetation varies greatly on the peninsula, with plants falling into four main categories: aquatic and subaquatic vegetation, and humid and subhumid forest vegetation. As you move inland from the coast, mangrove swamps are replaced first by a fairly dense forest of low deciduous trees, then by a more jungley zone with tall trees and climbing vegetation, and more than a few air plants (but without the soggy underbrush and multiple canopies you'd find further south). The taller trees of the peninsula's southern half harbor more than 100 species of orchid; for the really spectacular blooms, the avid orchid hunter will need to head into the highlands of Chiapas, where the exotic plants thrive at an elevation of about 1000m.

Tropical Mexico – The Ecotravellers' Wildlife Guide by Les Beletsky is a well-illustrated, informative guide to the land, air and sea life of southeastern Mexico.

Dispersed among the mango and avocado trees are many annuals and perennials, such as the aptly named *flamboyán* (royal poinciana), which bursts into bloom like a red-orange umbrella, and lavender-tinged jacaranda.

National Parks & Reserves

There are several national parks on the peninsula, some scarcely larger than the ancient Maya cities they contain – Parque Nacional Tulum is a good example of this. Others, such as Parque Nacional Isla Contoy, a bird sanctuary in northeastern Quintana Roo, are larger and have been designated to protect wildlife.

The fact that former president Ernesto Zedillo was an avid scuba diver was likely a factor in the creation of several *parques marinos nacionales* (national marine parks) off the coast of Quintana Roo: Arrecifes de Cozumel, Costa Occidental de Isla Mujeres, Punta Cancún y Nizuc, and Arrecifes de Puerto Morelos.

Very large national biosphere reserves surround Río Lagartos, Celestún (both in Yucatán state) and Banco Chinchorro (Quintana Roo), spreading across thousands of hectares. The Reservas de la Biosfera Ría Lagartos and Ría Celestún are well known for their diversity of bird and animal species, including large colonies of flamingos, while Banco Chinchorro contains a massive coral atoll, many shipwrecks and a host of marine species.

Even more impressive are the two colossal Unesco-designated biosphere reserves found in the Yucatán: the Reserva de la Biosfera Calakmul and the Reserva de la Biosfera Sian Ka'an. Calakmul, covering more than 7230 sq km in Campeche, Quintana Roo and Chiapas, as well as parts of Belize and Guatemala, is home to more than 300 bird species, plus jaguars, pumas, tapirs, coatis, peccaries and many other animals. Sian Ka'an, beginning 150km south of Cancún, covers 6000 sq km,

SMALL FOOTPRINTS, LARGE IMPACT: TIPS FOR STAYING GREEN

Travelers can help protect the Yucatán's environment by taking the following steps.

- Hire local guides. Not only does this provide local communities with a more ecologically sound way of supporting themselves, it also attaches value to nature and wildlife.
- Pack a water purifier or purifying tablets (chlorine dioxide) to avoid unnecessary waste of plastic bottles. Tourists the world over toss millions of plastic water bottles each day!
- Try to observe wildlife in its natural environment and do your best not to cause disturbances.
- Don't buy souvenirs made from endangered plants and animals that have been acquired illegally. By purchasing these items you aid in wildlife extinction.
- Don't carry off anything that you pick up at the site of an ancient city or out on a coral reef. Don't buy these products if offered by locals.
- When snorkeling or scuba diving, be careful what you touch and where you place your feet; not only can coral cut you, it's also extremely fragile and takes years to grow even a finger's length.
- Keep water use down, especially in areas that have signs requesting you to do so. Most of the Yucatán Peninsula has limited water reserves, and in times of drought the situation can become grave.
- Before plunging into a cenote make sure you're not using sunblock, lotions, perfumes, insect repellent or any other products that pollute the water system.

including 100 sq km of the Great Maya Barrier Reef. Its lifeforms range from more than 70 species of coral to 350 species of bird (by comparison, there are only 400 species of bird in all of Europe). Crocodiles, pumas, jaguars and jabirus are among the animals calling Sian Ka'an home.

Environmental Issues

Large-scale tourism developments are affecting and sometimes erasing fragile ecosystems, especially along the 'Riviera Maya' south of Cancún. Many hectares of vital mangrove swamp have been bulldozed, and beaches where turtles once laid eggs are now occupied by resorts and condo-mondos. Ironically, tourism development is a major contributor to coastal erosion, as was made evident when 2005's Hurricane Wilma swept away the beaches (many artificial) that attract hordes of tourists annually. And with the proliferation of new hotels comes the need for freshwater sources, increasing the danger of salinization of the water table. As employment-seekers converge on Quintana Roo's tourist zones, demand for building materials to construct makeshift housing for the burgeoning population is also a persistent issue.

Another key issue is the fragmentation of habitat. As patches of jungle shrink with new settlement and construction of new highways, they become isolated and species become trapped in smaller habitats. Animals' movements are restricted and the gene pool cannot flow beyond the borders of their fragmented habitat.

Also of concern is the need for effective waste management systems. Some places, for instance, do not have water treatment plants, which results in untreated sewage running through underground water systems and out to sea. The so-called *aguas negras* (black waters) contain nutrients that allow for mass algal growth. Unfortunately, these oxygen-depleting algae can have an asphyxiating effect on various forms of marine life, such as coral. For more information on this issue visit www.mexicoconservacion.org.

Mexico's largest oil field, the Cantarell complex, is in the Bay of Campeche, 85km off the shore of Ciudad del Carmen. In 2007 there was an 11,700-barrel oil spill in the bay, adversely affecting the area's marine flora and fauna. The Cantarell field is also yielding less oil than it did in the past, leading the company to seek new sources in the Alacranes reef off the coast of Progreso, and at Laguna de Términos, where further habitat destruction is feared.

Think before you drink! Around 2.7 million tons of plastic are used to bottle water each year. Stay green by asking your hotelier to provide water coolers or by carrying your own water filter.

The good news is that the level of protection on reserves and other important natural habitats has continued on a constant basis over the years. In 2012, 94,000 acres consisting of jungle area and coastline on Isla Cozumel's north and east sides were given protective status, and in 2009 some 1460 sq km of waters where whale sharks congregate (off the Quintana Roo coast) was declared a protected area. And in 2004, 370,000 acres of threatened forest in the Reserva de la Biosfera Calakmul was permanently protected. In Chiapas, Lagunas de Montebello National Park was designated a Unesco biosphere reserve in 2009, adding to the conservancy potential of the area.

But Yucatán's protected zones and reserves actually encompass private *ejidos* (communally owned land) occupied by *campesinos,* whose activities, particularly cattle raising and logging, may infringe upon the environment. Seeking a solution, some environmental organizations have begun training *ejido* inhabitants as guides for ecotourism activities, thus providing alternative livelihoods. Such programs are underway in the Reserva de la Biosfera Calakmul and on Isla Holbox and locals say the programs have worked out well because they provide a viable source of income.

Survival Guide

Directory A–Z

Accommodations

Accommodations in the Yucatán range from hammocks and *cabañas* (cabins)to hotels of every imaginable standard, including world-class resorts. In popular destinations for high season (Christmas through Easter, plus most of July and August), it's best to book in advance.

➡ Outside peak season, many midrange and top-end establishments in tourist destinations cut their room prices by 10% to 40%. They may also have special online offers.

➡ Some establishments (mostly top-end hotels) do not include a 14% to 17% tax charge in quoted prices. When in doubt, you can ask *'¿Están incluidos los impuestos?'* (Are taxes included?).

➡ In this book 'single' (abbreviated 's') signifies a room for one person, and 'double' ('d') means a room for two people. Mexicans sometimes use the phrase *'cuarto sencillo'* (literally, 'single room') to mean a room with one bed, which is often a *cama matrimonial* (double bed). A *cuarto doble* often means a room with two beds.

Price Categories

Room prices quoted in this book are high-season rates and subject to change. Rates do not reflect 'ultra' high-season prices that some midrange and top-end establishments charge from mid-December to early January, and during the two-week Easter vacation period. Budget accommodations usually keep prices the same year-round (bless their hearts!). Hotels in developed resort areas – such as Cancún and Playa del Carmen – may publish their rates in US dollars, so a flux in the peso-to-dollar exchange rate can mean a big swing in the actual on-the-ground price. Places that stick with the peso sometimes adjust their prices according to exchange-rate fluctuations.

BUDGET ($)

The Yucatán offers a mixed bag of affordable sleeping options, including hostels, *cabañas* (cabins), campgrounds, guesthouses and economical hotels. Rooms in this category are assumed to have bathrooms, unless otherwise stated. Recommended accommodations in this range will be simple and without frills but generally clean.

MIDRANGE ($$)

Midrange accommodations are chiefly hotels, but you'll also find many appealing B&Bs, guesthouses and bungalows in this price bracket. In some areas of the Yucatán, M$700 can get you a very comfortable and wonderfully atmospheric setup. Keep in mind that not all rooms are the same in many establishments (some are larger or have better views), so it's worth a look at several options before settling in.

TOP END ($$$)

Places in this category run from classy international hotels to deluxe coastal resorts and luxurious smaller establishments catering to travelers with a taste for comfort and beautiful design, and of course the deep pockets to pay for them.

Types of Accommodations

APARTMENTS & B&BS

In some places you can find *departamentos* (apartments) for tourists with fully equipped kitchens. Some are

BOOK YOUR STAY ONLINE

For more accommodations reviews by Lonely Planet authors, check out http://hotels.lonelyplanet.com. You'll find independent reviews, as well as recommendations on the best places to stay. Best of all, you can book online.

SLEEPING PRICE RANGES

The following price ranges refer to accommodations for two people in high season, including any taxes charged.

$ less than M$550

$$ M$550-1200

$$$ more than M$1200

very comfortable and they can be good value for three or more people. Tourist offices and advertisements in local newspapers (especially English-language newspapers) are good sources of information, as is www.locogringo.com.

In Yucatán B&Bs are generally upmarket guesthouses, often aimed at foreign tourists; they are usually comfortable and enjoyable places to stay.

CAMPING & TRAILER PARKS

Most organized campgrounds are actually trailer parks set up for people with camper vans and trailers (caravans) but are open to tent campers at lower rates. They're most common along the coast. Some are very basic, others area quite luxurious. Some restaurants and guesthouses in beach spots or country areas will let you pitch a tent on their patch for M$100 per person.

POSADAS & CASAS DE HUÉSPEDES

Posadas (inns), much like *casas de huéspedes* (guesthouses), are normally inexpensive and congenial, family-run accommodations with a relaxed atmosphere. More often than not, a *casa de huésped* is a home converted into simple guest lodgings, so it allows for plenty of interaction with the host family.

CABAÑAS

Cabañas are usually huts – of wood, brick, adobe and stone – with a palm-thatched roof. Some have dirt floors and nothing inside but a bed; others are deluxe, with electric light, mosquito net, fan, fridge, bar and decorations. Prices for simple *cabañas* cost M$300 to M$450. On the Caribbean some luxury *cabañas* can cost over M$1000.

HAMMOCKS

A hammock can be a very comfortable place to sleep in hot areas (but mosquito repellent or a net often comes in handy). You can rent a hammock and a place to hang it – usually under a palm roof outside a small guesthouse or beach restaurant – for M$50 to M$100. With your own hammock, the cost comes down a bit. It's easy enough to buy hammocks in the Yucatán; you'll find them for sale in Mérida and all along the Riviera Maya.

HOSTELS

Hostels exist in many of the towns and cities where backpackers congregate. They provide dorm accommodations (for about M$130 to M$180 per person), plus communal kitchens, bathrooms and living space and often private rooms. Standards of hygiene and security vary, but aside from being cheap, hostels are generally relaxed and good places to meet other travelers. **HostelWorld** (www.hostelworld.com) has listings.

There is a handful of hostels affiliated with Mexico's HI, **Hostelling International Mexico** (www.hostellingmexico.com). If you're an HI member, you get a dollar or two off the nightly rates at these places.

HOTELS

Yucatán has hotels in all price ranges, especially in developed areas. Before settling on a room, ask to see the range of options available. An additional M$150 or so in the budget and midrange categories may be the difference between a musty interior room and airy digs with a nice view. Top-end hotels offer rooms with varying degrees of luxury, depending on what you're willing to fork out.

RESORTS

A popular option for families, particularly in Cancún and the Riviera Maya, these sprawling hotels usually offer all-inclusive packages and provide most of everything you'll need within the confines of the property. There are also adults-only resorts, which put a premium on luxury and comfort. Shop around online and you can still find some resorts promoting cheaper European plans.

Activities

There's absolutely no shortage of things to do on the Yucatán Peninsula: some of the best scuba diving and snorkeling in the world is available here, beach lovers will find plenty of powdery white sand on which to sunbathe, and the ancient Maya cities that dot the landscape of the Yucatán are a thrill to explore.

Resources

AMTAVE (Mexican Association of Adventure Travel & Ecotourism; ☎1-800-654-4452; www.amtave.org) Has 79 member organizations.

Mexonline.com (www.mexonline.com) Includes listings of activities providers.

Planeta.com (www.planeta.com) Good resource on active and responsible tourism.

Climate

Cancún

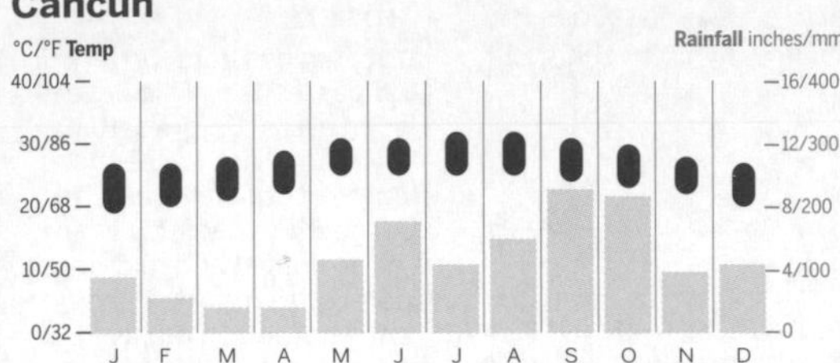

Cozumel

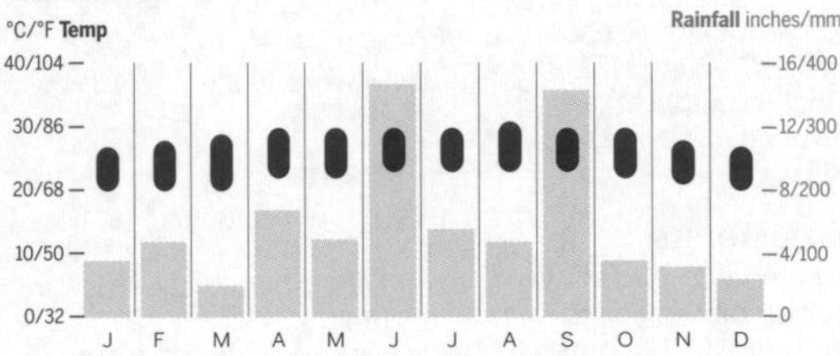

Mérida

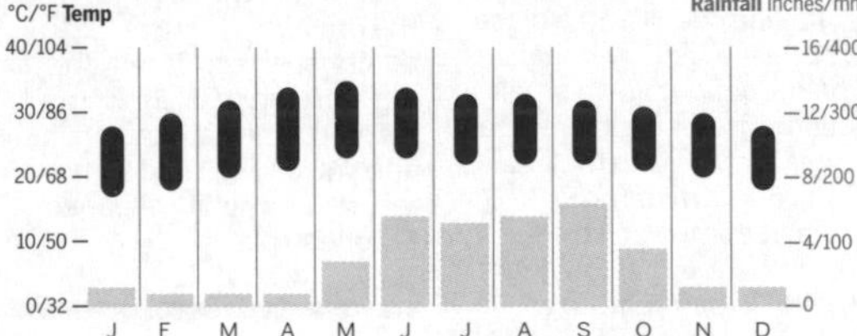

Courses

Taking classes can be a great way to meet people and get an inside angle on local life and culture. Mexican universities and colleges often offer classes. For long-term study in Mexico you'll need a student visa; contact a Mexican consulate for details. You can also arrange informal Spanish tutoring through most hostels. There are helpful links on the website of **Lonely Planet** (www.lonelyplanet.com).

- You can take language courses in Mérida, San Cristóbal de las Casas, Playa del Carmen and Puerto Morelos. See individual destinations for details.
- For cooking courses there's no better place to study than the culinary capital of Mérida. There are also classes in Puerto Morelos. See individual destinations for details.

Customs Regulations

Visitors are allowed to bring the following items into Mexico duty-free:

- two cameras
- up to 20 packs of cigarettes
- up to 3L of alcohol
- medicine for personal use, with prescription in the case of psychotropic drugs
- one laptop computer
- one digital music player

See www.aduanas.gob.mx for more details.

After handing in your customs declaration form, an automated system will determine whether your luggage will be inspected. A green light means pass, a red light means your bags will be searched.

Discount Cards

Reduced prices for students and seniors on Mexican buses and at museums and archaeological sites are usually only for those with Mexican residence or education credentials, but the following cards will sometimes get you a reduction (the ISIC is the most widely recognized). They are also recognized for reduced-price air tickets at student- and youth-oriented travel agencies:

- ISIC student card
- IYTC (under 26 card)
- ITIC card for teachers

Electricity

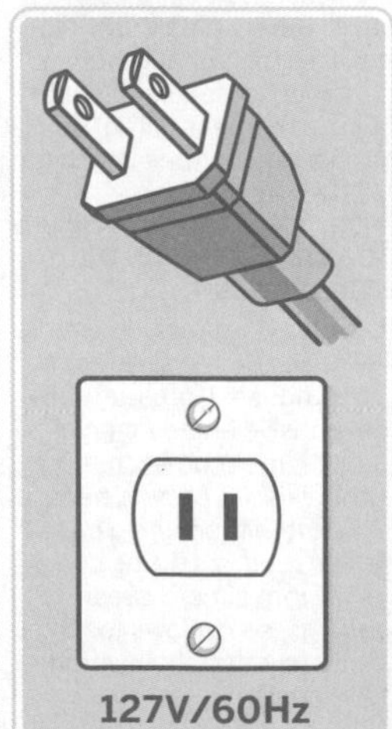

Embassies & Consulates

It's important to understand what your own embassy – the embassy of the country of which you are a citizen – can and can't do to help you if you get into trouble. Generally speaking, it won't be much help in emergencies if the trouble you're in is remotely your own fault. Remember that you are bound by the laws of the country you are in. In genuine emergencies you might get some assistance, such as a list of lawyers, but only if other channels have been exhausted.

Updated embassy details can be found at **Secretaría de Relaciones Exteriores** (www.sre.gob.mx) and **Embassyworld.com** (www.embassyworld.com).

Many embassies or their consular sections are in Mexico City (including Australia, Ireland and New Zealand); Cancún is home to several consulates, and there are some diplomatic outposts elsewhere as well.

Belizean Embassy (☎983-285-3511; Av Génova 369, Chetumal)

Canadian Embassy Cancún (☎998-883-3360; Blvd Kukulcán, Km 12, Centro Empresarial Oficina E7); Playa del Carmen (☎984-803-2411; crmen@international.gc.ca; Av 10 Sur, btwn Calles 3 & 5 Sur, in Plaza Paraíso Caribe)

Dutch Embassy Cancún (☎998-884-8672; Av Nichupte, in Pabellón Caribe); Mérida (☎999-924-3122; Calle 64 No 418)

French Embassy (☎999-930-1500; Calle 60 No 385, btwn Calles 41 & 43, Mérida)

German Embassy Cancún (☎998-884-1598; Punta Conoco 36, near Av Sunyaxchén); Mérida (☎999-944-3252; Calle 49 No 212, btwn Calles 31 & 33)

Guatemalan Embassy Ciudad Hidalgo (☎962-698-0184; 9a Calle Ote 9, Colonia San José); Comitán (☎963-110-6816; 1a Calle Sur Pte 35, Barrio de Guadalupe); Tapachula (☎962-626-1252; Central Poniente s/n, cnr Av 14 Sur, Edificio Consular)

Italian Embassy (☎998-884-1261; Alcatraces 39, SM22, Cancún)

UK Embassy (☎998-881-0100; Blvd Kukulcán, Km 13.5, The Royal Sands, Cancún)

US Embassy Cancún (☎998-883-0272; Blvd Kukulcán, Km 13, Despacho 301, Torre la Europea); Mérida (☎999-942-5700; Calle 60 No 338K, btwn Calles 29 & 31)

Gay & Lesbian Travelers

Mexico is more broad-minded about sexuality than you might expect. Gays and lesbians rarely attract open discrimination or violence. Discrimination based on sexual orientation has been illegal since 1999 and can be punished with up to three years in prison. Gay men have a more public profile than lesbians. Cancún has a small gay scene, and there are a number of gay-friendly establishments listed in Mérida at www.gaymexicomap.com. Here are some other good resources:

Gay Mexico (www.gaymexico.com.mx) Useful online guide for gay tourism in Mexico.

International Gay & Lesbian Travel Association (www.iglta.com) Provides information on the major travel providers in the gay sector.

PRACTICALITIES

- Mérida's **El Diario de Yucatán** (www.yucatan.com.mx) is one of the country's leading newspapers. **Yucatán Today** (www.yucatantoday.com) offers good English-language info on Yucatán state.
- Local TV is dominated by Televisa, which runs four of the six national channels; TV Azteca has the other two. A growing number of viewers have multichannel cable or satellite systems, such as Cablemás or Sky.
- Mexicans use the metric system for weights and measures.
- DVDs are encoded for Zone 4, the same as for Australia and New Zealand. Many DVDs sold in Mexico are illegal copies.
- Mexico has a ban on smoking in public indoor spaces, except in designated areas. Enforcement, however, is extremely patchy.

Out Traveler (www.out-traveler.com) Helpful general resource.

Health

Dr David Goldberg

Travelers to the Yucatán need to be careful chiefly about food- and water-borne diseases, though mosquito-borne infections can also be a problem. Most of these illnesses are not life threatening, but they can certainly impact on your trip. Besides getting the proper vaccinations, it's important that you bring a good insect repellent and exercise care in what you eat and drink.

Private hospitals give better care than public ones, but are more expensive. The US Consulate has listings of doctors and medical facilities in Cancún, Cozumel, Playa del Carmen and Campeche at http://merida.usconsulate.gov/hospitalsdoctors.html.

Before You Go

RECOMMENDED VACCINATIONS

Make sure all routine vaccinations are up to date and check whether all vaccines are suitable for children and pregnant women at wwwnc.cdc.gov. Since most vaccines don't produce immunity until at least two weeks after they're given, visit a physician four to eight weeks before departure.

Hepatitis A All travelers (not recommended for pregnant women or children under two); gamma globulin is the alternative.

Hepatitis B Long-term travelers in close contact with local population (requires three doses over a six-month period).

Rabies Recommended only for travelers who may have direct contact with stray dogs and cats, bats and wildlife.

Typhoid Recommended for all unvaccinated people, especially for those staying in small cities, villages and rural areas.

INTERNET RESOURCES

MD Travel Health (www.mdtravelhealth.com) Complete travel health recommendations for every country, updated daily.

Centers for Disease Control & Prevention (www.cdc.gov/travel) Official US website.

In the Yucatán

HEPATITIS A

Hepatitis A occurs throughout Central America. It's a viral infection of the liver usually acquired by ingestion of contaminated water, food or ice, though it may also be acquired by direct contact with infected persons. The illness occurs worldwide, but the incidence is higher in developing nations. Symptoms may include fever, malaise, jaundice, nausea, vomiting and abdominal pain. Most cases resolve uneventfully, though hepatitis A occasionally causes severe liver damage. There is no treatment.

➡ The vaccine for hepatitis A is extremely safe and highly effective. If you get a booster six to 12 months later, it lasts for at least 10 years. You should get it before you go to Mexico.

DENGUE FEVER

Dengue fever is a viral infection found throughout Central America. In Mexico, the risk is greatest along the Gulf coast, especially from July to September. Dengue is transmitted by Aedes mosquitoes, which bite preferentially during the day and are usually found close to human habitations, often indoors. They breed primarily in artificial water containers, such as barrels, cans, cisterns, metal drums and discarded tires. As a result, dengue is especially common in urban environments.

➡ Dengue usually causes flu-like symptoms, including fever, muscle aches, joint pains, headache and nausea and it's often followed by a rash.

➡ There is no vaccine and no specific treatment for dengue fever, except analgesics. Severe cases may require hospitalization.

MALARIA

Occurs in Chiapas and in rare cases, Quintana Roo. It's transmitted by mosquito bites, usually between dusk and dawn. The main symptom is high spiking fevers, which may be accompanied by chills, sweats, headache, body aches, general weakness, vomiting or diarrhea.

➡ Taking malaria pills is strongly recommended when visiting rural areas. For Mexico, the first-choice malaria pill is chloroquine.

➡ Protecting yourself against mosquito bites is just as important as taking malaria pills, as no pills are 100% effective. If you develop a fever after returning home, see a physician, as malaria symptoms may not occur for months. It can be diagnosed by a simple blood test.

TYPHOID FEVER

Typhoid fever is caused by ingestion of food or water contaminated by *Salmonella typhi*. Fever occurs in virtually all cases. Other symptoms may include headache, malaise, muscle aches, dizziness, loss of appetite, nausea and abdominal pain. Either diarrhea or constipation may occur.

➡ The drug of choice for typhoid fever is usually a quinolone antibiotic, such as ciprofloxacin (Cipro) or levofloxacin (Levaquin).

MOSQUITO BITES

➡ To prevent bites, wear long sleeves, long pants, hats and shoes (rather than sandals). In areas with *chaquistes* (gnatlike sand flies that can leave nasty welts), avoid exposing your flesh at dusk and dawn when the tiny buggers are out in full force.

➡ Don't sleep with the window open unless there is a functional screen. Use a good insect repellent, preferably one containing DEET, which should be applied to exposed skin and clothing, but don't use DEET-containing compounds on children under two.

➡ Insect repellents containing certain botanical products, including eucalyptus oil and soybean oil, are effective but last only 1½ to two hours. Where there is a high risk of malaria, use DEET-containing repellents. Products based on citronella are not effective.

➡ If sleeping outdoors or in accommodations that allows entry of mosquitoes, use a mosquito coil or a bed net treated with permethrin.

SNAKE & SCORPION BITES

Venomous snakes in the Yucatán generally do not attack without provocation, but may bite humans who accidentally come too close. Coral snakes are somewhat retiring and tend not to bite humans unless considerably provoked.

➡ In the event of a venomous snake or scorpion bite, place the victim at rest, keep the bitten area immobilized and move them immediately to the nearest medical facility. Avoid using tourniquets, which are no longer recommended.

➡ To prevent scorpion stings, be sure to inspect and shake out clothing, shoes and sleeping bags before use. If stung, apply ice or cold packs.

SUNBURN & HEAT EXHAUSTION

To protect yourself from excessive sun exposure, you should stay out of the mid-day sun, wear sunglasses and a wide-brimmed hat, and apply sunscreen with SPF 15 or higher, providing both UVA and UVB protection.

➡ Sunscreen should be applied to all exposed parts of the body approximately 30 minutes before sun exposure and be reapplied after swimming or vigorous activity.

➡ Do not apply sunscreen prior to swimming in cenotes (limestone sinkholes) – it pollutes the water!

➡ Drink plenty of fluids and avoid strenuous exercise when the temperature is high. Heat exhaustion is characterized by dizziness, weakness, headache, nausea or profuse sweating. Salt tablets or rehydration salts may help, but fluids, rest and shade are essential.

WATER

Tap water is generally not safe to drink.

➡ Vigorous boiling for one minute is the most effective means of water purification.

➡ Another option is to disinfect water with iodine pills. Instructions are usually provided and should be carefully followed.

➡ Numerous water filters are on the market. Those with smaller pores (reverse osmosis filters) provide the best protection, but they are relatively large and readily plugged by debris. Those with somewhat larger pores (microstrainer filters) are ineffective against viruses, although they do remove other organisms. Manufacturers' instructions must be carefully followed.

Insurance

A travel-insurance policy to cover theft, loss and medical problems is a good idea. Some policies specifically exclude dangerous activities such as scuba diving, motorcycling and even trekking.

You may prefer a policy that pays medical costs directly rather than requiring you to pay on the spot and claim later. If you have to claim later, keep all documentation. Check that the policy covers ambulances and emergency flights home.

Worldwide medical insurance for travelers is available online at www.lonelyplanet.com/travel-insurance/

Internet Access

Internet cafes (which charge about M$10 per hour) abound in the Yucatán. Many have webcams, headphones and Skype.

Many places (hotels, bars and restaurants) have wi-fi available, but in some hotels the signal only reaches the lobby. In this book the wi-fi icon means the signal reaches at least some part of the premises, while the internet icon means the establishment has internet-available computers for guests.

Legal Matters

Mexican law presumes an accused person is guilty until proven innocent.

➡ As in most other countries, the purchase of controlled medication requires a doctor's prescription.

➡ It's against Mexican law to take firearms or ammunition into the country (even unintentionally).

➡ A law passed in 2009 decriminalized the possession of small amounts of certain drugs for personal use – including marijuana (up to 5g), cocaine (500mg), heroin (50mg) and methamphetamine (40mg). The law states that first-time offenders do not face criminal prosecution. Selling drugs remains illegal, and people found in possession may still have to appear before a prosecutor to prove that the drugs are truly for personal use. The easiest way to stay out of trouble is to avoid drugs all together.

Maps

- Free city and regional maps of varying quality are given away by tourist offices around the peninsula.
- Quality regional maps include the highly detailed **ITMB** (www.itmb.ca) 1:500,000 *Yucatán Peninsula Travel Map* and the sketchier **Guía Roji** (www.guiaroji.com.mx) 1:1,000,000 scale *Maya World* (M$90) showing all of the peninsula and parts of Tabasco and Chiapas.
- Guía Roji also publishes maps of each Mexican state (M$50) and an annually updated national road atlas called *Mapa Turístico Carreteras de Mexico* (M$99). It's widely available throughout Mexico and can be bought from the website.
- *Riviera Maya, Cancún, Cozumel, Isla Mujeres, Chichén Itzá* and *Playa del Carmen* foldout maps are published by the US couple behind **Can-Do Maps** (www.cancunmap.com), aka MapChick.
- **Inegi** (Instituto Nacional de Estadística, Geografía e Informática; ☎800-490-4200; www.inegi.gob.mx) sells large-scale and topographical maps at its Centros de Información in the peninsula's principal cities (listed on the website) for M$50 to M$100 each.
- A good internet source is **Maps of Mexico** (www.maps-of-mexico.com), with detailed maps of all the states.

Money

Mexico's currency is the peso, usually denoted by the 'M$' sign. The peso is divided into 100 centavos. Coins come in denominations of 10, 20 and 50 centavos and one, two, five and 10 pesos; notes come in 20, 50, 100, 200 and 500 (and occasionally 1000) pesos.

The most convenient form of money is a major international credit or debit card – preferably two cards. Visa, MasterCard and American Express cards can be used to obtain cash easily from ATMs in Mexico, and are accepted for payment by most airlines, car-rental companies, travel agents, many upmarket hotels, and some restaurants and shops. Visa is the most universally accepted. Occasionally there's a surcharge for paying by card, or a discount for paying cash. Making a purchase by credit card normally gives you a more favorable rate than exchanging money at a bank, but you'll normally have to pay your card issuer a 'foreign exchange' transaction fee of around 2.5%.

As a backup to credit or debit cards, it's a good idea to take a little cash – best in US dollars, the most easily exchangeable foreign currency in Mexico. Euros, British pounds and Canadian dollars, in cash or traveler's checks, are accepted by most banks and some *casas de cambio* (money-exchange offices), but acceptance is less certain outside the main cities and tourist centers.

ATMs

ATMs (*caja permanente* or *cajero automático*) are plentiful in the Yucatán, and are the easiest source of cash. You can use major credit cards and some bank cards, such as those on the Cirrus and Plus systems, to withdraw pesos (or dollars) from ATMs. The exchange rate that banks use for ATM withdrawals is normally better than the 'tourist rate' – though that advantage may be negated by handling fees, interest charges and other methods that banks have of taking your money. Use ATMs during daylight hours, and, whenever possible, in secure indoor locations.

Banks & Casas de Cambio

You can change currency in banks or at *casas de cambio* (money-exchange offices). Banks go through a more time-consuming procedure than *casas de cambio* and usually have shorter hours. *Casas de cambio* can easily be found in just about every large or medium-size town and in some smaller ones. They're quick and often open on evenings or weekends, but be aware that some don't accept traveler's checks.

International Transfers

Should you need money wired to you in Mexico, an easy and quick method is through **Western Union** (☎inUSA 800-225-5227; www.westernunion.com). The service is offered by thousands of bank branches and other businesses around Mexico,

TAXES

Mexico's value-added tax (IVA) is levied at 16%. By law the tax must be included in prices quoted to you and should not be added afterward. Signs in shops and notices on restaurant menus often state '*IVA incluido.*' Occasionally they state instead that IVA must be added to the quoted prices. In Quintana Roo, IVA is 11% (a reduced rate set for some border states).

Hotel rooms are also subject to a lodging tax (ISH) of 2% or 3%, depending on the state.

identified by black-and-yellow signs. Your sender pays the money online or at a Western Union branch, along with a fee, and gives the details on who is to receive it and where. When you pick it up, take along photo identification. Western Union has offices worldwide.

US post offices (☎888-368-4669; www.usps.com) offer reasonably cheap money transfers to branches of Bancomer bank in Mexico. The service is called *Dinero Seguro*.

Tipping & Bargaining

Workers in tourism and service industries often depend on tips to supplement miserable basic wages. Here's what you should leave:

Restaurants About 15% unless service comes included in the check.

Hotels From 5% to 10% of your room cost.

Taxis Drivers don't expect tips unless a special service is provided.

Gas station and parking attendants M$5 or M$10.

Baggers in supermarkets M$3 or M$5.

Hotel and airport porters M$20 per bag.

Opening Hours

Standard hours are as follows (exceptions are noted in listings in this book):

Banks 9am to 4pm Monday to Friday, 10am to 2pm Saturday; some banks do not open Saturday, and weekend hours vary.

Casas de Cambio (currency exchange offices) 9am to 7pm daily

Stores/Shops 9am to 8pm Monday to Saturday; some shops close 2pm to 4pm. Supermarkets usually open from 9am to 10pm daily.

Museums Many close on Monday.

Photography & Video

Most Mexicans don't mind having their pictures taken but it's always a good idea to ask beforehand. Some indigenous people can be especially sensitive about this.

Be forewarned that a M$45 fee for use of video cameras is charged at many ruins.

Post

- An airmail letter or postcard weighing up to 20g costs M$11.50 to send to the USA or Canada, M$13.50 to Europe or South America, and M$16.50 to the rest of the world.
- Delivery takes 15 to 20 days, or five to to eight days if you pay for express service.
- If you're sending a package internationally from Mexico, be prepared to open it for inspection at the post office; take packing materials with you and don't seal it till you get there.
- For assured and speedy delivery, you can use one of the more expensive international courier services, such as **UPS** (☎800-902-9200; www.ups.com), **FedEx** (☎800-900-1100; www.fedex.com) or Mexico's **Estafeta** (☎800-903-3500; www.estafeta.com). A 1kg package typically costs about M$600 to the USA or Canada, and M$800 to Europe.

Public Holidays

Banks, post offices, government offices and many shops throughout Mexico are closed on the following national holidays:

Año Nuevo (New Year's Day) January 1

Día de la Constitución (Constitution Day) February 5

Día del Nacimiento de Benito Juárez (Anniversary of Benito Juárez' birth) March 21

Día del Trabajo (Labor Day) May 1

Día de la Independencia (Independence Day) September 16

Día de la Revolución (Revolution Day) November 20

Día de Navidad (Christmas Day) December 25

In addition, many offices and businesses close on the following optional holidays:

Día de la Bandera (Day of the National Flag) February 24

Viernes Santo (Good Friday) Two days before Easter Sunday

Cinco de Mayo (Anniversary of Mexico's victory over the French at Puebla) May 5

Día de la Raza (Columbus' discovery of the New World) October 12

Día de Muertos (Day of the Dead) November 1 & 2

Día de Nuestra Señora de Guadalupe (Day of Our Lady of Guadalupe) December 12

Safe Travel

Despite often-alarming media reports and official warnings for Mexico in general, the Yucatán Peninsula remains a very safe place to travel. Since most of the drug-related violence occurs between rival cartels or gangs, tourists are rarely caught up in the disputes. What's more, the Yucatán has managed to distance itself from the kind of turf wars occurring in other parts of Mexico, so it's one of the safest places in the country.

Foreign affairs departments can supply a variety of useful data about travel to Mexico.

Australia (☎outside Australia 612-6261-3305; www.dfat.gov.au)

Canada (☎in Canada 800-267-8376, outside Canada 613-944-4000; www.dfait-maeci.gc.ca)

UK (☎in UK 020-7008-1500; www.gov.uk/fco)

USA (☎in USA 808-407-4747, outside USA 202-501-4444; www.travel.state.gov)

Theft & Robbery

Pickpocketing and bag-snatching remain minor risks in crowded buses and bus stations, airports, markets or anywhere frequented by large numbers of tourists. Mugging is less common than purse-snatching, but more serious: resistance may be met with violence (do *not* resist). Usually these robbers will not harm you: they just want your money, fast.

➡ Don't go where there are few other people in the vicinity; this includes camping in secluded places. A simple rule: if there are women and children around, you're probably safe.

➡ Don't leave any valuables unattended while you swim. Run-and-grab thefts by people lurking in the woods are a common occurrence.

➡ If your hotel has a safe, leave most of your money, important documents and smaller valuables there in a sealed, signed envelope. Leave valuables in a locker when staying at a hostel.

➡ Carry only a small amount of money – enough for an outing – in a pocket. If you do have to carry valuables, keep them hidden in a money belt underneath your clothing.

➡ Don't keep money, credit or debit cards, wallets or bags in open view any longer than you have to. At ticket counters, keep a hand or foot on your bag at all times.

➡ Do not leave anything valuable-looking in a parked vehicle.

➡ Be careful about accepting drinks from overly social characters in bars, especially in tourist-heavy zones; there have been cases of drugging followed by robbery and assault.

➡ Be wary of attempts at credit-card fraud. One method is when the cashier swipes your card twice (once for the transaction and once for nefarious purposes). Keep your card in sight at all times.

Telephone

Call Offices

Costs in *casetas de teléfono* and *locutorios* (phone cabins) are often lower than those for Telmex card phones, and since you call from a booth you eliminate the street noise you get when calling from an exterior pay phone.

Cell Phones

Using your own cell phone (brought from home) in Mexico can be extremely expensive due to high roaming fees. **Roaming Zone** (www.roamingzone.com) is a useful source on roaming arrangements. Alternatively, you can insert a Mexican SIM card into your phone, but your phone needs to be unlocked for international use. Some Mexican cell-phone companies will unlock it for you for a fee. The easiest option is to simply buy a new Mexican cell phone: they're inexpensive (about M$400) and come with free credit. You'll often see cell phones on sale in convenience stores, where you can also buy more credit. Cell-phone service providers **Telcel** (www.telcel.com) and **Movistar** (www.movistar.com.mx) have the best coverage in the Yucatán region.

Like other Mexican phone numbers, every cell-phone number has an area code (usually the code of the city where the phone was bought). Here's how to make calls to and from Mexican cell phones.

➡ From local cell phone to cell phone, just dial the 10-digit number.

➡ From cell phone to landline, dial the landline's area code and number (also 10 digits).

➡ From landline to cell phone, dial ☎044 before the 10 digits if the cell phone's area code is the same as the area code you're dialing from, or ☎045 if the cell has a different area code.

➡ From another country to a Mexican cell phone, dial your international access code, the Mexican country code (☎52), then ☎1 plus the 10-digit number.

Credit on Mexican cell phones or SIM cards burns fast, especially when making calls outside the phone's area code. How do you think Telcel boss Carlos Slim became the world's richest man?

Collect Calls

Una llamada por cobrar (collect call) can cost the receiving party much more than if they call you, so you may prefer for the other party to call. You can make collect

USEFUL NUMBERS

Domestic Operator ☎020

Emergency ☎066

International Operator ☎090

Mexican directory information ☎040

Mexican toll-free numbers ☎800 followed by seven digits; always require the 01 long-distance prefix

calls from card phones without a card. Call an operator at 020 for domestic calls, or 090 for international calls. The Mexican term for 'home country direct' is *país directo:* but don't count on Mexican international operators knowing the access codes for all countries.

Some call offices and hotels will make collect calls for you, but they usually charge for the service.

Landlines

Telefonos fijos (Mexican landlines) have two- or three-digit area codes, which are listed in town headings throughout this book.

- From a landline to another landline in the same town, just dial the local number (seven or eight digits).
- From a landline to a landline in a different Mexican town, dial the long-distance prefix 01, then the area code, then the local number.
- To make an international call, dial the international prefix 00, then the country code (1 for the US and Canada, 44 for the UK etc), then area code and local number.
- To call a Mexican landline from another country, dial your international access code, then the Mexico country code 52, then the area code and number.

Long-Distance Discount Cards

Available at many newspaper stands, usually in denominations of M$100 and M$200, *tarjetas telefónicas de descuento* (discount phone cards) offer substantial savings on long-distance calls from landlines. You can use them from most public card phones.

Public Card Phones

These are common in towns and cities; you'll usually find some at airports and bus stations. The most common are those of the country's biggest phone company, Telmex. To use a Telmex card phone you need a phone card known as a *tarjeta Ladatel*. These are sold at kiosks and shops everywhere in denominations of M$30, M$50 and M$100.

Calls from Telmex card phones cost M$3 for unlimited time for local calls (M$1.50 per minute to cell phones); M$2.50 per minute for long-distance within Mexico (M$3 per minute to cell phones); M$5 per minute to the continental US, Canada and Central America; and M$10 per minute to anywhere else.

VOIP

Voice Over Internet Protocol (VOIP) services such as **Skype** (www.skype.com) are a very economical option for travelers who have a computer and the required software. You can also use Skype at internet cafes.

Time

The entire Yucatán Peninsula observes the Hora del Centro, which is the same as US Central Time – GMT minus six hours in winter, and GMT minus five hours during daylight-saving time (*horario de verano,* summer time), which runs from the first Sunday in April to the last Sunday in October. Clocks go forward one hour in April and back one hour in October.

Tourist Information

Just about every town of interest to tourists in the Yucatán has a state or municipal tourist office. They are generally helpful with maps, brochures and questions, and often some staff members speak English.

You can call the Mexico City office of the national tourism ministry **Sectur** (078; www.sectur.gob.mx) at any time – 24 hours a day, seven days a week – for information or help in English or Spanish.

Here are the contact details for the head tourism offices of each state:

Campeche (800-900-2267, 981-811-9229; www.campeche.travel)

Chiapas (800-280-3500, 961-617-0550; www.turismochiapas.gob.mx)

Quintana Roo (998-881-9000, 983-835-0860; sedetur.qroo.gob.mx)

Tabasco (800-216-0842, 993-316-8271; www.visitetabasco.com)

Yucatán state (999-930-3760; www.yucatan.travel)

Travelers with Disabilities

Yucatán Peninsula lodgings generally don't cater for travelers with disabilities, though some hotels and restaurants (mostly toward the top end of the market) and some public buildings now provide wheelchair access. The absence of institutionalized facilities is largely compensated for, however, by Mexicans' accommodating attitudes toward others, and special arrangements are gladly improvised.

Mobility is easiest in the major tourist resorts. Bus transportation can be difficult; flying or taking a taxi is easier. The following websites have useful information for disabled travelers:

Access-able Travel Source (www.access-able.com)

Mobility International USA (in USA 541-343-1284; www.miusa.org)

MossRehab ResourceNet (www.mossresourcenet.org)

Radar (in USA 020-7250-3222; www.radar.org.uk)

Visas

Every tourist must have a Mexican government tourist

permit, which is easily obtainable. Some nationalities also need to obtain visas.

➡ Citizens of the USA, Canada, EU countries, Australia, New Zealand, Iceland, Israel, Japan, Norway and Switzerland are among those who do not require visas to enter Mexico as tourists.

➡ The website of the **Instituto Nacional de Migración** (INM, National Migration Institute; ☎800-004-6264; www.inm.gob.mx) lists countries that must obtain a visa to travel to Mexico. If the purpose of your visit is to work (even as a volunteer), to report, to study, or to participate in humanitarian aid or human-rights observation, you may well need a visa, whatever your nationality. Visa procedures can take several weeks and you may be required to apply in your country of citizenship or residence.

➡ US citizens traveling by land or sea can enter Mexico and return to the US with a passport card, but if traveling by air will need a passport. Non-US citizens passing (even in transit) through the US on the way to or from Mexico should check well in advance on the US's complicated visa rules. Consult a US consulate, the **US State Department** (www.travel.state.gov), or **US Customs and Border Protection** (www.cbp.gov) websites.

➡ The regulations sometimes change. It's wise to confirm them with a Mexican embassy or consulate. Good sources for information on visa and similar matters are the **London consulate** (consulmex.sre.gob.mx/reinounido) and the **Washington consulate** (consulmex.sre.gob.mx/washington). Rules are also summarized on the INM website.

Tourist Permit & Fee

The Mexican tourist permit (tourist card; officially the *forma migratoria multiple* or FMM) is a brief paper document that you must fill out and get stamped by Mexican immigration when you enter Mexico and keep till you leave. It's available at official border crossings, international airports, ports, and often from airlines and Mexican consulates. At land borders you won't usually be given one automatically – you have to ask for it.

A tourist permit only permits you to engage in what are considered to be tourist activities (including sports, health, artistic and cultural activities).

➡ The maximum possible stay is 180 days for most nationalities but immigration officers will sometimes put a lower number (as little as 15 or 30 days in some cases) unless you tell them specifically what you need.

➡ The fee for the tourist permit, called the *derecho para no inmigrante* (DNI; nonimmigrant fee), is M$294, but it's free for people entering by land who stay less than seven days. If you enter Mexico by air, however, the fee is included in your airfare.

➡ If you enter by land, you must pay the fee at a bank in Mexico at any time before you reenter the frontier zone on your way out of Mexico (or before you check in at an airport to fly out of Mexico). Most Mexican border posts have on-the-spot bank offices where you can pay the DNI fee. When you pay at a bank, your tourist permit will be stamped to prove that you have paid.

➡ Look after your tourist permit because it may be checked when you leave the country. You can be fined for not having it.

➡ Tourist permits (and fees) are not necessary for visits within border zones (the territory between the border itself and INM's control points on highways leading into the Mexican interior, which is usually about 20km to 30km from the border).

EXTENSIONS & LOST CARDS

If the number of days given on your tourist permit is less than the maximum for your nationality (90 or 180 days in most cases), its validity may be extended one or more times, up to the maximum days.

To get a permit extended you have to apply to the INM, which has offices in many towns and cities. They're listed at www.inm.gob.mx under 'contact us.' You'll need your passport, tourist permit, photocopies of them and, at some offices, proof of 'sufficient' bank funds or a major credit card. Most INM offices will not extend a permit until a few days before it's due to expire.

If you lose your card, contact your nearest INM office, which will issue a duplicate for M$294.

Volunteering

Volunteering is a great way of giving back to local communities. In the Yucatán there are various organizations that welcome any help they can get, from environmental and wildlife-conservation NGOs to social programs. You can always look for opportunities at your local hostel or language school, some of which offer part-time volunteering opportunities. Most programs require a minimum commitment of at least a month, and some charge fees for room and board.

Volunteer Directories

Go Abroad (www.goabroad.com)

Go Overseas (www.gooverseas.com)

Idealist (www.idealist.org)

The Mexico Report (themexicoreport.com/non-profits-in-mexico)

Transitions Abroad (www.transitionsabroad.com)

Yucatán-based Programs

Centro Ecológico Akumal (www.ceakumal.org) Accepts volunteers for its environmental and protection programs.

Flora, Fauna y Cultura (www.florafaunaycultura.org) You can help with turtle conservation in Xcacel from May to October.

Junax (www.junax.org.mx) Works with indigenous communities in Chiapas; volunteers must speak Spanish.

Pronatura (www.pronaturappy.org.mx) Mérida-based environmental organization seeks volunteers to work at various projects in the Yucatán.

Women Travelers

Women can have a great time in the Yucatán, whether traveling with companions or traveling solo. Gender equality has come a long way in Mexico, and *yucatecos* (people from the Yucatán) are generally a very polite people, but lone women may still be subject to some whistles, loud comments and annoying attempts to chat them up.

Don't put yourself in peril by doing things that Mexican women would not do, such as drinking alone in a cantina, hitchhiking, walking alone through empty streets at night, or going alone to isolated places. Keep a clear head. Excessive alcohol will make you vulnerable. To keep yourself in the company of other travelers, head for accommodations such as hostels and popular hotels, where you're likely to join group excursions and activities.

On the streets of inland cities and towns, such as in Mérida and Valladolid, you'll notice that women cover up and don't display too much leg, midriff or even their shoulders. This also makes it easier to keep valuables out of sight.

Transportation

GETTING THERE & AWAY

Entering the Region

Immigration officers usually won't keep you waiting any longer than it takes to flick through your passport and enter your length of stay on your tourist permit. Anyone traveling to Mexico via the USA should be sure to check US visa and passport requirements. US citizens traveling by land or sea can enter Mexico and return to the US with a passport card, but if traveling by air will need a passport. Citizens of other countries need their passports to enter Mexico. Some nationalities also need a visa (see p287). Flights and tours can be booked online at www.lonelyplanet.com/bookings.

Air

Most visitors to the Yucatán arrive by air. Direct flights normally originate from an airline's hub city and connecting flights often go through Mexico City.

Airports & Airlines

The majority of flights into the peninsula arrive at busy **Aeropuerto Internacional de Cancún** (CUN; ☎998-848-7200; www.asur.com.mx; Carretera Cancún-Chetumal, Km 22; 📶). The region's other gateways are **Cozumel airport** (CZM; ☎987-872-2081; www.asur.com.mx; Av 65 & Blvd Aeropuerto; 📶), **Mérida** (MID; ☎999-940-6090; www.asur.com.mx), Campeche (CPE), Ciudad del Carmen, Chetumal and **Tuxtla Gutiérrez** (☎961-153-6068), which services San Cristóbal de las Casas in Chiapas.

Mexico's flagship airline is **Aeroméxico** (☎800-021-4000; www.aeromexico.com). Its safety record is comparable to major US and European airlines.

AIRLINES FLYING TO/FROM THE YUCATÁN

Aeroméxico (☎800-021-4000; www.aeromexico.com)

Air France (☎800-123-1628; www.airfrance.com)

AirTran Airways (☎in USA 800-247-8726; www.airtran.com)

American Airlines (☎800-904-6000; www.aa.com)

British Airways (☎in USA 866-835-4133; www.britishairways.com)

Delta Airlines (☎800-123-4710; www.delta.com)

Frontier Airlines (☎in USA 800-432-1359; www.flyfrontier.com)

Interjet (☎800-011-2345; www.interjet.com)

Magnicharters (☎800-201-1404; www.magnicharters.com.mx)

CLIMATE CHANGE & TRAVEL

Every form of transport that relies on carbon-based fuel generates CO_2, the main cause of human-induced climate change. Modern travel is dependent on airplanes, which might use less fuel per kilometer per person than most cars but travel much greater distances. The altitude at which aircraft emit gases (including CO_2) and particles also contributes to their climate change impact. Many websites offer 'carbon calculators' that allow people to estimate the carbon emissions generated by their journey and, for those who wish to do so, to offset the impact of the greenhouse gases emitted with contributions to portfolios of climate-friendly initiatives throughout the world. Lonely Planet offsets the carbon footprint of all staff and author travel.

DEPARTURE TAXES

An airport departure tax is usually included in your ticket cost, but if it isn't you must pay in cash during airport check-in. It varies from airport to airport and costs between US$18 to US$29 for international flights and a little less for domestic flights. This tax is separate from the fee for your tourist permit, which is also included in airfares.

There are two taxes on domestic flights: IVA, the value-added tax (16%), and TUA, an airport tax of about US$16. In Mexico, the taxes are normally included in quoted fares and paid when you buy the ticket. But if you bought the ticket outside Mexico you will have to pay the TUA when you check-in in Mexico.

Spirit Airlines (☎in USA 801-401-2200; www.spiritair.com)
Sun Country Airlines (☎in USA 800-359-6786; www.suncountry.com)
TACA Airlines (☎800-400-8222; www.taca.com)
United Airlines (☎800-900-5000; www.united.com)
US Airways (☎in USA 800-428-4322; www.usairways.com)
VivaAerobus (☎Mexico City 554-777-5050, USA 888-935-9848; www.vivaaerobus.com)
Volaris (☎800-122-8000; www.volaris.com)
WestJet (☎USA 855-547-2451; www.westjet.com)

Land

Mexico

➡ Mexico can be entered from the USA at around 40 official road-crossing points. Major entry points are San Ysidro/Tijuana and Calexico/Mexicali, from California; El Paso/Ciudad Juárez and Laredo/Nuevo Laredo, from Texas; and Nogales/Nogales, from Arizona.

➡ Buses departing from Oaxaca City and the southern Oaxaca coast town of Puerto Escondido go to San Cristóbal de las Casas and Tuxtla Gutiérrez, in Chiapas. If you have a vehicle, take Hwy 190 from Oaxaca City or Hwy 200 along the coast and follow the signs to Tuxtla Gutiérrez.

➡ From Villahermosa, the state capital of Tabasco, Palenque is just a 2½-hour bus ride away, or if you'd like to explore more of Mexico beyond the peninsula, buses leave frequently to the port city of Veracruz. Hwy 180 runs north from Villahermosa, then it heads along the coast to Campeche and makes its way inland toward Mérida.

Belize

➡ Crossing from Mexico to Belize at the southern tip of Quintana Roo is easy for most tourists and there are no special fees for such a visit.

➡ Each person leaving Belize for Mexico needs to pay a BZ$30 exit fee for stays of less than 24 hours and BZ$37.50 for longer stays. All fees must be paid in cash, in Belizean or US currency – officials usually won't have change for US currency.

➡ Frequent buses run from Chetumal to the Belizean towns of Corozal (M$35 to M$40, one hour) and Orange Walk (M$35 to M$50, two hours). The buses depart from the Nuevo Mercado Lázaro Cárdenas and some continue on to Belize City.

➡ Alternatively, **Gibson's Tours & Transfers** (☎501-423-8006; www.gibsonstoursandtransfers.com; Santa Elena-Corozal border) provides ground transportation to Corozal for M$290 and it offers transport to other Beilzean destinations as well. Gibson's also can help you get a special permit that's needed to cross the border with a rental car.

Guatemala

➡ The borders at La Mesilla/Ciudad Cuauhtémoc, Ciudad Tecún Umán/Ciudad Hidalgo and El Carmen/Talismán are all linked to Guatemala City, and nearby cities within Guatemala and Mexico, by plentiful buses and/or *combis* (minibuses).

➡ Agencies in San Cristóbal de las Casas offer daily van service to the Guatemalan cities of Quetzaltenango, Panajachel and Antigua.

➡ Additionally, there's a daily bus departing from the San Cristóbal de las Casas bus station that goes to the Ciudad Cuauhtémoc border, where you can catch Guatemalan buses on the other side in the border town of La Mesilla.

➡ **Transportes Palenque** (cnr Allende & Av 20 de Noviembre) runs vans out of Palenque to Tenosique, Tabasco, where you'll find onward connections to Guatemala.

➡ Travelers with their own vehicles can travel by road between Tenosique and Flores (Guatemala), via the border at El Ceibo.

➡ Rental car companies do not allow you to cross the Mexico-Guatemala border with their vehicles.

Sea

You can hire a boat at the **XTC Dive Center** (www.xtc-divecenter.com; Coast road, Km 0.3; 2-tank dives to Banco Chinchorro M$2580, snorkeling trips M$325) in Xcalak for M$780 per person (maximum eight people) to take you to San Pedro, Belize. There are also San Pedro–bound boats departing from Chetumal's Muelle Fiscal (dock) on Boulevard Bahía. See www.sanpedrowatertaxi.com for schedule and rates.

Mahahual, Puerto Chiapas, Progreso and Isla Cozumel are ports of call for cruise ships. The following are some of the lines serving them:

Carnival Cruise Lines (☎ in USA 800-764-7619; www.carnival.com)

Crystal Cruises (☎in USA 888-722-0021; www.crystalcruises.com)

Norwegian Cruise Lines (☎in USA 866-234-7350; www.ncl.com)

P&O Cruises (☎in UK 0843-374-0111; www.pocruises.com)

Princess Cruises (☎in USA 800-774-6237; www.princess.com)

Royal Caribbean International (☎in Mexico 800-700-2129, in USA 866-562-7625; www.royalcaribbean.com)

GETTING AROUND

Boat

Round-trip fares for frequent ferries running from the mainland to the islands are as follows:

Isla Holbox M$80

Isla Cozumel M$310

Isla Mujeres M$140 (from Puerto Juárez dock)

For more information about schedules, points of departure and car ferries, see www.granpuerto.com.mx and transcaribe.net. The Holbox ferries do not have websites. Also see individual destinations for details.

Bus

The Yucatán Peninsula has a good road and bus network, and comfortable, frequent, reasonably priced bus services connect all cities. Most cities and towns have one main bus terminal where all long-distance buses arrive and depart. It may be called the Terminal de Autobuses, Central de Autobuses, Central Camionera or simply La Central (not to be confused with *el centro,* the city center!). If there is no single main terminal, different bus companies will have separate terminals scattered around town. **Grupo ADO** (☎800-900-0105; www.ado.com.mx) operates most of the bus lines that you'll be using.

Classes

DELUXE & EXECUTIVE

De lujo (deluxe) services, and the even more comfortable *ejecutivo* (executive), run mainly on the busy routes. They are swift, modern and comfortable, with reclining seats, adequate leg room, air-con, few or no stops, toilets on board (but not necessarily toilet paper), and sometimes drinks or snacks. Deluxe buses usually show movies on video screens and may offer headphones.

ADO Platino (☎800-737-5856; www.adoplatino.com.mx), **ADO GL** (☎800-900-0105; www.adogl.com.mx) and **OCC** (☎800-900-0105; www.occbus.com.mx) provide luxury services. You can buy tickets to these services in the bus station before boarding.

1ST CLASS

On *primera (1a) clase* (1st-class) buses, standards of comfort are adequate at the very least. The buses usually have air-con and a toilet, and they stop infrequently. They always show movies (often bad ones, unless Vin Diesel films are your idea of cinematic glory) for most of the trip.

Bring a sweater or jacket to combat over-zealous air-conditioning. As with deluxe buses, you buy your ticket in the bus station before boarding. ADO sets the 1st-class standard.

2ND CLASS

Segunda (2a) clase (2nd-class) buses serve small towns and villages, and provide cheaper, slower travel on some intercity routes. A few are almost as quick, comfortable and direct as 1st-class buses. Others are old, slow and shabby.

Many 2nd-class services have no ticket office; you just pay your fare to the conductor. These buses tend to take slow, nontoll roads in and out of big cities and will stop anywhere to pick up passengers: if you board midroute you might make some of the trip standing. The small amount of money you save by traveling 2nd class is not usually worth the discomfort or extra journey time entailed, though traveling on these buses is a great way to meet locals and see less-traveled parts of the countryside.

Second-class buses can also be less safe than 1st-class or deluxe buses, for reasons of maintenance, driver standards, or because they are more vulnerable to being boarded by bandits on quiet roads. In the remote areas, however, you'll often find that 2nd-class buses are the only buses available.

Microbuses or '*micros*' are small, usually fairly new, 2nd-class buses with around 25 seats, often running short routes between nearby towns. The biggest 2nd-class companies are Mayab, Oriente and **Noreste** (☎800-280-1010; www.noreste.com.mx).

Costs

First-class buses typically cost around M$60 to M$70 per hour of travel (70km to 80km). Deluxe buses may cost just 10% or 20% more than 1st class, while *ejecutivo* services can be as much as 50% more. Second-class buses cost about 20% less than 1st class.

Reservations

For trips of up to four or five hours on busy routes, you can usually just go to the bus terminal, buy a ticket and head out without much delay. For longer trips, or routes with infrequent services, buy a ticket a day or more in advance. Deluxe and 1st-class bus companies have computerized ticket systems that allow you to select your seat when you buy your ticket.

Seats on deluxe and 1st-class lines such as ADO and OCC can be booked through **Boletotal** (☎800-009-9090; www.boletotal.mx), a reservations service with offices in Mérida, Cancún, Cozumel, Campeche and Ciudad del Carmen and San Cristóbal de las Casas. Boletotal adds a 10% surcharge to the cost of the ticket so you can save a little money by simply purchasing tickets at the bus terminal.

If you pay for a bus ticket in cash, cash refunds of 80% to 100% are available from many bus companies if you return your ticket more than an hour or two before the departure time.

Car & Motorcycle

Driving in Mexico is not as easy as it is north of the border, and rentals are more expensive, but having your own vehicle gives you extra flexibility and freedom. To reach some of the peninsula's most remote beaches – such as Punta Allen, the stretch of coast east of Progreso, or Xcalak – having a car makes life much easier.

Drivers should know some Spanish and have basic mechanical knowledge, reserves of patience and access to extra cash for emergencies. Very big cars are unwieldy on narrow roads, particularly in the peninsula's rural areas. A sedan with a trunk (boot) provides safer storage than a station wagon or hatchback. Tires (including a spare), shock absorbers and suspension should be in good condition. For security, have something to immobilize the steering wheel.

Motorcycling around the Yucatán is not for the fainthearted. Roads and traffic can be rough, and parts and mechanics hard to come by. Scooters are a good option for getting around on Isla Mujeres and Isla Cozumel. Helmets are required by Mexican law.

Bringing Your Own Vehicle

Unless you're planning on spending a lot of time touring the Yucatán and other parts of Mexico, you're better off with a rental car. Of course, if you're planning on bringing diving equipment or other cumbersome luggage, the long drive from the US or elsewhere may be worth your while.

You can check the full requirements for bringing a vehicle into Mexico with the **American Automobile Association** (AAA; www.aaa.com), a Mexican consulate or **Mexican Tourist Information** (☎in USA & Canada 866-640-0597).

DRIVER'S LICENSE

To drive a motor vehicle in Mexico you need a valid driver's license from your home country.

FUEL

All *gasolina* (gasoline) and diesel fuel in Mexico is sold by the government-owned Pemex (Petróleos Mexicanos). All major cities and most midsize towns in the Yucatán have gas stations. If you're heading to a remote coastal town or jungle region, you should fill up before leaving and wherever you can along the way.

The gasoline on sale is all *sin plomo* (unleaded). There are two varieties: *magna sin* (roughly equivalent to US regular unleaded), and premium (roughly equivalent to US super unleaded). At the time of research, *magna sin* cost about M$10.80 per liter, and premium about M$11.40. Diesel fuel is widely available at around M$11.20 per liter. Regular Mexican diesel has a higher sulfur content than US diesel, but there is a '*diesel sin*' with less sulfur.

Pump attendants at gas stations appreciate a tip of M$3 to M$5.

INSURANCE

It is very foolish to drive anywhere in Mexico without Mexican liability insurance. If you are involved in an accident, you can be jailed and have your vehicle impounded while responsibility and restitution is assessed. If you are to blame for an accident causing injury or death, you

THE GREEN ANGELS

The Mexican tourism ministry, Sectur, maintains a network of Ángeles Verdes (Green Angels) – bilingual mechanics in green uniforms and green trucks who patrol 60,000km of major highways throughout the country daily during daylight hours looking for tourists in trouble. They make minor repairs, change tires, provide fuel and oil, and arrange towing and other assistance if necessary. Service is free; parts, gasoline and oil are provided at cost. If you are near a telephone when your car has problems, you can call its **24-hour hotline** (☎078) or contact the network through the national **24-hour tourist-assistance service** (☎800-006-8839) in Mexico City.

may be detained until you guarantee restitution to the victims and payment of any fines. This could take weeks or months!

Adequate Mexican insurance coverage is the only real protection – it is regarded as a guarantee that restitution will be paid. Mexican law recognizes only Mexican *seguro* (motor insurance), so US or Canadian policy, even if it provides coverage, is not acceptable to Mexican officialdom. You can buy Mexican motor insurance online through the well-established **Sanborn's** (☎in USA 800-222-0158; www.sanbornsinsurance.com) and other companies.

Short-term insurance is about US$15 a day for full coverage on a car worth under US$10,000; liability-only insurance costs around half the full coverage cost.

MAPS

Signposting can be poor, especially along the Yucatán's non-toll roads, and decent maps are essential. Regional road maps such as Guia Roji's *Mundo Maya* (M$90) or ITMB's *Yucatán Peninsula Travel Reference Map* (US$12.95) are good options, or if you plan on visiting other parts of Mexico, Guia Roji's *Por las Carreteras de México* (M$200) will serve you well. Guia Roji maps are sold at bookstores, some newsstands and online at www.guiaroji.com.mx.

RENTALS

Auto rental in the Yucatán is expensive by US or European standards, but is not hard to organize. You can book by internet, phone or in person, and pick up cars at city offices, airports and many of the big hotels. You'll save money by booking ahead of time over the internet. Read the small print of the rental agreement.

➡ Renters must provide a valid driver's license (your home license is OK), passport and major credit card, and are usually required to be at least 21 years old (sometimes 25, or if you're aged 21 to 24 you may have to pay a surcharge).

➡ In addition to the basic rental rate, you pay tax and insurance to the rental company, and the full insurance that rental companies encourage can almost double the base cost. You'll usually have the option of taking liability-only insurance at a lower rate: about M$130 per day. Ask exactly what the insurance options cover: theft and damage insurance may only cover a percentage of costs. It's best to have plenty of liability coverage: Mexican law permits the jailing of drivers after an accident until they have met their obligations to third parties.

➡ The complimentary car-rental insurance offered with some US credit cards does not always cover Mexico. Call your card company ahead of time to check.

➡ Most rental agencies offer unlimited kilometers. Local firms may or may not be cheaper than the big international ones. In most places the cheapest car available (often a Volkswagen Beetle) costs M$400 to M$500 a day including unlimited kilometers, insurance and tax. If you rent by the week or month, the per-day cost can come down by 20% to 40%. You can also cut costs by avoiding airport pickups and drop-offs, for which 10% can be added to your total check. The extra charge for drop-off in another city, when available, is usually about M$4 per kilometer.

➡ Remember that you cannot take a rental car out of Mexico unless you have obtained a special permit.

➡ Motorcycles or scooters are available for rent in several tourist centers. You're usually required to have a driver's license and credit card. It's advisable to look particularly carefully into insurance arrangements here: some renters do not offer any insurance at all. Note that a locally acquired motorcycle license is not valid under some travel-insurance policies. Check the bike carefully for dings and scratches before taking it out or you may get hit with repair costs.

➡ The following are some major car-rental agencies in the Yucatán:

STAYING AWARE OF YOUR SURROUNDINGS

Here are several important tips to consider if you've got wheels:

➡ Fast-approaching vehicles from behind will often shine their brights or use their left-turn signal to indicate that you should change lanes and let them pass.

➡ Some streets may suddenly change direction without warning: pay close attention to the road or you may find yourself driving against the flow of traffic.

➡ Liability insurance does not include theft coverage: something to think about when parking your car overnight.

➡ Spare tires get swiped fairly regularly in Mexico: if you're going somewhere where you may need it, make sure it's still there before leaving.

Alamo (☎800-849-8001; www.alamo.com)
Budget (☎800-700-1700; www.budget.com.mx)
Easy Way (☎800-327-9929; www.easywayrentacar.com)
Europcar (☎800-201-2084; www.europcar.com.mx)
Hertz (☎800-709-5000; www.hertz.com)
National (☎800-716-6625; www.nationalcar.com.mx)
Thrifty (☎55-5207-1100; www.thrifty.com.mx)

ROAD CONDITIONS

There are three major toll roads (mostly four-lane) in the Yucatán that connect the major cities. They are generally in much better condition and a lot quicker than the alternative free roads.

Driving during the rainy season (usually from May to October) can be challenging to say the least, especially along dirt roads in rural and coastal areas.

Be especially wary of Alto (Stop) signs and speed bumps (called *topes, vibradores* or *reductores de velocidad*) and holes in the road. They are often not where you'd expect and missing one can cost you a traffic fine or car damage. Speed bumps are also used to slow traffic on highways that pass through built-up areas – they are not always signed and some of them are severe!

Driving on a dark night is best avoided since unlit vehicles, rocks, pedestrians and animals on the roads are common. Also, hijacks and robberies can occur (stay particularly alert while driving in the vicinity of the Mexico-Guatemala border).

ROAD RULES

Drive on the right-hand side of the road.

One-way streets are the rule in cities. Priority at street intersections is indicated by thin black and red rectangles containing white arrows. A black rectangle facing you means you have priority; a red one means you don't. The white arrows indicate the direction of traffic on the cross street; if the arrow points both ways, it's a two-way street.

Speed limits range between 80km/h and 120km/h on open highways (less when highways pass through built-up areas), and between 30km/h and 50km/h in towns and cities. Seat belts are obligatory for all occupants of a car, and children under five must be strapped into safety seats in the rear. Traffic laws and speed limits rarely seem to be enforced on the highways. Obey the rules in the cities so you don't give the police an excuse to demand a 'fine' that's payable on the spot.

Although less frequent in the Yucatán, there is always the chance that you will be pulled over by traffic police for an imaginary infraction. If this happens, stay calm and polite and don't be in a hurry. You don't have to pay a bribe, and corrupt cops would rather not work too hard to obtain one. You can also ask to see documentation about the law you have supposedly broken, ask for the officer's identification, ask to speak to a superior, and/or note the officer's name, badge number, vehicle number and department (federal, state or municipal). Pay any traffic fines at a police station and get a receipt, then if you wish to make a complaint head for a state tourist office.

Hitchhiking

Hitchhiking is never entirely safe in any country and even in Mexico's relatively safe Yucatán region it's best avoided. Travelers who decide to hitch should understand that they are taking a small, but potentially serious, risk. Keep in mind that kidnappings for ransom can – and do – happen in Mexico. People who do choose to hitch will be safer if they travel in pairs and let someone know where they are planning to go. A woman traveling alone certainly should not hitchhike in Mexico, and even two women together is not advisable, especially when traveling near the Chiapas–Guatemala border.

However, some people do choose to hitchhike, and it's not an uncommon way of getting to some of the off-the-beaten-track archaeological sites and other places that are poorly served by bus. If you do hitchhike, keep your wits about you and don't accept a lift if you have any misgivings.

In Mexico it's customary for the hitchhiker to offer to pay for the ride, especially if the ride is in a work or commercial vehicle. As a general rule, offer about M$10 per person for every 30 minutes of the ride, but not less than M$20 total, and never more than M$100. If you're driving a vehicle and making stops in rural areas, it's not uncommon for Mexican townspeople to ask for a lift. Most folks in these parts are harmless and they are only asking for a ride because there is infrequent bus service, but by no means should you feel obligated to pick them up, especially if the person has been drinking or has an odd vibe.

Local Transportation

Bus

Generally known as *camiones*, local buses are usually the cheapest way to get around cities and out to nearby towns and villages. They run frequently and fares in cities are dirt cheap.

Buses usually halt only at fixed *paradas* (bus stops), though in some places you can hold out your hand to stop one at any street corner. Not all bus drivers carry change.

Bicycle

Bicycling is becoming a more common mode of transportation in some cities. Having said that, never assume that motorists will give you the right of way and be particularly careful on narrow roads. A few areas, such as Valladolid, now have bicycle paths. In Mérida, a main downtown street is closed to traffic on Sundays for morning rides, and on Wednesday nights a group of bicycle activists organize mass rides. You can rent bikes in many towns for about M$25 per hour or M$100 per day.

It's possible to purchase a bicycle in the Yucatán. Indeed, if you plan to stay on the peninsula for a few months and want to get around by bike or at least exercise on one, purchasing isn't a bad option, as there are many inexpensive models available in the big cities.

Colectivo, Combi & Camión

On much of the peninsula, a variety of vehicles – often Volkswagen, Ford or Chevrolet vans – operate shuttle services between some towns, especially on short-haul routes and those linking rural settlements. These vehicles usually leave whenever they are full. Fares are typically a little less than those of 1st-class buses. *Combi* is a term often used for the Volkswagen variety; *colectivo* refers to any van type. *Taxi colectivo* may mean either public or private transport, depending on the location.

More basic than the *combis* are passenger-carrying *camiones* (trucks) and *camionetas* (pickups), usually with benches lining the sides. Standing in the back of a lurching truck with a couple of dozen *campesinos* (farm workers) and their machetes and animals is at least an experience to remember. Fares are similar to 2nd-class bus fares.

Taxis

Taxis are common in towns and cities, and are surprisingly economical. City rides usually cost around M$20 for a short trip. If a taxi has a meter you can ask the driver if it's working *('Funciona el taxímetro?')* If there's no meter, agree on a price before getting in the cab.

Many airports and some bus terminals have a system of authorized taxis: you buy a fixed-price ticket to your destination from a booth and then hand it over to the driver instead of paying cash. Fares are higher than what you'd pay on the street but these cabs offer guaranteed safety.

Renting a taxi for a daylong, out-of-town jaunt generally costs something similar to a rental car – M$600 to M$800.

Language

Although the predominant language of Mexico is Spanish, about 50 indigenous languages are spoken as a first language by more than seven million people throughout the country. There are more than 30 Maya languages still spoken today. In Chiapas the most widely spoken ones are Tzeltal, Tzotzil and Chol. Yucatec Maya is the most widely spoken indigenous language of the Yucatán.

SPANISH

Mexican Spanish pronunciation is easy, as most sounds have equivalents in English. Note that kh is a throaty sound (like the 'ch' in the Scottish *loch*), v and b are both pronounced like a soft English 'v' (between a 'v' and a 'b'), and r is strongly rolled. Also keep in mind that in some parts of Mexico the letters *ll* and *y* are pronounced like the 'll' in 'million', but in most areas they are pronounced like the 'y' in 'yes', and this is how they are represented in our pronunciation guides. If you read our colored pronunciation guides as if they were English, you'll be understood just fine. The stressed syllables are indicated with italics.

Where both polite and informal options are given in this chapter, they are indicated by the abbreviations 'pol' and 'inf'. Masculine and feminine forms of words are included where relevant and separated with a slash, eg *perdido/a* (m/f).

Basics

Hello.	*Hola.*	o·la
Goodbye.	*Adiós.*	a·*dyos*
How are you?	*¿Qué tal?*	ke tal
Fine, thanks.	*Bien, gracias.*	byen *gra*·syas
Excuse me.	*Perdón.*	per·*don*
Sorry.	*Lo siento.*	lo *syen*·to
Please.	*Por favor.*	por fa·*vor*
Thank you.	*Gracias.*	*gra*·syas
You're welcome.	*De nada.*	de *na*·da
Yes./No.	*Sí./No.*	see/no

My name is ...
Me llamo ... — me *ya*·mo ...

What's your name?
¿Cómo se llama Usted? — *ko*·mo se *ya*·ma oo·*ste* (pol)
¿Cómo te llamas? — *ko*·mo te *ya*·mas (inf)

Do you speak English?
¿Habla inglés? — *a*·bla een·*gles* (pol)
¿Hablas inglés? — *a*·blas een·*gles* (inf)

I don't understand.
Yo no entiendo. — yo no en·*tyen*·do

Accommodations

I'd like a ... room.	*Quisiera una habitación ...*	kee·*sye*·ra *oo*·na a·bee·ta·*syon* ...
single	*individual*	een·dee·vee·*dwal*
double	*doble*	*do*·ble

How much is it per night/person?
¿Cuánto cuesta por noche/persona? — *kwan*·to *kwes*·ta por *no*·che/per·*so*·na

Does it include breakfast?
¿Incluye el desayuno? — een·*kloo*·ye el de·sa·*yoo*·no

Numbers

1	*uno*	*oo*·no
2	*dos*	dos
3	*tres*	tres
4	*cuatro*	*kwa*·tro
5	*cinco*	*seen*·ko
6	*seis*	seys
7	*siete*	*sye*·te
8	*ocho*	o·cho
9	*nueve*	*nwe*·ve
10	*diez*	dyes
20	*veinte*	*veyn*·te
30	*treinta*	*treyn*·ta
40	*cuarenta*	kwa·*ren*·ta
50	*cincuenta*	seen·*kwen*·ta
60	*sesenta*	se·*sen*·ta
70	*setenta*	se·*ten*·ta
80	*ochenta*	o·*chen*·ta
90	*noventa*	no·*ven*·ta
100	*cien*	syen
1000	*mil*	meel

air-con	*aire acondicionado*	*ai*·re a·kon·dee·syo·*na*·do
bathroom	*baño*	*ba*·nyo
bed	*cama*	*ka*·ma
campsite	*terreno de cámping*	te·*re*·no de *kam*·peeng
hotel	*hotel*	o·*tel*
guesthouse	*pensión*	pen·*syon*
window	*ventana*	ven·*ta*·na
youth hostel	*albergue juvenil*	al·*ber*·ge khoo·ve·*neel*

Directions

Where's ...?
¿Dónde está ...? — *don*·de es·*ta* ...

What's the address?
¿Cuál es la dirección? — kwal es la dee·rek·*syon*

Could you please write it down?
¿Puede escribirlo, por favor? — *pwe*·de es·kree·*beer*·lo por fa·*vor*

Can you show me (on the map)?
¿Me lo puede indicar (en el mapa)? — me lo *pwe*·de een·dee·*kar* (en el *ma*·pa)

at the corner	*en la esquina*	en la es·*kee*·na
at the traffic lights	*en el semáforo*	en el se·*ma*·fo·ro
behind ...	*detrás de ...*	de·*tras* de ...
far	*lejos*	*le*·khos
in front of ...	*enfrente de ...*	en·*fren*·te de ...
left	*izquierda*	ees·*kyer*·da
near	*cerca*	*ser*·ka
next to ...	*al lado de ...*	al *la*·do de ...
opposite ...	*frente a ...*	*fren*·te a ...
right	*derecha*	de·*re*·cha
straight ahead	*todo recto*	*to*·do *rek*·to

Eating & Drinking

Can I see the menu, please?
¿Puedo ver el menú, por favor? — *pwe*·do ver el me·*noo* por fa·*vor*

What would you recommend?
¿Qué recomienda? — ke re·ko·*myen*·da

I don't eat (meat).
No como (carne). — no *ko*·mo (*kar*·ne)

That was delicious!
¡Estaba buenísimo! — es·*ta*·ba bwe·*nee*·see·mo

Cheers!
¡Salud! — sa·*loo*

The bill, please.
La cuenta, por favor. — la *kwen*·ta por fa·*vor*

I'd like a table for ...	*Quisiera una mesa para ...*	kee·*sye*·ra *oo*·na *me*·sa *pa*·ra ...
(eight) o'clock	*las (ocho)*	las (*o*·cho)
(two) people	*(dos) personas*	(dos) per·*so*·nas

Key Words

bottle	*botella*	bo·*te*·ya
breakfast	*desayuno*	de·sa·*yoo*·no
cold	*frío*	*free*·o
dessert	*postre*	*pos*·tre
dinner	*cena*	*se*·na
fork	*tenedor*	te·ne·*dor*
glass	*vaso*	*va*·so
hot (warm)	*caliente*	kal·*yen*·te
knife	*cuchillo*	koo·*chee*·yo
lunch	*comida*	ko·*mee*·da
plate	*plato*	*pla*·to
restaurant	*restaurante*	res·tow·*ran*·te
spoon	*cuchara*	koo·*cha*·ra

Meat & Fish

beef	*carne de vaca*	*kar*·ne de *va*·ka
chicken	*pollo*	*po*·yo

crab	*cangrejo*	kan·*gre*·kho
lamb	*cordero*	kor·*de*·ro
lobster	*langosta*	lan·*gos*·ta
oysters	*ostras*	*os*·tras
pork	*cerdo*	*ser*·do
shrimp	*camarones*	ka·ma·*ro*·nes
squid	*calamar*	ka·la·*mar*
veal	*ternera*	ter·*ne*·ra

Fruit & Vegetables

apple	*manzana*	man·*sa*·na
apricot	*albaricoque*	al·ba·ree·*ko*·ke
banana	*plátano*	*pla*·ta·no
beans	*frijoles*	free·*kho*·les
cabbage	*col*	kol
capsicum	*pimiento*	pee·*myen*·to
carrot	*zanahoria*	sa·na·o·rya
cherry	*cereza*	se·*re*·sa
corn	*maíz*	ma·*ees*
cucumber	*pepino*	pe·*pee*·no
grape	*uvas*	*oo*·vas
lettuce	*lechuga*	le·*choo*·ga
mushroom	*champiñón*	cham·pee·*nyon*
nuts	*nueces*	*nwe*·ses
onion	*cebolla*	se·*bo*·ya
orange	*naranja*	na·*ran*·kha
peach	*melocotón*	me·lo·ko·*ton*
pineapple	*piña*	*pee*·nya
potato	*patata*	pa·*ta*·ta
spinach	*espinacas*	es·pee·*na*·kas
strawberry	*fresa*	*fre*·sa
tomato	*tomate*	to·*ma*·te
watermelon	*sandía*	san·*dee*·a

Other

bread	*pan*	pan
cake	*pastel*	pas·*tel*
cheese	*queso*	*ke*·so
eggs	*huevos*	*we*·vos
French fries	*papas fritas*	*pa*·pas *free*·tas
honey	*miel*	myel
ice cream	*helado*	e·*la*·do
jam	*mermelada*	mer·me·*la*·da
pepper	*pimienta*	pee·*myen*·ta
rice	*arroz*	a·*ros*
salad	*ensalada*	en·sa·*la*·da
salt	*sal*	sal
soup	*caldo/sopa*	*kal*·do/*so*·pa
sugar	*azúcar*	a·*soo*·kar

Drinks

beer	*cerveza*	ser·*ve*·sa
coffee	*café*	ka·*fe*
juice	*zumo*	*soo*·mo
milk	*leche*	*le*·che
smoothie	*licuado*	lee·*kwa*·do
tea	*té*	te
(mineral) water	*agua (mineral)*	*a*·gwa (mee·ne·*ral*)
(red/white) wine	*vino (tinto/ blanco)*	*vee*·no (*teen*·to/ *blan*·ko)

Emergencies

Help!	*¡Socorro!*	so·*ko*·ro
Go away!	*¡Vete!*	*ve*·te

Call ...!	*¡Llame a ...!*	*ya*·me a ...
a doctor	*un médico*	oon *me*·dee·ko
the police	*la policía*	la po·lee·*see*·a

I'm lost.
Estoy perdido/a. es·*toy* per·*dee*·do/a (m/f)

Where are the toilets?
¿Dónde están los baños? *don*·de es·*tan* los *ba*·nyos

I'm ill.
Estoy enfermo/a. es·*toy* en·*fer*·mo/a (m/f)

I'm allergic to (antibiotics).
Soy alérgico/a a (los antibióticos). soy a·*ler*·khee·ko/a a (los an·tee·*byo*·tee·kos) (m/f)

Shopping & Services

I'd like to buy ...
Quisiera comprar ... kee·sye·ra kom·*prar* ...

I'm just looking.
Sólo estoy mirando. so·lo es·*toy* mee·*ran*·do

Can I look at it?
¿Puedo verlo? *pwe*·do *ver*·lo

How much is it?
¿Cuánto cuesta? *kwan*·to *kwes*·ta

Signs

Abierto	Open
Cerrado	Closed
Entrada	Entrance
Hombres/Varones	Men
Mujeres/Damas	Women
Prohibido	Prohibited
Salida	Exit
Servicios/Baños	Toilets

That's too expensive.
Es muy caro. es mooy *ka*·ro

There's a mistake in the bill.
Hay un error en la cuenta. ai oon e·*ror* en la *kwen*·ta

ATM	*cajero automático*	ka·*khe*·ro ow·to·*ma*·tee·ko
market	*mercado*	mer·*ka*·do
post office	*correos*	ko·*re*·os
tourist office	*oficina de turismo*	o·fee·*see*·na de too·*rees*·mo

Time & Dates

What time is it?	*¿Qué hora es?*	ke o·ra es
It's (10) o'clock.	*Son (las diez).*	son (las dyes)
It's half past (one).	*Es (la una) y media.*	es (la *oo*·na) ee *me*·dya

morning	*mañana*	ma·*nya*·na
afternoon	*tarde*	*tar*·de
evening	*noche*	*no*·che
yesterday	*ayer*	a·*yer*
today	*hoy*	oy
tomorrow	*mañana*	ma·*nya*·na

Monday	*lunes*	*loo*·nes
Tuesday	*martes*	*mar*·tes
Wednesday	*miércoles*	*myer*·ko·les
Thursday	*jueves*	*khwe*·ves
Friday	*viernes*	*vyer*·nes
Saturday	*sábado*	*sa*·ba·do
Sunday	*domingo*	do·*meen*·go

Transportation

boat	*barco*	*bar*·ko
bus	*autobús*	ow·to·*boos*
plane	*avión*	a·*vyon*
train	*tren*	tren

Question Words

How?	*¿Cómo?*	*ko*·mo
What?	*¿Qué?*	ke
When?	*¿Cuándo?*	*kwan*·do
Where?	*¿Dónde?*	*don*·de
Who?	*¿Quién?*	kyen
Why?	*¿Por qué?*	por ke

A ... ticket, please.	*Un billete de ..., por favor.*	oon bee·*ye*·te de ... por fa·*vor*
1st-class	*primera clase*	pree·*me*·ra *kla*·se
2nd-class	*segunda clase*	se·*goon*·da *kla*·se
one-way	*ida*	ee·da
return	*ida y vuelta*	ee·da ee *vwel*·ta

What time does it arrive/leave?
¿A qué hora llega/sale? a ke o·ra *ye*·ga/*sa*·le

Does it stop at ...?
¿Para en ...? pa·ra en ...

What stop is this?
¿Cuál es esta parada? kwal es *es*·ta pa·*ra*·da

Please tell me when we get to ...
¿Puede avisarme cuando lleguemos a ...? *pwe*·de a·vee·*sar*·me *kwan*·do ye·*ge*·mos a ...

I want to get off here.
Quiero bajarme aquí. *kye*·ro ba·*khar*·me a·*kee*

airport	*aeropuerto*	a·e·ro·*pwer*·to
bus stop	*parada de autobuses*	pa·*ra*·da de ow·to·*boo*·ses
ticket office	*taquilla*	ta·*kee*·ya
timetable	*horario*	o·*ra*·ryo
train station	*estación de trenes*	es·ta·*syon* de *tre*·nes

I'd like to hire a ...	*Quisiera alquilar ...*	kee·*sye*·ra al·kee·*lar* ...
bicycle	*una bicicleta*	*oo*·na bee·see·*kle*·ta
car	*un coche*	oon *ko*·che
motorcycle	*una moto*	*oo*·na *mo*·to

helmet	*casco*	*kas*·ko
mechanic	*mecánico*	me·*ka*·nee·ko
petrol/gas	*gasolina*	ga·so·*lee*·na
service station	*gasolinera*	ga·so·lee·*ne*·ra

Is this the road to ...?
¿Se va a ... por esta carretera? se va a ... por es·ta ka·re·*te*·ra

(How long) Can I park here?
¿(Cuánto tiempo) Puedo aparcar aquí? (*kwan*·to *tyem*·po) *pwe*·do a·par·*kar* a·*kee*

I've run out of petrol.
Me he quedado sin gasolina. me e ke·*da*·do seen ga·so·*lee*·na

I have a flat tyre.
Tengo un pinchazo. *ten*·go oon peen·*cha*·so

YUCATEC MAYA

Yucatec Maya, spoken primarily in the Yucatán, Campeche and Quintana Roo, and in the northern and western parts of Belize, belongs to the Amerindian languages, spoken by Native American people across North America. This means that Yucatec Maya (commonly called 'Yucatec' by scholars and 'Maya' by local speakers) is related to many indigenous languages spoken in the southeastern United States, as well as far-off California and Oregon (eg Costanoan, Klamath and Tsimshian). Yucatec is just one of about 30 languages in the Maya family (together with Quiché, Mam, Kekchi and Cakchiquel), but it probably has the largest number of speakers, estimated at more than half a million people.

You can hear Yucatec spoken in the markets and occasionally by hotel staff in cities throughout the peninsula. To hear Yucatec spoken by monolingual Maya speakers, you must travel to some of the peninsula's more remote villages. Maya speakers will not assume that you know any of their language. If you attempt to say something in Maya, however, people will usually respond quite favorably.

Pronunciation

The principles of Maya pronunciation are similar to those found in Spanish. Just follow the colored pronunciation guides included next to the Maya phrases in this section and read them as if they were English.

Maya consonants followed by an apostrophe (b', ch', k', p', t') are similar to regular consonants, but they should be pronounced more forcefully and 'explosively'. On the other hand, an apostrophe following a vowel indicates a glottal stop (similar to the sound between the two syllables in 'uh-oh').

Maya is a tonal language, which means that some words have different meanings when pronounced with a high tone or a low tone. For example, *aak* said with a high tone means 'turtle', but when said with a low tone it means 'grass' or 'vine'.

In many Maya place names the word stress falls on the last syllable. In written language, Spanish rules for indicating word stress with accent marks are often followed for these words. This practice varies, however; in this book we have tried to include accent marks whenever possible. Note also that the stressed syllable is always indicated with italics in our pronunciation guides.

Note also that words borrowed from Spanish, even if they are common ones, tend to be stressed differently in Yucatec Maya, eg *amigo* (Spanish for 'friend') is pronounced 'a·*mee*·go' in Spanish and '*a*·mee·go' in Yucatec.

Basics

Note that Maya speakers often reiterate what is said to them, instead of saying 'yes'; eg 'Are you going to the store?' – 'I'm going'.

Hello.	*Hola.*	o·la
Good day.	*Buenos dias.*	*bwe*·nos *dee*·as
How are you?	*Bix a beel?*	beesh a bail
How are you? (less formal)	*Bix yanikech?*	beesh yaw·nee·*kech*
OK./Well.	*Maalob.*	*ma*·lobe
Bye./See you tomorrow.	*Hasta saamal.*	*as*·ta *sa*·mal
Goodbye.	*Pa'atik kin bin.*	*pa'a*·teek keen been
Thank you.	*Dios Bo'otik.*	dyos *boe'o*·teek
Yes.	*Haa./He'ele.*	haa/*he'e*·le
No.	*Ma'.*	ma'
expensive	*ko'o*	*ko'*·o
pretty	*ki'ichpam*	*kee'*·eech·pam

What's your name?
Bix a k'aaba? — beesh a *k'aa*·ba

My name is ...
In kaabae' ... — een ka·ba·e' ...

I don't speak Maya.
Ma tin na'atik mayat'aani. — ma' teen *na'*·a·teek ma·ya·*taa*·nee

Do you speak Spanish?
Teche', ka t'aanik wa castellano t'aan? — *te*·che' ka *t'a*·neek wa ka·stay·*ya*·no t'an

I want to drink water.
Tak in wukik ha'. — tak een woo·*keek* ha'

I'm hungry.
Wiihen. — wee·*hen*

It's (very) tasty.
(Hach) Ki'. — (hach) kee'

How much is that/this one?
Baux lelo'/lela'? — ba·*hoosh* le·*lo'*/le·*la'*

Where is the ...?	*Tu'ux yaan le ...?*	*too'*·oosh yan le ...
bathroom	*baño*	*ba'*·nyo
doctor	*médico*	*me*·dee·ko
hotel	*hotel*	o·*tel*
road to ...	*u be ti' ...*	u be tee ...

1	*un peel*	oom pail
2	*ka peel*	ka pail
3	*ox peel*	osh pail

When counting animate objects, such as people, replace *peel* with *tuul* (pronounced 'tool'). Beyond three, use Spanish numbers.

GLOSSARY

Words specific to food, restaurants and eating are listed on p263.

Ah Tz'ib – Maya scribes. They penned the Chilam Balam and still practice their craft today.
alux (s), **aluxes** (pl) – Maya 'leprechauns,' benevolent 'little people'
Ángeles Verdes – 'Green Angels;' bilingual mechanics in green trucks who patrol major highways, offering breakdown assistance

baluartes – bastions, bulwarks or ramparts
barrio – district, neighborhood

cacique – indigenous chief; also used to describe a provincial warlord or strongman
cafetería – literally 'coffee-shop,' it refers to any informal restaurant with waiter service; it is not usually a self-service restaurant
cajero automático – Automated Teller Machine (ATM)
camión (s), **camiones** (pl) – truck; bus
camioneta – pickup
campechanos – citizens of Campeche
campesinos – countryfolk, farm workers
casa de cambio – currency-exchange office
casetas de teléfono – call offices where an on-the-spot operator connects the call for you, often shortened to *casetas*
Caste War – bloody 19th-century Maya uprising in the Yucatán
cenote – a deep limestone sinkhole containing water
cerveza – beer
Chac – Maya god of rain
chac-mool – Maya sacrificial stone sculpture
chenes – name for cenotes (limestone sinkholes) in the Chenes region
chultún (s), **chultunes** (pl) – Maya cistern found at Puuc archaeological sites south of Mérida
coctelería – seafood shack specializing in shellfish cocktails as well as *ceviche*
cocina – cookshop (literally 'kitchen'), a small, basic restaurant usually run by one woman, often located in or near a municipal market; also seen as *cocina económica* (economical kitchen) or *cocina familiar* (family kitchen); see also *lonchería*
colectivo – literally, 'shared,' a car, van (VW combi, Ford or Chevrolet) or minibus that picks up and drops off passengers along its set route; also known as *taxi colectivo*
combi – a catch-all term used for taxi, van and minibus services regardless of vehicle type
comida corrida – set meal, meal of the day
conquistador – explorer-conqueror of Latin America from Spain
costera – waterfront avenue
criollo – a person of pure Spanish descent born in Spanish America
cuota – toll road

daños a terceros – third-party car insurance
de lujo – deluxe class of bus service
DNI – Derecho para No Inmigrante; nonimmigrant fee charged to all foreign tourists and business travelers visiting Mexico

ejido – communal landholding, though laws now allow sale of *ejido* land to outside individuals
encomienda – a grant made to a conquistador, consisting of labor by or tribute from a group of indigenous people; the conquistador was supposed to protect and convert them, but usually treated them as little more than slaves

feria – fair or carnival, typically occurring during a religious holiday

gringo/a – male/female US or Canadian visitor to Latin America (sometimes applied to any visitor of European heritage); can be used derogatorily but more often is a mere statement of fact
gruta – cave, grotto
guayabera – man's thin fabric shirt with pockets and appliquéd designs on the front, over the shoulders and down the back; often worn in place of a jacket and tie

hacienda – estate; Hacienda (capitalized) is the Treasury Department
henequen – agave fiber used to make rope, grown particularly around Mérida
h-menob – Maya shaman still practicing their trade in the Yucatán today.
huipil (s), **huipiles** (pl) – indigenous women's sleeveless white tunic, usually intricately and colorfully embroidered

iglesia – church
INAH – Instituto Nacional de Arqueología e Historia; the body in charge of most ancient sites and some museums
INM – Instituto Nacional de Migración (National Immigration Institute)
Itzamná – lord of the heavens; a popular figure on the wooden panels of contemporary architecture
IVA – *impuesto al valor agregado* or 'ee-bah,' a 15% value-added tax added to many items in Mexico
Ixchel – Maya goddess of the moon and fertility

jarana – a folkloric dance that has been performed by Yucatecans for centuries
jipijapa – an alternative name for panama hats (which are made from *jipijapa* palm fronds)
Kukulcán – Maya name for the Aztec-Toltec plumed serpent Quetzalcóatl

lagunas – small lakes, lagoons
lonchería – from English 'lunch'; a simple restaurant that may in fact serve meals all day (not just lunch); often seen near municipal markets. See also *cocina*.
lotería – Mexico's version of bingo

machismo – maleness, masculine virility or bravura
malecón – waterfront boulevard
mariachi – small ensemble of Mexican street musicians; strolling mariachi bands often perform in restaurants
méridanos – citizens of Mérida
mestizo – also known as *ladino*, a person of mixed indigenous and European blood; the word now more commonly means 'Mexican'
metate – flattish stone on which corn is ground with a cylindrical stone roller
mezcal – a distilled alcoholic drink made from the agave plant

na – thatched Maya hut
nortes – relatively cold storms bringing wind and rain from the north
Nte – abbreviation for *norte* (north), used in street names

Ote – abbreviation for *oriente* (east), used in street names

palapa – thatched, palm-leaf-roofed shelter usually with open sides
Popol Vuh – painted Maya book containing sacred legends and stories; equivalent to the Bible
porfiriato – the name given to the era of Porfirio Diaz's 35-year rule as president-dictator (1876–1911), preceding the Mexican Revolution
PRI – Partido Revolucionario Institucional (Institutional Revolutionary Party); the controlling force in Mexican politics for much of the 20th century
primera (1a) clase – 1st class of bus service

Quetzalcóatl – plumed serpent god of the Aztecs and Toltecs

retablo – altarpiece (usually an ornate gilded, carved wooden decoration in a church)
ría – estuary
roofcomb – a decorative stonework lattice atop a Maya pyramid or temple

sacbé (s), **sacbeob** (pl) – ceremonial limestone avenue or path between great Maya cities
segunda (2a) clase – 2nd class of bus service
Semana Santa – Holy Week, the week from Palm Sunday to Easter Sunday; Mexico's major holiday period
stela (s), **stelae** (pl) – standing stone monument, usually carved
sur – south; often seen in street names

temazcal – bathhouse, sweat lodge
templo – in Mexico, a church; anything from a wayside chapel to a cathedral
tequila – clear, distilled liquor produced, like pulque and *mezcal,* from the maguey cactus
topes – speed bumps, sometimes indicated by a highway sign depicting a row of little bumps
torito – a vivacious song that evokes the fervor of a bullfight
tranvía – tram or motorized trolley

vaquería – a traditional Yucatecan party where couples dance in unison to a series of songs; the parties are often held in town halls or on haciendas

Xibalbá – in Maya religious belief, the secret world or underworld
xtabentún – a traditional Maya spirit in the Yucatán; an anise-flavored liqueur made by fermenting honey

yucateco – someone or something of the Yucatán Peninsula

Behind the Scenes

SEND US YOUR FEEDBACK

We love to hear from travelers – your comments keep us on our toes and help make our books better. Our well-traveled team reads every word on what you loved or loathed about this book. Although we cannot reply individually to postal submissions, we always guarantee that your feedback goes straight to the appropriate authors, in time for the next edition. Each person who sends us information is thanked in the next edition – the most useful submissions are rewarded with a selection of digital PDF chapters.

Visit **lonelyplanet.com/contact** to submit your updates and suggestions or to ask for help. Our award-winning website also features inspirational travel stories, news and discussions.

Note: We may edit, reproduce and incorporate your comments in Lonely Planet products such as guidebooks, websites and digital products, so let us know if you don't want your comments reproduced or your name acknowledged. For a copy of our privacy policy visit lonelyplanet.com/privacy.

OUR READERS

Many thanks to the travelers who used the last edition and wrote to us with helpful hints, useful advice and interesting anecdotes:

Fernanda Adame, Jeanne Bouteaud, Fiona Campbell, Katie Carey, Ross Edwards, Jennifer King, Mariana Kopfsguter, Katherine Krabel, Benjamin Meredith-Davies, Susan Mulholland, Lisanne Petracca, Lewis Phillips, Gina Restivo, Lars Schmeink

AUTHOR THANKS

John Hecht

Many thanks to all the good folks in the Yucatán who helped make this wonderful journey possible. Special gratitude goes out to commissioning editor Cat Craddock-Carrillo, co-author Sandra Bao, the book's previous writers, Raul LiCausi, Pepe Treviño and my loyal buddy, el campeon. Last but certainly not least, all my love to my wife Laura and a big hug for Carlos, the bravest person I've ever known.

Sandra Bao

Thanks to coordinating author John Hecht for his patience, and commissioning editor Cat Craddock-Carrillo for finally giving me a shot. A big shout out to BK for being the perfect driver and travel companion during my research. Also a big help to me were Rick and Diane, Nicolás Feldman and Rafael Tunesi. Finally, lots of love to my supportive family – mom, dad and Daniel – and especially to my husband, Ben Greensfelder.

ACKNOWLEDGMENTS

Climate map data adapted from Peel MC, Finlayson BL & McMahon TA (2007) 'Updated World Map of the Köppen-Geiger Climate Classification', *Hydrology and Earth System Sciences*, 11, 163344.

Chichén Itzá illustration, Michael Weldon.

Cover photograph: Tulum beach and El Castillo, Steve Allen/Getty Images.

THIS BOOK

This 6th edition of Lonely Planet's *Cancún, Cozumel & the Yucatán* guidebook was researched and written by John Hecht (coordinating author) and Sandra Bao. The previous two editions were written by Greg Benchwick.

This guidebook was commissioned in Lonely Planet's Oakland office, and produced by the following:

Commissioning Editor Catherine Craddock-Carrillo

Coordinating Editors Paul Harding, Fionnuala Twomey

Managing Cartographer Anita Banh

Coordinating Layout Designer Nicholas Colicchia

Managing Editor Bruce Evans

Senior Editors Andi Jones, Karyn Noble

Senior Cartographer Alison Lyall

Managing Layout Designer Chris Girdler

Assisting Editors Amy Karafin, Joanne Newell, Gabrielle Stefanos, Saralinda Turner

Cartographers Alex Leung, Gabriel Lindquist, Chris Tsismetzis

Cover Research Naomi Parker

Internal Image Research Gerard Walker

Language Content Branislava Vladisavljevic

Thanks to Ryan Evans, Larissa Frost, Mark Griffiths, Genesys India, Jouve India, Annelies Mertens, Trent Paton, Kerrianne Southway, Gerard Walker

Index

Map Pages **000**
Photo Pages **000**

D

Map Pages **000**
Photo Pages **000**

N

O

P

Map Pages **000**
Photo Pages **000**

R

S

T

Map Legend

Sights
- Beach
- Bird Sanctuary
- Buddhist
- Castle/Palace
- Christian
- Confucian
- Hindu
- Islamic
- Jain
- Jewish
- Monument
- Museum/Gallery/Historic Building
- Ruin
- Sento Hot Baths/Onsen
- Shinto
- Sikh
- Taoist
- Winery/Vineyard
- Zoo/Wildlife Sanctuary
- Other Sight

Activities, Courses & Tours
- Bodysurfing
- Diving/Snorkelling
- Canoeing/Kayaking
- Course/Tour
- Skiing
- Snorkelling
- Surfing
- Swimming/Pool
- Walking
- Windsurfing
- Other Activity

Sleeping
- Sleeping
- Camping

Eating
- Eating

Drinking & Nightlife
- Drinking & Nightlife
- Cafe

Entertainment
- Entertainment

Shopping
- Shopping

Information
- Bank
- Embassy/Consulate
- Hospital/Medical
- Internet
- Police
- Post Office
- Telephone
- Toilet
- Tourist Information
- Other Information

Geographic
- Beach
- Hut/Shelter
- Lighthouse
- Lookout
- Mountain/Volcano
- Oasis
- Park
- Pass
- Picnic Area
- Waterfall

Population
- Capital (National)
- Capital (State/Province)
- City/Large Town
- Town/Village

Transport
- Airport
- Border crossing
- Bus
- Cable car/Funicular
- Cycling
- Ferry
- Metro station
- Monorail
- Parking
- Petrol station
- Subway/Subte station
- Taxi
- Train station/Railway
- Tram
- Underground station
- Other Transport

Note: Not all symbols displayed above appear on the maps in this book

Routes
- Tollway
- Freeway
- Primary
- Secondary
- Tertiary
- Lane
- Unsealed road
- Road under construction
- Plaza/Mall
- Steps
- Tunnel
- Pedestrian overpass
- Walking Tour
- Walking Tour detour
- Path/Walking Trail

Boundaries
- International
- State/Province
- Disputed
- Regional/Suburb
- Marine Park
- Cliff
- Wall

Hydrography
- River, Creek
- Intermittent River
- Canal
- Water
- Dry/Salt/Intermittent Lake
- Reef

Areas
- Airport/Runway
- Beach/Desert
- Cemetery (Christian)
- Cemetery (Other)
- Glacier
- Mudflat
- Park/Forest
- Sight (Building)
- Sportsground
- Swamp/Mangrove

OUR STORY

A beat-up old car, a few dollars in the pocket and a sense of adventure. In 1972 that's all Tony and Maureen Wheeler needed for the trip of a lifetime – across Europe and Asia overland to Australia. It took several months, and at the end – broke but inspired – they sat at their kitchen table writing and stapling together their first travel guide, *Across Asia on the Cheap*. Within a week they'd sold 1500 copies. Lonely Planet was born.

Today, Lonely Planet has offices in Melbourne, London and Oakland, with more than 600 staff and writers. We share Tony's belief that 'a great guidebook should do three things: inform, educate and amuse'.

OUR WRITERS

John Hecht

Coordinating author; Plan Your Trip, Cancún & Around, Isla Mujeres, Isla Cozumel, Riviera Maya, Costa Maya & the Southern Caribbean Coast, Yucatán State & the Maya Heartland, Understand Cancún, Cozumel & Yucatán (except Yucatán Cuisine), Survival Guide John headed down Mexico way more than two decades ago and, much to mom's disappointment, he's still there. He spent the early years in Guadalajara, studying Spanish and practicing his new language skills in the neighborhood *cantinas*. Several years later he bid farewell to the mariachi capital to take a reporting job at an English-language newspaper in Mexico City. Next he turned freelance and one of his first gigs was a travel writing assignment in the Yucatán. He has now done several jobs in and around Cancún, including a series of short videos shot for Lonely Planet TV. Additionally, he has written for two editions of the Lonely Planet *Mexico* guide and he co-authored *Puerto Vallarta & Pacific Mexico*.

Read more about John at:
lonelyplanet.com/members/johnhecht

Sandra Bao

Campeche, Chiapas Sandra is a Chinese-American born in Argentina who has traveled to nearly 60 countries on six continents. In 1990, while on vacation, she drove to Mexico with her future husband Ben Greensfelder and fell in love with the country; nine years later she scored her first guidebook-writing gig for Lonely Planet, researching Chiapas. Since then she's travelled all around Mexico and especially Yucatán, and is constantly amazed by the wonders this beautiful region has to offer. Over the last 12 years Sandra has contributed to a few dozen Lonely Planet titles to countries like Argentina, Venezuela, Mexico and the USA.

Read more about Sandra at:
lonelyplanet.com/members/sandrabao

CONTRIBUTING AUTHOR

Mauricio Velázquez de León was born in Mexico City, where he was given boiled chicken feet and toasted corn tortillas to sooth his teething pains. He is the author of *My Foodie ABC: A Little Gourmet's Guide* (Duo Press, 2010) and lives in Maryland with his wife and twin sons, whose teething pains were soothed with toasted corn tortillas. He wrote the Yucatán Cuisine chapter in this book.

Published by Lonely Planet Publications Pty Ltd
ABN 36 005 607 983
6th edition – Sep 2013
ISBN 978 174220 014 9

10 9 8 7 6 5 4 3 2 1
Printed in China